International Accounting and Auditing Trends

Volume 1

CIFAR

Center for International
Financial Analysis & Research, Inc.
Princeton, New Jersey, USA

International Accounting and Auditing Trends

by Vinod B. Bavishi

Project Staff

Project Managers	Arlene W. Goldhammer	Haksu Kim
Database Developers	Marianne C. Owens, Manager	Sanjiv Vyas
Principal Research Associates	Monica Quill Kusakabe	Mercedes Paratje
	Alejandro del Riccio	Francis Schneider
	Sandeep Shroff	Eartha Vorswijk
Editorial Coordinators	Deborah A. McEvoy	Maureen M. O'Reilly
Research Associates	Yogesh Borkar	Sadanandan Nair
	Geun-Jin Lee	Yoshiko Okuda
	Neema Majmudar	Peter Sanders
	George Musonge	Chetan Shah
Information Services Associates	Karen L. Fiorello	Ana Maria Mangas
	Edward Gershman	M. Beth Troy, Manager
	Rekha Kak	Costa Sideridis

CIFAR

Center for International
Financial Analysis & Research, Inc.
Princeton, New Jersey, USA

ISBN No. 1-877587-02-8

The information presented in this study has been drawn from the sources indicated in the research design sections of the various chapters. The CIFAR project staff and the author have undertaken painstaking quality controls to assure the reasonableness of the information. Given the massive amount of collected data, the project staff, author and CIFAR cannot take responsibility for inadvertent errors or omissions.

FUTURE UPDATES:

The next edition of International Accounting and Auditing Trends will be published in October 1990. We would like to continue to improve this publication in future editions. Though much time and effort has been spent making sure that this study is a comprehensive and high quality research publication, we would sincerely appreciate receiving any comments and suggestions users have about this study. Please send your input to the following address:

Center for International
Financial Analysis & Research, Inc.
601 Ewing Street
Princeton, NJ 08540 USA

Phone: (609) 921-0910
FAX: (609) 921-0216
Telex: 6716479

ACKNOWLEDGMENTS

The Center for International Financial Analysis and Research (CIFAR) was founded in 1984 to facilitate the better understanding of international financial statements and to study global trends in international accounting and auditing. With the publication of International Accounting and Auditing Trends, I believe we have achieved this objective.

This publication is the culmination of the considerable efforts of many people over a period of more than four years. I am fortunate to have received the encouragement, assistance and support of many colleagues, organizations and my family. I would like to take this opportunity to acknowledge their contribution.

First of all, a study of this nature requires a dedicated team of colleagues. I am immensely grateful to the CIFAR team, listed above, who contributed to every step of this project and made the study a reality.

Secondly, five international accounting firms provided seed money for the initial phases of this study as well as invaluable data verification on the client database of International Accounting Firms (Chapter 10). The firms also gave us absolute independence to pursue this project as we deemed appropriate. We would like to convey our sincere appreciation for the support, patience and cooperation of the following international accounting firms which played an instrumental role in the successful completion of this study.

Arthur Andersen & Co.
Deloitte Haskins & Sells
Ernst & Whinney
Klynveld Peat Marwick Goerdeler
Price Waterhouse

Thirdly, we are very grateful to the following eight international accounting firms which helped us verify the client data. In many instances these firms went beyond verification of information and made requests to their colleagues around the world in order to provide us with more complete information.

Arthur Young International
BDO Binder
Coopers and Lybrand
Dunwoody Robson McGladrey & Pullen
Horwath & Horwath International
Moores Rowland International
Touche Ross International
Spicer & Oppenheim

The CIFAR team would like to convey their thanks to the librarians of the following organizations for allowing us to use their tremendous reference resources and, in some cases, providing us with copies of annual reports which were not in the CIFAR library:

American Institute of Certified Public Accountants Library (New York)
Banque Bruxelles Lambert Library (Brussels)
Bechtel Information Services (Rockville, Maryland)
Brooklyn Public Library (New York)
City Library (London)
Columbia Business School Library (New York)
DAFSA Library (Paris)
Disclosure, Inc. (Bethesda, Maryland)
Dresdner Bank Library (Frankfurt)
Financial Times Information Services (London)
Government Publications Center (Tokyo)
HWWA Institut fuer Wirtschaftsforschung (Hamburg)
Library of Congress (Washington, DC)
London Business School Library
Micromedia, Ltd. (Toronto)
Moody's Investors Service Library (New York)
New York Public Library
Princeton University, Firestone Library
Rider College Library (Lawrenceville, New Jersey)
Union Bank of Switzerland Library (Zurich)
University of Amsterdam Library
University of Connecticut Library (Stamford, Connecticut)
University of Singapore Business School Library
University of Toronto: School of Management Library
Wharton School's Lippincott Library (Philadelphia)
Wright Investors' Service Library (Bridgeport, Connecticut)

Professors Dick Van Offeren, of the University of Amsterdam, and Donald Wygal, of Rider College, helped us considerably by providing a peer review of the drafts of this study as well as helping us with writing and editing earlier drafts of several chapters when they were visiting research fellows at CIFAR during 1987-1988.

My sincere appreciation goes to Mr. Peter Donovan, President, and Mr. Harivadan Kapadia, Senior Vice President, at Wright Investors' Service for jointly developing with us the "Worldscope Database" which served as the foundation for many of the chapters in this study. Their support over the last three years is highly appreciated.

Since the establishment of CIFAR in July, 1984, I have had the privilege of many discussions on topics of mutual interest with professionals from various organizations (major investment firms, multinational banks, multinational corporations and international portfolio managers) who have helped CIFAR in its formative years by serving on the CIFAR steering committee, by providing funding for various research projects, and encouraging us to continue moving ahead despite all the difficulties involved in establishing a research group. Though numerous to list them all here, I am grateful to them for their kind support. "Analyzing International Financial Statements: Issues and Answers" (Chapter 6), reflects the insight we have gained from these international capital market participants.

I am indebted conceptually to Professors Harold E. Wyman of the University of Connecticut and Frederick D.S. Choi of New York University. I learned a great deal from both of these fine scholars of international accounting while working with them on joint publications as well as in preparing working papers for presentation at various conferences from 1979 to 1983. I am most grateful to them for their guidance.

Finally, I want to convey my gratitude and appreciation to my wife, Trishala and our children, Ami and Jay for their understanding, selfless support and patience over the last four years.

V.B.B.
May 19, 1989
Princeton, New Jersey

Background Information About the Research Group

The Center

Established in July 1984, the Center for International Financial Analysis and Research, Inc. (CIFAR) is an independent research group. Leading universities, financial institutions, international accounting firms and multinational corporations support CIFAR's research, educational and information dissemination programs.

CIFAR maintains financial information on ten thousand corporations from fifty countries and has compiled an extensive reference library on international accounting and capital markets worldwide.

Current research projects at CIFAR include a global financial analysis of companies worldwide in selected industries, (Banks, Insurance, Chemicals/Pharmaceuticals and Electronics), and the development of a financial database on 1,000 companies in twenty developing countries.

Research Team

CIFAR's team of fifteen researchers and five colleagues in the library/computer department is drawn from many universities and countries. The majority of these colleagues have advanced degrees in accounting or finance and are multilingual. Five CIFAR team members hold the professional qualifications of either Certified Public Accountant or Chartered Accountant.

Author

Vinod B. Bavishi is the founder of CIFAR and teaches finance and international accounting at the Business School of the University of Connecticut (USA).

Professor Bavishi directed and co-authored Who Audits the World: Trends in the Worldwide Accounting Profession, published by the University of Connecticut, 1983. More recently at CIFAR, he co-edited the Worldscope Company Profiles series, an eight-volume reference work which analyzes the financial statements of the world's leading 4,000 companies from the industrial countries.

Professor Bavishi holds an MBA in Finance, a Masters in Accounting and a Ph.D. in International Finance, as well as the CPA, CMA and CFA designations.

TABLE OF CONTENTS AND APPENDICES

Volume 1

INTERNATIONAL ACCOUNTING TRENDS

INTERNATIONAL AUDITING TRENDS

APPENDICES

Volume 2

CHAPTER 1

INTERNATIONAL ACCOUNTING TRENDS
INTRODUCTION AND RESEARCH DESIGN

Table of Contents

INTERNATIONAL ACCOUNTING TRENDS
INTRODUCTION AND RESEARCH DESIGN

The study is divided into two broad sections:

1. International Accounting Trends (Chapters 1 through 7)

2. International Auditing Trends (Chapters 8 through 14)

I. INTRODUCTION

The analysis of companies across national boundaries has become very important today for several reasons:

- Key capital markets are becoming internationally integrated.

- Competitive pressures in many global industries are increasing, thus requiring the analysis of international competitors.

- Money managers are building portfolios from a global list of securities.

In view of these trends, a consistent method is needed to analyze the performance of companies globally, and herein lies the role of accounting. Measuring performance within a particular country is not a problem, because each country establishes rules which facilitate the comparison of companies within that country. These rules constitute, collectively, the accounting principles and practices of that country. They are unique to that country and are a reflection of the social and economic environment from which they are derived.

The problem, however, is that there are as many sets of principles and practices as there are countries or regions in the world. Consequently, an analyst faces the monumental task of understanding the diversity in reporting practices and the meaning of the financial data generated by international companies. The goal is to reduce or eliminate the differences so that the performance of leading companies in a given industry can be compared on a worldwide basis.

Several international organizations have made progress toward the goal of eliminating differences in principles and practices. The International Accounting Standards Committee (IASC), European Community (EC), Organization for Economic Cooperation and Development (OECD), United Nations (UN), and International Federation of Accountants (IFAC) have recommended various accounting and auditing standards which have been wholly or partially adopted by individual companies and/or institutions responsible for setting accounting standards as a supplement to national and local standards. However, differences still exist!

The primary objective of Chapters 2 through 7 is to provide a further understanding of the discrepancies in accounting standards and financial disclosures, as evidenced in the annual reports of companies from 24 countries.

II. OVERVIEW OF CHAPTERS 2 THROUGH 7

Chapter 2 contains an analysis of the accounting standards (or accounting methods) followed by industrial companies in 24 countries.

Chapter 3 contains an analysis of the financial reporting and disclosure practices of industrial companies in 24 countries.

Chapter 4 presents an analysis of the accounting standards and financial reporting and disclosure practices of banks and insurance companies in 22 countries.

Chapter 5 presents an analysis of interim financial statements for industrial companies located in 20 countries.

Chapter 6 summarizes the difficulties associated with the analysis of companies' financial statements internationally and provides possible solutions to overcome these difficulties.

Chapter 7 presents the major findings from the observation of international accounting trends and identifies for the preparers, users and auditors of international financial statements, several implications for the future.

III. RESEARCH OBJECTIVES

The following research questions are addressed in Chapters 2 through 6:

Chapter 2 Accounting Standards: Industrial Companies

2-1 What are the key accounting standards or methods followed by the leading industrial corporations worldwide?

2-2 What are the implications of international differences in accounting standards for the valuation of assets and income determination of the industrial companies being analyzed?

2-3 To what extent has the international harmonization of accounting standards followed by industrial companies been achieved?

Chapter 3 Financial Statement Disclosures: Industrial Companies

3-1 What are the financial disclosure practices of industrial companies in various countries?

3-2 To what extent has the international harmonization of financial disclosures for industrial companies been achieved?

3-3 What financial disclosures should be included in annual reports of industrial companies published for an international audience?

Chapter 4 Accounting Standards and Financial Reporting Practices: Banks and Insurance Companies

4-1 What are the key accounting standards or methods followed by leading banks and insurance companies worldwide?

4-2 What are the implications of international differences in accounting standards for the valuation of assets and income determination of the banks and insurance companies analyzed?

4-3 To what extent has the international harmonization of accounting standards for banks and insurance companies been achieved?

4-4 What are the financial disclosure practices of banks and insurance companies by country?

4-5 To what extent has the international harmonization of financial disclosures for banks and insurance companies been achieved?

4-6 What financial disclosures should be included in the annual reports of banks and insurance companies published for an international audience?

Chapter 5 Interim Financial Statements: Industrial Companies

5-1 How frequently are interim financial statements published by industrial companies internationally?

5-2 What items are usually disclosed in interim financial statements worldwide?

5-3 To what extent has the international harmonization of financial disclosures been achieved in interim reporting?

5-4 What financial disclosures should be included in interim reports published for an international audience?

Chapter 6 Analyzing Financial Statements

6-1 What are the major difficulties which users face in analyzing international financial statements?

6-2 What are the major accounting differences among leading companies in 24 countries?

6-3 How do the annual reports of non-US companies prepared under local accounting standards compare to reports of non-US companies prepared under US accounting standards?

6-4 How can users of international financial statements reconcile accounting differences and overcome other difficulties encountered in analyzing international financial statements?

6-5 How can users of international financial statements use capital market-generated information?

IV. RESEARCH DESIGN

The basic approach for each of these chapters (2 through 6) was to develop relevant research questions, identify necessary information, select an appropriate sample of companies to study, extract data, build a chapter-specific database, analyze the data, and then draw conclusions.

Chapters 2 through 6 are based on the following data sources:

1. The Worldscope Database (jointly developed by CIFAR and Wright Investors' Service, Bridgeport, CT)

   This database includes country-specific data on 32 accounting policy variables, extensive footnotes and over 200 financial variables for approximately 5,000 companies in 24 countries.

2. Annual reports of selected companies from CIFAR's International Annual Reports Collection of 10,000 companies worldwide

3. CIFAR's previous work on projects undertaken with several major investment and financial organizations, which involved a global comparison of accounting differences in major industries

Since each chapter had a different focus and scope, the sample of companies used in Chapters 2 through 6 was modified appropriately. A more complete discussion of the research design is provided in each chapter.

Table 1-1 provides a list of the countries examined in Chapters 2 through 5. Though we focused on 24 countries for each of the chapters in our study of international accounting trends, several countries were excluded from Chapters 4 and 5 in cases where there were not enough companies to draw meaningful conclusions.

TABLE 1-1 COUNTRY COVERAGE FOR INTERNATIONAL ACCOUNTING TRENDS					
	Chapter 2	Chapter 3	Chapter 4		Chapter 5
			Accounting Standards/ Financial Reporting		
Country	Accounting Standards	Financial Reporting Practices	Banks	Insurance	Interim Reports
Australia	Y	Y	Y	Y	Y
Austria	Y	Y	Y	Y	N
Belgium	Y	Y	Y	Y	N
Canada	Y	Y	Y	Y	Y
Denmark	Y	Y	Y	Y	Y
Finland	Y	Y	Y	Y	Y
France	Y	Y	Y	Y	Y
Germany, West	Y	Y	Y	Y	Y
Hong Kong	Y	Y	Y	Y	Y
Italy	Y	Y	Y	Y	Y
Japan	Y	Y	Y	Y	Y
Korea, South	Y	Y	Y	Y	N
Malaysia	Y	Y	Y	Y	Y
Mexico	Y	Y	N	N	N
Netherlands	Y	Y	Y	Y	Y
New Zealand	Y	Y	N	N	Y
Norway	Y	Y	Y	Y	Y
Singapore	Y	Y	Y	Y	Y
South Africa	Y	Y	Y	Y	Y
Spain	Y	Y	Y	Y	Y
Sweden	Y	Y	Y	Y	Y
Switzerland	Y	Y	Y	Y	Y
United Kingdom	Y	Y	Y	Y	Y
United States	Y	Y	Y	Y	Y

KEY:

Y = included
N = not included

V. RESEARCH DESIGN LIMITATIONS

A project of this magnitude required considerable data collection, quality control and analysis. Several limitations need to be identified:

1. Country Coverage

   Our focus in the "International Accounting Trends" section has been on 24 countries selected on the basis of data availability, interest by international users in companies from capital markets in these countries and the research expertise of the CIFAR team.

   We hope to include other countries, primarily ones in the emerging capital markets, in the next edition of this study, scheduled for publication in October 1990.

2. Development of Research Design

   With varied sources and a large quantity of data involved, it was necessary to divide the project into chapters. This made the overall project more manageable but necessitated the selection of a set of companies for each chapter adequate to address the research questions at hand.

   Though the company selection was always done from the same pool of 10,000 leading companies worldwide, the total number of companies utilized varied between chapters. While in some cases we used a very large sample of companies and in others we used a smaller subset of companies, we are confident that in each case the sample of companies utilized is sufficient to identify country norms for the research questions addressed.

3. Analysis Techniques

   There is a distinct difference in the level of statistical analysis between the "International Accounting Trends" (Chapters 1 through 7) and "International Auditing Trends" (Chapters 8 through 14) sections.

   "International Accounting Trends" required more qualitative analysis as differences between groups of companies or countries were not apparent. Furthermore, accounting differences between industrial and financial companies, between annual and interim reports, and between annual reports for shareholders and government filings were not always clear. In many instances, the necessary information was simply not disclosed in the annual reports. Definitive analysis was rather difficult; therefore, the practices were categorized into the broad groups of 80-100%, 40-80%, or minority practice.

   On the other hand, the research questions addressed in "International Auditing Trends" were more readily answered without the use of such a broad range of data. We were able to build a data set on auditors and clients, offices and partners of the 16 leading international accounting firms, collect data on audit fees from annual reports in nine countries, and review auditors' reports for attributes we were interested in analyzing. Given the nature of quantitative data, the statistical analysis and conclusions are more precise in this section.

These limitations notwithstanding, we believe the study will benefit preparers, auditors, users and researchers of international financial statements.

VI. BENEFITS OF THE STUDY (CHAPTERS 2 THROUGH 7)

The study will benefit potential users by:

- Analyzing global accounting standards presently in use both in the industrial and financial sectors
- Identifying those standards which are not widely comparable by country and industry
- Analyzing worldwide trends across countries in financial statement disclosures
- Analyzing the contents of interim financial statements
- Identifying the difficulties involved in analyzing international financial statements and providing suggestions on how to overcome these difficulties

VII. POTENTIAL USERS (CHAPTERS 2 THROUGH 7)

- Controllers and financial executives of corporations worldwide
- Students and researchers studying international accounting trends
- Stock exchanges and other organizations responsible for setting accounting requirements
- Money managers investing in companies worldwide
- Lending officers of commercial banks worldwide
- Partners and managers of international accounting firms

VIII. APPENDICES: A THROUGH D

With the growth of international markets for goods, services, and capital, many companies may find it advantageous to prepare financial statements for use outside the domestic market. To assist such companies, the CIFAR project staff has examined hundreds of annual reports worldwide to identify the most appropriate reporting practices. From this analysis, guidelines have been developed to assist interested users in the development of annual reports for an international audience.

The four appendices at the end of the study address the following topics:

Appendix A provides guidelines for the preparation of an annual report for a multinational industrial company.

Appendix B provides guidelines for the preparation of an annual report for a multinational commercial bank.

Appendix C provides guidelines for the preparation of an annual report for a multinational insurance company.

Appendix D provides an accounting lexicon in eight languages (Dutch, French, German, Italian, Korean, Japanese, Portuguese and Spanish) with English translation.

CHAPTER 2

ACCOUNTING STANDARDS IN PRACTICE IN ANNUAL REPORTS OF INDUSTRIAL COMPANIES IN 24 COUNTRIES

Table of Contents

I. INTRODUCTION

The CIFAR project staff's discussions with users of international financial statements (i.e., portfolio managers, lenders, corporate strategic planners, investment bankers and consultants) have led to the conclusion that there is a need for a synthesis of the accounting standards currently in practice worldwide. Such a synthesis should also include an identification of key accounting differences. This will assist users in reconciling these differences in order to make accurate assessments and comparisons of international companies' performances.

A comprehensive review of the accounting standards in practice internationally is useful for the following reasons:

- Accounting standards published by national, regional and international organizations serve as minimum requirements and in many instances provide several alternative methods from which to choose.

- Various publications by international accounting firms include information on country-specific accounting standards, but a global analysis of a comprehensive list of standards is not provided.

- Analysis of a large number of annual reports from various countries provides a country norm of accounting methods based on actual practices.

II. RESEARCH OBJECTIVES

2-1 What are the key accounting standards followed by the leading industrial corporations worldwide?

2-2 What are the implications of the international differences in accounting standards for the valuation of assets and income determination of the industrial companies being analyzed?

2-3 To what extent has the international harmonization of accounting standards followed by the industrial companies been achieved?

III. RESEARCH DESIGN

This chapter presents information collected on accounting standards in use by industrial companies in 24 countries. Current practices, summarized by country, were analyzed through a series of questions regarding key accounting standards. For each question, the single practice which best reflects the predominant treatment (that employed by 80-100% of the companies) in each country is given. A second category of 40-80% of companies following a given practice was also used. If no disclosures were made in the annual reports or if a particular method was a minority practice, the corresponding response is indicated.

Exhibit 2-1 provides the list of questions used to summarize our findings.

Data were extracted from the Worldscope Database as well as from annual reports in the CIFAR library. Table 2-1 provides the total number of companies included by country and industry.

IV. FINDINGS

Empirical findings on accounting standards in practice by country are presented in Exhibit 2-2.

Key accounting differences which have an impact on valuation of assets and income determination internationally are:

A. Cost Basis of Financial Statements

The financial statements of most companies are based, in one way or another, on the historical cost of itemized assets. Among companies in Canada, Japan, South Africa, the US, and several European countries (Austria, West Germany and Switzerland) the basis is historical cost entirely. Those in Malaysia, the Netherlands, New Zealand, Norway, Singapore, Spain, Sweden and the UK use historical cost with price level adjustments. Companies in Australia, Belgium, Denmark, Finland, France, Hong Kong, Italy and South Korea base statements on historical cost with some revaluation. The financial statements of companies in Mexico are based on current cost data entirely.

B. Consolidation Practices

In a little less than half of the countries studied, including Australia, Canada, Hong Kong, Malaysia, the Netherlands, Singapore, South Africa, Sweden, the UK and the US, between 80 and 100% of the companies studied issue consolidated statements. In Japan, Mexico, New Zealand and much of Europe (Denmark, Finland, France, West Germany, Norway and Switzerland), 40-80% of the companies consolidate, and in Austria, Belgium, Italy, South Korea and Spain, a minority consolidate.

C. Accounting Methods for Long-Term Investments

Long-term investments of between 20 and 50% (of equity) are usually accounted for by either the cost method or the equity method. The former is most widely used by companies in Austria, Finland, West Germany and South Korea, the latter in Australia, Canada, Denmark, France, Mexico, the Netherlands, New Zealand, Singapore, South Africa, the UK and the US (in Australia such investments are often partially consolidated). Either the cost or equity method is used by companies in Belgium, Hong Kong, Italy, Japan, Malaysia, Norway, Spain, Sweden and Switzerland.

TABLE 2-1

NUMBER OF COMPANIES INCLUDED BY COUNTRY & INDUSTRY

Country	Number of Companies
Australia	48
Austria	16
Belgium	33
Canada	151
Denmark	28
Finland	32
France	126
Germany, West	151
Hong Kong	20
Italy	36
Japan	300
Korea, South	14
Malaysia	25
Mexico	15
Netherlands	42
New Zealand	20
Norway	28
Singapore	18
South Africa	60
Spain	25
Sweden	63
Switzerland	25
United Kingdom	232
United States	1,270
Total	2,778

Industry	Number of Companies
Consumer Goods	
-Apparel/Textiles	91
-Food & Beverage	210
-Pharmaceuticals/ Cosmetics	106
-Printing/Publishing	72
-Hotels & Recreation	90
-Retailing	260
-Tobacco	24
Capital Goods	
-Aerospace	26
-Automotive	78
-Construction	246
-Electronics	345
-Machinery & Equipment	162
-Metal Producers	240
Basic Industry	
-Chemicals	184
-Petroleum/Mining	184
-Paper	110
Other Industries	
-Diversified	117
-Miscellaneous Industries	233
Total	2,778

D. Accounting for Goodwill

In the majority of countries (including Japan, South Korea, all of North America and most of Europe), goodwill is capitalized and amortized by most companies. In the Netherlands, Switzerland and the majority of the Commonwealth, it is more common for companies to take goodwill to reserves, although they occasionally use other methods. While companies in Hong Kong, Malaysia, the Netherlands, Singapore, Switzerland and the UK almost exclusively take goodwill to reserves, in Australia it might also be capitalized, or in New Zealand and South Africa expensed. In France, companies usually either capitalize or expense goodwill.

E. Inventory Valuation Methods

The two most widely used methods for valuation of inventories are the first-in, first-out (FIFO) and average cost methods. The former is used by the overwhelming majority of companies in over three-quarters of the countries studied. These include companies in France, the Netherlands, South Africa, the Commonwealth (excluding Singapore), North America and Scandinavia. The average cost method is used by companies in West Germany, Japan, South Korea, Singapore, Spain and Switzerland. In Mexico a majority of companies use the replacement cost method.

F. Depreciation Method

A majority of companies in West Germany use mixed depreciation methods. Those in Japan and South Korea use accelerated depreciation. Most companies in all other countries studied use the straight-line method of depreciation.

G. Allowance of Excess Depreciation

Approximately one-half of the countries studied allow companies to carry excess depreciation of fixed assets while the other half prohibits it. Excess depreciation for financial reporting purposes is allowed in Austria, Belgium, Denmark, Finland, France, West Germany, South Korea, Mexico, the Netherlands, Norway, South Africa and Sweden. Excess depreciation is not allowed for financial reporting purposes in Australia, Hong Kong, Italy, Japan, Malaysia, New Zealand, Singapore, Spain, Switzerland, the UK or the US.

H. Foreign Currency Translation Method

Companies in most countries use the current rate method or its equivalent to translate financial statements from foreign to local currency. Only in Japan (where a majority use the current/non-current method) and West Germany (where most companies use the temporal method) is the current method not predominant.

I. Accounting for Foreign Currency Translation Gains and Losses

The majority of companies in slightly over half of the countries studied disclose foreign currency translation gains or losses on the income statement and/or in shareholders' equity. This practice is followed by companies in Australia, Belgium, Denmark, France, West Germany, Hong Kong, the Netherlands, New Zealand, South Africa, Sweden, the UK and the US. The second most widely used method is that of either taking the gains or losses to income or deferring them. This method is practiced by companies in Canada, Finland, Italy, Japan, South Korea and Spain. In Malaysia, Norway and Singapore, gains and losses are taken to the income statement and in Switzerland to shareholders' equity.

J. Deferral of Recorded Taxes

When accounting income is not equal to taxable income, deferred taxes are recorded by companies in Australia, Canada, Denmark, France, Hong Kong, Malaysia, Mexico, the Netherlands, New Zealand, Singapore, South Africa, the UK and the US. They are not recorded by companies in Austria, Belgium, Finland, West Germany, Italy, Japan, South Korea, Norway, Spain, Sweden or Switzerland.

K. Use of Discretionary Reserves

Companies make use of discretionary reserves in about one-third of the countries studied (all of which are in Europe), but do not use them in the other two-thirds.

L. Inclusion of Pension Fund Assets and Liabilities on the Company Balance Sheet

Companies in Belgium, Canada, France, Hong Kong, Italy, New Zealand, Norway, South Africa, Spain, the UK and the US do not carry pension fund assets and liabilities on the balance sheet, while those in Australia, Austria, West Germany, South Korea, Malaysia, Mexico, Singapore and Sweden do.

M. Revaluation of Assets

Most countries permit companies to revalue their assets. The exceptions are Japan, South Africa and the US.

V. SUMMARY AND CONCLUSIONS

In this chapter, differences and similarities in international accounting standards gleaned from an examination of annual reports of industrial companies in 24 countries were presented. Our analysis focused on the differences in key accounting standards in use as they affect valuation of assets and liabilities and income determination. The following key differences have been identified:

- Not all subsidiaries of which the parent company owns 50% or more are consistently consolidated, thus giving an incomplete picture of the company's performance. Furthermore, different methods of accounting for long-term investments make net income less comparable.

- Inventory valuation methods vary, affecting the cost of goods sold figure and inventory values.

- The methods used in depreciating fixed assets render depreciation expenses and net fixed assets noncomparable, particularly when the economic life of an asset is not considered and tax laws allow much faster depreciation.

- Differing approaches to the revaluation of fixed assets for price changes affect depreciation expenses, net fixed assets and shareholders' equity (since revaluation reserves are usually reported in the shareholders' equity section).

- Local rules allowing discretionary or general purpose reserves reduce the comparableness of the true performances of companies internationally.

- Due to differences in foreign currency translation methods and the treatment of resulting gains or losses, net income and affected balance sheet items are not comparable.

As was mentioned before, the international user's primary concerns regarding the use of international financial statements lie primarily in how reporting and accounting differences affect the valuation of assets and liabilities and the determination of income and expenses. But due to variations in the concepts of accounting standards internationally (i.e., tax base vs. capital market oriented) as well as the process itself (accounting standards set by professional accountants, stock exchange authorities, government agencies or a combination thereof), users cannot expect accounting standards worldwide to be uniform. Nevertheless, users would like to compare financial statements of companies from various countries, in global industries at least, so that a relative ranking of individual company performances can be derived.

We recommend that preparers of annual reports for industrial companies worldwide provide additional details in their financial statements to better facilitate analysis of international financial statements. In Chapter 6 of this study, "Analyzing International Annual Reports: Issues and Answers", we have provided suggestions to users on how to compensate for international accounting differences.

EXHIBIT 2-1

QUESTIONS AND ANSWERS FOR ACCOUNTING STANDARDS IN PRACTICE

Q1 FINANCIAL STATEMENTS COST BASIS

1 HISTORICAL COST ENTIRELY
2 HIST COST W/PRICE LEVEL ADJST
3 HIST COST W/CURR COST DATA
4 CURRENT COST DATA ENTIRELY
5 HIST COST WITH SOME REVALUATION
9 NOT DISCLOSED

Q2 CONSOLIDATED INFORMATION PROVIDED BY

1 80-100%
2 40-80%
3 MINORITY
9 NOT DISCLOSED

Q3 CONSOLIDATION PRACTICES FOR SUBSIDIARIES BY MAJORITY

1 ALL SUBSIDIARIES CONSOLIDATED
2 DOMESTIC CONS., OTHERS AT COST
3 DOMESTIC CONS., OTHERS AT EQUITY
4 FOREIGN CONS., OTHERS AT COST
5 FOREIGN CONS., OTHERS AT EQUITY
6 NO CONSOLIDATION
9 NOT DISCLOSED

Q4 INTER-COMPANY ACCOUNTS

1 ELIMINATED UPON CONSOLIDATION
2 NOT ELIMINATED
3 NOT DETERMINABLE
9 NOT DISCLOSED

Q5 ACCTG. METHOD FOR LONG-TERM INV'TS BETW 20-50% EQUITY

1 COST METHOD
2 EQUITY METHOD
3 COST OR EQUITY METHOD
4 EQUITY; PARTIALLY CONSOLIDATED
9 NOT DISCLOSED

Q6 CONSOLIDATION OF 20%<LT INV'T<50% DEPENDING ON INFLUENCE

1 YES, BY 80-100%
2 YES, BY 40-80%
3 MINORITY PRACTICE
4 NOT DONE
9 NOT DISCLOSED

Q7 ACCTG. METHOD FOR LONG-TERM INV'TS LESS THAN 20% OF EQUITY

1 COST METHOD
2 EQUITY METHOD
3 LOWER OF COST OR INTRINSIC VAL
4 MARKET
5 COST AND/OR EQUITY
9 NOT DISCLOSED

Q8 MARKETABLE SECURITIES CLASSIFIED BY MAJORITY AT

1 LOWER OF COST OR MARKET
2 MARKET VALUE
3 HISTORICAL COST
4 AVERAGE
5 COST WITH REVALUATION
9 NOT DISCLOSED

Q9 ACCOUNTING METHODS FOR ACQUISITIONS

1 POOLING METHOD BY 80-100%
2 POOLING METHOD BY 40-80%
3 PURCHASE METHOD BY 80-100%
4 PURCHASE METHOD BY 40-80%
5 MIXED METHODS BY 80-100%
6 MIXED METHODS BY 40-80%
7 METHOD DISCLOSED BY MINORITY
9 NOT DISCLOSED

Q10 ACCOUNTING FOR GOODWILL

1 CAPITALIZED & AMORTIZED
2 CAPITALIZED PERMANENTLY
3 EXPENSED
4 TAKEN TO RESERVES
5 AMORTIZED/TAKEN TO RESERVES
6 EXPENSED/TAKEN TO RESERVES
7 CAPITALIZED/TAKEN TO RESERVES
8 CAPITALIZED/EXPENSED
9 NOT DISCLOSED

Q11 ACCOUNTING FOR OTHER INTANGIBLES

1 AMORTIZED
2 CAPITALIZED
3 EXPENSED
4 TAKEN TO RESERVES
9 NOT DISCLOSED

Q12 MINORITY INTEREST EFFECT ON BALANCE SHEET

1 INCLUDED IN OWNERS' EQUITY
2 EXCLUDED FROM OWNERS' EQUITY
3 REPORTED ELSEWHERE ON B/S
9 NOT SPECIFIED

Q13 MINORITY INTEREST EFFECT IN INCOME STATEMENT

1 BEFORE BOTTOM LINE ON I/S
2 IN RET. EARN. AFTER BOTTOM LINE
3 NOT SPECIFIED IN I/S
9 NOT DISCLOSED

Q14 TREASURY STOCK EXISTENCE ALLOWED

1 YES
2 NO
3 MINORITY PRACTICE
9 NOT DISCLOSED

Q15 TREASURY STOCK GAINS & LOSSES

1 TAKEN TO INCOME STATEMENT
2 TAKEN TO SHAREHOLDERS' EQUITY
3 CAPITALIZED
8 NOT APPLICABLE
9 NOT DISCLOSED

Q16 TREASURY STOCK POSITION ON BALANCE SHEET

1 DEDUCTED FROM OWNERS' EQUITY
2 AS A PART OF L/T INVESTMENTS
3 AS A PART OF CURRENT ASSETS
4 AS A PART OF OTHER ASSETS
8 NOT APPLICABLE
9 NOT DISCLOSED

Q17 PROVISION MADE FOR UNCOLLECTIBLE ACCOUNTS

1 YES, AS DEDUCTION ON ASSET SIDE
2 YES, AS A CONTRA ITEM
3 NO PROVISION MADE
4 MIXED
9 NOT DISCLOSED

Q18 INVENTORY COSTING METHOD UTILIZED BY MAJORITY

1 FIFO
2 LIFO
3 AVERAGE
4 MIXED
5 REPLACEMENT COST
6 LAST PURCHASE PRICE PAID
7 A METHOD ADJUSTED BY INFLATION
8 OTHER METHOD
9 NOT DISCLOSED

Q19 MANUFACTURING OVERHEAD INCLUDED IN YEAR-END INVENTORY

1 PREDOMINANT PRACTICE
2 NOT INCLUDED IN INVENTORY
9 NOT DISCLOSED

Q20 YEAR-END INVENTORY CLASSIFIED AT

1 LOWER OF COST OR MARKET
2 CURRENT MARKET VALUE
3 HISTORICAL COST
4 EITHER HIST COST OR LCM
5 OTHER METHOD
9 NOT DISCLOSED

Q21 DEPRECIATION METHOD

1 STRAIGHT LINE
2 ACCELERATED
3 MIXED DEPRECIATION METHODS
4 SINKING FUND
5 UNIT OF PRODUCTION
6 NO DEPRECIATION COMPUTED
9 NOT DISCLOSED

Q22 ACCUMULATED DEPRECIATION DISCLOSED

1 NETTED ABAINST F/A DR SIDE B/S
2 NETTED AGAINST F/A OUTSIDE B/S
3 AS A CONTRA ITEM ON LIAB. SIDE
4 NO MAJORITY
9 NOT DISCLOSED

Q23 EXCESS DEPRECIATION

1 ALLOWED
2 NOT ALLOWED
9 NOT DISCLOSED

Q24 FOREIGN CURRENCY TRANSLATION METHOD

1 TEMPORAL
2 CURRENT RATE METHOD
3 MIXED
4 MONETARY/NON-MONETARY
5 CURRENT/NON-CURRENT
9 NOT DISCLOSED

Q25 ACCOUNTING FOR FOREIGN CURRENCY TRANSLATION GAINS OR LOSSES

1 TAKEN TO INCOME STATEMENT
2 TAKEN TO OWNERS' EQUITY
3 DEFERRED
4 TAKEN TO INCOME &/OR DEFERRED
5 TAKEN TO I/S &/OR OWNERS' EQ.
9 NOT DISCLOSED

Q26 RESEARCH & DEVELOPMENT COSTS

1 EXPENSED CURRENTLY
2 CAPITALIZED & AMORTIZED LATER
3 EXPENSED & CAPITALIZED LATER
4 MIXED
9 NOT DISCLOSED

Q27 DEFERRED TAXES RECORDED WHEN ACCOUNTING INCOME IS NOT EQUAL TO TAXABLE INCOME

1 YES
2 NO
3 NOT AVAILABLE
9 NOT DISCLOSED

Q28 ACCOUNTING FOR LONG-TERM FINANCIAL LEASES

1 CAPITALIZED
2 EXPENSED CURRENTLY
3 CAPITALIZED AND/OR EXPENSED
9 NOT DISCLOSED

Q29 CONTINGENT LIABILITIES DISCLOSED BY

1 80-100%
2 40-80%
3 MINORITY
9 NOT DISCLOSED

Q30 PREDOMINANT CONTINGENT LIABILITY REPORTED

1 LITIGATION
2 GUARANTEES/WARRANTIES
3 POLITICAL UNCERTAINTIES
4 UNFUNDED VESTED BENEFITS
5 GOVERNMENT LOANS
6 LEASES
7 OTHER
9 NOT DISCLOSED

Q31 DISCRETIONARY/NON-EQUITY RESERVES

1 GENERAL PURPOSE RESERVES EXOST
2 SOME SPECIFIC RESERVES EXIST
9 NO DISC/NON-EQTY RESERVES EXIST

Q32 PENSION EXPENSES ARE

1 PROVIDED REGULARLY
2 NOT PROVIDED REGULARLY
9 NOT DISCLOSED

Q33 PENSION FUNDS ARE OFF THE COMPANY'S B/S

1 YES
2 NO
3 NO MAJORITY
4 PARTIALLY FUNDED OUTSIDE
9 NOT DISCLOSED

Q34 EXPENSES FOR DISMISSAL INDEMNITIES RECORDED WHEN?

1 PAY AS YOU GO
2 ACCRUAL SET UP
9 NOT DISCLOSED

Q35 REVALUATION OF ACCOUNTS ALLOWED

1 YES
2 NO
9 NOT DISCLOSED

Q36 SUPPLEMENTARY CURRENT COST INFORMATION PRESENTED BY

1 80-100%
2 40-80%
3 MINORITY
9 NOT DISCLOSED

Accounting Standards in Practice in 24 Countries

NO.	ACCOUNTING & AUDITING ITEMS	Australia	Austria	Belgium
Q1	FINANCIAL STATEMENTS COST BASIS	HIST COST W/SOME REVALUATION	HISTORICAL COST ENTIRELY	HIST COST W/SOME REVALUATION
Q2	CONSOLIDATED INFORMATION PROVIDED BY	80-100%	MINORITY	MINORITY
Q3	CONSOLIDATION PRACTICES FOR MAJORITY-OWNED SUBSIDIARIES	ALL SUBSIDIARIES CONSOLIDATED	ALL SUBSIDIARIES CONSOLIDATED	ALL SUBSIDIARIES CONSOLIDATED
Q4	INTER-COMPANY ACCOUNTS	ELIMINATED UPON CONSOLIDATION	NOT DETERMINABLE	ELIMINATED UPON CONSOLIDATION
Q5	ACCTG. METHOD FOR LONG-TERM INV'TS BETW 20 - 50% OF EQUITY	EQUITY;PARTIALLY CONSOLIDATED	COST METHOD	COST OR EQUITY METHOD
Q6	CONSOLIDATION OF 20%<LT INV'T<50% DEPENDING ON INFLUENCE	MINORITY PRACTICE	NOT DONE	MINORITY PRACTICE
Q7	ACCTG. METHOD FOR LONG-TERM INV'TS LESS THAN 20% OF EQUITY	COST METHOD	COST METHOD	COST AND/OR EQUITY
Q8	MARKETABLE SECURITIES CLASSIFIED BY MAJORITY AT	LOWER OF COST OR MARKET	HISTORICAL COST	LOWER OF COST OR MARKET
Q9	ACCOUNTING METHOD FOR ACQUISITIONS	PURCHASE METHOD BY 80-100%	NOT DISCLOSED	PURCHASE METHOD BY 40-80%
Q10	ACCOUNTING FOR GOODWILL	CAPITALIZED/TAKEN TO RESERVES	CAPITALIZED & AMORTIZED	CAPITALIZED & AMORTIZED
Q11	ACCOUNTING FOR OTHER INTANGIBLES	AMORTIZED	AMORTIZED	AMORTIZED
Q12	MINORITY INTEREST EFFECT ON BALANCE SHEET	EXCLUDED FROM OWNERS' EQUITY	NOT SPECIFIED	EXCLUDED FROM OWNERS' EQUITY
Q13	MINORITY INTEREST EFFECT ON INCOME STATEMENT	BEFORE BOTTOM LINE ON I/S	NOT SPECIFIED ON I/S	BEFORE BOTTOM LINE ON I/S
Q14	TREASURY STOCK EXISTENCE ALLOWED	MINORITY PRACTICE	MINORITY PRACTICE	YES
Q15	TREASURY STOCK GAINS & LOSSES	NOT DISCLOSED	NOT DISCLOSED	NOT DISCLOSED
Q16	TREASURY STOCK POSITION ON BALANCE SHEET	DEDUCTED FROM OWNERS' EQUITY	AS A PART OF CURRENT ASSETS	AS A PART OF CURRENT ASSETS
Q17	PROVISION MADE FOR UNCOLLECTIBLE ACCOUNTS	YES,AS DEDUCTION ON ASSET SIDE	YES, AS A CONTRA ITEM	YES, AS A CONTRA ITEM
Q18	INVENTORY COSTING METHOD UTILIZED BY MAJORITY	FIFO	NOT DISCLOSED	MIXED
Q19	MANUFACTURING OVERHEAD INCLUDED IN YEAR-END INVENTORY	PREDOMINANT PRACTICE	PREDOMINANT PRACTICE	PREDOMINANT PRACTICE
Q20	YEAR-END INVENTORY CLASSIFIED AT	LOWER OF COST OR MARKET	LOWER OF COST OR MARKET	LOWER OF COST OR MARKET
Q21	DEPRECIATION METHOD	STRAIGHT LINE	STRAIGHT LINE	STRAIGHT LINE
Q22	ACCUMULATED DEPRECIATION DISCLOSED	NETTED AGAINST F/A OUTSIDE B/S	NETTED AGAINST F/A DR SIDE B/S	NETTED AGAINST F/A OUTSIDE B/S
Q23	EXCESS DEPRECIATION	NOT ALLOWED	ALLOWED	ALLOWED

Accounting Standards in Practice in 24 Countries

NO.	ACCOUNTING & AUDITING ITEMS	Australia	Austria	Belgium
Q24	FOREIGN CURRENCY TRANSLATION METHOD	CURRENT RATE METHOD	CURRENT RATE METHOD	CURRENT RATE METHOD
Q25	ACCOUNTING FOR FOREIGN CURRENCY TRANSLATION GAINS OR LOSSES	TAKEN TO I/S &/OR OWNERS' EQ.	NOT DISCLOSED	TAKEN TO I/S &/OR OWNERS' EQ.
Q26	RESEARCH & DEVELOPMENT COSTS	EXPENSED CURRENTLY	NOT DISCLOSED	EXPENSED CURRENTLY
Q27	DEFERRED TAXES RECORDED WHEN ACCOUNTING INCOME IS NOT EQUAL TO TAXABLE INCOME	YES	NO	NO
Q28	ACCOUNTING FOR LONG-TERM FINANCIAL LEASES	CAPITALIZED	NOT DISCLOSED	CAPITALIZED
Q29	CONTINGENT LIABILITIES DISCLOSED BY	40-80%	MINORITY	MINORITY
Q30	PREDOMINANT CONTINGENT LIABILITY REPORTED	GUARANTEES/WARRANTIES	GUARANTEES/WARRANTIES	GUARANTEES/WARRANTIES
Q31	DISCRETIONARY/NON-EQUITY RESERVES	SOME SPECIFIC RESERVES EXIST	GENERAL-PURPOSE RESERVES EXIST	GENERAL-PURPOSE RESERVES EXIST
Q32	PENSION EXPENSES ARE	PROVIDED REGULARLY	PROVIDED REGULARLY	PROVIDED REGULARLY
Q33	PENSION FUNDS ARE OFF THE COMPANY'S B/S	NO	NO	YES
Q34	EXPENSES FOR DISMISSAL INDEMNITIES RECORDED WHEN?	NOT DISCLOSED	PAY AS YOU GO	NOT DISCLOSED
Q35	REVALUATION OF ACCOUNTS ALLOWED	YES	YES	YES
Q36	SUPPLEMENTARY CURRENT COST INFORMATION PRESENTED BY	NOT DISCLOSED	NOT DISCLOSED	NOT DISCLOSED

Accounting Standards in Practice in 24 Countries

NO.	ACCOUNTING & AUDITING ITEMS	Canada	Denmark	Finland
Q1	FINANCIAL STATEMENTS COST BASIS	HISTORICAL COST ENTIRELY	HIST COST W/SOME REVALUATION	HIST COST W/SOME REVALUATION
Q2	CONSOLIDATED INFORMATION PROVIDED BY	80-100%	40-80%	40-80%
Q3	CONSOLIDATION PRACTICES FOR MAJORITY-OWNED SUBSIDIARIES	ALL SUBSIDIARIES CONSOLIDATED	ALL SUBSIDIARIES CONSOLIDATED	ALL SUBSIDIARIES CONSOLIDATED
Q4	INTER-COMPANY ACCOUNTS	ELIMINATED UPON CONSOLIDATION	ELIMINATED UPON CONSOLIDATION	ELIMINATED UPON CONSOLIDATION
Q5	ACCTG. METHOD FOR LONG-TERM INV'TS BETW 20 - 50% OF EQUITY	EQUITY METHOD	EQUITY METHOD	COST METHOD
Q6	CONSOLIDATION OF 20%<LT INV'T<50% DEPENDING ON INFLUENCE	MINORITY PRACTICE	MINORITY PRACTICE	NOT DONE
Q7	ACCTG. METHOD FOR LONG-TERM INV'TS LESS THAN 20% OF EQUITY	COST AND/OR EQUITY	COST AND/OR EQUITY	COST METHOD
Q8	MARKETABLE SECURITIES CLASSIFIED BY MAJORITY AT	HISTORICAL COST	MARKET VALUE	HISTORICAL COST
Q9	ACCOUNTING METHOD FOR ACQUISITIONS	PURCHASE METHOD BY 40-80%	PURCHASE METHOD BY 40-80%	PURCHASE METHOD BY 40-80%
Q10	ACCOUNTING FOR GOODWILL	CAPITALIZED & AMORTIZED	CAPITALIZED & AMORTIZED	CAPITALIZED & AMORTIZED
Q11	ACCOUNTING FOR OTHER INTANGIBLES	AMORTIZED	AMORTIZED	AMORTIZED
Q12	MINORITY INTEREST EFFECT ON BALANCE SHEET	EXCLUDED FROM OWNERS' EQUITY	EXCLUDED FROM OWNERS' EQUITY	EXCLUDED FROM OWNERS' EQUITY
Q13	MINORITY INTEREST EFFECT ON INCOME STATEMENT	BEFORE BOTTOM LINE ON I/S	BEFORE BOTTOM LINE ON I/S	BEFORE BOTTOM LINE ON I/S
Q14	TREASURY STOCK EXISTENCE ALLOWED	YES	YES	NOT DISCLOSED
Q15	TREASURY STOCK GAINS & LOSSES	TAKEN TO SHAREHOLDERS' EQUITY	NOT DISCLOSED	NOT APPLICABLE
Q16	TREASURY STOCK POSITION ON BALANCE SHEET	DEDUCTED FROM OWNERS' EQUITY	DEDUCTED FROM OWNERS' EQUITY	NOT APPLICABLE
Q17	PROVISION MADE FOR UNCOLLECTIBLE ACCOUNTS	YES,AS DEDUCTION ON ASSET SIDE	YES,AS DEDUCTION ON ASSET SIDE	YES, AS A CONTRA ITEM
Q18	INVENTORY COSTING METHOD UTILIZED BY MAJORITY	FIFO	FIFO	FIFO
Q19	MANUFACTURING OVERHEAD INCLUDED IN YEAR-END INVENTORY	PREDOMINANT PRACTICE	NOT INCLUDED IN INVENTORY	NOT INCLUDED IN INVENTORY
Q20	YEAR-END INVENTORY CLASSIFIED AT	LOWER OF COST OR MARKET	LOWER OF COST OR MARKET	LOWER OF COST OR MARKET
Q21	DEPRECIATION METHOD	STRAIGHT LINE	STRAIGHT LINE	STRAIGHT LINE
Q22	ACCUMULATED DEPRECIATION DISCLOSED	NETTED AGAINST F/A OUTSIDE B/S	NETTED AGAINST F/A OUTSIDE B/S	NETTED AGAINST F/A OUTSIDE B/S
Q23	EXCESS DEPRECIATION	NOT ALLOWED	ALLOWED	ALLOWED

Accounting Standards in Practice in 24 Countries

NO.	ACCOUNTING & AUDITING ITEMS	Canada	Denmark	Finland
Q24	FOREIGN CURRENCY TRANSLATION METHOD	CURRENT RATE METHOD	CURRENT RATE METHOD	CURRENT RATE METHOD
Q25	ACCOUNTING FOR FOREIGN CURRENCY TRANSLATION GAINS OR LOSSES	TAKEN TO INCOME &/OR DEFERRED	TAKEN TO I/S &/OR OWNERS' EQ.	TAKEN TO INCOME &/OR DEFERRED
Q26	RESEARCH & DEVELOPMENT COSTS	EXPENSED CURRENTLY	EXPENSED CURRENTLY	EXPENSED CURRENTLY
Q27	DEFERRED TAXES RECORDED WHEN ACCOUNTING INCOME IS NOT EQUAL TO TAXABLE INCOME	YES	YES	NO
Q28	ACCOUNTING FOR LONG-TERM FINANCIAL LEASES	CAPITALIZED	CAPITALIZED	CAPITALIZED
Q29	CONTINGENT LIABILITIES DISCLOSED BY	80-100%	40-80%	40-80%
Q30	PREDOMINANT CONTINGENT LIABILITY REPORTED	LITIGATION	GUARANTEES/WARRANTIES	GUARANTEES/WARRANTIES
Q31	DISCRETIONARY/NON-EQUITY RESERVES	NO DISC/NON-EQY RESERVES EXIST	GENERAL-PURPOSE RESERVES EXIST	GENERAL-PURPOSE RESERVES EXIST
Q32	PENSION EXPENSES ARE	PROVIDED REGULARLY	PROVIDED REGULARLY	PROVIDED REGULARLY
Q33	PENSION FUNDS ARE OFF THE COMPANY'S B/S	YES	NO MAJORITY	NO MAJORITY
Q34	EXPENSES FOR DISMISSAL INDEMNITIES RECORDED WHEN?	NOT DISCLOSED	NOT DISCLOSED	NOT DISCLOSED
Q35	REVALUATION OF ACCOUNTS ALLOWED	YES	YES	YES
Q36	SUPPLEMENTARY CURRENT COST INFORMATION PRESENTED BY	NOT DISCLOSED	NOT DISCLOSED	NOT DISCLOSED

Accounting Standards in Practice in 24 Countries

NO.	ACCOUNTING & AUDITING ITEMS	France	West Germany	Hong Kong
Q1	FINANCIAL STATEMENTS COST BASIS	HISTORICAL COST ENTIRELY	HISTORICAL COST ENTIRELY	HIST COST W/SOME REVALUATION
Q2	CONSOLIDATED INFORMATION PROVIDED BY	40-80%	40-80%	80-100%
Q3	CONSOLIDATION PRACTICES FOR MAJORITY-OWNED SUBSIDIARIES	ALL SUBSIDIARIES CONSOLIDATED	DOMESTIC CONS.,OTHERS AT COST	ALL SUBSIDIARIES CONSOLIDATED
Q4	INTER-COMPANY ACCOUNTS	ELIMINATED UPON CONSOLIDATION	ELIMINATED UPON CONSOLIDATION	ELIMINATED UPON CONSOLIDATION
Q5	ACCTG. METHOD FOR LONG-TERM INV'TS BETW 20 - 50% OF EQUITY	EQUITY METHOD	COST METHOD	COST OR EQUITY METHOD
Q6	CONSOLIDATION OF 20%<LT INV'T<50% DEPENDING ON INFLUENCE	MINORITY PRACTICE	NOT DONE	NOT DONE
Q7	ACCTG. METHOD FOR LONG-TERM INV'TS LESS THAN 20% OF EQUITY	COST METHOD	COST METHOD	COST METHOD
Q8	MARKETABLE SECURITIES CLASSIFIED BY MAJORITY AT	LOWER OF COST OR MARKET	LOWER OF COST OR MARKET	LOWER OF COST OR MARKET
Q9	ACCOUNTING METHOD FOR ACQUISITIONS	PURCHASE METHOD BY 40-80%	PURCHASE METHOD BY 80-100%	PURCHASE METHOD BY 40-80%
Q10	ACCOUNTING FOR GOODWILL	CAPITALIZED/EXPENSED	CAPITALIZED & AMORTIZED	TAKEN TO RESERVES
Q11	ACCOUNTING FOR OTHER INTANGIBLES	AMORTIZED	AMORTIZED	AMORTIZED
Q12	MINORITY INTEREST EFFECT ON BALANCE SHEET	EXCLUDED FROM OWNERS' EQUITY	REPORTED ELSEWHERE ON B/S	EXCLUDED FROM OWNERS' EQUITY
Q13	MINORITY INTEREST EFFECT ON INCOME STATEMENT	BEFORE BOTTOM LINE ON I/S	BEFORE BOTTOM LINE ON I/S	BEFORE BOTTOM LINE ON I/S
Q14	TREASURY STOCK EXISTENCE ALLOWED	MINORITY PRACTICE	MINORITY PRACTICE	NOT DISCLOSED
Q15	TREASURY STOCK GAINS & LOSSES	TAKEN TO SHAREHOLDERS' EQUITY	NOT DISCLOSED	NOT DISCLOSED
Q16	TREASURY STOCK POSITION ON BALANCE SHEET	DEDUCTED FROM OWNERS' EQUITY	AS A PART OF CURRENT ASSETS	NOT APPLICABLE
Q17	PROVISION MADE FOR UNCOLLECTIBLE ACCOUNTS	YES, AS A CONTRA ITEM	YES,AS DEDUCTION ON ASSET SIDE	YES,AS DEDUCTION ON ASSET SIDE
Q18	INVENTORY COSTING METHOD UTILIZED BY MAJORITY	FIFO	AVERAGE	FIFO
Q19	MANUFACTURING OVERHEAD INCLUDED IN YEAR-END INVENTORY	PREDOMINANT PRACTICE	PREDOMINANT PRACTICE	PREDOMINANT PRACTICE
Q20	YEAR-END INVENTORY CLASSIFIED AT	LOWER OF COST OR MARKET	LOWER OF COST OR MARKET	LOWER OF COST OR MARKET
Q21	DEPRECIATION METHOD	STRAIGHT LINE	MIXED DEPRECIATION METHODS	STRAIGHT LINE
Q22	ACCUMULATED DEPRECIATION DISCLOSED	NETTED AGAINST F/A DR SIDE B/S	NO MAJORITY	NETTED AGAINST F/A OUTSIDE B/S
Q23	EXCESS DEPRECIATION	ALLOWED	ALLOWED	NOT ALLOWED

Accounting Standards in Practice in 24 Countries

NO.	ACCOUNTING & AUDITING ITEMS	France	West Germany	Hong Kong
Q24	FOREIGN CURRENCY TRANSLATION METHOD	CURRENT RATE METHOD	TEMPORAL	CURRENT RATE METHOD
Q25	ACCOUNTING FOR FOREIGN CURRENCY TRANSLATION GAINS OR LOSSES	TAKEN TO I/S &/OR OWNERS' EQ.	TAKEN TO I/S &/OR OWNERS' EQ.	TAKEN TO I/S &/OR OWNERS' EQ.
Q26	RESEARCH & DEVELOPMENT COSTS	EXPENSED CURRENTLY	EXPENSED CURRENTLY	NOT DISCLOSED
Q27	DEFERRED TAXES RECORDED WHEN ACCOUNTING INCOME IS NOT EQUAL TO TAXABLE INCOME	YES	NO	YES
Q28	ACCOUNTING FOR LONG-TERM FINANCIAL LEASES	CAPITALIZED	CAPITALIZED	CAPITALIZED
Q29	CONTINGENT LIABILITIES DISCLOSED BY	40-80%	80-100%	40-80%
Q30	PREDOMINANT CONTINGENT LIABILITY REPORTED	GUARANTEES/WARRANTIES	GUARANTEES/WARRANTIES	GUARANTEES/WARRANTIES
Q31	DISCRETIONARY/NON-EQUITY RESERVES	GENERAL-PURPOSE RESERVES EXIST	GENERAL-PURPOSE RESERVES EXIST	SOME SPECIFIC RESERVES EXIST
Q32	PENSION EXPENSES ARE	PROVIDED REGULARLY	PROVIDED REGULARLY	PROVIDED REGULARLY
Q33	PENSION FUNDS ARE OFF THE COMPANY'S B/S	YES	NO	YES
Q34	EXPENSES FOR DISMISSAL INDEMNITIES RECORDED WHEN?	PAY AS YOU GO	NOT DISCLOSED	PAY AS YOU GO
Q35	REVALUATION OF ACCOUNTS ALLOWED	YES	YES	YES
Q36	SUPPLEMENTARY CURRENT COST INFORMATION PRESENTED BY	NOT DISCLOSED	NOT DISCLOSED	NOT DISCLOSED

Accounting Standards in Practice in 24 Countries

NO.	ACCOUNTING & AUDITING ITEMS	Italy	Japan	South Korea
Q1	FINANCIAL STATEMENTS COST BASIS	HIST COST W/SOME REVALUATION	HISTORICAL COST ENTIRELY	HIST COST W/SOME REVALUATION
Q2	CONSOLIDATED INFORMATION PROVIDED BY	MINORITY	40-80%	MINORITY
Q3	CONSOLIDATION PRACTICES FOR MAJORITY-OWNED SUBSIDIARIES	ALL SUBSIDIARIES CONSOLIDATED	DOMESTIC CONS.,OTHERS AT COST	DOMESTIC CONS.,OTHERS AT COST
Q4	INTER-COMPANY ACCOUNTS	ELIMINATED UPON CONSOLIDATION	ELIMINATED UPON CONSOLIDATION	NOT DETERMINABLE
Q5	ACCTG. METHOD FOR LONG-TERM INV'TS BETW 20 - 50% OF EQUITY	COST OR EQUITY METHOD	COST OR EQUITY METHOD	COST METHOD
Q6	CONSOLIDATION OF 20%<LT INV'T<50% DEPENDING ON INFLUENCE	MINORITY PRACTICE	MINORITY PRACTICE	NOT DONE
Q7	ACCTG. METHOD FOR LONG-TERM INV'TS LESS THAN 20% OF EQUITY	COST METHOD	COST METHOD	COST METHOD
Q8	MARKETABLE SECURITIES CLASSIFIED BY MAJORITY AT	LOWER OF COST OR MARKET	LOWER OF COST OR MARKET	LOWER OF COST OR MARKET
Q9	ACCOUNTING METHOD FOR ACQUISITIONS	PURCHASE METHOD BY 40-80%	PURCHASE METHOD BY 40-80%	PURCHASE METHOD BY 80-100%
Q10	ACCOUNTING FOR GOODWILL	CAPITALIZED & AMORTIZED	CAPITALIZED & AMORTIZED	CAPITALIZED & AMORTIZED
Q11	ACCOUNTING FOR OTHER INTANGIBLES	AMORTIZED	AMORTIZED	AMORTIZED
Q12	MINORITY INTEREST EFFECT ON BALANCE SHEET	EXCLUDED FROM OWNERS' EQUITY	EXCLUDED FROM OWNERS' EQUITY	EXCLUDED FROM OWNERS' EQUITY
Q13	MINORITY INTEREST EFFECT ON INCOME STATEMENT	BEFORE BOTTOM LINE ON I/S	BEFORE BOTTOM LINE ON I/S	BEFORE BOTTOM LINE ON I/S
Q14	TREASURY STOCK EXISTENCE ALLOWED	YES	YES	YES
Q15	TREASURY STOCK GAINS & LOSSES	NOT DISCLOSED	NOT DISCLOSED	NOT DISCLOSED
Q16	TREASURY STOCK POSITION ON BALANCE SHEET	DEDUCTED FROM OWNERS' EQUITY	DEDUCTED FROM OWNERS' EQUITY	AS A PART OF CURRENT ASSETS
Q17	PROVISION MADE FOR UNCOLLECTIBLE ACCOUNTS	YES, AS A CONTRA ITEM	YES, AS A CONTRA ITEM	YES, AS A CONTRA ITEM
Q18	INVENTORY COSTING METHOD UTILIZED BY MAJORITY	MIXED	AVERAGE	AVERAGE
Q19	MANUFACTURING OVERHEAD INCLUDED IN YEAR-END INVENTORY	PREDOMINANT PRACTICE	PREDOMINANT PRACTICE	PREDOMINANT PRACTICE
Q20	YEAR-END INVENTORY CLASSIFIED AT	LOWER OF COST OR MARKET	LOWER OF COST OR MARKET	LOWER OF COST OR MARKET
Q21	DEPRECIATION METHOD	STRAIGHT LINE	ACCELERATED	ACCELERATED
Q22	ACCUMULATED DEPRECIATION DISCLOSED	AS A CONTRA ITEM ON LIAB. SIDE	NETTED AGAINST F/A DR SIDE B/S	NETTED AGAINST F/A DR SIDE B/S
Q23	EXCESS DEPRECIATION	NOT ALLOWED	NOT ALLOWED	ALLOWED

Accounting Standards in Practice in 24 Countries

NO.	ACCOUNTING & AUDITING ITEMS	Italy	Japan	South Korea
Q24	FOREIGN CURRENCY TRANSLATION METHOD	CURRENT RATE METHOD	CURRENT/NON-CURRENT	NOT DISCLOSED
Q25	ACCOUNTING FOR FOREIGN CURRENCY TRANSLATION GAINS OR LOSSES	TAKEN TO INCOME &/OR DEFERRED	TAKEN TO INCOME &/OR DEFERRED	TAKEN TO INCOME &/OR DEFERRED
Q26	RESEARCH & DEVELOPMENT COSTS	EXPENSED CURRENTLY	EXPENSED CURRENTLY	EXPENSED CURRENTLY
Q27	DEFERRED TAXES RECORDED WHEN ACCOUNTING INCOME IS NOT EQUAL TO TAXABLE INCOME	NO	NO	NO
Q28	ACCOUNTING FOR LONG-TERM FINANCIAL LEASES	NOT DISCLOSED	CAPITALIZED	NOT DISCLOSED
Q29	CONTINGENT LIABILITIES DISCLOSED BY	MINORITY	40-80%	MINORITY
Q30	PREDOMINANT CONTINGENT LIABILITY REPORTED	GUARANTEES/WARRANTIES	GUARANTEES/WARRANTIES	GUARANTEES/WARRANTIES
Q31	DISCRETIONARY/NON-EQUITY RESERVES	GENERAL-PURPOSE RESERVES EXIST	SOME SPECIFIC RESERVES EXIST	SOME SPECIFIC RESERVES EXIST
Q32	PENSION EXPENSES ARE	PROVIDED REGULARLY	PROVIDED REGULARLY	PROVIDED REGULARLY
Q33	PENSION FUNDS ARE OFF THE COMPANY'S B/S	YES	PARTIALLY FUNDED OUTSIDE	NO
Q34	EXPENSES FOR DISMISSAL INDEMNITIES RECORDED WHEN?	PAY AS YOU GO	ACCRUAL SET UP	NOT DISCLOSED
Q35	REVALUATION OF ACCOUNTS ALLOWED	YES	NO	YES
Q36	SUPPLEMENTARY CURRENT COST INFORMATION PRESENTED BY	NOT DISCLOSED	NOT DISCLOSED	NOT DISCLOSED

Accounting Standards in Practice in 24 Countries

NO.	ACCOUNTING & AUDITING ITEMS	Malaysia	Mexico	Netherlands
Q1	FINANCIAL STATEMENTS COST BASIS	HIST COST W/PRICE LEVEL ADJST	CURRENT COST DATA ENTIRELY	HIST COST W/PRICE LEVEL ADJST
Q2	CONSOLIDATED INFORMATION PROVIDED BY	80-100%	40-80%	80-100%
Q3	CONSOLIDATION PRACTICES FOR MAJORITY-OWNED SUBSIDIARIES	ALL SUBSIDIARIES CONSOLIDATED	ALL SUBSIDIARIES CONSOLIDATED	ALL SUBSIDIARIES CONSOLIDATED
Q4	INTER-COMPANY ACCOUNTS	ELIMINATED UPON CONSOLIDATION	ELIMINATED UPON CONSOLIDATION	ELIMINATED UPON CONSOLIDATION
Q5	ACCTG. METHOD FOR LONG-TERM INV'TS BETW 20 - 50% OF EQUITY	COST OR EQUITY METHOD	EQUITY METHOD	EQUITY METHOD
Q6	CONSOLIDATION OF 20%<LT INV'T<50% DEPENDING ON INFLUENCE	NOT DONE	NOT DONE	MINORITY PRACTICE
Q7	ACCTG. METHOD FOR LONG-TERM INV'TS LESS THAN 20% OF EQUITY	COST METHOD	COST METHOD	COST AND/OR EQUITY
Q8	MARKETABLE SECURITIES CLASSIFIED BY MAJORITY AT	LOWER OF COST OR MARKET	HISTORICAL COST	LOWER OF COST OR MARKET
Q9	ACCOUNTING METHOD FOR ACQUISITIONS	PURCHASE METHOD BY 40-80%	PURCHASE METHOD BY 40-80%	PURCHASE METHOD BY 40-80%
Q10	ACCOUNTING FOR GOODWILL	TAKEN TO RESERVES	CAPITALIZED & AMORTIZED	TAKEN TO RESERVES
Q11	ACCOUNTING FOR OTHER INTANGIBLES	AMORTIZED	AMORTIZED	AMORTIZED
Q12	MINORITY INTEREST EFFECT ON BALANCE SHEET	EXCLUDED FROM OWNERS' EQUITY	EXCLUDED FROM OWNERS' EQUITY	EXCLUDED FROM OWNERS' EQUITY
Q13	MINORITY INTEREST EFFECT ON INCOME STATEMENT	BEFORE BOTTOM LINE ON I/S	BEFORE BOTTOM LINE ON I/S	BEFORE BOTTOM LINE ON I/S
Q14	TREASURY STOCK EXISTENCE ALLOWED	YES	NOT DISCLOSED	MINORITY PRACTICE
Q15	TREASURY STOCK GAINS & LOSSES	NOT DISCLOSED	NOT APPLICABLE	TAKEN TO SHAREHOLDERS' EQUITY
Q16	TREASURY STOCK POSITION ON BALANCE SHEET	DEDUCTED FROM OWNERS' EQUITY	NOT APPLICABLE	DEDUCTED FROM OWNERS' EQUITY
Q17	PROVISION MADE FOR UNCOLLECTIBLE ACCOUNTS	YES,AS DEDUCTION ON ASSET SIDE	YES,AS DEDUCTION ON ASSET SIDE	YES,AS DEDUCTION ON ASSET SIDE
Q18	INVENTORY COSTING METHOD UTILIZED BY MAJORITY	FIFO	REPLACEMENT COST	FIFO
Q19	MANUFACTURING OVERHEAD INCLUDED IN YEAR-END INVENTORY	PREDOMINANT PRACTICE	NOT DISCLOSED	PREDOMINANT PRACTICE
Q20	YEAR-END INVENTORY CLASSIFIED AT	LOWER OF COST OR MARKET	CURRENT MARKET VALUE	LOWER OF COST OR MARKET
Q21	DEPRECIATION METHOD	STRAIGHT LINE	STRAIGHT LINE	STRAIGHT LINE
Q22	ACCUMULATED DEPRECIATION DISCLOSED	NETTED AGAINST F/A OUTSIDE B/S	NO MAJORITY	NETTED AGAINST F/A OUTSIDE B/S
Q23	EXCESS DEPRECIATION	NOT ALLOWED	ALLOWED	ALLOWED

Accounting Standards in Practice in 24 Countries

NO.	ACCOUNTING & AUDITING ITEMS	Malaysia	Mexico	Netherlands
Q24	FOREIGN CURRENCY TRANSLATION METHOD	CURRENT RATE METHOD	NOT DISCLOSED	CURRENT RATE METHOD
Q25	ACCOUNTING FOR FOREIGN CURRENCY TRANSLATION GAINS OR LOSSES	TAKEN TO INCOME STATEMENT	NOT DISCLOSED	TAKEN TO I/S &/OR OWNERS' EQ.
Q26	RESEARCH & DEVELOPMENT COSTS	EXPENSED CURRENTLY	NOT DISCLOSED	EXPENSED CURRENTLY
Q27	DEFERRED TAXES RECORDED WHEN ACCOUNTING INCOME IS NOT EQUAL TO TAXABLE INCOME	YES	YES	YES
Q28	ACCOUNTING FOR LONG-TERM FINANCIAL LEASES	CAPITALIZED	CAPITALIZED	CAPITALIZED
Q29	CONTINGENT LIABILITIES DISCLOSED BY	MINORITY	80-100%	40-80%
Q30	PREDOMINANT CONTINGENT LIABILITY REPORTED	GUARANTEES/WARRANTIES	UNFUNDED VESTED BENEFITS	GUARANTEES/WARRANTIES
Q31	DISCRETIONARY/NON-EQUITY RESERVES	SOME SPECIFIC RESERVES EXIST	NO DISC/NON-EQY RESERVES EXIST	NO DISC/NON-EQY RESERVES EXIST
Q32	PENSION EXPENSES ARE	PROVIDED REGULARLY	PROVIDED REGULARLY	PROVIDED REGULARLY
Q33	PENSION FUNDS ARE OFF THE COMPANY'S B/S	NO	NO	NO MAJORITY
Q34	EXPENSES FOR DISMISSAL INDEMNITIES RECORDED WHEN?	ACCRUAL SET UP	PAY AS YOU GO	NOT DISCLOSED
Q35	REVALUATION OF ACCOUNTS ALLOWED	YES	YES	YES
Q36	SUPPLEMENTARY CURRENT COST INFORMATION PRESENTED BY	NOT DISCLOSED	40-80%	MINORITY

Accounting Standards in Practice in 24 Countries

NO.	ACCOUNTING & AUDITING ITEMS	New Zealand	Norway	Singapore
Q1	FINANCIAL STATEMENTS COST BASIS	HIST COST W/PRICE LEVEL ADJST	HIST COST W/PRICE LEVEL ADJST	HIST COST W/PRICE LEVEL ADJST
Q2	CONSOLIDATED INFORMATION PROVIDED BY	40-80%	40-80%	80-100%
Q3	CONSOLIDATION PRACTICES FOR SUBSIDIARIES BY MAJORITY	ALL SUBSIDIARIES CONSOLIDATED	ALL SUBSIDIARIES CONSOLIDATED	ALL SUBSIDIARIES CONSOLIDATED
Q4	INTER-COMPANY ACCOUNTS	ELIMINATED UPON CONSOLIDATION	ELIMINATED UPON CONSOLIDATION	ELIMINATED UPON CONSOLIDATION
Q5	ACCTG. METHOD FOR LONG-TERM INV'TS BETW 20 - 50% OF EQUITY	EQUITY METHOD	COST OR EQUITY METHOD	EQUITY METHOD
Q6	CONSOLIDATION OF 20%<LT INV'T<50% DEPENDING ON INFLUENCE	NOT DONE	NOT DONE	NOT DONE
Q7	ACCTG. METHOD FOR LONG-TERM INV'TS LESS THAN 20% OF EQUITY	COST METHOD	COST METHOD	COST METHOD
Q8	MARKETABLE SECURITIES CLASSIFIED BY MAJORITY AT	HISTORICAL COST	LOWER OF COST OR MARKET	LOWER OF COST OR MARKET
Q9	ACCOUNTING METHOD FOR ACQUISITIONS	PURCHASE METHOD BY 40-80%	PURCHASE METHOD BY 40-80%	PURCHASE METHOD BY 40-80%
Q10	ACCOUNTING FOR GOODWILL	EXPENSED/TAKEN TO RESERVES	CAPITALIZED & AMORTIZED	TAKEN TO RESERVES
Q11	ACCOUNTING FOR OTHER INTANGIBLES	EXPENSED	AMORTIZED	AMORTIZED
Q12	MINORITY INTEREST EFFECT ON BALANCE SHEET	EXCLUDED FROM OWNERS' EQUITY	EXCLUDED FROM OWNERS' EQUITY	EXCLUDED FROM OWNERS' EQUITY
Q13	MINORITY INTEREST EFFECT ON INCOME STATEMENT	BEFORE BOTTOM LINE ON I/S	BEFORE BOTTOM LINE ON I/S	BEFORE BOTTOM LINE ON I/S
Q14	TREASURY STOCK EXISTENCE ALLOWED	NOT DISCLOSED	YES	NOT DISCLOSED
Q15	TREASURY STOCK GAINS & LOSSES	NOT APPLICABLE	NOT DISCLOSED	NOT APPLICABLE
Q16	TREASURY STOCK POSITION ON BALANCE SHEET	NOT APPLICABLE	DEDUCTED FROM OWNERS' EQUITY	NOT APPLICABLE
Q17	PROVISION MADE FOR UNCOLLECTIBLE ACCOUNTS	YES,AS DEDUCTION ON ASSET SIDE	YES,AS DEDUCTION ON ASSET SIDE	YES,AS DEDUCTION ON ASSET SIDE
Q18	INVENTORY COSTING METHOD UTILIZED BY MAJORITY	FIFO	FIFO	AVERAGE
Q19	MANUFACTURING OVERHEAD INCLUDED IN YEAR-END INVENTORY	PREDOMINANT PRACTICE	PREDOMINANT PRACTICE	PREDOMINANT PRACTICE
Q20	YEAR-END INVENTORY CLASSIFIED AT	LOWER OF COST OR MARKET	LOWER OF COST OR MARKET	LOWER OF COST OR MARKET
Q21	DEPRECIATION METHOD	STRAIGHT LINE	STRAIGHT LINE	STRAIGHT LINE
Q22	ACCUMULATED DEPRECIATION DISCLOSED	NETTED AGAINST F/A OUTSIDE B/S	NETTED AGAINST F/A OUTSIDE B/S	NETTED AGAINST F/A OUTSIDE B/S
Q23	EXCESS DEPRECIATION	NOT ALLOWED	ALLOWED	NOT ALLOWED

Accounting Standards in Practice in 24 Countries

NO.	ACCOUNTING & AUDITING ITEMS	New Zealand	Norway	Singapore
Q24	FOREIGN CURRENCY TRANSLATION METHOD	CURRENT RATE METHOD	CURRENT RATE METHOD	CURRENT RATE METHOD
Q25	ACCOUNTING FOR FOREIGN CURRENCY TRANSLATION GAINS OR LOSSES	TAKEN TO I/S &/OR OWNERS' EQ.	TAKEN TO INCOME STATEMENT	TAKEN TO INCOME STATEMENT
Q26	RESEARCH & DEVELOPMENT COSTS	EXPENSED CURRENTLY	EXPENSED CURRENTLY	NOT DISCLOSED
Q27	DEFERRED TAXES RECORDED WHEN ACCOUNTING INCOME IS NOT EQUAL TO TAXABLE INCOME	YES	NO	YES
Q28	ACCOUNTING FOR LONG-TERM FINANCIAL LEASES	CAPITALIZED	CAPITALIZED	CAPITALIZED
Q29	CONTINGENT LIABILITIES DISCLOSED BY	40-80%	40-80%	40-80%
Q30	PREDOMINANT CONTINGENT LIABILITY REPORTED	GUARANTEES/WARRANTIES	GUARANTEES/WARRANTIES	GUARANTEES/WARRANTIES
Q31	DISCRETIONARY/NON-EQUITY RESERVES	SOME SPECIFIC RESERVES EXIST	GENERAL-PURPOSE RESERVES EXIST	SOME SPECIFIC RESERVES EXIST
Q32	PENSION EXPENSES ARE	PROVIDED REGULARLY	PROVIDED REGULARLY	PROVIDED REGULARLY
Q33	PENSION FUNDS ARE OFF THE COMPANY'S B/S	YES	YES	NO
Q34	EXPENSES FOR DISMISSAL INDEMNITIES RECORDED WHEN?	NOT DISCLOSED	NOT DISCLOSED	NOT DISCLOSED
Q35	REVALUATION OF ACCOUNTS ALLOWED	YES	YES	YES
Q36	SUPPLEMENTARY CURRENT COST INFORMATION PRESENTED BY	NOT DISCLOSED	NOT DISCLOSED	NOT DISCLOSED

Accounting Standards in Practice in 24 Countries

NO.	ACCOUNTING & AUDITING ITEMS	South Africa	Spain	Sweden
Q1	FINANCIAL STATEMENTS COST BASIS	HISTORICAL COST ENTIRELY	HIST COST W/PRICE LEVEL ADJST	HIST COST W/PRICE LEVEL ADJST
Q2	CONSOLIDATED INFORMATION PROVIDED BY	80-100%	MINORITY	80-100%
Q3	CONSOLIDATION PRACTICES FOR SUBSIDIARIES BY MAJORITY	ALL SUBSIDIARIES CONSOLIDATED	ALL SUBSIDIARIES CONSOLIDATED	ALL SUBSIDIARIES CONSOLIDATED
Q4	INTER-COMPANY ACCOUNTS	ELIMINATED UPON CONSOLIDATION	ELIMINATED UPON CONSOLIDATION	ELIMINATED UPON CONSOLIDATION
Q5	ACCTG. METHOD FOR LONG-TERM INV'TS BETW 20 - 50% OF EQUITY	EQUITY METHOD	COST OR EQUITY METHOD	COST OR EQUITY METHOD
Q6	CONSOLIDATION OF 20%<LT INV'T<50% DEPENDING ON INFLUENCE	MINORITY PRACTICE	NOT DONE	MINORITY PRACTICE
Q7	ACCTG. METHOD FOR LONG-TERM INV'TS LESS THAN 20% OF EQUITY	COST METHOD	COST METHOD	COST METHOD
Q8	MARKETABLE SECURITIES CLASSIFIED BY MAJORITY AT	HISTORICAL COST	LOWER OF COST OR MARKET	LOWER OF COST OR MARKET
Q9	ACCOUNTING METHOD FOR ACQUISITIONS	PURCHASE METHOD BY 40-80%	PURCHASE METHOD BY 80-100%	PURCHASE METHOD BY 80-100%
Q10	ACCOUNTING FOR GOODWILL	EXPENSED/TAKEN TO RESERVES	CAPITALIZED & AMORTIZED	CAPITALIZED & AMORTIZED
Q11	ACCOUNTING FOR OTHER INTANGIBLES	AMORTIZED	AMORTIZED	AMORTIZED
Q12	MINORITY INTEREST EFFECT ON BALANCE SHEET	EXCLUDED FROM OWNERS' EQUITY	EXCLUDED FROM OWNERS' EQUITY	EXCLUDED FROM OWNERS' EQUITY
Q13	MINORITY INTEREST EFFECT ON INCOME STATEMENT	BEFORE BOTTOM LINE ON I/S	BEFORE BOTTOM LINE ON I/S	BEFORE BOTTOM LINE ON I/S
Q14	TREASURY STOCK EXISTENCE ALLOWED	NOT DISCLOSED	MINORITY PRACTICE	MINORITY PRACTICE
Q15	TREASURY STOCK GAINS & LOSSES	NOT APPLICABLE	TAKEN TO SHAREHOLDERS' EQUITY	NOT DISCLOSED
Q16	TREASURY STOCK POSITION ON BALANCE SHEET	NOT APPLICABLE	DEDUCTED FROM OWNERS' EQUITY	DEDUCTED FROM OWNERS' EQUITY
Q17	PROVISION MADE FOR UNCOLLECTIBLE ACCOUNTS	NOT DISCLOSED	MIXED	YES,AS DEDUCTION ON ASSET SIDE
Q18	INVENTORY COSTING METHOD UTILIZED BY MAJORITY	FIFO	AVERAGE	FIFO
Q19	MANUFACTURING OVERHEAD INCLUDED IN YEAR-END INVENTORY	PREDOMINANT PRACTICE	PREDOMINANT PRACTICE	PREDOMINANT PRACTICE
Q20	YEAR-END INVENTORY CLASSIFIED AT	LOWER OF COST OR MARKET	LOWER OF COST OR MARKET	LOWER OF COST OR MARKET
Q21	DEPRECIATION METHOD	STRAIGHT LINE	STRAIGHT LINE	STRAIGHT LINE
Q22	ACCUMULATED DEPRECIATION DISCLOSED	NETTED AGAINST F/A OUTSIDE B/S	NETTED AGAINST F/A DR SIDE B/S	NETTED AGAINST F/A OUTSIDE B/S
Q23	EXCESS DEPRECIATION	ALLOWED	NOT ALLOWED	ALLOWED

Accounting Standards in Practice in 24 Countries

NO.	ACCOUNTING & AUDITING ITEMS	South Africa	Spain	Sweden
Q24	FOREIGN CURRENCY TRANSLATION METHOD	CURRENT RATE METHOD	CURRENT RATE METHOD	CURRENT RATE METHOD
Q25	ACCOUNTING FOR FOREIGN CURRENCY TRANSLATION GAINS OR LOSSES	TAKEN TO I/S &/OR OWNERS' EQ.	TAKEN TO INCOME &/OR DEFERRED	TAKEN TO I/S &/OR OWNERS' EQ.
Q26	RESEARCH & DEVELOPMENT COSTS	EXPENSED CURRENTLY	NOT DISCLOSED	EXPENSED CURRENTLY
Q27	DEFERRED TAXES RECORDED WHEN ACCOUNTING INCOME IS NOT EQUAL TO TAXABLE INCOME	YES	NO	NO
Q28	ACCOUNTING FOR LONG-TERM FINANCIAL LEASES	CAPITALIZED	CAPITALIZED	CAPITALIZED
Q29	CONTINGENT LIABILITIES DISCLOSED BY	40-80%	40-80%	80-100%
Q30	PREDOMINANT CONTINGENT LIABILITY REPORTED	GUARANTEES/WARRANTIES	GUARANTEES/WARRANTIES	GUARANTEES/WARRANTIES
Q31	DISCRETIONARY/NON-EQUITY RESERVES	SOME SPECIFIC RESERVES EXIST	GENERAL-PURPOSE RESERVES EXIST	GENERAL-PURPOSE RESERVES EXIST
Q32	PENSION EXPENSES ARE	PROVIDED REGULARLY	PROVIDED REGULARLY	PROVIDED REGULARLY
Q33	PENSION FUNDS ARE OFF THE COMPANY'S B/S	YES	YES	NO
Q34	EXPENSES FOR DISMISSAL INDEMNITIES RECORDED WHEN?	PAY AS YOU GO	NOT DISCLOSED	NOT DISCLOSED
Q35	REVALUATION OF ACCOUNTS ALLOWED	NO	YES	YES
Q36	SUPPLEMENTARY CURRENT COST INFORMATION PRESENTED BY	MINORITY	NOT DISCLOSED	MINORITY

Accounting Standards in Practice in 24 Countries

NO.	ACCOUNTING & AUDITING ITEMS	Switzerland	United Kingdom	United States
Q1	FINANCIAL STATEMENTS COST BASIS	HISTORICAL COST ENTIRELY	HIST COST W/PRICE LEVEL ADJST	HISTORICAL COST ENTIRELY
Q2	CONSOLIDATED INFORMATION PROVIDED BY	40-80%	80-100%	80-100%
Q3	CONSOLIDATION PRACTICES FOR MAJORITY-OWNED SUBSIDIARIES	ALL SUBSIDIARIES CONSOLIDATED	ALL SUBSIDIARIES CONSOLIDATED	ALL SUBSIDIARIES CONSOLIDATED
Q4	INTER-COMPANY ACCOUNTS	ELIMINATED UPON CONSOLIDATION	ELIMINATED UPON CONSOLIDATION	ELIMINATED UPON CONSOLIDATION
Q5	ACCTG. METHOD FOR LONG-TERM INV'TS BETW 20 - 50% OF EQUITY	COST OR EQUITY METHOD	EQUITY METHOD	EQUITY METHOD
Q6	CONSOLIDATION OF 20%<LT INV'T<50% DEPENDING ON INFLUENCE	NOT DONE	NOT DONE	MINORITY PRACTICE
Q7	ACCTG. METHOD FOR LONG-TERM INV'TS LESS THAN 20% OF EQUITY	COST METHOD	COST METHOD	COST METHOD
Q8	MARKETABLE SECURITIES CLASSIFIED BY MAJORITY AT	LOWER OF COST OR MARKET	HISTORICAL COST	LOWER OF COST OR MARKET
Q9	ACCOUNTING METHOD FOR ACQUISITIONS	PURCHASE METHOD BY 40-80%	PURCHASE METHOD BY 80-100%	PURCHASE METHOD BY 80-100%
Q10	ACCOUNTING FOR GOODWILL	TAKEN TO RESERVES	TAKEN TO RESERVES	CAPITALIZED & AMORTIZED
Q11	ACCOUNTING FOR OTHER INTANGIBLES	AMORTIZED	AMORTIZED	AMORTIZED
Q12	MINORITY INTEREST EFFECT ON BALANCE SHEET	EXCLUDED FROM OWNERS' EQUITY	EXCLUDED FROM OWNERS' EQUITY	EXCLUDED FROM OWNERS' EQUITY
Q13	MINORITY INTEREST EFFECT ON INCOME STATEMENT	BEFORE BOTTOM LINE ON I/S	BEFORE BOTTOM LINE ON I/S	BEFORE BOTTOM LINE ON I/S
Q14	TREASURY STOCK EXISTENCE ALLOWED	NOT DISCLOSED	MINORITY PRACTICE	YES
Q15	TREASURY STOCK GAINS & LOSSES	NOT APPLICABLE	TAKEN TO SHAREHOLDERS' EQUITY	TAKEN TO SHAREHOLDERS' EQUITY
Q16	TREASURY STOCK POSITION ON BALANCE SHEET	NOT APPLICABLE	DEDUCTED FROM OWNERS' EQUITY	DEDUCTED FROM OWNERS' EQUITY
Q17	PROVISION MADE FOR UNCOLLECTIBLE ACCOUNTS	YES,AS DEDUCTION ON ASSET SIDE	YES,AS DEDUCTION ON ASSET SIDE	YES,AS DEDUCTION ON ASSET SIDE
Q18	INVENTORY COSTING METHOD UTILIZED BY MAJORITY	AVERAGE	FIFO	FIFO
Q19	MANUFACTURING OVERHEAD INCLUDED IN YEAR-END INVENTORY	PREDOMINANT PRACTICE	PREDOMINANT PRACTICE	PREDOMINANT PRACTICE
Q20	YEAR-END INVENTORY CLASSIFIED AT	LOWER OF COST OR MARKET	LOWER OF COST OR MARKET	LOWER OF COST OR MARKET
Q21	DEPRECIATION METHOD	STRAIGHT LINE	STRAIGHT LINE	STRAIGHT LINE
Q22	ACCUMULATED DEPRECIATION DISCLOSED	NETTED AGAINST F/A OUTSIDE B/S	NETTED AGAINST F/A OUTSIDE B/S	NO MAJORITY
Q23	EXCESS DEPRECIATION	NOT ALLOWED	NOT ALLOWED	NOT ALLOWED

Accounting Standards in Practice in 24 Countries

NO.	ACCOUNTING & AUDITING ITEMS	Switzerland	United Kingdom	United States
Q24	FOREIGN CURRENCY TRANSLATION METHOD	CURRENT RATE METHOD	CURRENT RATE METHOD	CURRENT RATE METHOD
Q25	ACCOUNTING FOR FOREIGN CURRENCY TRANSLATION GAINS OR LOSSES	TAKEN TO OWNERS' EQUITY	TAKEN TO I/S &/OR OWNERS' EQ.	TAKEN TO I/S &/OR OWNERS' EQ.
Q26	RESEARCH & DEVELOPMENT COSTS	EXPENSED CURRENTLY	EXPENSED CURRENTLY	EXPENSED CURRENTLY
Q27	DEFERRED TAXES RECORDED WHEN ACCOUNTING INCOME IS NOT EQUAL TO TAXABLE INCOME	NO	YES	YES
Q28	ACCOUNTING FOR LONG-TERM FINANCIAL LEASES	CAPITALIZED	CAPITALIZED	CAPITALIZED
Q29	CONTINGENT LIABILITIES DISCLOSED BY	40-80%	80-100%	40-80%
Q30	PREDOMINANT CONTINGENT LIABILITY REPORTED	GUARANTEES/WARRANTIES	GUARANTEES/WARRANTIES	LITIGATION
Q31	DISCRETIONARY/NON-EQUITY RESERVES	GENERAL-PURPOSE RESERVES EXIST	SOME SPECIFIC RESERVES EXIST	NO DISC/NON-EQY RESERVES EXIST
Q32	PENSION EXPENSES ARE	PROVIDED REGULARLY	PROVIDED REGULARLY	PROVIDED REGULARLY
Q33	PENSION FUNDS ARE OFF THE COMPANY'S B/S	PARTIALLY FUNDED OUTSIDE	YES	YES
Q34	EXPENSES FOR DISMISSAL INDEMNITIES RECORDED WHEN?	NOT DISCLOSED	NOT DISCLOSED	NOT DISCLOSED
Q35	REVALUATION OF ACCOUNTS ALLOWED	YES	YES	NO
Q36	SUPPLEMENTARY CURRENT COST INFORMATION PRESENTED BY	MINORITY	MINORITY	MINORITY

CHAPTER 3

FINANCIAL REPORTING PRACTICES IN ANNUAL REPORTS OF INDUSTRIAL COMPANIES IN 24 COUNTRIES

Table of Contents

I. INTRODUCTION

Users of international financial statements have, by and large, taken a passive role regarding the financial reporting practices of companies worldwide. They accept what is available within a country, rather than persuading the preparers of financial statements worldwide to provide a minimum amount of financial information to facilitate the evaluation of a company's performance on a global basis.

At the same time, the information disclosed in financial statements can depend on the corporate view of the user's needs. This leads to great diversity in the content of financial reports. For example, a detailed presentation of capital expenditures may be common in the reports of one country and rarely found in another. The background of the management and directors may be provided in great depth in one country, while only a brief list of names is given in another.

Cultural differences and marketing traditions also play a major role in the presentation of financial statements. In certain countries the annual reports are rather long, with pictures of commissioned art and many pages of text, while in other countries the annual report text is brief with few, if any, pictures. Each country's language and traditions influence the general layout of the annual reports of its companies.

Furthermore, for competitive reasons, companies would generally like to disclose as little information as possible. Any new requirements for additional disclosures raise the concern of added costs for preparers of financial statements; the cost versus benefits of extensive financial reporting should be evaluated.

Though several international accounting organizations have been working toward the harmonization of financial reporting practices, it appears that some of them have focused on either a particular region (e.g., the EC) or certain types of companies (e.g., the United Nations and OECD focusing on the financial reporting practices of multinational corporations). The International Accounting Standards Committee (IASC) has focused more on harmonizing international accounting standards than international financial reporting practices per se.

II. RESEARCH OBJECTIVES

3-1 What are the financial disclosure practices of industrial companies in various countries?

3-2 To what extent has the international harmonization of financial disclosures for industrial companies been achieved?

3-3 What financial disclosures should be included in annual reports of industrial companies published for an international audience?

III. RESEARCH DESIGN

This chapter examines current disclosure practices, summarized by country, through a series of questions and answers regarding key financial reporting practices in 24 countries. For each question, the single practice which best reflects the predominant treatment (that employed by 80 - 100% of the companies) in each country is given. Also used is a second category comprised of 40 - 80% of the companies following a given practice. In cases where no disclosures are made in the annual reports, or where a particular method is a minority practice, the corresponding response is indicated.

Exhibit 3-1 provides the list of questions and answers used to summarize the findings.

The Worldscope Database was used to extract data on items reported in income statements and balance sheets worldwide. The footnotes in Worldscope also provided useful data for analyzing differences in the reporting of each accounting item.

To supplement the Worldscope Database and to identify general trends in the form and content of annual reports, annual reports of 10 to 20 leading companies in each country (for a larger industrial country, 20 reports were used, for a small country, 10) were utilized. This sample selection has a bias toward large companies, because they tend to disclose more than small companies. However, we felt that international users might be more interested in larger foreign companies than smaller ones.

IV. FINDINGS

Empirical findings on financial reporting practices by country are presented in Exhibit 3-2.

The following summary highlights the findings on selected financial reporting items:

A. Basic Financial Statements

1. Income Statement Format

In roughly half of the countries studied, the most popular income statement format is that of "sales minus expenses". This format is used by a majority of companies in the following countries: Canada, Denmark, Finland, West Germany, Japan, South Korea, Mexico, the Netherlands, Norway, South Africa, Sweden, Switzerland and the US.

"Operating profit less interest and tax expense" is the prevalent format in the Commonwealth countries (with the exception of South Africa).

The debit/credit format is the most popular in Austria and Belgium, while in France, Italy and Spain both the sales minus expenses and debit/credit formats are used.

2. Comparative Income Statement Data

In virtually all countries, the overwhelming majority of companies disclose two years of comparative data on the income statement. In fact, many US companies cover three years. However, in Austria, West Germany and South Korea some companies provide only one year of comparative data.

3. Disclosure of Earnings Per Share (EPS) Data

EPS information is reported by a majority of companies in, Canada, Finland, Japan, the US and the Commonwealth countries (except New Zealand). Between 40 and 80% of the companies in Mexico, New Zealand and much of Europe (France, the Netherlands, Norway, Sweden and Switzerland) report EPS data. A minority of companies in the remaining countries (Austria, Belgium, Denmark, West Germany, Italy, South Korea and Spain) report EPS data.

Generally, companies in Canada, the US and the Commonwealth countries (except Australia and New Zealand) disclose EPS on the income statement, while in Australia, Japan, Mexico and in European countries where EPS information is disclosed (Finland, France, the Netherlands, Sweden and Switzerland), it appears elsewhere in the report.

4. Calculation of Earnings Per Share

Where reporting EPS is common practice (i.e., in Canada, Finland, France, Hong Kong, Japan, the Netherlands, New Zealand, Norway, Switzerland and the US) it is calculated based on net income after preferred dividends. In most Commonwealth countries (Australia, Malaysia, Singapore, South Africa, and the UK), it is calculated before extraordinary items, while in Sweden, EPS is calculated as earnings after financial income and expenses less minority interest and a 50% tax deduction.

5. Definition of the EPS Denominator

Where EPS disclosure is generally prevalent, it is usually based on the average number of outstanding shares for the period. This is true for companies in the following countries: Canada, Finland, Hong Kong, Malaysia, New Zealand, Norway, Singapore, South Africa, Sweden, the UK, and the US. Companies that use the number of shares at year-end as a basis for calculation are mainly those in Australia, France, Japan, Mexico, South Korea, Spain and Switzerland.

6. Disclosure of Dividends Per Share (DPS)

Between 80 and 100% of the companies in Canada, Finland, Japan, the US and the Commonwealth countries (except South Africa), report DPS. Between 40 and 80% of the companies in South Korea, Mexico, South Africa and virtually all of Europe report DPS. Only in Austria and Denmark is such disclosure a minority practice.

Dividends per share are disclosed net after withholding tax adjustments by companies in Belgium, France, West Germany, Malaysia, Singapore and Switzerland. Elsewhere, DPS does not include any tax adjustment for the shareholders.

7. Balance Sheet Format

The most popular balance sheet format, used by companies in two-thirds of the countries studied, is "total assets = total liabilities + stockholders' equity", presented on either one or two pages (the latter practice is more common than the former). It is used by companies in Canada, Japan, South Korea, Mexico, New Zealand, the US and Continental Europe.

Companies in most Commonwealth countries use the second most popular format: "fixed assets plus net working capital equals long-term debt plus stockholders' equity", which is almost always disclosed on a single page.

8. Comparative Balance Sheet Data

Over 80% of the companies in the majority of countries studied provide balance sheet data for the most recent two years, with the exception of Austria, West Germany and South Korea, where only 40-80% of the companies provide such data.

9. Arrangement of Balance Sheet Items

Without exception, all of the companies studied arranged items on the balance sheet in some type of liquidity order. In a little less than 50% of the cases, items were reported by decreasing degree of liquidity, i.e., from most liquid to least liquid. This was true for companies in Canada, Finland, Italy, Japan, South Korea, Mexico, Norway, Sweden, Switzerland, and the US. On the other hand, in slightly more than 50% of the cases, items were reported by increasing degree of liquidity, i.e., from least liquid to most liquid. This was the case among companies in the Commonwealth countries and in most of the countries of Continental Europe.

10. Statement of Changes in Shareholders' Equity

A statement of changes in shareholders' equity is reported by a majority of companies in Austria, Canada, France, Japan, South Korea and Mexico and by between 40 and 80% of companies in Belgium, Italy, Sweden and the US. In all other countries studied, a minority of companies include this statement in their reports.

11. Statement of Changes in Financial Position

A statement of changes in financial position (often referred to as a statement of cash flow) is reported by a majority of companies in Australia, Finland, Malaysia, New Zealand, Norway, Singapore, South Africa and North America. In most other countries (Denmark, France, Hong Kong, Italy, the Netherlands, Spain and Sweden), between 40 and 80% of the companies disclose this statement. A minority of companies in Austria, Belgium, West Germany, Switzerland, Japan and South Korea include this statement in their accounts.

12. Definition of Funds in Statement of Changes in Financial Position

In roughly half of the countries studied, a working capital method is used in the statement of changes in financial position. This is true for companies in the following countries: Australia, Finland, France, Hong Kong, Italy, Japan, South Korea, Malaysia, New Zealand, Norway, Singapore, and Spain. Several others (Mexico, the Netherlands and Sweden) use modified cash as the basis for this statement. In the UK, net borrowings are used and in the US and Canada, a cash basis is used. For companies in Denmark, West Germany, South Africa and Switzerland, there is no majority policy.

13. Notes to the Accounts

As a general rule, notes to the financial accounts are extensively utilized in the Commonwealth countries, North America, the Netherlands and Scandinavia (except Denmark). Notes are moderately utilized in Japan, South Korea, and most other European countries.

14. Disclosure of Outstanding Common Shares

The number of outstanding common shares is reported by a majority of companies in Canada, France, Italy, Japan, the Netherlands, Norway, Sweden, the US and all the Commonwealth countries. Between 40 and 80% of the companies in South Korea, Mexico and most other European countries report this item. A minority of companies in Austria and West Germany report the number of outstanding common shares.

15. Disclosure of Shareholdings' Information

Majority shareholdings are disclosed by most companies in Australia, Finland, Italy, Malaysia, New Zealand, Singapore, Spain and the US, and by 40 to 80% in Japan, South Korea, Norway, South Africa, Sweden and the UK. A minority of companies in France and the Netherlands disclose majority shareholdings, while none in Austria, Belgium, Denmark, West Germany, Hong Kong, Mexico or Switzerland disclose this information.

16. Disclosure of Subsequent Events in Annual Reports

In Malaysia, Singapore and North America, a majority of companies disclose subsequent events in their annual reports. Between 40 and 80% of the companies in Australia, Germany and the Netherlands disclose such information, while among companies in all other countries, information regarding subsequent events is either disclosed by a minority or not at all.

B. Supplementary Disclosures

1. Reporting of Subsidiary Company Information

In Hong Kong, Japan, Singapore, South Africa, the UK, the US and almost all European countries, a parent company will disclose, as a minimum, the name, headquarters and percentage of ownership held of its subsidiaries. In addition to this information, companies in Australia, Belgium and Italy also tend to disclose the summary financial results of their subsidiaries. In several other countries (South Korea, Malaysia, Mexico and Switzerland) only the subsidiaries' names, either with or without addresses, are disclosed. In Austria, Canada and New Zealand, disclosure of subsidiary information is not generally prevalent.

2. Disclosure of Segment Information

In virtually all cases in which segment information is disclosed, it includes sales by product line or division. In a majority of the countries studied (Australia, Japan, the UK, the US and most of Europe), most companies also disclose operating income by product line. A less common supplementary disclosure to the aforementioned sales figures is a list of total assets by product line/division. Assets and sales by product line/division are disclosed by companies in Canada, the Netherlands, New Zealand and Norway. Total assets by product line/division alone are disclosed by companies in Austria.

Disclosure of segment information is practiced by a minority of companies in Hong Kong, South Korea, Malaysia, Mexico, Singapore and South Africa.

3. Disclosure of Geographic Information

Disclosure of geographic information as a breakdown of sales is almost universal in companies with international business. Geographic sales and operating income breakdowns are disclosed primarily by European companies, although Hong Kong also follows this practice. A geographic breakdown of sales and total assets is practiced in Australia, Belgium, Canada, Japan, Malaysia, New Zealand, Singapore, South Africa and the US. Disclosure of geographic segment information is a minority practice in Austria, Italy, South Korea, Mexico and Spain.

4. Breakdown of Employees

A breakdown of the number of employees by function, geographic area or line of business is presented by between 40 and 80% of companies in Belgium, France, the Netherlands, South Africa, Sweden, Switzerland, the UK and the US. Only in some southern European countries (Spain and Italy) do a majority of companies disclose such information.

In all other countries studied, such a breakdown of employees is either not disclosed or presented by only a minority of companies.

5. Remuneration to Directors and Officers

A majority of companies in most Commonwealth countries (Australia, Hong Kong, Malaysia, New Zealand, Singapore, South Africa and the UK) disclose executive remuneration, as do companies in Finland. A smaller number of companies in several other European countries (Denmark, France, West Germany, the Netherlands and Norway) also disclose such information, as do a minority of companies in Sweden and Mexico. Companies in other countries, including those in Canada, Japan, South Korea, the US and the rest of Europe, do not disclose information about directors' or officers' remuneration in the annual report.

6. Discussion of Labor Relations

Companies in only four of the countries studied disclosed information on labor relations. A clear majority (80-100%) in Spain and Italy and between 40-80% in the Netherlands and the US disclosed this type of information. In all other cases information regarding labor relations was either discussed by only a minority of companies or not included.

7. Names and Titles of Principal Officers and Board Members

In roughly half of the countries studied, a majority of companies disclose the names and titles of principal officers. In Hong Kong, Mexico and New Zealand only a minority of companies disclose this information.

A large majority of companies in most countries studied disclose a list of board members and their outside affiliations. In South Korea and Singapore, however, the number of companies reporting such information ranges between 40 and 80 per cent.

8. Disclosure of Company Shares Held by Directors and Principal Officers

A majority of companies in the US, and some Commonwealth countries (Hong Kong, Malaysia, Singapore and the UK) disclose the number of company shares held by their directors and/or officers, as do a smaller number in Australia, New Zealand, Sweden and Norway. In Finland, the Netherlands and South Africa, a minority disclose shares held by directors/officers, while elsewhere there is no disclosure at all.

9. Research and Development (R & D) Costs

In Finland, Italy, South Africa and Switzerland 40-80% of the companies studied disclose worldwide R & D costs, while a majority of US companies disclose this information. The only other country in which companies disclose R & D costs is Spain, where it is majority practice to disclose domestic R & D costs. In all other countries, research and development costs are either disclosed by a minority of companies or not at all.

10. Disclosure of Capital Expenditures

In the vast majority of countries, over 80% of the companies studied disclose worldwide capital expenditures. In Canada, France, Italy, and Switzerland, between 40 and 80% of the companies disclose it, while in Belgium and South Korea, only a minority of companies do.

V. SUMMARY AND CONCLUSIONS

In this chapter principal similarities and differences in financial reporting practices gleaned from our examination of the annual reports of industrial companies in 24 countries have been highlighted. It can be seen that while financial disclosures in international annual reports vary considerably, in certain areas, harmonization of financial reporting practices appears to be occurring.

The financial reporting practices in which the fewest variations exist are the following:

- Format and contents of basic financial statements
- Information about management and board members
- Inclusion of the statement of changes in financial position
- Use of footnotes explaining financial items

The widest gaps in financial reporting practices worldwide are in:

- Reporting of subsidiary company information
- Disclosure of segment and geographic information
- Disclosure of R & D costs and capital expenditures
- Disclosure of earnings per share data

While doing research for this study, we have observed, despite these differences, considerable improvement in financial reporting practices and increased adherence to international accounting standards. The factors leading to these improvements are the globalization of capital markets and efforts of international, regional and national accounting regulatory bodies. We believe that financial reporting practices worldwide will converge even further due to increased interest in the international analysis of financial statements.

In the larger (and perhaps more efficient) capital markets, companies must provide comprehensive financial information to their users (i.e., shareholders, lenders, unions, key suppliers, etc.). For those companies with wider interests, more complete financial disclosure will result in less perceived risk about the firm, thus reducing its cost of capital. In short, capital markets tend to reward more extensive disclosure by issuers of securities.

In order to facilitate better financial reporting for international users, we have prepared "A Guide to Prepare Annual Reports for Multinational Industrial Companies", found in Appendix A of this study.

EXHIBIT 3-1

QUESTIONS AND ANSWERS FOR FINANCIAL REPORTING PRACTICES

Q1 LANGUAGE OF THE FINANCIAL STATEMENTS

1 LOCAL LANGUAGE, MINOR. ENGLISH
2 LOCAL LANGUAGE, 40-80% ENGLISH
3 ENGLISH
4 NOT AVAILABLE

Q2 SUMMARY FINANCIAL INFORMATION PRESENTED BY

1 80-100%
2 40-80%
3 MINORITY
9 NOT DISCLOSED

Q3 MAJOR FINANCIAL RATIOS COMPUTED AND REPORTED BY

1 80-100%
2 40-80%
3 MINORITY
9 NOT DISCLOSED

Q4 NOTES TO THE FINANCIAL ACCOUNTS ARE

1 EXTENSIVELY UTILIZED
2 MODERATELY UTILIZED
3 NOT UTILIZED
9 NOT DISCLOSED

Q5 INFLATION ADJUSTED DATA PROVIDED BY

1 NONE OF THE COMPANIES
2 MINORITY
3 40 - 80%
4 80 - 100%
5 ALL OF COMPANIES
9 NOT DETERMINABLE

Q6 MAJORITY OF COMPANIES REPORT THE SUBSIDIARIES'

1 NAME ONLY OR WITH DOMICILE
2 NAME, DOMICILE, FIN'L RESULTS
3 NAME, HDQTR, FIN'L RESULTS, % HELD
4 NAME, DOMICILE, % HELD
5 MINORITY PRACTICE
9 NOT DISCLOSED

Q7 SEGMENT INFORMATION DISCLOSED BY

1 80-100%
2 40-80%
3 MINORITY
9 NOT DISCLOSED

Q8 GEOGRAPHIC INFORMATION DISCLOSED BY

1 80-100%
2 40%-80%
3 MINORITY
9 NOT DISCLOSED

Q9 SEGMENT INFORMATION DISCLOSED BY MAJORITY AS

3 SALES/TOTAL ASSETS BY PRODUCT
4 SALES/OPER. INC BY PRODUCT LINE
5 TOTAL ASSETS BY PRODUCT LINE
6 MINORITY PRACTICE
7 OTHER
9 NOT DISCLOSED

Q10 GEOGRAPHIC INFORMATION DISCLOSED BY MAJORITY AS

3 SALES/OPER. INC./TOTAL ASSETS
4 SALES/OPER. INC
5 TOTAL ASSETS
6 MINORITY PRACTICE
7 OTHER
9 NOT DISCLOSED

Q11 MAJORITY OF COMPANIES REPORT EMPLOYEES

1 WORLDWIDE BY 80-100%
2 WORLDWIDE BY 40-80%
3 DOMESTIC BY 80-100%
4 DOMESTIC BY 40-80%
5 PARENT COMPANY BY 80-100%
6 PARENT COMPANY BY 40-80%
8 BY MINORITY
9 NOT DISCLOSED

Q12 A BREAKDOWN OF EMPLOYEES BY FUNCTION, GEOGRAPHICAL AREA OR LINE OF BUSINESS EXISTS FOR

1 80-100%
2 40-80%
3 MINORITY
9 NOT DISCLOSED

Q13 BREAKDOWN OF FULL TIME/PART TIME EMPLOYEES EXISTS FOR

1 80-100%
2 40-80%
3 MINORITY
9 NOT DISCLOSED

Q14 TOTAL REMUNERATION TO DIRECTORS/OFFICERS DISCLOSED BY

1 80-100%
2 40-80%
3 MINORITY
9 NOT DISCLOSED

Q15 LABOR RELATIONS DISCUSSED BY

1 80-100%
2 40-80%
3 MINORITY
9 NOT DISCLOSED

Q16 STOCK OPTION PLANS ARE

1 USED
2 NOT USED
3 NOT DETERMINABLE

Q17 NAMES AND TITLES OF PRINCIPAL OFFICERS DISCLOSED BY

1 80-100%
2 40-80%
3 MINORITY
9 NOT DISCLOSED

Q18 LIST OF BOARD MEMBERS AND THEIR AFFILIATIONS DISCLOSED BY

1 80-100%
2 40-80%
3 MINORITY
9 NOT DISCLOSED

Q19 COMPANY SHARES HELD BY DIRECTORS/OFFICERS DISCLOSED BY

1 80-100%
2 40-80%
3 MINORITY
9 NOT DISCLOSED

Q20 RESEARCH AND DEVELOPMENT COSTS DISCLOSED BY

1 BY 80-100% WORLDWIDE
2 BY 40-80% WORLDWIDE
3 BY 80-100% DOMESTIC
4 BY 40-80% DOMESTIC
5 BY 80-100% PARENT CO.
6 BY 40-80% PARENT CO.
8 MINORITY
9 NOT DISCLOSED

Q21 CAPITAL EXPENDITURES DISCLOSED BY

1 80-100% FOR WORLDWIDE
2 40-80% FOR WORLDWIDE
3 80-100% FOR DOMESTIC
4 40-80% FOR DOMESTIC
5 80-100% FOR PARENT CO.
6 40-80% FOR PARENT CO.
8 MINORITY
9 NOT DISCLOSED

Q22 EXPORTS REPORTED BY

1 80-100%
2 40-80%
3 MINORITY
9 NOT DISCLOSED

Q23 INCOME STATEMENT FORMAT

1 SALES LESS EXPENSES
2 DR./CR. FORMAT
3 SALES-EXP, DR./CR. FORMATS
4 OPER PROFIT LESS INT & TAX EXP
5 NOT PRESCRIBED

Q24 COMPARATIVE INCOME STATEMENT DATA PROVIDED BY

1 80-100%, TWO YEARS
2 40-80%, TWO YEARS
3 80-100%, MORE THAN TWO YEARS
4 40-80%, MORE THAN TWO YEARS
5 MINORITY
8 NO COMPARATIVE DATA AVAILABLE
9 NOT DISCLOSED

Q25 SALES REPORTED BY

1 80-100%
2 40-80%
3 MINORITY
9 NOT DISCLOSED

Q26 COST OF GOODS SOLD REPORTED BY

1 80-100%
2 40-80%
3 MINORITY
9 NOT DISCLOSED

Q27 SG & A REPORTED ON INCOME STATEMENT BY

1 80-100%
2 40-80%
3 MINORITY
9 NOT DISCLOSED

Q28 DEPRECIATION REPORTED ON INCOME STATEMENT BY

1 80-100%
2 40-80%
3 MINORITY
9 NOT DISCLOSED

Q29 OPERATING INCOME REPORTED ON INCOME STATEMENT BY

1 80-100%
2 40-80%
3 MINORITY
9 NOT DISCLOSED

Q30 FOREIGN EXCHANGE GAINS/LOSSES REPORTED ON INCOME STATEMENT

1 80-100%
2 40-80%
3 MINORITY
9 NOT DISCLOSED

Q31 EXTRAORDINARY GAINS/LOSSES REPORTED ON INCOME STATEMENT

1 80-100%
2 40-80%
3 MINORITY
9 NOT DISCLOSED

Q32 INCOME TAX EXPENSE REPORTED BY

1 80-100%
2 40-80%
3 MINORITY
9 NOT DISCLOSED

Q33 MINORITY INTEREST REPORTED ON INCOME STATEMENT BY

1 80-100%
2 40-80%
3 MINORITY
9 NOT DISCLOSED

Q34 NET INCOME DISCLOSED BY

1 80-100%
2 40-80%
3 MINORITY
9 NOT DISCLOSED

Q35 BALANCE SHEET FORMAT

1 (TOT AST = LIAB + OE); 2 PAGES
2 (TOT AST = LIAB + OE); 1 PAGE
3 ((FA+NWC)-LTD=SE); 1 PAGE
4 (T = L + E); 1 OR 2 PAGES
5 NO PRESCRIBED FORMAT
6 (FA + NWC = LTD + OE); 1 PAGE
7 NO MAJORITY

Q36 COMPARATIVE BALANCE SHEET DATA PROVIDED BY

1 80-100%, TWO YEARS
2 40-80%, TWO YEARS
3 80-100%, MORE THAN TWO YEARS
4 40-80%, MORE THAN TWO YEARS
5 MINORITY
9 NOT DISCLOSED

Q37 BALANCE SHEET ITEMS REPORTED IN

1 DECREASING LIQUIDITY ORDER
2 INCREASING LIQUIDITY ORDER
3 NO FORMAT DEFINED
9 NOT DISCLOSED

Q38 BALANCE SHEET PRESENTED

1 BEFORE APPR. TO RET. EARNINGS
2 AFTER APPR. TO RET. EARNINGS
3 BEF. & AFTER APPR. TO RET. EARN.
9 NOT DISCLOSED

Q39 SEPARATION OF CURRENT AND LONG TERM ASSETS PROVIDED BY

1 80-100%
2 40-80%
3 MINORITY
9 NOT DISCLOSED

Q40 CASH AND EQUIVALENTS REPORTED BY

1 80-100%
2 40-80%
3 MINORITY
9 NOT DISCLOSED

Q41 ACCOUNTS RECEIVABLE REPORTED BY

1 SEPARATING ST & LT, GROSS
2 SEPARATING ST & LT, NET
3 NO BRKDWN ST & LT, GROSS
4 NO BRKDWN ST & LT, NET
5 NOT SEPAR FR OTHER CURR ASSETS
9 NOT DETERMINABLE

Q42 INVENTORIES REPORTED BY

1 80-100%
2 40-80%
3 MINORITY
9 NOT DISCLOSED

Q43 CURRENT ASSETS REPORTED BY

1 80-100%
2 40-80%
3 MINORITY
9 NOT DISCLOSED

Q44 FIXED ASSETS IN ASSET SIDE ARE REPORTED

1 MAJORITY BEFORE ACC. DEP.
2 MAJORITY AFTER ACC.DEP.
3 NO MAJORITY
4 MINORITY
9 NOT DISCLOSED

Q45 GOODWILL AND OTHER INTANGIBLES DISCLOSED BY

1 80-100%
2 40-80%
3 MINORITY
9 NOT DISCLOSED

Q46 TOTAL ASSETS CAN BE DERIVED

1 DIRECTLY FROM B/S
2 INDIRECTLY FROM B/S
3 NO MAJORITY

Q47 SEPARATION OF SHORT-TERM AND LONG-TERM LIABILITIES

1 80-100%
2 40-80%
3 MINORITY
9 NOT DISCLOSED

Q48 CURRENT LIABILITIES REPORTED BY

1 80-100%, BRKDWN DISCLOSED
2 40-80%, BRKDWN DISCLOSED
3 80-100%, NO BRKDWN DISCLOSED
4 40-80%, NO BRKDWN DISCLOSED
5 MINORITY
9 NOT DISCLOSED

Q49 LONG-TERM DEBT REPORTED BY

1 80-100%, CURR. PART SEPARATED
2 40-80%, CURR. PART SEPARATED
3 80-100% CURR. PART NOT SEPARATED
4 40-80% CURR. PART NOT SEPARATED
5 MINORITY
9 NOT DISCLOSED

Q50 PREFERRED STOCK REPORTED BY

1 80-100%
2 40-80%
3 MINORITY
4 NOT USED
9 NOT DISCLOSED

Q51 RESERVES DISCLOSED

1 STATUTORY/LEGAL BY 80-100%
2 STATUTORY/LEGAL BY 40-80%
3 DISCRETIONARY BY 80-100%
4 DISCRETIONARY BY 40-80%
5 STAT./LEGAL/DISC. BY 80-100%
6 STAT./LEGAL/DISC. BY 40-80%
8 MINORITY
9 NOT DISCLOSED

Q52 STATEMENT OF CHANGES IN STOCKHOLDERS' EQUITY REPORTED BY

1 80-100%
2 40-80%
3 MINORITY
9 NOT DISCLOSED

Q53 APPROPRIATION OF RETAINED EARNINGS DISCLOSED BY

1 80-100%
2 40-80%
3 MINORITY
9 NOT DISCLOSED

Q54 STATEMENT OF CASH FLOW IS REPORTED BY

1 80-100%
2 40-80%
3 MINORITY
9 NOT DISCLOSED

Q55 FUNDS DEFINITION IN STATEMENT OF CASH FLOW

1 WORKING CAPITAL
2 CASH
3 MODIFIED WORKING CAPITAL
4 MODIFIED CASH
5 NET BORROWINGS
6 EXTERNAL FUNDS
7 NOT DETERMINABLE
8 MINORITY PRACTICES
9 NOT DISCLOSED

Q56 IF CASH FLOW IS REPORTED, TOTAL FUNDS FROM OPERATIONS ARE DISCLOSED BY

1 80-100%
2 40-80%
3 MINORITY
9 NOT DISCLOSED

Q57 IF CASH FLOW IS REPORTED, ADJUSTMENTS FOR NON-CASH ITEMS ARE DISCLOSED BY

1 80-100%
2 40-80%
3 MINORITY
9 NOT DISCLOSED

Q58 SUBSEQUENT EVENTS DISCLOSED IN ANNUAL REPORTS BY

1 80-100%
2 40-80%
3 MINORITY
9 NOT DISCLOSED

Q59 EARNINGS PER SHARE DATA REPORTED BY

1 80-100%
2 40-80%
3 MINORITY
9 NOT DISCLOSED

Q60 EARNINGS PER SHARE DISCLOSED BY MAJORITY

1 IN INCOME STATEMENT
2 IN NOTES TO THE ACCOUNTS
3 ELSEWHERE IN THE REPORT
8 NO EPS GIVEN BY MAJORITY
9 NOT DISCLOSED

Q61 MAJORITY OF COMPANIES REPORT EPS BASED ON NET INCOME AFTER PREFERRED DIVIDENDS

1 YES
2 BEFORE MINORITY INTEREST
3 BEFORE ALLOCATION TO RESERVES
4 BEFORE INCOME TAX
5 BEFORE EXTRAORDINARY ITEMS
6 BEFORE FOREIGN EXCHG GAIN/LOSS
7 OTHER
8 NO EPS GIVEN BY MAJORITY
9 NOT DISCLOSED

Q62 EPS DENOMINATOR DEFINED BY MAJORITY AS

1 AVERAGE SHARES DURING PERIOD
2 YEAR-END SHARES
3 OTHER
9 MAJORITY DO NOT DISCLOSE EPS

Q63 DILUTED EARNINGS PER SHARE REPORTED BY

1 80-100%
2 40-80%
3 MINORITY
9 NOT DISCLOSED

Q64 DIVIDEND PER SHARE REPORTED BY

1 80-100%
2 40-80%
3 MINORITY
9 NOT DISCLOSED

Q65 MAJORITY OF COMPANIES REPORT DIVIDEND PER SHARE

1 GROSS
2 NET AFTER TAX ADJ
9 NOT DISCLOSED

Q66 INTERIM DPS REPORTED IN ANNUAL REPORTS BY

1 80-100%
2 40-80%
3 MINORITY
9 NOT DISCLOSED

Q67 COMMON SHARES OUTSTANDING REPORTED BY

1 80-100%
2 40-80%
3 MINORITY
9 NOT DISCLOSED

Q68 COMMON SHARES OUTSTANDING DISCLOSED AS

1 AVERAGE OUTSTANDING SHARES
2 EQUIVALENT SHRS BASED ON PAR
3 EST BASED ON UNIFORM PAR VALUE
4 STOCK DATA NOT REPORTED
5 YEAR-END SHARES
9 NOT DISCLOSED

Q69 CHANGES IN CAPITAL MOST FREQUENTLY ACHIEVED THROUGH

1 NEW ISSUE OF STOCK
2 NEW ISSUES, STOCK SPLIT
3 NEW ISSUES, STOCK DIVIDEND
4 NEW ISSUES, RIGHTS ISSUE
5 COMBINATION THREE/MORE OPTION
6 NEW ISS, STK DVD, CONV SEC
7 NEW ISS, STK SPLT, RIGHTS ISS
8 NEW ISS, STK DVD, RIGHTS ISS
9 NOT DISCLOSED

Q70 PAR OR STATED VALUE OF EQUITY (COMMON STOCK) REPORTED BY

1 80-100%
2 40-80%
3 MINORITY
9 NOT DISCLOSED

Q71 STOCK EXCHANGE WHERE TRADING OCCURS DISCLOSED BY

1 80-100%
2 40-80%
3 MINORITY
8 SINGLE STK EXCH IN THE COUNTRY
9 NOT DISCLOSED

Q72 YEAR-END STOCK PRICE REPORTED IN ANNUAL REPORTS BY

1 80-100%
2 40-80%
3 MINORITY
9 NOT DISCLOSED

Q73 MULTIPLE CLASSES OF STOCK ALLOWED ARE

1 UTILIZED BY 80-100%
2 UTILIZED BY 40-80%
3 UTILIZED BY MINORITY
4 NOT ALLOWED
9 NOT DISCLOSED

Q74 MULTIPLE CLASSES OF STOCK ALLOWED IN THE COUNTRY HAVE DIFFERENT

1 VOTING RIGHTS
2 DIVIDENDS
3 PAR VALUE
4 DISSOLUTION RIGHTS
5 OTHER
6 RIGHTS/DIVIDEND/PAR
8 NO MULTIPLE STOCK ALLOWED
9 NOT DISCLOSED

Q75 ARE THERE DIFFERENT DIVIDENDS PAID FOR EACH CLASS OF COMMON STOCK?

1 YES
2 NO
3 NO MULTIPLE STOCK ALLOWED
9 NOT DISCLOSED

Q76 EPS FOR MULTIPLE CLASSES OF STOCKS PROVIDED BY

1 80-100%
2 40-80%
3 NO DIFF IN EPS BTW STOCKS
4 NO MULTIPLE STOCK ALLOWED
5 MINOR OBSERVATIONS
9 NO MULTIPLE SHARES

Q77 MAJORITY SHAREHOLDINGS DISCLOSED BY

1 80-100%
2 40-80%
3 MINORITY
9 NOT DISCLOSED

Q78 NAMES OF PRINCIPAL SHAREHOLDERS DISCLOSED

1 80-100%
2 40-80%
3 MINORITY
9 NOT DISCLOSED

Financial Reporting Practices in 24 Countries

NO.	ACCOUNTING & AUDITING ITEMS	Australia	Austria	Belgium
Q1	LANGUAGE OF THE FINANCIAL STATEMENTS	ENGLISH	LOCAL LANGUAGE, MINOR. ENGLISH	LOCAL LANGUAGE, MINOR. ENGLISH
Q2	SUMMARY FINANCIAL INFORMATION PRESENTED BY	80-100%	80-100%	80-100%
Q3	MAJOR FINANCIAL RATIOS COMPUTED AND REPORTED BY	MINORITY	MINORITY	40-80%
Q4	NOTES TO THE FINANCIAL ACCOUNTS ARE	EXTENSIVELY UTILIZED	MODERATELY UTILIZED	MODERATELY UTILIZED
Q5	INFLATION ADJUSTED DATA PROVIDED BY	NONE OF THE COMPANIES	NONE OF THE COMPANIES	NONE OF THE COMPANIES
Q6	MAJORITY OF COMPANIES REPORT THE SUBSIDIARIES'	NAME,HDQTR,FIN'L RESULTS,%HELD	MINORITY PRACTICE	NAME,HDQTR,FIN'L RESULTS,%HELD
Q7	SEGMENT INFORMATION DISCLOSED BY	80-100%	40-80%	40-80%
Q8	GEOGRAPHIC INFORMATION DISCLOSED BY	40%-80%	MINORITY	40%-80%
Q9	SEGMENT INFORMATION DISCLOSED BY MAJORITY AS	SALES/OPER.INC BY PRODUCT LINE	TOTAL ASSETS BY PRODUCT LINE	SALES/OPER.INC BY PRODUCT LINE
Q10	GEOGRAPHIC INFORMATION DISCLOSED BY MAJORITY AS	SALES/OPER.INC./TOTAL ASSETS	MINORITY PRACTICE	SALES/OPER.INC./TOTAL ASSETS
Q11	MAJORITY OF COMPANIES REPORT EMPLOYEES	DOMESTIC BY 80-100%	WORLDWIDE BY 80-100%	WORLDWIDE BY 80-100%
Q12	A BREAKDOWN OF EMPLOYEES BY FUNCTION, GEOGRAPHICAL AREA OR LINE OF BUSINESS EXISTS FOR	NOT DISCLOSED	NOT DISCLOSED	40-80%
Q13	A BREAKDOWN OF FULL TIME/PART TIME EMPLOYEES EXISTS FOR	NOT DISCLOSED	MINORITY	MINORITY
Q14	TOTAL REMUNERATION TO DIRECTORS/OFFICERS DISCLOSED BY	80-100%	NOT DISCLOSED	NOT DISCLOSED
Q15	LABOR RELATIONS DISCUSSED BY	MINORITY	NOT DISCLOSED	MINORITY
Q16	STOCK OPTION PLANS ARE	USED	NOT USED	NOT USED
Q17	NAMES AND TITLES OF PRINCIPAL OFFICERS DISCLOSED BY	80-100%	80-100%	80-100%
Q18	LIST OF BOARD MEMBERS AND THEIR AFFILIATIONS DISCLOSED BY	80-100%	80-100%	80-100%
Q19	COMPANY SHARES HELD BY DIRECTORS/OFFICERS DISCLOSED BY	40-80%	NOT DISCLOSED	NOT DISCLOSED
Q20	RESEARCH AND DEVELOPMENT COSTS DISCLOSED BY	MINORITY	MINORITY	NOT DISCLOSED
Q21	CAPITAL EXPENDITURES DISCLOSED BY	80-100% FOR WORLDWIDE	80-100% FOR WORLDWIDE	MINORITY
Q22	EXPORTS REPORTED BY	MINORITY	MINORITY	MINORITY

Financial Reporting Practices in 24 Countries

NO.	ACCOUNTING & AUDITING ITEMS	Australia	Austria	Belgium
Q23	INCOME STATEMENT FORMAT	OPER PROFIT LESS INT & TAX EXP	DR./CR. FORMAT	DR./CR. FORMAT
Q24	COMPARATIVE INCOME STATEMENT DATA PROVIDED BY	80-100%, TWO YEARS	40-80%, TWO YEARS	80-100%, TWO YEARS
Q25	SALES REPORTED BY	80-100%	40-80%	40-80%
Q26	COST OF GOODS SOLD REPORTED BY	MINORITY	40-80%	40-80%
Q27	SG & A EXPENSE REPORTED ON INCOME STATEMENT BY	MINORITY	80-100%	40-80%
Q28	DEPRECIATION REPORTED ON INCOME STATEMENT BY	40-80%	40-80%	40-80%
Q29	OPERATING INCOME REPORTED ON INCOME STATEMENT BY	40-80%	MINORITY	40-80%
Q30	FOREIGN EXCHANGE GAINS/LOSSES REPORTED ON INCOME STATEMENT	40-80%	NOT DISCLOSED	MINORITY
Q31	EXTRAORDINARY GAINS/LOSSES REPORTED ON INCOME STATEMENT	80-100%	80-100%	80-100%
Q32	INCOME TAX EXPENSE REPORTED BY	80-100%	40-80%	40-80%
Q33	MINORITY INTEREST REPORTED ON INCOME STATEMENT BY	40-80%	MINORITY	40-80%
Q34	NET INCOME DISCLOSED BY	80-100%	80-100%	80-100%
Q35	BALANCE SHEET FORMAT	((FA+NWC)-LTD=SE);1 PAGE	(TOT AST = LIAB + OE);2 PAGES	(TOT AST = LIAB + OE);1 PAGE
Q36	COMPARATIVE BALANCE SHEET DATA PROVIDED BY	80-100%, TWO YEARS	40-80%, TWO YEARS	80-100%, TWO YEARS
Q37	BALANCE SHEET ITEMS REPORTED IN	INCREASING LIQUIDITY ORDER	INCREASING LIQUIDITY ORDER	INCREASING LIQUIDITY ORDER
Q38	BALANCE SHEET PRESENTED	AFTER APPR. TO RET. EARNINGS	AFTER APPR. TO RET. EARNINGS	BEFORE APPR. TO RET.EARNINGS
Q39	SEPARATION OF CURRENT AND LONG TERM ASSETS PROVIDED BY	80-100%	80-100%	80-100%
Q40	CASH AND EQUIVALENTS REPORTED BY	80-100%	80-100%	80-100%
Q41	ACCOUNTS RECEIVABLE REPORTED BY	SEPARATING ST & LT, NET	NOT SEPAR FR OTHER CURR ASSETS	SEPARATING ST & LT, NET
Q42	INVENTORIES REPORTED BY	80-100%	80-100%	80-100%
Q43	CURRENT ASSETS REPORTED BY	80-100%	40-80%	80-100%
Q44	FIXED ASSETS IN ASSET SIDE ARE REPORTED	MAJORITY AFTER ACC.DEP.	MAJORITY AFTER ACC.DEP.	MAJORITY AFTER ACC.DEP.
Q45	GOODWILL AND OTHER INTANGIBLES DISCLOSED BY	40-80%	80-100%	80-100%

Financial Reporting Practices in 24 Countries

NO.	ACCOUNTING & AUDITING ITEMS	Australia	Austria	Belgium
Q46	TOTAL ASSETS CAN BE DERIVED	NO MAJORITY	DIRECTLY FROM B/S	DIRECTLY FROM B/S
Q47	SEPARATION OF SHORT-TERM AND LONG-TERM LIABILITIES	80-100%	40-80%	80-100%
Q48	CURRENT LIABILITIES REPORTED BY	80-100%, BRKDWN DISCLOSED	80-100%, BRKDWN DISCLOSED	80-100%, BRKDWN DISCLOSED
Q49	LONG TERM DEBT REPORTED BY	80-100% CURR PART NOT SEPARATE	80-100%, CURR. PART SEPARATED	80-100%, CURR. PART SEPARATED
Q50	PREFERRED STOCK REPORTED BY	MINORITY	MINORITY	NOT USED
Q51	RESERVES DISCLOSED	STATUTORY/LEGAL BY 80-100%	STAT./LEGAL/DISC. BY 80-100%	STATUTORY/LEGAL BY 80-100%
Q52	STATEMENT OF CHANGES IN STOCKHOLDERS' EQUITY REPORTED BY	MINORITY	80-100%	40-80%
Q53	APPROPRIATION OF RETAINED EARNINGS DISCLOSED BY	80-100%	80-100%	80-100%
Q54	STATEMENT OF CASH FLOW IS REPORTED BY	80-100%	MINORITY	MINORITY
Q55	FUNDS DEFINITION IN STATEMENT OF CASH FLOW	WORKING CAPITAL	NOT DETERMINABLE	NOT DISCLOSED
Q56	IF CASH FLOW IS REPORTED, TOTAL FUNDS FROM OPERATIONS ARE DISCLOSED BY	80-100%	MINORITY	MINORITY
Q57	IF CASH FLOW IS REPORTED, ADJUSTMENTS FOR NON-CASH ITEMS ARE DISCLOSED BY	40-80%	MINORITY	MINORITY
Q58	SUBSEQUENT EVENTS DISCLOSED IN ANNUAL REPORTS BY	40-80%	MINORITY	MINORITY
Q59	EARNINGS PER SHARE DATA REPORTED BY	80-100%	MINORITY	MINORITY
Q60	EARNINGS PER SHARE DISCLOSED BY MAJORITY	ELSEWHERE IN THE REPORT	NO EPS GIVEN BY MAJORITY	NO EPS GIVEN BY MAJORITY
Q61	MAJORITY OF COMPANIES REPORT EPS BASED ON NET INCOME AFTER PREFERRED DIVIDENDS	BEFORE EXTRAORDINARY ITEMS	NO EPS GIVEN BY MAJORITY	NO EPS GIVEN BY MAJORITY
Q62	EPS DENOMINATOR DEFINED BY MAJORITY AS	YEAR-END SHARES	MAJORITY DO NOT DISCLOSE EPS	MAJORITY DO NOT DISCLOSE EPS
Q63	DILUTED EARNINGS PER SHARE REPORTED BY	NOT DISCLOSED	NOT DISCLOSED	NOT DISCLOSED
Q64	DIVIDEND PER SHARE REPORTED BY	80-100%	MINORITY	40-80%
Q65	MAJORITY OF COMPANIES REPORT DIVIDEND PER SHARE	GROSS	GROSS	NET AFTER TAX ADJ
Q66	INTERIM DPS REPORTED IN ANNUAL REPORTS BY	MINORITY	NOT DISCLOSED	NOT DISCLOSED

Financial Reporting Practices in 24 Countries

NO.	ACCOUNTING & AUDITING ITEMS	Australia	Austria	Belgium
Q67	COMMON SHARES OUTSTANDING REPORTED BY	80-100%	MINORITY	40-80%
Q68	COMMON SHARES OUTSTANDING DISCLOSED	YEAR-END SHARES	EQUIVALENT SHRS BASED ON PAR	YEAR-END SHARES
Q69	CHANGES IN CAPITAL MOST FREQUENTLY ACHIEVED THROUGH	COMBINATION THREE/MORE OPTION	NEW ISSUE OF STOCK	NEW ISSUES, RIGHTS ISSUE
Q70	PAR OR STATED VALUE OF EQUITY (COMMON STOCK) REPORTED BY	80-100%	MINORITY	MINORITY
Q71	STOCK EXCHANGE WHERE TRADING OCCURS DISCLOSED BY	40-80%	SINGLE STK EXCH IN THE COUNTRY	NOT DISCLOSED
Q72	YEAR-END STOCK PRICE REPORTED IN ANNUAL REPORTS BY	40-80%	NOT DISCLOSED	NOT DISCLOSED
Q73	MULTIPLE CLASSES OF STOCK ALLOWED ARE	UTILIZED BY MINORITY	NOT ALLOWED	UTILIZED BY MINORITY
Q74	MULTIPLE CLASSES OF STOCK ALLOWED IN THE COUNTRY HAVE DIFFERENT	VOTING RIGHTS	NO MULTIPLE STOCK ALLOWED	DIVIDENDS
Q75	ARE THERE DIFFERENT DIVIDENDS PAID FOR EACH CLASS OF COMMON STOCK?	NO	NO MULTIPLE STOCK ALLOWED	YES
Q76	EPS FOR MULTIPLE CLASSES OF STOCKS PROVIDED BY	MINOR OBSERVATIONS	NO MULTIPLE STOCK ALLOWED	40-80%
Q77	MAJORITY SHAREHOLDINGS DISCLOSED BY	80-100%	NOT DISCLOSED	NOT DISCLOSED
Q78	NAMES OF PRINCIPAL SHAREHOLDERS DISCLOSED	80-100%	NOT DISCLOSED	NOT DISCLOSED

Financial Reporting Practices in 24 Countries

NO.	ACCOUNTING & AUDITING ITEMS	Canada	Denmark	Finland
Q1	LANGUAGE OF THE FINANCIAL STATEMENTS	ENGLISH	LOCAL LANGUAGE, 40-80% ENGLISH	LOCAL LANGUAGE, 40-80% ENGLISH
Q2	SUMMARY FINANCIAL INFORMATION PRESENTED BY	80-100%	80-100%	80-100%
Q3	MAJOR FINANCIAL RATIOS COMPUTED AND REPORTED BY	40-80%	40-80%	80-100%
Q4	NOTES TO THE FINANCIAL ACCOUNTS ARE	EXTENSIVELY UTILIZED	MODERATELY UTILIZED	EXTENSIVELY UTILIZED
Q5	INFLATION ADJUSTED DATA PROVIDED BY	MINORITY	NONE OF THE COMPANIES	NONE OF THE COMPANIES
Q6	MAJORITY OF COMPANIES REPORT THE SUBSIDIARIES'	MINORITY PRACTICE	NAME,DOMICILE,%HELD	NAME,DOMICILE,%HELD
Q7	SEGMENT INFORMATION DISCLOSED BY	80-100%	40-80%	80-100%
Q8	GEOGRAPHIC INFORMATION DISCLOSED BY	80-100%	40%-80%	80-100%
Q9	SEGMENT INFORMATION DISCLOSED BY MAJORITY AS	SALES/OPERINC/TOT.ASST BY PROD	SALES/OPER.INC BY PRODUCT LINE	SALES/OPER.INC BY PRODUCT LINE
Q10	GEOGRAPHIC INFORMATION DISCLOSED BY MAJORITY AS	SALES/OPER.INC./TOTAL ASSETS	SALES/OPER. INC.	SALES/OPER. INC.
Q11	MAJORITY OF COMPANIES REPORT EMPLOYEES	WORLDWIDE BY 40-80%	WORLDWIDE BY 80-100%	WORLDWIDE BY 80-100%
Q12	A BREAKDOWN OF EMPLOYEES BY FUNCTION, GEOGRAPHICAL AREA OR LINE OF BUSINESS EXISTS FOR	NOT DISCLOSED	MINORITY	MINORITY
Q13	A BREAKDOWN OF FULL TIME/PART TIME EMPLOYEES EXISTS FOR	NOT DISCLOSED	NOT DISCLOSED	MINORITY
Q14	TOTAL REMUNERATION TO DIRECTORS/OFFICERS DISCLOSED BY	NOT DISCLOSED	40-80%	80-100%
Q15	LABOR RELATIONS DISCUSSED BY	NOT DISCLOSED	MINORITY	NOT DISCLOSED
Q16	STOCK OPTION PLANS ARE	USED	NOT USED	NOT USED
Q17	NAMES AND TITLES OF PRINCIPAL OFFICERS DISCLOSED BY	80-100%	80-100%	80-100%
Q18	LIST OF BOARD MEMBERS AND THEIR AFFILIATIONS DISCLOSED BY	80-100%	80-100%	80-100%
Q19	COMPANY SHARES HELD BY DIRECTORS/OFFICERS DISCLOSED BY	NOT DISCLOSED	NOT DISCLOSED	MINORITY
Q20	RESEARCH AND DEVELOPMENT COSTS DISCLOSED BY	MINORITY	NOT DISCLOSED	BY 40-80% WORLDWIDE
Q21	CAPITAL EXPENDITURES DISCLOSED BY	40-80% FOR WORLDWIDE	80-100% FOR WORLDWIDE	80-100% FOR WORLDWIDE
Q22	EXPORTS REPORTED BY	40-80%	MINORITY	40-80%

Financial Reporting Practices in 24 Countries

NO.	ACCOUNTING & AUDITING ITEMS	Canada	Denmark	Finland
Q23	INCOME STATEMENT FORMAT	SALES LESS EXPENSES	SALES LESS EXPENSES	SALES LESS EXPENSES
Q24	COMPARATIVE INCOME STATEMENT DATA PROVIDED BY	80-100%, TWO YEARS	80-100%, TWO YEARS	80-100%, TWO YEARS
Q25	SALES REPORTED BY	80-100%	80-100%	80-100%
Q26	COST OF GOODS SOLD REPORTED BY	40-80%	40-80%	40-80%
Q27	SG & A EXPENSE REPORTED ON INCOME STATEMENT BY	40-80%	80-100%	80-100%
Q28	DEPRECIATION REPORTED ON INCOME STATEMENT BY	80-100%	40-80%	80-100%
Q29	OPERATING INCOME REPORTED ON INCOME STATEMENT BY	40-80%	MINORITY	80-100%
Q30	FOREIGN EXCHANGE GAINS/LOSSES REPORTED ON INCOME STATEMENT	MINORITY	MINORITY	40-80%
Q31	EXTRAORDINARY GAINS/LOSSES REPORTED ON INCOME STATEMENT	80-100%	40-80%	80-100%
Q32	INCOME TAX EXPENSE REPORTED BY	80-100%	80-100%	80-100%
Q33	MINORITY INTEREST REPORTED ON INCOME STATEMENT BY	MINORITY	40-80%	40-80%
Q34	NET INCOME DISCLOSED BY	80-100%	80-100%	80-100%
Q35	BALANCE SHEET FORMAT	(TOT AST = LIAB + OE);1 PAGE	(TOT AST = LIAB + OE);2 PAGES	(TOT AST = LIAB + OE);2 PAGES
Q36	COMPARATIVE BALANCE SHEET DATA PROVIDED BY	80-100%, TWO YEARS	80-100%, TWO YEARS	80-100%, TWO YEARS
Q37	BALANCE SHEET ITEMS REPORTED IN	DECREASING LIQUIDITY ORDER	INCREASING LIQUIDITY ORDER	DECREASING LIQUIDITY ORDER
Q38	BALANCE SHEET PRESENTED	AFTER APPR. TO RET. EARNINGS	AFTER APPR. TO RET. EARNINGS	BEFORE APPR. TO RET.EARNINGS
Q39	SEPARATION OF CURRENT AND LONG TERM ASSETS PROVIDED BY	80-100%	80-100%	80-100%
Q40	CASH AND EQUIVALENTS REPORTED BY	80-100%	80-100%	80-100%
Q41	ACCOUNTS RECEIVABLE REPORTED BY	SEPARATING ST & LT, NET	SEPARATING ST & LT, NET	NO BRKDWN ST & LT, GROSS
Q42	INVENTORIES REPORTED BY	80-100%	80-100%	80-100%
Q43	CURRENT ASSETS REPORTED BY	80-100%	80-100%	80-100%
Q44	FIXED ASSETS IN ASSET SIDE ARE REPORTED	MAJORITY AFTER ACC.DEP.	MAJORITY AFTER ACC.DEP.	MAJORITY AFTER ACC.DEP.
Q45	GOODWILL AND OTHER INTANGIBLES DISCLOSED BY	40-80%	40-80%	80-100%

Financial Reporting Practices in 24 Countries

NO.	ACCOUNTING & AUDITING ITEMS	Canada	Denmark	Finland
Q46	TOTAL ASSETS CAN BE DERIVED	DIRECTLY FROM B/S	DIRECTLY FROM B/S	DIRECTLY FROM B/S
Q47	SEPARATION OF SHORT-TERM AND LONG-TERM LIABILITIES	80-100%	80-100%	80-100%
Q48	CURRENT LIABILITIES REPORTED BY	80-100%, BRKDWN DISCLOSED	80-100%, BRKDWN DISCLOSED	80-100%, BRKDWN DISCLOSED
Q49	LONG TERM DEBT REPORTED BY	80-100% CURR PART NOT SEPARATE	80-100%, CURR. PART SEPARATED	80-100%, CURR. PART SEPARATED
Q50	PREFERRED STOCK REPORTED BY	80-100%	80-100%	40-80%
Q51	RESERVES DISCLOSED	STATUTORY/LEGAL BY 80-100%	STAT./LEGAL/DISC. BY 80-100%	STAT./LEGAL/DISC. BY 80-100%
Q52	STATEMENT OF CHANGES IN STOCKHOLDERS' EQUITY REPORTED BY	80-100%	MINORITY	MINORITY
Q53	APPROPRIATION OF RETAINED EARNINGS DISCLOSED BY	80-100%	40-80%	40-80%
Q54	STATEMENT OF CASH FLOW IS REPORTED BY	80-100%	40-80%	80-100%
Q55	FUNDS DEFINITION IN STATEMENT OF CASH FLOW	CASH	MINORITY PRACTICES	WORKING CAPITAL
Q56	IF CASH FLOW IS REPORTED, TOTAL FUNDS FROM OPERATIONS ARE DISCLOSED BY	80-100%	40-80%	40-80%
Q57	IF CASH FLOW IS REPORTED, ADJUSTMENTS FOR NON-CASH ITEMS ARE DISCLOSED BY	80-100%	40-80%	MINORITY
Q58	SUBSEQUENT EVENTS DISCLOSED IN ANNUAL REPORTS BY	80-100%	MINORITY	MINORITY
Q59	EARNINGS PER SHARE DATA REPORTED BY	80-100%	MINORITY	80-100%
Q60	EARNINGS PER SHARE DISCLOSED BY MAJORITY	IN INCOME STATEMENT	NO EPS GIVEN BY MAJORITY	ELSEWHERE IN THE REPORT
Q61	MAJORITY OF COMPANIES REPORT EPS BASED ON NET INCOME AFTER PREFERRED DIVIDENDS	YES	NO EPS GIVEN BY MAJORITY	YES
Q62	EPS DENOMINATOR DEFINED BY MAJORITY AS	AVERAGE SHARES DURING PERIOD	MAJORITY DO NOT DISCLOSE EPS	AVERAGE SHARES DURING PERIOD
Q63	DILUTED EARNINGS PER SHARE REPORTED BY	NOT DISCLOSED	NOT DISCLOSED	NOT DISCLOSED
Q64	DIVIDEND PER SHARE REPORTED BY	80-100%	MINORITY	80-100%
Q65	MAJORITY OF COMPANIES REPORT DIVIDEND PER SHARE	GROSS	GROSS	GROSS
Q66	INTERIM DPS REPORTED IN ANNUAL REPORTS BY	MINORITY	NOT DISCLOSED	NOT DISCLOSED

Financial Reporting Practices in 24 Countries

NO.	ACCOUNTING & AUDITING ITEMS	Canada	Denmark	Finland
Q67	COMMON SHARES OUTSTANDING REPORTED BY	80-100%	40-80%	40-80%
Q68	COMMON SHARES OUTSTANDING DISCLOSED	YEAR-END SHARES	EQUIVALENT SHRS BASED ON PAR	AVERAGE OUTSTANDING SHARES
Q69	CHANGES IN CAPITAL MOST FREQUENTLY ACHIEVED THROUGH	COMBINATION THREE/MORE OPTION	NEW ISSUE OF STOCK	NEW ISSUES, RIGHTS ISSUE
Q70	PAR OR STATED VALUE OF EQUITY (COMMON STOCK) REPORTED BY	40-80%	40-80%	80-100%
Q71	STOCK EXCHANGE WHERE TRADING OCCURS DISCLOSED BY	80-100%	NOT DISCLOSED	MINORITY
Q72	YEAR-END STOCK PRICE REPORTED IN ANNUAL REPORTS BY	40-80%	MINORITY	MINORITY
Q73	MULTIPLE CLASSES OF STOCK ALLOWED ARE	UTILIZED BY MINORITY	UTILIZED BY 40-80%	UTILIZED BY 40-80%
Q74	MULTIPLE CLASSES OF STOCK ALLOWED IN THE COUNTRY HAVE DIFFERENT	VOTING RIGHTS	RIGHTS/DIVIDEND/PAR	VOTING RIGHTS
Q75	ARE THERE DIFFERENT DIVIDENDS PAID FOR EACH CLASS OF COMMON STOCK?	NO	NO	NO
Q76	EPS FOR MULTIPLE CLASSES OF STOCKS PROVIDED BY	NO DIFF IN DIVD BTW STOCKS	NO DIFF IN DIVD BTW STOCKS	NO DIFF IN DIVD BTW STOCKS
Q77	MAJORITY SHAREHOLDINGS DISCLOSED BY	NOT DISCLOSED	NOT DISCLOSED	80-100%
Q78	NAMES OF PRINCIPAL SHAREHOLDERS DISCLOSED	NOT DISCLOSED	NOT DISCLOSED	80-100%

Financial Reporting Practices in 24 Countries

NO.	ACCOUNTING & AUDITING ITEMS	France	West Germany	Hong Kong
Q1	LANGUAGE OF THE FINANCIAL STATEMENTS	LOCAL LANGUAGE, MINOR. ENGLISH	LOCAL LANGUAGE, MINOR. ENGLISH	LOCAL LANGUAGE, 40-80% ENGLISH
Q2	SUMMARY FINANCIAL INFORMATION PRESENTED BY	80-100%	40-80%	80-100%
Q3	MAJOR FINANCIAL RATIOS COMPUTED AND REPORTED BY	MINORITY	MINORITY	MINORITY
Q4	NOTES TO THE FINANCIAL ACCOUNTS ARE	MODERATELY UTILIZED	MODERATELY UTILIZED	EXTENSIVELY UTILIZED
Q5	INFLATION ADJUSTED DATA PROVIDED BY	NONE OF THE COMPANIES	NONE OF THE COMPANIES	NONE OF THE COMPANIES
Q6	MAJORITY OF COMPANIES REPORT THE SUBSIDIARIES'	NAME,DOMICILE,%HELD	NAME,DOMICILE,%HELD	NAME,DOMICILE,%HELD
Q7	SEGMENT INFORMATION DISCLOSED BY	80-100%	40-80%	MINORITY
Q8	GEOGRAPHIC INFORMATION DISCLOSED BY	80-100%	40%-80%	40%-80%
Q9	SEGMENT INFORMATION DISCLOSED BY MAJORITY AS	SALES/OPER.INC BY PRODUCT LINE	SALES/OPER.INC BY PRODUCT LINE	MINORITY PRACTICE
Q10	GEOGRAPHIC INFORMATION DISCLOSED BY MAJORITY AS	SALES/OPER. INC.	SALES/OPER. INC.	SALES/OPER. INC.
Q11	MAJORITY OF COMPANIES REPORT EMPLOYEES	WORLDWIDE BY 80-100%	WORLDWIDE BY 80-100%	BY MINORITY
Q12	A BREAKDOWN OF EMPLOYEES BY FUNCTION, GEOGRAPHICAL AREA OR LINE OF BUSINESS EXISTS FOR	40-80%	NOT DISCLOSED	NOT DISCLOSED
Q13	A BREAKDOWN OF FULL TIME/PART TIME EMPLOYEES EXISTS FOR	MINORITY	40-80%	NOT DISCLOSED
Q14	TOTAL REMUNERATION TO DIRECTORS/OFFICERS DISCLOSED BY	40-80%	40-80%	80-100%
Q15	LABOR RELATIONS DISCUSSED BY	MINORITY	MINORITY	NOT DISCLOSED
Q16	STOCK OPTION PLANS ARE	NOT USED	NOT USED	USED
Q17	NAMES AND TITLES OF PRINCIPAL OFFICERS DISCLOSED BY	80-100%	80-100%	MINORITY
Q18	LIST OF BOARD MEMBERS AND THEIR AFFILIATIONS DISCLOSED BY	80-100%	80-100%	80-100%
Q19	COMPANY SHARES HELD BY DIRECTORS/OFFICERS DISCLOSED BY	NOT DISCLOSED	NOT DISCLOSED	80-100%
Q20	RESEARCH AND DEVELOPMENT COSTS DISCLOSED BY	MINORITY	MINORITY	NOT DISCLOSED
Q21	CAPITAL EXPENDITURES DISCLOSED BY	40-80% FOR WORLDWIDE	80-100% FOR WORLDWIDE	80-100% FOR WORLDWIDE
Q22	EXPORTS REPORTED BY	MINORITY	40-80%	40-80%

Financial Reporting Practices in 24 Countries

NO.	ACCOUNTING & AUDITING ITEMS	France	West Germany	Hong Kong
Q23	INCOME STATEMENT FORMAT	SALES-EXP, DR./CR. FORMATS	SALES LESS EXPENSES	OPER PROFIT LESS INT & TAX EXP
Q24	COMPARATIVE INCOME STATEMENT DATA PROVIDED BY	80-100%, TWO YEARS	40-80%, TWO YEARS	80-100%, TWO YEARS
Q25	SALES REPORTED BY	80-100%	40-80%	40-80%
Q26	COST OF GOODS SOLD REPORTED BY	40-80%	MINORITY	MINORITY
Q27	SG & A EXPENSE REPORTED ON INCOME STATEMENT BY	80-100%	80-100%	NOT DISCLOSED
Q28	DEPRECIATION REPORTED ON INCOME STATEMENT BY	80-100%	40-80%	40-80%
Q29	OPERATING INCOME REPORTED ON INCOME STATEMENT BY	40-80%	MINORITY	40-80%
Q30	FOREIGN EXCHANGE GAINS/LOSSES REPORTED ON INCOME STATEMENT	40-80%	MINORITY	MINORITY
Q31	EXTRAORDINARY GAINS/LOSSES REPORTED ON INCOME STATEMENT	80-100%	80-100%	80-100%
Q32	INCOME TAX EXPENSE REPORTED BY	80-100%	80-100%	40-80%
Q33	MINORITY INTEREST REPORTED ON INCOME STATEMENT BY	80-100%	40-80%	40-80%
Q34	NET INCOME DISCLOSED BY	80-100%	80-100%	80-100%
Q35	BALANCE SHEET FORMAT	(TOT AST = LIAB + OE);2 PAGES	(TOT AST = LIAB + OE);2 PAGES	((FA+NWC)-LTD=SE);1 PAGE
Q36	COMPARATIVE BALANCE SHEET DATA PROVIDED BY	80-100%, TWO YEARS	40-80%, TWO YEARS	80-100%, TWO YEARS
Q37	BALANCE SHEET ITEMS REPORTED IN	INCREASING LIQUIDITY ORDER	INCREASING LIQUIDITY ORDER	INCREASING LIQUIDITY ORDER
Q38	BALANCE SHEET PRESENTED	BEFORE APPR. TO RET.EARNINGS	AFTER APPR. TO RET. EARNINGS	BEFORE APPR. TO RET.EARNINGS
Q39	SEPARATION OF CURRENT AND LONG TERM ASSETS PROVIDED BY	80-100%	80-100%	80-100%
Q40	CASH AND EQUIVALENTS REPORTED BY	80-100%	80-100%	80-100%
Q41	ACCOUNTS RECEIVABLE REPORTED BY	NO BRKDWN ST & LT, GROSS	NO BRKDWN ST & LT, GROSS	SEPARATING ST & LT, NET
Q42	INVENTORIES REPORTED BY	80-100%	80-100%	80-100%
Q43	CURRENT ASSETS REPORTED BY	80-100%	80-100%	80-100%
Q44	FIXED ASSETS IN ASSET SIDE ARE REPORTED	MAJORITY AFTER ACC.DEP.	MAJORITY AFTER ACC.DEP.	MAJORITY AFTER ACC.DEP.
Q45	GOODWILL AND OTHER INTANGIBLES DISCLOSED BY	80-100%	80-100%	40-80%

Financial Reporting Practices in 24 Countries

NO.	ACCOUNTING & AUDITING ITEMS	France	West Germany	Hong Kong
Q46	TOTAL ASSETS CAN BE DERIVED	DIRECTLY FROM B/S	DIRECTLY FROM B/S	INDIRECTLY FROM B/S
Q47	SEPARATION OF SHORT-TERM AND LONG-TERM LIABILITIES	80-100%	80-100%	80-100%
Q48	CURRENT LIABILITIES REPORTED BY	80-100%, BRKDWN DISCLOSED	80-100%, BRKDWN DISCLOSED	40-80%, BRKDWN DISCLOSED
Q49	LONG TERM DEBT REPORTED BY	80-100%, CURR. PART SEPARATED	40-80%, CURR. PART SEPARATED	40-80%, CURR. PART SEPARATED
Q50	PREFERRED STOCK REPORTED BY	40-80%	NOT USED	MINORITY
Q51	RESERVES DISCLOSED	STATUTORY/LEGAL BY 80-100%	STAT./LEGAL/DISC. BY 80-100%	STATUTORY/LEGAL BY 80-100%
Q52	STATEMENT OF CHANGES IN STOCKHOLDERS' EQUITY REPORTED BY	80-100%	MINORITY	MINORITY
Q53	APPROPRIATION OF RETAINED EARNINGS DISCLOSED BY	80-100%	MINORITY	80-100%
Q54	STATEMENT OF CASH FLOW IS REPORTED BY	40-80%	MINORITY	40-80%
Q55	FUNDS DEFINITION IN STATEMENT OF CASH FLOW	WORKING CAPITAL	MINORITY PRACTICES	WORKING CAPITAL
Q56	IF CASH FLOW IS REPORTED, TOTAL FUNDS FROM OPERATIONS ARE DISCLOSED BY	40-80%	MINORITY	80-100%
Q57	IF CASH FLOW IS REPORTED, ADJUSTMENTS FOR NON-CASH ITEMS ARE DISCLOSED BY	80-100%	MINORITY	80-100%
Q58	SUBSEQUENT EVENTS DISCLOSED IN ANNUAL REPORTS BY	NOT DISCLOSED	40-80%	MINORITY
Q59	EARNINGS PER SHARE DATA REPORTED BY	40-80%	MINORITY	80-100%
Q60	EARNINGS PER SHARE DISCLOSED BY MAJORITY	ELSEWHERE IN THE REPORT	NO EPS GIVEN BY MAJORITY	IN INCOME STATEMENT
Q61	MAJORITY OF COMPANIES REPORT EPS BASED ON NET INCOME AFTER PREFERRED DIVIDENDS	YES	NO EPS GIVEN BY MAJORITY	YES
Q62	EPS DENOMINATOR DEFINED BY MAJORITY AS	YEAR-END SHARES	MAJORITY DO NOT DISCLOSE EPS	AVERAGE SHARES DURING PERIOD
Q63	DILUTED EARNINGS PER SHARE REPORTED BY	NOT DISCLOSED	NOT DISCLOSED	MINORITY
Q64	DIVIDEND PER SHARE REPORTED BY	40-80%	40-80%	80-100%
Q65	MAJORITY OF COMPANIES REPORT DIVIDEND PER SHARE	NET AFTER TAX ADJ	NET AFTER TAX ADJ	GROSS
Q66	INTERIM DPS REPORTED IN ANNUAL REPORTS BY	NOT DISCLOSED	NOT DISCLOSED	40-80%

Financial Reporting Practices in 24 Countries

NO.	ACCOUNTING & AUDITING ITEMS	France	West Germany	Hong Kong
Q67	COMMON SHARES OUTSTANDING REPORTED BY	80-100%	MINORITY	80-100%
Q68	COMMON SHARES OUTSTANDING DISCLOSED	YEAR-END SHARES	EST BASED ON UNIFORM PAR VALUE	YEAR-END SHARES
Q69	CHANGES IN CAPITAL MOST FREQUENTLY ACHIEVED THROUGH	NEW ISS, STK DVD, RIGHTS ISS	NEW ISSUE OF STOCK	NEW ISS, STK SPLT, RIGHTS ISS
Q70	PAR OR STATED VALUE OF EQUITY (COMMON STOCK) REPORTED BY	40-80%	MINORITY	80-100%
Q71	STOCK EXCHANGE WHERE TRADING OCCURS DISCLOSED BY	NOT DISCLOSED	NOT DISCLOSED	NOT DISCLOSED
Q72	YEAR-END STOCK PRICE REPORTED IN ANNUAL REPORTS BY	MINORITY	NOT DISCLOSED	NOT DISCLOSED
Q73	MULTIPLE CLASSES OF STOCK ALLOWED ARE	UTILIZED BY MINORITY	NOT ALLOWED	UTILIZED BY MINORITY
Q74	MULTIPLE CLASSES OF STOCK ALLOWED IN THE COUNTRY HAVE DIFFERENT	VOTING RIGHTS	NO MULTIPLE STOCK ALLOWED	RIGHTS/DIVIDEND/PAR
Q75	ARE THERE DIFFERENT DIVIDENDS PAID FOR EACH CLASS OF COMMON STOCK?	YES	NO MULTIPLE STOCK ALLOWED	NO
Q76	EPS FOR MULTIPLE CLASSES OF STOCKS PROVIDED BY	80-100%	NO MULTIPLE STOCK ALLOWED	NO DIFF IN DIVD BTW STOCKS
Q77	MAJORITY SHAREHOLDINGS DISCLOSED BY	MINORITY	NOT DISCLOSED	NOT DISCLOSED
Q78	NAMES OF PRINCIPAL SHAREHOLDERS DISCLOSED	MINORITY	NOT DISCLOSED	NOT DISCLOSED

Financial Reporting Practices in 24 Countries

NO.	ACCOUNTING & AUDITING ITEMS	Italy	Japan	South Korea
Q1	LANGUAGE OF THE FINANCIAL STATEMENTS	LOCAL LANGUAGE, MINOR. ENGLISH	LOCAL LANGUAGE, MINOR. ENGLISH	LOCAL LANGUAGE, MINOR. ENGLISH
Q2	SUMMARY FINANCIAL INFORMATION PRESENTED BY	40-80%	80-100%	MINORITY
Q3	MAJOR FINANCIAL RATIOS COMPUTED AND REPORTED BY	MINORITY	MINORITY	MINORITY
Q4	NOTES TO THE FINANCIAL ACCOUNTS ARE	MODERATELY UTILIZED	MODERATELY UTILIZED	MODERATELY UTILIZED
Q5	INFLATION ADJUSTED DATA PROVIDED BY	NONE OF THE COMPANIES	NONE OF THE COMPANIES	NONE OF THE COMPANIES
Q6	MAJORITY OF COMPANIES REPORT THE SUBSIDIARIES'	NAME,HDQTR,FIN'L RESULTS,%HELD	NAME,DOMICILE,%HELD	NAME ONLY OR WITH DOMICILE
Q7	SEGMENT INFORMATION DISCLOSED BY	40-80%	40-80%	MINORITY
Q8	GEOGRAPHIC INFORMATION DISCLOSED BY	MINORITY	40%-80%	MINORITY
Q9	SEGMENT INFORMATION DISCLOSED BY MAJORITY AS	SALES/OPER.INC BY PRODUCT LINE	SALES/OPER.INC BY PRODUCT LINE	MINORITY PRACTICE
Q10	GEOGRAPHIC INFORMATION DISCLOSED BY MAJORITY AS	MINORITY PRACTICE	SALES/OPER.INC./TOTAL ASSETS	MINORITY PRACTICE
Q11	MAJORITY OF COMPANIES REPORT EMPLOYEES	WORLDWIDE BY 40-80%	PARENT COMPANY BY 80-100%	PARENT COMPANY BY 40-80%
Q12	A BREAKDOWN OF EMPLOYEES BY FUNCTION, GEOGRAPHICAL AREA OR LINE OF BUSINESS EXISTS FOR	80-100%	MINORITY	NOT DISCLOSED
Q13	A BREAKDOWN OF FULL TIME/PART TIME EMPLOYEES EXISTS FOR	NOT DISCLOSED	NOT DISCLOSED	NOT DISCLOSED
Q14	TOTAL REMUNERATION TO DIRECTORS/OFFICERS DISCLOSED BY	NOT DISCLOSED	NOT DISCLOSED	NOT DISCLOSED
Q15	LABOR RELATIONS DISCUSSED BY	80-100%	NOT DISCLOSED	NOT DISCLOSED
Q16	STOCK OPTION PLANS ARE	NOT USED	NOT USED	NOT USED
Q17	NAMES AND TITLES OF PRINCIPAL OFFICERS DISCLOSED BY	80-100%	80-100%	40-80%
Q18	LIST OF BOARD MEMBERS AND THEIR AFFILIATIONS DISCLOSED BY	80-100%	80-100%	40-80%
Q19	COMPANY SHARES HELD BY DIRECTORS/OFFICERS DISCLOSED BY	NOT DISCLOSED	NOT DISCLOSED	NOT DISCLOSED
Q20	RESEARCH AND DEVELOPMENT COSTS DISCLOSED BY	BY 40-80% WORLDWIDE	MINORITY	MINORITY
Q21	CAPITAL EXPENDITURES DISCLOSED BY	40-80% FOR WORLDWIDE	40-80% FOR PARENT CO.	MINORITY
Q22	EXPORTS REPORTED BY	MINORITY	40-80%	40-80%

Financial Reporting Practices in 24 Countries

NO.	ACCOUNTING & AUDITING ITEMS	Italy	Japan	South Korea
Q23	INCOME STATEMENT FORMAT	SALES-EXP, DR./CR. FORMATS	SALES LESS EXPENSES	SALES LESS EXPENSES
Q24	COMPARATIVE INCOME STATEMENT DATA PROVIDED BY	80-100%, TWO YEARS	80-100%, TWO YEARS	40-80%, TWO YEARS
Q25	SALES REPORTED BY	80-100%	80-100%	80-100%
Q26	COST OF GOODS SOLD REPORTED BY	40-80%	80-100%	40-80%
Q27	SG & A EXPENSE REPORTED ON INCOME STATEMENT BY	40-80%	80-100%	80-100%
Q28	DEPRECIATION REPORTED ON INCOME STATEMENT BY	80-100%	MINORITY	MINORITY
Q29	OPERATING INCOME REPORTED ON INCOME STATEMENT BY	40-80%	80-100%	80-100%
Q30	FOREIGN EXCHANGE GAINS/LOSSES REPORTED ON INCOME STATEMENT	MINORITY	40-80%	40-80%
Q31	EXTRAORDINARY GAINS/LOSSES REPORTED ON INCOME STATEMENT	80-100%	40-80%	40-80%
Q32	INCOME TAX EXPENSE REPORTED BY	80-100%	80-100%	80-100%
Q33	MINORITY INTEREST REPORTED ON INCOME STATEMENT BY	80-100%	40-80%	MINORITY
Q34	NET INCOME DISCLOSED BY	80-100%	80-100%	80-100%
Q35	BALANCE SHEET FORMAT	(TOT AST = LIAB + OE);2 PAGES	(TOT AST = LIAB + OE);2 PAGES	(TOT AST = LIAB + OE);2 PAGES
Q36	COMPARATIVE BALANCE SHEET DATA PROVIDED BY	80-100%, TWO YEARS	80-100%, TWO YEARS	40-80%, TWO YEARS
Q37	BALANCE SHEET ITEMS REPORTED IN	DECREASING LIQUIDITY ORDER	DECREASING LIQUIDITY ORDER	DECREASING LIQUIDITY ORDER
Q38	BALANCE SHEET PRESENTED	BEFORE APPR. TO RET.EARNINGS	BEFORE APPR. TO RET.EARNINGS	BEFORE APPR. TO RET.EARNINGS
Q39	SEPARATION OF CURRENT AND LONG TERM ASSETS PROVIDED BY	40-80%	80-100%	80-100%
Q40	CASH AND EQUIVALENTS REPORTED BY	80-100%	80-100%	80-100%
Q41	ACCOUNTS RECEIVABLE REPORTED BY	SEPARATING ST & LT, GROSS	NO BRKDWN ST & LT, GROSS	NO BRKDWN ST & LT, GROSS
Q42	INVENTORIES REPORTED BY	80-100%	80-100%	80-100%
Q43	CURRENT ASSETS REPORTED BY	40-80%	80-100%	80-100%
Q44	FIXED ASSETS IN ASSET SIDE ARE REPORTED	MAJORITY BEFORE ACC. DEP.	MAJORITY AFTER ACC.DEP.	MAJORITY AFTER ACC.DEP.
Q45	GOODWILL AND OTHER INTANGIBLES DISCLOSED BY	40-80%	80-100%	80-100%

Financial Reporting Practices in 24 Countries

NO.	ACCOUNTING & AUDITING ITEMS	Italy	Japan	South Korea
Q46	TOTAL ASSETS CAN BE DERIVED	INDIRECTLY FROM B/S	DIRECTLY FROM B/S	DIRECTLY FROM B/S
Q47	SEPARATION OF SHORT-TERM AND LONG-TERM LIABILITIES	40-80%	80-100%	80-100%
Q48	CURRENT LIABILITIES REPORTED BY	40-80%, BRKDWN DISCLOSED	80-100%, BRKDWN DISCLOSED	40-80%, BRKDWN DISCLOSED
Q49	LONG TERM DEBT REPORTED BY	80-100%, CURR. PART SEPARATED	80-100%, CURR. PART SEPARATED	80-100%, CURR. PART SEPARATED
Q50	PREFERRED STOCK REPORTED BY	40-80%	NOT USED	NOT USED
Q51	RESERVES DISCLOSED	STAT./LEGAL/DISC. BY 80-100%	STATUTORY/LEGAL BY 80-100%	STATUTORY/LEGAL BY 80-100%
Q52	STATEMENT OF CHANGES IN STOCKHOLDERS' EQUITY REPORTED BY	40-80%	80-100%	80-100%
Q53	APPROPRIATION OF RETAINED EARNINGS DISCLOSED BY	40-80%	80-100%	80-100%
Q54	STATEMENT OF CASH FLOW IS REPORTED BY	40-80%	MINORITY	MINORITY
Q55	FUNDS DEFINITION IN STATEMENT OF CASH FLOW	WORKING CAPITAL	WORKING CAPITAL	WORKING CAPITAL
Q56	IF CASH FLOW IS REPORTED, TOTAL FUNDS FROM OPERATIONS ARE DISCLOSED BY	40-80%	80-100%	80-100%
Q57	IF CASH FLOW IS REPORTED, ADJUSTMENTS FOR NON-CASH ITEMS ARE DISCLOSED BY	40-80%	80-100%	80-100%
Q58	SUBSEQUENT EVENTS DISCLOSED IN ANNUAL REPORTS BY	NOT DISCLOSED	MINORITY	MINORITY
Q59	EARNINGS PER SHARE DATA REPORTED BY	MINORITY	80-100%	MINORITY
Q60	EARNINGS PER SHARE DISCLOSED BY MAJORITY	NO EPS GIVEN BY MAJORITY	ELSEWHERE IN THE REPORT	NO EPS GIVEN BY MAJORITY
Q61	MAJORITY OF COMPANIES REPORT EPS BASED ON NET INCOME AFTER PREFERRED DIVIDENDS	NO EPS GIVEN BY MAJORITY	YES	NO EPS GIVEN BY MAJORITY
Q62	EPS DENOMINATOR DEFINED BY MAJORITY AS	MAJORITY DO NOT DISCLOSE EPS	YEAR-END SHARES	MAJORITY DO NOT DISCLOSE EPS
Q63	DILUTED EARNINGS PER SHARE REPORTED BY	NOT DISCLOSED	NOT DISCLOSED	NOT DISCLOSED
Q64	DIVIDEND PER SHARE REPORTED BY	40-80%	80-100%	40-80%
Q65	MAJORITY OF COMPANIES REPORT DIVIDEND PER SHARE	GROSS	GROSS	GROSS
Q66	INTERIM DPS REPORTED IN ANNUAL REPORTS BY	MINORITY	80-100%	NOT DISCLOSED

Financial Reporting Practices in 24 Countries

NO.	ACCOUNTING & AUDITING ITEMS	Italy	Japan	South Korea
Q67	COMMON SHARES OUTSTANDING REPORTED BY	80-100%	80-100%	40-80%
Q68	COMMON SHARES OUTSTANDING DISCLOSED	YEAR-END SHARES	YEAR-END SHARES	YEAR-END SHARES
Q69	CHANGES IN CAPITAL MOST FREQUENTLY ACHIEVED THROUGH	NEW ISSUES, RIGHTS ISSUE	NEW ISS, STK DVD, CONV SEC	NEW ISS, STK DVD, CONV SEC
Q70	PAR OR STATED VALUE OF EQUITY (COMMON STOCK) REPORTED BY	80-100%	80-100%	40-80%
Q71	STOCK EXCHANGE WHERE TRADING OCCURS DISCLOSED BY	NOT DISCLOSED	40-80%	SINGLE STK EXCH IN THE COUNTRY
Q72	YEAR-END STOCK PRICE REPORTED IN ANNUAL REPORTS BY	MINORITY	40-80%	NOT DISCLOSED
Q73	MULTIPLE CLASSES OF STOCK ALLOWED ARE	UTILIZED BY MINORITY	NOT ALLOWED	NOT ALLOWED
Q74	MULTIPLE CLASSES OF STOCK ALLOWED IN THE COUNTRY HAVE DIFFERENT	RIGHTS/DIVIDEND/PAR	NO MULTIPLE STOCK ALLOWED	NO MULTIPLE STOCK ALLOWED
Q75	ARE THERE DIFFERENT DIVIDENDS PAID FOR EACH CLASS OF COMMON STOCK?	YES	NO MULTIPLE STOCK ALLOWED	NO MULTIPLE STOCK ALLOWED
Q76	EPS FOR MULTIPLE CLASSES OF STOCKS PROVIDED BY	80-100%	NO MULTIPLE STOCK ALLOWED	NO MULTIPLE STOCK ALLOWED
Q77	MAJORITY SHAREHOLDINGS DISCLOSED BY	80-100%	40-80%	40-80%
Q78	NAMES OF PRINCIPAL SHAREHOLDERS DISCLOSED	80-100%	40-80%	40-80%

Financial Reporting Practices in 24 Countries

NO.	ACCOUNTING & AUDITING ITEMS	Malaysia	Mexico	Netherlands
Q1	LANGUAGE OF THE FINANCIAL STATEMENTS	LOCAL LANGUAGE, 40-80% ENGLISH	LOCAL LANGUAGE, MINOR. ENGLISH	LOCAL LANGUAGE, 40-80% ENGLISH
Q2	SUMMARY FINANCIAL INFORMATION PRESENTED BY	80-100%	40-80%	80-100%
Q3	MAJOR FINANCIAL RATIOS COMPUTED AND REPORTED BY	40-80%	MINORITY	40-80%
Q4	NOTES TO THE FINANCIAL ACCOUNTS ARE	EXTENSIVELY UTILIZED	EXTENSIVELY UTILIZED	EXTENSIVELY UTILIZED
Q5	INFLATION ADJUSTED DATA PROVIDED BY	NONE OF THE COMPANIES	80 - 100%	NONE OF THE COMPANIES
Q6	MAJORITY OF COMPANIES REPORT THE SUBSIDIARIES'	NAME ONLY OR WITH DOMICILE	NAME ONLY OR WITH DOMICILE	NAME,DOMICILE,%HELD
Q7	SEGMENT INFORMATION DISCLOSED BY	MINORITY	MINORITY	40-80%
Q8	GEOGRAPHIC INFORMATION DISCLOSED BY	40%-80%	MINORITY	40%-80%
Q9	SEGMENT INFORMATION DISCLOSED BY MAJORITY AS	MINORITY PRACTICE	MINORITY PRACTICE	SALES/TOTAL ASSETS BY PRODUCT
Q10	GEOGRAPHIC INFORMATION DISCLOSED BY MAJORITY AS	SALES/OPER.INC./TOTAL ASSETS	MINORITY PRACTICE	SALES/OPER. INC.
Q11	MAJORITY OF COMPANIES REPORT EMPLOYEES	BY MINORITY	WORLDWIDE BY 40-80%	WORLDWIDE BY 40-80%
Q12	A BREAKDOWN OF EMPLOYEES BY FUNCTION, GEOGRAPHICAL AREA OR LINE OF BUSINESS EXISTS FOR	MINORITY	NOT DISCLOSED	40-80%
Q13	A BREAKDOWN OF FULL TIME/PART TIME EMPLOYEES EXISTS FOR	NOT DISCLOSED	NOT DISCLOSED	MINORITY
Q14	TOTAL REMUNERATION TO DIRECTORS/OFFICERS DISCLOSED BY	80-100%	MINORITY	40-80%
Q15	LABOR RELATIONS DISCUSSED BY	NOT DISCLOSED	MINORITY	40-80%
Q16	STOCK OPTION PLANS ARE	USED	NOT USED	USED
Q17	NAMES AND TITLES OF PRINCIPAL OFFICERS DISCLOSED BY	40-80%	MINORITY	80-100%
Q18	LIST OF BOARD MEMBERS AND THEIR AFFILIATIONS DISCLOSED BY	80-100%	80-100%	80-100%
Q19	COMPANY SHARES HELD BY DIRECTORS/OFFICERS DISCLOSED BY	80-100%	NOT DISCLOSED	MINORITY
Q20	RESEARCH AND DEVELOPMENT COSTS DISCLOSED BY	MINORITY	NOT DISCLOSED	MINORITY
Q21	CAPITAL EXPENDITURES DISCLOSED BY	80-100% FOR WORLDWIDE	80-100% FOR WORLDWIDE	80-100% FOR WORLDWIDE
Q22	EXPORTS REPORTED BY	40-80%	40-80%	40-80%

Financial Reporting Practices in 24 Countries

NO.	ACCOUNTING & AUDITING ITEMS	Malaysia	Mexico	Netherlands
Q23	INCOME STATEMENT FORMAT	OPER PROFIT LESS INT & TAX EXP	SALES LESS EXPENSES	SALES-EXP, DR./CR. FORMATS
Q24	COMPARATIVE INCOME STATEMENT DATA PROVIDED BY	80-100%, TWO YEARS	80-100%, TWO YEARS	80-100%, TWO YEARS
Q25	SALES REPORTED BY	80-100%	80-100%	80-100%
Q26	COST OF GOODS SOLD REPORTED BY	MINORITY	80-100%	40-80%
Q27	SG & A EXPENSE REPORTED ON INCOME STATEMENT BY	NOT DISCLOSED	80-100%	40-80%
Q28	DEPRECIATION REPORTED ON INCOME STATEMENT BY	40-80%	MINORITY	40-80%
Q29	OPERATING INCOME REPORTED ON INCOME STATEMENT BY	40-80%	80-100%	80-100%
Q30	FOREIGN EXCHANGE GAINS/LOSSES REPORTED ON INCOME STATEMENT	MINORITY	80-100%	MINORITY
Q31	EXTRAORDINARY GAINS/LOSSES REPORTED ON INCOME STATEMENT	80-100%	80-100%	80-100%
Q32	INCOME TAX EXPENSE REPORTED BY	80-100%	80-100%	40-80%
Q33	MINORITY INTEREST REPORTED ON INCOME STATEMENT BY	40-80%	80-100%	40-80%
Q34	NET INCOME DISCLOSED BY	80-100%	80-100%	80-100%
Q35	BALANCE SHEET FORMAT	((FA+NWC)-LTD=SE);1 PAGE	(TOT AST = LIAB + OE);2 PAGES	(T = L + E); 1 OR 2 PAGES
Q36	COMPARATIVE BALANCE SHEET DATA PROVIDED BY	80-100%, TWO YEARS	80-100%, TWO YEARS	80-100%, TWO YEARS
Q37	BALANCE SHEET ITEMS REPORTED IN	INCREASING LIQUIDITY ORDER	DECREASING LIQUIDITY ORDER	INCREASING LIQUIDITY ORDER
Q38	BALANCE SHEET PRESENTED	AFTER APPR. TO RET. EARNINGS	BEFORE APPR. TO RET.EARNINGS	AFTER APPR. TO RET. EARNINGS
Q39	SEPARATION OF CURRENT AND LONG TERM ASSETS PROVIDED BY	80-100%	80-100%	40-80%
Q40	CASH AND EQUIVALENTS REPORTED BY	80-100%	80-100%	80-100%
Q41	ACCOUNTS RECEIVABLE REPORTED BY	NO BRKDWN ST & LT, NET	SEPARATING ST & LT, GROSS	NO BRKDWN ST & LT, NET
Q42	INVENTORIES REPORTED BY	80-100%	80-100%	80-100%
Q43	CURRENT ASSETS REPORTED BY	40-80%	80-100%	80-100%
Q44	FIXED ASSETS IN ASSET SIDE ARE REPORTED	MAJORITY AFTER ACC.DEP.	NO MAJORITY	MAJORITY AFTER ACC.DEP.
Q45	GOODWILL AND OTHER INTANGIBLES DISCLOSED BY	MINORITY	MINORITY	40-80%

Financial Reporting Practices in 24 Countries

NO.	ACCOUNTING & AUDITING ITEMS	Malaysia	Mexico	Netherlands
Q46	TOTAL ASSETS CAN BE DERIVED	INDIRECTLY FROM B/S	DIRECTLY FROM B/S	DIRECTLY FROM B/S
Q47	SEPARATION OF SHORT-TERM AND LONG-TERM LIABILITIES	80-100%	80-100%	80-100%
Q48	CURRENT LIABILITIES REPORTED BY	80-100%, BRKDWN DISCLOSED	80-100%, BRKDWN DISCLOSED	80-100%, BRKDWN DISCLOSED
Q49	LONG TERM DEBT REPORTED BY	80-100%, CURR. PART SEPARATED	80-100%, CURR. PART SEPARATED	80-100%, CURR. PART SEPARATED
Q50	PREFERRED STOCK REPORTED BY	NOT USED	NOT USED	40-80%
Q51	RESERVES DISCLOSED	STATUTORY/LEGAL BY 80-100%	STATUTORY/LEGAL BY 80-100%	STATUTORY/LEGAL BY 80-100%
Q52	STATEMENT OF CHANGES IN STOCKHOLDERS' EQUITY REPORTED BY	MINORITY	80-100%	MINORITY
Q53	APPROPRIATION OF RETAINED EARNINGS DISCLOSED BY	80-100%	80-100%	80-100%
Q54	STATEMENT OF CASH FLOW IS REPORTED BY	80-100%	80-100%	40-80%
Q55	FUNDS DEFINITION IN STATEMENT OF CASH FLOW	WORKING CAPITAL	MODIFIED CASH	MODIFIED CASH
Q56	IF CASH FLOW IS REPORTED, TOTAL FUNDS FROM OPERATIONS ARE DISCLOSED BY	80-100%	80-100%	40-80%
Q57	IF CASH FLOW IS REPORTED, ADJUSTMENTS FOR NON-CASH ITEMS ARE DISCLOSED BY	80-100%	80-100%	40-80%
Q58	SUBSEQUENT EVENTS DISCLOSED IN ANNUAL REPORTS BY	80-100%	80-100%	40-80%
Q59	EARNINGS PER SHARE DATA REPORTED BY	80-100%	40-80%	40-80%
Q60	EARNINGS PER SHARE DISCLOSED BY MAJORITY	IN INCOME STATEMENT	ELSEWHERE IN THE REPORT	ELSEWHERE IN THE REPORT
Q61	MAJORITY OF COMPANIES REPORT EPS BASED ON NET INCOME AFTER PREFERRED DIVIDENDS	BEFORE EXTRAORDINARY ITEMS	NOT DISCLOSED	YES
Q62	EPS DENOMINATOR DEFINED BY MAJORITY AS	AVERAGE SHARES DURING PERIOD	MAJORITY DO NOT DISCLOSE EPS	YEAR-END SHARES
Q63	DILUTED EARNINGS PER SHARE REPORTED BY	NOT DISCLOSED	NOT DISCLOSED	NOT DISCLOSED
Q64	DIVIDEND PER SHARE REPORTED BY	80-100%	40-80%	40-80%
Q65	MAJORITY OF COMPANIES REPORT DIVIDEND PER SHARE	NET AFTER TAX ADJ	GROSS	GROSS
Q66	INTERIM DPS REPORTED IN ANNUAL REPORTS BY	MINORITY	NOT DISCLOSED	NOT DISCLOSED

Financial Reporting Practices in 24 Countries

NO.	ACCOUNTING & AUDITING ITEMS	Malaysia	Mexico	Netherlands
Q67	COMMON SHARES OUTSTANDING REPORTED BY	80-100%	40-80%	80-100%
Q68	COMMON SHARES OUTSTANDING DISCLOSED	YEAR-END SHARES	YEAR-END SHARES	YEAR-END SHARES
Q69	CHANGES IN CAPITAL MOST FREQUENTLY ACHIEVED THROUGH	NEW ISSUE OF STOCK	NEW ISSUES, STOCK DIVIDEND	NEW ISS, STK DVD, RIGHTS ISS
Q70	PAR OR STATED VALUE OF EQUITY (COMMON STOCK) REPORTED BY	80-100%	40-80%	80-100%
Q71	STOCK EXCHANGE WHERE TRADING OCCURS DISCLOSED BY	SINGLE STK EXCH IN THE COUNTRY	NOT DISCLOSED	NOT DISCLOSED
Q72	YEAR-END STOCK PRICE REPORTED IN ANNUAL REPORTS BY	NOT DISCLOSED	NOT DISCLOSED	MINORITY
Q73	MULTIPLE CLASSES OF STOCK ALLOWED ARE	NOT ALLOWED	UTILIZED BY MINORITY	UTILIZED BY 40-80%
Q74	MULTIPLE CLASSES OF STOCK ALLOWED IN THE COUNTRY HAVE DIFFERENT	NO MULTIPLE STOCK ALLOWED	VOTING RIGHTS	RIGHTS/DIVIDEND/PAR
Q75	ARE THERE DIFFERENT DIVIDENDS PAID FOR EACH CLASS OF COMMON STOCK?	NO MULTIPLE STOCK ALLOWED	NO	YES
Q76	EPS FOR MULTIPLE CLASSES OF STOCKS PROVIDED BY	MINOR OBSERVATIONS	MINOR OBSERVATIONS	MINOR OBSERVATIONS
Q77	MAJORITY SHAREHOLDINGS DISCLOSED BY	80-100%	NOT DISCLOSED	MINORITY
Q78	NAMES OF PRINCIPAL SHAREHOLDERS DISCLOSED	80-100%	NOT DISCLOSED	MINORITY

Financial Reporting Practices in 24 Countries

NO.	ACCOUNTING & AUDITING ITEMS	New Zealand	Norway	Singapore
Q1	LANGUAGE OF THE FINANCIAL STATEMENTS	ENGLISH	LOCAL LANGUAGE, 40-80% ENGLISH	ENGLISH
Q2	SUMMARY FINANCIAL INFORMATION PRESENTED BY	80-100%	80-100%	80-100%
Q3	MAJOR FINANCIAL RATIOS COMPUTED AND REPORTED BY	40-80%	80-100%	80-100%
Q4	NOTES TO THE FINANCIAL ACCOUNTS ARE	EXTENSIVELY UTILIZED	EXTENSIVELY UTILIZED	EXTENSIVELY UTILIZED
Q5	INFLATION ADJUSTED DATA PROVIDED BY	NONE OF THE COMPANIES	NONE OF THE COMPANIES	NONE OF THE COMPANIES
Q6	MAJORITY OF COMPANIES REPORT THE SUBSIDIARIES'	MINORITY PRACTICE	NAME,DOMICILE,%HELD	NAME,DOMICILE,%HELD
Q7	SEGMENT INFORMATION DISCLOSED BY	40-80%	40-80%	MINORITY
Q8	GEOGRAPHIC INFORMATION DISCLOSED BY	40%-80%	40%-80%	40%-80%
Q9	SEGMENT INFORMATION DISCLOSED BY MAJORITY AS	SALES/OPERINC/TOT.ASST BY PROD	SALES/OPER.INC BY PRODUCT LINE	MINORITY PRACTICE
Q10	GEOGRAPHIC INFORMATION DISCLOSED BY MAJORITY AS	SALES/OPER.INC./TOTAL ASSETS	SALES/OPER. INC.	SALES/OPER.INC./TOTAL ASSETS
Q11	MAJORITY OF COMPANIES REPORT EMPLOYEES	WORLDWIDE BY 40-80%	WORLDWIDE BY 80-100%	WORLDWIDE BY 40-80%
Q12	A BREAKDOWN OF EMPLOYEES BY FUNCTION, GEOGRAPHICAL AREA OR LINE OF BUSINESS EXISTS FOR	MINORITY	MINORITY	NOT DISCLOSED
Q13	A BREAKDOWN OF FULL TIME/PART TIME EMPLOYEES EXISTS FOR	NOT DISCLOSED	NOT DISCLOSED	NOT DISCLOSED
Q14	TOTAL REMUNERATION TO DIRECTORS/OFFICERS DISCLOSED BY	80-100%	40-80%	80-100%
Q15	LABOR RELATIONS DISCUSSED BY	NOT DISCLOSED	NOT DISCLOSED	MINORITY
Q16	STOCK OPTION PLANS ARE	NOT USED	NOT USED	NOT USED
Q17	NAMES AND TITLES OF PRINCIPAL OFFICERS DISCLOSED BY	MINORITY	80-100%	80-100%
Q18	LIST OF BOARD MEMBERS AND THEIR AFFILIATIONS DISCLOSED BY	80-100%	80-100%	40-80%
Q19	COMPANY SHARES HELD BY DIRECTORS/OFFICERS DISCLOSED BY	40-80%	40-80%	80-100%
Q20	RESEARCH AND DEVELOPMENT COSTS DISCLOSED BY	NOT DISCLOSED	MINORITY	NOT DISCLOSED
Q21	CAPITAL EXPENDITURES DISCLOSED BY	80-100% FOR WORLDWIDE	80-100% FOR WORLDWIDE	80-100% FOR WORLDWIDE
Q22	EXPORTS REPORTED BY	40-80%	40-80%	40-80%

Financial Reporting Practices in 24 Countries

NO.	ACCOUNTING & AUDITING ITEMS	New Zealand	Norway	Singapore
Q23	INCOME STATEMENT FORMAT	OPER PROFIT LESS INT & TAX EXP	SALES LESS EXPENSES	OPER PROFIT LESS INT & TAX EXP
Q24	COMPARATIVE INCOME STATEMENT DATA PROVIDED BY	80-100%, TWO YEARS	80-100%, TWO YEARS	80-100%, TWO YEARS
Q25	SALES REPORTED BY	80-100%	80-100%	80-100%
Q26	COST OF GOODS SOLD REPORTED BY	MINORITY	40-80%	MINORITY
Q27	SG & A EXPENSE REPORTED ON INCOME STATEMENT BY	MINORITY	MINORITY	NOT DISCLOSED
Q28	DEPRECIATION REPORTED ON INCOME STATEMENT BY	80-100%	40-80%	40-80%
Q29	OPERATING INCOME REPORTED ON INCOME STATEMENT BY	40-80%	80-100%	40-80%
Q30	FOREIGN EXCHANGE GAINS/LOSSES REPORTED ON INCOME STATEMENT	MINORITY	MINORITY	80-100%
Q31	EXTRAORDINARY GAINS/LOSSES REPORTED ON INCOME STATEMENT	80-100%	80-100%	80-100%
Q32	INCOME TAX EXPENSE REPORTED BY	80-100%	40-80%	80-100%
Q33	MINORITY INTEREST REPORTED ON INCOME STATEMENT BY	40-80%	40-80%	40-80%
Q34	NET INCOME DISCLOSED BY	80-100%	80-100%	80-100%
Q35	BALANCE SHEET FORMAT	(T = L + E); 1 OR 2 PAGES	(TOT AST = LIAB + OE);2 PAGES	((FA+NWC)-LTD=SE);1 PAGE
Q36	COMPARATIVE BALANCE SHEET DATA PROVIDED BY	80-100%, TWO YEARS	80-100%, TWO YEARS	80-100%, TWO YEARS
Q37	BALANCE SHEET ITEMS REPORTED IN	INCREASING LIQUIDITY ORDER	DECREASING LIQUIDITY ORDER	INCREASING LIQUIDITY ORDER
Q38	BALANCE SHEET PRESENTED	AFTER APPR. TO RET. EARNINGS	AFTER APPR. TO RET. EARNINGS	AFTER APPR. TO RET. EARNINGS
Q39	SEPARATION OF CURRENT AND LONG TERM ASSETS PROVIDED BY	80-100%	80-100%	80-100%
Q40	CASH AND EQUIVALENTS REPORTED BY	80-100%	80-100%	80-100%
Q41	ACCOUNTS RECEIVABLE REPORTED BY	SEPARATING ST & LT, NET	NO BRKDWN ST & LT, GROSS	SEPARATING ST & LT, NET
Q42	INVENTORIES REPORTED BY	80-100%	80-100%	80-100%
Q43	CURRENT ASSETS REPORTED BY	80-100%	80-100%	80-100%
Q44	FIXED ASSETS IN ASSET SIDE ARE REPORTED	MAJORITY AFTER ACC.DEP.	MAJORITY BEFORE ACC. DEP.	MAJORITY AFTER ACC.DEP.
Q45	GOODWILL AND OTHER INTANGIBLES DISCLOSED BY	40-80%	40-80%	40-80%

Financial Reporting Practices in 24 Countries

NO.	ACCOUNTING & AUDITING ITEMS	New Zealand	Norway	Singapore
Q46	TOTAL ASSETS CAN BE DERIVED	INDIRECTLY FROM B/S	INDIRECTLY FROM B/S	INDIRECTLY FROM B/S
Q47	SEPARATION OF SHORT-TERM AND LONG-TERM LIABILITIES	80-100%	80-100%	80-100%
Q48	CURRENT LIABILITIES REPORTED BY	80-100%, BRKDWN DISCLOSED	MINORITY	80-100%, BRKDWN DISCLOSED
Q49	LONG TERM DEBT REPORTED BY	80-100%, CURR. PART SEPARATED	80-100%, CURR. PART SEPARATED	80-100%, CURR. PART SEPARATED
Q50	PREFERRED STOCK REPORTED BY	MINORITY	NOT USED	NOT USED
Q51	RESERVES DISCLOSED	STATUTORY/LEGAL BY 80-100%	STAT./LEGAL/DISC. BY 80-100%	STATUTORY/LEGAL BY 80-100%
Q52	STATEMENT OF CHANGES IN STOCKHOLDERS' EQUITY REPORTED BY	MINORITY	MINORITY	MINORITY
Q53	APPROPRIATION OF RETAINED EARNINGS DISCLOSED BY	40-80%	80-100%	80-100%
Q54	STATEMENT OF CASH FLOW IS REPORTED BY	80-100%	80-100%	80-100%
Q55	FUNDS DEFINITION IN STATEMENT OF CASH FLOW	WORKING CAPITAL	WORKING CAPITAL	WORKING CAPITAL
Q56	IF CASH FLOW IS REPORTED, TOTAL FUNDS FROM OPERATIONS ARE DISCLOSED BY	80-100%	40-80%	80-100%
Q57	IF CASH FLOW IS REPORTED, ADJUSTMENTS FOR NON-CASH ITEMS ARE DISCLOSED BY	40-80%	40-80%	80-100%
Q58	SUBSEQUENT EVENTS DISCLOSED IN ANNUAL REPORTS BY	MINORITY	NOT DISCLOSED	80-100%
Q59	EARNINGS PER SHARE DATA REPORTED BY	40-80%	40-80%	80-100%
Q60	EARNINGS PER SHARE DISCLOSED BY MAJORITY	NO EPS GIVEN BY MAJORITY	NO EPS GIVEN BY MAJORITY	IN INCOME STATEMENT
Q61	MAJORITY OF COMPANIES REPORT EPS BASED ON NET INCOME AFTER PREFERRED DIVIDENDS	YES	YES	BEFORE EXTRAORDINARY ITEMS
Q62	EPS DENOMINATOR DEFINED BY MAJORITY AS	AVERAGE SHARES DURING PERIOD	AVERAGE SHARES DURING PERIOD	AVERAGE SHARES DURING PERIOD
Q63	DILUTED EARNINGS PER SHARE REPORTED BY	MINORITY	NOT DISCLOSED	NOT DISCLOSED
Q64	DIVIDEND PER SHARE REPORTED BY	80-100%	40-80%	80-100%
Q65	MAJORITY OF COMPANIES REPORT DIVIDEND PER SHARE	GROSS	GROSS	NET AFTER TAX ADJ
Q66	INTERIM DPS REPORTED IN ANNUAL REPORTS BY	MINORITY	NOT DISCLOSED	MINORITY

Financial Reporting Practices in 24 Countries

NO.	ACCOUNTING & AUDITING ITEMS	New Zealand	Norway	Singapore
Q67	COMMON SHARES OUTSTANDING REPORTED BY	80-100%	80-100%	80-100%
Q68	COMMON SHARES OUTSTANDING DISCLOSED	YEAR-END SHARES	YEAR-END SHARES	YEAR-END SHARES
Q69	CHANGES IN CAPITAL MOST FREQUENTLY ACHIEVED THROUGH	NEW ISSUES, STOCK DIVIDEND	NEW ISSUE OF STOCK	NEW ISSUES, STOCK DIVIDEND
Q70	PAR OR STATED VALUE OF EQUITY (COMMON STOCK) REPORTED BY	80-100%	80-100%	80-100%
Q71	STOCK EXCHANGE WHERE TRADING OCCURS DISCLOSED BY	SINGLE STK EXCH IN THE COUNTRY	MINORITY	SINGLE STK EXCH IN THE COUNTRY
Q72	YEAR-END STOCK PRICE REPORTED IN ANNUAL REPORTS BY	NOT DISCLOSED	40-80%	NOT DISCLOSED
Q73	MULTIPLE CLASSES OF STOCK ALLOWED ARE	NOT ALLOWED	UTILIZED BY MINORITY	NOT ALLOWED
Q74	MULTIPLE CLASSES OF STOCK ALLOWED IN THE COUNTRY HAVE DIFFERENT	NO MULTIPLE STOCK ALLOWED	VOTING RIGHTS	NO MULTIPLE STOCK ALLOWED
Q75	ARE THERE DIFFERENT DIVIDENDS PAID FOR EACH CLASS OF COMMON STOCK?	NO MULTIPLE STOCK ALLOWED	NO	NO MULTIPLE STOCK ALLOWED
Q76	EPS FOR MULTIPLE CLASSES OF STOCKS PROVIDED BY	NO MULTIPLE STOCK ALLOWED	NO DIFF IN DIVD BTW STOCKS	NO MULTIPLE STOCK ALLOWED
Q77	MAJORITY SHAREHOLDINGS DISCLOSED BY	80-100%	40-80%	80-100%
Q78	NAMES OF PRINCIPAL SHAREHOLDERS DISCLOSED	40-80%	40-80%	80-100%

Financial Reporting Practices in 24 Countries

NO.	ACCOUNTING & AUDITING ITEMS	South Africa	Spain	Sweden
Q1	LANGUAGE OF THE FINANCIAL STATEMENTS	ENGLISH	LOCAL LANGUAGE, MINOR. ENGLISH	LOCAL LANGUAGE, 40-80% ENGLISH
Q2	SUMMARY FINANCIAL INFORMATION PRESENTED BY	80-100%	80-100%	80-100%
Q3	MAJOR FINANCIAL RATIOS COMPUTED AND REPORTED BY	80-100%	MINORITY	40-80%
Q4	NOTES TO THE FINANCIAL ACCOUNTS ARE	EXTENSIVELY UTILIZED	MODERATELY UTILIZED	EXTENSIVELY UTILIZED
Q5	INFLATION ADJUSTED DATA PROVIDED BY	NONE OF THE COMPANIES	NONE OF THE COMPANIES	MINORITY
Q6	MAJORITY OF COMPANIES REPORT THE SUBSIDIARIES'	NAME,DOMICILE,%HELD	NAME,DOMICILE,%HELD	NAME,DOMICILE,%HELD
Q7	SEGMENT INFORMATION DISCLOSED BY	MINORITY	40-80%	40-80%
Q8	GEOGRAPHIC INFORMATION DISCLOSED BY	40%-80%	MINORITY	40%-80%
Q9	SEGMENT INFORMATION DISCLOSED BY MAJORITY AS	MINORITY PRACTICE	SALES/OPER.INC BY PRODUCT LINE	SALES/OPER.INC BY PRODUCT LINE
Q10	GEOGRAPHIC INFORMATION DISCLOSED BY MAJORITY AS	SALES/OPER.INC./TOTAL ASSETS	MINORITY PRACTICE	SALES/OPER. INC.
Q11	MAJORITY OF COMPANIES REPORT EMPLOYEES	WORLDWIDE BY 80-100%	DOMESTIC BY 80-100%	WORLDWIDE BY 80-100%
Q12	A BREAKDOWN OF EMPLOYEES BY FUNCTION, GEOGRAPHICAL AREA OR LINE OF BUSINESS EXISTS FOR	40-80%	80-100%	40-80%
Q13	A BREAKDOWN OF FULL TIME/PART TIME EMPLOYEES EXISTS FOR	NOT DISCLOSED	80-100%	MINORITY
Q14	TOTAL REMUNERATION TO DIRECTORS/OFFICERS DISCLOSED BY	80-100%	NOT DISCLOSED	MINORITY
Q15	LABOR RELATIONS DISCUSSED BY	MINORITY	80-100%	NOT DISCLOSED
Q16	STOCK OPTION PLANS ARE	USED	NOT USED	NOT USED
Q17	NAMES AND TITLES OF PRINCIPAL OFFICERS DISCLOSED BY	80-100%	80-100%	80-100%
Q18	LIST OF BOARD MEMBERS AND THEIR AFFILIATIONS DISCLOSED BY	80-100%	80-100%	80-100%
Q19	COMPANY SHARES HELD BY DIRECTORS/OFFICERS DISCLOSED BY	MINORITY	NOT DISCLOSED	40-80%
Q20	RESEARCH AND DEVELOPMENT COSTS DISCLOSED BY	BY 40-80% WORLDWIDE	BY 80-100% DOMESTIC	MINORITY
Q21	CAPITAL EXPENDITURES DISCLOSED BY	80-100% FOR WORLDWIDE	80-100% FOR DOMESTIC	80-100% FOR WORLDWIDE
Q22	EXPORTS REPORTED BY	40-80%	40-80%	40-80%

Financial Reporting Practices in 24 Countries

NO.	ACCOUNTING & AUDITING ITEMS	South Africa	Spain	Sweden
Q23	INCOME STATEMENT FORMAT	SALES LESS EXPENSES	SALES-EXP, DR./CR. FORMATS	SALES LESS EXPENSES
Q24	COMPARATIVE INCOME STATEMENT DATA PROVIDED BY	80-100%, TWO YEARS	80-100%, TWO YEARS	80-100%, TWO YEARS
Q25	SALES REPORTED BY	80-100%	80-100%	80-100%
Q26	COST OF GOODS SOLD REPORTED BY	MINORITY	40-80%	40-80%
Q27	SG & A EXPENSE REPORTED ON INCOME STATEMENT BY	MINORITY	40-80%	40-80%
Q28	DEPRECIATION REPORTED ON INCOME STATEMENT BY	40-80%	40-80%	40-80%
Q29	OPERATING INCOME REPORTED ON INCOME STATEMENT BY	40-80%	40-80%	80-100%
Q30	FOREIGN EXCHANGE GAINS/LOSSES REPORTED ON INCOME STATEMENT	MINORITY	MINORITY	40-80%
Q31	EXTRAORDINARY GAINS/LOSSES REPORTED ON INCOME STATEMENT	80-100%	40-80%	80-100%
Q32	INCOME TAX EXPENSE REPORTED BY	80-100%	MINORITY	80-100%
Q33	MINORITY INTEREST REPORTED ON INCOME STATEMENT BY	40-80%	MINORITY	40-80%
Q34	NET INCOME DISCLOSED BY	80-100%	MINORITY	80-100%
Q35	BALANCE SHEET FORMAT	(FA + NWC = LTD + OE);1 PAGE	(TOT AST = LIAB + OE);2 PAGES	(TOT AST = LIAB + OE);2 PAGES
Q36	COMPARATIVE BALANCE SHEET DATA PROVIDED BY	80-100%, TWO YEARS	80-100%, TWO YEARS	80-100%, TWO YEARS
Q37	BALANCE SHEET ITEMS REPORTED IN	INCREASING LIQUIDITY ORDER	INCREASING LIQUIDITY ORDER	DECREASING LIQUIDITY ORDER
Q38	BALANCE SHEET PRESENTED	AFTER APPR. TO RET. EARNINGS	BEF & AFTER APPR.TO RET.EARN	AFTER APPR. TO RET. EARNINGS
Q39	SEPARATION OF CURRENT AND LONG TERM ASSETS PROVIDED BY	80-100%	80-100%	80-100%
Q40	CASH AND EQUIVALENTS REPORTED BY	80-100%	80-100%	80-100%
Q41	ACCOUNTS RECEIVABLE REPORTED BY	SEPARATING ST & LT, NET	NO BRKDWN ST & LT, GROSS	SEPARATING ST & LT, GROSS
Q42	INVENTORIES REPORTED BY	80-100%	80-100%	80-100%
Q43	CURRENT ASSETS REPORTED BY	80-100%	80-100%	80-100%
Q44	FIXED ASSETS IN ASSET SIDE ARE REPORTED	MAJORITY AFTER ACC.DEP.	MAJORITY AFTER ACC.DEP.	MAJORITY AFTER ACC.DEP.
Q45	GOODWILL AND OTHER INTANGIBLES DISCLOSED BY	40-80%	40-80%	40-80%

Financial Reporting Practices in 24 Countries

NO.	ACCOUNTING & AUDITING ITEMS	South Africa	Spain	Sweden
Q46	TOTAL ASSETS CAN BE DERIVED	INDIRECTLY FROM B/S	DIRECTLY FROM B/S	DIRECTLY FROM B/S
Q47	SEPARATION OF SHORT-TERM AND LONG-TERM LIABILITIES	80-100%	80-100%	80-100%
Q48	CURRENT LIABILITIES REPORTED BY	80-100%, BRKDWN DISCLOSED	80-100%, BRKDWN DISCLOSED	80-100%, BRKDWN DISCLOSED
Q49	LONG TERM DEBT REPORTED BY	80-100%, CURR. PART SEPARATED	80-100%, CURR. PART SEPARATED	80-100%, CURR. PART SEPARATED
Q50	PREFERRED STOCK REPORTED BY	80-100%	NOT USED	NOT USED
Q51	RESERVES DISCLOSED	STATUTORY/LEGAL BY 80-100%	STATUTORY/LEGAL BY 80-100%	STAT./LEGAL/DISC. BY 80-100%
Q52	STATEMENT OF CHANGES IN STOCKHOLDERS' EQUITY REPORTED BY	MINORITY	MINORITY	40-80%
Q53	APPROPRIATION OF RETAINED EARNINGS DISCLOSED BY	80-100%	40-80%	80-100%
Q54	STATEMENT OF CASH FLOW IS REPORTED BY	80-100%	40-80%	40-80%
Q55	FUNDS DEFINITION IN STATEMENT OF CASH FLOW	MINORITY PRACTICES	WORKING CAPITAL	MODIFIED CASH
Q56	IF CASH FLOW IS REPORTED, TOTAL FUNDS FROM OPERATIONS ARE DISCLOSED BY	40-80%	MINORITY	40-80%
Q57	IF CASH FLOW IS REPORTED, ADJUSTMENTS FOR NON-CASH ITEMS ARE DISCLOSED BY	MINORITY	MINORITY	MINORITY
Q58	SUBSEQUENT EVENTS DISCLOSED IN ANNUAL REPORTS BY	MINORITY	NOT DISCLOSED	NOT DISCLOSED
Q59	EARNINGS PER SHARE DATA REPORTED BY	80-100%	MINORITY	40-80%
Q60	EARNINGS PER SHARE DISCLOSED BY MAJORITY	IN INCOME STATEMENT	NO EPS GIVEN BY MAJORITY	ELSEWHERE IN THE REPORT
Q61	MAJORITY OF COMPANIES REPORT EPS BASED ON NET INCOME AFTER PREFERRED DIVIDENDS	BEFORE EXTRAORDINARY ITEMS	NO EPS GIVEN BY MAJORITY	OTHER
Q62	EPS DENOMINATOR DEFINED BY MAJORITY AS	AVERAGE SHARES DURING PERIOD	MAJORITY DO NOT DISCLOSE EPS	AVERAGE SHARES DURING PERIOD
Q63	DILUTED EARNINGS PER SHARE REPORTED BY	NOT DISCLOSED	NOT DISCLOSED	MINORITY
Q64	DIVIDEND PER SHARE REPORTED BY	40-80%	40-80%	40-80%
Q65	MAJORITY OF COMPANIES REPORT DIVIDEND PER SHARE	GROSS	GROSS	GROSS
Q66	INTERIM DPS REPORTED IN ANNUAL REPORTS BY	MINORITY	NOT DISCLOSED	MINORITY

Financial Reporting Practices in 24 Countries

NO.	ACCOUNTING & AUDITING ITEMS	South Africa	Spain	Sweden
Q67	COMMON SHARES OUTSTANDING REPORTED BY	80-100%	40-80%	80-100%
Q68	COMMON SHARES OUTSTANDING DISCLOSED	YEAR-END SHARES	YEAR-END SHARES	YEAR-END SHARES
Q69	CHANGES IN CAPITAL MOST FREQUENTLY ACHIEVED THROUGH	NEW ISS, STK DVD, RIGHTS ISS	NEW ISS, STK DVD, RIGHTS ISS	NEW ISS, STK DVD, CONV SEC
Q70	PAR OR STATED VALUE OF EQUITY (COMMON STOCK) REPORTED BY	80-100%	80-100%	80-100%
Q71	STOCK EXCHANGE WHERE TRADING OCCURS DISCLOSED BY	40-80%	MINORITY	40-80%
Q72	YEAR-END STOCK PRICE REPORTED IN ANNUAL REPORTS BY	40-80%	MINORITY	40-80%
Q73	MULTIPLE CLASSES OF STOCK ALLOWED ARE	UTILIZED BY MINORITY	UTILIZED BY MINORITY	UTILIZED BY 40-80%
Q74	MULTIPLE CLASSES OF STOCK ALLOWED IN THE COUNTRY HAVE DIFFERENT	VOTING RIGHTS	VOTING RIGHTS	VOTING RIGHTS
Q75	ARE THERE DIFFERENT DIVIDENDS PAID FOR EACH CLASS OF COMMON STOCK?	NO	NO	NO
Q76	EPS FOR MULTIPLE CLASSES OF STOCKS PROVIDED BY	NO DIFF IN DIVD BTW STOCKS	NO DIFF IN DIVD BTW STOCKS	80-100%
Q77	MAJORITY SHAREHOLDINGS DISCLOSED BY	40-80%	80-100%	40-80%
Q78	NAMES OF PRINCIPAL SHAREHOLDERS DISCLOSED	40-80%	80-100%	40-80%

Financial Reporting Practices in 24 Countries

NO.	ACCOUNTING & AUDITING ITEMS	Switzerland	United Kingdom	United States
Q1	LANGUAGE OF THE FINANCIAL STATEMENTS	LOCAL LANGUAGE, 40-80% ENGLISH	ENGLISH	ENGLISH
Q2	SUMMARY FINANCIAL INFORMATION PRESENTED BY	80-100%	80-100%	80-100%
Q3	MAJOR FINANCIAL RATIOS COMPUTED AND REPORTED BY	80-100%	MINORITY	80-100%
Q4	NOTES TO THE FINANCIAL ACCOUNTS ARE	MODERATELY UTILIZED	EXTENSIVELY UTILIZED	EXTENSIVELY UTILIZED
Q5	INFLATION ADJUSTED DATA PROVIDED BY	NONE OF THE COMPANIES	MINORITY	40 - 80%
Q6	MAJORITY OF COMPANIES REPORT THE SUBSIDIARIES'	NAME ONLY OR WITH DOMICILE	NAME,DOMICILE,%HELD	NAME,DOMICILE,%HELD
Q7	SEGMENT INFORMATION DISCLOSED BY	40-80%	40-80%	80-100%
Q8	GEOGRAPHIC INFORMATION DISCLOSED BY	40%-80%	80-100%	80-100%
Q9	SEGMENT INFORMATION DISCLOSED BY MAJORITY AS	SALES/OPER.INC BY PRODUCT LINE	SALES/OPER.INC BY PRODUCT LINE	SALES/OPERINC/TOT.ASST BY PROD
Q10	GEOGRAPHIC INFORMATION DISCLOSED BY MAJORITY AS	SALES/OPER. INC.	SALES/OPER. INC.	SALES/OPER.INC./TOTAL ASSETS
Q11	MAJORITY OF COMPANIES REPORT EMPLOYEES	WORLDWIDE BY 80-100%	DOMESTIC BY 80-100%	WORLDWIDE BY 80-100%
Q12	A BREAKDOWN OF EMPLOYEES BY FUNCTION, GEOGRAPHICAL AREA OR LINE OF BUSINESS EXISTS FOR	40-80%	40-80%	40-80%
Q13	A BREAKDOWN OF FULL TIME/PART TIME EMPLOYEES EXISTS FOR	NOT DISCLOSED	MINORITY	MINORITY
Q14	TOTAL REMUNERATION TO DIRECTORS/OFFICERS DISCLOSED BY	NOT DISCLOSED	80-100%	NOT DISCLOSED
Q15	LABOR RELATIONS DISCUSSED BY	MINORITY	MINORITY	40-80%
Q16	STOCK OPTION PLANS ARE	NOT USED	USED	USED
Q17	NAMES AND TITLES OF PRINCIPAL OFFICERS DISCLOSED BY	80-100%	80-100%	80-100%
Q18	LIST OF BOARD MEMBERS AND THEIR AFFILIATIONS DISCLOSED BY	80-100%	80-100%	80-100%
Q19	COMPANY SHARES HELD BY DIRECTORS/OFFICERS DISCLOSED BY	NOT DISCLOSED	80-100%	80-100%
Q20	RESEARCH AND DEVELOPMENT COSTS DISCLOSED BY	BY 40-80% WORLDWIDE	MINORITY	BY 80-100% WORLDWIDE
Q21	CAPITAL EXPENDITURES DISCLOSED BY	40-80% FOR WORLDWIDE	80-100% FOR WORLDWIDE	80-100% FOR WORLDWIDE
Q22	EXPORTS REPORTED BY	MINORITY	40-80%	40-80%

Financial Reporting Practices in 24 Countries

NO.	ACCOUNTING & AUDITING ITEMS	Switzerland	United Kingdom	United States
Q23	INCOME STATEMENT FORMAT	SALES LESS EXPENSES	OPER PROFIT LESS INT & TAX EXP	SALES LESS EXPENSES
Q24	COMPARATIVE INCOME STATEMENT DATA PROVIDED BY	80-100%, TWO YEARS	80-100%, TWO YEARS	80-100%, MORE THAN TWO YEARS
Q25	SALES REPORTED BY	80-100%	80-100%	80-100%
Q26	COST OF GOODS SOLD REPORTED BY	MINORITY	80-100%	80-100%
Q27	SG & A EXPENSE REPORTED ON INCOME STATEMENT BY	80-100%	MINORITY	80-100%
Q28	DEPRECIATION REPORTED ON INCOME STATEMENT BY	40-80%	40-80%	80-100%
Q29	OPERATING INCOME REPORTED ON INCOME STATEMENT BY	80-100%	40-80%	80-100%
Q30	FOREIGN EXCHANGE GAINS/LOSSES REPORTED ON INCOME STATEMENT	MINORITY	MINORITY	40-80%
Q31	EXTRAORDINARY GAINS/LOSSES REPORTED ON INCOME STATEMENT	80-100%	80-100%	80-100%
Q32	INCOME TAX EXPENSE REPORTED BY	40-80%	80-100%	80-100%
Q33	MINORITY INTEREST REPORTED ON INCOME STATEMENT BY	MINORITY	80-100%	80-100%
Q34	NET INCOME DISCLOSED BY	80-100%	80-100%	80-100%
Q35	BALANCE SHEET FORMAT	(TOT AST = LIAB + OE);1 PAGE	((FA+NWC)-LTD=SE);1 PAGE	(TOT AST = LIAB + OE);1 PAGE
Q36	COMPARATIVE BALANCE SHEET DATA PROVIDED BY	80-100%, TWO YEARS	80-100%, TWO YEARS	80-100%, TWO YEARS
Q37	BALANCE SHEET ITEMS REPORTED IN	DECREASING LIQUIDITY ORDER	INCREASING LIQUIDITY ORDER	DECREASING LIQUIDITY ORDER
Q38	BALANCE SHEET PRESENTED	AFTER APPR. TO RET. EARNINGS	AFTER APPR. TO RET. EARNINGS	BEFORE APPR. TO RET.EARNINGS
Q39	SEPARATION OF CURRENT AND LONG TERM ASSETS PROVIDED BY	80-100%	80-100%	80-100%
Q40	CASH AND EQUIVALENTS REPORTED BY	80-100%	80-100%	80-100%
Q41	ACCOUNTS RECEIVABLE REPORTED BY	SEPARATING ST & LT, NET	SEPARATING ST & LT, NET	NO BRKDWN ST & LT, NET
Q42	INVENTORIES REPORTED BY	80-100%	80-100%	80-100%
Q43	CURRENT ASSETS REPORTED BY	80-100%	80-100%	80-100%
Q44	FIXED ASSETS IN ASSET SIDE ARE REPORTED	MAJORITY AFTER ACC.DEP.	MAJORITY AFTER ACC.DEP.	MAJORITY AFTER ACC.DEP.
Q45	GOODWILL AND OTHER INTANGIBLES DISCLOSED BY	MINORITY	MINORITY	80-100%

Financial Reporting Practices in 24 Countries

NO.	ACCOUNTING & AUDITING ITEMS	Switzerland	United Kingdom	United States
Q46	TOTAL ASSETS CAN BE DERIVED	DIRECTLY FROM B/S	INDIRECTLY FROM B/S	DIRECTLY FROM B/S
Q47	SEPARATION OF SHORT-TERM AND LONG-TERM LIABILITIES	80-100%	80-100%	80-100%
Q48	CURRENT LIABILITIES REPORTED BY	40-80%, NO BRKDWN DISCLOSED	80-100%, BRKDWN DISCLOSED	80-100%, BRKDWN DISCLOSED
Q49	LONG TERM DEBT REPORTED BY	80-100% CURR PART NOT SEPARATE	80-100%, CURR. PART SEPARATED	80-100%, CURR. PART SEPARATED
Q50	PREFERRED STOCK REPORTED BY	NOT USED	80-100%	80-100%
Q51	RESERVES DISCLOSED	STATUTORY/LEGAL BY 80-100%	STATUTORY/LEGAL BY 80-100%	STATUTORY/LEGAL BY 80-100%
Q52	STATEMENT OF CHANGES IN STOCKHOLDERS' EQUITY REPORTED BY	MINORITY	MINORITY	40-80%
Q53	APPROPRIATION OF RETAINED EARNINGS DISCLOSED BY	40-80%	40-80%	40-80%
Q54	STATEMENT OF CASH FLOW IS REPORTED BY	MINORITY	80-100%	80-100%
Q55	FUNDS DEFINITION IN STATEMENT OF CASH FLOW	MINORITY PRACTICES	NET BORROWINGS	CASH
Q56	IF CASH FLOW IS REPORTED, TOTAL FUNDS FROM OPERATIONS ARE DISCLOSED BY	40-80%	80-100%	80-100%
Q57	IF CASH FLOW IS REPORTED, ADJUSTMENTS FOR NON-CASH ITEMS ARE DISCLOSED BY	40-80%	80-100%	80-100%
Q58	SUBSEQUENT EVENTS DISCLOSED IN ANNUAL REPORTS BY	NOT DISCLOSED	MINORITY	80-100%
Q59	EARNINGS PER SHARE DATA REPORTED BY	40-80%	80-100%	80-100%
Q60	EARNINGS PER SHARE DISCLOSED BY MAJORITY	ELSEWHERE IN THE REPORT	IN INCOME STATEMENT	IN INCOME STATEMENT
Q61	MAJORITY OF COMPANIES REPORT EPS BASED ON NET INCOME AFTER PREFERRED DIVIDENDS	YES	BEFORE EXTRAORDINARY ITEMS	YES
Q62	EPS DENOMINATOR DEFINED BY MAJORITY AS	YEAR-END SHARES	AVERAGE SHARES DURING PERIOD	AVERAGE SHARES DURING PERIOD
Q63	DILUTED EARNINGS PER SHARE REPORTED BY	NOT DISCLOSED	MINORITY	80-100%
Q64	DIVIDEND PER SHARE REPORTED BY	40-80%	80-100%	80-100%
Q65	MAJORITY OF COMPANIES REPORT DIVIDEND PER SHARE	NET AFTER TAX ADJ	GROSS	GROSS
Q66	INTERIM DPS REPORTED IN ANNUAL REPORTS BY	NOT DISCLOSED	40-80%	80-100%

Financial Reporting Practices in 24 Countries

NO.	ACCOUNTING & AUDITING ITEMS	Switzerland	United Kingdom	United States
Q67	COMMON SHARES OUTSTANDING REPORTED BY	40-80%	80-100%	80-100%
Q68	COMMON SHARES OUTSTANDING DISCLOSED	YEAR-END SHARES	YEAR-END SHARES	YEAR-END SHARES
Q69	CHANGES IN CAPITAL MOST FREQUENTLY ACHIEVED THROUGH	NEW ISSUE OF STOCK	NEW ISS, STK SPLT, RIGHTS ISS	COMBINATION THREE/MORE OPTION
Q70	PAR OR STATED VALUE OF EQUITY (COMMON STOCK) REPORTED BY	80-100%	80-100%	80-100%
Q71	STOCK EXCHANGE WHERE TRADING OCCURS DISCLOSED BY	MINORITY	MINORITY	80-100%
Q72	YEAR-END STOCK PRICE REPORTED IN ANNUAL REPORTS BY	40-80%	NOT DISCLOSED	80-100%
Q73	MULTIPLE CLASSES OF STOCK ALLOWED ARE	UTILIZED BY 40-80%	UTILIZED BY MINORITY	NOT ALLOWED
Q74	MULTIPLE CLASSES OF STOCK ALLOWED IN THE COUNTRY HAVE DIFFERENT	RIGHTS/DIVIDEND/PAR	VOTING RIGHTS	NO MULTIPLE STOCK ALLOWED
Q75	ARE THERE DIFFERENT DIVIDENDS PAID FOR EACH CLASS OF COMMON STOCK?	YES	NO	NO MULTIPLE STOCK ALLOWED
Q76	EPS FOR MULTIPLE CLASSES OF STOCKS PROVIDED BY	80-100%	NO DIFF IN DIVD BTW STOCKS	NO MULTIPLE STOCK ALLOWED
Q77	MAJORITY SHAREHOLDINGS DISCLOSED BY	NOT DISCLOSED	40-80%	80-100%
Q78	NAMES OF PRINCIPAL SHAREHOLDERS DISCLOSED	NOT DISCLOSED	40-80%	80-100%

CHAPTER 4

TRENDS IN THE FINANCIAL STATEMENTS OF BANKS AND INSURANCE COMPANIES

Table of Contents

I. INTRODUCTION

In recent years there has been increased interest in the financial analysis of banks and insurance companies worldwide as a result of the following factors:

- Regulations in many countries have allowed banks and insurance companies to diversify into other financial services.
- The globalization of capital markets has created a need for global financial intermediaries, leading to the formation of global financial organizations.
- Many banks have become shareholder-owned due to privatization in several countries.
- Central banks, which are concerned with the capital adequacy of major commercial banks, are working together on a more uniform definition of capital in banks' financial statements.
- The European Community's efforts regarding the creation of a single internal market have encouraged the formation of more Europe-wide financial institutions.
- Mergers and acquisitions within financial service industries on an international basis have increased.
- As money managers internationally are investing in stocks across national boundaries, interest in the stocks of banks and insurance companies worldwide has also increased.

In this chapter, we will analyze the accounting standards in practice and financial reporting trends established by companies in the banking and insurance industries.

II. RESEARCH OBJECTIVES

4-1 What are the key accounting standards or methods followed by leading banks and insurance companies worldwide?

4-2 What are the implications of international differences in accounting standards for the valuation of assets and income determination of the banks and insurance companies analyzed?

4-3 To what extent has the international harmonization of accounting standards for banks and insurance companies been achieved?

4-4 What are the financial disclosure practices of banks and insurance companies by country?

4-5 To what extent has the international harmonization of financial disclosures of banks and insurance companies been achieved?

4-6 What financial disclosures should be included in the annual reports of banks and insurance companies published for an international audience?

III. RESEARCH DESIGN

Some of the general questions on accounting standards and financial reporting practices described in Chapters 2 and 3 are also applicable to banks and insurance companies. Consequently this chapter focuses only on questions uniquely applicable to banks and insurance companies.

The information collected on accounting standards practiced by banks and insurance companies in 22 countries is presented in this chapter. Presented are the current practices, summarized by country, and arrived at by means of a series of questions and answers regarding key accounting standards. For each question, the single practice which best reflects the predominant treatment (that employed by 80 - 100% of the companies) in each country is given. We also used a second category of 40 - 80% of the companies in each country following a given practice. In cases where no disclosures are made in the annual reports of a particular country, or where a particular method is a minority practice, that information is also indicated.

Exhibits 4-1 and 4-3 provide the lists of questions used to collect data for banks and insurance companies respectively.

We extracted data from the Worldscope Database, supplemented by annual reports in the CIFAR library. Table 4-1 provides the total number of companies studied by country and industry.

TABLE 4-1 NUMBER OF COMPANIES INCLUDED BY COUNTRY AND INDUSTRY		
Country	Banks	Insurance
Australia	5	5
Austria	3	2
Belgium	4	3
Canada	5	7
Denmark	8	5
Finland	4	0
France	14	7
Germany, West	19	17
Hong Kong	4	0
Italy	16	5
Japan	68	19
Korea, South	6	1
Malaysia	3	0
Netherlands	5	5
New Zealand	1	1
Norway	4	2
Singapore	4	0
South Africa	5	3
Spain	8	1
Sweden	5	4
Switzerland	7	7
United Kingdom	8	14
United States	88	47
Totals	294	155

IV. FINDINGS: BANKS

Empirical findings for banks in each of the 22 countries studied are presented by country and accounting standard in Exhibit 4-2. The following is a summary of the findings:

A. General

1. Primary Activity of Banks

With few exceptions, most banks around the world engage in universal banking, in which a single institution offers a wide variety of banking services under one roof. However, in Japan, South Korea, the UK and the US, commercial banks are prohibited by law from engaging in the sale or underwriting of securities. As a result, investment banks or securities brokerage houses exist in these four countries to carry out these activities.

2. Government vs. Shareholder Ownership

In about 75% of the countries studied, the majority of banks are shareholder-owned. Only in Europe, and principally in Italy and France, have the majority of banks come under government control. State ownership of banks is also evident, although to a lesser extent, in Austria, Belgium, Finland and West Germany. In both sets of countries, the larger banks tend to be government-owned.

B. Accounting Standards in Practice

1. Allowance for Loan Losses Fixed by Law

The amount to be reserved by banks to provide for potential loan losses seems quite arbitrary among the countries studied. The amount is fixed by law in Canada, Hong Kong, Japan, South Korea and several European countries (Finland, West Germany, Italy, Norway, Spain and Sweden). This is not the case, however, in Australia, Malaysia, Singapore, South Africa, the UK, the US or the rest of Europe.

2. Valuation of Marketable Securities

A majority of banks in nearly two-thirds of the countries studied value marketable securities at the lower of cost or market (LCM).

3. Valuation of Investment Assets

Banks in over half of the countries studied value investment assets at the original purchase price. These include banks in Australia, Canada, most European countries, Japan, South Korea, and the US. The second most popular method is valuation of assets at market value, which is practiced in Denmark, the Netherlands, South Africa and Sweden. Valuation at the purchase price adjusted by amortization of any applicable premium or discount is practiced in Hong Kong and Malaysia. The lower of cost or market method is used in Switzerland and the UK.

4. "Hidden" or "Non-Equity" Reserves

"Hidden reserves" are permitted by banking law in virtually every European country, but are prohibited elsewhere.

In North America, Asia, the Commonwealth and Belgium, banks generally do not keep non-equity reserves (i.e., various general purpose reserves). In countries that do keep non-equity reserves, their primary component is either a revaluation reserve (in Austria, Denmark, and the Netherlands), loan loss and employee benefit reserves (in Italy), loan loss and revaluation reserves (in Finland), a combination of loan loss, revaluation and amortization reserves (in France, Norway, Sweden and Switzerland) or an unspecified special reserve (in West Germany and Spain).

C. Financial Reporting Practices

1. Organization of Assets and Liabilities

The most common method of segregating assets and liabilities on the balance sheet is by type of asset or liability. In nearly 90% of the countries studied, the majority of companies used this method. Companies in Malaysia, Singapore and South Africa group items on both sides of the balance sheet according to liquidity.

2. Segregation of Loans

Segregation by maturity date and/or by type of borrower (e.g., commercial sector) are the most popular methods of presenting loans on the balance sheet. Segregation by the type of borrower alone is common in a few European countries (i.e., Austria, Belgium, Denmark, Italy, Sweden and the UK). The use of maturity date alone in classification is even less common (only in West Germany and Singapore), but separation according to both of the above criteria is quite common, and is practiced in Australia, New Zealand, North America and most of Europe. It should also be mentioned that banks in some countries (e.g., Japan, South Korea and Switzerland) choose to classify according to the type of security given for the loan. Finally, companies in some countries (Finland, Hong Kong and Malaysia) present all loans under a single heading.

3. Interbank Loans

On the whole, most banks separate interbank loans from customer loans, although those in Japan, South Korea and several Asian Commonwealth countries seem to present only a partial separation (e.g., call loans). In general, interbank loans represent between 20 and 50% of total loans for banks in Continental Europe, and less than 20% for banks elsewhere.

4. Non-Performing Loans

Outside of Canada, the UK and the US, where banks disclose information on non-performing loans as supplementary data, no information on these loans is presented.

5. Segregation of Investment Assets

Most banks classify investment assets according to type of security. In Hong Kong, however, banks do not seem to segregate investment assets, while in West Germany and Singapore, banks segregate their investment assets primarily by maturity date.

6. Segregation of Deposits

The most popular method of segregating deposits, utilized by a majority of banks in half of the countries studied, is by type of deposit (i.e., demand deposits, savings deposits and time deposits). This is practiced in Canada, several European countries, Japan, South Korea, South Africa, the UK and the US. Segregation by time period (i.e., according to the date the deposit comes due) is practiced by banks in Belgium, Denmark and Hong Kong. In West Germany, separation is by time period as well as by type of deposit. Classification of deposits by type of depositor is most common among banks in Norway, Singapore, Spain and Sweden; banks in Norway and Sweden also segregate by type of deposit. Finally, banks in Australia and Switzerland segregate deposits into interest-bearing and non-interest-bearing classes as well as classifying them by type.

7. Inclusion of Customers' Liabilities in Total Assets

Customers' liabilities for acceptances are incorporated into assets by banks in Japan, South Korea, North America and the Commonwealth (excluding the UK). They are partially included by banks in Austria, Denmark and West Germany. Banks in all other countries, that is the majority of countries in Europe, along with the UK, do not include customers' liabilities for acceptances as a component of total assets, but rather disclose them in a footnote to the financial statements.

In the vast majority of cases, customers' liabilities for acceptances make up less than 20% of adjusted total assets (i.e., total assets excluding customers' liabilities for acceptances). The only exceptions occur among banks in Finland, France, Italy and Singapore, where they comprise between 20 and 80% of adjusted total assets and among banks in Norway and Spain, where customer's liabilities often exceed the amount of adjusted total assets.

8. Disclosure of Interest Income and Expense

Banks in the majority of countries studied disclose both interest income and interest expense in gross amounts on the income statement. This includes those in Australia, Japan, South Korea, North America and virtually all countries in Continental Europe. In Sweden and the UK, on the other hand, net amounts are disclosed on the income statement and gross amounts in a footnote. The single European country in which banks observe neither of these practices is the Netherlands, where the only disclosure is that of net interest income on the income statement. Finally, in Hong Kong, Malaysia, Singapore and South Africa there is no disclosure of interest income or interest expense whatsoever.

9. Disclosure of Commissions Earned and Paid

In a slight majority of the countries studied, banks disclose commission income and commission expense in gross, while in virtually all others, banks disclose net commission income. As a general rule, disclosure in gross is practiced by banks in Japan, South Korea, the US and several countries in Europe (Belgium, France, West Germany, Italy, Sweden and Switzerland). Disclosure in net is practiced by banks in Australia, the UK and other countries in Europe (Austria, Denmark, Finland, Netherlands, Norway and Spain). In Canada, Hong Kong, Malaysia, Singapore and South Africa neither commission income nor expenses are disclosed separately from other operating income or expenses.

10. Foreign Exchange Profits and Commissions

Foreign exchange profits and commissions are composed of commission income for banks in South Korea, Switzerland, the UK and the US, of translation and revaluation gains and losses for banks in the Netherlands and Norway, and of both commission and translation income for banks in Canada, France, Denmark, Italy, Japan and Sweden. Banks in Australia, Austria, Belgium, Finland, West Germany, Hong Kong, Malaysia, Singapore, South Africa and Spain did not separately disclose information on foreign exchange gains or losses.

V. FINDINGS: INSURANCE COMPANIES

The primary objective of this section is to identify key accounting standards and financial reporting practices of leading insurance companies in the 22 countries listed in Exhibit 4-4. The following is a summary of findings:

A. General

1. Life vs. Non-Life Business

Only in Australia, Canada, Hong Kong, Japan, South Korea and South Africa are insurance companies legally prohibited from concurrently engaging in life and non-life business. In all other countries studied, local laws permit insurance companies to handle both lines of business together.

2. Ownership of Insurance Companies

In general, insurance companies in most countries can be owned only by stockholders. However, in Austria, Canada, Finland, Singapore, the UK and the US, either stockholders or policyholders may be owners. In Australia, Japan and South Korea ownership policy is established according to the type of company: non-life insurance companies may be owned only by shareholders and life insurance companies only by policyholders.

B. Accounting Standards in Practice

1. Valuation of Fixed-Income Securities

Valuation methods for fixed-income securities vary widely. In Australia, France, Malaysia, Singapore and Spain, insurance companies carry fixed-income securities at historical cost. In Canada, Denmark, Finland, West Germany, South Korea, the Netherlands, South Africa and the US, they are valued at amortized cost and in Belgium, Hong Kong, Italy, Japan, Norway, Sweden and Switzerland at the lower of cost or market. Only in the UK are fixed-income securities valued at market price.

2. Valuation of Equity Securities

For equity securities, as for fixed-income securities, valuation methods also vary widely. In Canada, France and Hong Kong, they are recorded at historical cost. Valuation at market price, the method used by most companies, is practiced in Australia, Belgium, Denmark, Finland, Malaysia, the Netherlands, Singapore, South Africa, the UK and the US. Companies in West Germany, Italy, Japan, South Korea, Norway, Sweden and Switzerland carry equity securities at the lower of cost or market (LCM).

3. "Hidden" or "Non-Equity" Reserves

In most cases, insurance companies in the countries studied either do not hold non-equity reserves or do not disclose them. It is principally in Europe (i.e., Austria, Belgium, Finland, France, the Netherlands, Norway and Sweden) that companies do hold and disclose non-equity reserves.

C. Financial Reporting Practices

1. Organization of Assets and Liabilities on the Balance Sheet

On the whole, most insurance companies organize their balance sheets according to type of asset or liability. However, in Denmark, Finland, Norway, Singapore and South Africa balance sheets are organized according to liquidity of the asset or liability.

2. Results of Reinsurance Business

The predominant method of disclosing the results of reinsurance business, that is, by net results only, is used by companies in most countries of Scandinavia (Denmark, Norway, Sweden) and Europe (Austria, France, West Germany, Italy, Spain, and Switzerland), as well as in Hong Kong, Malaysia, South Africa and the US. Itemized disclosure of net results is the prevalent method in Australia, Japan, South Korea, the UK, and other European countries (Belgium, Finland and the Netherlands). The results of reinsurance business are not disclosed explicitly in Canada or Singapore. This means premium income or other expenses are netted by reinsurance items before they are included in the income statement.

3. Disclosure of Unearned Premium Income

On the whole, insurance companies in most countries do disclose unearned premium income in the income statement. The few that do not are found in Canada, Denmark, Norway, Singapore and the US.

4. Disclosure of Underwriting Expenses

Disclosure practices for underwriting expenses divide almost equally into two categories. In the first, underwriting expenses are included as part of general and administrative expenses. This method is used by companies in Canada, Denmark, Hong Kong, Japan, South Korea, Norway, South Africa, Sweden, Switzerland, and the UK. Those companies in the second category disclose underwriting expenses separately, and are found in Australia, Malaysia, Singapore, the US, and the majority of countries in Europe.

VI. SUMMARY AND CONCLUSIONS

A. Banks

- With regard to balance sheet organization and the extent of disclosure, the accounting practices of banks in most countries are relatively uniform. Assets and liabilities are presented by type. Loans are segregated primarily by maturity date or type of borrower, sometimes both, and occasionally according to the type of security used to guarantee the loan.

- Interbank transactions are fully or partially separated from transactions with customers.

- Marketable securities are carried at either historical cost, current market price or the lower of the two.

- Investment assets are usually valued at purchase price or purchase price with some adjustments, although valuation at market value or the lower of cost or market is also often practiced.

- There are four principal methods of disclosing deposits: by type of deposit, time period of the deposit, whether or not the deposit bears interest and type of depositor. In the majority of banks, only the first method is used, although many other banks use either one of the other methods alone or a combination of methods.

- A variety of items classified under "customers' liabilities for acceptances" are included in or excluded from total assets in roughly an equal number of cases, although in some cases disclosure is only partial. Due to the large amounts represented by these accounts, figures for total assets and liabilities could be misleading in those countries where banks include these accounts on both sides of the balance sheet.

- Total revenue is not clearly defined by banks in many countries, most of which represent interest income and commission income in net. Such netting out of often unrelated items may restrict users from undertaking a separate analysis of revenues and expenses.

- Similarly, separation of results between operating activities and non-operating activities is not obvious in the reports of most banks, due to the diversity of operating activities.

B. Insurance Companies

- The balance sheet format of most insurance companies is quite similar to that of other financial companies. Most provide comparative data, list assets and liabilities by decreasing order of liquidity and separate current items from long-term items. Assets and liabilities are segregated by type in the majority of cases, and by liquidity in other cases.

- There is a great variety of valuation methods for both fixed-income securities and equity securities. Fixed-income securities may be valued (in order of preference) at the lower of cost or market (LCM), amortized cost, historical cost or market price and equity securities at LCM, market price or historical cost.

- In most companies revenue is usually disclosed on the income statement in gross and by component, and sometimes by component alone, though all the components of total revenue are not uniformly disclosed. Where applicable, income from life and non-life operations are segregated, and the results of any reinsurance business are reported either in net or in gross.

- Unearned premium income is usually reported, and underwriting expense is either disclosed separately or included as part of general and administrative expenses. Other major expenses, usually disclosed separately, include claims and loss expenses and long-term policyholders' charges.

In conclusion, compared to our analysis of accounting standards and financial reporting practices observed for industrial companies in Chapters 2 and 3, we found financial reporting practices vary more than accounting standards among banks and insurance companies worldwide. Perhaps the additional layers of regulations at the national level have contributed to the lack of uniformity in their financial reporting practices. Furthermore, international accounting organizations have focused their efforts more on industrial companies to date.

We recommend that preparers of annual reports of banks and insurance companies worldwide provide additional details in their financial statements to facilitate international comparison of accounting standards and financial reporting practices. In Chapter 6 of this study, "Analyzing International Annual Reports: Issues and Answers", we have provided suggestions to users concerning how to compensate for international accounting differences.

We have observed significant improvements in the financial reporting practices of banks and insurance companies worldwide. However, more uniformity would be useful for international users. Appendices B and C of this study are intended to provide further guidance in this respect to preparers of financial statements for banks and insurance companies worldwide.

EXHIBIT 4-1

QUESTIONS AND ANSWERS FOR FINANCIAL STATEMENTS OF BANKS

Q1 BANK'S PRIMARY ACTIVITY IS

1 UNIVERSAL BANKING
2 COMMERCIAL BANKING ONLY
3 COMM. BANK. & OTHER FIN. SERV.
9 NOT DETERMINABLE

Q2 CENTRAL BANKING FUNCTIONS ARE CARRIED OUT BY

1 SPECIAL GOVERNMENT INSTITUTION
2 GOV'T AND PRIVATE INSTITUTIONS
3 PRIVATE INSTITUTIONS
9 NOT DETERMINABLE

Q3 ARE BANKS GOVERNMENT-OWNED OR SHAREHOLDER-OWNED?

1 USUALLY OWNED BY GOV'T
2 MOST PRIVATE, BUT SOME GOV'T
3 VIRTUALLY ALL BY SHAREHOLDERS
9 NOT KNOWN

Q4 ASSETS AND LIABILITIES ARE ORGANIZED ON THE BALANCE SHEET BY

1 LIQUIDITY(CURRENT/NON-CURRENT)
2 TYPE OF ASSET OR LIABILITY
3 OTHER MEANS
9 NOT DETERMINABLE

Q5 LOANS ARE SEGREGATED BY

1 MATURITY DATE
2 TYPE OF BORROWER
3 CURRENCY OF LOAN DENOMINATION
4 TYPE OF SECURITY
5 MATURITY & TYPE OF BORROWER
9 NOT SEGREGATED

Q6 ARE INTERBANK TRANSACTIONS SEPARATED FROM TRANSACTIONS WITH CUSTOMERS?

1 YES
2 NO
3 PARTIALLY SEPARATED
9 NOT KNOWN

Q7 WHAT PERCENTAGE OF TOTAL LOANS DO INTERBANK LOANS REPRESENT?

1 LESS THAN 20%
2 BETWEEN 20% AND 50%
3 MORE THAN 50%
8 NOT SEPARATED
9 NOT DETERMINABLE

Q8 IS THE AMOUNT OF ALLOWANCE FOR LOAN LOSSES FIXED BY LAW?

1 YES
2 NO
9 NOT DETERMINABLE

Q9 THE ALLOWANCE FOR LOAN LOSSES IS USUALLY IN THE FORM OF

1 SPECIFIC PROVISION
2 GENERAL PROVISION
3 SPECIFIC AND GENERAL PROVISION
9 NOT DISCLOSED

Q10 ACTUAL LOAN LOSSES ARE CHARGED OFF BY BEING

1 TAKEN AGAINST RESERVES ON B/S
2 TAKEN AS SEPARATE ITEM ON I/S
3 EXPENSED DIR/TAKEN AGAINST RES
9 NOT DISCLOSED

Q11 NON-PERFORMING LOANS ARE DISCLOSED AS

1 SUPPLEMENTARY INFORMATION
2 PART OF TOTAL LOANS
9 NOT DISCLOSED

Q12 INVESTMENT ASSETS ARE SEGREGATED BY

1 MATURITY
2 TYPE OF SECURITY
3 CURRENCY OF DENOMINATION
9 NOT SEGREGATED

Q13 MARKETABLE SECURITIES ARE CARRIED AT

1 LOWER OF COST OR MARKET VALUE
2 CURRENT MARKET VALUE
3 HISTORICAL COST
4 MOVING AVERAGE
5 WEIGHTED AVERAGE
6 PERIODIC AVERAGE
7 COST W/ PERIODIC REEVALUATION
8 NOT APPLICABLE
9 NOT DISCLOSED

Q14 INVESTMENT ASSETS ARE VALUED AT

1 PURCHASE PRICE
2 PUR PRI ADJ BY AMORT PRM/DISC
3 PUR PRI PART ADJ BY MKT VAL
4 MARKET VALUE
5 LOWER OF COST OR MARKET PRICE
9 NOT DISCLOSED

Q15 DEPOSITS ARE SEGREGATED ACCORDING TO

1 INT VS. NON-INT BEARING
2 DEMAND VS. SAVINGS VS. TIME
3 BEARING OF INT AND BY TYPE
4 TIME PERIOD
5 TIME PERIOD AND BY TYPE
6 DEPOSITOR AND BY TYPE
7 DEPOSITOR
8 NOT SEGREGATED
9 NOT DISCLOSED

Q16 ARE "HIDDEN RESERVES" PERMITTED BY BANKING LAW?

1 YES
2 NO
9 NOT DETERMINABLE

Q17 NON-EQUITY RESERVES ARE TYPICALLY COMPOSED OF

1 REVALUATION RESERVE
2 UNSPECIFIED SPECIAL RESERVE
3 LOAN LOSS RESERVE
4 LOAN LOSS & REVALUATION RES
5 LOAN LOSS/REVAL/AMORT RESERVES
6 NO NON-EQUITY RESERVES
7 LOAN LOSS/EMPLOYEE BENEFIT RES
9 COMPONENTS NOT DETERMINABLE

Q18 "HIDDEN" NON-EQUITY RESERVES USUALLY

1 EXIST AND SEP ACCOUNTED FOR
2 EXIST BUT NOT SEP ACCOUNTED
3 DO NOT EXIST
4 PART OF SHAREHOLDER'S EQUITY
9 NOT DETERMINABLE

Q19 ARE NON-EQUITY RESERVES UTILIZED PRIMARILY FOR TAX PURPOSES?

1 YES
2 NO
3 NO NON-EQUITY RESERVES
9 NOT DETERMINABLE

Q20 ARE CUSTOMER'S LIAB FOR ACCEPTANCES INCLUDED IN ASSETS?

1 YES
2 NO, DISCLOSED IN FOOTNOTE
3 YES, BUT ONLY PARTIALLY
9 CUST LIAB NOT DISCLOSED

Q21 CUSTOMER'S LIAB FOR ACCEPTANCES AS A PERCENTAGE OF ADJUSTED TOTAL ASSETS

1 LESS THAN 20%
2 BETWEEN 20% AND 80%
3 BETWEEN 80% AND 100%
4 OVER 100%
5 NOT APPLICABLE
9 CUST LIAB NOT DISCLOSED

Q22 IS TOTAL REVENUE DISCLOSED IN GROSS, IN NET OR BY COMPONENT?

1 GROSS & BY COMPONENTS ON I/S
2 GROSS ON I/S COMPONENTS IN F/N
3 COMPONENTS ONLY ON I/S
4 PARTIAL INFORMATION IN F/N
5 NET REVENUE DISCLOSED ON I/S
9 NOT DISCLOSED

Q23 INTEREST INCOME AND INTEREST EXPENSE ARE DISCLOSED AS

1 GROSS ON THE INCOME STATEMENT
2 NET ON I/S GROSS AMTS IN F/N
3 NET ON THE INCOME STATEMENT
9 NOT DISCLOSED

Q24 COMMISSIONS EARNED AND COMMISSIONS PAID ARE DISCLOSED AS

1 GROSS
2 NET
8 NOT DETERMINABLE
9 NOT DISCLOSED

Q25 FOREIGN EXCHANGE PROFITS AND COMMISSIONS ARE COMPOSED OF

1 COMM AND TRANS INCOME
2 COMMISSION INCOME ONLY
3 TRANS/REVAL G/L ONLY
9 NOT DISCLOSED

Financial Statements of Banks in 22 Countries

NO.	ACCOUNTING & AUDITING ITEMS	Australia	Austria	Belgium
Q1	BANK'S PRIMARY ACTIVITY IS	UNIVERSAL BANKING	UNIVERSAL BANKING	UNIVERSAL BANKING
Q2	CENTRAL BANKING FUNCTIONS ARE CARRIED OUT BY	SPECIAL GOVERNMENT INSTITUTION	SPECIAL GOVERNMENT INSTITUTION	GOV'T AND PRIVATE INSTITUTIONS
Q3	ARE BANKS GOVERNMENT-OWNED OR SHAREHOLDER-OWNED?	VIRTUALLY ALL BY SHAREHOLDERS	MOST PRIVATE, BUT SOME GOV'T	MOST PRIVATE, BUT SOME GOV'T
Q4	ASSETS AND LIABILITIES ARE ORGANIZED ON THE BALANCE SHEET BY	TYPE OF ASSET OR LIABILITY	TYPE OF ASSET OR LIABILITY	TYPE OF ASSET OR LIABILITY
Q5	LOANS ARE SEGREGATED BY	MATURITY & TYPE OF BORROWER	TYPE OF BORROWER	TYPE OF BORROWER
Q6	ARE INTERBANK TRANSACTIONS SEPARATED FROM TRANSACTIONS WITH CUSTOMERS?	YES	YES	YES
Q7	WHAT PERCENTAGE OF TOTAL LOANS DO INTERBANK LOANS REPRESENT?	LESS THAN 20%	BETWEEN 20% AND 50%	BETWEEN 20% AND 50%
Q8	IS THE AMOUNT OF ALLOWANCE FOR LOAN LOSSES FIXED BY LAW?	NO	NOT DETERMINABLE	NO
Q9	THE ALLOWANCE FOR LOAN LOSSES IS USUALLY IN THE FORM OF	SPECIFIC AND GENERAL PROVISION	GENERAL PROVISION	SPECIFIC AND GENERAL PROVISION
Q10	ACTUAL LOAN LOSSES ARE CHARGED OFF BY BEING	TAKEN AGAINST RESERVES ON B/S	TAKEN AGAINST RESERVES ON B/S	TAKEN AGAINST RESERVES ON B/S
Q11	NON-PERFORMING LOANS ARE DISCLOSED AS	NOT DISCLOSED	NOT DISCLOSED	NOT DISCLOSED
Q12	INVESTMENT ASSETS ARE SEGREGATED BY	TYPE OF SECURITY	TYPE OF SECURITY	TYPE OF SECURITY
Q13	MARKETABLE SECURITIES ARE CARRIED AT	CURRENT MARKET VALUE	LOWER OF COST OR MARKET VALUE	HISTORICAL COST
Q14	INVESTMENT ASSETS ARE VALUED AT	PURCHASE PRICE	PURCHASE PRICE	PURCHASE PRICE
Q15	DEPOSITS ARE SEGREGATED ACCORDING TO	BEARING OF INT AND BY TYPE	DEMAND VS. SAVINGS VS. TIME	TIME PERIOD
Q16	ARE "HIDDEN RESERVES" PERMITTED BY BANKING LAW?	NO	YES	NO
Q17	NON-EQUITY RESERVES ARE TYPICALLY COMPOSED OF	NO NON-EQUITY RESERVES	REVALUATION RESERVE	NO NON-EQUITY RESERVES
Q18	"HIDDEN" NON-EQUITY RESERVES USUALLY	DO NOT EXIST	EXIST AND SEP ACCOUNTED FOR	DO NOT EXIST
Q19	ARE NON-EQUITY RESERVES UTILIZED PRIMARILY FOR TAX PURPOSES?	NO NON-EQUITY RESERVES	YES	NO NON-EQUITY RESERVES
Q20	ARE CUSTOMER'S LIAB FOR ACCEPTANCES INCLUDED IN ASSETS?	YES	YES, BUT ONLY PARTIALLY	NO, DISCLOSED IN FOOTNOTE
Q21	CUSTOMER'S LIAB FOR ACCEPTANCES AS A PERCENTAGE OF ADJUSTED TOTAL ASSETS	LESS THAN 20%	LESS THAN 20%	LESS THAN 20%
Q22	IS TOTAL REVENUE DISCLOSED IN GROSS, IN NET OR BY COMPONENT?	COMPONENTS ONLY ON I/S	COMPONENTS ONLY ON I/S	GROSS & BY COMPONENTS ON I/S

Financial Statements of Banks in 22 Countries

NO.	ACCOUNTING & AUDITING ITEMS	Australia	Austria	Belgium
Q23	INTEREST INCOME AND INTEREST EXPENSE ARE DISCLOSED AS	GROSS ON THE INCOME STATEMENT	GROSS ON THE INCOME STATEMENT	GROSS ON THE INCOME STATEMENT
Q24	COMMISSIONS EARNED AND COMMISSIONS PAID ARE DISCLOSED AS	NET	NET	GROSS
Q25	FOREIGN EXCHANGE PROFITS AND COMMISSIONS ARE COMPOSED OF	NOT DISCLOSED	NOT DISCLOSED	NOT DISCLOSED

Financial Statements of Banks in 22 Countries

NO.	ACCOUNTING & AUDITING ITEMS	Canada	Denmark	Finland
Q1	BANK'S PRIMARY ACTIVITY IS	UNIVERSAL BANKING	UNIVERSAL BANKING	UNIVERSAL BANKING
Q2	CENTRAL BANKING FUNCTIONS ARE CARRIED OUT BY	SPECIAL GOVERNMENT INSTITUTION	SPECIAL GOVERNMENT INSTITUTION	SPECIAL GOVERNMENT INSTITUTION
Q3	ARE BANKS GOVERNMENT-OWNED OR SHAREHOLDER-OWNED?	VIRTUALLY ALL BY SHAREHOLDERS	VIRTUALLY ALL BY SHAREHOLDERS	MOST PRIVATE, BUT SOME GOV'T
Q4	ASSETS AND LIABILITIES ARE ORGANIZED ON THE BALANCE SHEET BY	TYPE OF ASSET OR LIABILITY	TYPE OF ASSET OR LIABILITY	TYPE OF ASSET OR LIABILITY
Q5	LOANS ARE SEGREGATED BY	MATURITY & TYPE OF BORROWER	TYPE OF BORROWER	NOT SEGREGATED
Q6	ARE INTERBANK TRANSACTIONS SEPARATED FROM TRANSACTIONS WITH CUSTOMERS?	YES	YES	YES
Q7	WHAT PERCENTAGE OF TOTAL LOANS DO INTERBANK LOANS REPRESENT?	LESS THAN 20%	LESS THAN 20%	BETWEEN 20% AND 50%
Q8	IS THE AMOUNT OF ALLOWANCE FOR LOAN LOSSES FIXED BY LAW?	YES	NO	YES
Q9	THE ALLOWANCE FOR LOAN LOSSES IS USUALLY IN THE FORM OF	SPECIFIC AND GENERAL PROVISION	GENERAL PROVISION	SPECIFIC AND GENERAL PROVISION
Q10	ACTUAL LOAN LOSSES ARE CHARGED OFF BY BEING	TAKEN AGAINST RESERVES ON B/S	TAKEN AGAINST RESERVES ON B/S	EXPENSED DIR/TAKEN AGAINST RES
Q11	NON-PERFORMING LOANS ARE DISCLOSED AS	SUPPLEMENTARY INFORMATION	NOT DISCLOSED	NOT DISCLOSED
Q12	INVESTMENT ASSETS ARE SEGREGATED BY	TYPE OF SECURITY	TYPE OF SECURITY	TYPE OF SECURITY
Q13	MARKETABLE SECURITIES ARE CARRIED AT	CURRENT MARKET VALUE	CURRENT MARKET VALUE	LOWER OF COST OR MARKET VALUE
Q14	INVESTMENT ASSETS ARE VALUED AT	PURCHASE PRICE	MARKET VALUE	PURCHASE PRICE
Q15	DEPOSITS ARE SEGREGATED ACCORDING TO	DEMAND VS. SAVINGS VS. TIME	TIME PERIOD	DEMAND VS. SAVINGS VS. TIME
Q16	ARE "HIDDEN RESERVES" PERMITTED BY BANKING LAW?	NO	YES	YES
Q17	NON-EQUITY RESERVES ARE TYPICALLY COMPOSED OF	NO NON-EQUITY RESERVES	REVALUATION RESERVE	LOAN LOSS & REVALUATION RES
Q18	"HIDDEN" NON-EQUITY RESERVES USUALLY	DO NOT EXIST	PART OF SHAREHOLDER'S EQUITY	EXIST AND SEP ACCOUNTED FOR
Q19	ARE NON-EQUITY RESERVES UTILIZED PRIMARILY FOR TAX PURPOSES?	NO NON-EQUITY RESERVES	NO	YES
Q20	ARE CUSTOMER'S LIAB FOR ACCEPTANCES INCLUDED IN ASSETS?	YES	YES, BUT ONLY PARTIALLY	NO, DISCLOSED IN FOOTNOTE
Q21	CUSTOMER'S LIAB FOR ACCEPTANCES AS A PERCENTAGE OF ADJUSTED TOTAL ASSETS	LESS THAN 20%	LESS THAN 20%	BETWEEN 20% AND 80%
Q22	IS TOTAL REVENUE DISCLOSED IN GROSS, IN NET OR BY COMPONENT?	COMPONENTS ONLY ON I/S	COMPONENTS ONLY ON I/S	COMPONENTS ONLY ON I/S

Financial Statements of Banks in 22 Countries

NO.	ACCOUNTING & AUDITING ITEMS	Canada	Denmark	Finland
Q23	INTEREST INCOME AND INTEREST EXPENSE ARE DISCLOSED AS	GROSS ON THE INCOME STATEMENT	GROSS ON THE INCOME STATEMENT	GROSS ON THE INCOME STATEMENT
Q24	COMMISSIONS EARNED AND COMMISSIONS PAID ARE DISCLOSED AS	NOT DISCLOSED	NET	NET
Q25	FOREIGN EXCHANGE PROFITS AND COMMISSIONS ARE COMPOSED OF	COMM AND TRANS INCOME	COMM AND TRANS INCOME	NOT DISCLOSED

Financial Statements of Banks in 22 Countries

NO.	ACCOUNTING & AUDITING ITEMS	France	West Germany	Hong Kong
Q1	BANK'S PRIMARY ACTIVITY IS	UNIVERSAL BANKING	UNIVERSAL BANKING	UNIVERSAL BANKING
Q2	CENTRAL BANKING FUNCTIONS ARE CARRIED OUT BY	SPECIAL GOVERNMENT INSTITUTION	SPECIAL GOVERNMENT INSTITUTION	GOV'T AND PRIVATE INSTITUTIONS
Q3	ARE BANKS GOVERNMENT-OWNED OR SHAREHOLDER-OWNED?	USUALLY OWNED BY GOV'T	MOST PRIVATE, BUT SOME GOV'T	VIRTUALLY ALL BY SHAREHOLDERS
Q4	ASSETS AND LIABILITIES ARE ORGANIZED ON THE BALANCE SHEET BY	TYPE OF ASSET OR LIABILITY	TYPE OF ASSET OR LIABILITY	TYPE OF ASSET OR LIABILITY
Q5	LOANS ARE SEGREGATED BY	MATURITY & TYPE OF BORROWER	MATURITY DATE	NOT SEGREGATED
Q6	ARE INTERBANK TRANSACTIONS SEPARATED FROM TRANSACTIONS WITH CUSTOMERS?	YES	YES	PARTIALLY SEPARATED
Q7	WHAT PERCENTAGE OF TOTAL LOANS DO INTERBANK LOANS REPRESENT?	BETWEEN 20% AND 50%	BETWEEN 20% AND 50%	BETWEEN 20% AND 50%
Q8	IS THE AMOUNT OF ALLOWANCE FOR LOAN LOSSES FIXED BY LAW?	NO	YES	YES
Q9	THE ALLOWANCE FOR LOAN LOSSES IS USUALLY IN THE FORM OF	GENERAL PROVISION	SPECIFIC AND GENERAL PROVISION	SPECIFIC AND GENERAL PROVISION
Q10	ACTUAL LOAN LOSSES ARE CHARGED OFF BY BEING	TAKEN AGAINST RESERVES ON B/S	TAKEN AGAINST RESERVES ON B/S	TAKEN AGAINST RESERVES ON B/S
Q11	NON-PERFORMING LOANS ARE DISCLOSED AS	NOT DISCLOSED	NOT DISCLOSED	NOT DISCLOSED
Q12	INVESTMENT ASSETS ARE SEGREGATED BY	TYPE OF SECURITY	MATURITY	NOT SEGREGATED
Q13	MARKETABLE SECURITIES ARE CARRIED AT	LOWER OF COST OR MARKET VALUE	LOWER OF COST OR MARKET VALUE	LOWER OF COST OR MARKET VALUE
Q14	INVESTMENT ASSETS ARE VALUED AT	PURCHASE PRICE	PURCHASE PRICE	PUR PRI ADJ BY AMORT PRM/DISC
Q15	DEPOSITS ARE SEGREGATED ACCORDING TO	DEMAND VS. SAVINGS VS. TIME	TIME PERIOD AND BY TYPE	TIME PERIOD
Q16	ARE "HIDDEN RESERVES" PERMITTED BY BANKING LAW?	YES	YES	NO
Q17	NON-EQUITY RESERVES ARE TYPICALLY COMPOSED OF	LOAN LOSS/REVAL/AMORT RESERVES	UNSPECIFIED SPECIAL RESERVE	NO NON-EQUITY RESERVES
Q18	"HIDDEN" NON-EQUITY RESERVES USUALLY	EXIST AND SEP ACCOUNTED FOR	EXIST AND SEP ACCOUNTED FOR	DO NOT EXIST
Q19	ARE NON-EQUITY RESERVES UTILIZED PRIMARILY FOR TAX PURPOSES?	YES	YES	NO NON-EQUITY RESERVES
Q20	ARE CUSTOMER'S LIAB FOR ACCEPTANCES INCLUDED IN ASSETS?	NO, DISCLOSED IN FOOTNOTE	YES, BUT ONLY PARTIALLY	YES
Q21	CUSTOMER'S LIAB FOR ACCEPTANCES AS A PERCENTAGE OF ADJUSTED TOTAL ASSETS	BETWEEN 20% AND 80%	LESS THAN 20%	LESS THAN 20%
Q22	IS TOTAL REVENUE DISCLOSED IN GROSS, IN NET OR BY COMPONENT?	GROSS & BY COMPONENTS ON I/S	GROSS & BY COMPONENTS ON I/S	PARTIAL INFORMATION IN F/N

Financial Statements of Banks in 22 Countries

NO.	ACCOUNTING & AUDITING ITEMS	France	West Germany	Hong Kong
Q23	INTEREST INCOME AND INTEREST EXPENSE ARE DISCLOSED AS	GROSS ON THE INCOME STATEMENT	GROSS ON THE INCOME STATEMENT	NOT DISCLOSED
Q24	COMMISSIONS EARNED AND COMMISSIONS PAID ARE DISCLOSED AS	GROSS	GROSS	NOT DISCLOSED
Q25	FOREIGN EXCHANGE PROFITS AND COMMISSIONS ARE COMPOSED OF	COMM AND TRANS INCOME	NOT DISCLOSED	NOT DISCLOSED

Financial Statements of Banks in 22 Countries

NO.	ACCOUNTING & AUDITING ITEMS	Italy	Japan	South Korea
Q1	BANK'S PRIMARY ACTIVITY IS	UNIVERSAL BANKING	COMMERCIAL BANKING ONLY	COMMERCIAL BANKING ONLY
Q2	CENTRAL BANKING FUNCTIONS ARE CARRIED OUT BY	SPECIAL GOVERNMENT INSTITUTION	SPECIAL GOVERNMENT INSTITUTION	SPECIAL GOVERNMENT INSTITUTION
Q3	ARE BANKS GOVERNMENT-OWNED OR SHAREHOLDER-OWNED?	USUALLY OWNED BY GOV'T	VIRTUALLY ALL BY SHAREHOLDERS	VIRTUALLY ALL BY SHAREHOLDERS
Q4	ASSETS AND LIABILITIES ARE ORGANIZED ON THE BALANCE SHEET BY	TYPE OF ASSET OR LIABILITY	TYPE OF ASSET OR LIABILITY	TYPE OF ASSET OR LIABILITY
Q5	LOANS ARE SEGREGATED BY	TYPE OF BORROWER	TYPE OF SECURITY	TYPE OF SECURITY
Q6	ARE INTERBANK TRANSACTIONS SEPARATED FROM TRANSACTIONS WITH CUSTOMERS?	YES	PARTIALLY SEPARATED	PARTIALLY SEPARATED
Q7	WHAT PERCENTAGE OF TOTAL LOANS DO INTERBANK LOANS REPRESENT?	BETWEEN 20% AND 50%	LESS THAN 20%	LESS THAN 20%
Q8	IS THE AMOUNT OF ALLOWANCE FOR LOAN LOSSES FIXED BY LAW?	YES	YES	YES
Q9	THE ALLOWANCE FOR LOAN LOSSES IS USUALLY IN THE FORM OF	SPECIFIC AND GENERAL PROVISION	SPECIFIC AND GENERAL PROVISION	SPECIFIC AND GENERAL PROVISION
Q10	ACTUAL LOAN LOSSES ARE CHARGED OFF BY BEING	EXPENSED DIR/TAKEN AGAINST RES	EXPENSED DIR/TAKEN AGAINST RES	TAKEN AGAINST RESERVES ON B/S
Q11	NON-PERFORMING LOANS ARE DISCLOSED AS	NOT DISCLOSED	NOT DISCLOSED	NOT DISCLOSED
Q12	INVESTMENT ASSETS ARE SEGREGATED BY	TYPE OF SECURITY	TYPE OF SECURITY	TYPE OF SECURITY
Q13	MARKETABLE SECURITIES ARE CARRIED AT	LOWER OF COST OR MARKET VALUE	LOWER OF COST OR MARKET VALUE	LOWER OF COST OR MARKET VALUE
Q14	INVESTMENT ASSETS ARE VALUED AT	PURCHASE PRICE	PURCHASE PRICE	PURCHASE PRICE
Q15	DEPOSITS ARE SEGREGATED ACCORDING TO	DEMAND VS. SAVINGS VS. TIME	DEMAND VS. SAVINGS VS. TIME	DEMAND VS. SAVINGS VS. TIME
Q16	ARE "HIDDEN RESERVES" PERMITTED BY BANKING LAW?	YES	NO	NO
Q17	NON-EQUITY RESERVES ARE TYPICALLY COMPOSED OF	LOAN LOSS/EMPLOYEE BENEFIT RES	NO NON-EQUITY RESERVES	NO NON-EQUITY RESERVES
Q18	"HIDDEN" NON-EQUITY RESERVES USUALLY	EXIST AND SEP ACCOUNTED FOR	DO NOT EXIST	DO NOT EXIST
Q19	ARE NON-EQUITY RESERVES UTILIZED PRIMARILY FOR TAX PURPOSES?	NO	NO NON-EQUITY RESERVES	NO NON-EQUITY RESERVES
Q20	ARE CUSTOMER'S LIAB FOR ACCEPTANCES INCLUDED IN ASSETS?	NO, DISCLOSED IN FOOTNOTE	YES	YES
Q21	CUSTOMER'S LIAB FOR ACCEPTANCES AS A PERCENTAGE OF ADJUSTED TOTAL ASSETS	BETWEEN 20% AND 80%	LESS THAN 20%	LESS THAN 20%
Q22	IS TOTAL REVENUE DISCLOSED IN GROSS, IN NET OR BY COMPONENT?	GROSS & BY COMPONENTS ON I/S	GROSS & BY COMPONENTS ON I/S	GROSS & BY COMPONENTS ON I/S

Financial Statements of Banks in 22 Countries

NO.	ACCOUNTING & AUDITING ITEMS	Italy	Japan	South Korea
Q23	INTEREST INCOME AND INTEREST EXPENSE ARE DISCLOSED AS	GROSS ON THE INCOME STATEMENT	GROSS ON THE INCOME STATEMENT	GROSS ON THE INCOME STATEMENT
Q24	COMMISSIONS EARNED AND COMMISSIONS PAID ARE DISCLOSED AS	GROSS	GROSS	GROSS
Q25	FOREIGN EXCHANGE PROFITS AND COMMISSIONS ARE COMPOSED OF	COMM AND TRANS INCOME	COMM AND TRANS INCOME	COMMISSION INCOME ONLY

Financial Statements of Banks in 22 Countries

NO.	ACCOUNTING & AUDITING ITEMS	Malaysia	Netherlands	Norway
Q1	BANK'S PRIMARY ACTIVITY IS	UNIVERSAL BANKING	UNIVERSAL BANKING	UNIVERSAL BANKING
Q2	CENTRAL BANKING FUNCTIONS ARE CARRIED OUT BY	GOV'T AND PRIVATE INSTITUTIONS	SPECIAL GOVERNMENT INSTITUTION	SPECIAL GOVERNMENT INSTITUTION
Q3	ARE BANKS GOVERNMENT-OWNED OR SHAREHOLDER-OWNED?	VIRTUALLY ALL BY SHAREHOLDERS	VIRTUALLY ALL BY SHAREHOLDERS	VIRTUALLY ALL BY SHAREHOLDERS
Q4	ASSETS AND LIABILITIES ARE ORGANIZED ON THE BALANCE SHEET BY	LIQUIDITY(CURRENT/NON-CURRENT)	TYPE OF ASSET OR LIABILITY	TYPE OF ASSET OR LIABILITY
Q5	LOANS ARE SEGREGATED BY	NOT SEGREGATED	MATURITY & TYPE OF BORROWER	MATURITY & TYPE OF BORROWER
Q6	ARE INTERBANK TRANSACTIONS SEPARATED FROM TRANSACTIONS WITH CUSTOMERS?	PARTIALLY SEPARATED	YES	YES
Q7	WHAT PERCENTAGE OF TOTAL LOANS DO INTERBANK LOANS REPRESENT?	LESS THAN 20%	BETWEEN 20% AND 50%	LESS THAN 20%
Q8	IS THE AMOUNT OF ALLOWANCE FOR LOAN LOSSES FIXED BY LAW?	NO	NO	YES
Q9	THE ALLOWANCE FOR LOAN LOSSES IS USUALLY IN THE FORM OF	SPECIFIC AND GENERAL PROVISION	SPECIFIC AND GENERAL PROVISION	SPECIFIC AND GENERAL PROVISION
Q10	ACTUAL LOAN LOSSES ARE CHARGED OFF BY BEING	TAKEN AGAINST RESERVES ON B/S	TAKEN AGAINST RESERVES ON B/S	EXPENSED DIR/TAKEN AGAINST RES
Q11	NON-PERFORMING LOANS ARE DISCLOSED AS	NOT DISCLOSED	NOT DISCLOSED	NOT DISCLOSED
Q12	INVESTMENT ASSETS ARE SEGREGATED BY	TYPE OF SECURITY	TYPE OF SECURITY	TYPE OF SECURITY
Q13	MARKETABLE SECURITIES ARE CARRIED AT	LOWER OF COST OR MARKET VALUE	CURRENT MARKET VALUE	LOWER OF COST OR MARKET VALUE
Q14	INVESTMENT ASSETS ARE VALUED AT	PUR PRI ADJ BY AMORT PRM/DISC	MARKET VALUE	PURCHASE PRICE
Q15	DEPOSITS ARE SEGREGATED ACCORDING TO	NOT SEGREGATED	DEMAND VS. SAVINGS VS. TIME	DEPOSITOR AND BY TYPE
Q16	ARE "HIDDEN RESERVES" PERMITTED BY BANKING LAW?	YES	NO	YES
Q17	NON-EQUITY RESERVES ARE TYPICALLY COMPOSED OF	NO NON-EQUITY RESERVES	REVALUATION RESERVE	LOAN LOSS/REVAL/AMORT RESERVES
Q18	"HIDDEN" NON-EQUITY RESERVES USUALLY	DO NOT EXIST	PART OF SHAREHOLDER'S EQUITY	EXIST AND SEP ACCOUNTED FOR
Q19	ARE NON-EQUITY RESERVES UTILIZED PRIMARILY FOR TAX PURPOSES?	NO NON-EQUITY RESERVES	NO	YES
Q20	ARE CUSTOMER'S LIAB FOR ACCEPTANCES INCLUDED IN ASSETS?	YES	NO, DISCLOSED IN FOOTNOTE	NO, DISCLOSED IN FOOTNOTE
Q21	CUSTOMER'S LIAB FOR ACCEPTANCES AS A PERCENTAGE OF ADJUSTED TOTAL ASSETS	LESS THAN 20%	LESS THAN 20%	OVER 100%
Q22	IS TOTAL REVENUE DISCLOSED IN GROSS, IN NET OR BY COMPONENT?	PARTIAL INFORMATION IN F/N	COMPONENTS ONLY ON I/S	COMPONENTS ONLY ON I/S

Financial Statements of Banks in 22 Countries

NO.	ACCOUNTING & AUDITING ITEMS	Malaysia	Netherlands	Norway
Q23	INTEREST INCOME AND INTEREST EXPENSE ARE DISCLOSED AS	NOT DISCLOSED	NET ON THE INCOME STATEMENT	GROSS ON THE INCOME STATEMENT
Q24	COMMISSIONS EARNED AND COMMISSIONS PAID ARE DISCLOSED AS	NOT DISCLOSED	NET	NET
Q25	FOREIGN EXCHANGE PROFITS AND COMMISSIONS ARE COMPOSED OF	NOT DISCLOSED	TRANS/REVAL G/L ONLY	TRANS/REVAL G/L ONLY

Financial Statements of Banks in 22 Countries

NO.	ACCOUNTING & AUDITING ITEMS	Singapore	South Africa	Spain
Q1	BANK'S PRIMARY ACTIVITY IS	UNIVERSAL BANKING	UNIVERSAL BANKING	UNIVERSAL BANKING
Q2	CENTRAL BANKING FUNCTIONS ARE CARRIED OUT BY	GOV'T AND PRIVATE INSTITUTIONS	PRIVATE INSTITUTIONS	SPECIAL GOVERNMENT INSTITUTION
Q3	ARE BANKS GOVERNMENT-OWNED OR SHAREHOLDER-OWNED?	VIRTUALLY ALL BY SHAREHOLDERS	VIRTUALLY ALL BY SHAREHOLDERS	VIRTUALLY ALL BY SHAREHOLDERS
Q4	ASSETS AND LIABILITIES ARE ORGANIZED ON THE BALANCE SHEET BY	LIQUIDITY(CURRENT/NON-CURRENT)	LIQUIDITY(CURRENT/NON-CURRENT)	TYPE OF ASSET OR LIABILITY
Q5	LOANS ARE SEGREGATED BY	MATURITY DATE	MATURITY & TYPE OF BORROWER	MATURITY & TYPE OF BORROWER
Q6	ARE INTERBANK TRANSACTIONS SEPARATED FROM TRANSACTIONS WITH CUSTOMERS?	PARTIALLY SEPARATED	NO	YES
Q7	WHAT PERCENTAGE OF TOTAL LOANS DO INTERBANK LOANS REPRESENT?	BETWEEN 20% AND 50%	NOT SEPARATED	LESS THAN 20%
Q8	IS THE AMOUNT OF ALLOWANCE FOR LOAN LOSSES FIXED BY LAW?	NO	NO	YES
Q9	THE ALLOWANCE FOR LOAN LOSSES IS USUALLY IN THE FORM OF	SPECIFIC AND GENERAL PROVISION	SPECIFIC AND GENERAL PROVISION	SPECIFIC AND GENERAL PROVISION
Q10	ACTUAL LOAN LOSSES ARE CHARGED OFF BY BEING	TAKEN AGAINST RESERVES ON B/S	TAKEN AGAINST RESERVES ON B/S	TAKEN AGAINST RESERVES ON B/S
Q11	NON-PERFORMING LOANS ARE DISCLOSED AS	NOT DISCLOSED	NOT DISCLOSED	NOT DISCLOSED
Q12	INVESTMENT ASSETS ARE SEGREGATED BY	MATURITY	TYPE OF SECURITY	TYPE OF SECURITY
Q13	MARKETABLE SECURITIES ARE CARRIED AT	LOWER OF COST OR MARKET VALUE	CURRENT MARKET VALUE	LOWER OF COST OR MARKET VALUE
Q14	INVESTMENT ASSETS ARE VALUED AT	PUR PRI PART ADJ BY MKT VAL	MARKET VALUE	PUR PRI PART ADJ BY MKT VAL
Q15	DEPOSITS ARE SEGREGATED ACCORDING TO	DEPOSITOR	DEMAND VS. SAVINGS VS. TIME	DEPOSITOR
Q16	ARE "HIDDEN RESERVES" PERMITTED BY BANKING LAW?	NO	NO	YES
Q17	NON-EQUITY RESERVES ARE TYPICALLY COMPOSED OF	NO NON-EQUITY RESERVES	NO NON-EQUITY RESERVES	UNSPECIFIED SPECIAL RESERVE
Q18	"HIDDEN" NON-EQUITY RESERVES USUALLY	DO NOT EXIST	DO NOT EXIST	EXIST AND SEP ACCOUNTED FOR
Q19	ARE NON-EQUITY RESERVES UTILIZED PRIMARILY FOR TAX PURPOSES?	NO NON-EQUITY RESERVES	NO NON-EQUITY RESERVES	NO
Q20	ARE CUSTOMER'S LIAB FOR ACCEPTANCES INCLUDED IN ASSETS?	YES	YES	NO, DISCLOSED IN FOOTNOTE
Q21	CUSTOMER'S LIAB FOR ACCEPTANCES AS A PERCENTAGE OF ADJUSTED TOTAL ASSETS	BETWEEN 20% AND 80%	LESS THAN 20%	OVER 100%
Q22	IS TOTAL REVENUE DISCLOSED IN GROSS, IN NET OR BY COMPONENT?	PARTIAL INFORMATION IN F/N	NOT DISCLOSED	GROSS & BY COMPONENTS ON I/S

Financial Statements of Banks in 22 Countries

NO.	ACCOUNTING & AUDITING ITEMS	Singapore	South Africa	Spain
Q23	INTEREST INCOME AND INTEREST EXPENSE ARE DISCLOSED AS	NOT DISCLOSED	NOT DISCLOSED	GROSS ON THE INCOME STATEMENT
Q24	COMMISSIONS EARNED AND COMMISSIONS PAID ARE DISCLOSED AS	NOT DISCLOSED	NOT DISCLOSED	NET
Q25	FOREIGN EXCHANGE PROFITS AND COMMISSIONS ARE COMPOSED OF	NOT DISCLOSED	NOT DISCLOSED	NOT DISCLOSED

Financial Statements of Banks in 22 Countries

NO.	ACCOUNTING & AUDITING ITEMS	Sweden	Switzerland	United Kingdom
Q1	BANK'S PRIMARY ACTIVITY IS	UNIVERSAL BANKING	UNIVERSAL BANKING	COMMERCIAL BANKING ONLY
Q2	CENTRAL BANKING FUNCTIONS ARE CARRIED OUT BY	SPECIAL GOVERNMENT INSTITUTION	SPECIAL GOVERNMENT INSTITUTION	SPECIAL GOVERNMENT INSTITUTION
Q3	ARE BANKS GOVERNMENT-OWNED OR SHAREHOLDER-OWNED?	VIRTUALLY ALL BY SHAREHOLDERS	VIRTUALLY ALL BY SHAREHOLDERS	VIRTUALLY ALL BY SHAREHOLDERS
Q4	ASSETS AND LIABILITIES ARE ORGANIZED ON THE BALANCE SHEET BY	TYPE OF ASSET OR LIABILITY	TYPE OF ASSET OR LIABILITY	TYPE OF ASSET OR LIABILITY
Q5	LOANS ARE SEGREGATED BY	TYPE OF BORROWER	TYPE OF SECURITY	TYPE OF BORROWER
Q6	ARE INTERBANK TRANSACTIONS SEPARATED FROM TRANSACTIONS WITH CUSTOMERS?	YES	YES	YES
Q7	WHAT PERCENTAGE OF TOTAL LOANS DO INTERBANK LOANS REPRESENT?	BETWEEN 20% AND 50%	BETWEEN 20% AND 50%	LESS THAN 20%
Q8	IS THE AMOUNT OF ALLOWANCE FOR LOAN LOSSES FIXED BY LAW?	YES	NO	NO
Q9	THE ALLOWANCE FOR LOAN LOSSES IS USUALLY IN THE FORM OF	GENERAL PROVISION	SPECIFIC AND GENERAL PROVISION	SPECIFIC AND GENERAL PROVISION
Q10	ACTUAL LOAN LOSSES ARE CHARGED OFF BY BEING	EXPENSED DIR/TAKEN AGAINST RES	TAKEN AGAINST RESERVES ON B/S	TAKEN AGAINST RESERVES ON B/S
Q11	NON-PERFORMING LOANS ARE DISCLOSED AS	NOT DISCLOSED	NOT DISCLOSED	SUPPLEMENTARY INFORMATION
Q12	INVESTMENT ASSETS ARE SEGREGATED BY	TYPE OF SECURITY	TYPE OF SECURITY	TYPE OF SECURITY
Q13	MARKETABLE SECURITIES ARE CARRIED AT	LOWER OF COST OR MARKET VALUE	LOWER OF COST OR MARKET VALUE	CURRENT MARKET VALUE
Q14	INVESTMENT ASSETS ARE VALUED AT	MARKET VALUE	LOWER OF COST OR MARKET PRICE	LOWER OF COST OR MARKET PRICE
Q15	DEPOSITS ARE SEGREGATED ACCORDING TO	DEPOSITOR AND BY TYPE	BEARING OF INT AND BY TYPE	DEMAND VS. SAVINGS VS. TIME
Q16	ARE "HIDDEN RESERVES" PERMITTED BY BANKING LAW?	YES	YES	NO
Q17	NON-EQUITY RESERVES ARE TYPICALLY COMPOSED OF	LOAN LOSS/REVAL/AMORT RESERVES	LOAN LOSS/REVAL/AMORT RESERVES	NO NON-EQUITY RESERVES
Q18	"HIDDEN" NON-EQUITY RESERVES USUALLY	EXIST AND SEP ACCOUNTED FOR	EXIST AND SEP ACCOUNTED FOR	DO NOT EXIST
Q19	ARE NON-EQUITY RESERVES UTILIZED PRIMARILY FOR TAX PURPOSES?	YES	YES	NO NON-EQUITY RESERVES
Q20	ARE CUSTOMER'S LIAB FOR ACCEPTANCES INCLUDED IN ASSETS?	NO, DISCLOSED IN FOOTNOTE	NO, DISCLOSED IN FOOTNOTE	NO, DISCLOSED IN FOOTNOTE
Q21	CUSTOMER'S LIAB FOR ACCEPTANCES AS A PERCENTAGE OF ADJUSTED TOTAL ASSETS	LESS THAN 20%	LESS THAN 20%	LESS THAN 20%
Q22	IS TOTAL REVENUE DISCLOSED IN GROSS, IN NET OR BY COMPONENT?	COMPONENTS ONLY ON I/S	GROSS & BY COMPONENTS ON I/S	COMPONENTS ONLY ON I/S

Financial Statements of Banks in 22 Countries

NO.	ACCOUNTING & AUDITING ITEMS	Sweden	Switzerland	United Kingdom
Q23	INTEREST INCOME AND INTEREST EXPENSE ARE DISCLOSED AS	NET ON I/S GROSS AMTS IN F/N	GROSS ON THE INCOME STATEMENT	NET ON I/S GROSS AMTS IN F/N
Q24	COMMISSIONS EARNED AND COMMISSIONS PAID ARE DISCLOSED AS	GROSS	GROSS	NET
Q25	FOREIGN EXCHANGE PROFITS AND COMMISSIONS ARE COMPOSED OF	COMM AND TRANS INCOME	COMMISSION INCOME ONLY	COMMISSION INCOME ONLY

Financial Statements of Banks in 22 Countries

NO.	ACCOUNTING & AUDITING ITEMS	United States		
Q1	BANK'S PRIMARY ACTIVITY IS	COMMERCIAL BANKING ONLY		
Q2	CENTRAL BANKING FUNCTIONS ARE CARRIED OUT BY	SPECIAL GOVERNMENT INSTITUTION		
Q3	ARE BANKS GOVERNMENT-OWNED OR SHAREHOLDER-OWNED?	VIRTUALLY ALL BY SHAREHOLDERS		
Q4	ASSETS AND LIABILITIES ARE ORGANIZED ON THE BALANCE SHEET BY	TYPE OF ASSET OR LIABILITY		
Q5	LOANS ARE SEGREGATED BY	MATURITY & TYPE OF BORROWER		
Q6	ARE INTERBANK TRANSACTIONS SEPARATED FROM TRANSACTIONS WITH CUSTOMERS?	YES		
Q7	WHAT PERCENTAGE OF TOTAL LOANS DO INTERBANK LOANS REPRESENT?	LESS THAN 20%		
Q8	IS THE AMOUNT OF ALLOWANCE FOR LOAN LOSSES FIXED BY LAW?	NO		
Q9	THE ALLOWANCE FOR LOAN LOSSES IS USUALLY IN THE FORM OF	SPECIFIC AND GENERAL PROVISION		
Q10	ACTUAL LOAN LOSSES ARE CHARGED OFF BY BEING	TAKEN AGAINST RESERVES ON B/S		
Q11	NON-PERFORMING LOANS ARE DISCLOSED AS	SUPPLEMENTARY INFORMATION		
Q12	INVESTMENT ASSETS ARE SEGREGATED BY	TYPE OF SECURITY		
Q13	MARKETABLE SECURITIES ARE CARRIED AT	CURRENT MARKET VALUE		
Q14	INVESTMENT ASSETS ARE VALUED AT	PURCHASE PRICE		
Q15	DEPOSITS ARE SEGREGATED ACCORDING TO	DEMAND VS. SAVINGS VS. TIME		
Q16	ARE "HIDDEN RESERVES" PERMITTED BY BANKING LAW?	NO		
Q17	NON-EQUITY RESERVES ARE TYPICALLY COMPOSED OF	NO NON-EQUITY RESERVES		
Q18	"HIDDEN" NON-EQUITY RESERVES USUALLY	DO NOT EXIST		
Q19	ARE NON-EQUITY RESERVES UTILIZED PRIMARILY FOR TAX PURPOSES?	NO NON-EQUITY RESERVES		
Q20	ARE CUSTOMER'S LIAB FOR ACCEPTANCES INCLUDED IN ASSETS?	YES		
Q21	CUSTOMER'S LIAB FOR ACCEPTANCES AS A PERCENTAGE OF ADJUSTED TOTAL ASSETS	LESS THAN 20%		
Q22	IS TOTAL REVENUE DISCLOSED IN GROSS, IN NET OR BY COMPONENT?	COMPONENTS ONLY ON I/S		

Financial Statements of Banks in 22 Countries

NO.	ACCOUNTING & AUDITING ITEMS	United States		
Q23	INTEREST INCOME AND INTEREST EXPENSE ARE DISCLOSED AS	GROSS ON THE INCOME STATEMENT		
Q24	COMMISSIONS EARNED AND COMMISSIONS PAID ARE DISCLOSED AS	GROSS		
Q25	FOREIGN EXCHANGE PROFITS AND COMMISSIONS ARE COMPOSED OF	COMMISSION INCOME ONLY		

EXHIBIT 4-3

QUESTIONS AND ANSWERS FOR

FINANCIAL STATEMENTS OF INSURANCE COMPANIES

Q1 BY LAW, MAY A COMPANY ENGAGE IN BOTH LIFE AND NON-LIFE INSURANCE BUSINESS?

1 YES
2 NO
9 NOT KNOWN

Q2 DO LIFE INSURANCE COMPANIES ALSO ENGAGE IN PENSION FUND MANAGEMENT OR DO SEPARATE ENTITIES EXIST FOR THAT PURPOSE?

1 PERFORMED BY LIFE INS COS
2 SEPARATE ENTITIES EXIST
3 COMPS MANAGE OWN PENSION FUNDS
9 NOT KNOWN

Q3 INSURANCE RESERVES ARE REGULATED BY

1 GOVERNMENT
2 INSURANCE INDUSTRY
3 NOT REGULATED
9 NOT KNOWN

Q4 MOST INSURANCE COMPANIES IN THE COUNTRY CAN BE OWNED BY

1 STOCKHOLDERS
2 NON-LIFE BY SH, LIFE BY PH
3 STOCKHOLDERS A/O POLICYHOLDERS
9 NOT DISCLOSED

Q5 ASSETS AND LIABILITIES ARE ORGANIZED ON THE BALANCE SHEET BY

1 LIQUIDITY(CURRENT/NON-CURRENT)
2 TYPE OF ASSET OR LIABILITY
3 OTHER MEANS
9 NOT DETERMINABLE

Q6 INVESTMENT ASSETS ARE SEGREGATED BY

1 MATURITY DATE
2 TYPE OF INVESTMENT ASSET
3 ISSUING ENTITY
4 NO SEGREGATION
9 NOT DISCLOSED

Q7 FIXED-INCOME SECURITIES ARE VALUED AT

1 HISTORICAL COST
2 MARKET PRICE
3 LOWER OF COST OR MARKET PRICE
4 AMORTIZED COST
5 COST ADJUSTED BY MARKET VALUE
6 NOT DETERMINABLE
7 FACE VALUE
8 NO MAJORITY PRACTICE
9 NOT DISCLOSED

Q8 EQUITY SECURITIES ARE VALUED AT

1 HISTORICAL COST
2 MARKET PRICE
3 LOWER OF COST OR MARKET PRICE
4 LOWER COST + PART ADJ TO MKT OR MKT
5 NOT DETERMINABLE
8 NO MAJORITY PRACTICE
9 NOT DISCLOSED

Q9 ARE CLAIMS AND LOSS RESERVES SEGREGATED FROM TECHNICAL RESERVES?

1 YES
2 NO
9 NOT DISCLOSED

Q10 ARE POLICYHOLDER'S SURPLUS, DIVIDENDS OR EQUITY DISCLOSED?

1 YES
2 NO
3 NOT APPLICABLE
9 NOT DISCLOSED

Q11 IS TOTAL REVENUE DISCLOSED IN GROSS, IN NET OR BY COMPONENT?

1 GROSS AND BY COMPONENTS ON I/S
2 GROSS ON I/S COMPONENTS IN F/N
3 BY COMPONENTS ONLY ON I/S
4 THROUGH PARTIAL INFO IN F/N
5 NET REVENUE DISCLOSED ON I/S
9 NOT DISCLOSED

Q12 ARE INCOME FROM LIFE AND NON-LIFE OPERATIONS SEGREGATED?

1 YES
2 NO
8 NOT APPLICABLE
9 NOT DISCLOSED

Q13 RESULTS OF REINSURANCE BUSINESS DISCLOSED AS

1 SEPARATE REINS OPER RESULTS
2 NET REINSURANCE RESULTS ONLY
3 GROSS REINS RESULTS ITEMIZED
8 NOT APPLICABLE
9 NOT DISCLOSED

Q14 IS UNEARNED PREMIUM INCOME DISCLOSED?

1 YES
2 NO
8 NOT APPLICABLE
9 NOT DISCLOSED

Q15 UNDERWRITING EXPENSES ARE

1 DISCLOSED SEPARATELY
2 PART OF CLAIMS & LOSS RESERVES
3 PART OF L.T. POLICY RESERVES
4 PART OF GEN/ADMIN EXPENSES
9 NOT DISCLOSED

Q16 "HIDDEN" NON-EQUITY RESERVES

1 EXIST & SEP ACCOUNTED FOR
2 EXIST BUT NOT SEP ACCOUNTED
3 DO NOT EXIST
8 NOT APPLICABLE
9 NOT DISCLOSED

Financial Statements of Insurance Companies in 22 Countries

NO.	ACCOUNTING & AUDITING ITEMS	Australia	Austria	Belgium
Q1	BY LAW, MAY A COMPANY ENGAGE IN BOTH LIFE AND NON-LIFE INSURANCE BUSINESS?	NO	YES	YES
Q2	DO LIFE INSURANCE COMPANIES ALSO ENGAGE IN PENSION FUND MANAGEMENT OR DO SEPARATE ENTITIES EXIST FOR THAT PURPOSE?	PERFORMED BY LIFE INS COS	PERFORMED BY LIFE INS COS	PERFORMED BY LIFE INS COS
Q3	INSURANCE RESERVES ARE REGULATED BY	INSURANCE INDUSTRY	GOVERNMENT	GOVERNMENT
Q4	MOST INSURANCE COMPANIES IN THE COUNTRY CAN BE OWNED BY	NON-LIFE BY SH, LIFE BY PH	STOCKHOLDERS A/O POLICYHOLDERS	STOCKHOLDERS
Q5	ASSETS AND LIABILITIES ARE ORGANIZED ON THE BALANCE SHEET BY	TYPE OF ASSET OR LIABILITY	TYPE OF ASSET OR LIABILITY	TYPE OF ASSET OR LIABILITY
Q6	INVESTMENT ASSETS ARE SEGREGATED BY	TYPE OF INVESTMENT ASSET	TYPE OF INVESTMENT ASSET	TYPE OF INVESTMENT ASSET
Q7	FIXED-INCOME SECURITIES ARE VALUED AT	HISTORICAL COST	NOT DISCLOSED	LOWER OF COST OR MARKET PRICE
Q8	EQUITY SECURITIES ARE VALUED AT	MARKET PRICE	NOT DISCLOSED	MARKET PRICE
Q9	ARE CLAIMS AND LOSS RESERVES SEGREGATED FROM TECHNICAL RESERVES?	YES	YES	YES
Q10	ARE POLICYHOLDER'S SURPLUS, DIVIDENDS OR EQUITY DISCLOSED?	NO	YES	NO
Q11	IS TOTAL REVENUE DISCLOSED IN GROSS, IN NET OR BY COMPONENT?	BY COMPONENTS ONLY ON I/S	BY COMPONENTS ONLY ON I/S	BY COMPONENTS ONLY ON I/S
Q12	ARE INCOME FROM LIFE AND NON-LIFE OPERATIONS SEGREGATED?	YES	YES	YES
Q13	RESULTS OF REINSURANCE BUSINESS DISCLOSED AS	GROSS REINS RESULTS ITEMIZED	NET REINSURANCE RESULTS ONLY	GROSS REINS RESULTS ITEMIZED
Q14	IS UNEARNED PREMIUM INCOME DISCLOSED?	YES	YES	YES
Q15	UNDERWRITING EXPENSES ARE	DISCLOSED SEPARATELY	DISCLOSED SEPARATELY	DISCLOSED SEPARATELY
Q16	"HIDDEN" NON-EQUITY RESERVES	NOT DISCLOSED	EXIST & SEP ACCOUNTED FOR	EXIST & SEP ACCOUNTED FOR

Financial Statements of Insurance Companies in 22 Countries

NO.	ACCOUNTING & AUDITING ITEMS	Canada	Denmark	Finland
Q1	BY LAW, MAY A COMPANY ENGAGE IN BOTH LIFE AND NON-LIFE INSURANCE BUSINESS?	NO	YES	YES
Q2	DO LIFE INSURANCE COMPANIES ALSO ENGAGE IN PENSION FUND MANAGEMENT OR DO SEPARATE ENTITIES EXIST FOR THAT PURPOSE?	SEPARATE ENTITIES EXIST	SEPARATE ENTITIES EXIST	SEPARATE ENTITIES EXIST
Q3	INSURANCE RESERVES ARE REGULATED BY	INSURANCE INDUSTRY	GOVERNMENT	INSURANCE INDUSTRY
Q4	MOST INSURANCE COMPANIES IN THE COUNTRY CAN BE OWNED BY	STOCKHOLDERS A/O POLICYHOLDERS	STOCKHOLDERS	STOCKHOLDERS A/O POLICYHOLDERS
Q5	ASSETS AND LIABILITIES ARE ORGANIZED ON THE BALANCE SHEET BY	TYPE OF ASSET OR LIABILITY	LIQUIDITY(CURRENT/NON-CURRENT)	LIQUIDITY(CURRENT/NON-CURRENT)
Q6	INVESTMENT ASSETS ARE SEGREGATED BY	TYPE OF INVESTMENT ASSET	TYPE OF INVESTMENT ASSET	TYPE OF INVESTMENT ASSET
Q7	FIXED-INCOME SECURITIES ARE VALUED AT	AMORTIZED COST	AMORTIZED COST	AMORTIZED COST
Q8	EQUITY SECURITIES ARE VALUED AT	HISTORICAL COST	MARKET PRICE	MARKET PRICE
Q9	ARE CLAIMS AND LOSS RESERVES SEGREGATED FROM TECHNICAL RESERVES?	YES	YES	YES
Q10	ARE POLICYHOLDER'S SURPLUS, DIVIDENDS OR EQUITY DISCLOSED?	YES	NO	NO
Q11	IS TOTAL REVENUE DISCLOSED IN GROSS, IN NET OR BY COMPONENT?	GROSS AND BY COMPONENTS ON I/S	BY COMPONENTS ONLY ON I/S	BY COMPONENTS ONLY ON I/S
Q12	ARE INCOME FROM LIFE AND NON-LIFE OPERATIONS SEGREGATED?	NOT APPLICABLE	YES	YES
Q13	RESULTS OF REINSURANCE BUSINESS DISCLOSED AS	NOT DISCLOSED	NET REINSURANCE RESULTS ONLY	GROSS REINS RESULTS ITEMIZED
Q14	IS UNEARNED PREMIUM INCOME DISCLOSED?	NO	NO	YES
Q15	UNDERWRITING EXPENSES ARE	PART OF GEN/ADMIN EXPENSES	PART OF GEN/ADMIN EXPENSES	DISCLOSED SEPARATELY
Q16	"HIDDEN" NON-EQUITY RESERVES	NOT DISCLOSED	NOT DISCLOSED	EXIST & SEP ACCOUNTED FOR

Financial Statements of Insurance Companies in 22 Countries

NO.	ACCOUNTING & AUDITING ITEMS	France	West Germany	Hong Kong
Q1	BY LAW, MAY A COMPANY ENGAGE IN BOTH LIFE AND NON-LIFE INSURANCE BUSINESS?	YES	YES	NO
Q2	DO LIFE INSURANCE COMPANIES ALSO ENGAGE IN PENSION FUND MANAGEMENT OR DO SEPARATE ENTITIES EXIST FOR THAT PURPOSE?	PERFORMED BY LIFE INS COS	PERFORMED BY LIFE INS COS	PERFORMED BY LIFE INS COS
Q3	INSURANCE RESERVES ARE REGULATED BY	INSURANCE INDUSTRY	GOVERNMENT	INSURANCE INDUSTRY
Q4	MOST INSURANCE COMPANIES IN THE COUNTRY CAN BE OWNED BY	STOCKHOLDERS	STOCKHOLDERS	STOCKHOLDERS
Q5	ASSETS AND LIABILITIES ARE ORGANIZED ON THE BALANCE SHEET BY	TYPE OF ASSET OR LIABILITY	TYPE OF ASSET OR LIABILITY	TYPE OF ASSET OR LIABILITY
Q6	INVESTMENT ASSETS ARE SEGREGATED BY	TYPE OF INVESTMENT ASSET	TYPE OF INVESTMENT ASSET	TYPE OF INVESTMENT ASSET
Q7	FIXED-INCOME SECURITIES ARE VALUED AT	HISTORICAL COST	AMORTIZED COST	LOWER OF COST OR MARKET PRICE
Q8	EQUITY SECURITIES ARE VALUED AT	HISTORICAL COST	LOWER OF COST OR MARKET PRICE	HISTORICAL COST
Q9	ARE CLAIMS AND LOSS RESERVES SEGREGATED FROM TECHNICAL RESERVES?	YES	YES	YES
Q10	ARE POLICYHOLDER'S SURPLUS, DIVIDENDS OR EQUITY DISCLOSED?	NO	NO	NO
Q11	IS TOTAL REVENUE DISCLOSED IN GROSS, IN NET OR BY COMPONENT?	BY COMPONENTS ONLY ON I/S	GROSS AND BY COMPONENTS ON I/S	GROSS AND BY COMPONENTS ON I/S
Q12	ARE INCOME FROM LIFE AND NON-LIFE OPERATIONS SEGREGATED?	YES	YES	NOT APPLICABLE
Q13	RESULTS OF REINSURANCE BUSINESS DISCLOSED AS	NET REINSURANCE RESULTS ONLY	NET REINSURANCE RESULTS ONLY	NET REINSURANCE RESULTS ONLY
Q14	IS UNEARNED PREMIUM INCOME DISCLOSED?	YES	YES	YES
Q15	UNDERWRITING EXPENSES ARE	DISCLOSED SEPARATELY	DISCLOSED SEPARATELY	PART OF GEN/ADMIN EXPENSES
Q16	"HIDDEN" NON-EQUITY RESERVES	EXIST & SEP ACCOUNTED FOR	NOT DISCLOSED	NOT DISCLOSED

Financial Statements of Insurance Companies in 22 Countries

NO.	ACCOUNTING & AUDITING ITEMS	Italy	Japan	South Korea
Q1	BY LAW, MAY A COMPANY ENGAGE IN BOTH LIFE AND NON-LIFE INSURANCE BUSINESS?	YES	NO	NO
Q2	DO LIFE INSURANCE COMPANIES ALSO ENGAGE IN PENSION FUND MANAGEMENT OR DO SEPARATE ENTITIES EXIST FOR THAT PURPOSE?	PERFORMED BY LIFE INS COS	PERFORMED BY LIFE INS COS	PERFORMED BY LIFE INS COS
Q3	INSURANCE RESERVES ARE REGULATED BY	INSURANCE INDUSTRY	GOVERNMENT	GOVERNMENT
Q4	MOST INSURANCE COMPANIES IN THE COUNTRY CAN BE OWNED BY	STOCKHOLDERS	NON-LIFE BY SH, LIFE BY PH	NON-LIFE BY SH, LIFE BY PH
Q5	ASSETS AND LIABILITIES ARE ORGANIZED ON THE BALANCE SHEET BY	TYPE OF ASSET OR LIABILITY	TYPE OF ASSET OR LIABILITY	TYPE OF ASSET OR LIABILITY
Q6	INVESTMENT ASSETS ARE SEGREGATED BY	TYPE OF INVESTMENT ASSET	TYPE OF INVESTMENT ASSET	TYPE OF INVESTMENT ASSET
Q7	FIXED-INCOME SECURITIES ARE VALUED AT	LOWER OF COST OR MARKET PRICE	LOWER OF COST OR MARKET PRICE	AMORTIZED COST
Q8	EQUITY SECURITIES ARE VALUED AT	LOWER OF COST OR MARKET PRICE	LOWER OF COST OR MARKET PRICE	LOWER OF COST OR MARKET PRICE
Q9	ARE CLAIMS AND LOSS RESERVES SEGREGATED FROM TECHNICAL RESERVES?	YES	YES	YES
Q10	ARE POLICYHOLDER'S SURPLUS, DIVIDENDS OR EQUITY DISCLOSED?	NO	YES	NO
Q11	IS TOTAL REVENUE DISCLOSED IN GROSS, IN NET OR BY COMPONENT?	GROSS AND BY COMPONENTS ON I/S	GROSS AND BY COMPONENTS ON I/S	GROSS AND BY COMPONENTS ON I/S
Q12	ARE INCOME FROM LIFE AND NON-LIFE OPERATIONS SEGREGATED?	YES	NOT APPLICABLE	NOT APPLICABLE
Q13	RESULTS OF REINSURANCE BUSINESS DISCLOSED AS	NET REINSURANCE RESULTS ONLY	GROSS REINS RESULTS ITEMIZED	GROSS REINS RESULTS ITEMIZED
Q14	IS UNEARNED PREMIUM INCOME DISCLOSED?	YES	YES	YES
Q15	UNDERWRITING EXPENSES ARE	DISCLOSED SEPARATELY	PART OF GEN/ADMIN EXPENSES	PART OF GEN/ADMIN EXPENSES
Q16	"HIDDEN" NON-EQUITY RESERVES	NOT DISCLOSED	DO NOT EXIST	DO NOT EXIST

Financial Statements of Insurance Companies in 22 Countries

NO.	ACCOUNTING & AUDITING ITEMS	Malaysia	Netherlands	Norway
Q1	BY LAW, MAY A COMPANY ENGAGE IN BOTH LIFE AND NON-LIFE INSURANCE BUSINESS?	YES	YES	YES
Q2	DO LIFE INSURANCE COMPANIES ALSO ENGAGE IN PENSION FUND MANAGEMENT OR DO SEPARATE ENTITIES EXIST FOR THAT PURPOSE?	PERFORMED BY LIFE INS COS	PERFORMED BY LIFE INS COS	SEPARATE ENTITIES EXIST
Q3	INSURANCE RESERVES ARE REGULATED BY	INSURANCE INDUSTRY	INSURANCE INDUSTRY	GOVERNMENT
Q4	MOST INSURANCE COMPANIES IN THE COUNTRY CAN BE OWNED BY	STOCKHOLDERS	STOCKHOLDERS	STOCKHOLDERS
Q5	ASSETS AND LIABILITIES ARE ORGANIZED ON THE BALANCE SHEET BY	TYPE OF ASSET OR LIABILITY	TYPE OF ASSET OR LIABILITY	LIQUIDITY(CURRENT/NON-CURRENT)
Q6	INVESTMENT ASSETS ARE SEGREGATED BY	TYPE OF INVESTMENT ASSET	TYPE OF INVESTMENT ASSET	TYPE OF INVESTMENT ASSET
Q7	FIXED-INCOME SECURITIES ARE VALUED AT	HISTORICAL COST	AMORTIZED COST	LOWER OF COST OR MARKET PRICE
Q8	EQUITY SECURITIES ARE VALUED AT	MARKET PRICE	MARKET PRICE	LOWER OF COST OR MARKET PRICE
Q9	ARE CLAIMS AND LOSS RESERVES SEGREGATED FROM TECHNICAL RESERVES?	YES	YES	YES
Q10	ARE POLICYHOLDER'S SURPLUS, DIVIDENDS OR EQUITY DISCLOSED?	NOT APPLICABLE	NO	YES
Q11	IS TOTAL REVENUE DISCLOSED IN GROSS, IN NET OR BY COMPONENT?	GROSS AND BY COMPONENTS ON I/S	BY COMPONENTS ONLY ON I/S	GROSS AND BY COMPONENTS ON I/S
Q12	ARE INCOME FROM LIFE AND NON-LIFE OPERATIONS SEGREGATED?	YES	YES	YES
Q13	RESULTS OF REINSURANCE BUSINESS DISCLOSED AS	NET REINSURANCE RESULTS ONLY	GROSS REINS RESULTS ITEMIZED	NET REINSURANCE RESULTS ONLY
Q14	IS UNEARNED PREMIUM INCOME DISCLOSED?	YES	YES	NO
Q15	UNDERWRITING EXPENSES ARE	DISCLOSED SEPARATELY	DISCLOSED SEPARATELY	PART OF GEN/ADMIN EXPENSES
Q16	"HIDDEN" NON-EQUITY RESERVES	DO NOT EXIST	EXIST & SEP ACCOUNTED FOR	EXIST & SEP ACCOUNTED FOR

Financial Statements of Insurance Companies in 22 Countries

NO.	ACCOUNTING & AUDITING ITEMS	Singapore	South Africa	Spain
Q1	BY LAW, MAY A COMPANY ENGAGE IN BOTH LIFE AND NON-LIFE INSURANCE BUSINESS?	YES	NO	YES
Q2	DO LIFE INSURANCE COMPANIES ALSO ENGAGE IN PENSION FUND MANAGEMENT OR DO SEPARATE ENTITIES EXIST FOR THAT PURPOSE?	PERFORMED BY LIFE INS COS	PERFORMED BY LIFE INS COS	PERFORMED BY LIFE INS COS
Q3	INSURANCE RESERVES ARE REGULATED BY	INSURANCE INDUSTRY	INSURANCE INDUSTRY	INSURANCE INDUSTRY
Q4	MOST INSURANCE COMPANIES IN THE COUNTRY CAN BE OWNED BY	STOCKHOLDERS A/O POLICYHOLDERS	STOCKHOLDERS	STOCKHOLDERS
Q5	ASSETS AND LIABILITIES ARE ORGANIZED ON THE BALANCE SHEET BY	LIQUIDITY(CURRENT/NON-CURRENT)	LIQUIDITY(CURRENT/NON-CURRENT)	TYPE OF ASSET OR LIABILITY
Q6	INVESTMENT ASSETS ARE SEGREGATED BY	TYPE OF INVESTMENT ASSET	TYPE OF INVESTMENT ASSET	TYPE OF INVESTMENT ASSET
Q7	FIXED-INCOME SECURITIES ARE VALUED AT	HISTORICAL COST	AMORTIZED COST	HISTORICAL COST
Q8	EQUITY SECURITIES ARE VALUED AT	MARKET PRICE	MARKET PRICE	LOWER COST+PARTADJTOMKT OR MKT
Q9	ARE CLAIMS AND LOSS RESERVES SEGREGATED FROM TECHNICAL RESERVES?	NO	YES	YES
Q10	ARE POLICYHOLDER'S SURPLUS, DIVIDENDS OR EQUITY DISCLOSED?	NO	NO	NO
Q11	IS TOTAL REVENUE DISCLOSED IN GROSS, IN NET OR BY COMPONENT?	NET REVENUE DISCLOSED ON I/S	GROSS AND BY COMPONENTS ON I/S	GROSS AND BY COMPONENTS ON I/S
Q12	ARE INCOME FROM LIFE AND NON-LIFE OPERATIONS SEGREGATED?	YES	NOT APPLICABLE	YES
Q13	RESULTS OF REINSURANCE BUSINESS DISCLOSED AS	NOT DISCLOSED	NET REINSURANCE RESULTS ONLY	NET REINSURANCE RESULTS ONLY
Q14	IS UNEARNED PREMIUM INCOME DISCLOSED?	NO	YES	YES
Q15	UNDERWRITING EXPENSES ARE	DISCLOSED SEPARATELY	PART OF GEN/ADMIN EXPENSES	DISCLOSED SEPARATELY
Q16	"HIDDEN" NON-EQUITY RESERVES	DO NOT EXIST	NOT DISCLOSED	EXIST BUT NOT SEP ACCOUNTED

Financial Statements of Insurance Companies in 22 Countries

NO.	ACCOUNTING & AUDITING ITEMS	Sweden	Switzerland	United Kingdom
Q1	BY LAW, MAY A COMPANY ENGAGE IN BOTH LIFE AND NON-LIFE INSURANCE BUSINESS?	YES	YES	YES
Q2	DO LIFE INSURANCE COMPANIES ALSO ENGAGE IN PENSION FUND MANAGEMENT OR DO SEPARATE ENTITIES EXIST FOR THAT PURPOSE?	SEPARATE ENTITIES EXIST	PERFORMED BY LIFE INS COS	PERFORMED BY LIFE INS COS
Q3	INSURANCE RESERVES ARE REGULATED BY	GOVERNMENT	GOVERNMENT	INSURANCE INDUSTRY
Q4	MOST INSURANCE COMPANIES IN THE COUNTRY CAN BE OWNED BY	STOCKHOLDERS	STOCKHOLDERS	STOCKHOLDERS A/O POLICYHOLDERS
Q5	ASSETS AND LIABILITIES ARE ORGANIZED ON THE BALANCE SHEET BY	TYPE OF ASSET OR LIABILITY	TYPE OF ASSET OR LIABILITY	TYPE OF ASSET OR LIABILITY
Q6	INVESTMENT ASSETS ARE SEGREGATED BY	TYPE OF INVESTMENT ASSET	TYPE OF INVESTMENT ASSET	TYPE OF INVESTMENT ASSET
Q7	FIXED-INCOME SECURITIES ARE VALUED AT	LOWER OF COST OR MARKET PRICE	LOWER OF COST OR MARKET PRICE	MARKET PRICE
Q8	EQUITY SECURITIES ARE VALUED AT	LOWER OF COST OR MARKET PRICE	LOWER OF COST OR MARKET PRICE	MARKET PRICE
Q9	ARE CLAIMS AND LOSS RESERVES SEGREGATED FROM TECHNICAL RESERVES?	YES	YES	YES
Q10	ARE POLICYHOLDER'S SURPLUS, DIVIDENDS OR EQUITY DISCLOSED?	NO	NO	YES
Q11	IS TOTAL REVENUE DISCLOSED IN GROSS, IN NET OR BY COMPONENT?	BY COMPONENTS ONLY ON I/S	BY COMPONENTS ONLY ON I/S	BY COMPONENTS ONLY ON I/S
Q12	ARE INCOME FROM LIFE AND NON-LIFE OPERATIONS SEGREGATED?	YES	YES	YES
Q13	RESULTS OF REINSURANCE BUSINESS DISCLOSED AS	NET REINSURANCE RESULTS ONLY	NET REINSURANCE RESULTS ONLY	GROSS REINS RESULTS ITEMIZED
Q14	IS UNEARNED PREMIUM INCOME DISCLOSED?	YES	YES	YES
Q15	UNDERWRITING EXPENSES ARE	PART OF GEN/ADMIN EXPENSES	PART OF GEN/ADMIN EXPENSES	PART OF GEN/ADMIN EXPENSES
Q16	"HIDDEN" NON-EQUITY RESERVES	EXIST & SEP ACCOUNTED FOR	NOT DISCLOSED	DO NOT EXIST

Financial Statements of Insurance Companies in 22 Countries

NO.	ACCOUNTING & AUDITING ITEMS	United States		
Q1	BY LAW, MAY A COMPANY ENGAGE IN BOTH LIFE AND NON-LIFE INSURANCE BUSINESS?	YES		
Q2	DO LIFE INSURANCE COMPANIES ALSO ENGAGE IN PENSION FUND MANAGEMENT OR DO SEPARATE ENTITIES EXIST FOR THAT PURPOSE?	PERFORMED BY LIFE INS COS		
Q3	INSURANCE RESERVES ARE REGULATED BY	INSURANCE INDUSTRY		
Q4	MOST INSURANCE COMPANIES IN THE COUNTRY CAN BE OWNED BY	STOCKHOLDERS A/O POLICYHOLDERS		
Q5	ASSETS AND LIABILITIES ARE ORGANIZED ON THE BALANCE SHEET BY	TYPE OF ASSET OR LIABILITY		
Q6	INVESTMENT ASSETS ARE SEGREGATED BY	TYPE OF INVESTMENT ASSET		
Q7	FIXED-INCOME SECURITIES ARE VALUED AT	AMORTIZED COST		
Q8	EQUITY SECURITIES ARE VALUED AT	MARKET PRICE		
Q9	ARE CLAIMS AND LOSS RESERVES SEGREGATED FROM TECHNICAL RESERVES?	YES		
Q10	ARE POLICYHOLDER'S SURPLUS, DIVIDENDS OR EQUITY DISCLOSED?	YES		
Q11	IS TOTAL REVENUE DISCLOSED IN GROSS, IN NET OR BY COMPONENT?	GROSS AND BY COMPONENTS ON I/S		
Q12	ARE INCOME FROM LIFE AND NON-LIFE OPERATIONS SEGREGATED?	YES		
Q13	RESULTS OF REINSURANCE BUSINESS DISCLOSED AS	NET REINSURANCE RESULTS ONLY		
Q14	IS UNEARNED PREMIUM INCOME DISCLOSED?	NO		
Q15	UNDERWRITING EXPENSES ARE	DISCLOSED SEPARATELY		
Q16	"HIDDEN" NON-EQUITY RESERVES	DO NOT EXIST		

CHAPTER 5

ANALYSIS OF SIMILARITIES AND DIFFERENCES IN INTERIM FINANCIAL STATEMENTS OF INDUSTRIAL COMPANIES IN 20 COUNTRIES

Table of Contents

I. INTRODUCTION

Investors, creditors and other decision makers need information about the financial condition and earning power of companies on a continuous and timely basis. Thus, interim financial reports have become a vital source of information that allow a close monitoring of corporate performance. Issued on a semi-annual or quarterly basis, they are used as a means of updating yearly results.

However, as useful as interim reports are, they present problems and limitations that must be carefully evaluated and understood by users. These problems are inherent in the assumptions and procedures that are employed in preparing interim reports. Because of the limited association of auditors with interim data, there is a lack of assurance that the reasonableness of data has been verified.

Seasonal peaks and valleys, which affect the level of sales and their attendant costs and other expenses, are common to many companies. The shorter the period reflected in financial reports, the smaller the chance that the effects of such peaks and valleys will be evened out. This can distort inter-quarter comparisons. Furthermore, national economic conditions can change, making comparisons of companies even more difficult.

These limitations notwithstanding, interim reports provide timely information to users attempting to evaluate the financial performance of companies internationally. Furthermore, in recent years improvements have been made in the presentation of interim reports. In this chapter, similarities and differences in interim reports from 20 countries are examined.

II. RESEARCH OBJECTIVES

5-1 How frequently are interim financial statements published by industrial companies internationally?

5-2 What items are usually disclosed in interim financial statements worldwide?

5-3 To what extent has the international harmonization of financial disclosures been achieved in interim reporting?

5-4 What financial disclosures should be included in interim reports published for an international audience?

III. RESEARCH DESIGN

To identify general trends in form and content, interim reports of 10 to 20 leading companies in each country were utilized. For a large industrial country 20 reports were used, while for a small industrial country 10 reports were used. This sample selection, therefore, has a bias toward large companies, which tend to disclose more than small companies. However, as more companies begin to prepare interim reports in many countries where such publication has only recently been required, norms based on the practices of larger companies can reflect examples for newer companies to follow.

For the majority of these companies, 1988 interim reports to shareholders are used. Interim reports published in 1987 are used in a few cases, if a 1988 interim report was not readily available.

This chapter includes only industrial companies since a sufficient number of financial company interim reports were not available in many countries.

Exhibit 5-1 provides the list of questions and answers used to summarize the findings.

IV. FINDINGS

Exhibit 5-2 provides a summary of current practices in interim reporting by country. In this section, our findings are presented by key items disclosed in interim reports worldwide as well as by interim reporting practices for selected countries.

A. Contents of Interim Reports Worldwide

1. Frequency of Interim Reports

   In Canada, West Germany and the US, interim reports are issued almost exclusively on a quarterly basis. Companies in Commonwealth and Continental European countries, as a general rule, publish interims semi-annually, while most other countries seem to make equal use of both quarterly and semi-annual reports. An exception can be found in the case of Finland, Norway and Sweden, where companies seem to favor a four-month reporting period.

2. Interim Financial Highlights

   Interim highlights were reported in only about 20% of the countries studied. In some cases these highlights were presented by means of graphs and charts (e.g., Japan) while in others they were disclosed in a written summary (e.g., Italy).

3. Interim Segment Information

When segment information is disclosed, it is usually in a table separate from the body of the financial statements, but in some cases it is presented within the statements themselves. Such information is more commonly disclosed in the interim financial statements of companies in Continental Europe than in the statements of companies in the US or Commonwealth countries.

4. Consolidation of Interim Reports

In virtually all cases, companies issue interim reports with consolidated financial statements.

5. Interim Income Statement

In most countries, the majority of companies which provide interim financial statements include an interim income statement. In Switzerland and Germany, however, no majority practice is evident.

6. Interim Balance Sheet

The inclusion of a balance sheet in interim reports is a majority practice only in Italy, Japan, New Zealand, South Africa and the US. In Canada, West Germany, the Netherlands, Spain and Switzerland, a minority of companies provide an interim balance sheet while in other countries studied no interim balance sheet was included.

7. Interim Report of Earnings Per Share (EPS)

As a general rule, companies from North America and Commonwealth countries which provide interim statements usually disclose interim EPS, as do those from Japan and the Netherlands.

8. Interim Report of Dividends Per Share (DPS)

A majority of companies in Hong Kong, Japan, Malaysia, Singapore, South Africa, the UK and the US disclose interim DPS, while a minority of companies in Australia, Canada, the Netherlands, and New Zealand do so.

B. Findings by Country

1. Canada, Japan, US

Companies from Canada, Japan, and the US follow similar disclosure practices and seem to disclose the most information. Companies from these countries publish consolidated reports with accounting policies disclosed in the footnotes. The income statement, balance sheet, and statement of changes in financial position are published, with adequate formatting of revenues, expenses, assets, and liabilities. The statements also include quantitative and qualitative information as part of the management's report.

2. Australia, Hong Kong, UK

Companies from these countries publish interim reports on a consolidated basis either quarterly or semi-annually. An income statement is the only report published. The balance sheet, statement of changes in financial position and other quantitative or qualitative information including the management report and a summary of accounting policies, are not provided.

3. Denmark, Finland, Norway, Sweden

The period covered by interim reports for these countries usually varies between three, four and six months. The interim statements are consolidated and the only statement published is the income statement. It includes sales, cost of sales, general and administrative expenses and other operating expenses. Income taxes, earnings per share and quarterly dividends are not generally disclosed and accounting policies and footnotes are omitted. The statements may disclose additional quantitative and qualitative information as part of the management report.

4. Netherlands

Outside of those in Canada, Japan and the US, companies in the Netherlands seem to disclose the most information in their interim statements, which are published quarterly or semi-annually and presented on a consolidated basis. The income statement and balance sheet are provided. The income statement discloses sales, cost of sales, general and administrative expenses and other operating expenses. In addition, earnings per share and dividends per share are disclosed. The management report includes both qualitative and quantitative information. The statements do not, however, disclose accounting policies.

5. West Germany

Interim reports from companies based in West Germany contain the least amount of financial information, since only a partial income statement is published. The income statement is in the form of a summary of financial highlights with only sales/revenues disclosed. It does not disclose any operating expenses, earnings per share or dividends. A balance sheet, statement of changes in financial position and the footnotes thereto are also not disclosed. The statement is usually issued quarterly and presented on a consolidated basis.

6. France

Interim reports from France typically cover six months and are issued on a consolidated basis. Typically, only an income statement is published which includes sales, cost of sales, general and administrative expenses and other operating expenses. Additional non-financial and financial information is published as part of the management report. No accounting policies or footnotes are included.

V. SUMMARY AND CONCLUSIONS

In classifying the interim reports of different countries by breadth of disclosure the following conclusions can be drawn:

- Reports from Canadian, Japanese and US companies generally provide the most information.
- Continental European companies disclose slightly less information than their Canadian, Japanese or US counterparts.
- Companies in Commonwealth countries report even less information than in the countries noted above.

If we were to construct a model interim report, it would be issued quarterly and contain an income statement in which sales, cost of goods sold, operating income, income tax expenses and net income for the period covered by the report are disclosed. It should also include key accounts from the balance sheet, brief notes to the accounts, earnings per share and dividend per share figures for the period, with a discussion of the operating results, by geographic area and segment, for the period covered.

EXHIBIT 5-1

QUESTIONS AND ANSWERS FOR INTERIM FINANCIAL REPORTING PRACTICES

Q1 FREQUENCY OF INTERIM REPORTS

1 QUARTERLY
2 SEMIANNUALLY
3 EVERY FOUR MONTHS
4 QUARTERLY/SEMIANNUALLY
5 FREQUENCY NOT DEFINED
8 NO INFORMATION AVAILABLE
9 NOT DISCLOSED

Q2 INTERIM REPORTS SIGNED BY MANAGEMENT

1 YES
2 NO
3 MINORITY PRACTICE
8 NO INFORMATION AVAILABLE
9 NOT DISCLOSED

Q3 INTERIM FINANCIAL HIGHLIGHTS REPORTED

1 YES
2 NO
3 MINORITY PRACTICE
8 NO INFORMATION AVAILABLE
9 NOT DISCLOSED

Q4 INTERIM INFLATION-ADJUSTED DATA REPORTED

1 YES
2 NO
3 MINORITY PRACTICE
8 NO INFORMATION AVAILABLE
9 NOT DISCLOSED

Q5 INTERIM SEGMENT INFORMATION REPORTED

1 YES
2 NO
3 MINORITY PRACTICE
8 NO INFORMATION AVAILABLE
9 NOT DISCLOSED

Q6 INTERIM GEOGRAPHICAL INFORMATION REPORTED

1 YES
2 NO
3 MINORITY PRACTICE
8 NO INFORMATION AVAILABLE
9 NOT DISCLOSED

Q7 INTERIM REPORT CONSOLIDATED

1 YES
2 NO
3 MINORITY PRACTICE
8 NO INFORMATION AVAILABLE
9 NOT DISCLOSED

Q8 AUDITED INTERIM STATEMENTS

1 YES
2 NO
3 MINORITY PRACTICE
8 NO INFORMATION AVAILABLE
9 NOT DISCLOSED

Q9 ACCOUNTING POLICIES GIVEN IN INTERIM REPORT

1 YES
2 NO
3 MINORITY PRACTICE
8 NO INFORMATION AVAILABLE
9 NOT DISCLOSED

Q10 NOTES TO FINANCIAL ACCOUNTS GIVEN IN INTERIM REPORT

1 YES
2 NO
3 MINORITY PRACTICE
8 NO INFORMATION AVAILABLE
9 NOT DISCLOSED

Q11 INTERIM INCOME STATEMENT GIVEN

1 YES
2 NO
3 MINORITY PRACTICE
8 NO INFORMATION AVAILABLE
9 NOT DISCLOSED

Q12 INTERIM SALES GIVEN

1 YES
2 NO
3 MINORITY PRACTICE
8 NO INFORMATION AVAILABLE
9 NOT DISCLOSED

Q13 INTERIM COGS GIVEN

1 YES
2 NO
3 MINORITY PRACTICE
8 NO INFORMATION AVAILABLE
9 NOT DISCLOSED

Q14 INTERIM DEPRECIATION GIVEN

1 YES
2 NO
3 MINORITY PRACTICE
8 NO INFORMATION AVAILABLE
9 NOT DISCLOSED

Q15 INTERIM OPERATING INCOME GIVEN

1 YES
2 NO
3 MINORITY PRACTICE
8 NO INFORMATION AVAILABLE
9 NOT DISCLOSED

Q16 INTERIM REPORTING OF INTEREST EXPENSE GIVEN

1 YES
2 NO
3 MINORITY PRACTICE
8 NO INFORMATION AVAILABLE
9 NOT DISCLOSED

Q17 INTERIM REPORT OF FOREIGN EXCHANGE GAINS AND LOSSES

1 YES
2 NO
3 MINORITY PRACTICE
8 NO INFORMATION AVAILABLE
9 NOT DISCLOSED

Q18 INTERIM REPORT OF EXTRAORDINARY GAINS/LOSSES

1 YES
2 NO
3 MINORITY PRACTICE
8 NO INFORMATION AVAILABLE
9 NOT DISCLOSED

Q19 INTERIM REPORT OF INCOME TAX EXPENSE GIVEN

1 YES
2 NO
3 MINORITY PRACTICE
8 NO INFORMATION AVAILABLE
9 NOT DISCLOSED

Q20 INTERIM REPORT OF NET INCOME GIVEN

1 YES
2 NO
3 MINORITY PRACTICE
8 NO INFORMATION AVAILABLE
9 NOT DISCLOSED

Q21 INTERIM BALANCE SHEET GIVEN

1 YES
2 NO
3 MINORITY PRACTICE
8 NO INFORMATION AVAILABLE
9 NOT DISCLOSED

Q22 INTERIM CASH AND EQUIVALENTS REPORTED

1 YES
2 NO
3 MINORITY PRACTICE
8 NO INFORMATION AVAILABLE
9 NOT DISCLOSED

Q23 INTERIM REPORT OF ACCOUNTS RECEIVABLE

1 YES
2 NO
3 MINORITY PRACTICE
8 NO INFORMATION AVAILABLE
9 NOT DISCLOSED

Q24 INTERIM REPORT OF INVENTORIES GIVEN

1 YES
2 NO
3 MINORITY PRACTICE
8 NO INFORMATION AVAILABLE
9 NOT DISCLOSED

Q25 INTERIM REPORT OF CURRENT ASSETS GIVEN

1 YES
2 NO
3 MINORITY PRACTICE
8 NO INFORMATION AVAILABLE
9 NOT DISCLOSED

Q26 INTERIM REPORT OF FIXED ASSETS GIVEN

1 YES
2 NO
3 MINORITY PRACTICE
8 NO INFORMATION AVAILABLE
9 NOT DISCLOSED

Q27 INTERIM REPORT OF ACCUMULATED DEPRECIATION GIVEN

1 YES
2 NO
3 MINORITY PRACTICE
8 NO INFORMATION AVAILABLE
9 NOT DISCLOSED

Q28 INTERIM REPORT OF LONG-TERM INVESTMENTS GIVEN

1 YES
2 NO
3 MINORITY PRACTICE
8 NO INFORMATION AVAILABLE
9 NOT DISCLOSED

Q29 INTERIM REPORT OF INTANGIBLES GIVEN

1 YES
2 NO
3 MINORITY PRACTICE
8 NO INFORMATION AVAILABLE
9 NOT DISCLOSED

Q30 INTERIM REPORT OF TOTAL ASSETS GIVEN

1 YES
2 NO
3 MINORITY PRACTICE
8 NO INFORMATION AVAILABLE
9 NOT DISCLOSED

Q31 INTERIM REPORT OF CURRENT LIABILITIES GIVEN

1 YES
2 NO
3 MINORITY PRACTICE
8 NO INFORMATION AVAILABLE
9 NOT DISCLOSED

Q32 INTERIM REPORT OF LONG TERM DEBT GIVEN

1 YES
2 NO
3 MINORITY PRACTICE
8 NO INFORMATION AVAILABLE
9 NOT DISCLOSED

Q33 INTERIM REPORT OF MINORITY INTEREST GIVEN

1 YES
2 NO
3 MINORITY PRACTICE
8 NO INFORMATION AVAILABLE
9 NOT DISCLOSED

Q34 INTERIM REPORT OF SHAREHOLDERS' EQUITY GIVEN

1 YES
2 NO
3 MINORITY PRACTICE
8 NO INFORMATION AVAILABLE
9 NOT DISCLOSED

Q35 INTERIM REPORT OF STATEMENT CHANGES FINANCIAL POSITION

1 YES
2 NO
3 MINORITY PRACTICE
8 NO INFORMATION AVAILABLE
9 NOT DISCLOSED

Q36 INTERIM REPORT OF FUNDS FROM OPERATIONS GIVEN

1 YES
2 NO
3 MINORITY PRACTICE
8 NO INFORMATION AVAILABLE
9 NOT DISCLOSED

Q37 INTERIM REPORT OF EARNINGS PER SHARE GIVEN

1 YES
2 NO
3 MINORITY PRACTICE
8 NO INFORMATION AVAILABLE
9 NOT DISCLOSED

Q38 INTERIM REPORT OF DIVIDEND PER SHARE GIVEN

1 YES
2 NO
3 MINORITY PRACTICE
8 NO INFORMATION AVAILABLE
9 NOT DISCLOSED

Interim Financial Reporting Practices in 20 Countries

NO.	ACCOUNTING & AUDITING ITEMS	Australia	Canada	Denmark
Q1	FREQUENCY OF INTERIM REPORTS	QUARTERLY/SEMIANNUALLY	QUARTERLY	SEMIANNUALLY
Q2	INTERIM REPORTS SIGNED BY MANAGEMENT	YES	YES	NO
Q3	INTERIM FINANCIAL HIGHLIGHTS REPORTED	NO	MINORITY PRACTICE	NO
Q4	INTERIM INFLATION-ADJUSTED DATA REPORTED	NO	NO	NO
Q5	INTERIM SEGMENT INFORMATION REPORTED	NO	MINORITY PRACTICE	MINORITY PRACTICE
Q6	INTERIM GEOGRAPHICAL INFORMATION REPORTED	NO	NO	NO
Q7	INTERIM REPORT CONSOLIDATED	YES	YES	YES
Q8	AUDITED INTERIM STATEMENTS	NO	NO	NO
Q9	ACCOUNTING POLICIES GIVEN IN INTERIM REPORT	NO	NO	NO
Q10	NOTES TO FINANCIAL ACCOUNTS GIVEN IN INTERIM REPORT	NO	NO	NO
Q11	INTERIM INCOME STATEMENT GIVEN	YES	YES	YES
Q12	INTERIM SALES GIVEN	YES	MINORITY PRACTICE	YES
Q13	INTERIM COGS GIVEN	NO	MINORITY PRACTICE	NO
Q14	INTERIM DEPRECIATION GIVEN	MINORITY PRACTICE	MINORITY PRACTICE	NO
Q15	INTERIM OPERATING INCOME GIVEN	YES	YES	YES
Q16	INTERIM REPORTING OF INTEREST EXPENSE GIVEN	YES	YES	MINORITY PRACTICE
Q17	INTERIM REPORT OF FOREIGN EXCHANGE GAINS AND LOSSES	NO	NO	NO
Q18	INTERIM REPORT OF EXTRAORDINARY GAINS/LOSSES	MINORITY PRACTICE	MINORITY PRACTICE	MINORITY PRACTICE
Q19	INTERIM REPORT OF INCOME TAX EXPENSE GIVEN	YES	YES	MINORITY PRACTICE
Q20	INTERIM REPORT OF NET INCOME GIVEN	YES	YES	MINORITY PRACTICE
Q21	INTERIM BALANCE SHEET GIVEN	NO	MINORITY PRACTICE	NO
Q22	INTERIM CASH AND EQUIVALENTS REPORTED	NO	MINORITY PRACTICE	NO
Q23	INTERIM REPORT OF ACCOUNTS RECEIVABLE	NO	NO	NO

Interim Financial Reporting Practices in 20 Countries

NO.	ACCOUNTING & AUDITING ITEMS	Australia	Canada	Denmark
Q24	INTERIM REPORT OF INVENTORIES GIVEN	NO	NO	NO
Q25	INTERIM REPORT OF CURRENT ASSETS GIVEN	MINORITY PRACTICE	MINORITY PRACTICE	NO
Q26	INTERIM REPORT OF FIXED ASSETS GIVEN	NO	MINORITY PRACTICE	NO
Q27	INTERIM REPORT OF ACCUMULATED DEPRECIATION GIVEN	NO	NO	NO
Q28	INTERIM REPORT OF LONG-TERM INVESTMENTS GIVEN	NO	MINORITY PRACTICE	NO
Q29	INTERIM REPORT OF INTANGIBLES GIVEN	NO	NO	NO
Q30	INTERIM REPORT OF TOTAL ASSETS GIVEN	MINORITY PRACTICE	MINORITY PRACTICE	MINORITY PRACTICE
Q31	INTERIM REPORT OF CURRENT LIABILITIES GIVEN	NO	MINORITY PRACTICE	NO
Q32	INTERIM REPORT OF LONG-TERM DEBT GIVEN	NO	MINORITY PRACTICE	NO
Q33	INTERIM REPORT OF MINORITY INTEREST GIVEN	NO	MINORITY PRACTICE	NO
Q34	INTERIM REPORT OF SHAREHOLDERS' EQUITY GIVEN	NO	MINORITY PRACTICE	MINORITY PRACTICE
Q35	INTERIM REPORT OF STATEMENT OF CHANGES IN FINANCIAL POSITION	NO	YES	NO
Q36	INTERIM REPORT OF FUNDS FROM OPERATIONS GIVEN	NO	YES	NO
Q37	INTERIM REPORT OF EARNINGS PER SHARE GIVEN	MINORITY PRACTICE	YES	NO
Q38	INTERIM REPORT OF DIVIDEND PER SHARE GIVEN	MINORITY PRACTICE	MINORITY PRACTICE	NO

Interim Financial Reporting Practices in 20 Countries

NO.	ACCOUNTING & AUDITING ITEMS	Finland	France	West Germany
Q1	FREQUENCY OF INTERIM REPORTS	EVERY FOUR MONTHS	SEMIANNUALLY	FREQUENCY NOT DEFINED
Q2	INTERIM REPORTS SIGNED BY MANAGEMENT	YES	YES	YES
Q3	INTERIM FINANCIAL HIGHLIGHTS REPORTED	MINORITY PRACTICE	NO	MINORITY PRACTICE
Q4	INTERIM INFLATION-ADJUSTED DATA REPORTED	NO	NO	NO
Q5	INTERIM SEGMENT INFORMATION REPORTED	YES	YES	YES
Q6	INTERIM GEOGRAPHICAL INFORMATION REPORTED	NO	NO	YES
Q7	INTERIM REPORT CONSOLIDATED	YES	YES	YES
Q8	AUDITED INTERIM STATEMENTS	NO	NO	NO
Q9	ACCOUNTING POLICIES GIVEN IN INTERIM REPORT	NO	NO	NO
Q10	NOTES TO FINANCIAL ACCOUNTS GIVEN IN INTERIM REPORT	NO	NO	NO
Q11	INTERIM INCOME STATEMENT GIVEN	YES	YES	MINORITY PRACTICE
Q12	INTERIM SALES GIVEN	YES	YES	YES
Q13	INTERIM COGS GIVEN	NO	NO	NO
Q14	INTERIM DEPRECIATION GIVEN	MINORITY PRACTICE	MINORITY PRACTICE	NO
Q15	INTERIM OPERATING INCOME GIVEN	YES	MINORITY PRACTICE	NO
Q16	INTERIM REPORTING OF INTEREST EXPENSE GIVEN	MINORITY PRACTICE	MINORITY PRACTICE	MINORITY PRACTICE
Q17	INTERIM REPORT OF FOREIGN EXCHANGE GAINS AND LOSSES	NO	NO	NO
Q18	INTERIM REPORT OF EXTRAORDINARY GAINS/LOSSES	NO	MINORITY PRACTICE	NO
Q19	INTERIM REPORT OF INCOME TAX EXPENSE GIVEN	NO	YES	MINORITY PRACTICE
Q20	INTERIM REPORT OF NET INCOME GIVEN	NO	YES	MINORITY PRACTICE
Q21	INTERIM BALANCE SHEET GIVEN	NO	NO	MINORITY PRACTICE
Q22	INTERIM CASH AND EQUIVALENTS REPORTED	NO	NO	NO
Q23	INTERIM REPORT OF ACCOUNTS RECEIVABLE	NO	NO	NO

Interim Financial Reporting Practices in 20 Countries

NO.	ACCOUNTING & AUDITING ITEMS	Finland	France	West Germany
Q24	INTERIM REPORT OF INVENTORIES GIVEN	NO	NO	NO
Q25	INTERIM REPORT OF CURRENT ASSETS GIVEN	NO	NO	NO
Q26	INTERIM REPORT OF FIXED ASSETS GIVEN	NO	MINORITY PRACTICE	YES
Q27	INTERIM REPORT OF ACCUMULATED DEPRECIATION GIVEN	NO	NO	NO
Q28	INTERIM REPORT OF LONG-TERM INVESTMENTS GIVEN	NO	NO	NO
Q29	INTERIM REPORT OF INTANGIBLES GIVEN	NO	NO	NO
Q30	INTERIM REPORT OF TOTAL ASSETS GIVEN	NO	MINORITY PRACTICE	MINORITY PRACTICE
Q31	INTERIM REPORT OF CURRENT LIABILITIES GIVEN	NO	MINORITY PRACTICE	NO
Q32	INTERIM REPORT OF LONG-TERM DEBT GIVEN	NO	MINORITY PRACTICE	NO
Q33	INTERIM REPORT OF MINORITY INTEREST GIVEN	NO	NO	NO
Q34	INTERIM REPORT OF SHAREHOLDERS' EQUITY GIVEN	NO	MINORITY PRACTICE	MINORITY PRACTICE
Q35	INTERIM REPORT OF STATEMENT OF CHANGES IN FINANCIAL POSITION	NO	NO	NO
Q36	INTERIM REPORT OF FUNDS FROM OPERATIONS GIVEN	NO	NO	NO
Q37	INTERIM REPORT OF EARNINGS PER SHARE GIVEN	NO	NO	NO
Q38	INTERIM REPORT OF DIVIDEND PER SHARE GIVEN	NO	NO	NO

Interim Financial Reporting Practices in 20 Countries

NO.	ACCOUNTING & AUDITING ITEMS	Hong Kong	Italy	Japan
Q1	FREQUENCY OF INTERIM REPORTS	SEMIANNUALLY	SEMIANNUALLY	SEMIANNUALLY
Q2	INTERIM REPORTS SIGNED BY MANAGEMENT	YES	MINORITY PRACTICE	YES
Q3	INTERIM FINANCIAL HIGHLIGHTS REPORTED	YES	YES	YES
Q4	INTERIM INFLATION-ADJUSTED DATA REPORTED	NO	NO	NO
Q5	INTERIM SEGMENT INFORMATION REPORTED	NO	YES	MINORITY PRACTICE
Q6	INTERIM GEOGRAPHICAL INFORMATION REPORTED	NO	NO	NO
Q7	INTERIM REPORT CONSOLIDATED	YES	MINORITY PRACTICE	MINORITY PRACTICE
Q8	AUDITED INTERIM STATEMENTS	NO	NO	NO
Q9	ACCOUNTING POLICIES GIVEN IN INTERIM REPORT	NO	MINORITY PRACTICE	MINORITY PRACTICE
Q10	NOTES TO FINANCIAL ACCOUNTS GIVEN IN INTERIM REPORT	NO	YES	MINORITY PRACTICE
Q11	INTERIM INCOME STATEMENT GIVEN	YES	YES	YES
Q12	INTERIM SALES GIVEN	YES	YES	YES
Q13	INTERIM COGS GIVEN	NO	YES	YES
Q14	INTERIM DEPRECIATION GIVEN	NO	YES	NO
Q15	INTERIM OPERATING INCOME GIVEN	YES	YES	YES
Q16	INTERIM REPORTING OF INTEREST EXPENSE GIVEN	NO	YES	YES
Q17	INTERIM REPORT OF FOREIGN EXCHANGE GAINS AND LOSSES	NO	NO	MINORITY PRACTICE
Q18	INTERIM REPORT OF EXTRAORDINARY GAINS/LOSSES	MINORITY PRACTICE	MINORITY PRACTICE	MINORITY PRACTICE
Q19	INTERIM REPORT OF INCOME TAX EXPENSE GIVEN	YES	YES	YES
Q20	INTERIM REPORT OF NET INCOME GIVEN	YES	YES	YES
Q21	INTERIM BALANCE SHEET GIVEN	NO	YES	YES
Q22	INTERIM CASH AND EQUIVALENTS REPORTED	NO	YES	YES
Q23	INTERIM REPORT OF ACCOUNTS RECEIVABLE	NO	YES	YES

Interim Financial Reporting Practices in 20 Countries

NO.	ACCOUNTING & AUDITING ITEMS	Hong Kong	Italy	Japan
Q24	INTERIM REPORT OF INVENTORIES GIVEN	NO	YES	YES
Q25	INTERIM REPORT OF CURRENT ASSETS GIVEN	NO	YES	YES
Q26	INTERIM REPORT OF FIXED ASSETS GIVEN	NO	YES	YES
Q27	INTERIM REPORT OF ACCUMULATED DEPRECIATION GIVEN	NO	YES	YES
Q28	INTERIM REPORT OF LONG-TERM INVESTMENTS GIVEN	NO	YES	YES
Q29	INTERIM REPORT OF INTANGIBLES GIVEN	NO	YES	NO
Q30	INTERIM REPORT OF TOTAL ASSETS GIVEN	NO	YES	YES
Q31	INTERIM REPORT OF CURRENT LIABILITIES GIVEN	NO	YES	YES
Q32	INTERIM REPORT OF LONG-TERM DEBT GIVEN	NO	YES	YES
Q33	INTERIM REPORT OF MINORITY INTEREST GIVEN	NO	YES	MINORITY PRACTICE
Q34	INTERIM REPORT OF SHAREHOLDERS' EQUITY GIVEN	NO	YES	YES
Q35	INTERIM REPORT OF STATEMENT OF CHANGES IN FINANCIAL POSITION	NO	NO	MINORITY PRACTICE
Q36	INTERIM REPORT OF FUNDS FROM OPERATIONS GIVEN	NO	NO	MINORITY PRACTICE
Q37	INTERIM REPORT OF EARNINGS PER SHARE GIVEN	YES	NO	YES
Q38	INTERIM REPORT OF DIVIDEND PER SHARE GIVEN	YES	NO	YES

Interim Financial Reporting Practices in 20 Countries

NO.	ACCOUNTING & AUDITING ITEMS	Malaysia	Netherlands	New Zealand
Q1	FREQUENCY OF INTERIM REPORTS	SEMIANNUALLY	QUARTERLY/SEMIANNUALLY	SEMIANNUALLY
Q2	INTERIM REPORTS SIGNED BY MANAGEMENT	YES	YES	YES
Q3	INTERIM FINANCIAL HIGHLIGHTS REPORTED	NO	MINORITY PRACTICE	NO
Q4	INTERIM INFLATION-ADJUSTED DATA REPORTED	NO	NO	NO
Q5	INTERIM SEGMENT INFORMATION REPORTED	NO	MINORITY PRACTICE	NO
Q6	INTERIM GEOGRAPHICAL INFORMATION REPORTED	NO	MINORITY PRACTICE	NO
Q7	INTERIM REPORT CONSOLIDATED	YES	YES	YES
Q8	AUDITED INTERIM STATEMENTS	NO	NO	NO
Q9	ACCOUNTING POLICIES GIVEN IN INTERIM REPORT	MINORITY PRACTICE	NO	NO
Q10	NOTES TO FINANCIAL ACCOUNTS GIVEN IN INTERIM REPORT	MINORITY PRACTICE	YES	NO
Q11	INTERIM INCOME STATEMENT GIVEN	YES	YES	YES
Q12	INTERIM SALES GIVEN	YES	YES	YES
Q13	INTERIM COGS GIVEN	NO	YES	NO
Q14	INTERIM DEPRECIATION GIVEN	NO	YES	NO
Q15	INTERIM OPERATING INCOME GIVEN	YES	MINORITY PRACTICE	YES
Q16	INTERIM REPORTING OF INTEREST EXPENSE GIVEN	NO	YES	NO
Q17	INTERIM REPORT OF FOREIGN EXCHANGE GAINS AND LOSSES	NO	NO	NO
Q18	INTERIM REPORT OF EXTRAORDINARY GAINS/LOSSES	YES	MINORITY PRACTICE	YES
Q19	INTERIM REPORT OF INCOME TAX EXPENSE GIVEN	YES	YES	YES
Q20	INTERIM REPORT OF NET INCOME GIVEN	YES	YES	YES
Q21	INTERIM BALANCE SHEET GIVEN	NO	MINORITY PRACTICE	YES
Q22	INTERIM CASH AND EQUIVALENTS REPORTED	NO	MINORITY PRACTICE	MINORITY PRACTICE
Q23	INTERIM REPORT OF ACCOUNTS RECEIVABLE	NO	MINORITY PRACTICE	MINORITY PRACTICE

Interim Financial Reporting Practices in 20 Countries

NO.	ACCOUNTING & AUDITING ITEMS	Malaysia	Netherlands	New Zealand
Q24	INTERIM REPORT OF INVENTORIES GIVEN	NO	MINORITY PRACTICE	MINORITY PRACTICE
Q25	INTERIM REPORT OF CURRENT ASSETS GIVEN	NO	MINORITY PRACTICE	YES
Q26	INTERIM REPORT OF FIXED ASSETS GIVEN	NO	MINORITY PRACTICE	MINORITY PRACTICE
Q27	INTERIM REPORT OF ACCUMULATED DEPRECIATION GIVEN	NO	NO	NO
Q28	INTERIM REPORT OF LONG-TERM INVESTMENTS GIVEN	NO	MINORITY PRACTICE	MINORITY PRACTICE
Q29	INTERIM REPORT OF INTANGIBLES GIVEN	NO	NO	NO
Q30	INTERIM REPORT OF TOTAL ASSETS GIVEN	NO	MINORITY PRACTICE	YES
Q31	INTERIM REPORT OF CURRENT LIABILITIES GIVEN	NO	MINORITY PRACTICE	MINORITY PRACTICE
Q32	INTERIM REPORT OF LONG-TERM DEBT GIVEN	NO	MINORITY PRACTICE	MINORITY PRACTICE
Q33	INTERIM REPORT OF MINORITY INTEREST GIVEN	NO	MINORITY PRACTICE	MINORITY PRACTICE
Q34	INTERIM REPORT OF SHAREHOLDERS' EQUITY GIVEN	NO	MINORITY PRACTICE	YES
Q35	INTERIM REPORT OF STATEMENT OF CHANGES IN FINANCIAL POSITION	NO	NO	NO
Q36	INTERIM REPORT OF FUNDS FROM OPERATIONS GIVEN	NO	NO	NO
Q37	INTERIM REPORT OF EARNINGS PER SHARE GIVEN	YES	YES	MINORITY PRACTICE
Q38	INTERIM REPORT OF DIVIDEND PER SHARE GIVEN	YES	MINORITY PRACTICE	MINORITY PRACTICE

Interim Financial Reporting Practices in 20 Countries

NO.	ACCOUNTING & AUDITING ITEMS	Norway	Singapore	South Africa
Q1	FREQUENCY OF INTERIM REPORTS	EVERY FOUR MONTHS	SEMIANNUALLY	QUARTERLY/SEMIANNUALLY
Q2	INTERIM REPORTS SIGNED BY MANAGEMENT	YES	NO	NO
Q3	INTERIM FINANCIAL HIGHLIGHTS REPORTED	NO	NO	MINORITY PRACTICE
Q4	INTERIM INFLATION-ADJUSTED DATA REPORTED	NO	NO	NO
Q5	INTERIM SEGMENT INFORMATION REPORTED	MINORITY PRACTICE	NO	MINORITY PRACTICE
Q6	INTERIM GEOGRAPHICAL INFORMATION REPORTED	NO	NO	NO
Q7	INTERIM REPORT CONSOLIDATED	YES	YES	YES
Q8	AUDITED INTERIM STATEMENTS	NO	NO	NO
Q9	ACCOUNTING POLICIES GIVEN IN INTERIM REPORT	NO	NO	NO
Q10	NOTES TO FINANCIAL ACCOUNTS GIVEN IN INTERIM REPORT	NO	NO	NO
Q11	INTERIM INCOME STATEMENT GIVEN	YES	YES	YES
Q12	INTERIM SALES GIVEN	MINORITY PRACTICE	YES	MINORITY PRACTICE
Q13	INTERIM COGS GIVEN	NO	NO	NO
Q14	INTERIM DEPRECIATION GIVEN	YES	MINORITY PRACTICE	MINORITY PRACTICE
Q15	INTERIM OPERATING INCOME GIVEN	YES	YES	MINORITY PRACTICE
Q16	INTERIM REPORTING OF INTEREST EXPENSE GIVEN	YES	MINORITY PRACTICE	MINORITY PRACTICE
Q17	INTERIM REPORT OF FOREIGN EXCHANGE GAINS AND LOSSES	NO	NO	NO
Q18	INTERIM REPORT OF EXTRAORDINARY GAINS/LOSSES	YES	YES	MINORITY PRACTICE
Q19	INTERIM REPORT OF INCOME TAX EXPENSE GIVEN	NO	YES	YES
Q20	INTERIM REPORT OF NET INCOME GIVEN	NO	YES	YES
Q21	INTERIM BALANCE SHEET GIVEN	NO	NO	YES
Q22	INTERIM CASH AND EQUIVALENTS REPORTED	NO	NO	MINORITY PRACTICE
Q23	INTERIM REPORT OF ACCOUNTS RECEIVABLE	NO	NO	MINORITY PRACTICE

Interim Financial Reporting Practices in 20 Countries

NO.	ACCOUNTING & AUDITING ITEMS	Norway	Singapore	South Africa
Q24	INTERIM REPORT OF INVENTORIES GIVEN	NO	NO	NO
Q25	INTERIM REPORT OF CURRENT ASSETS GIVEN	NO	NO	YES
Q26	INTERIM REPORT OF FIXED ASSETS GIVEN	NO	NO	YES
Q27	INTERIM REPORT OF ACCUMULATED DEPRECIATION GIVEN	NO	NO	NO
Q28	INTERIM REPORT OF LONG-TERM INVESTMENTS GIVEN	NO	NO	MINORITY PRACTICE
Q29	INTERIM REPORT OF INTANGIBLES GIVEN	NO	NO	NO
Q30	INTERIM REPORT OF TOTAL ASSETS GIVEN	NO	NO	YES
Q31	INTERIM REPORT OF CURRENT LIABILITIES GIVEN	NO	NO	YES
Q32	INTERIM REPORT OF LONG-TERM DEBT GIVEN	NO	NO	YES
Q33	INTERIM REPORT OF MINORITY INTEREST GIVEN	NO	NO	MINORITY PRACTICE
Q34	INTERIM REPORT OF SHAREHOLDERS' EQUITY GIVEN	NO	NO	MINORITY PRACTICE
Q35	INTERIM REPORT OF STATEMENT OF CHANGES IN FINANCIAL POSITION	NO	NO	NO
Q36	INTERIM REPORT OF FUNDS FROM OPERATIONS GIVEN	NO	NO	NO
Q37	INTERIM REPORT OF EARNINGS PER SHARE GIVEN	NO	YES	YES
Q38	INTERIM REPORT OF DIVIDEND PER SHARE GIVEN	NO	YES	YES

Interim Financial Reporting Practices in 20 Countries

NO.	ACCOUNTING & AUDITING ITEMS	Spain	Sweden	Switzerland
Q1	FREQUENCY OF INTERIM REPORTS	QUARTERLY/SEMIANNUALLY	FREQUENCY NOT DEFINED	SEMIANNUALLY
Q2	INTERIM REPORTS SIGNED BY MANAGEMENT	MINORITY PRACTICE	YES	NO
Q3	INTERIM FINANCIAL HIGHLIGHTS REPORTED	MINORITY PRACTICE	YES	NO
Q4	INTERIM INFLATION-ADJUSTED DATA REPORTED	NO	NO	NO
Q5	INTERIM SEGMENT INFORMATION REPORTED	NO	YES	YES
Q6	INTERIM GEOGRAPHICAL INFORMATION REPORTED	NO	NO	NO
Q7	INTERIM REPORT CONSOLIDATED	MINORITY PRACTICE	YES	YES
Q8	AUDITED INTERIM STATEMENTS	NO	NO	NO
Q9	ACCOUNTING POLICIES GIVEN IN INTERIM REPORT	NO	NO	MINORITY PRACTICE
Q10	NOTES TO FINANCIAL ACCOUNTS GIVEN IN INTERIM REPORT	MINORITY PRACTICE	NO	MINORITY PRACTICE
Q11	INTERIM INCOME STATEMENT GIVEN	YES	YES	MINORITY PRACTICE
Q12	INTERIM SALES GIVEN	YES	YES	YES
Q13	INTERIM COGS GIVEN	YES	YES	NO
Q14	INTERIM DEPRECIATION GIVEN	YES	YES	MINORITY PRACTICE
Q15	INTERIM OPERATING INCOME GIVEN	YES	YES	MINORITY PRACTICE
Q16	INTERIM REPORTING OF INTEREST EXPENSE GIVEN	YES	YES	MINORITY PRACTICE
Q17	INTERIM REPORT OF FOREIGN EXCHANGE GAINS AND LOSSES	MINORITY PRACTICE	MINORITY PRACTICE	NO
Q18	INTERIM REPORT OF EXTRAORDINARY GAINS/LOSSES	MINORITY PRACTICE	MINORITY PRACTICE	NO
Q19	INTERIM REPORT OF INCOME TAX EXPENSE GIVEN	NO	NO	NO
Q20	INTERIM REPORT OF NET INCOME GIVEN	MINORITY PRACTICE	NO	MINORITY PRACTICE
Q21	INTERIM BALANCE SHEET GIVEN	MINORITY PRACTICE	NO	MINORITY PRACTICE
Q22	INTERIM CASH AND EQUIVALENTS REPORTED	NO	NO	MINORITY PRACTICE
Q23	INTERIM REPORT OF ACCOUNTS RECEIVABLE	MINORITY PRACTICE	NO	MINORITY PRACTICE

Interim Financial Reporting Practices in 20 Countries

NO.	ACCOUNTING & AUDITING ITEMS	Spain	Sweden	Switzerland
Q24	INTERIM REPORT OF INVENTORIES GIVEN	MINORITY PRACTICE	NO	MINORITY PRACTICE
Q25	INTERIM REPORT OF CURRENT ASSETS GIVEN	MINORITY PRACTICE	NO	MINORITY PRACTICE
Q26	INTERIM REPORT OF FIXED ASSETS GIVEN	YES	NO	MINORITY PRACTICE
Q27	INTERIM REPORT OF ACCUMULATED DEPRECIATION GIVEN	NO	NO	NO
Q28	INTERIM REPORT OF LONG-TERM INVESTMENTS GIVEN	NO	NO	NO
Q29	INTERIM REPORT OF INTANGIBLES GIVEN	NO	NO	NO
Q30	INTERIM REPORT OF TOTAL ASSETS GIVEN	YES	NO	MINORITY PRACTICE
Q31	INTERIM REPORT OF CURRENT LIABILITIES GIVEN	MINORITY PRACTICE	NO	MINORITY PRACTICE
Q32	INTERIM REPORT OF LONG-TERM DEBT GIVEN	YES	NO	MINORITY PRACTICE
Q33	INTERIM REPORT OF MINORITY INTEREST GIVEN	NO	NO	NO
Q34	INTERIM REPORT OF SHAREHOLDERS' EQUITY GIVEN	YES	NO	MINORITY PRACTICE
Q35	INTERIM REPORT OF STATEMENT OF CHANGES IN FINANCIAL POSITION	NO	NO	NO
Q36	INTERIM REPORT OF FUNDS FROM OPERATIONS GIVEN	NO	NO	NO
Q37	INTERIM REPORT OF EARNINGS PER SHARE GIVEN	NO	NO	MINORITY PRACTICE
Q38	INTERIM REPORT OF DIVIDEND PER SHARE GIVEN	NO	NO	NO

Interim Financial Reporting Practices in 20 Countries

NO.	ACCOUNTING & AUDITING ITEMS	United Kingdom	United States	
Q1	FREQUENCY OF INTERIM REPORTS	SEMIANNUALLY	QUARTERLY	
Q2	INTERIM REPORTS SIGNED BY MANAGEMENT	YES	YES	
Q3	INTERIM FINANCIAL HIGHLIGHTS REPORTED	YES	NO	
Q4	INTERIM INFLATION-ADJUSTED DATA REPORTED	NO	NO	
Q5	INTERIM SEGMENT INFORMATION REPORTED	MINORITY PRACTICE	MINORITY PRACTICE	
Q6	INTERIM GEOGRAPHICAL INFORMATION REPORTED	MINORITY PRACTICE	NO	
Q7	INTERIM REPORT CONSOLIDATED	YES	YES	
Q8	AUDITED INTERIM STATEMENTS	NO	NO	
Q9	ACCOUNTING POLICIES GIVEN IN INTERIM REPORT	MINORITY PRACTICE	NO	
Q10	NOTES TO FINANCIAL ACCOUNTS GIVEN IN INTERIM REPORT	MINORITY PRACTICE	NO	
Q11	INTERIM INCOME STATEMENT GIVEN	YES	YES	
Q12	INTERIM SALES GIVEN	YES	YES	
Q13	INTERIM COGS GIVEN	NO	YES	
Q14	INTERIM DEPRECIATION GIVEN	NO	NO	
Q15	INTERIM OPERATING INCOME GIVEN	YES	YES	
Q16	INTERIM REPORTING OF INTEREST EXPENSE GIVEN	YES	YES	
Q17	INTERIM REPORT OF FOREIGN EXCHANGE GAINS AND LOSSES	NO	NO	
Q18	INTERIM REPORT OF EXTRAORDINARY GAINS/LOSSES	YES	YES	
Q19	INTERIM REPORT OF INCOME TAX EXPENSE GIVEN	YES	YES	
Q20	INTERIM REPORT OF NET INCOME GIVEN	YES	YES	
Q21	INTERIM BALANCE SHEET GIVEN	NO	YES	
Q22	INTERIM CASH AND EQUIVALENTS REPORTED	NO	YES	
Q23	INTERIM REPORT OF ACCOUNTS RECEIVABLE	NO	YES	

Interim Financial Reporting Practices in 20 Countries

NO.	ACCOUNTING & AUDITING ITEMS	United Kingdom	United States	
Q24	INTERIM REPORT OF INVENTORIES GIVEN	NO	YES	
Q25	INTERIM REPORT OF CURRENT ASSETS GIVEN	NO	YES	
Q26	INTERIM REPORT OF FIXED ASSETS GIVEN	NO	YES	
Q27	INTERIM REPORT OF ACCUMULATED DEPRECIATION GIVEN	NO	NO	
Q28	INTERIM REPORT OF LONG-TERM INVESTMENTS GIVEN	NO	NO	
Q29	INTERIM REPORT OF INTANGIBLES GIVEN	NO	NO	
Q30	INTERIM REPORT OF TOTAL ASSETS GIVEN	NO	YES	
Q31	INTERIM REPORT OF CURRENT LIABILITIES GIVEN	NO	YES	
Q32	INTERIM REPORT OF LONG-TERM DEBT GIVEN	NO	YES	
Q33	INTERIM REPORT OF MINORITY INTEREST GIVEN	NO	NO	
Q34	INTERIM REPORT OF SHAREHOLDERS' EQUITY GIVEN	NO	YES	
Q35	INTERIM REPORT OF STATEMENT OF CHANGES IN FINANCIAL POSITION	NO	MINORITY PRACTICE	
Q36	INTERIM REPORT OF FUNDS FROM OPERATIONS GIVEN	NO	MINORITY PRACTICE	
Q37	INTERIM REPORT OF EARNINGS PER SHARE GIVEN	YES	YES	
Q38	INTERIM REPORT OF DIVIDEND PER SHARE GIVEN	YES	YES	

CHAPTER 6

ANALYZING INTERNATIONAL FINANCIAL STATEMENTS:

ISSUES AND ANSWERS

Table of Contents

CHAPTER 6

Tables

CHAPTER 6

Tables
(Continued)

I. INTRODUCTION

Users in the financial community would like to compare a vast number of companies internationally, however, a complete restatement of each foreign company's accounts in a particular user's accounting conventions would be neither cost effective nor timely. Since users in the investment community are particularly interested in the relative differences found through examining the performances of companies, the approaches discussed in this chapter are meant to identify differences among annual reports worldwide and provide suggestions for resolving some of these differences.

II. RESEARCH OBJECTIVES

The objective of this chapter is to address the following research questions:

6-1 What are the major difficulties users face in analyzing international financial statements?

6-2 What are the major accounting differences among leading companies in 24 countries?

6-3 How do annual reports of non-US companies prepared under local accounting standards compare to reports of non-US companies prepared under US accounting standards?

6-4 How can users of international financial statements reconcile accounting differences and overcome other difficulties encountered in analyzing international financial statements?

6-5 How can users of international financial statements use capital market-generated information?

III. RESEARCH DESIGN

Data sources include the Worldscope Database, jointly developed by CIFAR and Wright Investors' Service, of Bridgeport, CT, and CIFAR's reference library of over 10,000 international annual reports. (See Chapter 1, Section IV).

The problems encountered in undertaking research and analyzing international annual reports have been divided into four sections:

- Administrative problems
- Problems with procedural accounting matters
- Differences in accounting standards
- Difficulties in merging fundamental accounting data with capital market-generated information

In each category we identify problems, discuss why these problems make international financial analysis more difficult, and provide suggestions, where possible, for resolving some of these difficulties.

We have drawn from research performed elsewhere in this study in order to provide a comprehensive examination of the issues involved in analyzing international financial statements.

IV. ADMINISTRATIVE PROBLEMS

In undertaking any international research, one is bound to encounter some general difficulties. In this section, these difficulties are identified as they pertain to the analysis of international financial statements.

A. Identification of a Global List of Companies

PROBLEMS:

- There is no single source which provides a comprehensive list of traded securities worldwide; this makes it difficult for a given user to systematically select a set of companies to employ in analysis. (Table 6-1 provides the number of domestic companies listed on selected exchanges in 24 countries.)
- In some instances, subsidiaries, whose reports are more difficult to analyze due to various transactions with parent companies, are also listed on stock exchanges.
- Stock exchange listings change considerably every year.
- In Europe, many prominent companies are not listed or are government-owned.

SOLUTIONS:

- Leading company listings, as well as company directories, are available for most stock exchanges.
- Stock exchange publications provide comprehensive information on the companies listed.
- One can construct a database, with a few key variables (such as country, company name, industry classification, sales, assets and market value of shares), to produce a global list of traded companies. Non-traded companies should also be included in such a list so that major companies in a given industry are analyzed together, even though the user's focus may be on traded companies.

B. Difficulties in Obtaining Information

PROBLEM:

In general, the availability of published corporate data on local companies is quite good, but information sources on foreign companies is not readily available.

SOLUTIONS:

- One potential way to improve the accessibility of information on international companies is to establish collections of international annual reports at leading public and academic libraries. In addition, users in need of annual reports from specific foreign firms may want to obtain them directly from companies of interest. Directories of foreign companies are available in the reference sections of major public and academic libraries worldwide.

- Another possible solution involves using any of the international financial data services listed in Table 6-2.

C. Delays in Receiving Financial Information

PROBLEM:

Companies in many countries take longer than three months after the fiscal year-end date to publish financial statements.

Some of the reasons for this delay are:

- Stock exchanges and government authorities in many countries allow a longer lead time to file annual reports.

- An English-language version of a foreign annual report is produced later than the local language version.

- Similarly, the consolidated version of an annual report is available later than the non-consolidated version.

Table 6-3 provides a classification of countries in terms of the average number of days elapsed between the year-end date of the financial statements and the date of the annual report's publication. Our information is based on our experience in receiving international annual reports for fiscal year 1987.

SOLUTIONS:

- The application of competitive pressure on companies worldwide, where the investment community demands timely information, may cause them to publish more quickly.

- Users may want to use press releases and news clippings to obtain key information, as these sources are available much sooner than the full text annual financial statements. Possible sources for this type of information are The Financial Times, Economist and The Wall Street Journal, as well as other leading financial and business publications worldwide.

- An increasing number of European companies publish preliminary annual results which provide key financial data and information on major developments long before their annual report is published.

D. Language Constraints

PROBLEM:

- Of the 5,000 non-US annual reports reviewed for this study, approximately 30% were not published in English.

- As English is becoming an accepted common denominator in international financial communication, international users may experience difficulty in using annual reports which are not published in English.

Table 6-4 identifies the availability of annual reports in English by country.

SOLUTIONS:

- Use accounting dictionaries or lexicons to translate foreign-language accounting terms into English. Appendix D of this study provides a lexicon in eight languages. (i.e., Dutch, French, German, Italian, Japanese, Korean, Portuguese and Spanish).

- Set up a computerized table to permit the printing of financial statements in multiple languages.

- Use professional translators to translate key financial pages.

- Recruit multilingual colleagues. In our experience of recruiting from business schools in the US and in Europe, we have been able to locate business graduates with multilingual expertise. Many MBA programs have an international focus and require foreign language skills in order for students to complete their degrees.

E. Financial Statements Expressed in Domestic Currency

PROBLEM:

Another perceived information barrier is the fact that figures in annual reports are expressed in domestic currency. In the present study, almost 100% of the financial statements studied were expressed in local currency.

SOLUTIONS:

Financial ratios that transform nominal measurements to percentage relationships are independent of currency denomination. A current ratio computed from ABC Plc's balance sheet in pounds or from a Spanish balance sheet expressed in pesetas is no different from a current ratio computed from ABC Plc's financial statements translated into Japanese yen.

For readers preferring a single currency framework, foreign currency translations can be accomplished simply by restating foreign currency balances in a user's domestic currency equivalents, using a rate equal to the exchange rate prevailing at the financial statement date. Such a translation would also allow users to rank companies worldwide in a given industry by sales, assets or market value.

To judge the true performance of an entity in a particular country, local currency results are preferable, as they are more useful in analyzing the financial history of a company vis-a-vis local competitors as well as in analyzing financial trends.

F. Different Fiscal Year-end Dates

PROBLEM:

Calendar year-end dates are not widely used as fiscal year-end dates in many countries. This makes it difficult to compare the reporting periods of companies, causing a problem in analysis if a user is studying a cyclical industry.

Table 6-5 provides a list of year-end dates used by companies in different countries.

SOLUTION:

The use of companies' quarterly reports may facilitate standardization where quarterly results from the previous year can be subtracted and quarterly results of the current year can be added, to obtain results for a common reporting period between various firms being analyzed.

TABLE 6-1

EXTENT OF LISTINGS ON STOCK EXCHANGES WORLDWIDE FOR COMMON SHARES

Country	Stock Exchange	Number of Domestic Companies Listed
North America		
Canada	Toronto	1147
Mexico	Mexico City	197
United States	American	818
	New York	1575
Asia/Pacific		
Australia	Sydney	1785
Hong Kong	Hong Kong	264
Japan	Tokyo	1532
Korea, South	Seoul	389
Malaysia	Kuala Lumpur	287
New Zealand	Wellington	274
Singapore	Singapore	127
Europe		
Austria	Vienna	69
Belgium	Brussels	192
Denmark	Copenhagen	272
Finland	Helsinki	49
France	Paris	481
Germany, West	Frankfurt	234
Italy	Milan	204
Netherlands	Amsterdam	226
Norway	Oslo	148
Spain	Madrid	312
Sweden	Stockholm	150
Switzerland	Zurich	166
United Kingdom (& Ireland)	London	2135
Africa/Middle East		
South Africa	Johannesburg	531
Total		13,564

Source: Various Stock Exchange Bulletins for 1986-1987

TABLE 6-2

SELECTED SOURCES OF INTERNATIONAL COMPANY INFORMATION

Service	Contact Address and Phone Number	Coverage	Format and Variables Available
Extel International Card Service	37-45 Paul Street London EC2A 4PB United Kingdom Ph: (01) 253-3400	22 Countries Over 4,500 Companies	Details of each company are published on an annual card, which shows a chairman's statement, identifies members of the board, and depicts profit and loss account, balance sheet, company capital (with history), subsidiaries and activities, dividend records, yields, earnings, etc. Cumulative news cards are issued regarding the announcement of dividends, interim or preliminary results or any other event concerning the company's capital, activities or organization. A monthly index and update is provided with the service.
Morgan Stanley Capital International Perspective	Morgan Stanley 1633 Broadway New York, NY 10019 USA Ph: (212) 703-2965	21 Countries 2,100 Companies	Published monthly and quarterly. Presents, in booklet form, share price information for the world's largest companies. Provides selected items from the balance sheet and income statement, and share data. National, regional and industry indices are also included.

TABLE 6-2
(Continued)
SELECTED SOURCES OF INTERNATIONAL COMPANY INFORMATION

Service	Contact Address and Phone Number	Coverage	Format and Variables Available
Moody's International Manual	Moody's Investors Service 99 Church Street New York, NY 10007 USA Ph: (212) 553-0300	Over 90 Countries excluding the US Nearly 5,000 Companies	Published annually in two volumes. Countries are listed alphabetically and each section includes a brief country profile followed by corporate profiles in which data from the income statement and balance sheet, financial and operating information, capital structure and capital stock data, company history and name of key managers are included. The coverage varies depending on whether a listed company pays for a detailed profile.
Worldscope Industrial Company Profiles and Worldscope Financial Service Profiles	CIFAR 601 Ewing Street Suite C-16 Princeton, NJ 08540 USA Ph: (609) 921-0910 and Wright Investors' Service 10 Middle Street Bridgeport, CT 06609 USA Ph: (203) 333-6666	5,000+ Companies in 24 Countries	Published in five-volume (Industrial Companies) and three-volume (Financial and other Service Companies) sets with quarterly updates. Provides comprehensive financial and capital market information, financial statement data, financial ratios, growth rates, per share data and investment ratios, five-year annual growth rates and identification of accounting practices used on a company-specific basis. Other features include a guide on how to analyze international financial statements. Also provides country and industry averages, and company rankings worldwide within a country, within a country by industry and within an industry.

TABLE 6-3
TIMELINESS OF PUBLICATION OF ANNUAL REPORTS
AVERAGE NUMBER OF DAYS ELAPSED BETWEEN FISCAL YEAR-END AND PUBLICATION OF ANNUAL REPORTS
FISCAL YEAR 1987 REPORTS

Country	60-150 days	151-180 days	181 and above
North America			
Canada	X		
Mexico		X	
United States	X		
Asia/Pacific			
Australia	X		
Hong Kong		X	
Japan	X		
Korea, South	X		
Malaysia		X	
New Zealand	X		
Singapore	X		
Europe			
Austria			X
Belgium			X
Denmark		X	
Finland	X		
France			X
Germany, West			X
Italy			X
Netherlands		X	
Norway		X	
Spain		X	
Sweden		X	
Switzerland		X	
United Kingdom	X		
Africa/Middle East			
South Africa	X		

TABLE 6-4

AVAILABILITY OF ENGLISH LANGUAGE FINANCIAL STATEMENTS - FISCAL YEAR 1987

Country	1987		
	All Companies Reporting in English	More than 50% Reporting In English	Less than 50% Reporting in English
<u>North America</u>			
Canada	X *		
Mexico			X
United States	X		
<u>Asia/Pacific</u>			
Australia	X		
Hong Kong	X		
Japan		X	
Korea, South			X
Malaysia	X		
New Zealand	X		
Singapore	X		
<u>Europe</u>			
Austria			X
Belgium			X
Denmark		X	
Finland		X	
France			X
Germany, West			X
Italy			X
Netherlands		X	
Norway		X	
Spain			X
Sweden		X	
Switzerland			X
United Kingdom	X		
<u>Africa/Middle East</u>			
South Africa	X		

* Less than 1% of Canadian companies publish annual reports only in French.

TABLE 6-5
YEAR-END DATES USED
FISCAL YEAR 1987
CLASSIFICATION OF COMPANIES BY FISCAL YEAR-END DATES

Country	Number of Companies	% of Companies with Year-End Dates Between: Jan. 1 to March 31	April 1 to June 30	July 1 to Sept. 30	Oct. 1 to Dec. 31
North America					
Canada	444	13%	5%	9%	73%
Mexico	34	-	6	12	82
United States	3,483	12	12	10	66
Asia/Pacific					
Australia	157	10	64	11	15
Hong Kong	145	28	17	3	52
Japan	510	75	7	6	12
Korea, South	51	21	18	4	57
Malaysia	70	20	21	6	53
New Zealand	34	50	32	9	9
Singapore	44	7	5	13	75
Europe					
Austria	67	-	-	-	100
Belgium	115	5	3	7	85
Denmark	96	2	6	6	86
Finland	85	4	1	7	88
France	317	3	1	3	93
Germany, West	548	2	4	8	86
Italy	158	2	3	1	94
Netherlands	252	3	2	5	90
Norway	84	2	1	-	97
Spain	72	-	3	-	97
Sweden	142	1	1	3	95
Switzerland	183	4	2	4	90
United Kingdom	702	29	9	11	51
Africa/Middle East					
South Africa	173	21	39	17	23
Total	7,966	16%	10%	8%	66%

V. PROBLEMS WITH PROCEDURAL ACCOUNTING MATTERS

This section focuses on accounting differences involved in the process of preparing financial statements. The difficulties arising from the application of differing accounting standards are discussed in the next section of this chapter.

A. Inadequate Disclosures

PROBLEM:

International financial statements vary in terms of what they disclose.

For example:

- A cash flow statement is not available in many countries.
- Segment and geographic information is widely available in North America, somewhat in Europe, and minimally in the Asia/Pacific region.
- Information on subsidiaries is extensive in Europe, but not as extensive in North America.
- Footnotes are extensive in reports from Commonwealth countries and Scandinavia but are not widely used in Japan or Continental Europe.

Chapter 3 provides further information on differences in financial reporting practices in 24 countries. Table 6-6 summarizes the key financial reporting items by country.

SOLUTION:

- Disclosing more information in financial statements depends on management's view of the user's needs. Therefore, capital market persuasion would improve disclosures.
- Local government agencies are demanding more disclosures. Government filings, which are in the public domain, such as Japanese companies' filings with the Japanese Ministry of Finance, and American companies' filings with the US Securities and Exchange Commission, usually provide more financial disclosure than those provided to shareholders.
- International governmental organizations (e.g., the Organization for Economic Cooperation and Development and the United Nations' Center on Transnational Corporations) are recommending that multinational corporations provide more financial information to users.

B. Differences in Auditing Standards and Audit Reports

PROBLEM:

Independent auditors help assure the integrity of financial information by reviewing financial statements and attesting to their reliability, fairness and general quality. National variations in auditing standards and practices are common and result primarily from differences in legal, political and economic factors.

It is important for international users, who may depend extensively on published financial statements, to understand these differences and their implications for reliance on the statements.

Table 6-7 highlights key differences in the auditors' reports included in the annual reports of companies from 24 countries. Chapter 12 provides further analysis of auditors' reports.

SOLUTION:

The international expansion of large public accounting firms represents a further harmonizing influence on local auditing practices. Table 6-8 shows the percentage of clients audited by international accounting firms in 24 countries.

Recent efforts toward the harmonization of auditing standards suggest that gaps in standards will narrow, at least in the major industrial nations. The European Community (EC), in its Fourth Directive, now requires all large public and private corporations to undergo an annual audit. The auditor is expected to disclose whether the annual accounts give a true and fair view of the financial position and of profit or loss. Recent efforts toward the harmonization of auditing standards have also been made by the International Federation of Accountants (IFAC).

C. Lack of Interim Data

PROBLEM:

As summarized in Table 6-9, interim reports are published on a varied frequency internationally, making a global comparison of the financial performance of companies in a given industry very difficult.

Interim financial statements often include several items from the income statement, but very few balance sheet items.

SOLUTION:

Capital market initiatives or regulatory changes requiring more frequent disclosure of financial data may persuade companies to provide interim information to users.

D. Differences in the Account Form of Financial Statements

PROBLEM:

Differences in international balance sheet and income statement formats can prove troublesome. Table 6-10 summarizes the differences in the 24 countries studied.

Income statement presentations appear standardized throughout most of the world. Differences occur primarily in a few European countries where the debit/credit format is commonly employed.

SOLUTION:

Because of the pervasiveness of the double-entry bookkeeping system internationally, similarity in the underlying structure of financial statements allows format differences to be reconciled readily. For example, current liabilities can be added back to net working capital to obtain current assets in an Australian company's balance sheet.

E. Variance in Definition of Accounting Terms

PROBLEM:

Some accounting terms have different meanings in various countries, leading to confusion.

For example:

North America	Commonwealth Countries
Inventories	Stock
Stock	Investments
Sales	Turnover
Leased Assets	Hired Purchased Assets
Accounts Receivable	Debtors
Accounts Payable	Creditors

SOLUTION:

The construction of a table of key terms and further familiarization with international reports usually resolves this problem.

The difficulties identified in this section are not insurmountable. With proper insight and experience, most of these problems can be overcome as many of them are mechanical in nature. In the next section, differences in accounting standards, which are more difficult to mitigate, are discussed.

TABLE 6-6

KEY DISCLOSURE DIFFERENCES: INDUSTRIAL COMPANIES

By Selected Countries	5 - 10 Years Financial Summary	Comparative Income Statement	Comparative Balance Sheet	Statement of Changes in SE Equity
North America				
Canada	E	2 Years	2 Years	E
Mexico	M	2 Years	2 Years	E
United States	E	2-3 Years	2 Years	M
Asia/Pacific				
Australia	E	2 Years	2 Years	L
Hong Kong	E	2 Years	2 Years	L
Japan	E	2 Years	2 Years	E
Korea, South	L	1-2 Years	1-2 Years	E
Malaysia	E	2 Years	2 Years	L
New Zealand	E	2 Years	2 Years	L
Singapore	E	2 Years	2 Years	L
Europe				
Austria	E	1-2 Years	1-2 Years	E
Belgium	E	2 Years	2 Years	M
Denmark	E	2 Years	2 Years	L
Finland	E	2 Years	2 Years	L
France	E	2 Years	2 Years	E
Germany, West	M	1-2 Years	1-2 Years	L
Italy	M	2 Years	2 Years	M
Netherlands	E	2 Years	2 Years	L
Norway	E	2 Years	2 Years	L
Spain	E	2 Years	2 Years	L
Sweden	E	2 Years	2 Years	M
Switzerland	E	2 Years	2 Years	L
United Kingdom	E	2 Years	2 Years	L
Africa/Middle East				
South Africa	E	2 Years	2 Years	L

Key:
E Extensively Disclosed
M Moderately Disclosed
L Less Frequently Disclosed

TABLE 6-6
(Continued)
KEY DISCLOSURE DIFFERENCES: INDUSTRIAL COMPANIES

By Selected Countries	Statement of Cash Flow	Notes to Financial Statement	Segment Information	Geographic Information
<u>North America</u>				
Canada	E	E	S/OI/TA	S/OI/TA
Mexico	E	E	MP	MP
United States	E	E	S/OI/TA	S/OI/TA
<u>Asia/Pacific</u>				
Australia	E	E	S/OI/TA	S/OI/TA
Hong Kong	M	E	MP	S/OI
Japan	L	M	S/OI/TA	S/OI/TA
Korea, South	L	M	MP	MP
Malaysia	E	E	MP	S/OI/TA
New Zealand	E	E	S/OI/TA	S/OI/TA
Singapore	E	E	MP	S/OI/TA
<u>Europe</u>				
Austria	L	M	TA	MP
Belgium	L	M	S/OI	S/OI/TA
Denmark	M	M	S/OI	S/OI
Finland	E	E	S/OI	S/OI
France	M	M	S/OI	S/OI
West Germany	L	M	S/OI	S/OI
Italy	M	M	S/OI	MP
Netherlands	M	E	S/OI/TA	S/OI
Norway	E	E	S/OI/TA	S/OI
Spain	M	M	S/OI	MP
Sweden	M	E	S/OI	S/OI
Switzerland	L	M	S/OI	S/OI
United Kingdom	E	E	S/OI	S/OI
<u>Africa/Middle East</u>				
South Africa	E	E	MP	S/OI/TA

Key:
S/OI/TA Sales, Operating Income and Total Assets by Product Line or by Area
S/OI Sales and Operating Income by Product Line or by Area
TA Total Assets by Product Line or by Area
MP Minority Practice

E Extensively Disclosed
M Moderately Disclosed
L Less Frequently Disclosed

TABLE 6-7

KEY CHARACTERISTICS OF AUDITORS' REPORTS

	Key Conclusion Words Used			Audit Report Coverage		
Country	True and Fair View	In Conformity With the Law	Fair and Conforms with GAAP	Identified Sections Only	Entire Report Covered	Percentage of Audit Reports Qualified
<u>North America</u>						
Canada			X	X		35%
Mexico			X	X		33
United States			X	X		4
<u>Asia/Pacific</u>						
Australia *				X		48
Hong Kong	X			X		4
Japan			X	X		21
Korea, South			X	X		0
Malaysia	X			X		0
New Zealand	X			X		0
Singapore	X			X		4
<u>Europe</u>						
Austria		X			X	0
Belgium			X	X		13
Denmark	X				X	0
Finland	X				X	0
France	X			X		12
Germany, West		X			X	0
Italy			X	X		10
Netherlands			X	X		0
Norway	X				X	4
Spain			X	X		37
Sweden	X				X	2
Switzerland		X		X		0
United Kingdom	X			X		3
<u>Africa/Middle East</u>						
South Africa	X			X		1

* Auditors' reports in Australia use "Properly Drawn Up" as the key conclusion phrase.

TABLE 6-8
PERCENTAGE OF COMPANIES AUDITED BY LEADING INTERNATIONAL ACCOUNTING FIRMS

Country	% of Clients Audited by	
	Sixteen Int'l. Acctg. Firms*	Audit Firms not Affiliated With Sixteen Int'l. Accounting Firms
<u>North America</u>		
Canada	97%	3%
Mexico	96	4
United States	100	0
<u>Asia/Pacific</u>		
Australia	95	5
Hong Kong	96	4
Japan	71	29
Korea, South	70	30
Malaysia	70	30
New Zealand	87	13
Singapore	99	1
<u>Europe</u>		
Austria	53	47
Belgium	45	55
Denmark	76	24
Finland	97	3
France	70	30
Germany, West	88	12
Italy	96	4
Netherlands	99	1
Norway	91	9
Spain	97	3
Sweden	95	5
Switzerland	56	44
United Kingdom	97	3
<u>Africa/Middle East</u>		
South Africa	97	3

* For a listing of the Sixteen International Accounting Firms, please refer to Chapter 10 in this study.

TABLE 6-9

FREQUENCY OF INTERIM FINANCIAL STATEMENTS
FISCAL YEAR 1988

	Majority Practice			Interims Published By Few Companies
Country	Quarterly	Every Four Months	Semi-Annually	
North America				
Canada	x			
Mexico				x
United States	x			
Asia/Pacific				
Australia			x	
Hong Kong			x	
Japan			x	
Korea, South				x
Malaysia			x	
New Zealand			x	
Singapore			x	
Europe				
Austria				x
Belgium				x
Denmark			x	
Finland		x		
France			x	
Germany, West			x	
Italy			x	
Netherlands	x			
Norway		x		
Spain	x			
Sweden		x		
Switzerland				x
United Kingdom			x	
Africa/Middle East				
South Africa			x	

TABLE 6-10

DIFFERENCES IN THE FORM OF FINANCIAL STATEMENTS
INDUSTRIAL COMPANIES

	Balance Statement			Income Statement		
Country	TA = TL + SE	FA + NWC Less LTD = SE	FA + NWC = LTD + SE	Sales Less Expenses	Debit = Credit	Op. Prof. Less Int. & Tax Exp.
North America						
Canada	X			X		
Mexico	X			X		
United States	X			X		
Asia/Pacific						
Australia		X				X
Hong Kong		X				X
Japan	X			X		
Korea, South	X			X		
Malaysia		X				X
New Zealand	X					X
Singapore		X				X
Europe						
Austria	X				X	
Belgium	X				X	
Denmark	X			X		
Finland	X			X		
France	X			X	X	
Germany, West	X			X		
Italy	X			X	X	
Netherlands	X			X	X	
Norway	X			X		
Spain	X			X	X	
Sweden	X			X		
Switzerland	X			X		
United Kingdom		X				X
Africa/Middle East						
South Africa			X	X		

Key:

TA = TL + SE	Total Assets = Total Liabilities + Shareholders' Equity
FA + NWC - LTD = SE	Fixed Assets + Net Working Capital - Long-Term Debt = Shareholders' Equity
FA + NWC = LTD + SE	Fixed Assets + Net Working Capital = Long-Term Debt + Shareholders' Equity
Op. Prof. - Int. & Tax Exp.	Operating Profits - Interest and Tax Expenses

VI. DIFFERENCES IN ACCOUNTING STANDARDS

On the surface, a user may find many accounting differences while reviewing the annual reports of companies worldwide. All of these differences, however, may not necessarily have an impact on earnings and balance sheet totals. Some of the differences can be easily reconciled.

The awareness of major differences in the underlying accounting principles of companies located in different countries is an important prerequisite for the analysis of international financial statements. With such knowledge, a user of financial statements may be able to at least take into account the magnitude of such differences.

To facilitate the comparison of companies internationally, the discussion of accounting differences has been divided into four sections:

A. Format differences
B. Accounting differences with a small impact on earnings/valuation
C. Accounting differences with a large impact on earnings/valuation
D. Methods of reconciling accounting differences

A. Format Differences

PROBLEMS:

- Due to the double entry bookkeeping system, which is widely accepted around the world, the income statement format is standardized as revenues minus expenses. However, expense classifications vary considerably. For example, the cost of goods sold is not defined consistently, and earnings per share are computed using different earnings numbers.

- The balance sheet has many such format differences from country to country.

  Some examples:

  - Contra accounts such as accumulated depreciation and treasury stock may or may not be netted out.

  - Contingent liabilities are sometimes included on both sides of the balance sheet, and as a result, assets and liabilities are overstated.

  - Sub-classifications, such as current assets and current liabilities, are not comparable.

Tables 6-11A through 6-11E report some of the format differences found in the annual reports of companies in selected countries.

SOLUTIONS:

Restate numbers to make them format compatible. For example, depreciation reserves can be subtracted from fixed assets; treasury stock can be subtracted from current assets, thereby effectively reducing shareholders' equity. Thus, format differences do not involve many changes in the figures. (The figures are regrouped into a format that will conform to the reporting practices of other countries.)

For example, US companies show earnings per share as net income minus preferred dividends, divided by the average number of common shares outstanding. UK companies, on the other hand, take net income before extraordinary items, and then divide that by the average number of total shares outstanding. An extraordinary loss would decrease the net income figure but would not show up in earnings per share. Comparing earnings per share for UK and US companies, therefore, simply means recalculating for extraordinary items.

B. Varying Application of Uniform Accounting Standards

PROBLEM:

Though accounting differences between companies worldwide are numerous, there are certain uniform accounting standards. However, differences still exist in the application of these standards.

For instance, the amortization of goodwill is common among all countries. However, there may be differences in the length of the period over which amortization takes place. European and other countries use a maximum of ten years. The United States prescribes a maximum period of forty years, but many US companies have used periods that fall substantially below forty years. It is clear, then, that the impact of yearly amortization expense on net income does vary, but not necessarily substantially.

Table 6-12 provides a list of a few of the accounting standards in this category.

SOLUTION:

The effect of accounting differences in this category are not of a large magnitude, and we believe that over a longer time period their effect would be nullified.

C. Major Differences in Accounting Standards

PROBLEMS:

Differences in international accounting standards which can have a great impact on earnings and various balance sheet totals are a major barrier for users of international financial statements. Some of these major differences in accounting policies are:

1. Depreciation Methods: Depreciation methods differ from industry to industry, country to country, and even within a country.

2. Inventory Methods: Although FIFO is widely accepted, companies in some countries use the weighted average or LIFO method for inventory valuation.

3. Deferred Taxes: Accounting rules differ from tax rules in some countries. The difference between the tax expense and the tax liability can be substantial.

4. Consolidation Principles: Quite frequently, only domestic or significant subsidiaries are consolidated. In addition, the cost basis of accounting for investments is used in many countries for investments of greater than 20% in a subsidiary.

5. Discretionary Reserves: In many countries, allocations to and from reserves, which can often distort income, can be made at management's discretion. For banks and insurance companies, allocations to such reserves constitute a large percentage of operating revenues.

6. Inflation Adjustments: The periodic revaluations of fixed assets and inventories are common in some countries, resulting in a revaluation reserve in the balance sheet and extra charges in the income statement.

7. Foreign Currency Gains/Losses and Translation Method: The current rate method is widely accepted, but currency translation gains and losses may either be reflected in the income statement or recorded as a change in reserves in the balance sheet.

8. Valuation of Fixed Income and Equity Securities: For banks and insurance companies, alternative methods of valuing their security portfolios are used (i.e., cost, market, or lower of cost or market).

Table 6-13 provides a summary of these major accounting differences among industrial companies in 24 countries.

Table 6-14 provides a summary of these major accounting differences among banks in 22 countries.

Table 6-15 provides a summary of these major accounting differences among insurance companies in 22 countries.

SOLUTIONS:

The ideal solution would be to have the leading companies in global industries prepare financial statements under a single accounting convention. Since this will not occur in the near future, we would like to suggest some practical approaches to the analysis of companies across national boundaries.

The user should exercise caution since all of these adjustments do not necessarily make annual reports completely comparable internationally. However, the approaches suggested in this section do minimize the impact of accounting differences so that a global view can be taken in evaluating companies:

1. Use Stock Market-Determined Financial Ratios:

   The investment community is very conversant with financial indicators derived from stock market data items such as market price per share, dividend per share, and the risk identification of each security. Stock market averages are also available on each of these items:

a. Dividend Yield = $\frac{\text{Total cash dividends to common shareholders}}{\text{Total market capitalization}}$

b. Annual Rate of Return to Stockholders = Dividend Yield ±Appreciation or Loss

c. Excess Returns = Annual Rate of Return to stockholders on a given company Less Risk Adjusted Rate of Return on that company

   Users can easily compare the financial performance of large international companies by using the above financial ratios.

   This approach is advantageous because the results are unaffected by accounting differences. In addition, financial analysis by users is facilitated by the availabilty and timeliness of the data.

   A major disadvantage of this approach, however, is that the underlying fundamental characteristics of each firm will not be evaluated.

2. Use Growth-Related Financial Ratios:

   Financial ratios, which are not affected by accounting differences, can be used. Year to year growth in sales, operating income, dividends, net worth, total assets, earnings per share, dividends per share, and book value per share can be computed. This approach allows for easier computation of global industry averages, thus facilitating global evaluation of international companies.

   The argument in favor of such an approach would be that large companies do not change their accounting standards each year. Therefore, year to year changes in key accounts can provide important signals about a particular firm's financial performance and position.

A problem with this approach would be that in several countries, due to various tax incentives, companies report a very low net income. Thus, a percentage change in earnings may not reflect actual performance.

3. Use Cash Flow Statements:

Use cash flow statements where charges to discretionary reserves and other non-cash expenses such as depreciation can be added back to net income to obtain true cash generated by the company, and thereby minimize the influence of accounting differences.

The financial community has recently expressed a preference for cash flow-related indicators, such as cash flow per share and cash flow generated as a percentage of sales, as unbiased indicators of a firm's performance.

4. Obtain Annual Reports Restated in User's GAAP:

In an attempt to better serve the information needs of foreign investors, a number of multinational companies have begun to experiment with alternative reporting modes. For example, in reporting to their US shareholders, Philips of the Netherlands not only presents English translations of its annual reports, but also restates the key items of its balance sheet and income statement according to US GAAP. Many large multinational firms in Japan go a step further and entirely restate their financial statements according to US GAAP. Swedish companies provide a reconciliation of the cost method of accounting for investments with the equity method, to reflect international accounting standards.

We obtained and analyzed the restatements of financial statements into US GAAP, which were published by selected companies in the United Kingdom, Sweden and Japan. Though only a few companies from these countries published financial statements according to US GAAP, the comparisons may be of use in identifying differences between the accounting standards of the US and each of these countries.

a. United Kingdom

The major reconciliation items, compared with the general practice in the United States, are summarized in Table 6-16.

The financial results of five UK companies under two sets of accounting standards are illustrated in Table 6-17. Shareholders' equity is significantly different when a company has very high foreign operations or purchases a business, which result in foreign currency translation adjustments and goodwill, respectively. Thus, the effects of the differences in standards can be either favorable or unfavorable.

b. Sweden

The major differences in accounting practices between Sweden and the United States are summarized in Table 6-18 and the financial results for selected companies in Table 6-19. The most significant differences in accounting practices between Sweden and the United States are the appropriation of earnings to untaxed reserves and related items in the balance sheet.

c. Japan

The restatements of Japanese companies are slightly different from those analyzed in the United Kingdom and Sweden. Japanese restatements focus mainly on the consolidated financial statements. Consolidation of financial data is a recent accounting practice in Japan. Since the 1970's, the Securities Exchange Law of Japan has required public companies to report consolidated financial statements based upon guidelines provided by the Japanese Institute of Certified Public Accountants. About 50% of the companies listed in the first section of the Tokyo Stock Exchange filed consolidated financial statements in 1987. However, the guidelines for consolidation have some flexibility. About 20% of the consolidated financial statements are restated to help foreign users understand them better, especially in terms of US GAAP. The restated financial statements are reported to the Ministry of Finance, as well as to the foreign users of English reports, together with unconsolidated financial statements.

A few companies provide two different consolidated financial statements: consolidation under pure Japanese accounting standards for the Ministry of Finance, and consolidation under the accounting standards partially modified to US GAAP for the foreign users of English-language reports. The most important items modified are summarized in Table 6-20. However, the modification of a few accounting standards is insufficient to explain the current norm of a higher price-earnings ratio for Japanese companies. For example, depreciation expense, which is a major expense in manufacturing companies, is based upon the accelerated depreciation method for both financial and tax reporting as permitted by Japanese tax regulations. Deferred income tax will also be affected by the depreciation method if a straight-line method, which is common in the US or EC countries, is applied for financial reporting purposes.

Table 6-21 illustrates the differences between the financial results of a few companies which report two different consolidated financial statements. It is difficult to draw a definite conclusion from the table.

Table 6-22 approaches the problem from a different angle. Thirty-one companies were selected from the electronics industry, of which 15 companies report consolidated financial information under Japanese GAAP, while the other 16 companies report under adjusted US GAAP. The latest financial information, taken from annual reports for fiscal years ending as recently as April 1988, has been analyzed. It is assumed that these companies have similar types of assets since they are in the same industry.

Depreciation expense-related ratios are similar for these two groups, with the result that they use the same method to calculate depreciation expenses.

Deferred income tax is not used under Japanese GAAP, but is used under US GAAP. For example, in the US, an accelerated depreciation method is used for tax purposes and a straight-line depreciation method for financial reporting purposes. This is not the case in Japan.

Pension expenses are another issue, but their significance to the cost of goods sold and selling, general and administrative expenses is very small. It is difficult to say whether the use of different accounting practices to determine pension expenses will affect the operating margin significantly.

The effects of foreign currency translation are not specified on the income statement; however, accumulated adjustments have affected the shareholders' equity negatively in recent years, particularly for companies under US GAAP.

Operating results under US GAAP are much higher than those under Japanese GAAP in terms of return on assets or return on equity. Price to earnings or price over book value per share ratios are also realistic compared to averages in other countries.

To summarize, Japanese adjustments to US GAAP are published only for outside users. The adjustments are done partially. Further research in the areas of depreciation expense, pension expenses, inclusion of smaller subsidiaries and their related accounting practices will be necessary, in order to fully reconcile Japanese GAAP to US GAAP.

5. Create Subtotals of Key Accounts Which are Format Compatible:

Users can minimize differences in accounting terminology, stock price format, statement format and language through the use of standardized company profile accounts. Research into the accounting standards and practices of each country can be done prior to the actual extraction of financial data. Efforts can then be made to streamline the coding of accounts to make them comparable across countries for each company. Valuation provisions/charges and contra items that tend to inflate or deflate total assets can be adjusted against the respective asset accounts, thereby reducing the effect of over or understatement. Although this approach does not eliminate accounting differences, it does make key accounts such as operating income, current assets, total assets, and owners' equity more comparable internationally.

6. Restate Financial Statements of Companies in a Given Industry Worldwide:

Identify specific differences in accounting principles between companies of interest, and determine the direction and magnitude of the impact of these accounting changes on the earnings and valuations of the companies. As an illustration, we have highlighted such differences in Table 6-23 for selected companies in the electronics industry.

Here are some suggestions regarding the adjustment of key accounting differences:

a. Depreciation:

To harmonize discrepancies, an equalization method can be utilized whereby equal percentages are applied to depreciate assets when an equal number of years is taken for the estimated asset life.

b. Differences in Income Tax Expense & Deferred Taxes:

To compensate for tax differences, one may want to ignore taxes altogether and focus on pre-tax income in order to compare true operating income.

c. Discretionary Reserves:

To neutralize this variable, a user can either focus on income before reserves, or add the reserves back to pre-tax income.

d. Inventory Cost Methods:

Many companies adopt one inventory approach, but footnote what the costs would have been had they used another formula. This procedure allows for easy comparison.

If alternative inventory cost numbers are not reported, one can compare the results of companies that use different inventory costing methods by calculating the cost of goods sold as a percentage of sales.

e. Results of Non-consolidated Subsidiaries:

Many companies in Europe disclose key financial variables of non-consolidated subsidiaries (i.e. sales, net earnings, total assets) in their parent company reports.

To restate parent company statements for non-consolidated subsidiaries, the user should subtract the dividend earnings of non-consolidated subsidiaries from the parent company report and add back the total earnings of non-consolidated subsidiaries. If there are any minority holdings in these subsidiaries, an appropriate portion of earnings should be subtracted to reflect the share of minority holders.

7. Keep Abreast of International Accounting Developments:

Regular users of international financial statements may want to keep abreast of international accounting developments so that the impact of various changes in international accounting standards can be reflected in their analysis. Table 6-24 provides various sources of information on current international accounting developments.

TABLE 6-11A

FORMAT DIFFERENCES IN REPORTING FROM SELECTED COUNTRIES

ITEM:	COST OF GOODS SOLD (COGS) IN INCOME STATEMENT
Australia	-No cost of goods sold is disclosed. Trading profit from operations before taxation is disclosed. COGS is sometimes disclosed in the footnotes.
Canada	-Cost of sales provided. Also administration and depreciation expenses are provided separately.
France	-COGS not given. In its place a company will disclose operating expense accounts that include depreciation and interest expense. Other operating expenses may not be included but disclosed elsewhere.
W. Germany	-Not given. A list of operating expense accounts is given and can be used to approximate COGS. These expenses include depreciation.
Italy	-COGS not given, but a list of operating expense accounts is provided.
Japan	-Provided.
Sweden	-Not given, but a list of operating expense accounts that include depreciation is given.
Switzerland	-Not given, but a list of operating expenses is provided.
UK	-Usually provided, and is the actual cost of the goods sold; does not include interest expense and depreciation.
US	-Provided.

TABLE 6-11B

FORMAT DIFFERENCES IN REPORTING FROM SELECTED COUNTRIES

ITEM:	EARNINGS PER SHARE (EPS)
Australia	-Disclosed in financial highlights, not in I/S* Basis of computation usually not disclosed. Computed after extraordinary items are considered.
Canada	-Usually basic EPS are disclosed but could also be fully diluted. Based on weighted average number of shares. Calculated before and after extraordinary items.
France	-Basic EPS. Calculated after preferred dividends. Effect of extraordinary items is included. Calculated on the basis of total shares outstanding.
W. Germany	-Basic EPS. Calculated after preferred dividends and extraordinary items and based on weighted average number of shares.
Italy	-Rarely disclosed.
Japan	-Basic EPS. Based on weighted average number of shares. Could be stated per unit of 100 shares. Computed after effect of extraordinary items.
Sweden	-Basic EPS. Calculated after preferred dividends (though preferred equity is rare), but before extraordinary items. Based on weighted average number of shares.
Switzerland	-Not disclosed on I/S - disclosed in financial summary. Basis of computation is usually disclosed.
UK	-Basic EPS. Calculated after preferred dividends but before extraordinary items. Based on weighted average number of shares.
US	-Basic and diluted EPS calculated after preferred dividends; before and after extraordinary items. Weighted average shares are used.

* I/S = Income Statement

TABLE 6-11C

FORMAT DIFFERENCES IN REPORTING FROM SELECTED COUNTRIES

ITEM:	CURRENT ASSETS
Australia	-Shown in descending order of liquidity. Individual accounts are net of valuation or contra items.
Canada	-Shown in descending order of liquidity. Net of valuation or contra accounts
France	-Shown in ascending order of liquidity. Valuation accounts may be shown on liability side. Inventory may be shown as separate item.
W. Germany	-Shown in ascending order of liquidity. No netting, valuation accounts are on liability side. Could include treasury stock.
Italy	-Shown in descending order of liquidity. Individual accounts in gross amount, valuation or contra accounts on liability side.
Japan	-Shown in descending order of liquidity. Individual accounts are net of valuation or contra accounts. May include treasury stock.
Sweden	-Shown in descending order of liquidity. Valuation accounts netted out.
Switzerland	-Shown in descending order of liquidity. Net of valuation or contra accounts.
UK	-Shown in ascending order of liquidity. Shown net of current liabilities.
US	-Shown in descending order of liquidity. Individual accounts are net of any valuation or contra accounts.

TABLE 6-11D

FORMAT DIFFERENCES IN REPORTING FROM SELECTED COUNTRIES

ITEM:	PROPERTY, PLANT AND EQUIPMENT
Australia	-Shown net. Accumulated depreciation shown in footnotes.
Canada	-Shown net. Accumulated depreciation disclosed in footnotes.
France	-Shown gross with accumulated depreciation. Subject to revaluation. Accumulated depreciation may be shown under liabilities.
W. Germany	-Shown gross on asset side with accumulated depreciation on liability side.
Italy	-Shown gross; accumulated depreciation on liability side.
Japan	-Shown gross, but accumulated depreciation is deducted to arrive at net fixed assets.
Sweden	-Shown net of accumulated depreciation.
Switzerland	-Shown gross with accumulated depreciation, additions and disposals.
UK	-Shown net of accumulated depreciation.
US	-Shown gross, but accumulated depreciation is deducted to arrive at net figure.

TABLE 6-11E

FORMAT DIFFERENCES IN REPORTING FROM SELECTED COUNTRIES

ITEM:	TREASURY STOCK
Australia	-Reduction of shareholders' equity.
Canada	-Reduction of shareholders' equity.
France	-Not disclosed.
West Germany	-Included in current assets.
Italy	-Included in current assets.
Japan	-Reduction of shareholders' equity in consolidated version. Included in current assets in unconsolidated version.
Sweden	-Reduction of shareholders' equity.
Switzerland	-Included in current assets.
UK	-Reduction of shareholders' equity.
US	-Reduction of shareholders' equity.

TABLE 6-12

ACCOUNTING DIFFERENCES WITH A SMALL IMPACT ON EARNINGS/VALUATION
INDUSTRIAL COMPANIES FROM SELECTED COUNTRIES

STANDARD	AUSTRALIA	CANADA	FRANCE	W. GERMANY	ITALY	JAPAN
R & D Costs Expensed Currently?	Yes	Yes	Yes	ND	ND	ND
Pension Fund Contributions Provided Regularly?	Yes	Yes	Yes	Yes	Yes	Yes
Accounting for Investments Less than 20% -Cost Method?	Mixed	Yes	ND	Yes	Mixed	Yes
Acquisition Method -Purchase?	Yes	Yes	Yes	Yes	ND	Yes
Accounting for Goodwill -Amortized ?	Yes	Yes	Yes	Mixed	ND	Yes
Accounting for Minority Interest -Before Bottom Line on Income Statement; Excluded from Stock-holders' Equity?	Yes	ND	Yes	Yes	Yes	Yes

KEY

Yes - most common practice
No - not commonly adhered to; small number may adhere to standard
Mixed - more than one method used considerably
ND - not disclosed; majority of companies do not disclose method

TABLE 6-12
(Continued)
ACCOUNTING DIFFERENCES WITH A SMALL IMPACT ON EARNINGS/VALUATION
INDUSTRIAL COMPANIES FROM SELECTED COUNTRIES

STANDARD	NETH.	SWEDEN	SWITZ.	UK	US
R & D Costs Expensed Currently?	ND	ND	ND	Yes	Yes
Pension Fund Contributions Provided Regularly?	Yes	Yes	ND	Yes	Yes
Accounting for Investments Less than 20% -Cost Method?	Yes	Mixed	ND	ND	Yes
Acquisition Method -Purchase?	Yes	Yes	Yes	Yes	Yes
Accounting for Goodwill -Amortized ?	Mixed	Yes	ND	No	Yes
Accounting for Minority Interest -Before Bottom Line on Income Statement; Excluded from Stock-holders Equity?	Yes	Yes	Yes	Yes	Yes

KEY

Yes - most common practice
No - not commonly adhered to; small number may adhere to standard
Mixed - more than one method used considerably
ND - not disclosed; majority of companies do not disclose method

TABLE 6-13
MAJOR ACCOUNTING DIFFERENCES AMONG COUNTRIES
INDUSTRIAL COMPANIES

Country	Revaluation Allowed	Consolidated Financial Data	Valuation Long-Term Investments 20% - 50%	Inventory Valuation Methods
North America				
Canada	Yes	E	Equity	FIFO
Mexico	Yes	M	Equity	Rep. Cost
United States	No	E	Equity	FIFO
Asia/Pacific				
Australia	Yes	E	Eq/PC	FIFO
Hong Kong	Yes	E	Cost/Eq	FIFO
Japan	No	M	Cost/Eq	Average
Korea, South	Yes	L	Cost	Average
Malaysia	Yes	E	Cost/Eq	FIFO
New Zealand	Yes	M	Equity	FIFO
Singapore	Yes	E	Equity	Average
Europe				
Austria	Yes	L	Cost	Not. Disc
Belgium	Yes	L	Cost/Eq	Mixed
Denmark	Yes	M	Equity	FIFO
Finland	Yes	M	Cost	FIFO
France	Yes	M	Equity	FIFO
Germany, West	Yes	M	Cost	Average
Italy	Yes	L	Cost/Eq	Mixed
Netherlands	Yes	E	Equity	FIFO
Norway	Yes	M	Cost/Eq	FIFO
Spain	Yes	L	Cost/Eq	Average
Sweden	Yes	E	Cost/Eq	FIFO
Switzerland	Yes	M	Cost/Eq	Average
United Kingdom	Yes	E	Equity	FIFO
Africa/Middle East				
South Africa	No	E	Equity	FIFO

Key:

Consolidated Financial Data

E Extensively Disclosed
M Moderately Disclosed
L Less Frequently Disclosed

Valuation of Long-Term Investments 20-50%

Eq/PC Equity Method; partially consolidated
Cost/Eq Cost Method or Equity Method

Inventory Valuation Methods

FIFO	First in First Out
Rep. Cost	Replacement Cost
Average	Average Cost
Mixed	No Majority Practice, one of several methods used

TABLE 6-13 (Continued) MAJOR ACCOUNTING DIFFERENCES AMONG COUNTRIES: INDUSTRIAL COMPANIES				
Country	Deferred Income Taxes	Discretionary and/or Non-Equity Reserves	Currency Translation G/L Taken To	Depreciation Methods
<u>North America</u>				
Canada	Used	Not Used	IS/Defer	SL
Mexico	Used	Not Used	ND	SL
United States	Used	Not Used	IS/SE	SL
<u>Asia/Pacific</u>				
Australia	Used	Not Used*	IS/SE	SL
Hong Kong	Used	Not Used*	IS/SE	SL
Japan	Not Used	Not Used*	IS/Defer	AM
Korea, South	Not Used	Not Used*	IS/Defer	AM
Malaysia	Used	Not Used*	IS	SL
New Zealand	Used	Not Used*	IS/SE	SL
Singapore	Used	Not Used*	IS	SL
<u>Europe</u>				
Austria	Not Used	Used	ND	SL
Belgium	Not Used	Used	IS/SE	SL
Denmark	Used	Used	IS/SE	SL
Finland	Not Used	Used	IS/Defer	SL
France	Used	Used	IS/SE	SL
Germany, West	Not Used	Used	IS/SE	Mixed
Italy	Not Used	Used	IS/Defer	SL
Netherlands	Used	Not Used	IS/SE	SL
Norway	Used	Used	IS	SL
Spain	Not Used	Used	IS/Defer	SL
Sweden	Not Used	Used	IS/SE	SL
Switzerland	Not Used	Used	SE	SL
United Kingdom	Used	Not Used*	IS/SE	SL
<u>Africa/Middle East</u>				
South Africa	Used	Not Used*	IS/SE	SL

Key:

<u>Depreciation Methods</u>

SL Straight Line Method
AM Accelerated Method

<u>Currency Translation Gains/Losses Taken to:</u>

IS Income Statement
SE Shareholders' Equity
IS/Defer Income Statement and/or Deferred
IS/SE Income Statement and/or Shareholders' Equity
ND Not Disclosed

*Specific items such as replacement reserves or excess depreciation used.

TABLE 6-14 MAJOR ACCOUNTING DIFFERENCES AMONG COUNTRIES: BANKS				
Country	Valuation of Marketable Securities	Allow. Loan Losses Fixed By Law	Valuation of Long-Term Investment	Hidden or Non-Equity Reserves
North America				
Canada	MV	Yes	PP	No
United States	MV	No	PP	No
Asia/Pacific				
Australia	MV	No	PP	No
Hong Kong	LCM	Yes	PP/Amort	No
Japan	LCM	Yes	PP	No
Korea, South	LCM	Yes	PP	No
Malaysia	LCM	No	PP/Amort	No
Singapore	LCM	No	PP/MV	No
Europe				
Austria	LCM	ND	PP	Sep'd
Belgium	HC	No	PP	No
Denmark	MV	No	MV	SE
Finland	LCM	Yes	PP	Sep'd
France	LCM	No	PP	Sep'd
Germany, West	LCM	Yes	PP	Sep'd
Italy	LCM	Yes	PP	Sep'd
Netherlands	MV	No	MV	SE
Norway	LCM	Yes	PP	Sep'd
Spain	LCM	Yes	PP/MV	Sep'd
Sweden	LCM	Yes	MV	Sep'd
Switzerland	LCM	No	LCM	Sep'd
United Kingdom	MV	No	LCM	No
Africa/Middle East				
South Africa	MV	No	MV	No

KEY:

Valuation of Marketable Securities

MV	Market Value
HC	Historical Cost
LCM	Lower of Cost or Market
ND	Not Determinable

Valuation of Long-Term Investments

PP	Purchase Price
PP/Amort	Purchase Price Adjusted by Amortization of Premiums or Discounts
PP/MV	Purchase Price Adjusted by Market Value
MV	Market Value
LCM	Lower of Cost or Market

Hidden or Non-equity Reserves

NO	Do Not Exist
Sep'd	Exist and Separately Accounted For
SE	Exist and Accounted for as a Part of Shareholders' Equity

TABLE 6-14 (Continued) MAJOR ACCOUNTING DIFFERENCES AMONG COUNTRIES: BANKS			
Country	Customers' Liability For Acceptances	Interest Inc/Exp Disclosed	Commissions Earned/Paid Disclosed
North America			
Canada	TA	Gross	ND
United States	TA	Gross	Gross
Asia/Pacific			
Australia	TA	Gross	Net
Hong Kong	TA	ND	ND
Japan	TA	Gross	Gross
Korea, South	TA	Gross	Gross
Malaysia	TA	ND	ND
Singapore	TA	ND	ND
Europe			
Austria	TA/pt	Gross	Net
Belgium	FN	Gross	Gross
Denmark	TA/pt	Gross	Net
Finland	FN	Gross	Net
France	FN	Gross	Gross
Germany, West	TA/pt	Gross	Gross
Italy	FN	Gross	Gross
Netherlands	FN	Net	Net
Norway	FN	Gross	Net
Spain	FN	Gross	Net
Sweden	FN	Net/FN	Gross
Switzerland	FN	Gross	Gross
United Kingdom	FN	Net/FN	Net
Africa/Middle East			
South Africa	TA	ND	ND

Key:

Customers Liability for Acceptances

TA	As a Part of Total Assets
TA/pt	Partially as a Part of Total Assets
FN	Disclosed Only in a Footnote

Commissions Earned/Paid Disclosed

Gross	Gross Amounts on Income Statement
Net	Net Amounts on Income Statement
Net/FN	Net Amounts on Income Statement and Gross Amounts on a Footnote
ND	Not Disclosed Separately

TABLE 6-15 MAJOR ACCOUNTING DIFFERENCES AMONG COUNTRIES: INSURANCE COMPANIES						
Country	Life/ Non-Life by the Same Company	Fixed Income Securities Valuation	Equity Securities Valuation	Reinsurance Business	Underwriting Expenses Disclosed	Hidden or Non-Equity Reserves
<u>North America</u>						
Canada	No	AC	HC	ND	GAE	ND
United States	Yes	AC	MP	Net	Sep	NE
<u>Asia/Pacific</u>						
Australia	No	HC	MP	Gross	Sep	ND
Hong Kong	No	LCM	HC	Net	GAE	ND
Japan	No	LCM	LCM	Gross	GAE	NE
Korea, South	No	AC	LCM	Gross	GAE	NE
Malaysia	Yes	HC	MP	Net	Sep	NE
Singapore	Yes	HC	MP	ND	Sep	NE
<u>Europe</u>						
Austria	Yes	ND	ND	Net	Sep	Sep
Belgium	Yes	LCM	MP	Gross	Sep	Sep
Denmark	Yes	AC	MP	Net	GAE	ND
Finland	Yes	AC	MP	Gross	Sep	Sep
France	Yes	HC	HC	Net	Sep	Sep
Germany, West	Yes	AC	LCM	Net	Sep	ND
Italy	Yes	LCM	LCM	Net	Sep	ND
Netherlands	Yes	AC	MP	Gross	Sep	Sep
Norway	Yes	LCM	LCM	Net	GAE	Sep
Spain	Yes	HC	LACM	Net	Sep	Not Sep
Sweden	Yes	LCM	LCM	Net	GAE	Sep
Switzerland	Yes	LCM	LCM	Net	GAE	ND
United Kingdom	Yes	MP	MP	Gross	GAE	NE
<u>Africa/Middle East</u>						
South Africa	No	AC	MP	Net	GAE	ND

Key:

<u>Fixed Income and Equity Securities Valuation</u>

AC	Amortized Cost
HC	Historical Cost
MP	Market Price
LCM	Lower of Cost or Market
ND	Not Disclosed
LACM	Lower Cost and Partial Adjustment to Market

<u>Reinsurance Business</u>

Gross	Gross Amounts on Individual Accounts are Disclosed
Net	Only Net Reinsurance Results are Disclosed

<u>Underwriting Expenses Disclosed</u>

GAE	Part of General Administrative Expenses
Sep	Separately Disclosed

<u>Hidden or Non-Equity Reserves</u>

NE	Do Not Exist
Sep	Exist and Separately Accounted For
Not Sep	Exist but Not Separately Accounted For
ND	Not Disclosed

TABLE 6-16

MAJOR DIFFERENCES IN ACCOUNTING STANDARDS
BETWEEN THE UNITED KINGDOM AND THE UNITED STATES

Items	United Kingdom GAAP	United States GAAP
1. Deferred Income Taxes		
• Method Used	• Liability Method	• Deferral Method
• Coverage	• Partially Used (Only if probable to be payable in foreseeable future)	• Fully Used
2. Property Revaluation	• Allowed Under Certain Circumstances	• Not Allowed
3. Dividends	• Proposed Amounts	• Declared Amounts
4. Gain or Loss on Foreign Currency Forward Exchange Contracts	• Not Allowed	• Allowed
5. Extraordinary Items	• Broad Definition	• Narrow Definition
6. Discontinued Operation	• Part of Extraordinary Items	• Separate Item
7. Foreign Currency Translation of Income Statement Items	• Fiscal Year-End Rate	• Average Rate
8. Goodwill	• Write-down Against Reserve	• 40 Years of Amortization
9. Convertible Cumulative Redeemable Preferred Shares	• As a Part of Shareholders' Equity	• Separate Item
10. Capitalization of Interest Expenses on Long-Term Contracts	• Not Capitalized	• Deferred and Amortized
11. Exceptional Pension Contributions	• Charged When Payable	• Deferred and Amortized

TABLE 6-17

MAJOR FINANCIAL ITEMS UNDER
UNITED KINGDOM AND UNITED STATES ACCOUNTING STANDARDS
FOR SELECTED UK-BASED COMPANIES
FISCAL YEAR 1987

	Net Income (£ in MM)		Earnings (£ Per Share)		Shareholders' Equity (£ in MM)	
UK-based Companies	UK GAAP	US GAAP	UK GAAP	US GAAP	UK GAAP	US GAAP
British Airways	148	155	.205	.220	605	410
Beecham Group Plc	199	189	.271	.250	1,276	1,372
Glaxo Holdings Plc	496	481	.670	.650	1,450	1,460
Reuters Holdings Plc	109	93	.260	.221	218	384
Saatchi & Saatchi Co. Ltd	67	33	.459	.215	40	628

TABLE 6-18

MAJOR DIFFERENCES IN ACCOUNTING STANDARDS
BETWEEN SWEDISH GAAP AND US GAAP

Items	Swedish GAAP	United States GAAP
1. Special Reserves and Provisions (Allocations to untaxed reserves)	• Allowed	• Not Allowed
2. Deferred Income Taxes	• Not Allowed	• Allowed
3. Classification of Accumulated Foreign Currency Translation Adjustment	• Distribute Them Between Restricted and Unrestricted Retained Earnings	• Separate Item as a Part of Shareholders' Equity
4. Revaluation of Assets	• Allowed in Certain Circumstances	• Not Allowed
5. Valuation of Investment Assets	• Write-up and Write-down	• Only Write-down
6. Capitalization of Interest Expenses for Construction	• Not Allowed	• Allowed
7. Early Termination Benefits	• Capitalized and Amortized	• Expensed in the Year
8. Revenue Recognition of Long-Term Contracts	• Completion Method	• Percentage of Completion
9. Equity Earnings of Associated Companies (20-50%)	• Generally Cost Method (recently some use equity method)	• Equity Method
10. Earnings Per Share Calculation	• Income Before Extraordinary Items	• After Extraordinary Items

TABLE 6-19

MAJOR FINANCIAL ITEMS UNDER
SWEDISH AND UNITED STATES ACCOUNTING STANDARDS
FOR SELECTED SWEDISH COMPANIES
FISCAL YEAR 1987

	Net Income (In Millions of Swedish Kronor)		Earnings (Per Share in Swedish Kronor)		Shareholders' Equity (in Millions of Swedish Kronor)	
Swedish Companies	Swedish GAAP	US GAAP	Swedish GAAP	US GAAP	Swedish GAAP	US GAAP
Atlas Copco AB	459	634	15.40	27.00	3,258	3,820
Electrolux AB	1,282	1,833	25.6 *	25.0*	9,914	11,340
Ericsson (LM) Telefon AB	495	657	17.9	17.22	7,468	8,684
SKF AB	739	288	20.9	10.65	9,632	9,125
Volvo AB	3,291	1,345	57.80	59.70	12,264	20,092

*Fully Diluted

TABLE 6-20

ACCOUNTING STANDARDS MODIFICATION TO US GAAP
FOR FOREIGN USERS OF THE CONSOLIDATED FINANCIAL STATEMENTS
IN JAPAN

Items	Japanese GAAP	Adjustment to US GAAP
1. Deferred Income Taxes	• Not Used	• Partially Applied
2. Compensated Absences	• Expensed when Paid	• Partially Accrued
3. Foreign Currency Translation Adjustments	• Modified Temporal Method	• Mainly Current Rate Method
4. Valuation of Marketable Equity Securities	• Lower of Cost or Market (Individual Basis)	• Lower of Cost or Market (Aggregate Basis)
5. Classification of Business Tax	• As a Part of Selling, General, and Administrative Expenses	• As a Part of Income Taxes
6. Appropriation for Special Reserves	• Allowed	• Not Allowed

TABLE 6-21

MAJOR FINANCIAL ITEMS UNDER
JAPANESE ACCOUNTING STANDARDS AND US GAAP MODIFICATION
FOR SELECTED JAPANESE COMPANIES

1987 OPERATING RESULTS

Japanese Companies	Net Income (In Millions of Japanese Yen)		Earnings Per Share (In Japanese Yen)		Shareholders' Equity (In Millions of Japanese Yen)	
	Japan	US GAAP	Japan	US GAAP	Japan	US GAAP
Denny's Japan Co. Ltd	2,557	2,528	95.63	94.5	33,964	26,584
Nitto Electric Ind.	8,275	8,107	56.22	52.91	117,173	115,545
Seven-Eleven Japan	18,390	18,937	150.49	155.0	82,757	85,107
Sumitomo Corp.	28,924	30,184	37.22	37.01	342,368	335,580
Uny Co. Ltd.	9,672	8,454	62.90	52.36	128,776	130,746

TABLE 6-22

COMPARISON OF FINANCIAL DATA BETWEEN COMPANIES UNDER PURE JAPANESE GAAP AND US GAAP ADJUSTMENTS FOR SELECTED COMPANIES IN THE ELECTRONICS INDUSTRY

	Japanese GAAP*	US GAAP Adjustment**
Financial Data	Average	Average
1. Depreciation Expenses		
Depreciable Assets/ Total Assets	19.5%	17.5%
Accumulated Depreciation/ Gross Depreciable Assets	59.9%	60.6%
Depreciation Expense/ COGS and SGA	5.5%	6.0%
2. Effective Tax Rate	63.3%	58.3%
3. Operating Margin	4.2%	8.6%
4. Cumulative Foreign Currency Adjustments to Shareholders' Equity	-0.88%	-3.7%
5. Return on Assets	1.87%	2.9%
6. Return on Equity	4.8%	6.3%
7. Price/Earnings	78.1 Times	45.1 Times
8. Price/Book Value	3.18 Times	2.61 Times

Key:

* Average of 15 Japanese Electronics Companies' Financial Statements Prepared under Japanese Accounting Standards

Alps Electric Company, Ltd.
Citizen Watch Co., Ltd.
Hattori, Seiko Co., Ltd.
Konica Corp.
Matsushita Electric Works Ltd.
Minolta Camera Co. Ltd.
Nikon Corp.
Nippondenso Co., Ltd.
Oki Electric Ind. Co. Ltd.
Sharp Corporation
Sumitomo Electric Industries, Ltd.
Tokyo Electric Co. Ltd. (TEC)
Victor Company of Japan Ltd.
Yamaha Corporation
Yokagowa Electric Corp.

** Average of 16 Japanese Electronics Companies' Financial Statements Prepared under US Accounting Standards

Canon Inc.
Casio Computer Company Ltd.
Fuji Photo Film Co., Ltd.
Hitachi Ltd.
Makita Electric Works Ltd.
Matsushita Electric Industrial Co.
Mitsubishi Electric Corporation
Murata Manufacturing Co. Ltd.
NEC Corporation
Olympus Optical Co., Ltd.
Omron Tateisi Electronics Co. Ltd.
Ricoh Co. Ltd.
Sanyo Electric Co. Ltd.
Sony Corporation
TDK Corporation
Toshiba Corporation

TABLE 6-23

ACCOUNTING DIFFERENCES WITH LARGE IMPACT ON EARNINGS
SELECTED COMPANIES IN THE ELECTRONICS INDUSTRY

Accounting Standards	FRANCE Thomson	WEST GERMANY Siemens	ITALY Olivetti	JAPAN Hitachi Ltd.	NETHERLANDS Philips	UK Plessey	US Hewlett-Packard
Financial Statement Cost Basis:							
-Historical Cost?	Yes	Yes	No	Yes	No	No	Yes
-Historical Cost with Revaluation of Assets?	No	No	Yes	No	Yes	Yes	No
Depreciation:							
-Straight Line Method?	Mixed	Mixed	Yes	Accel.	Yes	Yes	Accel.
-Excess Depreciation Used	No	Yes	No	No	No	No	No
Accounting for Long-Term Investments Greater than 50%: -Full Consolidation?	Yes	No	Yes	No	Yes	Yes	Yes

TABLE 6-23
(Continued)
ACCOUNTING DIFFERENCES WITH LARGE IMPACT ON EARNINGS
SELECTED COMPANIES IN THE ELECTRONICS INDUSTRY

Accounting Standards	FRANCE Thomson	WEST GERMANY Siemens	ITALY Olivetti	JAPAN Hitachi Ltd.	NETHERLANDS Philips	UK Plessey	US Hewlett-Packard
Accounting for Long-Term Investments between 21 - 50%: -Equity Method	No, at cost	No, at cost	Yes	Yes	Yes	Yes	Yes
Inventory Cost Method?	Mixed	Not Discl.	Mixed	Mixed	Current Cost	Not Discl.	FIFO
Deferred Taxes Reported?	Yes	No	Yes	Yes	Yes	Yes	Yes
Discretionary Reserves Used?	Yes	Yes	Not Discl.	Yes	Yes	Yes	No
Currency Translation: -Current Method?	Yes	Temporal	Yes	Mixed	Yes	Yes	Not Discl.
-Gains/Losses Reflected in Current Income?	Yes	Yes and/or deferred	Yes	Yes, and to S/E	Yes, and to S/E	Yes, also in S/E	Yes

TABLE 6-24

INTERNATIONAL ACCOUNTING PUBLICATIONS/CONFERENCES

A. International Accounting Organizations:

1. IASC News:
International Accounting Standards Committee (IASC)
41 Kingsway
London WC 2B 6YU
United Kingdom

2. IFAC News & Annual Report:
International Federation of Accountants (IFAC)
540 Madison Avenue
New York, NY 10020

B. Governmental Organizations Involved in International Accounting Standards

1. Bulletin of the European Communities
Official Journal of the European Communities:
(Please contact the nearest EC office)
or write to:
Commission of the European Community
200 Rue de la Loi
B1040 Brussels
Belgium

2. OECD Observer:
Organization for Economic Cooperation and Development
(Please contact the nearest OECD office)
or write to:
OECD
2 Rue Andre Pascal
75775 Paris Cedex 16
France

3. CTC Reporter:
United Nations Centre on Transnational Corporations (UNCTC)
Room DC2-1312
New York, NY 10017
USA

C. Monthly International Accounting Publications

1. International Accounting Bulletin:
Lafferty Publications Ltd.
Axe & Bottel Court, 70 Newcomen St.
London SE1 1YT
United Kingdom

2. World Accounting Report:
Financial Times Business Information Ltd.
Tower House
Southhampton Street
London WC2E 7HA
United Kingdom

Table 6-24
(Continued)

INTERNATIONAL ACCOUNTING PUBLICATIONS/CONFERENCES

D. Publications of International Accounting Firms:

Many of the sixteen international accounting firms studied in this research project publish reference manuals and newsletters on international accounting and auditing standards as well as individual country guides, although the frequency of publication is not regular. We recommend that users request current publications on international accounting topics from the local offices of international accounting firms.

E. Conferences of Academic Organizations:

1. Newsletter: International Accounting Section:
American Accounting Association
5717 Bessie Drive
Sarasota, FL 34233
USA
(Annual conference usually held in August)

2. Center on International Education & Research in Accounting Newsletter:
Center for International Education & Research in Accounting
University of Illinois at Urbana-Champaign
320 Commerce Building (West)
1206 South Sixth Street
Urbana, IL 61820
USA
(Annual conference usually held in April)

3. EAA Newsletter:
European Accounting Association (EAA)
c/o EFMD
40 rue Washington
B-1050 Brussels
Belgium
(Annual conference usually held in April)

VII. DIFFICULTIES IN MERGING FUNDAMENTAL ACCOUNTING DATA WITH CAPITAL MARKET-GENERATED INFORMATION

Users need to combine accounting information with additional information from capital markets in order to complete their assessment of a foreign company's performance. There are some difficulties in obtaining this information and combining it with company-specific accounting data. This section discusses those difficulties.

A. Inconsistent Reporting of International Stock Prices

PROBLEM:

A principal difficulty we have found is that the format for the reporting of stock prices worldwide is not always consistent.

- Though most newspapers list companies in alphabetical order, some newspapers list individual companies under industry classifications (e.g., Financial Times and some Japanese newspapers), thus requiring prior knowledge about the industry classification of companies of interest.
- Identification of different securities (i.e., common stock, preferred stock, long-term securities) is sometimes not clear.
- In some cases, dividends are reported before taxes and, in other cases, they are reported after taxes.

Table 6-25 summarizes the information listed in the stock price sections of the leading newspapers of 24 countries.

SOLUTION:

The preparation of an in-house guide on how to use reported stock prices will improve financial analysis of international companies.

B. Lack of Capital Change Information

PROBLEM:

Information about capital changes of international companies (stock splits, stock dividends and rights offerings) is not readily available on a timely basis.

SOLUTION:

- Multiple sources must be utilized to compile this information, such as:

    - printed services on corporate news worldwide
    - the financial press
    - stock exchange bulletins
    - databases on international stock prices

- Users should persuade stock markets to publish capital change information regularly.

C. Multiple Classes of Common Stock

PROBLEM:

- More than one type of common stock is permitted in several countries, which makes computation of stock-related ratios difficult. Table 6-26 provides a general overview of the various classes of common stock in existence in selected countries.

- In many of these countries, one class of common stock may be "more common" than another. In most cases, the annual report includes selected information for the class which should be considered "common" (such as the earnings per share computations). The other "common shares" are mostly held by related parties and are not traded regularly.

SOLUTION:

Compute common stock-related ratios (such as price/earnings, price/book value, dividend yield and dividend payout), based on the aggregate value of the shares of the different classes of stocks traded.

D. Lack of Information on Local Capital Market Behavior

PROBLEM:

The final problem in this category is that little information is available on domestic capital market preferences. In other words, it is difficult to know how key players in each market use financial data.

The following questions will help illustrate this problem:

- When do companies in different countries increase dividends? An examination of dividend growth vs. earnings growth, will reveal different trends in different countries. For example, US companies tend to reward stockholders sooner, while Japanese companies usually increase dividends only after earnings growth has been maintained.

- Which financial ratios are important in which markets? Current ratios and interest coverage are very important in the US, but not as important in Japan.

- What would be an acceptable limit to the amount of debt companies carry? Japanese and European companies have high leverage ratios compared to US companies.

Tables 6-27, 6-28 and 6-29 provide selected financial ratios for companies from selected countries in the industrial, banking and insurance sectors.

SOLUTIONS:

- Familiarity with the financial environment of the company whose financial ratios are being examined is a logical remedy to the problem of capital market differences. Again, using Japan as an example, an understanding of the locally accepted business practice of banks serving both creditors and stockholders, and the practice of interlocking ownership, enables readers to interpret Japanese financial statement ratios more intelligently. While direct experience with a country is an invaluable means of acquiring environmental familiarity, reading programs (e.g., country guides, articles in the financial press, etc.), and continuing education seminars provide alternative sources of information.

- Cross-tabulate historical results to identify patterns, such as growth in assets vs. growth in net worth, to see to what degree growth is financed by equity.

In summary, international users of company-specific financial data need to analyze a company's stock market performance vis-a-vis the performance indicated by accounting variables such as earnings per share, return on equity, etc. Many users prefer combining both sources of information by computing the price/earnings ratio or market/book value ratio. Though the preparers or auditors are not responsible for providing capital market-related variables, it is useful to discuss these difficulties as they relate to the interpretation of international financial statements.

TABLE 6-25

VARIATIONS IN STOCK PRICE REPORTING FOUND IN NEWSPAPERS FROM SELECTED COUNTRIES

Country/Newspaper	Yearly High/ Low	Amount of Last Dividend Paid	Dividend Yield %	P / E	Previous Day's Volume	Previous Day's High/Low	Previous Day's Closing Price	Net Change
Australia Sydney Morning Herald		X	X	X	X	X	X	X
Yearly data based on calendar year. Includes closing buy/sell offers.								
Austria Die Presse					X		X	
Also includes closing price from two most recent trading sessions.								
Belgium Le Soir							X	
Lists the closing price from two most recent trading sessions.								
Canada Financial Times of Canada	X	X	X	X	X		X	X
Also discloses dates on which latest interim and fiscal year earnings were declared.								
Denmark Berlinske Tidende	X	X	X	X	X	X	X	X
Yearly high and low prices are based on the calendar year. Also includes total capitalization.								
Finland Helsingin Sonomat			X	X	X	X	X	X
Includes final "buy" and "sell" offers, par value of share.								
France Le Monde							X	X
Also lists the closing price from two most recent trading sessions.								
West Germany Frankfurter Allgemeine Zeitung		X					X	
Also includes closing price from two most recent trading sessions.								

TABLE 6-25 (Continued)

VARIATIONS IN STOCK PRICE REPORTING FOUND IN NEWSPAPERS FROM SELECTED COUNTRIES

Country/Newspaper	Yearly High/ Low	Amount of Last Dividend Paid	Dividend Yield %	P / E	Previous Day's Volume	Previous Day's High/Low	Previous Day's Closing Price	Net Change
Hong Kong South China Morning Post	X	X	X	X	X	X	X	X
Gross yield disclosed; yearly comparisons based on calendar year to date.								
Italy Corriere della Sera	X				X		X	X
Two days previous closing price also listed.								
Japan The Japan Times							X	X
No other information disclosed.								
Korea, South Korea Herald				X	X		X	X
No other information disclosed.								
Malaysia New Straits Times	X				X		X	X
Yearly high and low prices are for calendar year to date.								
Mexico Excelsior							X	X
Final "buy" and "sell" offers for day's trading also included.								
Netherlands De Volksrant	X					X	X	
Closing price for previous year and dates of high/low prices also included.								
New Zealand The Evening Post					X		X	X
No other information disclosed.								

TABLE 6-25 (Continued)

VARIATIONS IN STOCK PRICE REPORTING FOUND IN NEWSPAPERS FROM SELECTED COUNTRIES

Country/Newspaper	Yearly High/ Low	Amount of Last Dividend Paid	Dividend Yield %	PE	Volume	Previous Day's High/Low	Previous Day's Closing Price	Net Change
Norway Aftenposten	X				X	X	X	X
Includes final "buy" and "sell" offers. Also includes return over last 12 months.								
Singapore The Straits Times	X		X		X	X	X	X
Yearly high and low prices are for the calendar year.								
South Africa Die Burger		X			X	X	X	X
Also includes EPS figures and closing "buy" and "sell" offers.								
Spain El Pais	X				X	X	X	
Par value of share, closing price for two days previous also disclosed. Yearly high/low prices given for calendar year. Number of days traded for current year given.								
Sweden Svenska Dagbladet	X	X	X		X	X	X	X
Also disclosed are 12 and 24-month percentage changes in price and 5-year average growth rates in price, dividend and EPS.								
Switzerland Neue Zuercher Zeitung							X	
Also disclosed is closing price for two days previous.								
United Kingdom Financial Times		X	X				X	
Other disclosures include date last dividend paid, total market capitalization.								
United States The Wall Street Journal	X	X	X	X	X	X	X	X
Yearly high and low prices are for the preceding 52-week period.								

TABLE 6-26

CHARACTERISTICS OF MULTIPLE CLASSES OF COMMON STOCKS FOR SELECTED COUNTRIES

	Belgium	Denmark	Finland	Mexico	Spain	Sweden	Switzerland
Total Companies Studied	49	47	41	15	45	83	44
Number of Companies With Multiple Classes of Common Stocks	24	18	15	4	5	42	35
% of Companies With Multiple Stocks	49	38	37	27	11	51	80
<u>Characteristic of Multiple Classes of Common Stocks</u>							
Number of Different Classes	4	2	7	2	2	4	4
Different Voting Rights	no	yes	yes	no	no	yes	yes
Different Dividends Paid	yes	yes	yes	no	ND	no	ND
Different Tax Treatment	yes	no	no	no	no	ND	no
Different Market Prices	yes	ND	yes	ND	ND	yes	yes
Different Par Values	yes	no	ND	no	no	ND	yes
Different Ownership Rights	no	ND	ND	yes	yes	yes	yes

ND Not Disclosed

TABLE 6-27
CAPITAL MARKET DIFFERENCES: SELECTED RATIOS
INDUSTRIAL COMPANIES
FISCAL YEAR 1987

Oper. Margin %	Eff. Tax Rate %	Return on Assets %	Return on Equity %	Total Assets Turn-over	Country	No. of Companies	Current Ratio	Common Equity % Assets	Price/ Earnings Ratio	Price/ Book Value Ratio	Dividend Payout %
					North America						
9.2	44.3	4.7	12.8	1.0	Canada	151	1.5	34.3	15.0	1.9	27.9
19.2	28.8	17.0	42.1	0.5	Mexico	15	1.9	44.0	8.5	1.2	6.0
10.1	43.8	5.6	13.7	1.1	United States	1270	1.6	39.2	15.2	2.0	48.6
					Asia/Pacific						
9.5	37.4	5.8	14.4	0.9	Australia	48	1.3	42.1	14.9	1.8	42.5
19.5	14.0	13.6	21.8	0.4	Hong Kong	20	1.4	63.7	7.8	1.3	26.6
2.6	58.9	1.5	5.8	1.3	Japan	300	1.2	25.9	54.9	2.9	79.9
5.0	30.5	2.4	13.6	1.8	Korea, South	14	0.9	17.8	8.2	0.9	23.0
8.4	45.1	3.9	7.0	0.6	Malaysia	25	1.4	54.5	20.8	1.4	63.4
10.8	15.5	9.1	22.2	0.8	New Zealand	20	1.6	41.8	10.5	1.7	17.1
10.1	29.2	6.1	10.2	0.5	Singapore	18	1.8	57.8	19.6	1.8	30.3
					Europe						
-1.2	42.1	0.9	4.4	1.1	Austria	16	1.4	20.2	23.7	1.0	114.6
5.7	34.2	3.9	13.1	1.3	Belgium	33	1.4	32.3	14.8	1.8	47.8
4.3	33.4	3.7	12.1	1.3	Denmark	28	1.5	31.0	11.0	1.3	40.7
6.3	17.5	2.9	16.7	0.9	Finland	32	1.5	18.1	15.7	2.1	26.6
3.9	42.4	3.6	20.0	1.2	France	126	1.3	19.9	9.7	1.6	21.5
2.7	52.8	2.7	10.2	1.4	Germany, West	151	1.8	26.1	22.1	2.2	45.1
7.6	24.6	4.7	17.7	0.8	Italy	36	1.3	21.4	8.0	1.4	23.7
5.5	21.6	4.5	14.2	1.3	Netherlands	42	1.5	30.8	6.1	0.9	34.6
4.4	29.9	2.7	17.2	1.1	Norway	28	1.2	15.1	10.8	1.8	36.9
5.5	21.3	3.1	8.0	0.9	Spain	25	1.3	40.7	18.8	1.2	38.8
6.4	34.6	3.4	19.9	1.2	Sweden	63	1.6	19.0	18.9	3.1	31.3
16.3	71.8	4.3	9.1	0.9	Switzerland	25	2.2	48.5	11.1	1.0	25.9
8.7	36.6	7.4	17.5	1.2	United Kingdom	232	1.5	42.9	12.1	2.0	35.4
					Africa/Middle East						
13.1	39.6	8.5	18.2	1.1	South Africa	60	1.6	47.7	12.3	2.0	43.3

Source: Worldscope Industrial Company Profiles (1989)

TABLE 6-28
CAPITAL MARKET DIFFERENCES: SELECTED RATIOS
BANKS
FISCAL YEAR 1987

Return on Assets %	Return on Equity %	Eff. Tax Rate %	Total Int. Inc. % Earning Assets	Reserve for Loan Loss-% Total Loans	Country	No. of Companies	Earning Assets % Total Assets	Equity % Total Assets	Price/ Earnings Ratio	Price/ Book Value Ratio	Dividend Payout %
					North America						
-0.3	-8.6	36.9	9.0	1.8	Canada	5	89.0	3.5	NC	1.0	NC
-0.3	-6.1	n/a	10.5	3.3	United States	88	84.4	4.5	NC	1.0	NC
					Asia/Pacific						
0.6	13.6	51.4	17.1	1.7	Australia	5	75.6	4.7	15.0	1.7	34.5
0.3	12.5	54.4	6.3	0.9	Japan	68	72.5	2.1	76.1	8.4	21.9
0.1	5.0	34.2	6.9	1.5	Korea, South	6	65.6	2.9	30.9	1.3	45.4
					Europe						
0.5	8.3	21.7	11.1	n/a	Denmark	8	74.5	6.4	8.3	0.6	36.4
0.3	13.0	35.7	10.7	5.3	France	14	93.5	2.6	9.1	1.0	22.4
0.2	6.6	54.3	6.8	n/a	Germany, West	19	91.4	3.1	29.1	1.8	69.0
0.5	11.9	40.7	9.9	3.6	Italy	16	81.4	4.4	9.4	1.0	27.2
0.4	10.5	27.5	2.2	n/a	Netherlands	5	95.8	4.0	10.1	0.9	47.4
0.9	19.0	20.8	12.3	4.2	Spain	8	80.8	4.8	15.3	2.7	34.1
0.4	30.6	38.2	2.5	0.5	Sweden	5	93.3	1.3	16.8	4.1	53.3
0.5	7.9	33.3	5.3	n/a	Switzerland	6	89.5	6.0	19.5	1.4	65.9
nom	-0.6	n/a	12.5	4.4	United Kingdom	8	86.1	5.0	NC	0.9	NC
					Africa/Middle East						
0.7	12.7	41.7	n/a	n/a	South Africa	5	80.9	4.4	8.9	1.2	42.1

Source: Worldscope Financial and Service Company Profiles (1988)

NC = Not Computed due to negative earnings per share

TABLE 6-29
CAPITAL MARKET DIFFERENCES: SELECTED RATIOS
INSURANCE COMPANIES
FISCAL YEAR 1987

Return on Assets %	Return on Equity %	Eff. Tax Rate %	Net Premium Written % Equity	Benefit & Loss Reserve % Total Cap	Country	No. of Companies	Equity % Total Assets	Equity Sec. & Real Estate % Inv't Assets	Price/ Earnings Ratio	Price/ Book Value Ratio	Dividend Payout %
					North America						
0.2	0.1	16.6	286.5	721.3	Canada	7	7.1	15.8	n/a*	n/a*	n/a*
2.4	16.6	12.5	224.5	183.3	United States	47	13.5	7.2	7.7	1.2	26.2
					Asia/Pacific						
0.2	25.9	88.7	1590.0	n/a	Australia	5	1.1	79.6	n/a	n/a	n/a
0.3	3.2	20.1	285.1	24.6	Japan	19	10.6	41.2	73.9	1.9	33.6
					Europe						
0.6	6.8	37.9	115.2	552.1	Denmark	5	9.7	9.2	15.7	1.0	18.3
2.1	21.7	12.0	386.0	627.7	France	7	8.6	42.3	7.0	1.3	15.6
0.4	8.7	47.2	498.3	920.3	Germany, West	17	5.0	29.3	106.3	7.7	51.5
1.6	12.5	35.9	228.6	344.1	Italy	5	12.9	31.9	71.5	8.6	36.0
1.0	9.8	24.6	157.9	410.6	Netherlands	5	9.8	18.4	19.4	1.8	51.2
0.6	7.6	28.1	399.8	760.1	Switzerland	7	7.9	20.2	77.2	5.1	57.8
1.0	16.9	30.9	364.9	287.5	United Kingdom	14	5.9	57.4	16.7	2.6	48.2

Source: Worldscope Financial and Service Company Profiles (1988)

*n/a - not applicable

VIII. SUMMARY AND CONCLUSIONS

The "answers" provided above represent specific approaches to international financial statement analysis. Ultimately, a more coherent, systematic approach to financial analysis at the international level must be developed.

After the accounting numbers of companies from different countries in a given industry have been made comparable, it is easier to construct industry averages within a region or worldwide. A practical framework is needed for users to analyze the financial statements of companies in a given industry across national boundaries. The following steps are suggested to aid in the development of a comprehensive global industry analysis system:

A. Develop a standard chart of accounts to facilitate format compatibility of data internationally.

B. Compile company-specific accounting practices so accounting differences can be analyzed by company, industry and country.

C. Compute financial ratios by:
- Industry within country
- Country averages
- Industry within region
- Regional averages
- Industry globally

D. Develop computer software logic to allow users to convert financial data on any company from one country's accounting standards, currency and language, into another country's accounting standards, currency and language.

In conclusion, this chapter has attempted to provide some suggestions on how to compensate for accounting differences internationally. Further research is needed to empirically document the impact of accounting differences on earnings and balance sheet accounts in order for users to restate financial statements fully in the accounting conventions of their home country.

CHAPTER 7

INTERNATIONAL ACCOUNTING TRENDS SUMMARY AND CONCLUSIONS

I. SUMMARY RESEARCH DESIGN

The primary objective of Chapters 1 through 7 has been to examine international accounting trends. Over the last four years we have been studying the financial statements of over 5,000 companies in 24 countries. Depending on the scope of a chapter or the research question which needed to be addressed, we used either the full data base of companies or a subset. In order to provide timely data, we focused on annual reports from fiscal year 1987 and interim reports from fiscal year 1988.

II. MAJOR FINDINGS

This final chapter of "International Accounting Trends" summarizes the major conclusions drawn in Chapters 2 through 6 of this study.

A. Accounting Standards Practiced by Industrial Companies in 24 Countries

Our analysis focused on differences in accounting standards in use as they affect the valuation of assets and liabilities and income determination. In the process, major differences have been identified as follows:

- Not all subsidiaries of which the parent company owns 50% or more are consistently consolidated, thus giving an incomplete picture of the company's performance. Furthermore, different methods of accounting for long-term investments make net income less comparable.
- Inventory valuation methods vary, affecting the cost of goods sold figure and inventory values.
- Various methods used in depreciating fixed assets make depreciation expenses and net fixed assets noncomparable, particularly when the economic lives of assets are not considered and tax laws allow much faster depreciation.
- Differing approaches to the revaluation of fixed assets for price changes affect depreciation expenses, net fixed assets and shareholders' equity (since revaluation reserves are usually reported in the shareholders' equity section).
- Local rules allowing discretionary or general purpose reserves reduce the comparableness of the true performances of companies internationally.
- Due to differences in foreign currency translation methods and the treatment of resulting gains or losses, net income and affected balance sheet items are not comparable.

B. Financial Reporting Practices of Industrial Companies in 24 Countries

The financial reporting practices in which the fewest variations exist are the following:

- Format and content of basic financial statements (i.e., income statement, balance sheet and statement of changes in financial position)
- Information about management and board members
- Use of footnotes explaining financial items

The widest gaps in financial reporting practices worldwide are in:

- Reporting of subsidiary company information
- Disclosure of segment and geographic information
- Disclosure of earnings per share data

C. Financial Statements of Banks and Insurance Companies in 22 Countries

We found that financial reporting practices vary more than accounting standards among banks and insurance companies worldwide. For industrial companies the reverse was true.

- There are many valuation methods for both fixed-income securities and equity securities (either historical cost, current market price or "lower of cost or market" are used).

- For banks, a variety of items classified under "customers' liabilities for acceptances" are included in or excluded from total assets in roughly an equal number of cases.

- For both banks and insurance companies components of total revenues are not clearly segregated in many countries. For example, commission income and commission expenses are often netted in some countries.

D. Interim Financial Statements of Industrial Companies in 20 Countries

Interim reporting across national boundaries can be categorized into four groups:

- Reports from Canadian, Japanese and US companies generally provide the most information.

- Continental European companies disclose slightly less information than their Canadian, Japanese or US counterparts.

- Companies in the Commonwealth countries report less information than those in the countries noted above.

III. IMPLICATIONS FOR THE FUTURE

Based on our research, numerous discussions with users of international financial statements and our observation of the progress made toward the harmonization of accounting standards and financial reporting practices worldwide, we believe that international accounting will move in the direction summarized below:

A. International Listings Will Increase

Companies are increasingly listing their securities on stock exchanges outside of their home country along with their domestic exchange. As a result of this increase in international listings, the number of international shareholders will also rise. Preparers will need to expand annual reports to provide additional information which international users need. These internationally listed firms will also provide restated key financial numbers under several countries' accounting standards (depending on the locations of their shareholders) to facilitate better understanding of their performance among these international users.

B. Investment in Foreign Securities by Institutional Investors Will Increase

Trustees of pension funds and other institutional money managers are increasingly investing in foreign securities in order to diversify their portfolios and obtain better returns. In addition, in some countries (e.g., Japan and Switzerland) pension funds have been allowed to be invested in foreign equity securities. This increase in the number of worldwide users of international financial statements has in turn helped to expedite the process of improved financial reporting and harmonization of accounting standards. These users in many cases are institutional investors with large resources from which to invest. Thus, their collective voice can exert considerable influence on preparers and accounting standard setters.

C. Globalization of Brokerage Firms' Research

We believe that the prices of international stocks purchased by international investors will be determined internationally rather than on the listed company's local stock exchange. Therefore, company and industry research being done at international brokerage firms must also be globalized. Brokerage firms usually have their analysts follow companies in a particular industry, so a cadre of global industry analysts (or in some instances regional analysts) will emerge.

Such globalization of brokerage firms' research should pinpoint a lack of information on companies from certain countries. Given the importance of these international capital market intermediaries, preparers of financial statements will need to provide these analysts with necessary information. We predict that ultimately the annual reports in those countries will expand in scope to include these additional items.

D. Accounting Standard Setters Will Reduce Available Alternatives of Accounting Standards

Efforts are under way at the International Accounting Standards Committee (IASC) to reduce, and in some instances, eliminate the alternatives existing in various accounting standards. In the near future, the focus of international, regional and national institutions responsible for setting accounting standards will be to streamline the existing body of accounting standards.

E. Increased Cooperation Between Stock Exchanges to Harmonize Filings

There will be more discussion among stock exchanges and national capital market regulators at least in major markets in the near future leading to reciprocal acceptance of annual and other filings by listed companies (i.e., home country filings will be acceptable to other capital markets).

Due to the integration of capital markets within the EC, such efforts will take place in Europe first, but similar action will be taken between Canada, Japan, the UK and the US.

In conclusion, harmonization efforts will continue in the future. International and regional standard setting groups such as the IASC and the EC are facilitating the harmonization of accounting standards and financial reporting practices. In our view, however, the movement toward international harmonization will be driven by users, and to a certain extent preparers, of financial statements, rather than by standard setters.

The role of leading international accounting firms is crucial in harmonizing accounting standards worldwide for several reasons. First, further development and harmonization of international auditing practices are important for international users. Second, these firms can facilitate the harmonization of accounting standards by assisting preparers of annual reports with the adoption of international accounting standards. Third, they can draw upon their vast resources to assist users in analyzing international financial statements.

The second section of this study examines the major accounting firms worldwide and identifies international auditing trends.

CHAPTER 8

INTERNATIONAL AUDITING TRENDS
INTRODUCTION AND RESEARCH DESIGN

Table of Contents

CHAPTER 8

INTERNATIONAL AUDITING TRENDS
INTRODUCTION AND RESEARCH DESIGN

This study is divided into two broad sections:

1. International Accounting Trends (Chapters 1 through 7)

2. International Auditing Trends (Chapters 8 through 14)

I. INTRODUCTION

The objective of Chapters 9 through 14 is to further define the areas of competition among international accounting firms, and to examine the recent trends in audit fees and auditors' reports in order to draw conclusions about trends in the global accounting services industry. Specifically, we wish to determine the elements of global competition and identify the principal international accounting firms which compete in an increasingly complex international environment.

II. OVERVIEW OF CHAPTERS 9 THROUGH 14

Chapter 9 presents an analysis of the global organizations of the leading sixteen international accounting firms based on their offices and number of partners worldwide.

Chapter 10 contains an analysis of the global client base of the leading international accounting firms.

Chapter 11 presents factors which determine audit fees, based on data available in the annual reports of client companies in 9 countries.

Chapter 12 compares differences in auditors' reports and promptness in completing the external audit in 24 countries.

Chapter 13 explains how to undertake a global competitive analysis, utilizing a questionnaire approach.

Chapter 14 presents major findings on global competition among the 16 leading international accounting firms.

III. RESEARCH QUESTIONS

The following questions are addressed in Chapters 9 through 13:

Chapter 9 Global Competitive Analysis of International Accounting Firms Based on Organization

9-1 Where are the offices of the international accounting firms located throughout the world?

9-2 How have leading international accounting firms organized their offices worldwide under their international name, under a combined name or under the local name?

9-3 Which regions, countries and major cities have the highest number of offices and partners among leading international accounting firms?

9-4 What is the average number of partners per office for each of these international accounting firms worldwide?

9-5 How have the leading international accounting firms grown globally in recent years?

9-6 How are the top international accounting firms ranked globally?

9-7 How has the 1987 merger of Klynveld Main Goerdeler (KMG) and Peat Marwick Mitchell & Co. (PMM) affected the international competitive rankings of accounting firms globally and regionally?

9-8 Where and when have mergers between local firms of leading international firms been most active? Which firms have been most active in mergers?

Chapter 10 Global Competitive Analysis Based on Clients Audited

10-1 Who are the leading accounting firms worldwide based on the number and size of clients they audit?

10-2 Do international accounting firms audit most of the multinational corporations worldwide?

10-3 What is the composition of the client base of the international accounting firms in terms of countries, regions, economy types and common markets?

10-4 Do international accounting firms have any industry concentration on a worldwide, regional or country basis?

10-5 Within specific countries, what is the presence of the leading international accounting firms in terms of client size, as measured by client company sales or assets?

10-6 To what extent are large subsidiaries audited by the parent company's auditor?

10-7 How do partner and office demographics for the international accounting firms relate to client statistics for these firms?

Chapter 11 Audit Fees

11-1 What client company characteristics (i.e., type of industry, multinational operations, size) determine the amount of audit fees paid to external auditors (in countries where audit fee information is published)?

11-2 Are there significant audit fee differences within a country?

11-3 Are there significant cross-national differences in the determination of audit fees as a percentage of sales or assets?

11-4 What has been the trend in audit fees as a percentage of sales or assets in terms of countries and industries over the past six years?

Chapter 12 Audit Opinions

12-1 How do auditors' reports, included in annual reports, compare globally in terms of format and content?

12-2 What are the reasons audit opinions are qualified internationally?

12-3 Is the audit process completed on a timely basis internationally?

Chapter 13 Global Competitive Analysis

13-1 What are some key areas which an international accounting firm should study in order to compare itself with global competitors and position itself for the future?

IV. RESEARCH DESIGN

The basic approach for each of these chapters (9 through 13) was to develop relevant research questions, identify necessary information, select an appropriate sample of companies to study, extract data, build a chapter-specific database, analyze the data, and draw conclusions.

Chapters 9 through 13 are based on the following data sources:

1. Annual reports of selected companies from CIFAR's International Annual Reports Collection of 10,000 companies worldwide.

2. The current office directories of the 16 leading international accounting firms. (Table 8-1 provides a list of these firms.)

3. Auditor data provided by the local offices of international accounting firms for Chapter 10.

4. International company directories and leading company listings.

Because each chapter had a different focus and scope, the sample of companies used in Chapters 9 through 13 was modified appropriately. A more complete discussion of the research design is provided in each chapter. Similarly, a list of countries was modified on the basis of data availability.

TABLE 8-1

LIST OF SIXTEEN INTERNATIONAL ACCOUNTING FIRMS COVERED IN THE STUDY

	Abbreviations Used
Big-8 International Accounting Firms	
1 Arthur Andersen & Company	AA
2 Arthur Young International	AYI
3 Coopers & Lybrand	CL
4 Deloitte Haskins & Sells International	DHSI
5 Ernst & Whinney	EW
6 Klynveld Peat Marwick Goerdeler	KPMG
7 Price Waterhouse	PW
8 Touche Ross International	TRI
Small-8 International Accounting Firms	
9 BDO Binder	BDO
10 Dunwoody Robson McGladrey & Pullen	DRMP
11 Grant Thornton International	GTI
12 Hodgson Landau Brands	HLB
13 Horwath & Horwath International	HHI
14 Moores Rowland International	MRI
15 Pannell Kerr Forster	PKF
16 Spicer & Oppenheim	SO

V. BENEFITS OF THE STUDY (CHAPTERS 9 THROUGH 14)

The study will benefit potential users by:

- Documenting the international networks of leading accounting firms
- Facilitating comparison of the worldwide client base of leading international accounting firms
- Identifying key factors for determining audit fees
- Identifying worldwide trends in auditors' reports

VI. POTENTIAL USERS (CHAPTERS 9 THROUGH 14)

- Partners and managers of international accounting firms
- Strategic planning executives of accounting firms worldwide
- Controllers and financial executives of corporations worldwide
- Students and researchers studying international accounting firms
- Prospective employees of international accounting firms

VII. APPENDICES: E THROUGH H

In addition to the chapters identified above, the second section of this study is supplemented by Appendices E through H. These appendices provide readers with country-specific, industry specific or firm-specific information for the topics covered in Chapters 9, 10, and 11.

The four appendices at the end of the study address the following topics:

Appendix E provides the total number of partners for sixteen international accounting firms by country and city.

Appendix F provides a list of over 16,000 clients of the sixteen leading international accounting firms by country and alphabetical order of client name. Information on sales, assets, fiscal year of sales and assets and industry description are provided. If the client company is a subsidiary, it is identified as such and its parent listed as a foreign or domestic company.

Appendix G provides a list of audit fees, sales, assets, industry description and international auditors for 1,100 clients in nine countries (where audit fees are disclosed in annual reports). The list is arranged by country and alphabetically by client name within the country.

Appendix H provides profiles of the sixteen leading international accounting firms. Partners and the total clients they audit are listed by country and region. Clients are also grouped by industry.

CHAPTER 9
ANALYSIS OF THE GLOBAL NETWORK OF THE OFFICES AND PARTNERS OF SIXTEEN INTERNATIONAL ACCOUNTING FIRMS

Table of Contents

CHAPTER 9

Tables

Tables
(Continued)

I. RESEARCH OBJECTIVES

Our research on the global network of the leading sixteen international accounting firms focused on the following questions:

9-1. Where are the offices of the international accounting firms located throughout the world?

9-2. How have leading international accounting firms organized their offices worldwide: under their international name, a combined name or the local name?

9-3. Which regions, countries and major cities have the highest number of offices and partners among leading international accounting firms?

9-4. What is the average number of partners per office for each of these international accounting firms worldwide?

9-5. How have the leading international accounting firms grown globally in recent years?

9-6. How are the top international accounting firms ranked globally?

9-7. How has the 1987 merger of Klynveld Main Goerdeler (KMG) and Peat Marwick Mitchell & Co. (PMM) affected the international competitive rankings of accounting firms globally and regionally?

9-8. Where and when have mergers between local firms of leading international firms been most active? Which firms have been most active in mergers?

II. RESEARCH DESIGN

A. Variables of Interest

When this project commenced four years ago, the preliminary research resulted in a set of sixteen international accounting firms classified as the big eight and the small eight.

The international office directories of the sixteen largest accounting firms were consulted for the analysis of the firms' global organization. The following data were extracted for each office listed in each firm's directory: country, city, local firm name, organizational structure, and number of partners.

An office was counted for each separate location listed in the directory. A satellite office with a separate address was counted as one office. Special care was taken not to duplicate partners listed for more than one office. In cases where a partner was listed for two or more offices, the partner was counted for the office of the larger city.

Table 9-1 provides a list of the international firms, their abbreviated names and the year of the office directories utilized. The 1982 office directories for the big eight firms were also used for the six-year trend analysis. The abbreviated names will be used to refer to the firms throughout the chapter.

B. Definition of Organizational Structure

Each firm's office was placed into one of four categories of organizational structure. The determination of the structure was based on how the firm's local practice was listed in the directory.

The types of organizational structure used are defined as follows:

1. International Name or Combination of Names

    - The international accounting firm uses its international name to practice in a foreign country or has created a joint name. The joint name combines a firm's international name with the name of a local firm which is fully affiliated with the international firm (such as Thorne, Ernst & Whinney in Canada).

    - The international name and local firm name are used together for a national practice (such as Arthur Young, Clarkson, Gordon Co. in Canada).

    - A country or a local designation (such as Ltd. or S.A.) is added to the firm's international name.

    The international/combined name structure suggests a stronger relationship between the international and local firm.

2. Local Name

    - An international name is used mainly for coordination purposes among member firms and the local name is used exclusively for the local practice.

3. Multiple Affiliations

    - Local accounting firms are affiliated with more than one international accounting firm.

    The total number of offices and partners in multiple affiliation firms were excluded from our totals in order to avoid duplication of numbers, and because the total number was not significant regionally or globally. However, there was some significance in the number of firms with multiple affiliations in Japan, South Korea, Singapore, Thailand and the Philippines.

    A further study of multiple affiliation firms is presented in Section I of this chapter, and the location of these offices can be found in Appendix E.

4. Correspondent Firms

    - A local firm has a relationship with the international firm, mainly through the exchange of client assignments from the international firm. The correspondent is only partially affiliated and generally is not represented on the administrative board.

We excluded correspondent or representative offices listed in the office directories of the sixteen international accounting firms from our analysis of total offices and partners of international firms because these firms do not have full affiliation with the international accounting firms.

A further study of correspondent firms is presented in Section J of this chapter, and the location of the correspondents can be found in Appendix E.

C. Data Difficulties:

1. Each of the sixteen firms publishes its directory at a different time during the year, thus, this analysis reflects a firm at only one point in time in 1982 and 1988. However, each firm publishes its directory around the same time from year to year and, therefore, the 1982 and 1988 comparisons indicate the growth of each firm over the same period of time.

2. Mergers occurring after the publication of the 1988 office directories of the sixteen international accounting firms have not been included.

3. Though most office directories have clearly identified participating principals which were included in the partner count, several directories did not clearly make this distinction.

4. The total number of professional staff may be a better measure for determining the relative standings of international accounting firms, but this number was not published by the office in each country for most international accounting firms. Therefore, we used the total number of partners per city, country, region and worldwide for each of the sixteen accounting firms. It was assumed that in a competitive environment, the ratio of partners to audit staff should be fairly uniform among international accounting firms and the number of partners assigned to a particular office should reflect the level of client practice the firm has at that office.

We believe that the conclusions drawn in this chapter would not be materially different if all of these limitations were resolved; thus the chapter provides a useful comparison of sixteen international accounting firms worldwide based on the number of offices and partners.

TABLE 9-1

SIXTEEN INTERNATIONAL ACCOUNTING FIRMS STUDIED

NAME OF THE ACCOUNTING FIRM	ABBREVIATION	YEAR OF OFFICE DIRECTORY USED
Big Eight		
1. Arthur Andersen & Company	AA	1988
2. Arthur Young International	AYI	1988
3. Coopers & Lybrand	CL	1988
4. Deloitte Haskins & Sells International	DHSI	1988
5. Ernst & Whinney	EW	1988
6. Klynveld Peat Marwick Goerdeler Int'l.	KPMG	1988
7. Price Waterhouse	PW	1988
8. Touche Ross International	TRI	1988
Small Eight		
9. BDO Binder	BDO	1988
10. Dunwoody Robson McGladrey & Pullen	DRMP	1988
11. Grant Thornton International	GTI	1988
12. Horwath & Horwath International	HHI	1988
13. Hodgson Landau Brands International	HLB	1988
14. Moores Rowland International	MRI	1988
15. Pannell Kerr Forster	PKF	1988
16. Spicer & Oppenheim International	SO	1988

III. ANALYSIS

An analysis of the international accounting firms is presented in this section:

A. World Summary

Table 9-2 lists the total number of offices, partners, and average partners per office for each of the sixteen firms. KPMG had the most partners worldwide (5161), while CL was second with 3341, followed by TRI with 2792, and EW with 2721. As shown in Table 9-2, the firms ranging from fourth to eighth in the number of partners were all within 1% of each other in terms of the ratio of each firm's partners to the total number of partners of the sixteen leading accounting firms analyzed. The number of partners of the small eight firms ranged between 1% and 4.5% of the world total.

An analysis of the total number of offices worldwide for all sixteen firms indicates that KPMG had the most offices (641), followed by CL with 565, and TRI with 515.

The highest average number of partners per office was associated with AA (9.83), followed by KPMG (8.05) and EW (7.20). The average number of partners per office was significantly lower for HLB (3.17), DRMP (3.70), and BDO (4.00), in comparison with the other international firms.

Table 9-2 also shows the accounting firms analyzed by number of partners and organizational structure. The total number of partners worldwide was 31,751. The majority (69%) worked in firms which practiced under an international or combined name worldwide, while among individual firms with a majority working under international or combined name, this percentage varied from approximately 51% for GTI to 100% for KPMG.

The remaining 31% of the total number of partners worldwide had the local name structure. It was used by TRI (59.63%) of the big eight and was more commonly used by DRMP, HLB, MRI and SO of the small eight.

B. US and Non-US

Table 9-3 lists the total number of US and non-US offices and partners for each of the sixteen international accounting firms. The international accounting firms with the highest number of partners in the US were KPMG (1794), AA (1351), and EW (1230). KPMG also had the most offices (137), followed by EW (119) and DHSI (113). The firms with the highest number of partners outside the US were KPMG (3367), CL (2174), and TRI (1957). KPMG had the most offices outside the US (504), followed by CL (466) and TRI (428).

The average number of partners per office tended to be higher in the US than outside the US. AA had the highest average number of partners per office in the US, followed by KPMG, CL and SO.

In the small eight, DRMP led in the US with 470 partners, followed by HHI (455) and GTI (376). BDO had the largest number of partners outside the US (1081). Three of the small eight firms, BDO, MRI and GTI, have more partners outside of the US than AA of the big eight.

C. Industrial and Developing Countries

Table 9-4 classifies the total number of offices, partners and the average number of partners per office for each of the sixteen international firms into industrial and developing country classifications. The list of countries included in this study is provided in Table 9-4A. Industrial countries form 86.82% of the total partners worldwide in international accounting firms. The international accounting firms with the highest number of partners in industrial countries included KPMG (4541), CL (2791) and EW (2480). KPMG, with 471 offices, and CL with 397, also led the other firms with the most offices in industrial countries. In the small eight category, BDO (1225), GTI (1179) and MRI (1034) lead in total partners in industrial countries.

Only 13.18% of the total partners in international firms practiced in developing countries. KPMG (620 partners), CL (550 partners) and PW (541 partners) have the most partners and offices in these countries. Among the small eight, HHI (177), BDO (172) and MRI (159) led in terms of the number of partners in the developing countries.

In general, international firms have an average of 6.46 partners per office in industrial countries. Comparatively, in the developing countries, the overall average number of partners per office was 3.23. AA had the highest average of 11.13 partners per office in industrial countries and HHI had the highest average of 5.36 partners per office in developing countries.

D. Regions of the World

The data were analyzed and grouped into the following five regions:

- North America
- Europe
- Asia/Pacific
- Africa/Middle East
- South America/Caribbean

The analysis of the number of offices, partners and average partners per office for the sixteen leading firms in each region appears in Tables 9-5 through 9-7 and is described in the following pages. The countries included in each region are listed in Table 9-7A.

North America (Table 9-5)

The total of 14,886 partners in North America (as shown in Table 9-5) represents 46.9% of the world total. The first eight firms constituted 77.2% of the total partners in North America, while the small eight firms constituted the remaining 22.8% in North America.

KPMG had the largest number of partners, 14.0% of the total partners in North America, followed by EW with 11.8%, CL with 9.9% and AA with 9.7%. EW and DHSI had the most offices, 190 and 176, respectively. AA had the highest average number of partners per office in North America (13.44). KPMG and CL also maintained high averages of 11.97 and 11.35, respectively. Among the small eight, GTI, DRMP and BDO led in the number of offices and partners.

Europe (Table 9-6)

According to our analysis, the total of 10,233 partners located in Europe represents 32.23% of total partners worldwide. KPMG had the most partners (20.8%), followed by CL (9.2%), AYI (9.0%) and TRI (8.0%). The firms with the highest number of offices were KPMG, CL and TRI with 272, 225, and 191, out of a total of 2122 offices in the region. KPMG (7.81), AA (6.92) and PW (6.10) had the highest average number of partners per office. Among the small eight, BDO, MRI and GTI had the most offices and partners in this region.

Asia/Pacific (Table 9-6)

CL had the largest number of partners, with 16.0% of the total partners in this region. It was followed by KPMG (13.7%), TRI (13.0%), and PW (10.1%). Many of the big eight firms had more than 9% of the total partners in the Asia/Pacific region. However, AA (3.3%) ranked below SO (4.0%), HHI (3.9%) and BDO (3.7%), the leading firms among the small eight, in the percentage of total partners in the Asia/Pacific region.

CL also had the highest percentage of offices (15.4%) in the region, followed by TRI with 13.5%, and KPMG (11.4%). DRMP (6.3%) and SO (5.0%) led in the number of offices among the small eight.

The average number of partners per office was highest for AA (7.41), KPMG (6.09) and PW (5.89).

Africa/Middle East (Table 9-7)

Africa and the Middle East have 5.37% of the total partners of the leading sixteen firms. Within this region, KPMG had the highest number of partners (14.4%), followed by CL (10.7%), and DHSI (10.3%). In the small eight, MRI (7.9%) had a higher percentage of total partners than EW (7.6%), PW (7.5%), AYI (6.7%) and AA (2.1%) in the big eight. KPMG, CL, TRI and DHSI had the greatest number of offices in the region. HHI (10.71) had the highest average of partners per office.

South America/Caribbean (Table 9-7)

The leading accounting firms in South America and the Caribbean had 3.33% of total partners worldwide. Based on the total number of partners in this region, PW had 20.2%, followed by KPMG (17.0%) and CL (11.7%). PW and KPMG had a significant margin over other firms in the region. PW also had more offices (56) in the region than KPMG (44) and CL (38).

E. European Community (EC)

Table 9-8 provides an analysis of offices and partners of the accounting firms in the European Community. Twenty-seven percent of total partners worldwide in leading international accounting firms were located within the EC. KPMG had the most partners in the EC (21.4% of the EC total), more than twice the number of CL (8.6%), AYI (8.4%), TRI (7.6%) and PW (7.3%). Out of a total of 1500 EC offices, KPMG had the highest number (197), followed by TRI (138), and AYI (123). MRI and BDO had more offices than four of the big eight international firms and more partners than AA and EW. KPMG had the highest average number of partners per office (9.29), followed by AA with 7.51, and PW with 7.35.

F. Top Ten Countries

The organizational networks of the sixteen largest firms were analyzed by country to determine which countries were of major importance to the firms, measured in terms of the total number of partners. The ten most significant countries for these firms appear in Tables 9-9 through 9-11. Since North America was the most significant region, it is not surprising that the United States had more offices and partners than the other countries (22% of the total 5,567 offices and 35% of the worldwide total of 31,751 partners). For all sixteen firms, the UK was second in number of partners (12%) and third in number of offices (9%). Canada ranked third in number of partners (11%) and second in number of offices (10%).

In Europe, the UK, France and the Netherlands had the highest number of partners. In terms of number of offices, the UK, the Netherlands and West Germany were the leaders. In the Asia/Pacific region, Australia had a significant lead over New Zealand and Japan in terms of the number of offices and partners affiliated with international accounting firms.

KPMG led in seven of the top ten countries in the number of partners, except for Canada, the Netherlands and Japan. EW led in Canada, AYI led in the Netherlands and TRI led in Japan.

Among the small eight firms, in terms of the number of partners, country rankings are as follows: DRMP led in the US; GTI led in the UK and Canada; PKF led in Australia, BDO led both in the Netherlands and West Germany; HLB in France; SO in New Zealand. MRI, a small eight firm, was second to KPMG in South Africa (118 and 122 partners, respectively), and HHI ranked fifth in Japan among all sixteen firms.

An analysis of the average number of partners per office indicated that Japan (9.70 partners per office), France (9.34 partners per office) and the US (9.08 partners per office) led over the other major countries. With the exception of South Africa, a sizeable difference exists in the partners per office between big eight and small eight firms. (Table 9-11)

G. Organizational Structure by Region and Countries

Several trends in organizational structure can be noted in Table 9-12. Globally, 69% of the firms practiced under the international or combined name rather than the local name. North America had 81%, Asia/Pacific had 64% and Europe had 59% of the region's partners in this category.

An analysis of the organizational structures of firms in industrial and developing countries indicates that more than 71% of the total partners in industrial countries practice under an international name, as opposed to 56% in developing countries.

Ninety percent of US partners practice under the international or combined name. Other countries with a similar practice include the UK (84%), New Zealand (85%), Australia (73%) and Canada (56%). On the other hand, in Japan (61%), France (43%), the Netherlands (67%) and West Germany (87%), more than one-third of partners are practicing under the local name. This may reflect local regulations concerning the firm's name.

In addition, analysis of the European Community (EC) indicates that 63% of partners in the community practiced under an international or combined name.

H. Top 25 Cities

In the global grouping of partners in the sixteen largest international accounting firms, 36% were located in the 25 major cities listed in Table 9-13. New York and London led the world in terms of the number of partners per city, with New York ahead by fourteen partners, followed by Chicago, Toronto and Los Angeles. KPMG, CL and PW were the leading firms in both New York and London.

I. Accounting Firms with Multiple International Affiliations

A firm was classified as having a multiple affiliation when more than one international accounting firm listed the same local firm as part of its group. The total number of partners and offices of the local accounting firms with multiple international affiliations is excluded from the analysis in this chapter because of the difficulty in allocating partners among the affiliated international firms.

In this section, we have, however, examined the extent of multiple affiliations worldwide. Table 9-14 presents local accounting firms which have multiple affiliations with international accounting firms. Except for the larger firms, most multiple affiliated firms were correspondent or representative firms and nearly half were in the Asia/Pacific region. PKF, DHSI and DRMP had the most multiple affiliations. Asahi Shinwa in Japan, and the SGV Group in Asia/Pacific were the largest firms with multiple affiliations.

J. Use of Correspondents by International Firms

As indicated earlier, correspondent firms were excluded from our analysis because they are not fully affiliated with the international accounting firms. However, we have analyzed the scope of the relationship with correspondents and identified the largest ones. The number of offices and partners by international accounting firm can be seen in Table 9-15.

In general, the correspondent relationship was not significant on a worldwide basis for the big sixteen international accounting firms, though EW in the big eight and HHI in the small eight have used correspondent firms more extensively than other international accounting firms.

In Table 9-16, correspondent firms with six or more partners are listed by country, local firm name and affiliated international accounting firm.

K. PMM & KMG Merger

Table 9-17 is an analysis of the merger between Peat Marwick Mitchell & Co. (PMM) and Klynveld Main Goerdeler & Co. (KMG), which was announced on January 1, 1987 and became effective April 1, 1987. In this analysis, data for 1988 on the merged entity, KPMG, was compared with 1986 information on the two firms prior to the merger to examine the effects of the merger.

KPMG in 1988 had 98% of the combined total partners of PMM and KMG in 1986. The greatest gain was in Europe, where it grew 12% and in South America and the Caribbean where it grew 2%. This gain is also reflected in the EC countries where KPMG gained 11% over the combined totals for PMM and KMG in 1986.

The new firm benefited most in France (+50%) and the United Kingdom (+14%) and lost the largest number of partners in Canada (-40%) and Japan (-48%). In Canada, KPMG lost its affiliation with Thorne Riddell, which joined EW just prior to the PMM and KMG merger, while in Japan, KPMG lost its affiliation with Sanwa Audit Corporation. Sanwa Tokyo Marunouchi & Co. merged with Tohmatsu Awoki & Co. to form Tohmatsu Awoki Sanwa, which is affiliated with TRI.

The comparison of the combined pre-merger total number of offices to the number of 1988 offices of KPMG indicates a reduction. This may be due to the combining of duplicate offices in various cities. A look at the growth in average partners per office indicates an overall growth of 11%, supporting the conclusion that the merger resulted in larger combined offices with more partners.

Despite the various gains and losses of partners and offices, the merger of KMG and PMM resulted in the emergence of the largest international firm in terms of the number of partners and offices in the world. The merger also allowed the combined firm to strengthen its overall presence worldwide, though it lost some strength in affiliations in Japan and Canada.

L. Other Mergers and Acquisitions

This section gives a summary analysis of the mergers which occurred in the last eight years between local accounting firms and the leading international accounting firms.

The following publications were surveyed for 1982-1988 to obtain data for this section:

World Accounting Report
Public Accounting Report
International Accounting Bulletin
Wall Street Journal Indexes
Financial Times Indexes

The dates, company names and countries were recorded and a frequency analysis was made. It was found that the countries where mergers occurred most frequently were:

	Country	Number of Mergers During 1982-1988
1.	US	34
2.	Japan	21
3.	Canada	18
4.	Australia	15
5.	United Kingdom	14

Among the leading international firms, the firms expanding most actively were:

Firm	Number of Mergers During 1982-1988
KPMG	32 (PMM-KMG was counted as 1 of these 32 mergers)
TRI	28
DHSI	22
PW	18
EW	17

Mergers occurred most frequently in the following years:

Year	Number of Mergers
1988	55
1987	46
1985	40

Merger activity has accelerated in recent years with KPMG, TRI and DHSI as the top firms in terms of merger activities. The industrial countries, particularly Japan, continue to lead in mergers and acquisitions.

M. Other Smaller International Accounting Groups

In addition to the initial sample of the top sixteen firms (i.e., big eight and small eight) selected for analysis in this study, recently, a third group of eight other international firms which have grown in importance was identified.

The 1988 international office directories for the following eight firms were obtained:

1. Accounting Firms Associated, Inc. (AFAI)
2. Clark Kenneth Leventhal (CKL)
3. DFK International (DFK)
4. Jeffrey Henry International (JHI)
5. The International Group of Accounting Firms (IGAF)
6. Midsnell International (MI)
7. Moore Stephens (MS)
8. Summit International Associates, Inc. (SIAI)

Table 9-18 summarizes the operations of these firms worldwide and by region. Seven out of eight directories listed all partners' and principals' names. JHI, however, only listed the contact partner for each office and is therefore not fully represented in our comparison.

A summary of the second group of eight international accounting firms reveals that MS was the largest with 171 offices and 630 partners. SIAI was second in partners. MI was second in number of offices and third in number of partners.

SIAI, AFAI and IGAF had more than half of their partners in North America, while MS and DFK had greater concentration in Europe.

The emergence of this third group of international accounting firms warrants continued monitoring. The next edition of International Accounting and Auditing Trends will examine these firms more closely.

N. Six-Year Trends

An analysis of six-year trends in the global networks of the leading international accounting firms was made by comparing data from 1982 and 1988. The factors for comparison were organizational structure, five major regions, EC, US and non-US, industrial and developing countries, major countries and cities. The 1982 office directories for international firms were used to extract comparative data. For comparison with KPMG, figures for KMG and PMM and the combined totals are also shown.

Sufficient information was not available for the eight smaller firms to present a relevant comparison and, therefore, they were excluded from this section.

Each region, area and organization is analyzed comparatively by number of offices, number of partners and average number of partners per office. Areas of growth and reduction are also identified.

1. World Summary (Tables 9-19 and 9-20)

   CL led the list in terms of the number of partners worldwide in 1982. In 1988, KPMG took the lead with the highest number of partners (5161) and CL was ranked second (3341 partners). TRI was third in 1988 (2792 partners).

   In the ranking of the average number of partners per office in 1982, AA (9.28 partners) and AYI (7.94 partners) topped the list with notably higher averages than the other firms. While in 1988, AA (9.83), KPMG (8.05) and EW (7.20) were the highest ranking firms.

   As shown in Table 9-20, many of the leading firms which had the majority of their partners using only an international name in 1982 have continued to globalize their local practice by forming combined names and/or inviting their local firms to use their international name. However, international name structure remained an established practice among the big eight in 1988.

2. US and Non-US (Tables 9-21 and 9-22)

   In 1982, the three firms with the largest number of partners in the US were PMM (1148), AA (984) and CL (836). In 1988, KPMG (1794), which resulted from the PMM and KMG merger, and AA (1351) were still ranked the highest with EW (1230) replacing CL in third place. The three firms at the top of the ranks for the largest number of US offices were EW (113), PMM (96) and DHSI (95) in 1982. They remained in the lead in 1988 with a change in the order of ranking as follows: KPMG (137), EW (119) and DHSI (113) in 1988.

Outside the US, the top three firms with the largest number of partners were KMG (1781), CL (1446) and TRI (1333) in 1982. In 1988, the top three remained the same: KPMG (3367), CL (2174) and TRI (1957). However, there were changes in the rankings by number of offices. In 1982, the top three firms were CL (339), TRI (307) and KMG (280), while in 1988, KPMG ranked first with 504, followed by CL (466) and TRI (428).

3. Industrial and Developing Countries (Tables 9-23 and 9-24)

In 1982, KMG, CL and PMM had the largest number of partners in the industrial countries. However, the merger of KMG and PMM resulted in a large lead and the top position in 1988 for KPMG (4541 partners), with CL (2791 partners) ranking second, and EW third with 2480 partners. The KMG-PMM merger had a similar effect in the developing countries, with KPMG leading with 620 partners in 1988. CL moved from first place (345 partners) in 1982, to second (550 partners) in 1988. PW held the second position in developing countries in 1982 and the third in 1988.

In terms of the number of offices, KPMG led in the industrial countries in 1988 and KMG led in 1982. In industrial countries, CL was second in 1982 and 1988 but was first in number of offices in developing countries in 1982. TRI was third in 1982 and was replaced by DHSI in 1988. In developing countries, KPMG took the lead.

Developing countries grew more than industrial both in the number of offices and partners.

4. Regional Analyses (Tables 9-25 through 9-29)

North America

In North America (Table 9-25), the top position in terms of the total number of partners was claimed by PMM in 1982 (15%), and by KPMG in 1988 with 18%. CL (13% in 1982) fell from second to third place with 13% of the total number of partners in 1988, while EW was second in number of partners with 15% in 1988. The highest average number of partners per office was retained by AA with 12.95 in 1982 and 13.44 in 1988. In 1982, the second and third positions were held by AYI (11.2) and PMM (11.2). In 1988, these positions were held by KPMG (11.97) and CL (11.35).

Europe

The European region (Table 9-26) saw the strengthening of first-place for KMG (1125 partners in 1982) to KPMG (2124 partners in 1988). CL increased its number of partners by 64% over the six-year period and stayed in second place. AYI also increased its partners, by 75%, and was again third in 1988. KMG (7.8), AA (6.02) and AYI (5.9) had the highest average number of partners per office in 1982. KPMG (7.8), AA (6.92) and PW (6.10) were the top three firms in 1988.

Asia/Pacific

In the Asia/Pacific region (Table 9-27), CL retained its leadership with the highest number of partners (17% of total partners in 1982 and 21% in 1988), as well as the largest number of offices. In 1982, TRI (334 partners) closely followed CL (342 partners); PW held the third position. In 1988, KPMG took second place and TRI dropped to third. In 1982, the average number of partners per office was highest for AYI (7.7), DHSI (6.7) and KMG (5.3), while in 1988, AA (7.4), KPMG (6.1) and PW (5.9) led in average number of partners.

Africa/Middle East

KPMG is the new leader in the Africa/Middle East region, both in number of partners (21% of the regional total) and number of offices (18%). In 1982, TRI and DHSI, both with 145 partners, tied for first place (16%) with CL ranking third. In 1988, the second position was held by CL (15%) and third place by DHSI. In terms of the number of offices, CL (51 offices) moved from first place in 1982, to second place (55 offices) in 1988, after KPMG. TRI moved from second position in 1982 to third. The regional figure for the average number of partners per office was very low compared with other regions in both 1982 and 1988; the average grew modestly (11%).

South America/Caribbean

In the South America/Caribbean region (Table 9-29), PW retained its lead in number of partners, comprising 25% in both 1982 and 1988. In 1982, CL (14%) and PMM (14%) were second in the number of the total partners in the region. In 1988, KPMG (21%), was second and CL (15%) third. PW remained first in number of offices. This region also had a low average number of partners per office in comparison with other regions, with 3.46 partners per office in 1988.

5. European Community (EC)

The EC countries had a total of 3988 partners (23% of the worldwide total for the big eight firms) in 1982. In 1988, the EC (Table 9-8) represented 25% of the total 23,623 partners worldwide for the big eight firms. The top position in the EC with 1010 partners was held by KMG in 1982 and by KPMG with 1830 partners in 1988 (Table 9-30). CL held second place in both 1982 and 1988. In 1988, AYI, with 712 partners, replaced TRI which held third place with 462 partners in 1982.

In terms of the number of EC offices, KPMG (formerly KMG) remained on top, followed by TRI, and CL in 1982.

In the EC countries, the number of offices and the number of partners for the big eight international accounting firms has grown by 38% and 48%, respectively, between 1982 and 1988.

6. Major Countries (Table 9-31 and 9-32)

A comparison between 1982 and 1988 of the top five countries, determined by the number of partners, indicates various trends among the big eight accounting firms. Table 9-31 is a comparison based on the number of offices, and Table 9-32 illustrates changes in the number of partners, in the United States, United Kingdom, Canada, Australia and France.

The largest growth in the US in the number of offices was achieved by AA and AYI (both 37%), while EW grew most rapidly in terms of number of partners (55%).

In the United Kingdom, TRI grew the most in number of offices (55%) and PW in number of partners (100%).

In Canada, the largest change took place for EW. EW grew phenomenally (632%) in number of partners and 318% in number of offices. This is partly due to the merger of EW and Thorne Riddell, which was affiliated with KMG in 1982. For much the same reason, KPMG shows a 50% decrease in partners and a reduction of 59% in number of offices. Also TRI achieved significant growth in number of partners(113%).

CL, which grew 24%, held the lead in Australia. EW also advanced in Australia, with a growth of 107% in number of partners and 78% in number of offices. Although AA gained only one office, it increased its number of partners by 162%.

EW had the greatest growth in terms of partners in France. CL increased its number of offices there by 367% and partners by 205%, giving it second place in France after KPMG, which had by far the most partners (596).

7. Changes in Number of Partners by Major Cities

A look at the change in the number of partners in recent years by major cities (Table 9-33) indicates that Tokyo experienced the greatest growth (116%). Atlanta (56%), Cleveland (51%), Stockholm (48%) and Paris (48%) also had a considerable amount of growth in recent years.

In comparing the three leading firms from 1982 and 1988, KPMG moved into first place in eight out of 20 cities in 1988, whereas in 1982, KMG and PMM led in only five out of 20 cities. AA was second, taking the lead in four cities and second place in four of the top 20 cities in 1988.

In London, PW moved from third to first in number of partners, and moved into third position over AYI in New York. KPMG and CL remained in first and second place in New York. In Chicago, AA remained first, and KPMG was second.

TRI gained strength in Tokyo, where it moved from second to first place in the six-year period. In Montreal, DHSI took the leading position, even though it was not in the top three in 1982. KPMG remained first in Los Angeles, Paris and Washington DC. It gained the lead in Johannesburg, Dallas, and Melbourne. CL was first in Philadelphia and Boston. EW held its lead in Cleveland, where it is headquartered.

TABLE 9-2
WORLD SUMMARY
TOTAL NUMBER OF OFFICES, PARTNERS, AVERAGE PARTNERS PER OFFICE, AND ORGANIZATIONAL STRUCTURES WORLDWIDE BY INTERNATIONAL FIRM

					% of Total Partners by Organizational Structure	
Number of Offices	Total Partners	% of Total Partners	Average Partners Per Office	Firms	Int'l. or Combined Name	Local Name
				Big Eight		
217	2133	6.72	9.83	AA	83.83	16.17
418	2562	8.07	6.13	AYI	53.12	46.88
565	3341	10.52	5.91	CL	72.97	27.03
471	2345	7.39	4.98	DHSI	72.20	27.80
378	2721	8.57	7.20	EW	89.86	10.14
641	5161	16.25	8.05	KPMG	100.0	0
424	2568	8.09	6.06	PW	92.48	7.52
515	2792	8.79	5.42	TRI	40.37	59.63
3629	23623	74.40	6.51	Sub-Total	77.84	22.16
				Small Eight		
349	1397	4.40	4.00	BDO	99.79	0.21
281	1041	3.28	3.70	DRMP	0.00	100.00
302	1294	4.08	4.28	GTI	50.77	49.23
196	1042	3.28	5.32	HHI	57.49	42.51
145	459	1.45	3.17	HLB	0.00	100.00
293	1193	3.76	4.07	MRI	0.00	100.00
197	828	2.61	4.20	PKF	81.16	18.84
175	874	2.75	4.99	SO	36.84	63.16
1938	8128	25.60	4.19	Sub-Total	44.83	55.17
5567	31751	100.00	5.70	Total	69.39	30.61

TABLE 9-3

TOTAL NUMBER OF OFFICES, PARTNERS AND AVERAGE PARTNERS PER OFFICE US AND NON-US

US					Non-US			
No. of Offices	Total Ptnrs.	% of Total Partners Worldwide	Average Ptnrs. Per Office	Firms	No. of Offices	Total Ptnrs.	% of Total Partners Worldwide	Avg. Ptnrs. Per Office
				Big Eight				
97	1351	4.25	13.93	AA	120	782	2.46	6.52
97	792	2.49	8.16	AYI	320	1770	5.57	5.51
99	1167	3.68	11.79	CL	466	2174	6.85	4.67
113	800	2.52	7.08	DHSI	358	1545	4.87	4.32
119	1230	3.87	10.34	EW	259	1491	4.70	5.76
137	1794	5.65	13.09	KPMG	504	3367	10.60	6.68
109	881	2.77	8.08	PW	315	1687	5.31	5.36
87	835	2.63	9.60	TRI	428	1957	6.16	4.57
857	8850	27.87	10.31	Sub-Total	2771	14773	46.53	5.33
				Small Eight				
49	316	1.00	6.45	BDO	300	1081	3.40	3.60
89	470	1.48	5.28	DRMP	192	571	1.80	2.97
58	376	1.18	6.48	GTI	244	918	2.89	3.76
58	455	1.43	7.84	HHI	138	587	1.85	4.25
13	50	0.16	3.85	HLB	132	409	1.29	3.10
46	239	0.75	5.20	MRI	247	954	3.00	3.86
36	175	0.55	4.86	PKF	161	653	2.06	4.06
9	104	0.33	11.56	SO	166	770	2.43	4.64
358	2185	6.88	6.10	Sub-Total	1580	5943	18.72	3.76
1216	11035	34.75	9.07	Total	4351	20716	65.25	4.76

TABLE 9-4

TOTAL NUMBER OF OFFICES, PARTNERS, AND AVERAGE PARTNERS PER OFFICE BY INDUSTRIAL AND DEVELOPING COUNTRIES AND INT'L ACCOUNTING FIRMS

INDUSTRIAL COUNTRIES					DEVELOPING COUNTRIES			
No. of Offices	Total Ptnrs.	% of Total Partners Worldwide	Average Ptnrs. Per Office	Firms	No. of Offices	Total Ptnrs.	% of Total Partners Worldwide	Average Ptnrs. Per Office
				Big Eight				
174	1936	6.10	11.13	AA	43	197	0.62	4.58
328	2275	7.17	6.94	AYI	90	287	0.90	3.19
397	2791	8.79	7.03	CL	168	550	1.73	3.27
368	2020	6.36	5.49	DHSI	103	325	1.02	3.16
296	2480	7.81	8.38	EW	82	241	0.76	2.94
471	4541	14.30	9.64	KPMG	170	620	1.95	3.65
264	2027	6.38	7.68	PW	160	541	1.70	3.38
363	2362	7.44	6.51	TRI	152	430	1.35	2.83
2661	20432	64.35	7.68	Sub-Total	968	3191	10.05	3.30
				Small Eight				
297	1225	3.86	4.12	BDO	52	172	0.54	3.31
242	944	2.97	3.90	DRMP	39	97	0.31	2.49
163	1179	3.71	4.42	GTI	35	115	0.36	3.29
118	865	2.72	5.31	HHI	33	177	0.56	5.36
248	412	1.30	3.49	HLB	27	47	0.15	1.74
139	1034	3.26	4.17	MRI	45	159	0.50	3.53
135	736	2.32	5.29	PKF	58	92	0.29	1.59
140	739	2.33	5.47	SO	40	135	0.43	3.38
1609	7134	22.47	4.43	Sub-Total	329	994	3.13	3.02
4270	27566	86.82	6.46	Total	1297	4185	13.18	3.23

TABLE 9-4A
LISTING OF INDUSTRIAL AND DEVELOPING COUNTRIES INCLUDED IN STUDY OF PARTNERS OF INTERNATIONAL ACCOUNTING FIRMS

Industrial Countries:

Australia	Finland	Japan	Spain
Austria	France	Netherlands	Sweden
Belgium	Germany, West	New Zealand	Switzerland
Canada	Ireland	Norway	United Kingdom
Denmark	Italy	South Africa	United States

Note: Iceland, Liechtenstein, Luxembourg and Monaco were also included as industrial countries

Developing Countries:

Andorra	Guinea	Philippines
Angola	Guyana	Portugal
Antigua	Haiti	Puerto Rico
Argentina	Honduras	Qatar
Aruba	Hong Kong	Saudi Arabia
Bahamas	India	Senegal
Bahrain	Indonesia	Seychelles
Barbados	Iran	Sierra Leone
Belize	Iraq	Singapore
Benin	Israel	Solomon Islands
Bermuda	Ivory Coast	Sri Lanka
Bolivia	Jamaica	St. Kitts-Nevis-Anguilla
Botswana	Jordan	St. Lucia
Brazil	Kenya	St. Vincent
British Virgin Islands	Korea, South	Sudan
Brunei	Kuwait	Surinam
Cameroon	Lebanon	Swaziland
Cayman Islands	Lesotho	Syria
Chile	Liberia	Tahiti
China	Libya	Tanzania
China, Taiwan	Macau	Thailand
Colombia	Malawi	Togo
Congo	Malaysia	Trinidad and Tobago
Cook Islands	Maldives	Tunisia
Costa Rica	Malta	Turkey
Cyprus	Mauritius	Turks and Caicos Islands
Dominica	Mexico	Uganda
Dominican Republic	Morocco	United Arab Emirates
Ecuador	Montserrat	Virgin Islands (US)
Egypt	Namibia	Uruguay
El Salvador	Nepal	Vanuatu
Fiji	Netherlands Antilles	Venezuela
Gabon	New Caledonia	Western Samoa
Gambia	Niger	Yemen
Ghana	Nigeria	Zaire
Gibraltar	Northern Mariana Islands	Zambia
Greece	Oman	Zimbabwe
Greenland	Pakistan	
Grenada	Panama	
Guam	Papua New Guinea	
Guatemala	Paraguay	
Peru		

TABLE 9-5

TOTAL NUMBER OF OFFICES, PARTNERS, AND AVERAGE PARTNERS PER OFFICE BY REGION AND INTERNATIONAL ACCOUNTING FIRM

NORTH AMERICA*

Firms	No. of Offices	Total Partners	% of Total Partners	Average Partners Per Office
Big Eight				
AA	107	1438	9.7	13.44
AYI	127	1217	8.2	9.58
CL	130	1475	9.9	11.35
DHSI	176	1136	7.6	6.45
EW	190	1764	11.8	9.28
KPMG	174	2082	14.0	11.97
PW	142	1161	7.8	8.18
TRI	140	1214	8.2	8.67
Sub-Total Big 8	1186	11487	77.2	9.69
Small Eight				
BDO	136	574	3.9	4.22
DRMP	123	604	4.1	4.91
GTI	144	654	4.4	4.54
HHI	68	529	3.6	7.78
HLB	19	79	0.5	4.16
MRI	86	476	3.2	5.53
PKF	64	343	2.3	5.36
SO	15	140	0.9	9.33
Sub-Total Small 8	655	3399	22.8	5.19
Total	1841	14886	100.0%	8.09

*North America: Countries listed in Table 9-7A

TABLE 9-6

TOTAL NUMBER OF OFFICES, PARTNERS, AND AVERAGE PARTNERS PER OFFICE BY REGION AND INTERNATIONAL ACCOUNTING FIRM

EUROPE*					ASIA/PACIFIC**			
No. of Offices	Total Ptnrs.	% of Total Ptnrs.	Average Ptnrs. Per Office	Firms	No. of Offices	Total Ptnrs.	% of Total Ptnrs.	Average Ptnrs. Per Office
				Big Eight				
64	443	4.3	6.92	AA	17	126	3.3	7.41
188	925	9.0	4.92	AYI	42	244	6.3	5.81
225	940	9.2	4.18	CL	117	619	16.0	5.29
172	718	7.0	4.17	DHS	48	240	6.2	5.00
74	437	4.3	5.91	EW	64	368	9.5	5.75
272	2124	20.8	7.81	KPMG	87	530	13.7	6.09
111	677	6.6	6.10	PW	66	389	10.1	5.89
191	821	8.0	4.30	TRI	103	503	13.0	4.88
1297	7085	69.2	5.46	Sub-Total	544	3019	78.0	5.55
				Small Eight				
147	574	5.6	3.90	BDO	30	144	3.7	4.80
85	269	2.6	3.16	DRMP	48	99	2.6	2.06
118	496	4.8	4.20	GTI	13	54	1.4	4.15
80	244	2.4	3.05	HHI	30	152	3.9	5.07
95	302	3.0	3.18	HLB	8	42	1.1	5.25
145	492	4.8	3.39	MRI	28	89	2.3	3.18
60	296	2.9	4.93	PKF	23	117	3.0	5.09
95	475	4.6	5.00	SO	38	154	4.0	4.05
825	3148	30.8	3.82	Sub-Total	218	851	22.0	3.90
2122	10233	100.0	4.82	Total	762	3870	100.0	5.08

* Europe: Countries listed in Table 9-7A

**Asia/Pacific: Countries listed in Table 9-7A

TABLE 9-7

TOTAL NUMBER OF OFFICES, PARTNERS AND AVERAGE PARTNERS PER OFFICE BY REGION AND INTERNATIONAL ACCOUNTING FIRM

AFRICA/MIDDLE EAST*					SOUTH AMERICA/CARIBBEAN**			
No. of Offices	Total Ptnrs.	% of Total Ptnrs.	Average Ptnrs. Per Office	Firms	No. of Offices	Total Ptnrs.	% of Total Ptnrs.	Average Ptnrs. Per Office
				Big Eight				
13	36	2.1	2.77	AA	16	90	8.5	5.62
36	115	6.7	3.19	AYI	25	61	5.8	2.44
55	183	10.7	3.33	CL	38	124	11.7	3.26
50	175	10.3	3.50	DHSI	25	76	7.2	3.04
38	129	7.6	3.39	EW	12	23	2.2	1.92
64	246	14.4	3.84	KPMG	44	179	17.0	4.07
49	128	7.5	2.61	PW	56	213	20.2	3.80
52	173	10.1	3.33	TRI	29	81	7.7	2.79
357	1185	69.5	3.32	Sub-Total	245	847	80.2	3.46
				Small Eight				
22	71	4.1	3.23	BDO	14	34	3.2	2.43
7	28	1.6	4.00	DRMP	18	41	3.9	2.28
15	57	3.3	3.80	GTI	12	33	3.1	2.75
7	75	4.4	10.71	HHI	11	42	4.0	3.82
15	24	1.4	1.60	HLB	8	12	1.1	1.50
33	135	7.9	4.09	MRI	1	1	***	1.00
34	39	2.3	1.15	PKF	16	33	3.1	2.06
22	92	5.4	4.18	SO	5	13	1.2	2.60
155	521	30.5	3.36	Sub-Total	85	209	19.8	2.46
512	1706	100.0	3.33	Total	330	1056	100.0	3.20

*Africa/Middle East: Countries listed in Table 9-7A
**South America/Caribbean: Countries listed in Table 9-7A

*** = Less than 1%

TABLE 9-7A

LISTING OF COUNTRIES INCLUDED IN THE REGIONAL ANALYSIS OF PARTNERS

<u>North America</u>

Canada	Mexico	USA	

<u>Europe</u>

Andorra	Germany (West)	Luxembourg	Portugal
Austria	Gibraltar	Malta	Spain
Belgium	Greece	Monaco	Sweden
Cyprus	Iceland	Netherlands	Switzerland
Denmark	Ireland	Norway	Turkey
Finland	Italy		United Kingdom
France	Liechtenstein		

*Includes the Channel Islands

<u>Asia/Pacific</u>

Australia	Hong Kong	Nepal	Singapore
Brunei	India	New Caledonia	Solomon Islands
People's Republic of China	Indonesia	New Zealand	Sri Lanka
	Japan	Nortern Mariana Islands	Tahiti
China (Taiwan)	Korea (South)		Thailand
Cook Islands	Macau	Pakistan	Western Samoa
Fiji	Malaysia	Papua New Guinea	Vanuatu
Guam	Maldives	Philippines	

<u>Africa/Middle East</u>

Angola	Iraq	Morocco	Swaziland
Bahrain	Israel	Namibia	Syria
Benin	Ivory Coast	Niger	Tanzania
Botswana	Jordan	Nigeria	Togo
Cameroon	Kenya	Oman	Tunisia
Congo	Kuwait	Qatar	Uganda
Egypt	Lebanon	Saudi Arabia	United Arab Emirates
Gabon	Lesotho	Senegal	Yemen
Gambia	Liberia	Seychelles	Zaire
Ghana	Libya	Sierra Leone	Zambia
Guinea	Malawi	South Africa**	Zimbabwe
Iran	Mauritius	Sudan	

**Includes Bophuthatswana, Ciskei, Transkei

<u>South America/Caribbean</u>

Antigua	Cayman Islands	Guatemala	Puerto Rico
Argentina	Chile	Guyana	St. Kitts-Nevis-Anguilla
Aruba	Colombia	Haiti	St. Lucia
Bahamas	Costa Rica	Honduras	St. Vincent
Barbados	Dominica	Jamaica	Surinam
Belize	Dominican Republic	Montserrat	Trinidad and Tobago
Bermuda	Ecuador	Netherlands Antilles	Turks and Caicos Islands
Bolivia	El Salvador	Panama	Virgin Islands (US)
Brazil	Greenland	Paraguay	Uruguay
British Virgin Islands	Grenada	Peru	Venezuela

TABLE 9-8

TOTAL NUMBER OF OFFICES, PARTNERS AND AVERAGE PARTNERS PER OFFICE BY EC AND INTERNATIONAL ACCOUNTING FIRM

EC*

Firms	Number of Offices	Total Partners	% of Total Partners	Average Partners Per Office
Big Eight				
AA	53	398	4.7	7.51
AYI	123	712	8.4	5.79
CL	122	739	8.6	6.06
DHSI	89	530	6.2	5.96
EW	68	424	5.0	6.24
KPMG	197	1830	21.4	9.29
PW	85	625	7.3	7.35
TRI	138	653	7.6	4.73
Sub-Total Big Eight	875	5911	69.1	6.76
Small Eight				
BDO	92	439	5.1	4.77
DRMP	75	245	2.9	3.27
GTI	87	426	5.0	4.90
HHI	42	174	2.0	4.14
HLB	82	261	3.0	3.18
MRI	122	464	5.4	3.80
PKF	51	252	3.0	4.94
SO	74	377	4.4	5.09
Sub-Total Small Eight	625	2638	30.9	4.22
Total	1500	8549	100.0	5.70

*Countries included: Belgium, Denmark, France, West Germany, Greece, Ireland, Italy, Luxembourg, Netherlands, Portugal, Spain, United Kingdom

TABLE 9-9

NUMBER OF OFFICES BY TOP TEN COUNTRIES AND INTERNATIONAL ACCOUNTING FIRMS

	United States		Canada		United Kingdom		Australia		Netherlands	
Firms	No. of Offices	%	No. of Offices	%	No. of Offices	%	No. of Offices	%	No. of Offices	%
Big Eight										
AA	97	8	7	1	12	3	6	2	3	1
AYI	97	8	25	5	22	5	13	5	43	18
CL	99	8	24	4	40	8	34	13	3	1
DHSI	113	9	60	11	21	4	14	5	23	10
EW	119	10	71	13	25	5	16	6	2	1
KPMG	137	11	28	5	57	12	23	9	27	11
PW	109	9	24	4	23	5	19	7	4	2
TRI	87	7	42	8	31	6	21	8	33	14
Sub Total	858	71	281	51	231	48	146	55	138	58
Small Eight										
BDO	49	4	86	15	34	7	11	4	19	8
DRMP	89	7	32	6	26	5	34	13	21	9
GTI	58	5	86	15	53	11	12	5	0	0
HHI	58	5	5	1	9	2	10	4	19	8
HLB	12	1	4	1	20	4	7	3	18	7
MRI	46	4	38	7	53	11	10	4	18	7
PKF	36	3	25	4	32	7	15	6	5	2
SO	9	1	3	0	24	5	15	6	3	1
Sub Total	357	29	279	49	251	52	114	45	103	42
Total	1215	100	560	100	482	100	260	100	241	100

TABLE 9-9
(Continued)
NUMBER OF OFFICES BY TOP TEN COUNTRIES AND INTERNATIONAL ACCOUNTING FIRMS

	West Germany		South Africa		New Zealand		France		Japan	
Firms	No. of Offices	%	No. of Offices	%	No. of Offices	%	No. of Offices	%	No. of Offices	%
Big Eight										
AA	7	4	3	2	0	0	3	3	3	5
AYI	12	7	12	7	11	8	9	7	*	*
CL	15	9	12	7	18	13	14	11	10	15
DHSI	11	6	17	11	15	11	4	3	3	5
EW	4	2	16	10	12	9	2	2	10	15
KPMG	33	20	18	11	16	12	28	23	4	6
PW	6	4	13	8	7	5	12	10	7	10
TRI	16	10	13	8	17	13	7	6	14	20
Sub Total	104	62	104	64	96	71	79	65	51	76
Small Eight										
BDO	17	10	11	7	7	5	2	2	0	0
DRMP	1	1	3	2	1	1	10	8	1	2
GTI	5	3	11	7	0	0	4	3	0	0
HHI	1	1	3	2	6	5	1	1	7	10
HLB	11	6	1	1	1	1	12	10	0	0
MRI	13	8	20	13	4	3	2	2	8	12
PKF	3	2	0	0	3	2	1	1	0	0
SO	12	7	6	4	16	12	10	8	0	0
Sub Total	63	38	55	36	38	29	42	35	16	24
Total	167	100	159	100	134	100	121	100	67	100

* AYI's affiliate in Japan was excluded from this table because it also has affiliation with two other international accounting firms.

TABLE 9-10

NUMBER OF PARTNERS BY TOP TEN COUNTRIES AND INTERNATIONAL ACCOUNTING FIRMS

Firms	United States		United Kingdom		Canada		Australia		France	
Big Eight	Total Ptnrs.	%	Total Ptnrs.	%	Total Ptnrs.	%	Total Ptnrs.	%	Total Ptnrs.	%
AA	1351	12	131	3	57	2	68	4	55	5
AYI	792	7	214	6	397	11	83	5	55	5
CL	1167	11	364	10	245	7	199	13	58	5
DHSI	800	7	257	7	328	9	91	6	25	2
EW	1230	11	253	7	534	15	124	8	39	3
KPMG	1794	16	500	13	257	7	233	15	596	52
PW	881	8	364	10	242	7	163	10	48	4
TRI	835	8	237	6	334	9	124	8	46	5
Sub-Total	8850	80	2320	61	2394	67	1085	69	922	82
Small Eight										
BDO	316	3	227	6	249	7	68	4	38	3
DRMP	470	4	117	3	127	4	72	5	38	3
GTI	376	3	276	7	278	8	47	3	23	2
HHI	455	4	105	3	57	2	54	3	5	1
HLB	50	1	90	2	23	1	32	2	53	5
MRI	239	2	248	7	229	6	52	3	10	1
PKF	175	2	183	5	161	4	85	6	8	1
SO	104	1	211	6	31	1	80	5	33	3
Sub-Total	2185	20	1457	39	1155	33	490	31	208	18
TOTAL	11035	100	3777	100	3549	100	1575	100	1130	100

TABLE 9-10
(Continued)
NUMBER OF PARTNERS BY TOP TEN COUNTRIES AND INTERNATIONAL ACCOUNTING FIRMS

Firms	Netherlands		South Africa		West Germany		New Zealand		Japan	
Big Eight	Total Ptnrs.	%	Total Ptnrs.	%	Total Ptnrs.	%	Total Ptnrs.	%	Total Ptnrs.	%
AA	18	2	19	2	31	4	0	0	29	4
AYI	242	24	61	6	72	9	90	13	*	*
CL	24	2	81	9	102	13	95	13	175	27
DHSI	108	11	84	9	41	5	78	11	22	3
EW	10	1	87	9	19	2	61	9	106	16
KPMG	212	21	122	13	185	24	103	15	50	8
PW	22	2	61	6	31	4	46	7	37	6
TRI	143	14	101	11	70	9	90	13	179	28
Sub-Total	779	78	616	65	551	70	563	80	598	92
Small Eight										
BDO	55	5	43	5	60	8	23	3	0	0
DRMP	41	4	21	2	6	0	4	1	2	0
GTI	0	0	41	4	26	3	0	0	0	0
HHI	29	3	49	5	3	0	19	3	43	7
HLB	36	4	4	0	28	4	7	1	0	0
MRI	42	4	118	13	59	8	16	2	8	1
PKF	11	1	0	1	17	2	19	3	0	0
SO	12	1	59	6	36	5	54	8	0	0
Sub-Total	226	22	335	35	235	30	142	20	53	8
TOTAL	1005	100	951	100	786	100	705	100	651	100

* AYI's affiliate in Japan was excluded from this table because it also has affiliation with two other international accounting firms.

TABLE 9-11
AVERAGE NUMBER OF PARTNERS PER OFFICE
BY TOP TEN COUNTRIES AND INTERNATIONAL ACCOUNTING FIRMS

United States	United Kingdom	Canada	Australia	France	Firms	Netherlands	South Africa	Japan	West Germany	New Zealand
					Big Eight					
13.93	10.92	8.14	11.33	18.33	AA	6.00	6.33	9.67	4.43	0.00
8.16	9.73	15.88	6.38	6.11	AYI	5.63	5.08	*	6.00	8.18
11.79	9.10	10.21	5.85	4.14	CL	8.00	6.75	17.50	6.80	5.28
7.14	12.24	5.47	6.50	6.25	DHSI	4.70	4.94	7.33	3.73	5.20
10.34	10.12	7.52	7.75	19.50	EW	5.00	5.44	10.60	4.75	5.08
13.09	8.77	9.18	10.13	21.29	KPMG	7.85	6.78	12.50	5.61	6.44
8.08	15.83	10.08	8.58	4.00	PW	5.50	4.69	5.14	5.17	6.57
9.60	7.65	7.95	5.90	6.57	TRI	4.33	7.77	12.79	4.38	5.29
10.31	10.04	8.52	7.43	11.67	Sub-Total	5.64	5.92	11.71	5.30	5.86
					Small Eight					
6.45	6.68	2.89	6.18	19.00	BDO	2.90	3.91	0.00	3.53	3.29
5.28	4.50	3.97	2.12	3.80	DRMP	1.95	7.00	2.00	6.00	4.00
6.48	5.21	3.23	3.92	5.75	GTI	0.00	3.73	0.00	5.20	0.00
7.84	11.67	11.40	5.40	5.00	HHI	1.53	16.33	6.14	3.00	3.17
4.17	4.50	5.75	4.57	4.42	HLB	2.00	4.00	0.00	2.55	7.00
5.20	4.60	6.03	5.20	5.00	MRI	2.33	5.90	1.00	4.54	4.00
4.86	5.72	6.44	5.67	8.00	PKF	2.20	0.00	0.00	5.67	6.33
11.56	8.79	10.33	5.33	3.30	SO	4.00	9.83	0.00	3.00	3.38
5.99	5.80	4.14	4.30	4.95	Sub-Total	2.19	6.09	3.31	3.73	3.74
9.08	7.84	6.34	6.06	9.34	Avg.	4.17	5.98	9.70	4.71	5.26

* AYI's affiliate in Japan was excluded from this table because it also has affiliation with two other international accounting firms.

TABLE 9-12
SUMMARY OF ORGANIZATIONAL STRUCTURE
USED BY SIXTEEN INTERNATIONAL ACCOUNTING FIRMS

% Of Total Partners by Organizational Structure

Various Regional Classifications	Int'l. or Combined Name	Local Name
World	69%	31%
Regions		
North America	81%	19%
Europe	59%	41%
Asia/Pacific	64%	36%
Africa/Middle East	58%	42%
South America/Caribbean	54%	46%
Industrial/Developing		
Industrial	71%	29%
Developing	56%	44%
US/Non-US		
US	90%	10%
Non-US	58%	42%
Major Countries		
US	90%	10%
United Kingdom	84%	16%
Canada	56%	44%
Australia	73%	27%
France	57%	43%
Netherlands	33%	67%
South Africa	58%	42%
Germany, West	13%	87%
Japan	39%	61%
New Zealand	85%	15%
Common Market		
EC	63%	37%

TABLE 9-13

TOP TWENTY-FIVE CITIES BY TOTAL PARTNERS
AND LEADING THREE INTERNATIONAL ACCOUNTING FIRMS

	City	Country	Total Big 16 Partners by City	Leading Big 16 Firms (% of Total Partners in the City)		
				1	2	3
1.	New York	United States	1448	KPMG (16%)	CL (13%)	PW (11%)
2.	London	United Kingdom	1434	PW (15%)	KPMG (12%)	CL (11%)
3.	Chicago	United States	839	AA (32%)	KPMG (11%)	EW (9%)
4.	Toronto	Canada	757	AYI (23%)	EW (17%)	KPMG/PW(10%)
5.	Los Angeles	United States	521	KPMG (16%)	AA (12%)	EW (11%)
6.	Paris	France	509	KPMG (27%)	AA (10%)	CL (9%)
7.	Sydney	Australia	488	KPMG (14%)	PW (13%)	CL (12%)
8.	Montreal	Canada	464	DHSI (13%)	MRI (13%)	GTI (12%)
9.	Tokyo	Japan	438	TRI (29%)	CL (22%)	EW (12%)
10.	Washington DC	United States	396	KPMG (18%)	AA/EW(14%)	CL (10%)
11.	Boston	United States	349	CL (19%)	KPMG (13%)	AA (11%)
12.	Johannesburg	South Africa	344	KPMG (16%)	EW (11%)	TRI (10%)
13.	Houston	United States	330	AA (22%)	KPMG (15%)	EW (9%)
14.	Melbourne	Australia	324	KPMG (14%)	PW (12%)	CL (10%)
15.	Dallas	United States	319	KPMG (18%)	AA (16%)	EW (11%)
16.	San Francisco	United States	306	AA (17%)	KPMG (16%)	CL (12%)
17.	Philadelphia	United States	305	CL (20%)	HHI (19%)	KPMG (14%)
18.	Stockholm	Sweden	280	DHSI (18%)	KPMG/(11%) TRI	CL (8%)
19.	Atlanta	United States	260	AA (21%)	KPMG (15%)	EW (13%)
20.	Cleveland	United States	253	EW (46%)	AA (8%)	KPMG/MRI(8%)
21.	Copenhagen	Denmark	248	KPMG (26%)	MRI (10%)	CL (8%)
22.	Vancouver	Canada	247	EW (20%)	TRI (11%)	CL (10%)
23.	Dublin	Ireland	227	KPMG (16%)	PW (14%)	CL (12%)
24.	Amsterdam	Netherlands	223	KPMG (35%)	AYI (19%)	DHSI (13%)
25.	Calgary	Canada	210	AYI (15%)	EW (14%)	TRI (13%)
	Total Partners		11519 (36% of the World Total)			

TABLE 9-14

LOCAL ACCOUNTING FIRMS HAVING MULTIPLE
AFFILIATIONS WITH INTERNATIONAL ACCOUNTING FIRMS

		International Accounting Firms															
Country	Local Accounting Firm	AA	AYI	BDO	CL	DHSI	DRMP	EW	GTI	HHI	HLB	KPMG	MRI	PKF	PW	SO	TRI
Australia	Garrott & Garrott		C											C			
Barbados	Pannell Kerr Forster		C											C			
Bermuda	Rawlinson, Hunter, Butterfield & Co					C										C	
Bermuda	S. Arthur Morris						C		C	C				C			
Brunei	Ting Wong & Co. (SGV Group)		C	C													
Cameroon	Kooh et Mure				C								C				
Cayman Islands	Morris Brankin & Co.						C		C	C				C			
Cayman Islands	Rawlinson, Hunter, Butterfield					C										C	
Channel Island	Reads & Co. (UK)											C				B	
Cyprus	Savvides Shakallis Papakyriacou						C							C			
Egypt	Saleh, Barsoum & Abel Aziz			C									C				
Fiji	G. Lal & Co.					C								C			
Finland	Oy Forsstrom & Hallback AB					B		B						B			
Indonesia	Drs. Siddharta & Co.				C									C			
Indonesia	Drs. Utomo & Co. (SGV Group)	B				B											
Jamaica	Pannel Kerr Forster		C											C			
Japan	Asahi Shinwa		A	A					A								
Japan	Shinko Audit Corp.													C	C	C	
Kenya	Muchekehu & Co.										C		C				
Korea, South	Ahn, Kwon & Co.					B	B							B			
Korea, South	Sae Dong & Co.								B								B
Luxembourg	Hoogewerf & Co.								C	C							
Malaysia	Baharom-Jasani								C		C						
Malaysia	Kassam Chan & Co.					B	B										
Monaco	Hoogewerf & Co.								C	C							C
Pakistan	Ford Rhodes Robson & Morrow		C		C	C	C										
Philippines	Sycip Gorres Velayo (SGV) & Co.	A					A	A						C			
Singapore	Foo Kon & Tan (SGV Group)								C		C					C	
Sri Lanka	Ford Rhodes Thornton & Co.					B	B					B					
Taiwan	Diwan & Company		C	C													
Taiwan	T.N. Soong & Co. (SGV Group)	B				B	B	B						B			
Thailand	SGV - Na Thalang & Co. (SGV Group)	B				B	B									C	
Turkey	Cevdet Suner, Ltd.							C					C				
Turks &																	
Calico Islands	Morris, Cottingham & Co.						C		C								
Zimbabwe	Pim Goldby												C				C

Key: A - 50 or more partners B - 10-50 partners C - Less than 10 partners

TABLE 9-15

TOTAL NUMBER OF OFFICES AND PARTNERS IN CORRESPONDENT FIRMS BY INTERNATIONAL ACCOUNTING FIRM

Number of Correspondent Offices	Firms	Total Partners at Correspondent Firms
	Big Eight	
0	AA	0
0	AYI	0
5	CL	16
8	DHSI	17
54	EW	177
16	KPMG	45
7	PW	19
0	TRI	0
90	Sub-Total	274
	Small Eight	
0	BDO	0
0	DRMP	0
40	GTI	85
53	HHI	187
7	HLB	20
17	MRI	19
26	PKF	90
29	SO	94
172	Sub-Total	495
262	Total	769

TABLE 9-16

MAJOR CORRESPONDENT FIRMS USED BY SIXTEEN INTERNATIONAL ACCOUNTING FIRMS

Country	Local Firm Serving As a Correspondent	International Firm
Bangladesh	A. Qasam & Co.	CL
Belgium	Andre Hoste & Co.	HHI
Canada	Henderson Partners	PKF
Chile	Bakovic y Balic	EW
Cyprus	Kyprianides & Stylianou	HLB
Denmark	Revisionsfirmaet Askgaard Olesen	HHI
Denmark	Revisor Centret I/S	EW
Germany, West	AWT Allgemeine Wirtschaftstreuhand GmbH	HHI
Germany, West	Dr. Lipfert GmbH	HHI
Germany, West	Dres.Bronner Treuhand-Revision GmbH	HHI
Germany, West	Hanseatische Mercator Treuhand GmbH	HHI
Iceland	Loggiltir Endurskodendur hf.	HHI
India	A. F. Ferguson & Co.	KPMG
India	P. K. Chopra & Co.	HHI
India	Ratan S. Mama & Co.	PKF
India	S. B. Billimoria & Co.	EW
India	S. N. Dhawan & Co.	PKF
Indonesia	Drs Machdjud Modopuro & Co.	HHI
Iran	Agahan and Company	CL
Korea, South	Dongsuh Accounting Corporation	EW
Korea, South	Samduk Accounting Corporation	SO
Mexico	Gossler S. C.	SO
Mexico	Despacho Freyssinier Morin	EW
New Zealand	Chambers Nicholls	GTI
Norway	Johannessen, Andersen & Co.	EW
Pakistan	A. F. Ferguson & Co.	PW
Spain	Audihispania, S. A.	SO
Sweden	Bertil Olsson Revisionsbyra A/B	EW
Turkey	Denet A. S.	KPMG
United Kingdom	Crichton Associates	HHI
United Kingdom	Jackson Fox	HLB
Venezuela	Perez - Mena & Everts	EW
Venezuela	Couto Alen y Asociados, S. C.	PKF

TABLE 9-17

PMM & KMG MERGER

Various Area Classifications	No. of Offices					No. of Partners					Average Partners/Office				
	1986			1988	Inc	1986			1988	Inc	1986			1988	Inc
	PMM	KMG	TOTAL	KPMG	(Dec)	PMM	KMG	TOTAL	KPMG	(Dec)	PMM	KMG	TOTAL	KPMG	(Dec)
World	368	355	723	641	(11%)	2621	2639	5260	5161	(2%)	7.1	7.4	7.3	8.1	11%
Regions															
No. America	138	95	233	174	(25%)	1532	745	2277	2082	(9%)	11.1	7.8	9.8	14.0	43%
Europe	84	170	254	272	7%	466	1437	1903	2124	12%	5.5	8.5	7.5	7.8	4%
Asia/Pacific	68	31	99	87	(12%)	379	254	633	530	(16%)	5.6	8.2	6.4	6.1	(5%)
Africa/Mid East	45	36	81	64	(21%)	137	127	264	246	(7%)	3.0	3.5	3.3	3.8	15%
South America/ Caribbean	33	23	56	44	(21%)	107	76	183	179	2%	3.2	3.3	3.3	4.1	24%
Ind/Developing															
Industrial	253	279	532	471	(12%)	2249	2350	4599	4541	(2%)	8.9	8.4	8.6	9.6	12%
Developing	115	76	191	170	(11%)	372	289	661	620	(6%)	3.2	3.8	3.4	3.7	9%
US/Non-US															
United States	111	72	183	137	(25%)	1293	514	1807	1794	(1%)	11.6	7.1	9.9	13.1	33%
Non-US	257	283	540	504	(7%)	1328	2125	3453	3367	(3%)	5.2	7.5	6.4	6.7	5%
Common Markets															
EC	77	117	194	197	2%	450	1206	1656	1830	11%	5.8	10.3	8.5	9.3	9%
Major Countries															
United States	111	72	183	137	(25%)	1293	514	1807	1794	(1%)	11.6	7.1	9.9	13.1	33%
United Kingdom	45	19	64	57	(11%)	273	166	439	500	14%	6.1	8.7	6.9	8.8	28%
Canada	23	18	41	28	(13%)	218	211	429	257	(40%)	9.5	11.7	10.5	9.2	(12%)
Australia	23	10	33	23	(30%)	144	91	235	233	(1%)	6.3	9.1	7.1	10.1	42%
France	3	27	30	28	7%	10	387	397	596	50%	3.3	14.3	13.2	21.3	61%
Netherlands	3	26	29	27	(7%)	19	199	218	212	(3%)	6.3	7.7	7.5	7.9	5%
South Africa	10	17	27	18	(33%)	45	84	129	122	(5%)	4.5	4.9	4.8	6.8	42%
Japan	4	3	7	4	(43%)	45	51	96	50	(48%)	11.3	17.0	13.7	12.5	(9%)
Germany, West	6	16	22	33	50%	50	206	256	185	(28%)	8.3	12.9	11.6	5.6	(52%)
New Zealand	12	11	23	16	30%	89	55	144	103	(29%)	7.4	5.5	6.3	6.4	2%

TABLE 9-18

OTHER SMALLER INTERNATIONAL ACCOUNTING FIRMS
TOTAL PARTNERS WORLDWIDE AND BY REGIONS

Worldwide					% of Partners by Region for Each Firm					
Other Eight Firms	Number of Countries	Number of Affiliates	Total Offices	Total Partners	North America	Europe	Asia/ Pacific	South America/ Caribbean	Africa/ Middle East	Total
AFAI	19	75	124	383	63%	27%	9%	0	1%	100%
CKL	30	36	93	392	30%	40%	20%	3%	7%	100%
DFK	48	64	157	486	35%	45%	16%	1%	3%	100%
JHI*	22	42	43	*	*	*	*	*	*	*
IGAF	40	81	123	474	56%	22%	12%	4%	6%	100%
MI	55	80	168	519	29%	40%	19%	6%	6%	100%
MS	51	72	171	630	29%	47%	9%	9%	6%	100%
SIAI	25	50	120	594	71%	25%	2%	0	2%	100%
TOTAL	n/a	500	999	3478	44%	36%	12%	4%	4%	100%

* Office directory listed contact partners name only.

n/a - not applicable

TABLE 9-19

RECENT CHANGES IN NUMBER OF OFFICES, NUMBER OF PARTNERS AND AVERAGE PARTNERS PER OFFICE BY INTERNATIONAL ACCOUNTING FIRMS
1982 - 1988

	Change in No. of Offices			Change in No. of Partners			Change in Average Partners per Officers		
	No. of Offices		% of Growth	Total Partners		% of Growth	Avg. Partners		% of Growth
Firms	1982	1988	(Reduction)	1982	1988	(Reduction)	1982	1988	(Reduction)
AA	155	217	40%	1438	2133	48%	9.28	9.83	6%
AYI	247	418	69%	1960	2562	31%	7.94	6.13	(23%)
CL	424	565	33%	2282	3341	46%	5.38	5.91	10%
DHSI	313	471	50%	1785	2345	31%	5.70	4.98	(13%)
EW	283	378	34%	1479	2721	84%	5.23	7.20	38%
KMG	362	n/a	n/a	2254	n/a	n/a	6.23	n/a	n/a
PMM	311	n/a	n/a	2143	n/a	n/a	6.89	n/a	n/a
KPMG	673*	641	(5%)	4397*	5161	17%	6.53*	8.05	23%
PW	326	424	30%	1677	2568	53%	5.14	6.06	18%
TRI	384	515	34%	2046	2792	36%	5.33	5.42	2%
Total	2805	3629	29%	17064	23623	38%	6.08	6.51	7%

* 1982 figures of KMG & PMM were summed for KPMG but are not included in the totals.

n/a - not applicable

TABLE 9-20

RECENT CHANGES IN ORGANIZATION STRUCTURE USED BY INTERNATIONAL ACCOUNTING FIRMS

1982			1988	
% of Total Partners by Organizational Structure			% of Total Partners by Organizational Structure	
International or Combined Name	Local Name	Firms	International or Combined Name	Local Name
		Big Eight		
99.17	.83	AA	83.83	16.17
47.45	52.55	AYI	53.12	46.88
75.77	24.23	CL	72.97	27.03
82.18	17.82	DHSI	72.20	27.80
93.91	6.09	EW	89.86	10.14
22.76	77.24	KMG	n/a	n/a
95.66	4.34	PMM	n/a	n/a
62.59*	37.41*	KPMG	100.00	0
95.23	4.77	PW	92.48	7.52
61.83	38.17	TRI	40.37	59.63
72.47%	27.53%	Total	77.80%	22.20%

* 1982 figures for PMM and KMG were summed for comparison to the new firm, KPMG, but are not included in the totals.

n/a - not applicable

TABLE 9-21

RECENT CHANGES IN TOTAL NUMBER OF OFFICES, PARTNERS AND AVERAGE PARTNERS PER OFFICE OF INTERNATIONAL ACCOUNTING FIRMS IN THE US

Firms	Number of Offices		% of Growth (Reduction)	Number of Partners		% of Growth (Reduction)	Average Partners Per Office		% of Growth (Reduction)
Big Eight	1982	1988		1982	1988		1982	1988	
AA	71	97	37%	984	1351	37%	13.86	13.93	0%
AYI	70	97	39%	707	792	12%	10.10	8.16	(19%)
CL	85	99	16%	836	1167	40%	9.84	11.79	20%
DHSI	95	113	19%	643	800	24%	6.77	7.08	5%
EW	113	119	5%	794	1230	55%	7.03	10.34	47%
KMG	82	n/a	n/a	473	n/a	n/a	5.77	n/a	n/a
PMM	96	n/a	n/a	1148	n/a	n/a	11.96	n/a	n/a
KPMG	178*	137	(23%)	1621*	1794	11%	9.11*	13.09	44%
PW	83	109	31%	580	881	52%	6.99	8.08	16%
TRI	77	87	13%	713	835	17%	9.26	9.60	4%
TOTAL	772	858	11%	6878	8850	29%	8.91	10.31	16%

TABLE 9-22

RECENT CHANGES IN TOTAL NUMBER OF OFFICES, PARTNERS AND AVERAGE PARTNERS PER OFFICE OF INTERNATIONAL ACCOUNTING FIRMS IN NON-US COUNTRIES

Firms	Number of Offices		% of Growth (Reduction)	Number of Partners		% of Growth (Reduction)	Average Partners Per Office		% of Growth (Reduction)
Big Eight	1982	1988		1982	1988		1982	1988	
AA	84	120	43%	454	782	72%	5.40	6.52	21%
AYI	177	321	81%	1253	1770	41%	7.08	5.51	(22%)
CL	339	466	37%	1446	2174	50%	4.27	4.67	9%
DHSI	218	358	64%	1142	1545	35%	5.24	4.32	(18%)
EW	170	259	52%	685	1491	118%	4.03	5.76	43%
KMG	280	n/a	n/a	1781	n/a	n/a	6.36	n/a	n/a
PMM	215	n/a	n/a	995	n/a	n/a	4.63	n/a	n/a
KPMG	495*	504	2%	2776*	3367	21%	5.61*	6.68	19%
PW	243	315	30%	1097	1687	54%	4.51	5.36	19%
TRI	307	428	39%	1333	1957	47%	4.34	4.57	5%
TOTAL	2033	2771	36%	10186	14773	45%	5.01	5.33	6%

*1982 figure for PMM and KMG were summed for comparison with the new firm, KPMG, but is not included in the totals.

n/a - not applicable

TABLE 9-23
RECENT CHANGES IN TOTAL NUMBER OF OFFICES, PARTNERS AND AVERAGE PARTNERS PER OFFICE OF INTERNATIONAL ACCOUNTING FIRMS IN INDUSTRIAL COUNTRIES

	Change in No. of Offices			Change in No. of Partners			Change in Average Partners		
	No. of Offices		% of Growth (Reduction)	Total Partners		% of Growth (Reduction)	Average Ptnrs. Per Office		% of Growth (Reduction)
Firms	1982	1988		1982	1988		1982	1988	
Big Eight									
AA	126	174	38%	1332	1936	45%	10.57	11.13	5%
AYI	209	328	57%	1822	2275	25%	8.72	6.94	(20%)
CL	297	397	34%	1937	2791	44%	6.52	7.03	8%
DHSI	243	368	51%	1618	2020	25%	6.66	5.49	(18%)
EW	210	296	41%	1316	2480	88%	6.27	8.38	34%
KMG	316	n/a	n/a	2151	n/a	n/a	6.81	n/a	n/a
PMM	223	n/a	n/a	1912	n/a	n/a	8.57	n/a	n/a
KPMG	539*	471	(13%)	4063*	4541	12%	15.38	9.64	(37%)
PW	211	264	25%	1345	2027	51%	6.37	7.68	20%
TRI	272	363	33%	1772	2362	33%	6.51	6.51	0%
Total	2107	2661	26%	15205	20432	34%	7.22	7.68	6%

TABLE 9-24
RECENT CHANGES IN TOTAL NUMBER OF OFFICES, PARTNERS AND AVERAGE PARTNERS PER OFFICE OF INTERNATIONAL ACCOUNTING FIRMS IN DEVELOPING COUNTRIES

	Change in No. of Offices			Change in No. of Partners			Change in Average Partners		
	No. of Offices		% of Growth (Reduction)	Total Partners		% of Growth (Reduction)	Average Ptnrs. Per Office		% of Growth (Reduction)
Firms	1982	1988		1982	1988		1982	1988	
Big Eight									
AA	29	43	48%	106	197	86%	3.66	4.58	25%
AY	38	90	137%	138	287	108%	3.63	3.19	(12%)
CL	127	168	32%	345	550	59%	2.72	3.27	21%
DHSI	70	103	47%	167	325	95%	2.39	3.16	32%
EW	73	82	12%	163	241	48%	2.23	2.94	32%
KMG	46	n/a	n/a	103	n/a	n/a	2.24	n/a	n/a
PMM	88	n/a	n/a	231	n/a	n/a	2.63	n/a	n/a
KPMG	134*	170	27%	334*	620	86%	4.86	3.65	(25%)
PW	115	160	39%	332	541	63%	2.89	3.38	17%
TRI	112	152	36%	274	430	57%	2.45	2.83	24%
Total	698	968	39%	1859	3191	72%	2.66	3.30	13%

* 1982 figures of KMG and PMM were summed to compare the growth of the new firm, KPMG, but were not included in the totals.

n/a - not applicable

TABLE 9-25

RECENT CHANGES IN TOTAL NUMBER OF OFFICES, PARTNERS AND AVERAGE PARTNERS PER OFFICE BY REGION AND INTERNATIONAL ACCOUNTING FIRM
NORTH AMERICA

	No. of Offices		% of Growth	Total Partners		% of Growth	Ptnrs. Per Off.		% of Growth
Firms	1982	1988	(Reduction)	1982	1988	(Reduction)	1982	1988	(Reduction)
Big Eight									
AA	81	107	32%	1049	1438	37%	12.95	13.44	4%
AYI	94	127	35%	1054	1217	15%	11.21	9.58	(15%)
CL	112	130	16%	1134	1475	30%	10.12	11.35	12%
DHSI	129	176	36%	883	1136	29%	6.84	6.45	(6%)
EW	150	190	27%	910	1764	94%	6.07	9.28	53%
KMG	136	n/a	n/a	804	n/a	n/a	5.91	n/a	n/a
PMM	121	n/a	n/a	1359	n/a	n/a	11.23	n/a	n/a
KPMG	257*	174	(32%)	2163*	2082	(4%)	8.42*	11.97	42%
PW	109	142	30%	772	1161	50%	7.08	8.18	15%
TRI	110	140	27%	974	1214	25%	8.85	8.67	(3%)
Total	1042	1186	14%	8939	11487	29%	8.58	9.69	13%

TABLE 9-26

RECENT CHANGES IN TOTAL NUMBER OF OFFICES, PARTNERS AND AVERAGE PARTNERS PER OFFICE BY REGION AND INTERNATIONAL ACCOUNTING FIRM
EUROPE

	No. of Offices		% of Growth	Total Partners		% of Growth	Average Ptnrs. Per Office		% of Growth
Firms	1982	1988	(Reduction)	1982	1988	(Reduction)	1982	1988	(Reduction)
Big Eight									
AA	41	64	56%	247	443	79%	6.02	6.92	15%
AYI	89	188	111%	528	925	75%	5.93	4.92	(17%)
CL	135	225	67%	573	940	64%	4.24	4.18	(2%)
DHSI	77	172	123%	456	718	57%	5.92	4.17	(30%)
EW	62	74	19%	329	437	33%	5.31	5.91	11%
KMG	144*	n/a	n/a	1125*	n/a	n/a	7.81	n/a	n/a
PMM	67	n/a	n/a	332	n/a	n/a	4.96	n/a	n/a
KPMG	211*	272	29%	1457*	2124	46%	6.91*	7.81	16%
PW	70	111	59%	369	677	83%	5.27	6.10	16%
TRI	126	191	52%	521	821	58%	4.13	4.30	4%
Total	811	1297	60%	4480	7085	58%	5.52	5.46	(1%)

*1982 figures of KMG and PMM were summed to compare the growth of the new firm, KPMG, but were not included in the totals.

n/a - not applicable

TABLE 9-27

RECENT CHANGES IN TOTAL NUMBER OF OFFICES, PARTNERS AND AVERAGE PARTNERS PER OFFICE BY REGION AND INTERNATIONAL ACCOUNTING FIRM
ASIA/PACIFIC

Firms	No. of Offices 1982	No. of Offices 1988	% of Growth (Reduction)	Total Partners 1982	Total Partners 1988	% of Growth (Reduction)	Average Ptnrs. Per Office 1982	Average Ptnrs. Per Office 1988	% of Growth (Reduction)
Big Eight									
AA	10	17	70%	51	126	147%	5.10	7.41	45%
AYI	31	42	35%	238	244	3%	7.68	5.81	(24%)
CL	94	117	24%	342	619	81%	3.64	5.29	45%
DHSI	35	48	37%	235	240	2%	6.71	5.00	(26%)
EW	29	64	121%	107	368	244%	3.69	5.75	56%
KMG	35	n/a	n/a	187	n/a	n/a	5.34	n/a	n/a
PMM	52	n/a	n/a	252	n/a	n/a	4.85	n/a	n/a
KPMG	87*	87	0%	439*	530	21%	5.05*	6.09	21%
PW	65	66	2%	273	389	42%	4.20	5.89	40%
TRI	74	103	39%	334	503	51%	4.51	4.88	8%
Total	425	544	28%	2019	3019	50%	4.75	5.55	17%

*1982 figures of KMG and PMM were summed to compare the growth of the new firm, KPMG, but were not included in the totals.

n/a - not applicable

TABLE 9-28
RECENT CHANGES IN TOTAL NUMBER OF OFFICES, PARTNERS AND AVERAGE PARTNERS PER OFFICE
BY REGION AND INTERNATIONAL ACCOUNTING FIRM
AFRICA/MIDDLE EAST

Firms	No. of Offices 1982	No. of Offices 1988	% of Growth (Reduction)	Total Partners 1982	Total Partners 1988	% of Growth (Reduction)	Average Ptnrs. Per Office 1982	Average Ptnrs. Per Office 1988	% of Growth (Reduction)
Big Eight									
AA	9	13	44%	24	36	50%	2.67	2.77	4%
AYI	18	36	100%	82	115	40%	4.56	3.19	(30%)
CL	51	55	8%	137	183	34%	2.69	3.33	24%
DHSI	46	50	9%	145	175	21%	3.15	3.50	11%
EW	31	38	23%	109	129	18%	3.52	3.39	(3%)
KMG	32	n/a	n/a	96	n/a	n/a	3.00	n/a	n/a
PMM	38	n/a	n/a	106	n/a	n/a	2.79	n/a	n/a
KPMG	70*	64	(9%)	202*	246	22%	2.89*	3.84	34%
PW	38	49	29%	91	128	41%	2.39	2.61	9%
TRI	47	52	11%	145	173	19%	3.09	3.33	8%
Total	310	357	15%	935	1185	27%	3.02	3.32	10%

TABLE 9-29
RECENT CHANGES IN TOTAL NUMBER OF OFFICES, PARTNERS AND AVERAGE PARTNERS PER OFFICE
BY REGION AND INTERNATIONAL ACCOUNTING FIRM
SOUTH AMERICA/CARIBBEAN

Firms	No. of Offices 1982	No. of Offices 1988	% of Growth (Reduction)	Total Partners 1982	Total Partners 1988	% of Growth (Reduction)	Average Ptnrs. Per Office 1982	Average Ptnrs. Per Office 1988	% of Growth (Reduction)
Big Eight									
AA	14	16	14%	67	90	34%	4.79	5.62	18%
AYI	15	25	67%	58	61	5%	3.87	2.44	(37%)
CL	32	38	19%	96	124	29%	3.00	3.26	9%
DHSI	26	25	(4%)	66	76	15%	2.54	3.04	20%
EW	11	12	9%	24	23	(4%)	2.18	1.92	(12)%
KMG	15	n/a	n/a	42	n/a	n/a	2.80	n/a	n/a
PMM	33	n/a	n/a	94	n/a	n/a	2.85	n/a	n/a
KPMG	48*	44	(8%)	136*	179	32%	2.83*	4.07	44%
PW	44	56	27%	172	213	24%	3.91	3.80	(3%)
TRI	27	29	7%	72	81	13%	2.67	2.79	5%
Total	217	245	13%	691	847	23%	3.18	3.46	9%

* 1982 figures of KMG and PMM were summed to compare the growth of the new firm, KPMG, but were not included in the totals.

n/a - not applicable

TABLE 9-30

RECENT CHANGES IN TOTAL NUMBER OF OFFICES, PARTNERS AND AVERAGE PARTNERS PER OFFICE BY INTERNATIONAL ACCOUNTING FIRM
EC

Firms	No. of Offices		% of Growth (Reduction)	Total Partners		% of Growth (Reduction)	Partners Per Office		% of Growth (Reduction)
	1982	1988		1982	1988		1982	1988	
Big Eight									
AA	34	53	56%	213	398	87%	6.26	7.51	20%
AYI	66	123	86%	459	712	55%	6.95	5.79	(17%)
CL	77	122	58%	470	739	57%	6.10	6.06	(1%)
DHSI	62	89	44%	389	530	36%	6.27	5.96	(5%)
EW	58	68	17%	319	424	33%	5.50	6.24	13%
KMG	114	n/a	n/a	1010	n/a	n/a	8.86	n/a	n/a
PMM	64	n/a	n/a	325	n/a	n/a	5.08	n/a	n/a
KPMG	178*	197	11%	1335*	1830	37%	7.50*	9.29	24%
PW	59	85	44%	341	625	83%	5.78	7.35	27%
TRI	102	138	35%	462	653	41%	4.53	4.73	4%
Total	636	875	38%	3988	5911	48%	6.27	6.76	8%

*1982 figures of KMG and PMM were summed to compare the growth of the new firm, KPMG, but were not included in the totals.

n/a - not applicable

TABLE 9-31 RECENT CHANGES IN TOTAL NUMBER OF OFFICES OF BIG EIGHT INTERNATIONAL ACCOUNTING FIRMS IN MAJOR COUNTRIES															
	United States			United Kingdom			Canada			Australia			France		
Firms	82	88	% Chg.	82	88	% Chg.	82	88	% Chg.	82	88	% Chg.	82	88	% Chg.
AA	71	97	37	9	12	33	7	7	0	5	6	20	2	3	50
AYI	70	97	37	18	22	22	21	25	19	7	13	86	2	9	350
CL	85	99	17	33	40	21	22	24	9	37	34	(8)	3	14	367
DHSI	95	113	14	29	21	(28)	32	60	88	15	14	(7)	3	4	33
EW	113	119	5	27	25	(7)	17	71	318	9	16	78	2	2	0
KMG	82	n/a	n/a	19	n/a	n/a	46	n/a	n/a	21	n/a	n/a	26	n/a	n/a
PMM	96	n/a	n/a	39	n/a	n/a	22	n/a	n/a	20	n/a	n/a	1	n/a	n/a
KPMG*	177	137	(23)	56	57	(2%)	68	28	(59)	41	23	(44)	27	28	4
PW	83	109	31	17	23	35	22	24	9	26	19	(27)	5	12	140
TRI	77	87	13	20	31	55	28	42	50	16	21	31	6	7	17
Total	772	858	11%	209	231	11%	217	281	30	156	146	(6)	50	79	58%

TABLE 9-32 RECENT CHANGES IN TOTAL NUMBER OF PARTNERS OF BIG EIGHT INTERNATIONAL ACCOUNTING FIRMS IN MAJOR COUNTRIES															
	United States			United Kingdom			Canada			Australia			France		
Firms	82	88	% Chg.	82	88	% Chg.	82	88	% Chg.	82	88	% Chg.	82	88	% Chg.
AA	984	1351	37	92	131	42	48	57	19	26	68	162	23	55	139
AYI	707	792	12	168	214	27	331	397	20	75	83	11	28	55	96
CL	836	1167	40	224	364	63	251	245	(2)	160	199	24	19	58	205
DHSI	643	800	24	250	257	3	231	328	42	140	91	(35)	14	25	79
EW	794	1230	55	229	253	10	73	534	632	60	124	107	10	39	290
KMG	473	n/a	n/a	166	n/a	n/a	314	n/a	n/a	87	n/a	n/a	374	n/a	59
PMM	1148	n/a	n/a	190	n/a	n/a	199	n/a	n/a	121	n/a	n/a	8	n/a	n/a
KPMG*	1615	1794	11	356	500	40	513	257	(50)	208	233	12	382	596	56
PW	580	881	52	182	364	100	182	242	33	139	163	17	27	48	78
TRI	713	835	17	157	237	51	157	334	113	107	124	16	22	46	109
Total	6878	8850	29	1658	2320	40	1786	2394	34	915	1085	19	525	922	76

* 1982 figures for PMM and KMG were summed for comparison to the new firm, but are not included in the totals.

n/a - not applicable

TABLE 9-33

RECENT CHANGES IN TOTAL NUMBER OF PARTNERS BY MAJOR CITIES AND LEADING THREE FIRMS

Total Partners of Big Eight Firms				1982 3 Leading Firms			1988 3 Leading Firms		
1982	1988	% CHANGE	LEADING CITIES	1	2	3	1	2	3
1078	1202	12%	New York, U.S.A.	PMM	CL	AYI	KPMG	CL	PW
866	1066	23%	London, U.K.	CL	EW	PW	PW	KPMG	CL
566	674	19%	Chicago, U.S.A.	AA	PMM	EW	AA	KPMG	EW
592	630	6%	Toronto, Canada	AYI	TRI	CL	AYI	EW	KPMG/PW
187	404	116%	Tokyo, Japan	AYI	TRI	KMG	TRI	CL	EW
315	346	10%	Sydney, Australia	DHSI	PW	CL	KPMG	PW	CL
295	276	(6%)	Montreal, Canada	CL*	TRI	AYI	DHSI	EW*	TRI*
328	423	29%	Los Angeles, U.S.A.	PMM	AA	AYI	KPMG	AA	EW
263	389	48%	Paris, France	KMG	PMM	AYI	KPMG	AA	CL
254	357	41%	Washington DC, U.S.A.	PMM	AA	CL	KPMG	EW/AA	PW
210	250	19%	Johannesburg, S. Africa	DHSI	KMG	EW	KPMG	EW	TRI
279	274	2%	Houston, U.S.A.	AA	PMM	TRI	AA	KPMG	EW
234	277	18%	Dallas, U.S.A.	AYI	PMM	AA	KPMG	AA	EW
229	236	3%	Melbourne, Australia	DHSI	PW	CL	KPMG	PW	CL
195	251	29%	San Francisco, U.S.A.	AA	CL	TRI	AA	KPMG	CL
244	219	(10%)	Philadelphia, U.S.A.	CL	KMG	PMM	CL	KPMG*	AA
213	276	30%	Boston, U.S.A.	CL	AA	PMM	CL	KPMG	AA
118	175	48%	Stockholm, Sweden	KMG	DHSI	TRI	DHSI	KPMG/TRI	CL
141	220	56%	Atlanta, U.S.A.	AA	TRI	EW	AA	KPMG	EW
168	253	51%	Cleveland, U.S.A.	EW	AA/TRI	PW	EW	AA	KPMG

*Note: If small eight firms had been included, GTI was first in 1982 in Montreal, and MRI was second and GTI was third in 1988 in the same city. HHI was second in Philadelphia in 1988.

IV. SUMMARY AND CONCLUSIONS

Where are the international accounting firms located throughout the world?

- The top sixteen firms are located in 152 countries and territories of the world.

- More partners were in North America than any other single region; Europe was the second most important region.

- Less than one-fourth of the total partners were located in the three other major regions of the world (Asia/Pacific, Africa/Middle East, and South America/Caribbean), even though three out of the top ten countries were in the Asia/Pacific regions.

How have leading international accounting firms organized their offices worldwide?

- The majority of partners practiced under the international or combined international and local name, particularly in the industrial countries. Out of all big eight firms, PW used the international or combined name the most, though recently, KPMG and BDO have begun to add their international initials to the local names of each of their offices worldwide. Of the top eight firms, TRI and AYI practiced under local name most often.

- Practicing under the local name was more common outside the US and UK and was almost exclusively used in France and Japan, where local regulations limit the use of international accounting firm names.

Which were the leading countries and cities in terms of number of offices and partners?

- The US, UK and Canada led in both number of offices and partners.

- New York, London and Chicago had the greatest number of partners, followed by Toronto, Los Angeles and Paris.

  Appendix E provides a global chart of the number of partners of the sixteen international accounting firms by region, country and city.

How many partners per office, on the average, were there for the international accounting firms?

- AA led worldwide in number of partners per office with almost twice the world average. KPMG and EW also had a high average. The big eight firms generally had larger averages than the small eight firms. Also, industrial countries had more than twice the average partners per office than developing countries. In North America the average was much higher than in other regions.

How has the 1987 merger of Klynveld Main Goerdeler (KMG) and Peat Marwick Mitchell & Co. (PMM) affected the international competitive rankings of accounting firms globally and regionally?

- Globally, the merger has pushed KPMG ahead of CL, which led in number of partners in 1982. It did not have much effect on their overall competitive standing in North America and Europe since the pre-merged firms already led in these regions. The merger also helped the firm take a lead in the Africa/Middle East region, where it gained over CL and DHSI.

Where and when have mergers between local firms and leading international firms been most active? What firms have been most active in mergers?

- Mergers have been most frequent in 1987 and 1988 in the US, Japan and Canada with KPMG, TRI and DHSI identified as the most active firms.

How have the leading international accounting firms grown globally in recent years?

- The firms in the Europe and Asia/Pacific regions had the overall largest percentage growth in comparison to the firms in other regions.

- Although the merger of PMM and KMG created the largest firm in terms of number of offices and partners, EW had the largest percentage growth in partners over the past six years and AYI increased its number of offices most. EW's growth was chiefly outside the US where it grew 118% over the number of partners it had in 1982.

- AYI grew the most rapidly in number of partners in developing countries.

- PW had a high percentage of growth in number of partners in Europe.

- AA and EW grew over 100% in the Asia/Pacific region.

What are the competitive standings of leading international accounting firms in the world, various regions, countries and cities?

- KPMG led the firms globally by ranking first in three major regions and second in the Asia/Pacific region, where CL ranked the highest, and in the South America/Caribbean region, where PW dominated. TRI also had a strong presence in the Asia/Pacific and Africa/Middle East regions.

- CL had a strong distribution of partners in the widest range of areas, including the developing countries, particularly in the Asia/Pacific and Africa/Middle East regions.

- PW showed good coverage in the developing countries, particularly in the Asia/Pacific and Africa/Middle East regions.

- In number of partners, KPMG led in seven out of the top ten countries. EW led in Canada, AYI in the Netherlands and TRI in Japan.

- KPMG, CL and PW were the leading firms in both London and New York. KPMG led in New York and PW in London. AA, with headquarters in Chicago, led in the third-ranked city. AYI led in Toronto (the fourth city), KPMG in Los Angeles (the fifth city) and in Paris (the sixth city).

The data summarized in this chapter has provided an overview of the global networks of the sixteen leading international accounting firms. The next chapter provides a similar analysis based on clients audited by these sixteen international accounting firms.

CHAPTER 10

ANALYSIS OF CLIENTS AUDITED BY LEADING INTERNATIONAL ACCOUNTING FIRMS

Table of Contents

CHAPTER 10

TABLES

I. INTRODUCTION

The multinational networks which large accounting firms are developing through restructuring and expanding in an increasingly competitive marketplace are the result of client needs and market forces. In fact, the changing structure of the accounting profession as a whole has been affected by the increasing globalization of capital markets. This chapter presents the results of a global competitive analysis of the client base of the sixteen leading international accounting firms.

The client profiles presented in various tables and summaries reflect how the major international accounting firms have responded to the challenges of the marketplace. They also show what measures these firms have taken to integrate their resources in order to establish strategically advantageous alliances to break down international barriers and capture market shares. At the same time, the profiles will allow for the identification of gaps in representation among the international accounting firms in various industries and geographic locations.

II. RESEARCH OBJECTIVES

In this global competitive analysis of the client base of the leading international accounting firms, the following research questions will be addressed:

10-1 Who are the leading international accounting firms worldwide based on the number and size of clients they audit?

10-2 Do the international accounting firms audit most of the multinational corporations worldwide?

10-3 What is the composition of the client base of the international accounting firms in terms of countries, regions, economy types and common markets?

10-4 Do the international accounting firms have any industry concentration on a worldwide, regional or country basis?

10-5 Within specific countries, what is the presence of the leading international accounting firms in terms of client size, as measured by client company sales or assets?

10-6 To what extent are large subsidiaries audited by the parent company's auditor?

10-7 How do partner and office demographics for the international accounting firms worldwide relate to client statistics for these firms?

III. RESEARCH DESIGN

Identifying the Client Base

The client data set consisted of approximately 13,000 non-US and 3,600 US companies, identified primarily from CIFAR's extensive annual reports collection, and further enhanced by leading global, regional and country-specific reference sources, financial directories, stock exchange publications and leading company and industry-specific listings published in local business-related magazines, journals and newspapers.

The comprehensive collection of international reference materials in the Brooklyn Public Library (Brooklyn, New York) and the City Business Library (London), as well as sources from several other private, public and academic accounting and business libraries were consulted to verify and expand upon the data where company annual reports were unavailable.

Input from the sixteen leading international accounting firms also helped to identify new companies within the various countries. A size criterion for new company inclusion based on sales or assets was established according to whether the company in question was from a country considered to be in the "large industrial", "smaller industrial" or "emerging market" category. It follows that in the emerging market countries many relatively smaller companies, in terms of sales and assets, have been included.

In certain smaller emerging market countries there is an overall lack of company financial and auditor data. We chose to omit these countries (e.g., Egypt, Iceland, Indonesia and Jordan) from the analysis in this chapter. However, this will not significantly alter worldwide conclusions.

Variables Extracted

Data was extracted from the client company 1987 annual report whenever it was available. However, for 37 % of the clients 1986 data was used, because 1987 data was unavailable at the time.

The data for the sales and assets of the majority of the US companies included was extracted from the Worldscope Database, co-developed by CIFAR and Wright Investors' Service.

Whenever possible, the following information was extracted for each client company:

1. Country and Company Name
2. Industry Classification
3. Parent or Subsidiary Classification
4. Multinationality Status (For the Leading 2,000 Companies Worldwide)
5. Ownership Status (Government vs. Shareholder-owned)
6. Fiscal Year of Financial Information
7. Consolidated Sales in Local Currency for Clients in Manufacturing Sectors (Non-consolidated sales were used if consolidated sales were not available.)
8. Consolidated Assets in Local Currency for Client Groups in both Manufacturing and Service Sectors (Non-consolidated assets were used if consolidated assets were not available.)
9. Auditor(s) or Auditing Firm(s), derived from the Auditor's Report included in the Annual Report

Appendix F presents the companies included in our client database.

Auditor Identification

In creating the client data set, every effort was made to identify relevant external auditors and auditing firms and to establish proper links between these external auditors and the sixteen international accounting firms. We have chosen to focus on only the top 16 international accounting firms because of the large gap in the number of clients audited between this group and the rest. The sixteenth firm was a logical cut-off point for in-depth analysis and summarization.

Due to constant restructuring within firms, affiliation changes among local firms, and newly formed alliances of major audit firms on local levels, there are often local firm name changes which accompany these new associations. Every effort has been made to identify the most up-to-date local auditor name based on entries in the 1988 office directories of the international accounting firms. If there was a discrepancy between the auditor's name as it appeared in the client's annual report and in the latest office directory, the latter name has generally established as the most current. The summary totals attributed to each of the international accounting firms represent all the various local firm names and individual partners identified as operating within the particular international accounting firm's organizational structure.

Information found in recent international accounting newsletters and bulletins was also utilized to identify changes in firm affiliations not yet reflected in the firm's office directories.

Individual Auditors

Quite frequently, the audit opinions in client company annual reports are signed by individual partners rather than by an accounting firm. Every effort was made to assign proper credit to the international firms by matching partners listed in firm office directories with individual partner signatures. Direct input from accounting firms also identified previously unknown affiliate links.

Non-Affiliated Firms

Even though major international accounting firms are capturing an increasingly larger share of the audit market, there are still a significant number of firms in various countries that have remained independent of the sixteen major international accounting firms. In order to present a truly competitive analysis of accounting firms on a global basis, it is necessary to examine who these independent firms are, where they are located, and the strength of their client base in terms of sales or assets within a particular country. Major non-affiliated firms are listed in Table 10-21.

In the tables and appendix listings of all clients, all individual auditors and non-affiliated firms have been merged into one category: "NAFF" (not affiliated with one of the sixteen large international accounting firms). This NAFF category also includes local auditing firms which have multiple affiliations with the sixteen international accounting firms.

Smaller International Accounting Groups

We have also looked at the clients in our database which are audited by the other smaller international accounting groups referred to in Chapter 9. If we had included them among our large international accounting firms, our rankings would not have changed. The client base of these other eight firms overall is small. Perhaps non-audit services are more important to these smaller firms, compared to big eight and small eight firms.

Joint Auditors

There are several countries in which the use of joint auditors is common, often as a result of legal requirements for company audits. In France, for example, more than one auditor is required to audit companies that publish consolidated financial reports. The sales or assets totals in the summaries for these companies have been divided in proportion to the number of auditors. The countries in which this practice is prevalent are summarized in Table 10-23.

Government Auditors

In the summary tables as well as in Appendix F, "Client Companies by Country," government companies which are audited by government auditors have been excluded, as by definition they are not part of the audit marketplace. However, government-owned companies with independent auditors are included in this study and are summarized in Table 10-24.

No Disclosure of External Auditors

Occasionally, audit opinions do not identify the external auditor. The "auditor not identified" description has been assigned in these instances (NADT). This designation is also used in cases where auditors were very difficult to identify. However, as can be seen in Table 10-1, this rarely occurs. (For less than 1% of 16,600 clients the external auditor could not be identified.)

Sales and Assets

In order to facilitate global comparisons, all local sales and assets figures have been converted into US dollars, expressed in millions. For sales, the exchange rate used was an average computed from rates for the 12-month period prior to the fiscal year-end. For assets, the fiscal year-end exchange rate corresponding to the fiscal year-end date of the particular company's financial reports was used.

Each client company has also been assigned a "DSum" or dollar sum figure which represents either total sales or assets, depending on the type of industry in which the company is engaged: i.e., sales for industrials, transportation and utilities, assets for financials. The DSum figure found in many of the tables is a single combined total of the composite sales and/or assets for the particular group of companies being examined. Many of the summary tables provide rankings based on this DSum calculation.

Size of Clients

Five size categories, based on sales or assets, were established for the various clients. The size was defined by sales or assets, depending upon the client's industry classification.

Banks, insurance companies and other financial services are grouped by assets. Companies in all other industries are grouped according to sales. The categories, all in US$, were assigned as follows:

1. 1-100 million
2. 101-500 million
3. 501 million-1 billion
4. 1-10 billion
5. 10 billion and over

The summary data regarding the size of clients will provide insight into exactly which firms are auditing the largest companies worldwide.

Multinationality

To whatever extent possible, the leading client companies were classified into various categories of multinationality. For the purpose of this analysis, the distinction is purely one of non-multinationality versus multinationality on the basis of whether the company has subsidiaries in three or more countries. We will focus on the top 2,000 multinational and non-multinational companies worldwide.

US and Non-US Clients

The US has the largest concentration of clients, accounting firm offices and partners worldwide. Thus, comparing the US with the rest of the world will point out the differences between US and non-US based audit practices among the large international accounting firms.

Industrial and Emerging Market Countries

Due to the increasing global importance of "developing countries" in the marketplace, clients in these countries will be grouped and contrasted with clients in "industrialized" countries.

Regions

Regional groupings of the client companies will be used to identify geographic strengths and weaknesses among the large accounting firms and provide additional insights for them to strengthen international networks in previously untapped locations.

European Community (EC)

Client data will also be analyzed in terms of the EC, which includes some of the world's most industrialized countries. As the EC member countries are planning to substantially reduce internal trade barriers by the year 1992, a separate analysis of this market is appropriate.

Leading Countries

In order to facilitate analysis of the representation of the large international accounting firms in specific countries, tabulations will include summary totals of sales and assets within the top ten countries around the world.

Industries

In the various industry tables, client company industries are grouped into six general industry categories (consumer goods, capital goods, basic industries, financials, utilities and transportation, other) and thirty specific industry categories.

A complete list of the specific industries which belong to each of the six broader categories may be found in Table 10-4A. The summaries will assist the reader in observing the distribution of accounting firms within particular industries, and in evaluating industry-specific concentrations.

Subsidiaries

Efforts were made to determine whether listed clients are, in fact, subsidiaries (defined as a company of which 50% or more of equity is owned by another company) of parent companies already in the data set and then whether these linked companies are audited by the same auditing firm. The auditors of these parent and subsidiary companies can be compared on two levels: (1) when parent and subsidiary are both located in the same country, and (2) when parent and subsidiary are located in two different countries.

Accounting Firm Input

If the necessary information was not available regarding auditors of selected client companies in annual reports and various reference sources, assistance was solicited from accounting firms to identify missing information, particularly missing auditor information and any known international auditor affiliations. The information received from local branches of international firms helped greatly in accurately identifying auditors.

Direct contact with the local offices of five randomly selected international firms in approximately twenty countries made the data set more complete where (1) the client auditors were generally individuals not linked with any major firms, (2) the client auditors were unaffiliated firms or (3) information was lacking on client auditors.

Local and International Auditors in Japan

A situation found exclusively in Japan was that local language annual reports submitted to the Japanese Ministry of Finance are signed by local Japanese auditors while those in English for the same companies are signed by large international accounting firms. We used local Japanese auditors as primary auditors for our study.

Table 10-22 summarizes the Japanese client companies in our data set which have independent international accounting firms as auditors of their English language version reports and different local auditors who sign the Japanese reports.

Treatment of Subsidiaries

Our data set consists of 2,458 subsidiary companies, for which we have corresponding client parent companies. Most of our summary rankings are based on percentage of market share in dollar sum. Overstating the dollar sum impact for international accounting firms from both the subsidiary and consolidated parent company financial figures has been avoided by excluding the dollar sum figures for subsidiary companies from those of the parent company. The consolidated parent company figures would, by definition, include sales and assets of all subsidiary companies.

On a worldwide basis, we have deducted all DSum amounts for all subsidiary companies from parent DSum figures regardless of worldwide location of parent and subsidiaries and regardless of whether the subsidiary and parent have the same accounting firm affiliate (Table 10-2).

On a regional basis, the subsidiary DSum has been deducted from the parent company DSum only if the subsidiary and parent are located in the same region (Tables 10-10, 10-11, 10-12).

In the European Community the subsidiary DSum has been deducted from the parent company DSum only if the subsidiary is also located within the European Community (Table 10-16).

On a country basis, the subsidiary DSum amount is deducted from the parent DSum only if a subsidiary is located in the same country as the parent (Tables 10-15 and 10-18).

On a worldwide industry basis, if the parent and subsidiary are in the same broad industry group, the subsidiary DSum figure is deducted from the parent DSum (Table 10-4).

The fact that we have made these adjustments will be footnoted in the particular tables affected, together with indications of how the rankings would have changed had subsidiary DSum not been excluded from parent company auditors' DSum.

Companies with Dual Home Countries

For Shell and Unilever, we have preserved parent company status for both the Dutch and British holding companies (i.e., we have taken separately the sales or assets of these particular companies from consolidated reports for each home country).

Recent Mergers

Where recent mergers have taken place, only the surviving company has been tabulated for our purposes. Since it is not yet apparent whether the merged companies actually retain "subsidiary" status or are defunct, no assumptions have been made.

We have not reflected takeovers which occurred during 1988 in the database because the impact of such activities, in terms of variables of interest for both the acquired and the target company, would not be reflected in the 1987 annual report, but in 1988 data.

US Credit Companies

There are several US credit companies with large assets bases which are not consolidated with their parent companies, and, therefore, we have chosen not to classify these companies as subsidiaries. Thus, they have not been excluded from the totals for ranking purposes.

Financial Services/Holding Companies

If a manufacturing company's sales figure consisted mostly of investment income and the assets base was disproportionately high, we have reclassified this company into the "Financial Services/Holding Companies" industry.

Limited Data on Subsidiaries

In many instances, it was particularly difficult to obtain auditor information on subsidiaries because they do not publish separate annual reports.

Quality Control Measures Taken

The entire data set was verified several times to accurately reflect company names and industries, private and government-owned enterprises, subsidiary and parent linkages, mergers, defunct companies, sales and assets figures, including increases or decreases in sales and/or assets from 1986 to 1987, currency conversion factors and identify 1987 auditors of client companies.

Table 10-1 provides an overall picture, by percentage, of how many auditors and corresponding sales or assets figures have been identified for the total representative sample of companies in each country. Companies for which auditors were not disclosed account for less than 1% of the total client data base and 13% of total sales or assets. We feel that this small amount of unavailable information has not significantly affected the analysis or conclusions of this chapter.

TABLE 10-1

COUNTRIES AND NUMBER OF CLIENT COMPANIES INCLUDED

Region/Country	No. of Companies Included	Auditors Identified %	Sales or Assets Identified %
North America			
Canada	1327	100%	61%*
Mexico	108	95	92
United States	3639	100	99
Sub-Total	5074	100%	89%
Europe			
Austria	96	99%	89%
Belgium	155	100	89
Denmark	235	100	97
Finland	119	99	90
France	446	100	91
Germany, West	745	100	96
Greece	18	94	94
Ireland	50	98	86
Italy	366	96	77
Luxembourg	42	98	86
Netherlands	375	99	80
Norway	129	97	92
Portugal	32	97	72
Spain	119	90	91
Sweden	337	100	74
Switzerland	262	93	92
Turkey	24	80	58
United Kingdom	1147	100	87
Sub-Total	4697	99%	87%
Asia			
Australia	528	100%	83%
China, Taiwan	117	99	79
Hong Kong	337	99	81
India	406	100	72
Japan	1889	100	99
Korea, South	244	100	98
Malaysia	254	99	74
New Zealand	181	100	73
Pakistan	78	100	95
Philippines	251	99	22
Singapore	123	100	59
Thailand	145	97	79
Sub-Total	4553	100%	84%

* Our coverage for the leading 500 Canadian companies was 99% complete. In the total sample of 1327 companies there were many small mining/petroleum companies whose sales or assets were not readily available.

TABLE 10-1
(Continued)

COUNTRIES AND NUMBER OF CLIENT COMPANIES INCLUDED

Country	No. of Companies Included	Auditors Identified %	Sales or Assets Identified %
Africa/Middle East			
Israel	43	95%	88%
Kenya	13	100	62
Kuwait	20	90	95
Nigeria	25	92	68
South Africa	362	99	77
United Arab Emirates	15	100	53
Zimbabwe	17	82	88
Sub-Total	495	98%	77%
South America			
Argentina	66	97	92
Brazil	244	93	95
Chile	67	99	91
Colombia	109	98	61
Peru	19	100	84
Venezuela	34	100	71
Sub-Total	539	96%	86%
Grand Total	15358*	99%	87%

* The total number of companies in this table does not match the total worldwide number of companies as stated in Table 10-2 because for each country in Table 10-1, each company is counted only once, but, in Table 10-2, and other subsequent tables, companies which are jointly audited are counted as an audit client for each of the auditors involved. However, the sales or assets are divided proportionally.

IV. ANALYSIS

This section will provide tabulation, summarization and different levels of analysis of the data gathered on the sixteen international accounting firms based on the client companies they audit. The large sample size allows some general conclusions to be drawn about major players in international accounting.

A. Worldwide

It is useful to first look at the worldwide presence of the sixteen major international accounting firms in terms of clients audited. Table 10-2 provides such a picture. The major sixteen firms, plus unaffiliated firms, individuals, and multiple affiliated auditors (all grouped together as NAFF), are classified by total number and size of clients. The size of clients is determined on the basis of total sales or assets. As previously described, either sales or assets were extracted for summary table totals based on the particular industry of the client company. Assets were used for banks, insurance companies and other financial industries; sales for all other industries. The client company listings in Appendix F provide both sales and assets, where applicable. As depicted in Table 10-2, the sixteen largest international accounting firms have captured 76% (12,607 clients) of the worldwide audit market of companies represented in this study. These 12,607 companies in turn account for 85% of the worldwide total sales or assets of all the companies analyzed.

A closer look reveals that the big eight of the sixteen firms, as a group, audits 69% of the total client base, which represents 81% of combined sales or assets. The small eight audits 7% of the client companies representing 4% of total sales or assets.

A relatively large group of companies (3,899), 23% of the total, are audited by firms or individuals clearly unaffiliated with the big sixteen firms. They account for 15% of the total sales or assets variable.

On a firm-specific level in this overall worldwide analysis, KPMG has the most audit clients, both in terms of number of clients audited (14% of the total) and size of clients as defined by the sum of total sales or assets (17%). It should be kept in mind that the formation of this firm is the result of the 1987 merger of two large international accounting firms, Klynveld Main Goerdeler and Peat, Marwick, Mitchell & Co. CL ranks second in terms of client number (10%) followed closely by PW (10%). However, in total sales or assets, PW is second (12%) and EW third (11%).

In terms of global totals, the top ranked firm among the small eight firms, BDO, with 2% of all clients worldwide and 2% of total sales or assets, ranks significantly below the eighth ranked firm of the big eight in both categories.

It is quite apparent that whether analyzing by client number statistics or by sales or assets statistics on a worldwide basis, the big eight firms have created and maintained a significant overall dominance in the auditing of major companies throughout the world. There is definitely a significant distance between the big eight and the small eight firms. The impact of the multitude of international affiliations which the sixteen firms have established, as outlined in Chapter Nine, is certainly reflected in these worldwide client totals. The big eight, in particular, have capitalized upon global and multinational opportunities which exist in the marketplace to enhance the breadth and diversification of their client base.

To the greatest extent possible, we have classified client companies into categories of multinationality and non-multinationality. We have decided to focus on the top 2,000 companies, 1,000 from each group, as we felt the degree of multinationality would decrease thereafter considerably. Our perception of multinationality is structural - the criterion is having subsidiaries in three or more countries. Table 10-3 summarizes the relevant findings.

Eighty-four percent of the top 1,000 multinational companies are audited by a big eight affiliated firm, compared with 76% of the non-multinational companies. These firms account for 86% and 80% of sales or assets totals, respectively. On the average, the top 1,000 multinational companies are larger than the top 1,000 non-multinational companies.

Among the big eight firms auditing multinational companies, KPMG, CL and PW rank first, second and third, respectively, in terms of total clients. In terms of total sales or assets, the highest are KPMG, EW and PW. Among the big eight auditors for non-multinational companies, based on number of clients, KPMG is first, followed by EW and CL. Based on dollar sum, KPMG is first, followed by PW and CL.

Among the small eight firms, BDO audits the most multinational and non-multinational companies. For the small eight group of accounting firms, the multinational companies are on the average smaller in terms of sales or assets than the non-multinational companies. Eleven percent of all multinational companies in this sample are audited by unaffiliated firms or individuals as opposed to 15% of non-multinational companies.

The industries included in the scope of this analysis have been classified into six broad groupings:

1. Consumer Goods
2. Capital Goods
3. Basic Industries
4. Financials
5. Utilities and Transportation
6. Other

A list of the specific industries which belong to each of the categories may be found in Table 10-4A.

Table 10-4 shows, on a global basis, the relative market position held by each of the 16 international accounting firms within the six broad industry groups, based on total dollar sum of representative companies. This table is to be viewed on an industry-specific basis.

In the consumer goods industries, the highest position in terms of dollar sum is held by TRI, followed by KPMG and CL.

Among companies engaged in capital goods industries, KPMG leads on audits of total dollar sum with CL and EW ranking second and third, respectively.

In the basic industries category, the ranking among the top three firms is as follows: PW, CL, EW.

For financial companies, KPMG is the strongest, followed by EW and PW.

In the transportation and utilities sectors, CL leads in terms of dollar sum audited, followed by AA, and then PW.

In each of the industry groups, the big eight firms audit at least 75% of all clients, based on dollar sum.

The variations in market share of the top 16 firms illustrates the strengths which certain firms possess in specific industries. As the large international accounting firms continue to formulate their strategies for additional local audit firm alliances and the acquisition of accompanying corporate clients, they may choose to target previously untapped industries or attempt to grow in industries where they already have a significant market share.

Table 10-5 presents the worldwide distribution of client companies among the leading international accounting firms by size. As previously described in section III, five categories were established.

The top three firms in terms of number of clients worldwide (KPMG, CL, PW) maintain one of the top three positions in each of the individual size categories, with a slight variation in the "over 10 billion" category, where KPMG is number one, followed by PW and EW. KPMG led in all the dollar sum categories.

Research indicates that the larger the size category, the greater the number of clients audited by the big eight accounting firms.

TABLE 10-2

INTERNATIONAL ACCOUNTING FIRMS
AND THE CLIENTS THEY AUDIT
WORLDWIDE

Number of Companies	%	Firms	Total Sales or Assets*	%
		Big Eight		
1130	6.80	AA	1695	5.83
1004	6.04	AYI	1701	5.85
1721	10.35	CL	3155	10.86
1214	7.30	DHSI	2388	8.22
1345	8.09	EW	3314	11.41
2248	13.52	KPMG	4994	17.19
1679	10.10	PW	3349	11.53
1123	6.75	TRI	2821	9.71
11464	68.95	Sub-Total	23418	80.63
		Small Eight		
352	2.12	BDO	513	1.76
86	.52	DRMP	64	.21
174	1.05	GTI	256	.88
156	.94	HHI	72	.24
39	.23	HLB	8	.02
134	.81	MRI	71	.24
85	.51	PKF	82	.28
117	.70	SO	124	.42
1143	6.88	Sub-Total	1191	4.09
3899	23.45	NAFF	4380	15.08
123	.74	NADT	54	.18
4022	24.19	Sub-Total	4435	15.26
16629	100	Total	29044	100

*Rounded in $US Billions

Note: As explained in the "Treatment of Subsidiaries" section of the Research Design, for this table, we have excluded subsidiary figures from parent company auditor DSum figures, but we have not reduced the corresponding number of clients per accounting firm. The rankings would have been the same for the big eight firms had we not deducted subsidiary DSum figures from parent companies.

TABLE 10-3
INTERNATIONAL ACCOUNTING FIRMS AND THE CLIENTS THEY AUDIT
MULTINATIONAL VS. NON-MULTINATIONAL COMPANIES

MNC				Non-MNC		
Number of Companies	Total Sales or Assets*	%	Firms	Number of Companies	Total Sales or Assets*	%
76	733	5.23	AA	62	663	5.62
68	986	7.03	AYI	58	596	5.05
136	1630	11.63	CL	100	1270	10.77
79	1056	7.53	DHSI	74	1065	9.03
116	1937	13.82	EW	102	1112	9.43
174	2578	18.39	KPMG	182	2130	18.08
130	1778	12.68	PW	90	1392	11.81
65	1338	9.55	TRI	93	1249	10.60
844	12036	85.90	Sub-Total	761	9477	80.44
21	260	1.85	BDO	15	183	1.55
2	23	.16	DRMP	2	10	.08
5	15	.10	GTI	11	174	1.47
3	12	.08	HHI	5	32	.27
1	2	.01	HLB	0	0	0
2	6	.04	MRI	4	37	.31
6	33	.23	PKF	3	22	.18
3	43	.30	SO	5	63	.53
43	393	2.80	Sub-Total	45	520	4.41
113	1582	11.29	NAFF	191	1770	15.02
0	0	0	NADT	3	13	.11
113	1582	11.29	Sub-Total	194	1784	15.14
1000	14011	100	Total	1000	11781	100

*Rounded in $US Billions

Note: This table focuses on only the top 2,000 companies in our client data base, 1,000 multinational and 1,000 non-multinational.

TABLE 10-4 INTERNATIONAL ACCOUNTING FIRM MARKET SHARES WITHIN SIX INDUSTRY GROUPS WORLDWIDE							
Consumer Goods	Capital Goods	Basic Industries	Firm	Financials	Utilities Transportation	Other Industries	Total - All Industry Groups
DSum %	DSum %	DSum %		DSum %	DSum %	DSum %	DSum %
6.47	6.82	10.42	AA	4.63	14.85	13.48	5.83
4.17	6.48	9.11	AYI	5.65	5.49	8.57	5.85
11.28	12.69	13.73	CL	10.01	17.02	10.97	10.86
9.16	8.86	5.81	DHSI	8.16	10.49	9.65	8.22
7.80	12.14	12.64	EW	11.80	8.28	9.67	11.41
13.48	14.28	9.11	KPMG	19.51	8.65	11.17	17.19
7.96	11.59	22.99	PW	11.00	10.80	16.53	11.53
15.26	6.48	4.16	TRI	10.12	5.68	5.44	9.71
75.58	79.34	87.97	Sub-Total	80.88	81.26	85.48	80.63
1.11	1.90	1.46	BDO	1.93	.87	1.73	1.76
.17	.45	.06	DRMP	.20	.06	.70	.21
.73	.32	.48	GTI	1.02	.31	.94	.88
.51	.31	.38	HHI	.19	.39	.56	.24
.11	.08	.03	HLB	.01	.04	.07	.02
.26	.55	.33	MRI	.12	1.55	.62	.24
.80	.42	.39	PKF	.20	.05	.70	.28
.43	.22	.37	SO	.49	.11	.17	.42
4.12	4.25	3.50	Sub-Total	4.16	3.38	5.49	4.09
20.02	16.27	8.29	NAFF	14.76	14.98	8.44	15.08
.29	.13	.24	NADT	.15	.39	.59	.18
20.31	16.40	8.53	Sub-Total	14.91	15.37	9.03	15.26
100	100	100		100	100	100	100

Note: As explained in the "Treatment of Subsidiaries" section of the Research Design, for this table we have excluded subsidiary figures from parent company auditor DSum figures. Had we not deducted subsidiary DSum figures among the top three auditors in each industry group, the only changes would have been - PW as number three in the Capital Goods category and DHSI as number three in the Utilities/Transportation category.

TABLE 10-4A

Industry Groups

1. Consumer Goods	2. Capital Goods
Food/Beverages	Metal Manufacturing/Metal Products
Textiles/Apparel	Electronics
Tobacco	Transportation Equipment/Aerospace
Publishing/Printing	Indust/Farm Equipment
Pharmaceuticals	Construction
Broadcasting	
Retailing/Trading	
Hotels	
3. Basic Industries	**4. Financials**
Mining/Petroleum	Banking
Forest Products	Insurance
Chemicals	Commercial Finance
Rubber/Plastics	Personal Loans
Glass/Concrete	Leasing/Rental
	Financial Services and/or Holding Co.
	Real Estate
5. Utilities & Transportation	**7. Other**
Utilities	Other Industries
Transportation	Multiple Industries
	Industry Unknown

TABLE 10-5 INTERNATIONAL ACCOUNTING FIRMS AND SIZE OF THEIR CLIENTS WORLDWIDE						
Large DSum %				Small DSum %		
over $10 Billion DSum %	$1 - $10 Billion DSum %	$501 Million $1 Billion DSum %	Firms	$101 - $500 Million DSum %	$1 - $100 Million DSum %	Total All Size Groups DSum %
			Big Eight			
4.61	8.22	8.27	AA	8.02	5.72	5.83
6.11	5.66	6.74	AYI	6.72	5.49	5.85
10.81	11.81	10.37	CL	11.15	8.77	10.86
8.49	7.89	7.73	DHSI	7.86	5.81	8.22
12.28	9.78	7.69	EW	8.55	6.84	11.41
18.68	16.69	14.25	KPMG	13.65	13.49	17.19
12.84	10.18	10.82	PW	9.13	11.40	11.53
10.95	7.16	7.43	TRI	6.78	7.10	9.71
84.77	77.39	73.30	Sub-Total	71.86	64.62	80.63
			Small Eight			
1.70	1.81	2.04	BDO	1.91	2.28	1.76
.10	.32	.69	DRMP	.43	.40	.21
.71	.97	1.19	GTI	.89	1.19	.88
.07	.49	.59	HHI	.96	1.31	.24
0	.03	.10	HLB	.36	.22	.02
.12	.39	.43	MRI	.64	.69	.24
.12	.56	.56	PKF	.37	.40	.28
.46	.29	.67	SO	.68	.82	.42
3.28	4.86	6.27	Sub-Total	6.24	7.32	4.09
11.95	17.40	19.76	NAFF	20.81	27.40	15.08
0	.37	.66	NADT	1.08	.67	.18
11.95	17.77	20.42	Sub-Total	21.89	28.07	15.26
100	100	100	Total	100	100	100

B. US/Non-US

Table 10-6 sub-groups the data set to show the US in relation to the rest of the world. The US has the largest concentration of offices of international accounting firms and the most partners overall as described in Chapter 9. Twenty-two percent of all companies analyzed for auditor data in this study are located in the US (or 29% of the world's total combined sales or assets).

Looking at each major international accounting firm in terms of client numbers and combined sales or assets reveals the degree of the firm's strength within the US and overseas.

In the US, the big eight firms have clearly established a foothold in dominating the audit market. This group in the US, as auditors of 94% of all companies studied, also accounts for 99% of the country's combined company sales or assets. The same eight firms account for 62% of all non-US companies examined, as well as 75% of the total sales or assets.

The small eight have a negligible presence in the US when viewed individually or as a group in relation to their US big eight counterparts. Among non-US clients, however, the small eight presence is slightly more significant.

On an individual firm basis in the US, KPMG ranks first with regard to both number of clients audited and combined sales or assets of its clients. It is followed by AA and then EW in terms of client numbers, but by PW and EW in terms of sales or assets.

In the non-US marketplace, KPMG is the leading auditor based on number of clients and client size, followed by CL and then PW.

In analyzing the big eight international firms, DHSI, TRI and AYI are the smallest in the US in terms of client size and number of clients, while in the non-US realm TRI, AYI and AA are the smallest based on number of clients and DHSI, AYI and AA are the smallest based on client size.

As expected, the smaller firms which are non-US based (BDO, MRI, HLB) have a stronger non-US than US client base, but the reverse does not hold true for the US based smaller eight firms.

Among non-US firms, the highest combined number of overall clients (30%) and combined sales or assets totals (20%) are attributed to unaffiliated auditors. The largest unaffiliated firms will be examined in depth in a later section of this chapter (Table 10-21). This category is, however, of minor significance in the US (2% of all US companies audited).

Table 10-7 identifies the international accounting firm market share by industry group in the US and in non-US countries. Overall, in comparing the six broad industry groups in the US and non-US markets, the big eight in the US audit at least 98% of all client companies in each of the industry groups, while percentages for big eight auditors in each industry category in non-US countries range from 66 - 83%.

On a specific industry group basis, for the consumer goods industry in the US, the three ranked highest are TRI, AA and PW. Outside the US, TRI, KPMG and CL are the leaders.

For capital goods in the US, the top three are PW, DHSI and CL. For this industry in the rest of the world, KPMG, CL and EW lead the rest.

In the basic industry group, PW is number one, followed by AA and AYI in the US, but in non-US markets, PW is followed by EW and CL.

For financial companies in the US, the top three are KPMG, EW and PW. For non-US companies, they are KPMG, PW and TRI.

In the US, the utilities/transportation sectors are dominated by AA, CL and DHSI, while outside the US the top three are PW, KPMG and EW.

In all of the industry groups, (with the exception of TRI in the consumer goods industry, PW in basic industries and KPMG in the financial sector), the top three rankings are not consistently held by the same firms in US and non-US audit markets, indicating that relative strengths established by firms in the US are not necessarily applicable in other markets.

The size of clients being audited can also be compared within and outside the US, as shown in Table 10-8.

In the smallest size category (1-100 million) in the US, the top three are as follows: KPMG, AA, EW. For the same category in the non-US domain, they are KPMG, PW and CL.

In the 101-500 million category for the US, AA is the leader, followed by KPMG, and EW, while for non-US countries the top three are KPMG, CL and PW.

In the middle size category (501 - 1 billion), the US market is dominated by KPMG, AA and PW. For non-US companies KPMG, CL and PW are the leaders.

For companies in the US with dollar sum in the $1 - 10 billion range, KPMG is the audit leader, followed by AA and EW. For non-US companies, KPMG also dominates, but is followed by CL and PW.

In the largest size category (over 10 billion), KPMG audits the most companies in the US, followed by PW and EW. For non-US companies, KPMG also leads, but is followed by EW and TRI.

KPMG leads in all US and non-US size categories, with the exception of the 101 - 500 million size category in the US.

AA and EW exhibit strengths in many of the size categories in the US, but CL and PW lead in more non-US than US size categories.

TABLE 10-6 INTERNATIONAL ACCOUNTING FIRMS AND TOTAL CLIENTS THEY AUDIT								
US					NON-US			
Number of Companies	%	Total Sales or Assets*	%	Firms	Number of Companies	%	Total Sales or Assets*	%
				Big Eight				
622	17.09	927	10.89	AA	508	3.91	969	4.20
266	7.31	662	7.78	AYI	738	5.68	1237	5.37
414	11.38	988	11.61	CL	1307	10.06	2513	10.91
356	9.78	926	10.89	DHSI	858	6.61	1671	7.25
467	12.83	1109	13.03	EW	878	6.76	2408	10.45
640	17.59	1808	21.25	KPMG	1608	12.38	3762	16.33
380	10.44	1277	15.01	PW	1299	10.00	2440	10.59
286	7.86	684	8.04	TRI	837	6.44	2299	9.98
3431	94.28	8380	98.53	Sub-Total	8033	61.84	17299	75.09
				Small Eight				
21	.58	11	.13	BDO	331	2.55	542	2.35
20	.55	14	.16	DRMP	66	.51	50	.21
41	1.13	21	.24	GTI	133	1.02	238	1.03
42	1.15	19	.22	HHI	114	.88	63	.27
5	.14	1	0	HLB	34	.26	8	.03
2	.05	0	0	MRI	132	1.02	76	.33
1	.03	0	0	PKF	84	.65	90	.39
2	.05	26	.30	SO	115	.89	108	.47
134	3.68	92	1.07	Sub-Total	1009	7.78	1176	5.10
74	2.03	33	.39	NAFF	3825	29.45	4503	19.54
0	0		0	NADT	123	.95	59	.25
74	2.03	33	.39	Sub-Total	3948	30.40	4561	19.80
3639	100	8505	100	Total	12990	100	23036	100

*Rounded in $US Billions

TABLE 10-7
INTERNATIONAL ACCOUNTING FIRM MARKET SHARES WITHIN SIX INDUSTRY GROUPS
US

Consumer Goods	Capital Goods	Basic Industries	Firm	Financials	Utilities Transportation	Other Industries	Total - All Industry Groups
DSum %	DSum %	DSum %		DSum %	DSum %	DSum %	DSum %
			Big Eight				
14.54	8.86	20.90	AA	6.67	30.78	21.36	10.89
5.97	7.67	11.59	AYI	7.70	6.06	10.78	7.78
11.32	15.88	10.82	CL	8.95	30.03	11.34	11.61
8.88	17.00	6.95	DHSI	10.30	14.12	10.52	10.89
12.55	10.40	5.87	EW	15.64	3.73	10.02	13.03
14.02	11.26	5.69	KPMG	28.45	5.66	9.30	21.25
14.49	20.03	35.33	PW	12.38	8.06	18.32	15.01
16.18	8.02	2.53	TRI	8.25	.71	6.02	8.04
97.95	99.12	99.68	Sub-Total	98.34	99.15	97.66	98.53
			Big Eight				
.13	.02	.04	BDO	.17	0	.25	.13
.28	.01	.01	DRMP	.20	0	.37	.16
.23	.35	.07	GTI	.25	.08	.69	.24
.94	.35	0	HHI	.04	.75	.38	.22
.06	0	0	HLB	0	0	.04	0
0	0	.03	MRI	0	0	0	0
0	.01	0	PKF	0	0	0	0
0	0	0	SO	.49	0	0	.30
1.64	.74	.15	Sub-Total	1.15	.83	1.73	1.07
.42	.16	.19	NAFF	.49	.01	.59	.39
0	0	0	NADT	0	0	0	0
.42	.16	.19	Sub-Total	.49	.01	.59	.39
100	100	100		100	100	100	100

TABLE 10-7 (continued)
INTERNATIONAL ACCOUNTING FIRM MARKET SHARES WITHIN SIX INDUSTRY GROUPS
NON-US

Consumer Goods	Capital Goods	Basic Industries	Firm	Financials	Utilities Transportation	Other Industries	Total - All Industry Groups
DSum %	DSum %	DSum %		DSum %	DSum %	DSum %	DSum %
			Big Eight				
2.92	6.50	6.02	AA	3.96	3.65	1.74	4.20
3.43	5.48	8.39	AYI	5.35	5.05	5.25	5.37
11.57	12.15	14.93	CL	10.39	9.70	10.26	10.91
9.34	6.44	4.63	DHSI	7.30	7.56	7.98	7.25
5.72	11.65	15.40	EW	10.43	10.74	10.60	10.45
12.91	16.69	12.56	KPMG	17.25	10.80	13.66	16.33
5.64	8.80	17.46	PW	10.74	12.30	13.25	10.59
14.51	5.43	4.16	TRI	10.58	8.99	4.32	9.98
66.04	73.14	83.55	Sub-Total	76.00	68.79	67.06	75.09
			Big Eight				
1.48	2.56	2.10	BDO	2.47	1.47	3.98	2.35
.11	.57	.07	DRMP	.19	.11	1.17	.21
.91	.26	.61	GTI	1.20	.45	1.29	1.03
.28	.24	.91	HHI	.23	.04	.81	.27
.16	.10	.04	HLB	.01	.07	.11	.03
.36	.69	.40	MRI	.17	2.61	1.55	.33
1.21	.54	.76	PKF	.24	.08	1.76	.39
.71	.29	.46	SO	.48	.18	.44	.47
5.22	5.25	5.35	Sub-Total	4.99	5.01	11.11	5.10
28.33	21.44	10.78	NAFF	18.74	25.57	20.35	19.54
.40	.17	.31	NADT	.22	.65	1.50	.25
28.73	21.61	11.09	Sub-Total	18.96	26.22	21.85	19.80
100	100	100		100	100	100	100

TABLE 10-8
INTERNATIONAL ACCOUNTING FIRMS AND SIZE OF THEIR CLIENTS
US

Large				Small		
over $10 Billion Dsum %	$1 - $10 Billion Dsum %	$501 - $1 Billion Dsum %	Firms	$101 - $500 Million Dsum %	$1 - $100 Million Dsum %	Total - All Size Groups Dsum %
			Big Eight			
6.58	16.19	18.12	AA	18.30	15.88	10.89
8.61	6.55	5.82	AYI	8.82	7.35	7.78
11.40	12.04	10.58	CL	12.12	10.53	11.61
11.34	10.51	8.22	DHSI	10.86	8.30	10.89
12.67	13.77	12.21	EW	12.77	11.84	13.03
22.38	20.39	19.30	KPMG	15.21	16.87	21.25
17.84	11.43	13.13	PW	8.52	10.16	15.01
8.66	7.19	7.93	TRI	6.58	10.27	8.04
99.48	98.07	95.30	Sub Total	93.18	91.20	98.53
			Small Eight			
0	.25	.44	BDO	.46	1.64	.13
0	.28	1.07	DRMP	.49	.66	.16
0	.36	1.50	GTI	1.39	1.31	.24
0	.40	.58	HHI	1.28	2.28	.22
0	0	0	HLB	.19	.39	0
0	0	0	MRI	.08	0	0
0	0	0	PKF	.03	0	0
.52	0	0	SO	.11	0	.30
.52	1.29	3.59	Sub Total	4.03	6.28	1.07
0	.65	1.12	NAFF	2.80	2.52	.39
0	0	0	NADT	0	0	0
0	.65	1.12	Sub Total	2.80	2.52	.39
100	100	100	Total	100	100	100

TABLE 10-8 (continued) INTERNATIONAL ACCOUNTING FIRMS AND SIZE OF THEIR CLIENTS NON-US						
Large				Small		
over $10 Billion Dsum %	$1 - $10 Billion Dsum %	$501 - $1 Billion Dsum %	Firms	$101 - $500 Million Dsum %	$1 - $100 Million Dsum %	Total - All Size Groups Dsum %
			Big Eight			
3.95	4.70	4.77	AA	4.27	2.79	4.20
5.27	5.27	7.07	AYI	5.96	4.95	5.37
10.61	11.71	10.30	CL	10.80	8.26	10.91
7.53	6.74	7.55	DHSI	6.77	5.09	7.25
12.15	8.02	6.08	EW	7.01	5.40	10.45
17.43	15.05	12.46	KPMG	13.08	12.52	16.33
11.15	9.63	10.01	PW	9.35	11.76	10.59
11.73	7.15	7.25	TRI	6.86	6.18	9.98
79.82	68.27	65.49	Sub Total	64.10	56.95	75.09
			Small Eight			
2.27	2.49	2.61	BDO	2.43	2.47	2.35
.13	.33	.56	DRMP	.40	.33	.21
.96	1.24	1.08	GTI	.71	1.16	1.03
.09	.53	.59	HHI	.85	1.04	.27
0	.04	.14	HLB	.43	.18	.03
.17	.56	.58	MRI	.85	.88	.33
.16	.81	.76	PKF	.50	.51	.39
.44	.41	.91	SO	.89	1.06	.47
4.22	6.41	7.23	Sub Total	7.06	7.63	5.10
15.98	24.80	26.39	NAFF	27.38	34.57	19.54
0	.53	.90	NADT	1.48	.86	.25
15.98	25.33	27.29	Sub Total	28.86	35.43	19.80
100	100	100	Total	100	100	100

C. Industrial/Developing Countries

Those countries considered to be emerging or developing markets have had significant growth in recent years. Much expansion among the large accounting firms has taken place in these countries and it is interesting to view the emerging markets in relation to the industrialized countries of the world. Findings regarding these two groups are shown in Table 10-9. A complete list of both the industrial and developing countries can be found in Table 10-9A.

The developing countries as a group represent only 20% of the entire client company data set and a much lower 6% of total combined sales or assets, indicating that the average size of client companies is smaller in developing countries.

Based on its worldwide totals, KPMG performs the most industrialized country audits ranked by client numbers and client size with CL second and PW third for total audits. Ranked by total sales and assets, PW and EW are second and third, respectively.

However, among the developing countries, PW is clearly the leader based on client numbers, followed by KPMG and CL. Based on client size, KPMG holds first place with PW second and CL third.

Overall, the presence of auditors who are non-affiliated with the big sixteen international accounting firms' auditors is higher in developing countries than in industrialized countries. In the industrialized world, 21% of the sample client companies are audited by unaffiliated individuals or firms as opposed to 33% in the developing countries. The corresponding DSum percentages are 14% and 27%.

The relatively large number of companies audited by unaffiliated firms in developing markets may have implications for larger international firms. To the extent that larger international firms wish to expand within developing market countries, they may choose to target additional local firms for affiliation.

TABLE 10-9 INTERNATIONAL ACCOUNTING FIRMS AND TOTAL CLIENTS THEY AUDIT								
INDUSTRIAL COUNTRIES					DEVELOPING COUNTRIES			
Number of Companies	%	Total Sales or Assets*	%	Firms	Number of Companies	%	Total Sales or Assets*	%
				Big Eight				
1015	7.66	1833	6.17	AA	115	3.41	62	3.32
893	6.74	1782	6.00	AYI	111	3.29	117	6.25
1461	11.02	3352	11.29	CL	260	7.71	150	7.98
1044	7.88	2539	8.55	DHSI	170	5.04	58	3.11
1130	8.53	3410	11.49	EW	215	6.37	106	5.65
1888	14.24	5272	17.77	KPMG	360	10.67	298	15.89
1182	8.92	3462	11.67	PW	497	14.73	255	13.60
977	7.37	2892	9.74	TRI	146	4.33	91	4.84
9590	72.36	24542	82.72	Sub-Total	1874	55.55	1138	60.68
				Small Eight				
216	1.63	528	1.77	BDO	136	4.03	25	1.35
77	.58	60	.20	DRMP	9	.27	4	.23
137	1.03	161	.54	GTI	37	1.10	98	5.24
108	.81	46	.15	HHI	48	1.42	36	1.91
34	.26	8	.02	HLB	5	.15	1	.04
84	.63	55	.18	MRI	50	1.48	21	1.12
76	.57	76	.25	PKF	9	.27	14	.76
69	.52	122	.41	SO	48	1.42	12	.62
801	6.03	1056	3.55	Sub-Total	342	10.14	212	11.29
2799	21.12	4022	13.55	NAFF	1100	32.60	514	27.41
65	.49	47	.16	NADT	58	1.72	11	.60
2864	21.61	4069	13.71	Sub-Total	1158	34.32	525	28.01
13255	100	29667	100	Total	3374	100	1874	100

*Rounded in $US Billions

TABLE 10-9A

LIST OF INDUSTRIAL AND DEVELOPING COUNTRIES INCLUDED IN STUDY OF CLIENTS OF INTERNATIONAL ACCOUNTING FIRMS

	Industrial Countries:	
Australia	Ireland	South Africa
Austria	Italy	Spain
Belgium	Japan	Sweden
Canada	Luxembourg	Switzerland
Denmark	Netherlands	United Kingdom
Finland	New Zealand	United States
France	Norway	
Germany, West		
	Developing Countries:	
Argentina	Kuwait	United Arab Emirates
Brazil	Malaysia	Venezuela
Chile	Mexico	Zimbabwe
China, Taiwan	Nigeria	
Colombia	Pakistan	
Greece	Peru	
Hong Kong	Philippines	
India	Portugal	
Israel	Singapore	
Kenya	Thailand	
Korea, South	Turkey	

D. Regions of the World

Client company data has also been grouped into five geographic regions (North America, Europe, Asia/Pacific, South America, Africa/Middle East) and the results are summarized in Tables 10-10 through 10-12. Analyzing each of the sixteen international accounting firms within and across these regions is quite revealing because different auditing firms display varying degrees of prominence worldwide, highlighting the fact that each firm has strengths that make it function more effectively in some regions than in others.

North America

Thirty-one percent of the world's client audits are performed within the North American region at a corresponding 31% of world total DSum. The North American market is dominated across both variables by KPMG. Second place is held by AA for client numbers and PW for total sales or assets. EW is third for both client numbers and sales or assets.

Europe

The big eight client groups in both North America and Europe hold a relatively comparable combined sales or assets total, although the total in Europe for this group is represented by fewer companies. This means that, overall, the big eight in Europe are auditing larger clients than in North America.

Overall, Europe comprises 39% of the entire world audit market in combined sales or assets.

More specifically, KPMG holds the lead in Europe with DHSI next in total audits and CL following close behind. Second place for dollar sum totals is held by PW, followed by CL.

The big eight handles 68% of the total European market in terms of total clients and 76% of the market in terms of total sales or assets. Unaffiliated firms and individuals make up 22% of the total audit client base in Europe or 16% of the sales or assets total.

Asia/Pacific

Companies in the Asia/Pacific region with total figures relatively similar to those in the North American region, generally have more audits performed by CL, but EW handles the largest company audits. Second place for number of audits and largest company audits is held by KPMG and TRI, respectively, and third place by PW and CL, respectively.

In Asia/Pacific, the big eight audit 52% of all companies, representing 71% of combined sales or assets.

Approximately 43% of the entire client base (or 28% of combined sales or assets) in Asia/Pacific is audited by an unaffiliated individual or firm. Many of the local accounting firms which have multiple affiliations with the large international accounting firms are located in this region. They have been incorporated into this unaffiliated category.

Among small eight firms in Asia/Pacific, BDO audits more clients than two of the big eight firms.

South America

The South American region represents 3% of total clients worldwide and a corresponding 1% of world sales and assets. In this region, PW leads in client numbers and in the total figures which these companies represent.

DHSI represents the next largest group of companies but AYI has the second highest sales or assets base. In third place is AA for total companies and KPMG for combined sales or assets. The big eight perform 69% of all South American audits, at an equivalent 60% of the entire region's sales or assets. GTI, in the small eight group, performs more audits in South America than two of the big eight and has the second highest sales or assets totals of all the sixteen firms for the region. This is due to the fact that the largest bank in Brazil is audited by GTI.

Twenty-two percent of all South American audits are carried out by firms or individuals not connected with the sixteen largest international firms, for 14% of the region's sales or assets.

Africa/Middle East

The Africa/Middle East region comprises 3% of the world clients and 1% of total world sales and assets. In this region, KPMG leads in overall audits, but EW performs audits of larger companies. TRI holds second place for both audit clients and combined sums. The third position is held by DHSI and KPMG in the respective categories.

The big eight firms audit 68% of companies in this region, or companies with 63% of total sales or assets. The smaller eight international accounting firms audit a higher percentage of companies in this region (18%) than in any other region.

An analysis by regions of the world can also be broken down into industry groups by region. Table 10-13 presents rankings of international accounting firms' performance in each of the broad industry groups on a regional basis. The top five firms within each of the industry groups are presented along with their corresponding dollar sum percentage. Rarely are there consistencies among firm rankings for the same industry group in different regions. An industry strength for a particular firm in one region is not necessarily an industry strength for that firm in a different region.

In Table 10-14 accounting firm partner demographics from Chapter 9 are compared with data on the clients audited by these partners. For each firm, the relationship is shown between the percentage of partners within the region and the regional dollar sum percentage.

Many of the percentages based on number of partners and dollar sum of audits are reasonably parallel. A disproportionate balance between partners and DSum, with partner percentages being the higher variable could indicate that the firm's partners are providing more non-audit services and are possibly auditing smaller firms overall. In general, the small eight firms have a larger percentage of partners than DSum percentage.

TABLE 10-10
INTERNATIONAL ACCOUNTING FIRMS AND THE CLIENTS THEY AUDIT

NORTH AMERICA*					EUROPE**			
Number of Companies	%	Total Sales or Assets***	%	Firms	Number of Companies	%	Total Sales or Assets***	%
				Big Eight				
684	13.41	876	9.75	AA	315	5.77	743	6.50
407	7.98	808	8.99	AYI	435	7.97	807	7.06
579	11.35	955	10.62	CL	495	9.07	1042	9.11
448	8.78	974	10.83	DHSI	513	9.40	959	8.39
641	12.56	1156	12.86	EW	248	4.54	680	5.94
723	14.17	1871	20.83	KPMG	884	16.20	1997	17.47
557	10.92	1338	14.89	PW	469	8.59	1786	15.63
400	7.84	820	9.12	TRI	313	5.73	661	5.78
4439	87.01	8798	97.93	Sub-Total	3672	67.27	8676	75.92
				Small Eight				
24	.47	11	.12	BDO	195	3.57	482	4.22
34	.67	14	.15	DRMP	43	.79	46	.39
73	1.43	45	.49	GTI	66	1.21	118	1.03
62	1.22	19	.21	HHI	45	.82	18	.15
5	.10	1	0	HLB	28	.51	7	.05
30	.59	4	.04	MRI	46	.84	52	.45
15	.29	2	.02	PKF	48	.88	64	.55
8	.16	26	.29	SO	55	1.01	88	.77
251	4.93	121	1.35	Sub-Total	526	9.63	873	7.64
401	7.86	63	.69	NAFF	1199	21.97	1834	16.05
11	.22	1	.01	NADT	61	1.12	43	.37
412	8.08	64	.71	Sub-Total	1260	23.09	1877	16.43
5102	100	8983	100	Total	5458	100	11427	100

* North America: Canada, Mexico, United States

**Europe: Austria, Belgium, Denmark, Finland, France, West Germany, Greece, Ireland, Italy, Luxembourg, Netherlands, Norway, Portugal, Spain, Sweden, Switzerland, Turkey, United Kingdom

***Rounded in $US Billions

Note: As explained in the "Treatment of Subsidiaries" section of the Research Design, for this table we have excluded subsidiary amounts from parent company auditor DSum figures, but we have not reduced the corresponding number of client companies per accounting firm. Had we not deducted DSum subsidiary figures from parent companies in both North America and Europe, the top three auditors would remain the same.

TABLE 10-11 INTERNATIONAL ACCOUNTING FIRMS AND THE CLIENTS THEY AUDIT								
ASIA/PACIFIC*					SOUTH AMERICA**			
Number of Companies	%	Total Sales or Assets***	%	Firms	Number of Companies	%	Total Sales or Assets***	%
				Big Eight				
56	1.13	61	.74	AA	52	9.58	21	5.33
110	2.22	37	.44	AYI	18	3.31	50	12.85
577	11.66	1180	14.25	CL	33	6.08	22	5.64
134	2.71	448	5.40	DHSI	59	10.87	18	4.58
396	8.00	1452	17.53	EW	8	1.47	1	.26
516	10.43	1162	14.02	KPMG	40	7.37	29	7.51
453	9.15	217	2.62	PW	157	28.91	92	23.54
343	6.93	1309	15.80	TRI	6	1.10	2	.40
2585	52.23	5865	70.83	Sub-Total	373	68.69	234	60.15
				Small Eight				
115	2.32	15	.18	BDO	9	1.66	3	.77
7	.14	3	.03	DRMP	2	.37	2	.46
8	.16	1	0	GTI	12	2.21	85	21.88
28	.57	15	.17	HHI	2	.37	0	.05
1	.02	0	0	HLB	0	0	0	0
16	.32	3	.03	MRI	0	0	0	0
20	.40	17	.20	PKF	0	0	0	0
37	.75	8	.09	SO	3	.55	2	.52
232	4.68	61	.73	Sub-Total	28	5.16	92	23.69
2119	42.82	2354	28.43	NAFF	120	22.10	56	14.47
13	.26	1	.01	NADT	22	4.05	7	1.67
2132	43.08	2355	28.44	Sub-Total	142	26.15	63	16.15
4949	100	8281	100	Total	543	100	389	100

* Asia/ Pacific: Australia, Hong Kong, India, Japan, South Korea, Malaysia, New Zealand, Pakistan, Philippines, Singapore, China (Taiwan), Thailand

**South America: Argentina, Brazil, Chile, Colombia, Peru and Venezuela

***Rounded in $US Billions

Note: As explained in the "Treatment of Subsidiaries" section of the Research Design, for this table we have excluded subsidiary amounts from parent company auditor DSum figures but we have not reduced the corresponding number of client companies per accounting firm. Had we not deducted DSum subsidiary figures from parent companies in Asia/Pacific, among the top three firms, KPMG would have been number three, rather than CL. In South America, there would be no change among the top three auditors.

TABLE 10-12
INTERNATIONAL ACCOUNTING FIRMS AND THE CLIENTS THEY AUDIT

AFRICA/MIDDLE EAST*

Number of Companies	%	Firms	Total Sales or Assets**	%
		Big Eight		
23	3.99	AA	16	4.00
34	5.89	AYI	20	4.99
37	6.41	CL	9	2.42
60	10.40	DHSI	33	8.40
52	9.01	EW	57	14.50
85	14.73	KPMG	37	9.55
43	7.45	PW	24	6.09
61	10.57	TRI	50	12.73
395	68.45	Sub-Total	245	62.72
		Small Eight		
9	1.56	BDO	5	1.25
0	0	DRMP	0	0
15	2.60	GTI	8	2.00
19	3.29	HHI	21	5.32
5	.87	HLB	1	.22
42	7.28	MRI	13	3.36
2	.35	PKF	1	.14
14	2.43	SO	1	.17
106	18.38	Sub-total	49	12.49
60	10.40	NAFF	94	23.97
16	2.77	NADT	3	.80
76	13.17	Sub-Total	97	24.78
577	100	Total	391	100

*Africa/Middle East: Israel, Kenya, Kuwait, Nigeria, South Africa, United Arab Emirates and Zimbabwe

**Rounded in $US Billions

Note: As explained in the "Treatment of Subsidiaries" section of the Research Design, for this table, we have excluded subsidiary amounts from parent company auditor DSum figures, but we have not reduced the corresponding number of client companies per accounting firm. Had we not deducted DSum subsidiary figures from parent companies in Africa/Middle East, the second and third place ranking for DSum would be switched to KPMG, second, and TRI, third.

TABLE 10-13
LEADING INTERNATIONAL ACCOUNTING FIRMS
BY BROAD INDUSTRY GROUPS AND REGION

Region	Industry Groups	Leading Five Firms (Based on DSum%)				
		1	2	3	4	5
North America	Consumer Goods	TRI (15.30)	PW (14.85)	EW (13.46)	AA (13.42)	KPMG (13.40)
	Capital Goods	PW (20.01)	DHSI (17.20)	CL (15.04)	KPMG (10.92)	AYI (8.71)
	Basic Industries	PW (33.14)	AA (18.97)	CL (12.72)	AYI (12.41)	EW (6.50)
	Financials	KPMG (27.09)	EW (14.92)	PW (11.58)	AYI (10.18)	DHSI (10.07)
	Utilities & Transportation	CL (28.79)	AA (28.56)	DHSI (13.53)	PW (8.33)	AYI (6.47)
Europe	Consumer Goods	KPMG (19.21)	NAFF (16.68)	CL (13.30)	DHSI (10.00)	PW (8.23)
	Capital Goods	KPMG (20.63)	CL (13.21)	NAFF (12.00)	PW (11.08)	AA (10.74)
	Basic Industries	PW (18.31)	KPMG (16.78)	EW (16.28)	CL (13.90)	AA (7.37)
	Financials	KPMG (18.28)	PW (16.52)	NAFF (16.27)	DHSI (8.29)	CL (8.12)
	Utilities & Transportation	PW (18.68)	NAFF (18.23)	CL (11.70)	DHSI (10.91)	KPMG (10.41)
Asia/Pacific	Consumer Goods	NAFF (40.01)	TRI (22.13)	CL (10.97)	KPMG (8.65)	DHSI (8.51)
	Capital Goods	NAFF (36.73)	EW (25.56)	KPMG (12.41)	CL (11.90)	TRI (7.80)
	Basic Industries	NAFF (30.54)	CL (18.57)	EW (16.43)	PW (12.76)	TRI (6.78)
	Financials	NAFF (24.30)	EW (18.36)	KPMG (16.36)	TRI (16.11)	CL (15.06)
	Utilities & Transportation	NAFF (42.17)	EW (22.17)	KPMG (13.08)	TRI (12.84)	CL (5.50)
South America	Consumer Goods	NAFF (28.96)	DHSI (19.13)	PW (15.23)	AYI (8.11)	AA (7.44)
	Capital Goods	PW (59.51)	NAFF (22.15)	DHSI (4.85)	KPMG (4.66)	AA (2.69)
	Basic Industries	PW (33.91)	AYI (33.28)	AA (9.76)	NAFF (9.00)	CL (6.89)
	Financials	GTI (37.43)	PW (17.10)	AYI (11.47)	KPMG (11.41)	NAFF (9.02)
	Utilities & Transportation	NAFF (41.23)	DHSI (14.50)	AYI (11.88)	PW (9.51	AA (9.03)
Africa/Middle East	Consumer Goods	KPMG (19.19)	AA (17.66)	SO (13.22)	EW (11.21)	AYI (9.44)
	Capital Goods	KPMG (23.65)	GTI (22.67)	EW (11.56)	NAFF (11.52)	PW (7.68)
	Basic Industries	EW (28.55)	DHSI (20.80)	KPMG (19.87)	TRI (8.13)	NAFF (7.57)
	Financials	NAFF (28.33)	TRI (14.22)	EW (13.18)	KPMG (7.54)	HHI (6.76)
	Utilities & Transportation	DHSI (50.46)	KPMG (48.60)	NAFF (.93)	n/a	n/a

n/a - not applicable

TABLE 10-14

REGIONAL SUMMARY OF THE INTERNATIONAL ACCOUNTING FIRMS

North America		Europe			Asia/Pacific		South America		Africa	
% of Partners	% of DSum	% of Partners	% of DSum	Firms	% of Partners	% of DSum	% of Partners	% of DSum	% of Partners	% of DSum
				Big Eight						
9.7	9.8	4.3	7.8	AA	3.3	1.0	8.5	6.4	2.1	5.4
8.2	9.0	9.0	8.5	AYI	6.3	.6	5.8	15.3	6.7	6.8
9.9	10.7	9.2	10.9	CL	16.0	19.9	11.7	6.8	10.7	3.0
7.6	10.9	7.0	10.0	DHSI	6.2	7.6	7.2	5.5	10.3	11.2
11.8	13.0	4.3	7.1	EW	9.5	24.5	2.2	.3	7.6	19.3
14.0	21.0	20.8	20.9	KPMG	13.7	19.6	17.0	8.9	14.4	12.5
7.8	15.0	6.6	18.7	PW	10.1	3.7	20.2	28.2	7.5	8.1
8.2	9.2	8.0	6.9	TRI	13.0	22.0	7.7	.6	10.1	16.9
77.2	98.6	69.2	90.8	Sub-Total	78.0	98.9	80.2	71.8	69.5	83.2
				Small Eight						
3.9	.1	5.6	5.1	BDO	3.7	.3	3.2	.9	4.1	1.7
4.1	.2	2.6	.5	DRMP	2.6	.1	3.9	.6	1.6	0
4.4	.5	4.8	1.2	GTI	1.4	0	3.1	26.1	3.3	2.7
3.6	.2	2.4	.2	HHI	3.9	.3	4.0	0	4.4	7.1
.5	0	3.0	.1	HLB	1.1	0	1.1	0	1.4	.3
3.2	0	4.8	.5	MRI	2.3	0	*	0	7.9	4.4
2.3	0	2.9	.7	PKF	3.0	.3	3.1	0	2.3	.3
.9	.3	4.6	.9	SO	4.0	.1	1.2	.6	5.4	.3
22.8	1.4	30.8	9.2	Sub-total	22.0	1.1	19.8	28.2	30.5	16.8
100	100	100	100	Total	100	100	100	100	100	100

Note: To make the percentage of partners comparable with the percentage of DSum, we have omitted "NAFF" and "NADT" DSum and recomputed the regional DSum percentage for each of the 16 firms.

* = Less than 1%

In Table 10-15, the international accounting firms are presented in terms of dollar sum percentage for each country in the study. This table is to be viewed on a country-specific basis only. Each country can be viewed as a separate audit market with a separate DSum percentage provided for each international accounting firm. Regional DSum percentages are also provided for each firm. For this table, as described in the Research Design section of this chapter, subsidiary DSum figures have been omitted from parent company DSum to capture a clear picture of each firm's strength within each country without overstating dollar sum amounts for parent company auditors.

Presentation by country allows the reader to identify the top ranking international accounting firms within each country and to identify countries where the percentage of non-affiliated auditors is high. It is interesting to note that in some countries the small eight firms have captured significant segments of the audit market. For example, among small eight firms ranked on the DSum dimension, in France, Portugal and Switzerland, BDO is number one. In Malaysia, PKF ranks first. HHI holds the number one position in Israel. In Brazil, GTI is number one, and in Peru, SO leads all firms.

It must also be noted that since we have incorporated all multiple affiliated auditors into the "NAFF" category, there are certain accounting firms within certain countries which will have low or non-existent DSum percentages because they are included in the NAFF DSum percentage for that country. In Table 10-15, these firms are designated with a "*". This should also be taken into consideration when viewing the regional totals for each firm. This situation exists almost exclusively in the Asia/Pacific countries.

TABLE 10-15
INTERNATIONAL ACCOUNTING FIRMS BY COUNTRY BASED ON TOTAL SALES OR ASSETS - DSUM %

Country	AA	AYI	CL	DHSI	EW	KPMG	PW	TRI	BDO	DRMP	GTI	HHI	HLB	MRI	PKF	SO	NAFF	NADT	Total
North America																			
Canada	3	24	5	10	9	14	10	19	0	0	2	0	0	0	0	0	3	0	100
Mexico	5	23	29	1	10	12	8	2	0	0	4	0	0	1	0	0	4	4	100
United States	11	7	11	11	13	22	16	9	0	0	0	0	0	0	0	0	0	0	100
Regional Total	10	9	11	11	13	21	15	9	0	0	0	0	0	0	0	0	1	0	100
Europe																			
Austria	0	0	0	0	0	37	0	0	9	0	0	0	0	0	0	6	47	0	100
Belgium	1	6	0	1	0	18	2	15	0	0	0	2	0	0	0	0	55	0	100
Denmark	2	10	7	16	11	15	1	4	0	0	8	0	0	1	1	0	25	0	100
Finland	0	1	36	2*	0*	20	10	23	4	0	2	0	0	0	0*	0	3	0	100
France	20	7	9	1	6	3	2	8	11	1	1	0	0	2	0	1	30	0	100
Germany, West	1	3	9	7	0	22	35	7	4	1	0	0	0	0	1	0	12	0	100
Greece	0	0	0	0	0	0	0	0	0	0	0	0	0	0	0	0	100	0	100
Ireland	0	1	37	13	20	8	1	0	0	0	2	0	0	0	0	0	19	1	100
Italy	14	6	7	11	8	21	22	2	0	0	5	0	0	0	0	0	2	3	100
Luxembourg	0	14	0	0	0	17	10	58	0	0	0	0	0	0	0	0	1	1	100
Netherlands	0	43	4	7	0	43	1	2	0	0	0	0	0	0	0	0	1	0	100
Norway	7	6	18	6	4	24	16	5	4	0	0	0	0	0	0	0	8	1	100
Portugal	4	1	0	0	1	0	1	0	5	0	0	0	0	0	0	0	85	2	100
Spain	46	1	2	20	3	12	12	1	0	0	0	0	0	1	0	0	1	2	100
Sweden	0	14	18	25	5	7	3	12	1	0	0	0	0	1	9	0	5	0	100
Switzerland	1	3	19	0	0	8	4	4	16	0	0	0	0	0	0	1	44	1	100
Turkey	27	13	0	0	0	5	32	0	0	0	0	0	0	0	0	0	20	3	100
United Kingdom	1	4	10	16	20	20	20	3	0	0	1	0	0	0	0	2	3	0	100
Regional Total	7	7	9	8	6	17	16	6	4	0	1	0	0	0	1	1	16	0	100

* Since multiple affiliated auditors have been incorporated into the "NAFF" category, certain firms within certain countries have a low Dsum percentage because they are included in the country-specific NAFF Dsum.

Note: This chart is to be read across each row so each country's Dsum = 100%. For example, AA audits 3% of all Canadian companies while AYI audits 24%, etc. As described in the "Treatment of Subsidiaries" section of the Research Design, subsidiary DSum figures have been deducted from parent company DSum figures.

TABLE 10-15 (Continued)
INTERNATIONAL ACCOUNTING FIRMS BY COUNTRY BASED ON TOTAL SALES OR ASSETS - DSUM %

Country	AA	AYI	CL	DHSI	EW	KPMG	PW	TRI	BDO	DRMP	GTI	HHI	HLB	MRI	PKF	SO	NAFF	NADT	Total
Asia/Pacific																			
Australia	3	5	8	23	2	23	15	15	0	0	0	0	0	0	1	1	5	0	100
China, Taiwan	27*	1	2	0*	1*	2	3	3	0	0*	0	0	0	0	0*	7	53	0	100
Hong Kong	1	0	0	1	1	45	42	0	5	0	0	0	0	1	0	0	4	0	100
India	0	6	6	0	2	3	1	7	2	1	0	3	0	1	2	0	67	0	100
Japan	0	0*	15	5	20	13	1	17	0*	0	0*	0	0	0	0	0	29	0	100
South Korea	0	3	18	0*	3	35	6	0*	0	0*	0*	4	0	0	0*	1	30	0	100
Malaysia	11	0	3	0*	21	6	6	0	0	0*	0	0	0	0	22	0	30	0	100
New Zealand	0	6	6	13	14	28	12	7	0	0	0	0	0	0	0	0	13	0	100
Pakistan	1	0*	0*	0*	0	18	14	0	1	0*	0	0	0	0	0	0	67	0	100
Philippines	0*	0	10	0	0*	0	0	0	0	0*	3	0	0	0	0*	0	87	0	100
Singapore	0	0	35	1	8	11	45	0	0	0	0*	0	0*	0	0	0	1	0	100
Thailand	0*	0	0	2*	0	4	1	51	0	0*	0	0	0	0	0	0*	41	1	100
Regional Total	1	0	14	5	18	14	3	16	0	0	0	0	0	0	0	0	28	0	100
Africa/Middle East																			
Israel	0	0	0	0	0	0	0	0	0	0	4	15	0	0	0	0	80	1	100
Kenya	0	0	4	4	0	49	0	0	0	0	0	0	0	0	43	0	0	0	100
Kuwait	0	19	0	0	49	0	10	9	0	0	1	0	0	0	0	0	13	0	100
Nigeria	0	0	0	4	1	27	1	49	0	0	0	0	0	0	0	0	15	3	100
South Africa	3	2	5	19	9	18	5	18	3	0	2	5	1	8	0	0	3	0	100
United Arab Emirates	29	0	0	0	43	0	7	16	0	0	0	0	0	0	0	0	5	0	100
Zimbabwe	0	5	14	12	0	0	11	5	0	0	0	0	0	0	0	0	0	53	100
Regional Total	4	5	2	8	15	10	6	13	1	0	2	5	0	3	0	0	24	1	100
South America/Caribbean																			
Argentina	2	0	10	12	1	3	45	0	1	0	0	0	0	0	0	0	19	7	100
Brazil	6	18	1	5	0	6	15	0	1	1	30	0	0	0	0	0	14	2	100
Chile	0	0	55	2	1	4	38	1	0	0	0	0	0	0	0	0	0	0	100
Colombia	17	4	0	1	0	17	38	0	0	0	0	0	0	0	0	0	19	3	100
Peru	27	4	10	3	0	0	0	0	0	0	0	0	0	0	0	36	20	0	100
Venezuela	0	0	0	0	2	16	50	2	0	0	7	0	0	0	0	0	24	0	100
Regional Total	5	13	6	5	0	8	24	0	1	0	22	0	0	0	0	1	14	2	100
Global Total	6	6	11	8	11	17	12	10	2	0	1	0	0	0	0	0	15	0	100

E. EC

As described in Table 10-16, in the European Community member nations as a group, KPMG audits the most clients, which also represent the highest overall combined sales or assets sum. PW ranks second in terms of client numbers and sales or assets total. DHSI is next in terms of both audit clients and combined sales or assets totals. In comparison with the European region (Table 10-10), the EC countries represent 79% of total company audits for Europe comprising 85% of combined sales or assets. The big eight perform the audits of 67% of the EC country companies, the small eight, 10%, and unaffiliated entities, 22%, once again demonstrating the prevalence of individual and unaffiliated firms in Europe. For Europe as a whole, the big eight also perform 67% of all client audits, the small eight, 10%.

A comparison of the EC, as a separate market, to Europe as a whole will reveal that there is some variation among the rankings of the big eight firms. This reveals that those firms which are the strongest within the EC are not necessarily the strongest among non-EC European countries (besides KPMG), and vice-versa. Within the EC, PW ranks second in terms of both client numbers and size of clients. These positions within all of Europe are held by DHSI and PW, respectively. The next in rank within the EC is DHSI for client numbers and for client size. For all of Europe, CL ranks third for both variables.

Table 10-17 focuses on firm strengths within the six industry classifications based on total dollar sum for each firm within the EC.

In three of the six industries, namely consumer goods, capital goods, and utilities and transportation, there is quite a large margin between the leading audit firm and the second-ranked firm.

Clients in the consumer goods industries are dominated by KPMG, then CL, followed by DHSI.

KPMG leads in the capital goods industries as well, but is followed here by AA and PW.

PW audits the largest companies in the basic industries, followed by EW and KPMG.

The rankings within the financial sector are as follows: KPMG, PW, DHSI.

PW audits the largest utilities and transportation companies, followed by CL, then DHSI.

The individual industry strengths within the EC for the top three firms are consistent with the overall European industry groups, with the exception of capital goods where CL is stronger than AA when viewing Europe as a whole.

TABLE 10-16 INTERNATIONAL ACCOUNTING FIRMS AND THE CLIENTS THEY AUDIT				
EC				
Number of Companies	%	Firms	Total Sales or Assets*	%
		Big Eight		
291	6.77	AA	767	7.91
328	7.63	AYI	718	7.40
298	6.93	CL	717	7.39
377	8.77	DHSI	816	8.41
221	5.14	EW	650	6.70
726	16.89	KPMG	1834	18.91
423	9.84	PW	1730	17.84
237	5.51	TRI	517	5.34
2901	67.48	Sub-Total	7750	79.92
		Small Eight		
142	3.30	BDO	306	3.16
41	.95	DRMP	37	.38
59	1.37	GTI	113	1.16
33	.77	HHI	21	.21
22	.51	HLB	7	.07
38	.88	MRI	46	.47
31	.72	PKF	24	.24
46	1.07	SO	64	.66
412	9.57	Sub-Total	618	6.37
949	22.08	NAFF	1288	13.28
36	.84	NADT	40	.40
985	22.92	Sub-Total	1328	13.69
4298	100	Total	9696	100

*Rounded in $US Billions

Countries Included: Belgium, Denmark, France, West Germany, Greece, Ireland, Italy, Luxembourg, Netherlands, Portugal, Spain, United Kingdom

Note: As explained in the "Treatment of Subsidiaries" section of the Research Design, for this table we have excluded subsidiary amounts from parent company auditor DSum figures but we have not reduced the corresponding number of client companies per accounting firm. Had we not deducted DSum subsidiary figures from parent companies in the EC, the top three ranked firms would remain the same.

TABLE 10-17

INTERNATIONAL ACCOUNTING FIRM MARKET SHARES WITHIN SIX INDUSTRY GROUPS - EC

Consumer Goods	Capital Goods	Basic Industries	Firm	Financials	Utilities and Transp.	Other Industries	Total All Industry Groups
DSum %	DSum %	DSum %		DSum %	DSum %	DSum %	DSum %
			Big Eight				
5.97	12.19	8.08	AA	7.22	6.27	2.58	7.59
6.28	6.57	5.96	AYI	7.37	6.32	3.37	7.08
10.96	11.21	12.45	CL	6.96	10.95	7.62	8.08
9.72	8.98	4.48	DHSI	8.91	10.27	6.16	8.67
4.92	2.77	17.85	EW	6.40	3.89	17.89	6.77
18.16	22.64	17.62	KPMG	18.99	9.19	19.20	18.90
9.01	11.80	19.70	PW	18.57	21.46	12.68	17.49
6.69	3.41	2.01	TRI	6.40	1.26	2.01	5.67
71.71	79.57	88.15	Sub-Total	80.82	69.61	71.51	80.29
			Small Eight				
3.21	4.71	2.56	BDO	3.00	2.07	2.69	3.10
.30	1.18	.13	DRMP	.37	.14	.46	.42
1.67	.16	.74	GTI	1.15	.77	.16	1.05
.57	.17	1.57	HHI	.09	.02	1.12	.22
.47	.21	.05	HLB	.01	.15	0	.06
.44	1.49	.36	MRI	.11	5.74	.82	.43
2.06	.40	1.12	PKF	.03	0	3.57	.28
1.57	.42	.22	SO	.63	.02	.17	.61
10.29	8.74	6.75	Sub-Total	5.39	8.91	8.99	6.20
17.72	11.52	4.95	NAFF	13.38	20.29	19.50	13.12
.29	.18	.16	NADT	.40	1.20	0	.37
18.01	11.70	5.11	Sub-Total	13.78	21.49	19.50	13.50
100	100	100		100	100	100	100

F. Leading Countries of the World

The top sixteen international accounting firms may be viewed from yet another perspective. For Table 10-18, we have selected the top ten countries of the world in terms of combined total sales or assets. In this ranking, we have excluded subsidiary DSum totals from parent company DSum figures when a parent company is located in the same country as the subsidiary. In descending order, these ten countries are as follows: United States, Japan, Germany, United Kingdom, France, Italy, Canada, Netherlands, Switzerland and Sweden. To this list of countries we have added three other countries which were among the top ten countries based on partner data in Chapter Nine, namely, Australia, South Africa and New Zealand. In this table, for each accounting firm we have juxtaposed the percentage of partners within the country with the DSum percentage represented by clients audited. Both dimensions will paint a clear picture of the international accounting firms' share of the marketplace.

In the United States, the rankings for DSum are as follows: KPMG, PW, EW. Based on partner numbers, KPMG is number one, AA number two and CL and EW tied for third place. In the United States, as presented previously, the big eight firms audit 98% of the country's dollar sum, and a corresponding 80% of the partners are from big eight firms.

In Japan, based on dollar sum, EW ranks first, then TRI, followed by CL. Based on partner percentage, the ranking is TRI, CL, EW. The big eight audit 71% of the total sales and assets at a corresponding 92% of total partners within the country.

In Germany, the big eight audit 83% of the country's DSum and have 70% of the country's partner base. Based on dollar sum, the rankings are PW, KPMG, CL. For partners, it changes to KPMG, CL, then AYI and TRI (both with 9%).

Within the United Kingdom, there is only a slight margin separating the top three firms based on dollar sum: EW, KPMG, PW. The big eight firms perform 92% of all audits in the sample set of companies, but a much lower 61% of the partners in the United Kingdom are from big eight firms. It is not surprising that 39% of the partners in the United Kingdom are from small eight firms since several of them are based there. Overall, however, these firms are auditing relatively smaller companies than their big eight counterparts. If subsidiary totals had not been excluded, DSum order for the top three would have been KPMG, PW, EW.

In France, the dollar sum contribution among big eight firms is only 55%, and partners from these eight firms make up 82% of total partners. The small eight firms audit 16% of the client company total sales or assets, this figure being derived primarily from the dollar sum impact of BDO. Based on dollar sum, the ranking is AA, BDO, CL. However, based on partner percentages, KPMG is number one, followed by five firms with the same percentage of partners within France (5%) - AA, AYI, CL, TRI and HLB. It appears that KPMG audits relatively small companies in France and its practice in that country is highly diversified in non-audit activities. In France, the presence of unaffiliated auditors is also significant.

In Italy, the big eight firms audit 91% of all client companies' sales or assets. Specifically, the top three audit firms are PW, KPMG and AA. At a corresponding 82% of partners, the order is AA, KPMG and CL (both with 13%), then AYI and PW (both with 10%). If subsidiary totals had not been excluded, DSum order for the top three would have been KPMG, PW, AA.

In Canada, the big eight audit 94% of all companies. AYI leads, based on dollar sum, followed by TRI and KPMG. However, based on partners, the order is EW, AYI, DHSI/TRI.

In the Netherlands, 99% of all client companies are audited by big eight firms. This high percentage consists primarily of KPMG and AYI with DHSI following by a wide margin. AYI has the most partners, followed by KPMG and TRI. If subsidiary totals had not been excluded, DSum order for the top three would have been AYI, KPMG, DHSI.

In Switzerland, CL is the firm auditing the largest clients, followed by BDO, then KPMG. This country has the highest percentage of dollar sum being audited by unaffiliated firms (44%). AYI has the highest percentage of partners, followed by KPMG and BDO.

In Sweden, the big eight audit 83% of client companies. The top three firms are DHSI, CL and AYI. Among partners, the rankings are DHSI, KPMG, AYI.

In Australia, where 93% of all clients are audited by big eight firms, DHSI is number one, followed very closely by KPMG, then TRI. KPMG has the most partners, then CL and PW. If subsidiary totals had not been excluded, DSum order for the top three would have been DHSI, KPMG, PW.

In South Africa, where 79% of dollar sum audits are performed by big eight firms, DHSI leads, followed by TRI and KPMG. KPMG has the most partners, followed by MRI and AYI (both with 13%). Among the 13 countries summarized in this table, the highest percentage of dollar sum among small eight firms is in South Africa (18%).

In New Zealand, where 86% of client dollar sums are audited by big eight firms, KPMG ranks first, followed by EW, then DHSI. Corresponding partner rankings are as follows: KPMG, then AYI, CL and TRI (all with 13%) and DHSI.

TABLE 10-18 LEADING COUNTRIES AMONG INTERNATIONAL ACCOUNTING FIRMS BASED ON % OF DSUM AND % OF PARTNERS*								
United States		Japan			Germany		United Kingdom	
% of Partners	% of DSum	% of Partners	% of DSum	Firms	% of Partners	% of DSum	% of Partners	% of DSum
				Big Eight				
12	10.56	4	.45	AA	4	.56	3	1.15
7	7.07	0	**	AYI	9	2.52	6	3.65
11	11.13	27	15.16	CL	13	9.13	10	9.66
7	11.23	3	5.14	DHSI	5	6.62	7	16.49
11	13.17	16	19.97	EW	2	.45	7	19.62
16	21.60	8	12.52	KPMG	24	21.75	13	19.55
8	15.56	6	.58	PW	4	34.83	10	19.48
8	8.17	28	17.25	TRI	9	6.73	6	2.61
80	98.49	92	71.07	Sub-Total	70	82.59	61	92.21
				Small Eight				
3	.14	0	0	BDO	8	4.08	6	.42
4	.17	0	0	DRMP	0	.72	3	.07
3	.24	0	0	GTI	3	0	7	.92
4	.23	7	0	HHI	0	.01	3	.12
1	.01	0	0	HLB	4	.02	2	.14
2	0	1	0	MRI	8	.06	7	.47
2	0	0	0	PKF	2	.58	5	.35
1	.32	0	0	SO	5	.02	6	2.10
20	1.11	8	0	Sub-total	30	5.49	39	4.59
n/a	.41	n/a	28.93	NAFF	n/a	11.92	n/a	3.20
n/a	0	n/a	0	NADT	n/a	0	n/a	0
n/a	.41	n/a	28.93	Sub-Total	n/a	11.92	n/a	3.20
100	100	100	100	Total	100	100	100	100

* As previously explained in the Research Design section of this chapter, to compile the data for this table, we have subtracted subsidiary dollar sum figures from parent company auditors to the extent that the subsidiary and parent companies are located in the same country.

** Since multiple affiliated auditors are not reflected separately but are incorporated in the "NAFF" category, the share of DSum which Asahi Shinwa contributes to AYI is not presented.

TABLE 10-18 (Continued)
LEADING COUNTRIES AMONG INTERNATIONAL ACCOUNTING FIRMS
BASED ON % OF DSUM AND % OF PARTNERS*

France		Italy			Canada		Netherlands	
% of Partners	% of DSum	% of Partners	% of DSum	Firms	% of Partners	% of DSum	% of Partners	% of DSum
				Big Eight				
5	19.84	20	14.25	AA	2	2.62	2	.30
5	6.62	10	5.81	AYI	11	24.32	24	42.47
5	8.83	13	6.50	CL	7	4.89	2	3.77
2	1.28	5	11.24	DHSI	9	9.65	11	6.68
3	5.56	4	8.24	EW	15	9.34	1	.28
52	3.28	13	20.71	KPMG	7	13.95	21	42.50
4	1.59	10	21.60	PW	7	10.31	2	1.07
5	8.06	7	2.32	TRI	9	18.94	14	1.71
82	55.06	82	90.67	Sub-Total	67	94.02	78	98.78
				Small Eight				
3	10.71	2	.03	BDO	7	0	5	.21
3	1.27	1	0	DRMP	4	0	4	0
2	.73	3	5.04	GTI	8	2.39	0	0
1	.24	3	0	HHI	2	.03	3	.05
5	.09	2	0	HLB	1	0	4	0
1	1.66	1	0	MRI	6	.33	4	.01
1	0	0	0	PKF	4	.21	1	0
3	.82	4	0	SO	1	0	1	0
18	15.52	16	5.07	Sub-total	33	2.96	22	.27
n/a	29.61	N/A	1.64	NAFF	n/a	2.93	n/a	.83
n/a	0	N/A	2.63	NADT	n/a	.09	n/a	.11
n/a	29.61	N/A	4.27	Sub-Total	n/a	3.02	n/a	.94
100	100	100	100	Total	100	100	100	100

* As previously explained in the Research Design section of this chapter, to compile the data for this table, we have subtracted subsidiary dollar sum figures from parent company auditors to the extent that the subsidiary and parent companies are located in the same country.

TABLE 10-18 (Continued)
LEADING COUNTRIES AMONG INTERNATIONAL ACCOUNTING FIRMS
BASED ON % OF DSUM AND % OF PARTNERS*

Switzerland		Sweden			Australia		South Africa		New Zealand	
% of Partners	% of DSum	% of Partners	% of DSum	Firms	% of Partners	% of DSum	% of Partners	% of DSum	% of Partners	% of DSum
				Big Eight						
4	.50	1	.22	AA	4	3.17	2	2.74	0	0
23	2.93	12	13.88	AYI	5	5.00	13	1.79	13	6.22
10	18.87	11	18.31	CL	13	8.28	9	5.47	13	5.62
3	.37	16	24.80	DHSI	6	22.87	9	18.86	11	12.69
2	0	0	4.64	EW	8	1.61	9	9.14	9	14.25
19	7.54	13	6.50	KPMG	15	22.48	15	17.71	15	28.08
3	3.94	2	2.98	PW	10	14.85	6	4.65	7	12.23
6	3.90	8	11.97	TRI	8	15.16	11	18.17	13	7.14
70	38.05	63	83.30	Sub-Total	69	93.42	65	78.53	80	86.23
				Small Eight						
15	16.45	6	.63	BDO	4	0	5	2.91	3	0
0	0	1	0	DRMP	5	0	2	0	1	0
0	0	7	.20	GTI	3	0	4	2.10	0	0
1	.03	7	.42	HHI	3	.01	5	4.56	3	0
2	0	3	.06	HLB	2	0	0	.52	1	0
1	0	3	1.13	MRI	3	.04	13	7.80	2	0
1	0	5	8.88	PKF	6	1.06	1	0	3	.07
9	1.47	5	.07	SO	5	.53	6	.34	8	.40
29	17.92	37	11.39	Sub-total	31	1.64	35	18.23	20	.47
n/a	43.50	n/a	5.31	NAFF	n/a	5.12	n/a	3.15	n/a	13.28
n/a	.51	n/a	0	NADT	n/a	0	n/a	.08	n/a	0
n/a	44.01	n/a	5.31	Sub-Total	n/a	5.12	n/a	3.23	n/a	13.28
100	100	100	100	Total	100	100	100	100	100	100

* As previously explained in the Research Design section of this chapter, to compile the data for this table, we have subtracted subsidiary dollar sum figures from parent company auditors to the extent that the subsidiary and parent companies are located in the same country.

G. <u>Analysis by International Accounting Firm</u>

Table 10-19 presents, on a firm by firm basis worldwide, the top five industries based on the dollar sum of clients audited. Presentation in this fashion will allow a firm to perform an industry assessment of its leading clients and identify strong industry niches it has established and wishes to continue to strengthen. The firm can also evaluate the strengths of its competitors.

For each of the big eight firms and many of the small eight firms, the highest percentage of dollar sum is always in the banking sector.

AA's next strengths lie in utilities and mining/petroleum.

For AYI, insurance and financial services/holding companies are dominant after banking.

For CL, subsequent strengths are in insurance and utilities.

DHSI is also strong in the insurance sector, followed by transportation equipment/aerospace.

EW has expertise in insurance, and mining/petroleum industries.

For KPMG, after banking, industry strengths are found in insurance, followed by electronics.

PW is strong in mining/petroleum and insurance.

TRI dominates in the insurance industry as well as in retailing/trading.

The reader can refer to the accounting firm profiles in Appendix H to further identify individual firm strengths and weaknesses.

Another approach to viewing the specific country total dollar sum data, which is found in Table 10-20, is to look at each firm and chart the top five countries in which each of the sixteen firms operates with their respective dollar sum market shares. This approach highlights the strength of the firm in each country based on dollar sum percentage data. The largest sum figure for big eight firms is always in the US or Japan.

For all firms, the combined dollar sum of its top five countries always comprises at least 75% of the total DSum of the firm.

With some exceptions among the small eight accounting firms, the majority of the top five countries for each firm are among the leading industrial countries.

TABLE 10-19

TOP FIVE INDUSTRIES AMONG INTERNATIONAL ACCOUNTING FIRMS
BASED ON TOTAL SALES OR ASSETS

AA		AYI		CL		DHSI	
Industry	DSum %	Industry	DSum %	Industry	DSum %	Industry	DSum %
1 Banking	(44)	1 Banking	(43)	1 Banking	(37)	1 Banking	(41)
2 Utilities	(8)	2 Insurance	(11)	2 Insurance	(15)	2 Insurance	(13)
3 Mining	(8)	3 Fin. Svs.	(10)	3 Utilities	(6)	3 Transp.	(14)
4 Fin. Svs.	(4)	4 Mining	(8)	4 Fin. Svs.	(5)	4 Retailing	(6)
5 Retailing	(4)	5 Electronics	(4)	5 Retailing	(4)	5 Fin. Svs.	(6)
Total	68%	Total	76%	Total	67%	Total	72%

EW		KPMG		PW		TRI	
Industry	DSum %	Industry	DSum %	Industry	DSum %	Industry	DSum %
1 Banking	(57)	1 Banking	(62)	1 Banking	(58)	1 Banking	(57)
2 Insurance	(12)	2 Insurance	(9)	2 Mining	(9)	2 Insurance	(12)
3 Mining	(5)	3 Electronics	(4)	3 Insurance	(5)	3 Retailing	(12)
4 Electronics	(4)	4 Retailing	(3)	4 Electronics	(4)	4 Transp.	(2)
5 Retailing	(3)	5 Comm. Fin.	(3)	5 Utilities	(3)	5 Electronics	(2)
Total	81%	Total	81%	Total	79%	Total	85%

BDO		DRMP		GTI		HHI	
Industry	DSum %	Industry	DSum %	Industry	DSum %	Industry	DSum %
1 Banking	(62)	1 Banking	(45)	1 Banking	(72)	1 Banking	(35)
2 Insurance	(11)	2 Insurance	(20)	2 Retailing	(5)	2 Insurance	(10)
3 Electronics	(3)	3 Transp.	(7)	3 Pers. Loan	(5)	3 Mining	(9)
4 Retailing	(3)	4 Construct.	(6)	4 Insurance	(2)	4 Retailing	(8)
5 Indus. Eqp.	(3)	5 Food/Bev.	(4)	5 Chemicals	(2)	5 Transp.	(6)
Total	82%	Total	82%	Total	86%	Total	68%

HLB		MRI		PKF		SO	
Industry	DSum %	Industry	DSum %	Industry	DSum %	Industry	DSum %
1 Food/Bev.	(34)	1 Utilities	(23)	1 Banking	(31)	1 Fin. Svs.	(43)
2 Fin. Svs.	(12)	2 Insurance	(19)	2 Retailing	(16)	2 Banking	(36)
3 Transp.	(9)	3 Transp.	(17)	3 Insurance	(9)	3 Food/Bev.	(6)
4 Indus. Eqp.	(7)	4 Banking	(12)	4 Forest Prd	(9)	4 Retailing	(2)
5 Mining	(7)	5 Fin. Svs.	(7)	5 Transp.	(8)	5 Metal	(2)
Total	69%	Total	78%	Total	73%	Total	89%

Note: The following abbreviations of industries were used:

Fin. Svs.	-	Financial Services/Holding Companies
Mining	-	Mining Petroleum
Transp.	-	Transportation Equipment/Aerospace
Retailing	-	Retailing/Trading
Comm. Fin.	-	Commercial Finance
Indus. Eqp.	-	Industrial Equipment/Farm Equipment
Pers. Loan	-	Personal Loans
Forest Prd.	-	Forest Products
Food/Bev.	-	Food/Beverages

TABLE 10-20

TOP FIVE COUNTRIES AMONG INTERNATIONAL ACCOUNTING FIRMS
BASED ON TOTAL SALES OR ASSETS

AA		AYI		CL		DHSI	
Country	DSum %	Country	DSum %	Country	DSum %	Country	DSum %
1 US	(49)	1 US	(33)	1 Japan	(33)	1 US	(37)
2 France	(22)	2 Neth.	(19)	2 US	(28)	2 Japan	(15)
3 Italy	(10)	3 Canada	(12)	3 Germany	(8)	3 UK	(14)
4 Spain	(9)	4 France	(7)	4 UK	(6)	4 Germany	(7)
5 Japan	(2)	5 UK	(4)	5 France	(5)	5 Italy	(5)
Total	92%	Total	75%	Total	80%	Total	78%

EW		KPMG		PW		TRI	
Country	DSum %	Country	DSum %	Country	DSum %	Country	DSum %
1 Japan	(42)	1 US	(34)	1 US	(36)	1 Japan	(42)
2 US	(32)	2 Japan	(17)	2 Germany	(27)	2 US	(23)
3 UK	(12)	3 Germany	(11)	3 UK	(12)	3 Germany	(6)
4 France	(3)	4 UK	(8)	4 Italy	(7)	4 Canada	(6)
5 Italy	(3)	5 Neth.	(6)	5 Canada	(3)	5 France	(5)
Total	92%	Total	76%	Total	85%	Total	82%

BDO		DRMP		GTI		HHI	
Country	DSum %	Country	DSum %	Country	DSum %	Country	DSum %
1 France	(38)	1 France	(38)	1 Brazil	(32)	1 US	(25)
2 Switz.	(24)	2 Germany	(31)	2 Italy	(23)	2 Israel	(18)
3 Germany	(21)	3 US	(21)	3 Canada	(8)	3 S. Korea	(13)
4 Austria	(5)	4 India	(4)	4 UK	(8)	4 Belgium	(12)
5 US	(2)	5 Brazil	(3)	5 US	(8)	5 S. Africa	(10)
Total	90%	Total	97%	Total	79%	Total	78%

HLB		MRI		PKF		SO	
Country	DSum %	Country	DSum %	Country	DSum %	Country	DSum %
1 UK	(35)	1 France	(44)	1 Sweden	(46)	1 UK	(35)
2 France	(20)	2 S. Africa	(18)	2 Germany	(19)	2 US	(20)
3 S. Africa	(11)	3 UK	(14)	3 Malaysia	(13)	3 Austria	(12)
4 US	(9)	4 Sweden	(7)	4 UK	(9)	4 France	(12)
5 Belgium	(9)	5 Canada	(4)	5 Australia	(4)	5 Switz.	(9)
Total	84%	Total	87%	Total	91%	Total	88%

H. Other Findings of Interest

1. Major Non-Affiliated Firms

In certain countries a significant number of companies are audited by various unaffiliated firms, and this comprises a substantial portion of the total number of audits done in that particular country. A sample of some of the larger firms in terms of the number and size of clients is shown in Table 10-21.

The countries included account for over 20% of total sales or assets for unaffiliated firms. The top unaffiliated firms selected in each country are the largest either in terms of the number of clients or dollar sum or both.

Several countries - Denmark, France, Japan, South Korea, Malaysia and Thailand - have large unaffiliated concentrations, in spite of the fact that there is a well-established big eight base co-existing in these countries.

In a few countries - Austria, Belgium, India, Pakistan, Philippines and Switzerland - the overall unaffiliated presence is larger than the big eight concentration. Israel is unique in that it has virtually no big eight foundation.

Some of the larger non-affiliated firms represent potential links for the large international accounting firms as they continue to expand globally.

2. Auditor Differences in Japanese/English Reports

Table 10-22 focuses on the auditor situation unique to Japan which was previously addressed in the Research Design section of this chapter. Twenty-six companies use local auditors in the Japanese-language annual report who differ in their affiliation from the independent accounting firms which audit the English language version of the same company's annual report.

3. Use of Joint Auditors

On a worldwide basis, the use of joint auditors, whereby two or more individuals or accounting firms have signed the audit opinion, is not extensive. This practice is most prevalent in the countries listed in Table 10-23. The use of joint auditors is often due to country-specific legal auditing requirements. As depicted in the table, for example, of all client companies located in Finland, 55% are audited by one auditor, 30% by two, 13% by three and 2% by four.

4. Non-Government Auditors of Government-Owned Firms

We have excluded from our study government companies audited by government auditors, as we did not consider them to be part of the audit market. However, in certain countries, there are a significant number of government companies that use independent auditors. We have selected those countries with at least five government clients audited by big eight, small eight or unaffiliated auditors where the total dollar sum of these government companies is at least 10% of the total dollar sum of that particular country. Table 10-24 summarizes our findings.

TABLE 10-21 MAJOR NON-AFFILIATED FIRMS			
Country (Total DSum by NAFF for the Country)	Number of Clients	* DSum	% of Sales or Assets of Country Totals
Austria (47.47%)			
Gesellschaft fuer Revision und Treuhaendige Verwaltung	6	33,428	12.29%
Treuberatung Gesellschaft mbh	4	22,619	8.84
Sparkassen Pruefungs - Verband Pruefungsstelle	6	19,015	6.99
Belgium (55.20%)			
V. Emons	11	107,871	27.10
D. Van Woensel	4	36,692	9.22
Huybrechts, Vaes, Verhagen, Wodon, Fallon & Co.	5	23,709	5.96
Denmark (24.47%)			
Revisionsfirmaet G.Bretlau	2	10,828	4.33
Revisionsfirmaet L. Larsen	3	9,454	3.78
Rigsrevision	5	9,048	3.62
France (29.61%)			
S.C.P. Berder-Viala-Buchalet et Autres- Secor Audit	7	99,405	5.26
Cabinet Robert Mazars	29	76,388	4.04
Guerard Delbor Vallas et Cie	13	53,866	2.85
Calan Ramolino et Associes	21	29,755	1.58
India (66.66%)			
Brahmayya & Co.	15	5,605	2.95
Arjun K.S. Aiyer & Co.	12	5,578	2.94
Israel (79.97%)			
Haft & Haft	8	45,192	51.26
Somekh Chaikin	9	18,287	20.74

* Rounded in millions of US$

** Non-Affiliated DSum in these countries also includes those firms having affiliations with several international accounting firms.

TABLE 10-21 (Continued) MAJOR NON-AFFILIATED FIRMS			
Country (DSum by NAFF)	Number of Clients	DSum %	% of Sales or Assets of Country Totals
Japan (28.93%) **			
Itoh Audit Corp.	19	85,619	1.21
Toyo Audit Corp.	33	485,48	.69
South Korea (29.72%) **			
Dong Sung Accounting Corp.	4	31,053	12.13
Malaysia (28.93%) **			
Hanafiah Raslan & Mohamad	31	10,140	20.91
Othman, Hew & Co.	6	444	.92
Pakistan (66.53%) **			
Hyder Bhimji & Co.	7	4,554	23.48
Philippines (87.07%) **			
Joaquin Cunanam & Co.	19	1,381	12.26
Switzerland (43.50%)			
Koreag Controll & Revisions AG	11	146,765	19.02
Bank Auditing Inc. (BAI)	10	129,563	16.79
Thailand (40.85%)			
Suphat & Co.	7	8,715	21.60
Thammakarn Accounting Office	11	201	.50

* Rounded in millions of US$

** Non-Affiliated DSum in these countries also includes those firms having affiliations with several international accounting firms.

TABLE 10-22

AUDITOR DIFFERENCES IN JAPANESE AND ENGLISH LANGUAGE ANNUAL REPORTS

Japanese Client Company	Local Auditor with International Affiliate in Japanese Annual Report Submitted to the Ministry of Finance		International Audit Firm in the English Version of the Annual Report
C. Itoh & Co., Ltd.	Tohmatsu Awoki & Sanwa	TRI	KPMG
Canon Inc.	Showa Ota & Co.	EW	KPMG
Dai Nippon Construction	Meiji Audit Corporation	NAFF	KPMG
Fuji Photo Film Co. Ltd.	Showa Ota & Co.	EW	PW
Fujisawa Pharmaceutical Co. Ltd.	Naniwa Audit Corp.; Koh, Toji	NAFF	PW
Honda Motor Co. Ltd.	Showa Ota & Co.	EW	KPMG
Komatsu Construciton Co., Ltd.	Asahi Shinwa & Co.	MULT	DHSI
Komatsu Forklift Co., Ltd.	Asahi Shinwa & Co.	MULT	AYI
Komatsu Ltd.	Asahi Shinwa & Co.	MULT	DHSI
Marui Co. Ltd.	Asahi Shinwa & Co.	MULT	AYI
Mitsubishi Electric Corporation	Showa Ota & Co.	EW	KPMG
Mitsui & Co. Ltd.	Tohmatsu Awoki & Sanwa	TRI	DHSI
NEC Corporation	Showa Ota & Co.	EW	PW
Nippon Meat Packers Inc.	Century Audit Corporation	KPMG	DHSI
Nippon Telegraph & Telephone Corp.	Asahi Shinwa & Co.	MULT	PW
Nitto Denko Corp.	Century Audit Corporation	KPMG	AA
Nomura Securities Co. Ltd.	Showa Ota & Co.	EW	PW
Olympus Optical Co. Ltd.	Asahi Shinwa & Co.	MULT	AA
Pioneer Electronic Corp.	Tohmatsu Awoki & Sanwa	TRI	PW
Prima Meat Packers Ltd.	Showa Ota & Co.	EW	PW
Q. P. Corp.	Century Audit Corporation	KPMG	AA
Stanley Electric Co. Ltd.	Chuo Shinko Audit Corporation	CL	AA
Sumitomo Corp.	Asahi Shinwa & Co.	MULT	TRI
TDK Corporation	Ishihara, Yasuhide;	NAFF	KPMG
	Nakshima, Kazuaki	NAFF	
Toshiba Corporation	Showa Ota & Co.	EW	PW
Uny Co., Ltd.	Chuo Shinko Audit Corporation	CL	EW

Key:

NAFF = Not affiliated with international accounting firms

MULT = Affiliations with several international accounting firms

TABLE 10-23

COUNTRIES WHERE THE USE OF JOINT AUDITORS IS PREVALENT

Country	Total No. of Clients	Percentage of Clients Using Number of Audit Firm(s)				
		1	2	3	4	5
Austria	106	82	15	3	0	0
Belgium	184	72	23	5	0	0
Denmark	369	30	66	3	0	0
Finland	166	55	30	13	2	0
France	783	20	69	10	1	0
Germany, West	787	92	6	2	0	0
Greece	31	10	90	0	0	0
Hong Kong	353	90	10	0	0	0
India	495	70	18	3	6	4
Ireland	53	85	15	0	0	0
Israel	45	87	13	0	0	0
Japan	2159	77	20	3	*	0
Kenya	14	86	14	0	0	0
Luxembourg	45	82	18	0	0	0
Nigeria	31	48	52	0	0	0
Pakistan	89	74	26	0	0	0
South Africa	409	78	22	0	0	0
Sweden	500	40	54	6	1	0
Switzerland	265	95	3	2	0	0
UAE	16	88	12	0	0	0

* Less than 1%

TABLE 10-24

NON-GOVERNMENT AUDITORS OF GOVERNMENT OWNED FIRMS

	Government-Owned Clients Audited by Non-Government Auditors				
		DSum % of Country Totals	Number of Clients Audited By		
Country	Number of Clients		Big Eight	Small Eight	NAFF
Austria	12	32%	2	2	8
Finland	9	18%	6	2	1
France	21	34%	11	4	6
Germany, West	41	30%	30	1	10
India	18	21%	4	2	12
Italy	18	29%	16	0	2
Norway	9	12%	6	2	1

I. Subsidiary vs. Parent Company Auditors

In Tables 10-25 and 10-27, we examine the subsidiary companies in our data base in terms of the location of parent and subsidiary companies and the correspondence between the parent and subsidiary's auditor.

In Table 10-25, the total number of subsidiaries identified in our data set of client companies are presented in a matrix based both on location and comparison of parent and subsidiary auditors.

Forty-nine percent of all subsidiary companies included in the study have the same auditor as their parent. Of that group of companies, a higher percentage are located in the same country as the parent. Fifty-one percent of the total number of subsidiary companies have parent auditors which differ.

In Table 10-26, we have presented each of the sixteen international accounting firms along with their representative number of subsidiary client companies, and have classified them according to whether the parent company is located in the home country or in a foreign country. The subsidiaries are then sub-classified based on whether or not they have the same auditors as the parents. The percentages provided will more precisely define the extent of same/different auditor usage among the accounting firms.

The big eight firms generally audit both the parent and corresponding subsidiary client companies, regardless of their location, more often than small eight firms.

In Table 10-27, we have arranged the data on subsidiaries for leading parent countries in order to present the total number of subsidiaries within each parent country and the categorization of these subsidiaries based on the location of their sub-categorization of same/different auditor relationships.

In general, different auditors are used more frequently when the parent company is located in a foreign country.

J. World Summary

Table 10-28 brings together demographics on number of offices, number of partners, and clients and dollar sum audited by these partners.

Overall, the big eight firms account for 74% of the number of audit partners worldwide, who in turn serve as auditors for 91% of total world clients, which represent 95% of the world's dollar sum.

The top three global rankings for each of the categories presented are as follows:

- Based on number of partners, KPMG is number one, followed by CL and TRI. For number of offices, KPMG leads, followed by CL and TRI.

- For worldwide number of clients, after KPMG, CL and PW are the leaders. For dollar sum, KPMG is followed by PW and EW.

- KPMG is clearly the leader in all of these dimensions worldwide. However, there are slight variations among the next in rank.

Worldwide, the small eight represent a fairly substantial share of the market based on the number of partners and total offices but, the corresponding dollar sum and client figures were much less proportional.

Table 10-29 is a general summary presenting each country in this chapter with the corresponding share of the audit market which the big eight, small eight and unaffiliated auditors exhibit.

This analysis allows for a better understanding of the specific country and regional strengths and weaknesses which the big eight firms, as a group, display.

Table 10-30 summarizes country and region-specific total partner percentages, dollar sum percentages and Gross National Product percentages worldwide. This table provides insight into the strengths of international accounting firms relative to the economic standing of the country.

International accounting firms are well-established in Australia, Canada, the Netherlands, New Zealand, South Africa, the UK and the US.

International accounting firms are not as well-established in Brazil, France, West Germany, Italy, Japan, South Korea and Spain.

Table 10-25

OVERALL SUMMARY OF PARENT-SUBSIDIARY COUNTRY AND AUDITOR RELATIONSHIPS

	Subsidiaries In Same Country as Parent Company		Subsidiaries In Different Country as Parent Company		Total	
Parent vs. Subsidiary Company Auditors	No. of Companies	%	No. of Companies	%	No. of Companies	%
Subsidiary Audited by the Same Auditor as the Parent Company	743	52%	466	46%	1209	49%
Subsidiary Audited by a Different Auditor than the Parent Company	695	48%	554	54%	1249	51%
Total	1438	100%	1020	100%	2458	100%

TABLE 10-26 AUDITORS OF PARENT AND SUBSIDIARY COMPANIES										
	Parent in the Same Country					Parent in a Foreign Country				
		Same Auditor For Parent		Different Auditor For Parent			Same Auditor For Parent		Different Auditor For Parent	
Sub-sidiary Auditor	Number of Sub-sidiaries	Number of Sub-sidiaries	%	Number of Sub-sidiaries	%	Number of Sub-sidiaries	Number of Sub-sidiaries	%	Number of Sub-sidiaries	%
AA	105	70	66%	35	34%	74	37	50%	37	50%
AYI	97	56	58	41	42	53	17	32	36	68
CL	174	101	58	73	42	105	62	59	43	41
DHSI	119	63	53	56	47	99	55	55	44	45
EW	128	73	57	55	43	55	21	38	34	62
KPMG	212	117	55	95	45	174	81	46	93	54
PW	125	76	60	49	40	276	172	62	104	38
TRI	84	38	45	46	55	38	10	26	28	74
Sub-Total	1044	594	57%	450	43%	874	455	52%	419	48%
BDO	36	10	27	26	73	9	0	0	9	100
DRMP	11	0	0	11	100	5	0	0	5	100
GTI	10	4	40	6	60	3	0	0	3	100
HHI	10	4	40	6	60	4	0	0	4	100
HLB	0	0	0	0	0	2	0	0	2	100
MRI	18	8	44	10	56	3	0	0	3	100
PKF	10	4	40	6	60	2	0	0	2	100
SO	12	6	50	6	50	5	1	20	4	80
Sub-Total	107	36	34%	71	66%	33	1	3%	32	97%
NAFF	287	113	39	174	61	113	10	9	103	91
NADT		0	0	0	0	0	0	0	0	0
Total	1438	743	52%	695	48%	1020	466	46%	554	54%

TABLE 10-27

AUDITOR AND PARENT/SUBSIDIARY RELATIONSHIPS
CLASSIFIED BY PARENT COUNTRIES

		Parent in the Home Country			Parent in Foreign Country		
Country	Total Number of Subsidiaries	Number of Companies With Same Auditor	Number of Companies With Different Auditor	% Using Different Auditor Than Parent	Number of Companies With Same Auditor	Number of Companies With Different Auditor	% Using Different Auditor Than Parent
Australia	95	34	38	53%	8	15	65%
Canada	117	52	38	42	13	14	52
France	266	68	134	66	6	58	91
Germany, West	233	85	79	48	23	46	66
Italy	61	16	23	65	4	18	81
Japan	216	90	60	40	10	56	85
Netherlands	76	12	5	29	21	38	64
New Zealand	34	9	22	71	1	2	67
South Africa	73	32	40	55	1	0	0
Sweden	89	17	32	65	12	28	70
Switzerland	70	6	10	62	12	42	78
United Kingdom	343	88	86	49	71	98	58
United States	567	154	62	29	264	87	25
Other Countries	218	80	66	45	20	52	72
Total	2458	743	695	48%	466	554	54%

TABLE 10-28 WORLD SUMMARY OF THE INTERNATIONAL ACCOUNTING FIRMS COMPARING PARTNERS, OFFICES AND CLIENTS							
		Total Offices					
Number of Partners	% of Total Partners	Offices	%	Firms	Number of Clients	%	Dollar Sum % of Clients Audited
				Big Eight			
2133	6.72	217	3.90	AA	1130	8.96	6.88
2562	8.07	418	7.51	AYI	1004	7.96	6.91
3341	10.52	565	10.15	CL	1721	13.65	12.82
2345	7.39	471	8.46	DHSI	1214	9.62	9.70
2721	8.57	378	6.79	EW	1345	10.66	13.46
5161	16.25	641	11.51	KPMG	2248	17.83	20.29
2568	8.09	424	7.62	PW	1679	13.31	13.60
2792	8.79	515	9.25	TRI	1123	8.90	11.46
23623	74.40	3629	65.19	Sub-Total	11464	90.93	95.16
				Small Eight			
1397	4.40	349	6.27	BDO	352	2.79	2.08
1041	3.28	281	5.05	DRMP	86	.68	.26
1294	4.08	302	5.42	GTI	174	1.38	1.04
1042	3.28	196	3.52	HHI	156	1.23	.29
459	1.45	145	2.60	HLB	39	.30	.03
1193	3.76	293	5.24	MRI	134	1.06	.28
828	2.61	197	3.54	PKF	85	.67	.33
874	2.75	175	3.14	SO	117	.92	.50
8128	25.60	1938	34.81	Sub-Total	1143	9.06	4.83
31751	100.00	5567	100.0	Total	12607	100.0	100.0

Note: To make the percentage of partners comparable with the percentage of DSum, we have omitted "NAFF" and "NADT" DSum and recomputed the world DSum % for each of the 16 firms.

TABLE 10-29

WORLD SUMMARY OF AUDITOR PERCENTAGES
BY REGION AND COUNTRY
BASED ON DSUM

Country	% of Big Eight Auditors	% of Small Eight Auditors	% of NAFF Auditors	% of NADT Auditors	Total*
North America					
Canada	94.03	2.95	2.93	.09	100.0
Mexico	90.24	5.79	3.74	.23	100.0
United States	98.48	1.11	.41	0	100.0
Sub-Total	97.93	1.35	.69	.01	100.0
Europe					
Austria	37.64	14.84	47.47	.05	100.0
Belgium	42.12	2.68	55.20	0	100.0
Denmark	65.74	9.79	24.47	0	100.0
Finland	90.83	5.68	3.40	.08	100.0
France	55.07	15.52	29.61	0	100.0
Germany, West	82.59	5.49	11.92	0	100.0
Greece	.11	0	99.80	.09	100.0
Ireland	79.07	1.64	18.58	.71	100.0
Italy	90.67	5.07	1.64	2.63	100.0
Luxembourg	98.03	0	.92	1.06	100.0
Netherlands	98.79	.27	.83	.11	100.0
Norway	86.53	3.88	8.37	1.21	100.0
Portugal	8.05	4.72	85.15	2.08	100.0
Spain	96.67	.82	.46	2.05	100.0
Sweden	83.29	11.40	5.31	0	100.0
Switzerland	38.04	17.95	43.50	.51	100.0
Turkey	76.90	0	19.74	3.36	100.0
United Kingdom	92.21	4.59	3.20	0	100.0
Sub-Total	75.92	7.64	16.05	.37	100.0
Asia					
Australia	93.41	1.64	5.12	0	100.0
China, Taiwan	39.08	7.33	53.36	.23	100.0
Hong Kong	89.60	6.40	3.99	0	100.0
India	24.51	8.79	66.66	.05	100.0
Japan	71.07	0	28.93	0	100.0
Korea, South	65.54	4.74	29.72	0	100.0
Malaysia	47.55	22.40	29.93	.13	100.0
New Zealand	86.24	.48	13.28	0	100.0
Pakistan	32.28	1.19	66.53	0	100.0
Philippines	10.10	2.57	87.07	.26	100.0
Singapore	99.22	0	.78	0	100.0
Thailand	57.53	.21	40.85	1.40	100.0
Sub-Total	70.83	.73	28.43	.01	100.0

* Rounded in some instances.

TABLE 10-29
(Continued)
WORLD SUMMARY OF AUDITOR PERCENTAGES
BY REGION AND COUNTRY
BASED ON DSUM

Country	% of Big Eight Auditors	% of Small Eight Auditors	% of NAFF Auditors	% of NADT Auditors	Total*
Africa/Middle East					
Israel	0	19.11	79.97	.92	100.0
Kenya	56.64	43.36	0	0	100.0
Kuwait	86.06	.99	12.84	.12	100.0
Nigeria	81.52	0	15.32	3.17	100.0
South Africa	78.53	18.23	3.15	.08	100.0
United Arab Emirates	95.13	0	4.87	0	100.0
Zimbabwe	47.49	0	0	52.51	100.0
Sub-Total	62.72	12.49	23.97	.80	100.0
South America/Caribbean					
Argentina	72.88	1.16	19.28	6.68	100.0
Brazil	52.56	31.85	13.83	1.75	100.0
Chile	99.68	.17	0	.14	100.0
Colombia	77.71	0	19.31	2.98	100.0
Peru	44.55	35.65	19.79	0	100.0
Venezuela	69.62	6.58	23.80	0	100.0
Sub-Total	60.15	23.69	14.47	1.67	100.0
Grand Total	80.63	4.09	15.08	.18	100.0

*Rounded in some instances.

TABLE 10-30

WORLD SUMMARY OF THE INTERNATIONAL ACCOUNTING FIRMS

Country	In Billions of US $ GNP*	% of Worldwide GNP	% of Total Partners**	% of Dollar Sum***
North America				
Canada	367.0	3.17	11.2	2.96
Mexico	126.0	1.09	1.0	.32
United States	4200.0	36.29	34.8	27.09
Sub-Total	4693.0	40.55	47.0	30.37
Europe				
Austria	94.7	.82	.3	.91
Belgium	111.0	.96	.9	1.33
Denmark	57.9	.50	1.7	.84
Finland	54.0	.47	.3	.62
France	724.0	6.26	3.6	6.33
Germany, West	898.0	7.76	2.5	9.16
Greece	32.8	.28	.1	.15
Ireland	21.3	.18	.9	.15
Italy	368.0	3.18	1.0	3.99
Luxembourg	4.9	.04	.1	.28
Netherlands	189.8	1.64	3.2	2.63
Norway	57.0	.49	.8	.53
Portugal	28.9	.25	.1	.09
Spain	187.6	1.62	1.0	1.11
Sweden	100.0	.86	2.1	1.44
Switzerland	126.2	1.09	1.4	2.59
Turkey	52.0	.45	.1	.08
United Kingdom	453.0	3.91	11.9	7.07
Sub-Total	3561.1	30.77	31.9	39.30
Asia				
Australia	153.0	1.32	5.0	1.10
China, Taiwan	72.6	.63	.1	.15
Hong Kong	41.8*	.36	.6	.59
India	194.0	1.68	.5	.64
Japan	1900.0	16.42	2.1	23.72
Korea, South	90.6	.78	.3	.86
Malaysia	29.0	.25	.3	.16
New Zealand	23.2	.20	2.2	.16
Pakistan	32.0	.28	.1	.07
Philippines	34.5	.30	.2	.04
Singapore	16.0	.14	.4	.17
Thailand	40.0	.35	.1	.14
Sub-Total	2626.7	22.70	11.8	27.80

* Source for GNP for Year 1985 or 1986 taken from 1989 World Almanac and Book of Facts (GDP was used for Hong Kong, Zimbabwe and Argentina)

** Percentage of total partners computed from country partner totals in Appendix E.

*** DSum by country as a percentage of Dsum worldwide

TABLE 10-30 (Continued) WORLD SUMMARY OF THE INTERNATIONAL ACCOUNTING FIRMS				
Country	In Billions of US $ GNP*	% of Worldwide GNP	% of Total Partners**	% of Dollar Sum ***
Africa/Middle East				
Israel	25.9	.22	.1	.30
Kenya	6.7	.06	.2	0
Kuwait	17.3	.15	1	.24
Nigeria	53.0	.46	.4	.07
South Africa	112.0	.97	3.0	.56
United Arab Emirates	24.0	.21	.1	.05
Zimbabwe	4.7*	.04	.3	0
Sub-Total	243.6	2.10	4.2	1.22
South America/Caribbean				
Argentina	77.2*	.67	.5	.06
Brazil	250.0	2.16	.7	.91
Chile	16.1	.14	.2	.10
Colombia	31.0	.27	.2	.05
Peru	17.0	.15	.1	.02
Venezuela	57.0	.49	.2	.15
Sub-Total	448.3	3.87	1.9	1.29
Other Countries			3.0	
Grand Total	11572.7	100	100	100

* Source for GNP for Year 1985 or 1986 taken from 1989 World Almanac and Book of Facts (GDP was used for Hong Kong, Zimbabwe and Argentina

** Percentage of total partners computed from country partner totals in Appendix E.

*** DSum by country as a percentage of Dsum worldwide

V. SUMMARY AND CONCLUSIONS

Which are the leading international accounting firms worldwide based on the number and size of clients they audit?

The big eight international accounting firms audit the vast majority of clients worldwide.

The small eight have significant presence in limited areas.

KPMG is almost consistently the audit leader worldwide with CL, PW and EW also among the top four firms.

National auditing firms not affiliated with international accounting firms are significant in Asia/Pacific and Africa/Middle East.

Do international accounting firms audit most of the multinational corporations worldwide?

Big eight international accounting firms audit a larger percentage of multinational companies than non-multinational companies.

What is the composition of the client base of the international accounting firms in terms of particular countries, regions, economy types and common markets?

The big eight have a dominant presence in the US (94% of all sample companies and 99% of the corresponding sales and assets).

Overall, in the rest of the world, the big eight presence is not as overwhelming (62% of all companies and 75% of the dollar sum).

In the US, the leaders are KPMG, AA, EW and PW, but generally outside the US, CL holds a prominent position, along with KPMG and PW.

PW audits the most clients in developing countries.

The big eight perform two-thirds of EC country audits with KPMG, PW and DHSI ranking at the top.

Overall rankings among regions vary:

In North America, KPMG, AA, PW and EW are among the strongest.

Europe is dominated by KPMG, DHSI, CL and PW.

CL, EW, KPMG, TRI and PW are most prominent in Asia/Pacific. The majority of multiple affiliated firms are located in this region.

In South America, PW, DHSI, AYI, AA and KPMG are most visible.

Africa is dominated by KPMG, EW, TRI and DHSI.

The small eight presence is most visible in South America and Africa.

Do the international accounting firms have any industry concentration on a worldwide basis? On a regional basis? On a country basis?

The top three audit firms vary in each of the broad industry classifications and do not consistently hold their strong industry positions globally.

Broad industry strengths within the US do not carry over to non-US countries for the international accounting firms, nor do they correspond on a regional basis.

All of the big eight firms hold dominant positions as auditors in the banking sector. Insurance, financial services, utilities, mining and petroleum also ranked consistently as prominent industries for these firms.

Within specific countries, what is the presence of the leading international accounting firms in terms of size of clients?

Among the leading ten countries, there is some variation in top audit firms among the big eight based on dollar sum.

In Japan and the UK, EW is most prominent with strong competition in the UK from DHSI, KPMG and PW.

In Germany and Italy, PW is the leader.

In France, AA is strongest. BDO ranks higher in France than the other seven of the big eight firms.

Canada is dominated by AYI.

In the Netherlands, KPMG emerges as the leader with AYI closely following.

Switzerland is dominated by CL. BDO is also quite strong there.

In Sweden, DHSI is the leader.

To what extent are large subsidiaries audited by the parent company's auditor?

In our sample of approximately 2500 subsidiary companies, 49% of these have the same auditor as the parent company and of these, 61% are also located in the same country as the parent.

How do partner demographics relate to client statistics for firms?

A high percentage of partners and a corresponding low dollar sum of clients may indicate an overall shift among firms away from traditional audit business.

The data summarized in the tables describes in general terms the spectrum of clients which constitute the global auditing market of the sixteen leading international accounting firms. The world audit market consists of an assortment of sub-markets which we have defined for our sample of client companies worldwide. The market which has emerged for audit services is competitive and the preceding tables have revealed interesting characteristics of audit firms and their clients. We hope that this study will contribute to a better understanding of the auditing industry and assist in firm re-appraisals of existing structures as each international accounting firm defines the role it wishes to play in the global audit marketplace.

CHAPTER 11

ANALYSIS OF AUDIT FEES IN NINE COUNTRIES

Table of Contents

CHAPTER 11

Tables

I. INTRODUCTION

This chapter examines the extent to which audit fees correlate with some of the key characteristics of client companies in a group of nine countries (i.e., Australia, Hong Kong, India, Ireland, Malaysia, New Zealand, Singapore, South Africa and the United Kingdom) where audit fee information is available.

II. RESEARCH OBJECTIVES

11-1 What client company characteristics (i.e., type of industry, multinational operations, size) determine the amount of audit fees paid to external auditors (in countries where audit fee information is published)?

11-2 Are there significant audit fee differences within a country?

11-3 Are there significant cross-national differences in the determination of audit fees as a percentage of assets?

11-4 What has been the trend in audit fees as a percentage of assets in terms of countries and industries over the past six years?

III. RESEARCH DESIGN

A. Selected Countries, Companies and Variables

. Information (i.e., audit fees, sales, assets) was collected from annual reports of companies in nine countries that require a disclosure of audit fees in their annual reports. Other countries were excluded because disclosure of audit fees was not available in their annual reports.

. Government-owned companies were excluded from the sample as our research focused on shareholder-owned companies. Subsidiary companies were included if an external auditor expressed an opinion on the financial statements of a subsidiary company.

B. Size Groups

. Companies were grouped by size of the company's sales or assets. For industrial companies (i.e., consumer products, capital goods, basic and other industries), total sales for 1987 was used as a size variable, while for financial and service companies (i.e., utilities and transportation) total assets was used.

- In order to facilitate the classification of companies from these nine countries into one set of size groups, all local sales and assets figures were converted to US dollars. For sales, the exchange rate which represented an average for the 12 months previous to the company's fiscal year-end was used. For assets, the year-end exchange rate corresponding to the fiscal year-end date of the particular company's financial report was used.

- The total number of companies included in this chapter is summarized by country and size group in Table 11-1.

C. Multinationality of Clients

- To whatever extent possible, client companies have been classified into various categories of multinationality. For the purpose of this analysis, the distinction is purely one of non-multinationality versus multinationality. A company is considered to be multinational if it has subsidiaries in three or more countries.

- Table 11-2 identifies the number of multinational companies by country.

D. Auditor Identified

- The international accounting firms which audited client companies for fiscal year 1987 were identified from the CIFAR database of clients (see Chapter 10 for further details). If the local audit firm was not affiliated with one of the international firms, we identified local firms as NAFF, meaning non-affiliated auditor.

- Table 11-3 lists the total number of client companies included in this chapter by international accounting firm and country.

- If a given company was audited by more than one audit firm, total sales, assets and audit fees were equally divided between auditors when analyzing the audit fee.

E. Type of Industry

- In order to categorize companies which would be considered similar in terms of accounting and auditing procedures, we classified companies into the following industry groups:

  - Consumer Goods
  - Capital Goods
  - Basic Industries
  - Financials
  - Utilities and Transportation
  - Other Industries

- Table 11-4 provides a detailed breakdown of the number of companies included in this study by industry and country.

TABLE 11-1

NUMBER OF COMPANIES INCLUDED BY SIZE
FOR FISCAL YEAR 1987

Size Groups In US $	Australia	Hong Kong	India	Ireland	Malaysia	New Zealand	Singapore	South Africa	United Kingdom	Total
Above 10 billion	4	2	0	1	1	0	1	0	27	36
1.1 - 10 billion	31	17	0	3	4	4	8	22	186	275
501 million - 1 billion	27	4	4	3	7	5	0	17	79	146
101 - 500 million	28	29	37	10	20	14	16	57	229	440
1 - 100 million	11	30	32	5	18	2	12	19	76	205
Total	101	82	73	22	50	25	37	115	597	1102

TABLE 11-2 NUMBER OF COMPANIES INCLUDED - MULTINATIONALITY VS. NON-MULTINATIONALITY FOR FISCAL YEAR 1987 - AUSTRALIA AND UNITED KINGDOM			
	Australia	United Kingdom	Total
Multinational	41	300	341
Non-Multinational	60	297	357
Total	101	597	698

Note: This analysis was not done for the other countries (i.e., Hong Kong, India, Ireland, Malaysia, New Zealand, Singapore and South Africa) as there was not a sufficient number of multinational companies in various size categories based in those countries.

TABLE 11-3

NUMBER OF COMPANIES INCLUDED BY AUDITING FIRM
FOR FISCAL YEAR 1987

Firms	Australia	Hong Kong	India	Ireland	Malaysia	New Zealand	Singapore	South Africa	United Kingdom	Total
Big Eight										
AA	6	1	0	0	2	0	0	5	24	38
AYI	8	0	2	1	1	5	0	6	36	59
CL	18	1	10	3	4	4	9	9	52	110
DHSI	7	2	0	2	0	2	3	21	72	109
EW	5	3	8	6	12	3	11	20	56	124
KPMG	19	25	17	3	8	8	5	28	140	253
PW	16	26	6	2	7	1	9	5	76	148
TRI	13	1	3	1	0	1	0	15	29	63
Sub-Total Big Eight	92	59	46	18	34	24	37	109	485	904
Small Eight										
BDO	0	17	4	0	0	0	0	0	21	42
DRMP	0	0	1	0	0	0	0	0	5	6
GTI	0	0	0	1	0	0	0	2	10	13
HHI	0	0	2	0	0	0	0	3	5	10
HLB	0	0	0	0	0	0	0	2	5	7
MRI	0	0	1	0	0	0	0	16	4	21
PKF	1	0	0	0	2	0	0	0	5	8
SO	1	0	2	0	0	1	0	2	16	22
Sub-Total Small Eight	2	17	10	1	2	1	0	25	71	129
NAFF	10	11	32	4	14	3	0	3	56	133
TOTAL	104*	87*	88*	23*	50	28*	37	137*	612*	1166*

* This total is higher than in earlier tables, reflecting those companies audited by more than one auditor.

TABLE 11-4

NUMBER OF COMPANIES INCLUDED BY INDUSTRY GROUP
FOR FISCAL YEAR 1987

Industry Groups *	Australia	Hong Kong	India	Ireland	Malaysia	New Zealand	Singapore	South Africa	United Kingdom	Total
Consumer Goods	19	13	30	7	8	8	9	20	168	282
Capital Goods	23	13	20	2	8	5	6	17	159	253
Basic Industries	20	1	15	3	11	6	0	38	67	161
Financials	33	47	0	8	18	5	15	33	157	316
Utilities & Transport.	4	7	6	1	1	1	4	0	15	39
Other	2	1	2	1	4	0	3	7	31	51
Total	101	82	73	22	50	25	37	115	597	1102

*Industries Included:

<u>Consumer Goods</u>
Food/Beverages
Textiles/Apparel
Tobacco
Publishing/Printing
Pharmaceuticals
Broadcasting
Retailing/Trading
Various Services
Hotels

<u>Other</u>
Other Industries
Multiple Industries

<u>Capital Goods</u>
Metal Mfg/Metal Prod
Electronics
Transp Eqp/Aerospace
Photo/Scient Equip
Indust/Farm Equip
Construction

<u>Utilities & Transportation</u>
Utilities
Transportation

<u>Basic Industries</u>
Mining/Petroleum
Forest Products
Chemicals
Rubber/Plastics
Building Materials

<u>Financials & Service Industries</u>
Banking
Insurance
Commercial Finance
Personal Loans
Leasing/Rental
Fin Svs/Holding Co.
Real Estate

F. Time Span

- Financial information was extracted for the fiscal years 1982 through 1987. Companies which were acquired or had merged during this period were retained to obtain historical trends, though data items for the years following their acquisition were not available.

- Information for analysis was collected mainly from annual reports (see Chapter 8, Section 4).

- In order for a company to be included in the sample, at least two consecutive years of financial information had to be available. Information for some years is missing either due to changes in the fiscal year-end of the client company or because the annual report for a particular year was not available.

- Table 11-5 summarizes the number of companies included in this chapter by year and country.

G. Audit Fee as Percentage of Sales or Assets

In order to compare audit fee norms, we computed an audit fee percentage which is defined as audit fees divided by total sales or total assets. Total sales was used as a divisor for companies in industrial groups (i.e., consumer, capital goods, basic and other industries), while total assets was used as a divisor for companies in financial, utilities and transportation groups.

To compute audit fees by group, the audit fees of each company included in the group (i.e., industry, size or country) were added and divided by the sum of either sales or assets of the same companies (depending on the industry group of the company).

H. Data Difficulties

Readers should be aware of the following constraints which made it difficult to compare the audit fee percentage across countries:

1. Inconsistent Reporting of Audit Fees

   The companies studied did not provide consistent audit fee data across countries. For example, most of the Australian companies provide precise information about the current year's audit fees, fees paid for other services received, and expenses. In the United Kingdom, companies usually provide only one caption, "auditor's remuneration", without disclosing the exact content of the account. However, within a country, we found consistent reporting of audit fees.

2. Holding Companies Treated as Finance Companies

   Several countries (e.g., Australia, South Africa and the United Kingdom) have holding companies which own various manufacturing companies. These holding companies do not report sales, but report investment income from their manufacturing subsidiaries. The audit fee thus reflects the total incurred by the entire group. Rather than classifying these holding companies as manufacturing firms (which would have resulted in a very high audit fee as a percentage of investment income), these companies were classified as financial companies and audit fee as a percentage of assets was used as a basis for comparison. Assuming that the audit fee incurred for these entities would also reflect the manufacturing nature of their subsidiaries, treating these holding companies as finance companies may have increased audit fees as a percentage of assets for the financial group.

3. Differences in Economic Environment Among the Nine Countries Studied

   The average chargeable rate for one hour of professional auditing work, inflation rates and competitiveness among international accounting firms vary from country to country, thus making cross-national comparisons less useful.

4. Other Determinants of Audit Fees Not Studied

   Audit fees are also influenced by other variables which we were unable to analyze in this chapter. Such variables include: the efforts of the client companies' internal audit staff in assisting the external auditors, whether it is the first year of audit for that accounting firm or a continuing audit, the number of active subsidiaries the client companies have, and the extent of computerization of the client companies' accounting records. Information about these items is not readily available in the public domain.

The above limitations notwithstanding, we have portrayed trends in audit fees within each country. Such an analysis will provide insight into audit fee norms in the nine countries studied, and will provide general findings which are applicable to other countries.

IV. FINDINGS

Simply identifying audit fees will provide no real benefit since it would be expected that larger companies would require more audit hours to complete the audit and, therefore, be charged a larger audit fee than smaller companies. The following analysis compares audit fees as a percentage of company sales or assets by various categories (e.g., size, industry groups, multinationality, etc.):

A. Audit Fee by Size of Client Companies

Table 11-6 shows an inverse relationship between the size and significance of audit fees. The larger the client company size, the lower the audit fee incurred by the client, measured as a percentage of sales or assets.

Table 11-6 also shows that the more developed countries (Australia, Ireland, New Zealand, South Africa and the United Kingdom) generally have higher audit fee percentages in relation to the sales or assets value of the client companies, than do developing countries (Hong Kong, India, Malaysia, and Singapore).

B. Audit Fee by Industry Group

Table 11-7 presents audit fee percentages according to six industry groups for the nine countries studied.

The financial and utilities and transportation segments show a substantially lower audit fee percentage than the rest of the industry groups. The nature of the assets involved and the standardized nature of the business transactions in these industries are considered the major factors for these lower-than-average audit costs. Another reason is that financial service companies carry a much larger asset base on average compared to sales levels for industrial companies. Thus, the audit fee as a percentage of total assets is smaller for companies in the financial, utilities and transportation segments.

The capital goods industry has a higher fee/sales ratio in Australia and the United Kingdom. The complexity of the manufacturing companies in this industry and the larger number of components involved in their production process which require larger inventories of raw material and work-in-process goods explain the higher audit fees.

C. Audit Fee by Size and Industry Group

Table 11-8 provides audit fee norms for both size and industry group by country. In general, its findings are consistent with those of the previous two tables, though there are some exceptions.

D. Audit Fee for Multinational Companies

Table 11-9 presents the audit fees for multinational and non-multinational companies and size groups for Australia and the United Kingdom. This analysis was not done for the other countries (i.e., Hong Kong, India, Ireland, Malaysia, New Zealand, Singapore and South Africa) as there was an insufficient number of multinational companies in various size categories based in those countries.

As expected, multinational companies have a higher fees/sales or assets ratio. The higher audit fees are caused by the larger number of subsidiaries involved in a multinational corporation. Furthermore, a more complex consolidation and foreign currency translation process is required for multinational operations.

E. Audit Fee Analyzed by Auditing Firm Classification

Tables 11-10, 11-11 and 11-12 illustrate that there are some differences, in terms of the ratio of fees to sales or assets, for the big eight firms in comparison to the small eight firms and non-affiliated firms, but trends are not conclusive. Based on our analysis of earlier tables, audit fees were determined mainly by the size and industry group of client companies.

F. Audit Fee Trends: Last Six Years

In Table 11-13, fees are compared for the period from 1982 to 1987 by country. In Table 11-14, yearly changes in audit fee percentage for 1982-1987 are provided. Generally, significant changes are not apparent in these tables. Most countries show a decreasing trend of audit fees as a percentage of sales or assets except for India and Ireland, which have increased audit fees in recent years.

This may indicate that it is difficult to increase audit fees due to rising competition among international accounting firms. The recent stagnation in the growth of audit services has increased pressure on audit firms to grow in other services such as consulting and tax and financial planning.

TABLE 11-5

NUMBER OF COMPANIES INCLUDED BY YEAR: BY COUNTRY
FOR FISCAL YEARS 1982-1987

Fiscal Year	Australia	Hong Kong	India	Ireland	Malaysia	New Zealand	Singapore	South Africa	United Kingdom	Total
1987	101	82	73	22	50	25	37	115	597	1102
1986	110	86	78	22	55	28	43	120	659	1201
1985	112	84	72	24	55	29	43	123	670	1212
1984	110	86	46	23	55	28	41	116	642	1147
1983	108	81	43	23	48	27	41	115	585	1071
1982	108	75	44	23	48	26	41	113	555	1033

TABLE 11-6

AUDIT FEES BY SIZE AND COUNTRY FOR FISCAL YEAR 1987

Size Groups	Australia		Hong Kong		India		Ireland		Malaysia		New Zealand		Singapore		South Africa		United Kingdom	
	N	Fee %	N	Fee %	N	Fee %	N	Fee %	N	Fee %	N	Fee %	N	Fee %	N	Fee %	N	Fee %
<u>US $</u>																		
Above 10 billion	4	.006	2	.007	0	0	1	.004	1	.004	0	0	1	.003	0	0	27	.008
1.1 - 10 billion	31	.043	17	.025	0	0	3	.016	4	.004	4	.052	8	.007	22	.026	186	.039
501 million - 1 billion	27	.068	4	.010	4	.006	3	.060	7	.030	5	.064	0	0	17	.065	79	.075
101 - 500 million	28	.063	29	.032	37	.007	10	.078	20	.032	14	.066	16	.068	57	.069	229	.095
1 - 100 million	11	.055	30	.053	32	.012	5	.138	18	.046	2	.174	12	.038	19	.175	76	.096
Country Average	101	.025	82	.014	73	.008	22	.040	50	.014	25	.057	37	.012	115	.039	597	.027

TABLE 11-7

AUDIT FEES BY INDUSTRY GROUPS AND COUNTRIES

Audit Fee as Percentage of Sales or Assets for Fiscal Year 1987																		
	Australia		Hong Hong		India		Ireland		Malaysia		New Zealand		Singapore		South Africa		United Kingdom	
	N	Fee %	N	Fee %	N	Fee %	N	Fee %	N	Fee %	N	Fee %	N	Fee %	N	Fee %	N	Fee %
Consumer Goods	19	.043	13	.099	30	.008	7	.088	8	.042	8	.052	9	.124	20	.062	168	.052
Capital Goods	23	.098	13	.071	20	.008	2	.114	8	.090	5	.060	6	.063	17	.117	159	.088
Basic Industries	20	.052	1	.050	15	.008	3	.101	11	.030	6	.063	0	0	38	.059	67	.057
Financial Industries	33	.010	47	.010	0	.000	8	.012	18	.006	5	.054	15	.006	33	.020	157	.007
Utilities & Transportation	4	.088	7	.033	6	.005	1	.026	1	.007	1	.114	4	.012	0	0	15	.022
Other Industry	2	.066	1	.149	2	.007	1	.151	4	.111	0	0	3	.180	7	.109	31	.075
Country Average	101	.025	82	.014	73	.008	22	.040	50	.014	25	.057	37	.012	115	.039	597	.027

TABLE 11-8

AUDIT FEES - FOR INDUSTRY GROUP BY SIZE

Audit Fee as Percentage of Sales or Assets for Fiscal Year 1987

	Consumer Goods		Capital Goods		Basic Industry		Finance Industry		Utilities Transport		Other Industry		Average for Size Group	
	N	Fee %	N	Fee %	N	Fee %	N	Fee %	N	Fee %	N	Fee %	N	Fee %
Australia														
Above 10 billion	0	0	0	0	0	0	4	.006	0	0	0	0	4	.006
1.1 - 10 billion	6	.037	4	.106	7	.049	10	.024	2	.094	2	.066	31	.043
501 million - 1 billion	6	.070	9	.083	3	.058	7	.048	2	.076	0	0	27	.068
101 - 500 million	7	.074	8	.118	5	.065	8	.015	0	0	0	0	28	.063
1 - 100 million	0	0	2	.144	5	.117	4	.025	0	0	0	0	11	.055
Industry Average for Australia	19	.043	23	.098	20	.052	33	.010	4	.088	2	.066	101	.025
Hong Kong														
Above 10 billion	0	0	0	0	0	0	2	.007	0	0	0	0	2	.007
1.1 - 10 billion	0	0	0	0	0	0	11	.012	5	.034	1	.149	17	.025
501 million - 1 billion	0	0	0	0	0	0	4	.010	0	0	0	0	4	.010
101 - 500 million	4	.110	5	.075	0	0	18	.026	2	.015	0	0	29	.032
1 - 100 million	9	.085	8	.066	1	.050	12	.037	0	0	0	0	30	.053
Industry Average for Hong Kong	13	.099	13	.071	1	.050	47	.010	7	.033	1	.149	82	.014
India														
Above 10 billion	0	0	0	0	0	0	0	0	0	0	0	0	0	0
1.1 - 10 billion	0	0	0	0	0	0	0	0	0	0	0	0	0	0
501 million - 1 billion	3	.006	1	.005	0	0	0	0	0	0	0	0	4	.006
101 - 500 million	10	.007	12	.008	9	.007	0	0	4	.005	2	.007	37	.007
1 - 100 million	17	.015	7	.010	6	.013	0	0	2	.005	0	0	32	.012
Industry Average for India	30	.008	20	.008	15	.008	0	0	6	.005	2	.007	73	.008

TABLE 11-8 (Continued)

AUDIT FEES - FOR INDUSTRY GROUP BY SIZE

Audit Fee as Percentage of Sales or Assets for Fiscal Year 1987	Consumer Goods		Capital Goods		Basic Industry		Finance Industry		Utilities Transport		Other Industry		Average for Size Group	
	N	Fee %	N	Fee %	N	Fee %	N	Fee %	N	Fee %	N	Fee %	N	Fee %
Ireland														
Above 10 billion	0	0	0	0	0	0	1	.004	0	0	0	0	1	.004
1.1 - 10 billion	0	0	0	0	1	.084	2	.003	0	0	0	0	3	.016
501 million - 1 billion	0	0	0	0	1	.096	2	.022	0	0	0	0	3	.060
101 - 500 million	5	.080	0	0	1	.164	3	.071	1	.026	0	0	10	.078
1 - 100 million	2	.159	2	.114	0	0	0	0	0	0	1	.151	5	.138
Industry Average for Ireland	7	.088	2	.114	3	.101	8	.012	1	.026	1	.151	22	.040
Malaysia														
Above 10 billion	0	0	0	0	0	0	1	.004	0	0	0	0	1	.004
1.1 - 10 billion	0	0	0	0	0	0	4	.004	0	0	0	0	4	.004
501 million - 1 billion	0	0	0	0	0	0	5	.011	1	.007	1	.123	7	.030
101 - 500 million	3	.025	4	.088	7	.027	5	.017	0	0	1	.058	20	.032
1 - 100 million	5	.087	4	.101	4	.057	3	.019	0	0	2	.043	18	.046
Industry Average for Malaysia	8	.042	8	.090	11	.030	18	.006	1	.007	4	.111	50	.014
New Zealand														
Above 10 billion	0	0	0	0	0	0	0	0	0	0	0	0	0	0
1.1 - 10 billion	0	0	0	0	1	.045	3	.054	0	0	0	0	4	.052
501 million - 1 billion	4	.050	0	0	1	.116	0	0	0	0	0	0	5	.064
101 - 500 million	3	.053	5	.060	4	.077	1	.060	1	.114	0	0	14	.066
1 - 100 million	1	.180	0	0	0	0	1	.133	0	0	0	0	2	.174
Industry Average for New Zealand	8	.052	5	.060	6	.063	5	.054	1	.114	0	0	25	.057

TABLE 11-8 (Continued)

AUDIT FEES - FOR INDUSTRY GROUP BY SIZE

Audit Fee as Percentage of Sales or Assets for Fiscal Year 1987

	Consumer Goods		Capital Goods		Basic Industry		Finance Industry		Utilities Transport		Other Industry		Average for Size Group	
	N	Fee %	N	Fee %	N	Fee %	N	Fee %	N	Fee %	N	Fee %	N	Fee %
Singapore														
Above 10 billion	0	0	0	0	0	0	1	.003	0	0	0	0	1	.003
1.1 - 10 billion	0	0	0	0	0	0	6	.007	2	.006	0	0	8	.007
501 million - 1 billion	0	0	0	0	0	0	0	0	0	0	0	0	0	0
101 - 500 million	4	.128	4	.062	0	0	4	.011	2	.041	2	.168	16	.068
1 - 100 million	5	.104	2	.066	0	0	4	.013	0	0	1	.226	12	.038
Industry Average for Singapore	9	.124	6	.063	0	0	15	.006	4	.012	3	.180	37	.012
South Africa														
Above 10 billion	0	0	0	0	0	0	0	0	0	0	0	0	0	0
1.1 - 10 billion	6	.052	0	0	2	.074	14	.016	0	0	0	0	22	.026
501 million - 1 billion	2	.043	2	.124	7	.055	2	.005	0	0	4	.110	17	.065
101 - 500 million	10	.103	11	.113	23	.037	10	.051	0	0	3	.101	57	.069
1 - 100 million	2	.085	4	.119	6	.055	7	.252	0	0	0	0	19	.175
Industry Average for South Africa	20	.062	17	.117	38	.059	33	.020	0	0	7	.109	115	.039
United Kingdom														
Above 10 billion	1	.052	0	0	2	.025	20	.005	3	.010	1	.045	27	.008
1.1 - 10 billion	57	.046	42	.076	15	.098	69	.009	1	.061	2	.058	186	.039
501 million - 1 billion	20	.073	22	.101	4	.087	20	.028	8	.115	5	.078	79	.075
101 - 500 million	69	.108	74	.144	35	.119	35	.028	1	.130	15	.162	229	.095
1 - 100 million	21	.113	21	.228	11	.170	13	.030	2	.109	8	.205	76	.096
Industry Average for United Kingdom	168	.052	159	.088	67	.057	157	.007	15	.022	31	.075	597	.027

TABLE 11-9

AUDIT FEES BY MNC AND SIZE
FOR AUSTRALIA AND THE UNITED KINGDOM

Audit Fee as Percentage of Sales or Assets for Fiscal Year 1987

	Multinational Companies		Non-Multinational Companies	
	N	Fee %	N	Fee %
Australia				
Size (in U.S. $)				
Above 10 billion	3	.006	1	.005
1.1 - 10 billion	15	.055	16	.028
501 million - 1 billion	15	.077	12	.055
101 - 500 million	8	.102	20	.047
1 - 100 million*	0	0	11	.055
United Kingdom				
Size (in U.S. $)				
Above 10 billion	20	.010	7	.002
1.1 - 10 billion	126	.056	60	.007
501 million - 1 billion	46	.100	33	.037
101 - 500 million	92	.118	137	.078
1 - 100 million	16	.106	60	.092

* There is no analysis of multinational companies in the size group US$ 1-100 million in Australia because there were only non-multinational companies in this size group.

TABLE 11-10

AUDIT FEES BY TYPE OF AUDIT FIRM AND COUNTRY

Audit Fee as Percentage of Sales or Assets for Fiscal Year 1987

	Australia		Hong Kong		India		Ireland		Malaysia		New Zealand		Singapore		South Africa		United Kingdom	
	N	Fee %	N	Fee %	N	Fee %	N	Fee %	N	Fee %	N	Fee %	N	Fee %	N	Fee %	N	Fee %
Big Eight	92	.023	59	.013	46	.008	18	.041	34	.029	24	.057	37	.012	109	.045	485	.027
Small Eight	2	.074	17	.018	10	.008	1	.096	2	.004	1	.027	0	0	25	.022	71	.033
NAFF	10	.043	11	.012	32	.007	4	.020	14	.008	3	.059	0	0	3	.011	56	.030

TABLE 11-11

AUDIT FEES BY COUNTRY, INDUSTRY GROUP AND TYPE OF AUDIT FIRM

Audit Fees as Percentage of Sales or Assets for Fiscal Year 1987

	Consumer Goods		Capital Goods		Basic Industry		Financial		Utilities Transport		Other	
	N	Fee %	N	Fee %	N	Fee %	N	Fee %	N	Fee %	N	Fee %
Australia												
Big Eight	14	.041	21	.105	20	.053	32	.009	3	.081	2	.066
Small Eight	1	.063	0	0	0	0	0	0	1	.117	0	0
NAFF	4	.039	2	.074	2	.041	2	.029	0	0	0	0
Hong Kong												
Big Eight	11	.100	7	.070	0	0	33	.010	7	.033	1	.149
Small Eight	0	0	6	.071	0	0	11	.013	0	0	0	0
NAFF	2	.083	1	.079	1	.050	7	.009	0	0	0	0
India												
Big Eight	18	.009	11	.008	9	.008	0	0	7	.005	1	.012
Small Eight	3	.009	2	.009	3	.007	0	0	1	.010	1	.006
NAFF	13	.007	12	.007	5	.006	0	0	1	.003	1	.006
Ireland												
Big Eight	5	.116	1	.087	3	.103	7	.014	1	.026	1	.151
Small Eight	0	0	0	0	1	.096	0	0	0	0	0	0
NAFF	2	.050	1	.147	0	0	1	.004	0	0	0	0
Malaysia												
Big Eight	5	.070	6	.104	8	.029	11	.012	0	0	4	.111
Small Eight	0	0	0	0	0	0	1	.004	1	.007	0	0
NAFF	3	.028	2	.065	3	.032	6	.004	0	0	0	0

TABLE 11-11 (Continued)

AUDIT FEES BY COUNTRY, INDUSTRY GROUP AND TYPE OF AUDIT FIRM

Audit Fees as Percentage of Sales or Assets for Fiscal Year 1987

	Consumer Goods		Capital Goods		Basic Industry		Financial		Utilities Transport		Other	
	N	Fee %	N	Fee %	N	Fee %	N	Fee %	N	Fee %	N	Fee %
<u>New Zealand</u>												
Big Eight	7	.055	4	.066	8	.063	5	.053	0	0	0	0
Small Eight	0	0	1	.027	0	0	0	0	0	0	0	0
NAFF	1	.035	0	0	0	0	1	.065	1	.114	0	0
<u>Singapore</u>												
Big Eight	9	.124	6	.063	0	0	15	.006	4	.012	3	.180
Small Eight	0	0	0	0	0	0	0	0	0	0	0	0
NAFF	0	0	0	0	0	0	0	0	0	0	0	0
<u>South Africa</u>												
Big Eight	18	.065	16	.119	39	.059	29	.024	0	0	7	.110
Small Eight	3	.054	3	.102	2	.070	16	.013	0	0	1	.080
NAFF	0	0	1	.043	0	0	2	.010	0	0	0	0
<u>United Kingdom</u>												
Big Eight	137	.054	129	.087	54	.056	131	.007	13	.019	22	.068
Small Eight	24	.047	17	.095	9	.070	16	.010	1	.179	4	.159
NAFF	14	.033	19	.113	4	.208	13	.004	1	.059	5	.084

TABLE 11-12

AUDIT FEES BY COUNTRY, SIZE GROUP AND TYPE OF AUDIT FIRM

Audit Fees as Percentage of Sales or Assets for Fiscal Year 1987										
	Above 10 Billion		1.1 - 10 Billion		501 Million - 1 Billion		101 - 500 Million		1 - 100 Million	
	N	Fee %	N	Fee %	N	Fee %	N	Fee %	N	Fee %
Australia										
Big Eight	4	.006	28	.043	24	.061	27	.064	9	.085
Small Eight	0	0	1	.063	1	.117	0	0	0	0
NAFF	0	0	4	.033	2	.107	2	.033	2	.023
Hong Kong										
Big Eight	3	.007	13	.030	3	.007	22	.036	18	.068
Small Eight	0	0	2	.010	1	.021	7	.019	7	.028
NAFF	0	0	2	.002	0	0	2	.058	7	.064
India										
Big Eight	0	0	0	0	4	.006	24	.008	18	.016
Small Eight	0	0	0	0	1	.007	5	.008	4	.012
NAFF	0	0	0	0	0	0	13	.006	19	.008
Ireland										
Big Eight	0	0	3	.016	3	.047	8	.085	4	.135
Small Eight	0	0	0	0	1	.096	0	0	0	0
NAFF	1	.004	0	0	0	0	2	.050	1	.147
Malaysia										
Big Eight	0	0	1	.004	4	.053	14	.034	15	.046
Small Eight	1	.004	0	0	1	.007	0	0	0	0
NAFF	0	0	3	.004	2	.005	6	.028	3	.049

TABLE 12 (Continued) AUDIT FEES BY COUNTRY, SIZE GROUP AND TYPE OF AUDIT FIRM										
Audit Fees as Percentage of Sales or Assets for Fiscal Year 1987										
	Above 10 Billion		1.1 - 10 Billion		501 Million - 1 Billion		101 - 500 Million		1 - 100 Million	
	N	Fee %	N	Fee %	N	Fee %	N	Fee %	N	Fee %
New Zealand										
Big Eight	0	0	5	.051	4	.070	13	.066	2	.174
Small Eight	0	0	0	0	0	0	1	.027	0	0
NAFF	0	0	1	.065	1	.035	1	.114	0	0
Singapore										
Big Eight	1	.003	8	.007	0	0	16	.068	12	.038
Small Eight	0	0	0	0	0	0	0	0	0	0
NAFF	0	0	0	0	0	0	0	0	0	0
South Africa										
Big Eight	0	0	19	.030	20	.069	53	.074	17	.194
Small Eight	0	0	9	.018	1	.004	11	.048	4	.103
NAFF	0	0	2	.010	0	0	0	0	1	.043
United Kingdom										
Big Eight	25	.008	171	.041	63	.078	178	.097	49	.086
Small Eight	2	.013	13	.026	7	.076	34	.085	15	.073
NAFF	1	.001	9	.018	10	.056	21	.102	15	.194

TABLE 11-13

TRENDS IN AUDIT FEES: LAST SIX YEARS

Audit Fees as Percentage of Sales or Assets for Each Year 1982-1987																			
	Australia		Hong Kong		India		Ireland		Malaysia		New Zealand		Singapore		South Africa		United Kingdom	
	N	Fee %	N	Fee %	N	Fee %	N	Fee %	N	Fee %	N	Fee %	N	Fee %	N	Fee %	N	Fee %
1987	101	.025	82	.014	73	.008	22	.040	50	.014	25	.057	37	.012	115	.039	597	.027
1986	110	.026	86	.013	78	.007	22	.023	55	.015	28	.052	43	.013	120	.041	659	.028
1985	112	.027	84	.015	72	.007	24	.027	55	.015	29	.059	43	.013	123	.042	670	.028
1984	110	.029	86	.014	46	.007	23	.025	55	.015	28	.065	41	.013	116	.042	642	.028
1983	108	.033	81	.014	43	.007	23	.026	48	.016	27	.072	41	.014	115	.047	585	.030
1982	108	.033	75	.014	44	.006	23	.025	48	.017	26	.076	41	.014	113	.047	555	.031
*	649	.028	494	.014	356	.007	137	.027	311	.015	163	.060	246	.013	702	.042	3708	.029

*Country Average

TABLE 11-14
PERCENTAGE CHANGE IN AUDIT FEES
YEAR TO YEAR AND SIX YEARS' TRENDS BY COUNTRY

	1987 over 1986		1986 over 1985		1985 over 1984		1984 over 1983		1983 over 1982		Overall 1987 Over 1982
	N	Fee %	N	Fee %	N	Fee %	N	Fee %	N	Fee %	Fee %
Australia	101	(3.50)*	110	(4.40)	112	(5.60)	110	(11.00)	108	(.59)	(23.00)
Hong Kong	82	.86	86	(8.90)	84	2.97	86	5.76	81	(1.20)	(1.10)
India	73	3.91	78	3.00	72	6.79	46	(6.50)	43	17.30	25.40
Ireland	22	72.40	22	(15.00)	24	9.95	23	(4.80)	23	4.29	60.30
Malaysia	50	(4.80)	55	2.67	55	(4.90)	55	(4.80)	48	(5.80)	(17.00)
New Zealand	25	8.29	28	(12.00)	29	(9.40)	28	(9.20)	27	(4.80)	(25.00)
Singapore	37	(1.60)	43	(3.60)	43	(.62)	41	(6.50)	41	.00	(12.00)
South Africa	115	(4.80)	120	(3.10)	123	1.68	116	(11.00)	115	(.57)	(17.00)
United Kingdom	597	(1.80)	659	(.49)	670	(1.00)	642	(4.30)	585	(4.10)	(11.00)

* Year to Year Percentage Change in Audit Fee was Computed Using the Following Formula:

$$\left[\frac{\dfrac{\text{Audit Fee 1987}}{\text{Sales or Assets 1987}} \text{ minus } \dfrac{\text{Audit Fee 1986}}{\text{Sales or Assets 1986}}}{\dfrac{\text{Audit Fee 1986}}{\text{Sales or Assets 1986}}}\right] \text{Multiplied by 100}$$

V. SUMMARY AND CONCLUSIONS

The following conclusions are based on our analysis of audit fee data of 1,100 companies in nine countries for the years 1982-1987:

- Audit fees are determined by the size and industry classification of the client company audited.
- Companies in the capital goods industry pay the highest audit fees of the six industry groups analyzed. Companies in the financial services and utilities and transportation industry groups pay the lowest audit fees.
- Multinational companies pay higher audit fees in comparison to domestic companies in the same industry and size group.
- Client companies located in industrial countries pay higher audit fees than companies in developing countries.
- The audit services industry is very competitive in large industrialized countries. If size and industry are considered constants, it can be concluded that clients pay similar audit fees in countries such as Australia and the United Kingdom.
- Audit fees as a percentage of sales or assets have not increased over a six-year period. On the contrary, they have actually decreased in seven of the nine countries studied in this chapter.

Ideally, this type of analysis would be conducted for more than nine countries. Such an analysis, however, will only be possible when the disclosure of audit fee data extends beyond the countries identified in this chapter.

CHAPTER 12

ANALYSIS OF SIMILARITIES AND DIFFERENCES IN AUDITORS' REPORTS IN 24 COUNTRIES

Table of Contents

Tables

I. INTRODUCTION

Independent auditors help assure the integrity of financial information by examining financial statements and attesting to their reliability, fairness and general quality. The auditor's report communicates to users what external auditors have concluded, as well as the standards and procedures which they followed to arrive at their conclusions.

Like accounting standards, requirements regarding auditors' reports differ from one country to another. It is important for international users, who may depend extensively on published financial statements, to understand these differences and their implications for the reliability of the statements.

II. RESEARCH OBJECTIVES

This chapter focuses on an analysis of the differences found among auditors' reports worldwide. The following questions concerning auditors' reports are addressed:

12-1 How do auditors' reports, included in annual reports, compare globally in terms of format and content?

12-2 What are the reasons audit opinions are qualified internationally?

12-3 Is the audit process completed on a timely basis internationally?

III. RESEARCH DESIGN

Each of the above mentioned research objectives was carried out by examining the auditors' reports included in the annual reports of companies from 24 countries. When a full annual report was available in English, the English report was used, otherwise the native language report was used. For Japanese companies, if an English report was not available, we used the annual report titled "Yukashoken Hokokusho Soran", filed with the Japanese Ministry of Finance.

To identify general trends in the form and content of auditors' opinions, the annual reports of ten leading companies in each country were identified. A small sample of companies was used because the auditor's report is presented in a fairly uniform manner within each country. A review of leading companies in each country provided a general overview of the form and content of the auditor's report for that particular country.

In order to identify the extent and variety of qualifications present in auditors' opinions internationally, the auditors' reports from the 1987 annual reports of 3,892 companies worldwide were reviewed.

In order to examine the time elapsed between year-end dates and auditors' reports dates, fiscal year 1987 annual reports of 1,957 companies were utilized. The objective was to obtain a representative sample large enough to cover various client characteristics such as different industry groups, size, multinationality and year-end dates.

IV. CHARACTERISTICS OF AUDITORS' REPORTS WORLDWIDE

Table 12-1 presents findings on the form and content of auditors' reports. The following observations highlight the differences found.

A. To Whom is the Auditor's Report Addressed?

The auditor's report is not specifically addressed to the board of directors or shareholders in many countries. In Australia, Hong Kong, Malaysia, New Zealand, Singapore and South Africa, for example, the report was addressed frequently to "the members" without explaining whether this referred to the members of the board of directors, the management, or the shareholders. In France and Belgium, the auditor's report was commonly addressed to "Ladies and Gentlemen." The majority of audit reports in Austria, Denmark, Finland, West Germany, the Netherlands, and Sweden had no addressee.

B. Is the Auditor's Address Provided?

Most auditors in South Korea and some auditors in Italy, Japan, Spain and the US provided full address in the auditor's report. Auditors from other countries only provided the name of the city where the audit firm is located.

C. Is the Audit Firm Identified?

Though the audit firm or individual auditor's name was always provided, we found that it was not always clear if all individuals listed in the auditor's report were external auditors. Similarly, audit firm identification was not clear in instances where only individual auditors were identified.

D. Where is the Auditor's Report Placed?

The auditor's report is not always listed in the table of contents of the annual report or located adjacent to the footnotes and schedules. Therefore, the report is often difficult to locate. The problem is even more complicated in some countries (e.g., Belgium, France) where more than one auditor's report is included.

TABLE 12-1
CHARACTERISTICS OF AUDITORS' REPORTS

Country	To Whom Addressed	Auditor's Address Provided	Is It Signed? *	Where is it located in the Annual Report?
Australia	Members of the Company	No	Yes (b)	After Financial Statements and Footnotes
Austria	Not Addressed	No	Yes (b)	Between Financial Statements
Belgium	Ladies and Gentlemen	No	Yes (d)	After Financial Statements and Footnotes
Canada	Shareholders	No	Yes (a)	No Majority Practice
Denmark	Not Addressed	No	Yes (b)	Before Financial Statements
Finland	Not Addressed	No	Yes (c)	After Financial Statements and Footnotes
France	Ladies and Gentlemen	No	Yes (b)	No Majority Practice
Germany, West	Not Addressed	No	Yes (b)	Between Financial Statements
Hong Kong	Members of the Company	No	Yes (a)	After Financial Statements and Footnotes
Italy	Shareholders	Minority Practice	Yes (b)	No Majority Practice
Japan	Board of Directors	Minority Practice	Yes (a)	After Financial Statements and Footnotes
Korea, South	Shareholders and Board of Directors	Majority Practice	Yes (a)	After Financial Statements and Footnotes
Malaysia	Members of the Company	No	Yes (b)	After Financial Statements and Footnotes
Mexico	Shareholders	No	Yes (b)	Before Financial Statements
Netherlands	Not Addressed	No	Yes (a)	After Financial Statements and Footnotes
New Zealand	Members of the Company	No	Yes (a)	After Financial Statements and Footnotes
Norway	Shareholders	No	Yes (b)	After Financial Statements
Singapore	Members of the Company	No	Yes (a)	After Financial Statements and Footnotes
South Africa	Members of the Company	No	Yes (a)	No Majority Practice
Spain	Shareholders and Board of Directors	Minority Practice	Yes (d)	No Majority Practice
Sweden	Not Addressed	No	Yes (c)	After Financial Statements and Footnotes
Switzerland	Shareholders	No	Yes (b)	No Majority Practice
United Kingdom	Members of the Company	No	Yes (a)	No Majority Practice
United States	Shareholders and/or Board of Directors	Minority Practice	Yes (a)	No Majority Practice

* Report is Signed by: a = Firm name alone
b = Firm name with names of individual auditors
c = Names of individual auditors alone (no affiliation)
d = No consistency (some by firm name alone and some by firm name with individual auditors)

TABLE 12-1 (Continued)
CHARACTERISTICS OF AUDITORS' REPORTS

Country	Audited Sections of Annual Reports Referred to in Auditors' Reports*									Key Conclusion Words Used**	Adherence to Auditing Standards Mentioned
	B	I	SCFP	FN	RET EARN	SH EQ	ACCT POL	MGT SECT	ANN ACT		
Australia	Y	Y		Y						properly drawn up	Yes
Austria									Y	in confo with law	Yes
Belgium	Y	Y	Y					Y		fairl, const, confo	Yes
Canada	Y	Y	Y		Y					fairl, const, confo	Yes
Denmark									Y	true, fair, confo	Yes
Finland									Y	true, fair, confo	Yes
France	Y	Y	Y	Y						true, fair, confo	Yes
Germany, West									Y	in confo with law	Yes
Hong Kong	Y	Y	Y	Y						true, fair, confo	Yes
Italy	Y	Y	Y	Y		Y				fairl, const, confo	Yes
Japan	Y	Y	Y		Y	Y				fairl, const, confo	Yes
Korea, South	Y	Y	Y		Y					fairl, const, confo	Yes
Malaysia	Y	Y	Y	Y						true, fair, confo	No
Mexico	Y	Y	Y			Y				fairl, const, confo	No
Netherlands	Y	Y	Y	Y						fairl, const, confo	No
New Zealand	Y	Y	Y	Y			Y			true, fair, confo	No
Norway									Y	true, fair, confo	Yes
Singapore	Y	Y	Y	Y						true, fair, confo	Yes
South Africa	Y	Y	Y				Y			fairly presents	No
Spain	Y	Y	Y		Y					fairl, const, confo	Yes
Sweden									Y	true, fair, confo	Yes
Switzerland	Y	Y						Y		in conform with law	No
United Kingdom	Y	Y	Y	Y			Y			true, fair, confo	Yes
United States	Y	Y	Y	Y		Y				fairl, const, confo	Yes

Key:

* Audited Sections of Annual Reports:

Y	Majority Practice
B	Balance Sheet
I	Income Statement
SCFP	Statement of Changes in Financial Position
FN	Footnotes
RET. EARN.	Retained Earnings
SH. EQ.	Shareholders' Equity
ACCT. POL.	Statement of Accounting Policy
MGT. SECT.	Management Sections
ANN. ACT.	Auditor's Report makes no mention of specific statements or sections audited, but rather refers to an audit of the "annual accounts" or annual report.

** Key Conclusion Words Used:

true, fair, confo	"true and fair view" and "in conformity with"
in confo with law	"in conformity with local legal requirements"
fairl, const, confo	"fairly presents", "consistently" "in conformity with"

E. Which Sections of Annual Reports are Audited?

In some European countries, such as Austria, Denmark, Finland, West Germany and Norway, the specific financial statements audited were not clearly identified. For instance, the terms "financial statements" and "annual report" were used without identifying which specific statements were included in the audit. This practice can leave the reader in doubt about the scope of the audit opinion, especially if there are supplementary statements such as value added which may or may not have been audited.

F. Which Key Words were Used for the Unqualified Opinion?

The data collected from the 24 countries studied can be classified into three groups. One group, which used phrases such as, "fairly presents", "consistently" and "in conformity with", included Belgium, Canada, Italy, Japan, South Korea, Mexico, the Netherlands, South Africa, Spain and the US. The second group, which predominantly used the phrases "true and fair view" and "in conformity with", consisted of Denmark, Finland, France, Hong Kong, Malaysia, New Zealand, Norway, Singapore, Sweden and the UK. The third group, which used only the phrase "in conformity with local legal requirements", included Austria, West Germany and Switzerland.

G. Were Local Auditing Standards Followed?

In the reports of most countries, the scope paragraph made reference to the fact that generally accepted auditing standards were followed. Auditors' reports in Malaysia, the Netherlands, New Zealand, South Africa and Switzerland made no mention of the application of local auditing standards.

References to auditing standards alone are not helpful to international users who may not be familiar with the auditing standards in a particular country. Hence, there is a need to expand the scope paragraph to disclose some of the methods and procedures used in the audit. For example, mention might be made as to whether key auditing principles were followed, physical inventory observation conducted or accounts receivable confirmation obtained.

V. ANALYSIS OF QUALIFIED AUDITORS' REPORTS

In our review of the audit opinions of 3,892 companies' 1987 international annual reports, we found 363 audit opinions (9% of the total) which were qualified.

For our analysis, reference to the work of other auditors in auditors' reports was not considered to be a qualification.

Table 12-2 provides the percentages of qualified auditors' reports by country. Table 12-3 details the reasons mentioned for issuing a qualified audit opinion in selected countries.

Independent auditors in Australia, Canada and Japan seem to issue qualified audit opinions more often than auditors in other countries. The main reasons these auditors issue qualified opinions are as follows:

AUSTRALIA

- Departure from GAAP, while auditor does not justify the departure
- Departure from GAAP, while auditors concur

CANADA

- Inconsistency in the application of principles
- Departure from GAAP, while auditors concur

JAPAN

- Departure from GAAP, while auditors concur
- Inconsistency in the application of accounting principles
- Scope limitation primarily dealing with financial statements restated in US standards

TABLE 12-2 NUMBER OF AUDITORS' REPORTS: UNQUALIFIED VS. QUALIFIED BY COUNTRY					
		Unqualified Reports		Qualified Reports	
COUNTRY	Number of Companies Studied	Number	% of Total	Number	% of Total
Australia	112	58	52 %	54	48 %
Austria	15	15	100	-	-
Belgium	31	27	87	4	13
Canada	227	147	65	80	35
Denmark	37	37	100	-	-
Finland	35	35	100	-	-
France	151	133	88	18	12
Germany, West	132	132	100	-	-
Hong Kong	27	26	96	1	4
Italy	21	19	90	2	10
Japan	523	415	79	108	21
Korea, South	10	10	100	-	-
Malaysia	32	32	100	-	-
Mexico	6	4	67	2	33
Netherlands	56	56	100	-	-
New Zealand	15	15	100	-	-
Norway	25	24	96	1	4
Singapore	27	26	96	1	4
South Africa	69	68	99	1	1
Spain	30	19	63	11	37
Sweden	63	62	98	1	2
Switzerland	33	33	100	-	-
United Kingdom	292	283	97	9	3
United States	1923	1853	96	70	4
Total	3892	3529	91 %	363	9 %

TABLE 12-3

MOST FREQUENT REASONS TO ISSUE A QUALIFIED AUDITOR'S REPORT FOR SELECTED COUNTRIES

	A	B	C	D	E	F	G	H	I	Total Qualified Opinions
Australia	23	-	4	-	3	24	-	-	-	54
Belgium	-	1	1	-	1	1	-	-	-	4
Canada	15	-	61	-	-	2	-	-	2	80
France	1	8	3	-	1	2	-	-	3	18
Japan	46	-	41	-	1	-	19	1	6	114
Spain	2	2	1	-	2	2	-	-	3	12
United Kingdom	-	-	3	1	1	4	-	-	-	9
United States	30	2	1	19	17	2	1	9	2	83
All other countries	2	1	-	1	2	-	-	1	-	7
Total	119	14	115	21	28	37	20	11	16	381*

Key:

A Departure from GAAP; auditor concurs
B Inconsistency; change in accounting principles
C Inconsistency in the application of principles
D Uncertainties due to litigation
E Uncertainties concerning the valuation of assets and liabilities or concerning sales or assets
F Departure from GAAP, unjustified
G Scope limitation
H Uncertainties regarding the going concern
I Other (less frequent) reasons

* The total in this table is higher than the total of qualified reports indicated in Table 12-2 since some auditor's reports included more than one reason for a qualified audit opinion.

VI. PROMPTNESS IN PREPARING AND PUBLISHING ANNUAL REPORTS

The publication of annual reports has to be timely in order for the reports to be of value to users. In general, promptness in publishing annual reports is a function of the following factors:

- How quickly a company's accounting system can produce financial statements
- How quickly auditors can audit the client company's statements
- How quickly printers can print the needed quantity of reports
- How quickly companies can prepare the mailings

It is difficult to quantify the timeliness of annual reports since an official publication date is not printed. The date of the auditor's report is used here as a benchmark for measuring timeliness computed as the number of days elapsed between the company's fiscal year-end and the auditor's report date. This measure would at least quantify the time required for the company to produce the needed financial information for its external auditors and for the external auditors to complete the audit. Such a measure can be compared internationally to evaluate promptness in preparing annual reports.

There may be some variation regarding the date placed on the auditor's report worldwide. For example, in the UK and Canada the auditor's report date reflects the end of the field work, while in many European countries this date refers to the date when the entire audit is completed.

The consolidated and English-language versions of international reports are published later than non-consolidated native language versions in many countries. However, the audit opinion date is still a valid measure for a comparison of the promptness of preparation of annual reports internationally since auditors would have completed the necessary audit work for consolidated reports by the opinion date noted in a non-consolidated version.

Table 12-4 provides overall findings regarding promptness in preparing annual reports by country, as well as by size of client company.

The audit process was completed most promptly (in less than 60 days) in Canada, South Korea, South Africa and the US. On the other hand, companies in Austria, France, West Germany, and Italy take longer than 100 days after the year-end to complete the audit process.

Large companies, with more than US$10 billion in either assets or sales (in the case of financial and non-financial companies respectively) generally completed their audit process in the shortest amount of time. Smaller companies with between US$1 million to 500 million in sales or assets took the longest amount of time to complete the audit process.

Timeliness was also examined in terms of industry type as shown in Table 12-5. It was concluded that, in general, companies in the financial service industries complete their audit process earliest, followed by companies in the basic industries. Companies in the utilities sector and capital goods industries seem to take the longest time.

Time elapsed as a function of the quarter in which the year-end date falls was also measured to see whether auditors of companies with non-calendar year-end dates complete audits sooner than those with calendar year-end dates. The results are presented in Table 12-6.

In general, the audit process for companies with non-calendar year-end dates is completed sooner than for those with calendar year-end dates, where calendar year-end dates are predominantly used. Where non-calendar year-end dates are used by a majority of companies (such as March 31 in Japan and June 30 in Australia), those companies with year-end dates which differ from the majority of companies completed their audit process faster.

A comparison was also made between multinational and non-multinational companies as shown in Table 12-7. Non-multinational companies seem to complete their audit process faster than multinational companies. One reason for this might be the fact that multinational firms have subsidiaries located in many countries with different legal requirements, and therefore may need more time to produce their annual reports.

TABLE 12-4

AVERAGE NUMBER OF DAYS ELAPSED BETWEEN FISCAL YEAR-END DATE & DATE OF AUDITOR'S REPORT BY COUNTRY AND SIZE OF CLIENT COMPANIES

Country	Total Sample		Average Number of Days Elapsed By Size Group*									
	N	Average Number of Days Elapsed	Size N	Grp=1 Days Elapsed	Size N	Grp=2 Days Elapsed	Size N	Grp=3 Days Elapsed	Size N	Grp=4 Days Elapsed	Size N	Grp=5 Days Elapsed
Australia	56	79	5	107	16	81	17	77	16	72	2	61
Austria	20	117	1	91	10	126	2	155	3	139	4	64
Belgium	25	95	2	83	6	88	2	100	12	107	3	66
Canada	116	46	8	50	35	45	25	48	44	45	4	45
Denmark	33	81	3	100	15	86	6	85	8	63	1	49
Finland	32	74	1	88	10	80	5	78	12	77	4	43
France	52	115	2	101	16	124	11	120	17	111	6	101
Germany, West	122	103	3	117	23	93	25	105	49	109	22	97
Hong Kong	17	83	5	104	4	79	-	36	7	71	1	75
Italy	32	108	-	-	8	102	6	127	14	105	4	106
Japan	515	96	8	88	114	95	92	96	242	99	56	89
Korea, South	15	45	1	44	3	42	2	44	4	55	5	41
Malaysia	24	105	8	94	11	107	2	103	1	148	1	134
Mexico	10	73	1	99	6	77	2	58	1	51	-	-
Netherlands	48	87	2	93	10	86	14	93	16	88	5	65
New Zealand	17	74	-	-	10	72	5	83	2	61	-	-
Norway	21	84	2	75	5	86	7	87	7	81	-	-
Singapore	22	84	9	75	8	91	-	134	4	98	1	68
South Africa	44	56	3	61	20	62	8	53	13	49	-	-
Spain	19	82	1	85	4	78	2	109	5	107	5	38
Sweden	55	85	-	97	19	89	13	86	18	85	5	69
Switzerland	31	79	-	74	5	74	4	77	16	87	6	64
United Kingdom	154	87	5	92	45	93	29	87	61	87	13	62
United States	477	41	1	56	29	41	86	44	262	40	99	40
Total No. of Co.'s and Avg. Days Elap.	1957	76	71	85	432	84	365	78	834	75	247	63

* SIZE CATEGORIES USED
Sales for manufacturing companies or assets for financial companies

1 = up to US$ 100 million
2 = US$ 101 - 500 million
3 = US$ 501 million - 1 billion
4 = US$ 1.001 billion - 10 billion
5 = US$ 10.001 billion or more

** Eight companies are missing due to a lack of sales figures.

TABLE 12-5

AVERAGE NUMBER OF DAYS ELAPSED BETWEEN FISCAL YEAR-END DATE & DATE OF AUDITOR'S OPINION BY COUNTRY AND INDUSTRY GROUPS

Country	N	Average Number of Days Elapsed	Average Number of Days Elapsed By Industry Group*									
			Consumer Goods		Capital Goods		Basic Industrials		Financials		Utilities/ Transport.	
			N	Days Elapsed	N	Days Elapsed	N	Days Elapsed	N	Days Elapsed	N	Days Elapsed
Australia	56	79	14	75	21	83	13	82	4	61	3	90
Austria	20	117	4	128	7	147	4	104	4	64	1	119
Belgium	25	95	3	101	5	95	6	96	5	76	5	108
Canada	116	46	28	51	19	41	38	45	3	27	24	47
Denmark	33	81	11	78	10	94	3	77	6	58	2	102
Finland	32	74	4	77	8	82	12	79	4	43	3	72
France	52	115	20	123	17	113	4	125	7	93	2	103
Germany, West	122	103	22	106	47	109	21	102	13	88	17	103
Hong Kong	17	83	3	120	5	83	-	62	4	63	5	76
Italy	32	108	8	116	12	115	3	91	7	94	2	112
Japan	515	96	122	96	225	97	87	100	39	86	34	101
Korea, South	15	45	4	40	2	59	4	50	5	41	-	-
Malaysia	24	105	5	106	3	116	10	96	3	138	-	-
Mexico	10	73	4	69	2	80	3	72	-	-	1	74
Netherlands	48	87	16	92	14	85	8	77	4	68	5	105
New Zealand	17	74	6	84	5	83	5	56	1	58	-	141
Norway	21	84	5	86	7	83	4	78	0	0	3	95
Singapore	22	84	7	84	8	78	0	0	3	80	3	110
South Africa	44	56	10	55	8	55	14	61	9	49	-	-
Spain	19	82	1	85	3	117	4	78	5	38	4	101
Sweden	55	85	9	88	21	86	15	89	5	48	5	101
Switzerland	31	79	6	65	11	97	4	83	5	56	5	75
United Kingdom	154	87	54	87	50	92	18	86	20	71	4	71
United States	477	41	102	42	111	40	72	43	117	36	47	47
Total No. of Co.'s and Avg. Days Elap.	1957	76	468	79	621	84	352	76	273	57	175	77

* 68 companies, which belong to the "other industry" category, are missing.

TABLE 12-6

AVERAGE NUMBER OF DAYS ELAPSED BETWEEN FISCAL YEAR-END DATE & DATE OF AUDITOR'S OPINION BY COUNTRY AND YEAR-END DATE GROUP

	Total Sample		Average Number of Days Elapsed By Fiscal Year-End Groups*							
			Quarter Group 1		Quarter Group 2		Quarter Group 3		Quarter Group 4	
Country	N	Average Number of Days Elapsed	N	Days Elapsed	N	Days Elapsed	N	Days Elapsed	N	Days Elapsed
Australia	56	79	6	70	38	85	6	64	6	66
Austria	20	117	-	-	-	-	-	-	20	117
Belgium	25	95	3	86	-	-	2	103	20	95
Canada	116	46	21	50	4	49	13	53	78	43
Denmark	33	81	2	82	3	100	2	56	26	80
Finland	32	74	3	80	-	-	2	88	27	73
France	52	115	3	120	-	-	1	125	48	115
Germany, West	122	103	3	94	8	129	18	105	93	101
Hong Kong	17	83	4	117	1	49	2	43	10	81
Italy	32	108	1	73	3	92	-	-	28	111
Japan	515	96	380	97	37	93	36	95	62	96
Korea, South	15	45	2	38	1	39	-	-	12	47
Malaysia	24	105	1	94	7	93	4	123	12	106
Mexico	10	73	-	-	1	103	1	42	8	73
Netherlands	48	87	2	73	2	81	2	108	42	87
New Zealand	17	74	9	71	5	76	2	77	1	89
Norway	21	84	-	-	-	-	-	-	21	84
Singapore	22	84	2	100	-	-	3	64	17	86
South Africa	44	56	10	57	11	68	10	39	13	59
Spain	19	82	-	-	1	85	-	-	18	82
Sweden	55	85	1	88	1	86	1	102	52	85
Switzerland	31	79	1	56	3	65	1	97	26	81
United Kingdom	154	87	64	82	14	92	32	91	44	90
United States	477	41	28	41	22	42	18	44	409	40
Total No. of Co.'s and Avg. Days Elap.	1957	76	546	89	162	81	156	80	1093	69

Fiscal Year-End Groups Used:

Quarter Group 1 = Client companies with fiscal year-end date between January 1 and March 31

Quarter Group 2 = Client companies with fiscal year-end date between April 1 and June 30

Quarter Group 3 = Client companies with fiscal year-end date between July 1 and September 30

Quarter Group 4 = Client companies with fiscal year-end date between October 1 and December 31

TABLE 12-7

AVERAGE NUMBER OF DAYS ELAPSED BETWEEN FISCAL YEAR-END DATE & DATE OF AUDITOR'S REPORT BY COUNTRY AND MULTINATIONALITY

Country	Total Sample		Average Number of Days Elapsed By Multinationality			
			Multinational Companies		Non-Multinational Companies	
	N	Average Number of Days Elapsed	N	Days Elapsed	N	Days Elapsed
Australia	56	79	32	75	24	84
Austria	20	117	6	129	14	112
Belgium	25	95	17	99	8	85
Canada	116	46	40	47	76	45
Denmark	33	81	18	81	15	80
Finland	32	74	18	76	14	71
France	52	115	33	117	19	113
Germany, West	122	103	64	108	58	98
Hong Kong	17	83	2	102	15	80
Italy	32	108	13	114	19	105
Japan	515	96	230	99	285	95
Korea, South	15	45	2	46	13	45
Malaysia	24	105	2	94	22	106
Mexico	10	73	2	47	8	79
Netherlands	48	87	38	84	10	98
New Zealand	17	74	7	60	10	85
Norway	21	84	15	82	6	88
Singapore	22	84	7	85	15	84
South Africa	44	56	6	48	38	57
Spain	19	82	6	85	13	81
Sweden	55	85	39	85	16	84
Switzerland	31	79	23	82	8	70
United Kingdom	154	87	128	88	26	79
United States	477	41	216	40	261	41
Total No. of Co.'s and Avg. Days Elap.	1957	76	964	79	993	74

VII. SUMMARY AND CONCLUSIONS

An analysis of the form and content of auditors' reports yields the following observations:

- The auditor's report is not specifically addressed in many countries.
- Audit firm identification was not always clear.
- The auditor's report is not always listed in the table of contents.
- Specific statements audited were not identified clearly.
- Different key words were used for the unqualified audit opinion.
- Reference to local auditing standards was not consistently made.

In studying qualified auditors' reports, we found that auditors in Australia, Canada and Japan seem to issue qualified audit opinions more often than auditors in other countries.

It can be further concluded that industry sector, company size, multinational status, and fiscal year-end date are factors which affect the length of time needed to complete the audit process.

We believe that recent harmonization efforts will narrow gaps in auditing standards, at least in the major industrial nations. The globalization of capital markets is increasing the need for the harmonization of accounting and auditing standards. If harmonization becomes a reality, companies raising capital outside their national boundaries will use international auditing firms and will publish annual reports on a more timely basis.

We also believe that as annual reports are relied upon more by users internationally, international accounting firms will begin to utilize international auditing standards, even though local auditing standards may not require their adoption.

CHAPTER 13

UNDERTAKING COMPETITIVE ANALYSIS AMONG INTERNATIONAL ACCOUNTING FIRMS: ISSUES AND ANSWERS

Table of Contents

I. INTRODUCTION

International accounting firms' competitive practices usually evolve through a recognition of opportunities and threats in the operating environment. For example, a strategy to expand internally can be developed through the allocation of firm resources as new opportunities are identified. The development of Management Advisory Services within a firm through the hiring of qualified personnel would be an example of this approach.

It is quite important, therefore, for the international accounting firm to be able to monitor conditions within the internal and external environment. In this regard, "knowing the competition" is necessary.

From a competitive point of view, the ability to perceive the forces which have an impact upon the marketplace can enable the decision maker to plan for a response to changing conditions. The purpose of this chapter is to provide guidance to the international accounting firm for monitoring its competitive position.

II. RESEARCH OBJECTIVE & DESIGN

13-1 What are some key areas which an international accounting firm should study in order to compare itself with global competitors and position itself for the future?

This chapter has been developed from the data gathered in other chapters of the study. It is also based on informal discussions with the strategic planners of major accounting firms and academic colleagues, and on observations of current developments as they affect international accounting firms.

III. SUGGESTED APPROACH TO GLOBAL COMPETITIVE ANALYSIS FOR INTERNATIONAL ACCOUNTING FIRMS

In order to evaluate the strengths and weaknesses of the international firm relative to the competition, it is useful to first identify the major characteristics involved. Such characteristics have been identified by the CIFAR project team and are the focus of the Global Competitive Analysis Questionnaire which is included at the end of this chapter as Exhibit 13-1.

It is possible for individual firms to approach this matter differently, and to include the use of the questionnaire at various levels of responsibility (and, therefore, for varying numbers of operating units). Thus, the questions identified in the following sections can be modified to accommodate the needs of individual firms.

The questions are arranged so that a given firm can answer them with reference to its own operations as well as those of competing firms. It is suggested, however, that careful attention is paid initially to an internal assessment since such information is reliable and more readily available than data concerning competitors. This provides a basis for the assessment of competitive strengths and weaknesses.

This section provides further discussion of items included in the "Global Competitive Analysis Questionnaire".

A. Personnel

A starting point for the assessment of an international public accounting firm is the identification of the composition of current personnel, accompanied by a review of personnel practices. Section A provides questions pertaining to current personnel statistics. A review of personnel practices is included in Section B.

1. Personnel Statistics

The questions address current staffing in terms of command (partners or partners and managers) and support staff. The questionnaire assumes the division of departments by functional area to include Audit, Management Advisory Services, and Tax. A category for Other is included to allow for specialized services which may differ from one firm to the next.

The latter questions on the schedule (A141 - A155) focus on changes in staff. Changes in the numbers of partners in the functional areas and changes in the support staff levels can reflect policy changes directed by the senior management of the firm. At the same time, changes could be taking place due to other reasons, e.g. attrition in a particular functional department due to competitive forces. An examination of staffing changes, therefore, can provide a basis for questioning the motivation for the observed change.

2. Recruiting, Training and Quality Control

Specific personnel practices are addressed in Section B. Their importance will be observed in relation to questions asked in other schedules. For example, perceived weaknesses due to staff attrition may be closely related to training or recruiting practices. The ability to act upon perceived future growth opportunities can be enhanced or constrained by such practices.

B. Generation of Revenues

Revenue generation can be examined in terms of present conditions and future strategies. A starting point is the Revenue Profile provided in Section C which examines existing revenues by functional department.

1. Revenues

An examination of fee income by functional departments sheds light on the relative share of revenue provided by each area. Section C also examines the growth in each of the functions. Management attention, therefore, can be directed accordingly to the following questions:

- Are areas of growth or stagnation apparent?
- Does this suggest the need to reexamine the relative "share of the pie" for each area?

2. Changes in Clientele

Section D allows for an examination of a firm's client base and recent changes which have occurred, a logical extension of the questions in Section C. The specific items in Section D allow for the classification of clients into Industrial and Service sectors. To the extent that the information is available, an additional refinement would be to identify client gains and losses for each functional area.

Sections C and D together can help establish a profile of existing revenue components and assist in identifying recent changes in composition. While information on other competing firms will be less readily available, an attempt should be made to examine the same questions for the competition. Patterns of change within the firm can then be matched with observations concerning competitors. Threats relating to the loss of clients or opportunities pertaining to client acquisition can then be noted, at least in a preliminary fashion.

3. Marketing Practices

Following the preliminary assessment of existing trends in the marketplace, Section E should be used to address the issue of how the firm has marketed itself. As with the previous schedules, initial self-assessment can then lead to an examination of the competition's marketing practices.

The items listed are designed to provide a focus on specific aspects of the marketing environment. Your response can enable the identification of strengths or weaknesses of the marketing effort and can also be related to the other schedules. For example, item E109 pertains to the support of the academic community. If your self-assessment is lower than desired, then additional questioning concerning your firm's support <u>for</u> the academic community would be warranted. What is your involvement with schools? Do you routinely include professors on the mailing list for firm publications (see Section F)? Have you participated in internship programs with schools in your area? To the extent that answers to these questions can play a role in the ability to recruit top quality students, the marketing of the firm to the academic community is important. Its importance can be assessed, as well, in light of the observable strengths and weaknesses relating to personnel practices in Section B.

The final question of Section E is designed to focus attention on specific strategies which your firm and its competitors have implemented. Given the importance of self-assessment, the following approach is suggested as an alternative to a single question (as shown in Section E):

- What types of special programs have you organized to attract new business?
- What types of special activities have been successful in this regard?
- What types of special programs have been attempted by competitors?
- What types of activities have been successful for competitors?

By identifying the special programs and activities which you have implemented and evaluated in terms of effectiveness, you are better able to assess the desirability of future efforts. The comparison of your efforts with those of the competition can help further define your plans.

4. Publications

Section F assists in the identification of various types of formal written communication. These can be extremely important to the promotion of the firm's image to the professional community. In addition, an assessment of the quality and frequency of a particular variable can be important when related to other schedules. For example, poor and/or infrequent reviews of new issues facing business may properly be viewed as a weakness in light of rapid changes noted elsewhere. On the other hand, highly regarded publications in the tax area (for example) could be channeled to new outlets to prospect for new business.

C. External Environment: Opportunities and Threats

The examination of personnel considerations and factors affecting revenue generation provide the opportunity internally to assess personnel strengths and weaknesses. The following schedules are specifically focused on the external environment: examination of industry characteristics, potential strategies for expansion, and the possible threat of additional competitive forces.

1. Industry Characteristics

Section G provides for an assessment of your firm's largest markets as well as the markets which exhibit the greatest growth potential. Your firm will identify the international accounting firms which lead in servicing the selected industries. A logical focal point will be your determination of where your firm stands in terms of a leadership role in these industries. After an identification of your firm's strengths and weaknesses with regard to personnel and marketing characteristics, you can better assess the potential for assuming or holding a leadership position. The potential for expansion in specialized functional areas is addressed in Section H.

2. Expansion Strategies

The ability to identify growth markets in relevant industries (per Section G) can be refined to denote specific areas of functional service growth within those industries. This is provided for in Section H.

The first part of Section H specifies certain types of specialized services which can be developed internally and offered to clients. The number of specialized services to be included will be determined by your past experience, the observed experience of competitors, and the nature of the industries identified in Section G. The items in Section H allow for an assessment of competitors' activities in these areas. As in previous sections, an initial self-assessment will be a useful basis for comparison.

Movement by your firm in any one of these areas, (or the lack of it), can be matched with the actions of competitors. Your ability to carve a niche in the industries noted in Section G can be affected by your development in the functional service areas of Section H. Similarly, competitor gains in specialized service development can threaten your advancement in those markets.

The items labeled H121 and H122 address the possibility of expansion through external acquisition, rather than internal development. To the extent that either audit or non-audit client services represent potential growth areas, these items are important. For example, it may be determined that a certain specialized area has high growth potential. One possible strategy could be to expand into this area internally, adding to existing staff and facilities. This approach may be more feasible for certain firms than for others. An alternative would be to expand via the acquisition of a firm which has known strengths in the area of growth which you have identified.

3. Other Competitive Forces

The final schedule for assessment pertains to other competitive forces. Sections G and H provide for the identification of growth areas in specific industries and specialized functional service areas. Potential threats from Big 8 competitors are also noted in these sections.

Section I provides for an examination of the importance of non-accounting firm competitors in your area.

Items I101 to I107 identify specific types of specialized practice firms and call for your assessment of their overall competitive threat. Certain specialty practices could be more or less threatening than others.

Completion of this section, in combination with sections G and H, enables a more comprehensive assessment of external threats to your firm. One additional advantage of assessing the threat of non-accounting firm competition is the potential to turn a perceived threat into an opportunity. An existing specialty practice which has already established itself in an area of high growth potential can be carefully studied to identify tactics which have been employed successfully by that firm. Also, as noted previously, a potential expansion strategy for your firm could be the acquisition of an established practice, including competitors presently identified as being threats to your firm.

IV. SUMMARY

The questionnaire sections identified in this chapter are designed to call attention to both the internal and external environments of the firm. Emphasis has been placed on the benefits of identifying the strengths and weaknesses of existing practices as well as opportunities and threats to the firm.

In that regard, the questions suggested can be employed to develop competitive strategies. However, the questionnaire sections are not intended to be a cookbook for policy-making: no single recipe exists for the development of strategies. Instead, the intention is to focus the attention of decision makers toward areas of strategic importance. Each of these areas represents an important aspect of business which deserves continued monitoring.

Such monitoring requires both the development of an internal profile of the firm and an assessment of the external characteristics of the competition. It can also lead to the identification of possible strategies for the future. These strategies can then set the agenda for the types of activities or events which should be monitored in the future.

In summary, the framework developed in this chapter provides a tool for the assessment of international accounting firms' competitive positions. A periodic review will lead to the identification of strategic goals for the firm, and for the future monitoring of progress toward these goals. This process can be undertaken globally, regionally and, with some modification to the questions, at a country level.

In the following chapter we have identified both obstacles and opportunities for international accounting firms in order to illustrate that periodic monitoring and assessment will be necessary to adapt to the dynamics of changing competitive positions.

EXHIBIT 13-1

A SAMPLE QUESTIONNAIRE FOR GLOBAL COMPETITIVE ANALYSIS OF INTERNATIONAL ACCOUNTING FIRMS

Conducted as of ______________________________

For __________ Worldwide ____________ Region __________________ Country ____________________

Prepared by: ____________________

Date: ____________________

Section		
	A	Personnel Statistics
	B	Recruiting, Training and Quality Control
	C	Revenues
	D	Current Client Base
	E	Marketing Profile
	F	Publications: Country-Specific
	G	Industry Characteristics
	H	Expansion Strategies
	I	Other Competitive Forces

Exhibit 13-1
Section A - Personnel Statistics

VARIABLES	AA	AYI	CL	DHSI	EW	KPMG	PW	TRI	Other	Other
A101 Professional Personnel - Audit Enter total number of professional personnel, including managers and partners, in the Audit Department.										
A102 Professional Personnel - MAS Enter total number of professional personnel, including managers and partners, in the MAS Department.										
A103 Professional Personnel - TAX Enter total number of professional personnel, including managers and partners, in the TAX Department.										
A104 Professional Personnel - Other (describe) This category includes departments established to perform specific services (eg. financial consulting services) or to serve specific segments of the market (e.g. small or emerging business services). Not all offices of a firm have established a separate department(s) to provide these services. Do not attempt to extract comparative data if these services are routinely performed by Audit, MAS or TAX.										
A105 Professional Personnel - Total Enter the total number of professional personnel. (Sum A101 + A102 + A103 + A104)										
A111 Partners - Audit Enter the total number of full-time partners dedicated to the Audit Dept.										
A112 Partners - MAS Enter the total number of full-time partners dedicated to the MAS Dept.										
A113 Partners - TAX Enter the total number of full-time partners dedicated to the TAX Dept.										
A114 Partners - Other Enter the total number of full-time partners dedicated to the other department(s) identified in A104.										

Exhibit 13-1

Section A - Personnel Statistics (Cont.)

VARIABLES	AA	AYI	CL	DHSI	EW	KPMG	PW	TRI	Other
A115 Partners - Total Enter the number of partners. (Sum of A111 + A112 + A113 + A114)									
A121 Total Staff - Audit Enter the number of staff personnel dedicated to the Audit Department. Staff personnel include administrative staff, clerical staff and all other personnel who are not engaged in direct client service.									
A122 Total Staff - MAS Enter the number of staff personnel dedicated to the MAS Department. Staff personnel include administrative staff, clerical staff and all other personnel who are not engaged in direct client service.									
A123 Total Staff - TAX Enter the number of staff personnel dedicated to the TAX Department. Staff personnel include administrative staff, clerical staff and all other personnel who are not engaged in direct client service.									
A124 Total Staff - Other Enter the number of staff personnel dedicated to the other department identified in A104. Staff personnel include administrative staff, clerical staff and all other personnel who are not engaged in direct client service.									
A125 Total Staff Total staff should include all staff personnel identified in A121-A124 and any additional general purpose staff that are not allocated to a specific department									
A131 Number of Offices Enter the number of offices this firm has in your authorized territory.									
A141 Number of New Partners Admitted - Audit Enter the number of new Audit partners admitted during the surveyed firm's last fiscal year.									
A142 Number of New Partners Admitted - MAS Enter the number of new MAS partners admitted during the surveyed firm's last fiscal year.									

EXHIBIT 13-1

Section A - Personnel Statistics (Cont.)

VARIABLES	AA	AYI	CL	DHSI	EW	KPMG	PW	TRI	Other
A143 Number of New Partners Admitted - TAX Enter the number of new TAX partners admitted during the surveyed firm's last fiscal year.									
A144 Number of New Partners Admitted - Other Enter the number of new other partners admitted during the surveyed firm's last fiscal year.									
A145 Number of New Partners Admitted - Total Enter the total number of new partners admitted during the surveyed firm's last fiscal year. (Sum of A141 + A142 + A143 + A144)									
A146 Staff Additions - Audit Enter the number of new audit staff added during the last fiscal year.									
A147 Staff Additions - MAS Enter the number of new MAS staff added during the last fiscal year.									
A148 Staff Additions - TAX Enter the number of new TAX staff added during the last fiscal year.									
A149 Staff Additions - Other Enter the number of new other staff added during the last fiscal year.									
A150 Total Staff Additions									
A151 Staff Attrition - Audit Enter the percentage of audit staff turnover during the last fiscal year.									
A152 Staff Attrition - MAS Enter the percentage of MAS staff turnover during the last fiscal year.									
A153 Staff Attrition - TAX Enter the percentage of TAX staff turnover during the last fiscal year.									
A154 Staff Attrition - Other Enter the Percentage of other staff turnover during the last fiscal year.									
A155 Total Staff - Percentage of Turnover during the last fiscal year.									

EXHIBIT 13-1

Section B - Recruiting, Training and Quality Control

VARIABLE	AA	AYI	CL	DHSI	EW	KPMG	PW	TRI	Other
B101 How many professional staff members were loaned (or temporarily transferred under training assignments) to foreign countries during the last fiscal year?									
B102 How many professional staff members were temporarily borrowed from foreign countries?									
B103 Use of outside experts in training programs (Yes/No)									
B104 Central training facilities in the country or region (Yes/No)									
B105 Does your firm regularly engage in internal peer review?									
B106 Does your firm regularly engage in external peer review?									
B107 Peer review - Internal (Y/N) Does competitor regularly engage in an internal peer review process?									
B108 Peer review - External (Y/N) Does competitor regularly engage in external peer review groups?									
B109 Lawsuits Enter the number of lawsuits brought by clients, within the last fiscal year.									

EXHIBIT 13-1
Section C - Revenues

VARIABLE	AA	AYI	CL	DHSI	EW	KPMG	PW	TRI	Other
C101 Fee Income - Audit Enter Audit fees (in millions of local currency) for the last fiscal year.									
C102 Fee Income - MAS Enter MAS fees (in millions of local currency) for the last fiscal year.									
C103 Fee Income - TAX Enter TAX fees (in millions of local currency) for the last fiscal year.									
C104 Fee Income - Other Enter fees (in millions of local currency) for the last fiscal year from services rendered by the other department identified in A104.									
C105 Fee Income - Total Enter total fee income (in millions of local currency) from the last fiscal year from the Audit, MAS, TAX and other deparments.									
C111 Fee Growth - Audit Enter the growth (in percent) in Audit fee income for the last fiscal year.									
C112 Fee Growth - MAS Enter the growth (in percent) in MAS fee income for the last fiscal year.									
C113 Fee Growth - TAX Enter the growth (in percent) in TAX fee income for the last fiscal year.									
C114 Fee Growth - Other Enter the growth (in percent) in fee income for the other department(s) identified in A104 for the last fiscal year.									
C115 Fee Growth - Total Enter the overall average growth (in percent) in fee income for the last fiscal year.									

EXHIBIT 13-1
Section D - Current Client Base

VARIABLE	AA	AYI	CL	DHSI	EW	KPMG	PW	TRI	Other
D101 Number of Clients by Industry Industry 1 ____ 2 ____ 3 ____ 4 ____ 5 ____ 6 ____ 7 ____ 8 ____									
D102 Number of Clients by size 1 ____ 2 ____ 3 ____ 4 ____ 5 ____									
D103 Clients by ownership 1 Listed on Stock Exchanges 2 Not Listed on Exchanges 3 Government Owned 4 Subsidiaries of Local Companies 5 Subsidiaries of Foreign Companies									
D104 Clients by Multinationality 1 Multinational Firms 2 Non-multinational Firms									

EXHIBIT 13-1
Section D - Changes in Clientele (Numbers)

CLIENTS IN INDUSTRIAL SECTORS:

VARIABLE	AA	AYI	CL	DHSI	EW	KPMG	PW	TRI	OTHER
D105 Clients gained (annual sales over__________) Enter the increase in clients attributable to the acquisition of new clients. General Instruction: Select a benchmark for annual sales appropriate to your firm's practice in a particular country, region or worldwide									
D106 Clients lost (annual sales over__________) Enter the decrease in clients attributable to the loss of clients.									

CLIENTS IN SERVICE SECTORS:

VARIABLE	AA	AYI	CL	DHSI	EW	KPMG	PW	TRI	OTHER
D107 Clients gained (over year-end assets of ________) Enter the increase in clients attributable to the acquisition of new clients.									
D108 Clients lost (over year-end assets of ________) Enter the decrease in clients attributable to the loss of clients.									

EXHIBIT 13-1
Section E - Marketing Profile

General Instructions:

For each of the Big-8 firms plus any other firm(s) identified in Section A, please answer the following questions (E101 - E109) using the key below.

Key:

1= Excellent
2= Above Average
3= Average
4= Below Average
5= Poor
6= No Opinion

Variables	AA	AYI	CL	DHSI	EW	KPMG	PW	TRI	Other
E101 Local visibility of international name									
102 Visibility of local name, if different									
E103 Leadership in local accounting professional organizations									
E104 Participation in Accounting Standard setting process									
E105 Leadership in International Accounting Organizations									
E106 Ability to win in competitive situations									
E107 Ability to win government assignments (if different from E106 above)									
E108 Ability to target prospects									
E109 Support of academic community									
E110 Extent of advertising activity									
E111 Overall effectiveness of marketing efforts									
E112 In your competitor's advertisements, what is the main theme promoted? List the appropriate codes from key below: (Add codes as considered necessary) Key: 1= low fees; 2= quality of service; 3= industry expertise; 4= variety of services; 5= internationalization; 6= other ________; 7= other ________									

EXHIBIT 13-1
Section E
Marketing Profiles (continued)

	AA	AYI	CL	DHSI	EW	KPMG	PW	TRI	Other
E113 What kinds of special events have been most successful in keeping and attracting new business for your competitors? Rank according to the appropriate codes given below. (Every code may not be applicable) Key: 1= educational seminars for client and non-clients 2= special publications 3= high visibility profile with professional societies 4= jointly sponsored events on current broad based issues 5= other ___________									

EXHIBIT 13-1

Section F - Publications: Country-Specific

General Instructions:

For each of the Big-8 firms plus any other firm(s) identified in Section A, answer the following questions (F101 - F107) using keys presented below:

Q = Quality:

F = Frequency:

D = Distribution

Quality:

1= Well done
2= Above Average
3= Average
4= Poor
5= Not done

Frequency:

1= Annually
2= Semi-annually
3= Quarterly
4= Monthly
5= Bi-Monthly
6= Weekly
7= Not Frequent
8= Not Known
9= Not Applicable

Distribution:

1= Given to Clients Only
2= Given to Clients & Prospective Clients
3= Widely Distributed

Variables			AA	AYI	CL	DHSI	EW	KPMG	PW	TRI	Other
F101	External Newsletters For Clients and the Public in General	Q									
		F									
		D									
F102	Accounting Standards	Q									
		F									
		D									
F103	Review of New Issues Facing Business	Q									
		F									
		D									
F104	Industry Analysis	Q									
		F									
		D									

EXHIBIT 13-1

Section F

Publications: Country-Specific (Continued)

Variables		AA	AYI	CL	DHSI	EW	KPMG	PW	TRI	Other
F105 Tax Publications	Q									
	F									
	D									
F106 Annual Report	Q									
	F									
	D									
F107 Other	Q									
	F									
	D									

EXHIBIT 13-1

Section G

Industry Characteristics

Key for G101 - G104

G101 Largest Accounting Services Markets
Rank (1 to 5) the top five largest industries in your territory. (Rank (1 TO 5) the top five largest industries in your territory. Rank one as the largest in terms of gross sales or turnover, two as the next largest and so forth.

G102 Accounting Firm Leaders
For each of the five industries identified in G101, enter, in rank order, the three accounting firms who best serve each of these industries in your territory. (1=Best; 2=2nd best; 3=3rd best)

G103 Future Growth Potential
Rank (1 to 5) the top five industries in your territory which have the greatest potential for future growth. (1=Highest; 2=2nd highest; etc.)

G104 Accounting Firm Leaders
For each of the five industries identified as having the greatest potential for future growth, enter in rank order the three accounting firms who are in the position to best serve each of these industries.

G101	G102			G103	G104		
Largest Industries	Accounting Firm Leaders 1	2	3	Future Growth Potential Industries	Future Growth Potential Industries Accounting Firm Leaders		
1 ______	___	___	___	1 ______	___	___	___
2 ______	___	___	___	2 ______	___	___	___
3 ______	___	___	___	3 ______	___	___	___
4 ______	___	___	___	4 ______	___	___	___
5 ______	___	___	___	5 ______	___	___	___

EXHIBIT 13-1

Section H

Expansion Strategies

General Instructions:

For each of the Big-8 plus any other firm(s) identified in Section A, evaluate questions H101 - H134 using the key provided below.

Key:
1. Aggressive
2. Average
3. Passive
4. None

Expansion into new areas: Internal

VARIABLE	AA	AYI	CL	DHSI	EW	KPMG	PW	TRI	Other
H101 Consulting Services Assess competitive firms' expansion in consulting services.									
H102 Mergers and Acquisitions Assess competitive firms' expansion in merger and acquisition services.									
H103 Small Business Assess competitive firms' expansion in small business services.									
H104 Government Service Assess competitive firms' expansion in government services.									
H105 Software Development Assess competitive firms' expansion in software development.									
H106 Executive Seminars Assess competitive firms' expansion in executive seminars.									
H107 Liquidation Services Assess competitive firms' expansion in liquidation services.									
H108 ____________ If the competition provides additional services, enter description of these services. (Examples may include personal financial consulting, executive search services etc.)									

EXHIBIT 13-1

Expansion Strategies (Continued)

Section H
Expansion: External

VARIABLE	AA	AYI	CL	DHSI	EW	KPMG	PW	TRI	Other
H121 Purchase of other traditional practices: Audit, Tax, MAS									
H122 Purchase of other non-traditional practices: Consulting, Service Bureaus, etc.									

EXHIBIT 13-1

Section I - Other Competitive Forces

General Instructions:

The purpose of Section I is to ascertain the impact of non-accounting firm competition on firm departments. Use the key below in answering questions I101 - I108. Enter the name of competitor(s) if choice 1 (aggressively threatening Big-8 market) or choice 2 (planning to increase their share) is made.

Key:
1. Aggressively threatening Big-8 market.
2. Planning to increase their market share of Big-8 market.
3. Not expanding into the accounting firm market.

	MAS	TAX	Other Services
I101 Large Consulting Firms ____________ Assess the impact of large consulting firms in your territory, on your Audit, MAS, TAX and other department(s).			
I102 Commercial Banks ____________ Assess the impact of commercial banks in your territory, on your Audit, MAS, TAX and other department(s).			
I103 Computer Service Bureaus ____________ Assess the impact of computer service bureaus in your territory, on your Audit, MAS, TAX and other department(s).			
I104 Law Firms ____________ Assess the impact of law firms in your territory, on your Audit, MAS, TAX and other department(s).			
I105 Appraisal Firms ____________ Assess the impact of appraisal firms in your territory, on your Audit, MAS, Tax and other department(s).			
I106 Investment Banking Firms ____________ Assess the impact of investment banking firms in your territory, on your Audit, MAS, Tax and other department(s).			
I107 Company Registrars ____________ Assess the impact of company registrars in your territory, on your Audit, MAS, Tax and other department(s).			
I108 Other ____________			

CHAPTER 14

INTERNATIONAL AUDITING TRENDS
SUMMARY AND CONCLUSIONS

I. SUMMARY OF RESEARCH DESIGN (CHAPTERS 9 THROUGH 13)

The basic objective of Chapters 9 through 13 has been to examine international auditing trends. Our primary sources were the following:

- CIFAR's collection of over 10,000 international annual reports (the 1987 fiscal year report was examined in the majority of cases)
- The current office directories of the sixteen leading international accounting firms (published during 1988)
- Data provided by the local offices of international accounting firms

Depending on the scope of a chapter or a research question which needed to be addressed, we used either the full database of companies or a subset.

II. MAJOR FINDINGS (CHAPTERS 9 THROUGH 13)

This final chapter of "International Auditing Trends" summarizes the major conclusions rendered in Chapters 9 through 13 of this study.

A. Global Competitive Analysis

1. Worldwide Strengths

   - Though the sixteen leading international accounting firms were examined, the big eight group clearly dominates the accounting services industry.
   - Within the big eight, KPMG (which was created by the merger of PMM and KMG in 1987) led all other big eight firms in total number of offices, partners, clients audited, and sales and assets of clients audited, followed by CL, PW, TRI and EW.

2. Regional/Country Strengths

   - Analyzing each of the sixteen international accounting firms within and across five geographic regions revealed that auditing firms display varying degrees of prominence in various regions of the world.
   - North America is the largest region for the auditing industry. KPMG, EW, PW, and CL are the strongest there among the big eight.
   - Europe is the second most important region for international accounting firms. KPMG, CL, PW, and AYI have the widest coverage in Europe, though within the European Community KPMG, PW and DHSI audit most sales and assets.

- CL, EW, KPMG and TRI have the widest coverage in the Asia/Pacific region.

- KPMG, EW, CL and TRI have the largest practices in the Africa/Middle East regions.

- PW, KPMG, and AYI lead other international firms in South America.

3. Country Strengths

   - In terms of the leading industrial countries (by GNP), the big eight international accounting firms have a dominant share of the audit services market in the US, the UK, Canada, West Germany, Italy, Spain, the Netherlands, and Australia.

   - International accounting firms audit nearly two-thirds of publicly listed companies, while national accounting firms not affiliated with international accounting firms audited almost one-third of the clients in other large industrial countries (i.e., France, Japan and Switzerland).

   - National accounting firms not affiliated with the leading sixteen international accounting firms are also dominant in several smaller countries in Europe (e.g., Austria, Belgium, Greece and Portugal) and in developing countries elsewhere (e.g., India, Israel, Pakistan, Philippines and Taiwan).

4. Industry Specialization

   - Different international accounting firms have developed concentrations in various industries.

   - Industry strengths of the leading international accounting firms do not hold true across regions.

5. Cities

   London, New York, Chicago, Toronto and Los Angeles are the leading cities for public accounting services, followed by Paris, Sydney, Montreal, Tokyo, and Washington, DC.

6. Growth 1982-1987

   - Over the last five years, the leading accounting firms have experienced the greatest growth in Europe and the Asia/Pacific regions.

   - An analysis of the growth patterns of the big eight firms shows:

     - EW has grown most outside of the US
     - AYI has had the greatest increase in number of offices worldwide
     - PW has grown most in Europe
     - AA and EW have experienced the greatest growth in the Asia/Pacific region

B. <u>Audit Fees</u>

- Audit fees are determined by the size and industry classification of the client company audited.

- Companies in the capital goods industry pay the highest audit fees of the six industry groups analyzed. Companies in the financial services, utilities and transportation industry groups pay the lowest audit fees.

- Multinational companies pay higher audit fees in comparison to domestic companies in the same industry and size group.

- Client companies located in industrial countries pay higher audit fees than companies in developing countries.

- If one considers size and industry group as constants, it can be concluded that clients pay similar audit fees in countries such as Australia and the United Kingdom.

- Audit fees as a percentage of sales or assets have not increased over the last six years.

C. Auditors' Reports

The format and content of auditors' reports vary considerably worldwide. Specifically, key conclusion words and indications of auditing standards used lack uniformity.

In studying qualified auditors' reports, we found that auditors in Australia, Canada and Japan seem to issue qualified audit opinions more often than those in other countries.

Industry sector, company size, multinational status and fiscal year-end date are factors which affect the length of time needed to complete the audit process.

III. IMPLICATIONS FOR THE FUTURE

In our research for this project over the last four years, we have observed both opportunities and obstacles to the growth of international accounting firms. A summary of these points follows:

A. Obstacles

Obstacle - 1 Legal Liabilities

In recent years, international accounting firms, in their role as external auditors, have been party to legal suits initiated by the shareholders and lenders of failed client firms. The courts have ruled that accounting firms can be held liable for damages. For the accounting firm, being held party to a suit can result in its bearing some of the financial burden for a failed client firm.

International accounting firms should obviously seek to avoid settlement losses. They can protect themselves from suits through paying the costs of escalating liability insurance premiums and by applying more rigorous and time-consuming review procedures while conducting the audit. Accounting firms will need to be more selective in acquiring new clients. While competitive pressures to expand the client base are great, indiscriminate acceptance of new clients could lead to heavy litigation expenses and settlement costs.

Obstacle - 2 Technological Change and its Impact on Audit Fees

Advancement in computer technology has greatly reduced the time required to complete an audit. However, revenue generated from auditing a client has typically been a function of billable hours. Today pressures are put upon the accounting firm to bill at the regular hourly rate but for fewer hours worked. Logic would suggest that a higher rate should be charged because of the accounting firm's investment in computer equipment and training. However, competitive pressures may not allow accounting firms to increase audit fees.

Obstacle - 3 Mergers and Acquisitions within the Client Base

In recent years, there has been a considerable increase in mergers and acquisitions in Canada, the UK, the US, and to a lesser extent, Australia, all of which are major markets for the services of international accounting firms. According to predictions in capital market circles, merger and acquisition activities will increase in the near future in Continental Europe, as well as in the Asia/Pacific region, as some of the regulations restricting mergers and acquisitions are removed worldwide.

After a merger, it is typical to employ only one external auditor to perform the audit of the merged company, even though a different auditors may have been utilized previously by each of the merged firms. The result can be beneficial for the accounting firm which prevails after the merger, but will require the second firm to look elsewhere for replacement revenues.

If the client base is not maintained, auditing as a revenue generating function will lose ground relative to the other functional activities of the accounting firm. As an alternative, firms can aggressively promote and add to the client base. The game is sometimes zero sum since a gain for one accounting firm represents the loss of a client for another.

B. Opportunities

Opportunity - 1 Europe 1992: Unified Market

Over the last 10 years, considerable progress has been made toward harmonizing the accounting and auditing standards of European Community (EC) member nations, primarily due to EC Directives. The next three years will be pivotal in terms of achieving the goal of a "one market concept" among the EC member nations.

The successful creation of a single internal market would reduce the competitive advantage of national accounting firms, whose local knowledge would no longer be critical. Firms with a Europe-wide network (which is the case for international accounting firms) would be able to service the European operations of a client rather than several national accounting firms servicing various segments. We have observed a considerable increase in the presence of international accounting firms in two EC countries, namely Italy and Spain over the last four years. We believe there are still opportunities for growth in Belgium, Denmark, France, Greece and Portugal.

Opportunity - 2 Globalization of Capital Markets

Capital markets, particularly larger ones, are becoming globally integrated. An increasing number of companies are using capital markets outside their home country to raise long-term capital, thus making it necessary for issuers of securities to prepare annual reports for international users. The audit and other related services provided by international accounting firms will be needed more than ever by these new participants in global capital markets.

Opportunity - 3 Increased Interest in Emerging Capital Markets

The international investment community has started investing in companies located in developing or emerging capital markets, as evidenced by various country specific mutual funds launched over the last three years. Furthermore, debt/equity swaps, which are being discussed to reduce the debt burdens of developing countries, would also increase international interest in the stocks and bonds of companies in developing countries.

An increasing interest in companies from emerging capital markets, (particularly in Argentina, Brazil, Chile, India, South Korea, Malaysia, Mexico, Philippines, Portugal, Taiwan and Thailand) should result in increased appointments of international accounting firms as external auditors as well as increased use of other related services offered by these firms.

In conclusion, we see the growth of international accounting firms as closely connected with the globalization of capital markets. As investors worldwide invest in foreign securities, more comprehensive financial statements will be needed, resulting in an increased need for the auditing and other services of international accounting firms.

INTRODUCTION TO APPENDICES A, B & C

Appendix A A GUIDE FOR PREPARING ANNUAL REPORTS FOR MULTINATIONAL INDUSTRIAL COMPANIES

Appendix B A GUIDE FOR PREPARING AN ANNUAL REPORT FOR A MULTINATIONAL COMMERCIAL BANK

Appendix C A GUIDE FOR PREPARING AN ANNUAL REPORT FOR A MULTINATIONAL INSURANCE COMPANY

If a finance director does not have information concerning a country's local requirements for preparing financial statements and would like to improve the presentation of his company's financial statements for international users, what are the items he should include?

In order to prepare a checklist of items which provide a common thread for international users, we identified 300 of the most international companies, and used the 1987 annual reports of these companies to summarize key attributes. The companies represent three basic types of businesses: Industrial, Banks, and Insurance.

The argument in favor of choosing such an international group was that these companies are already raising long-term funds across national boundaries and, therefore, are providing additional information to investors, lenders and other users worldwide.

Rather than providing content analysis, we decided to provide a comprehensive checklist of items included in international reports and include typical examples of good disclosures.

Though the checklist is most suitable for a larger company preparing an annual report for an international audience, there are many examples applicable to smaller companies with an audience in fewer countries.

Readers should keep in mind that this list is not all-inclusive. Readers should also note that not all of the points mentioned have to be followed, as some of these items may not be applicable to every company. Financial reporting rules may not allow such reporting.

General observations about preparing annual reports for international companies have been summarized in the next section. This will provide an introductory overview for each of the three appendices which follow. Appendix A provides a guide for industrial companies. Appendix B and Appendix C provide guidelines for banks and insurance companies, respectively.

Each annual report is generally composed of sections which convey information concerning the following categories: General Information, Financial Information, and Supplementary Information. These are outlined below.

General Information

- Financial Summary
- Group's Organization
- Officers
- Management Reports
- Other Important Operating Activities

Financial Information

- Auditor's Report
- Financial Statements: Income Statement, Balance Sheet, Statement of Changes in Financial Position and Statement of Changes in Shareholders' Equity
- Accounting Policies
- Notes to the Financial Statements

Supplementary Information

- Additional analysis of important financial data for each industry group (i.e., loans and deposits in banks, premium income and investment assets in insurance companies, sales and cost of goods sold in industrial companies)
- Quarterly Financial Data
- Inflation Accounting
- Subsidiary and Branch Information
- Shareholders' Information

GENERAL OBSERVATIONS ABOUT PREPARING ANNUAL REPORTS

Some of the points included in this section appear quite obvious but are sometimes overlooked. So, at the risk of appearing overly detailed, these points are included for the preparation of the annual reports.

1. Table of Contents

   The Table of Contents at the front of the annual report should include clear reference to the basic financial statements, footnotes to the financial statements, auditor's opinion, historical summary, and management's analysis of financial performance.

2. Auditor's Opinion:

   - The auditor's opinion should be visibly placed.

   - If local rules require the individual auditor's name to appear, the auditing firm's name in brackets would be useful.

   - If the auditor is affiliated with an international auditing firm, such identification should be listed also.

3. Directory of Key Locations

A list of key operations (i.e., plants, offices) would also be useful to international users for contacting local offices to obtain additional information. Company name, address, phone, telex and telefax should be provided for locations worldwide.

4. Cover

. The front cover should clearly indicate the name of the company and the fiscal year of the report.

. If the fiscal year covers a different time period than the calendar year (e.g., April 1, 1987 to March 31, 1988), the dates the report actually covers, rather than the year, should be listed on the cover.

5. Sequence of Years

. Throughout the report, a sequence of years should be consistently used, either in descending order or ascending order.

. Highlighting in bolder type or a different color background may help users focus on the current year.

6. To Facilitate Photocopying

. Copier machines and telefax are now used widely in the international business community, therefore, colors, graphics and photos which cannot be copied well (for example, light blue inks) should be avoided.

. Large tables (which fold out to 11" x 17" or longer) are difficult to use. Companies may want to reduce these tables to 8 1/2" by 11" or break them up into two pages.

. The company name and year of the report should be printed on each page of the annual report for easy identification of company and year if pages are copied and used by a number of people at one organization.

7. English Version of the Report

A full-text English translation is recommended for the international edition (rather than an abridged version). The following are variations of English versions provided by companies internationally:

. Some companies, particularly in Scandinavia, provide side by side translation (i.e., both local language and English terms are printed on the same page in different color ink or on each half of the page).

. Many companies in Hong Kong, Israel, Malaysia and South Africa provide both English and native language information bound in the same report.

- Many companies in Japan provide international reports restated into US accounting standards.

- If a company decides that the entire report should not be translated into English, then translating the financial section is the second best option.

- An accounting lexicon is prepared and included in Appendix D to facilitate translation of the financial section of international annual reports.

8. Rounded Numbers

Figures should be rounded into millions or billions rather than providing an exact number with decimals.

9. Number of Pages in Annual Report

As with any written communication, annual reports should be brief.

One booklet is more efficient than several separate booklets. (Producing separate booklets is a common practice in many European companies).

10. Glossary of Technical Terms

For industries which use many technical terms to describe their activities (such as Pharmaceuticals), a brief glossary of technical terms and their general meanings would be useful.

11. Brand Names

Consumer firms may want to list their major brand names and the countries in which these brands are marketed.

12. Timeliness of Report

- Annual reports should be made available to users as soon as possible after the fiscal year-end.

- There are three phases in preparing reports: the audit process, printing, and distribution of the report. Finance directors should work toward expediting each of these three phases so that reports are made available to international users in a timely fashion, within three to four months of the year-end date.

13. Comparability

For the sake of comparability, a minimum of two year's worth of data, including the current year's, should be provided. If possible, data from several previous years should also be supplied.

APPENDIX A

A GUIDE FOR PREPARING ANNUAL REPORTS

FOR MULTINATIONAL INDUSTRIAL COMPANIES

INTRODUCTION

This appendix provides a suggested format for preparing the annual report of a multinational industrial company. It is recommended that the reader should first review the Introduction to Appendices A, B & C before starting to read Appendix A.

The appendix includes an appropriate format for each section of the report. Where possible, descriptive or narrative comments have been avoided. In certain instances, descriptive comments are made to provide specific guidance. Readers are encouraged to consult local authorities concerning any areas for which further guidance is needed.

[inside of cover]

- Brief Description of Business
- Brief History
- Address of Headquarters

The ABC Industrial Company was founded in 1900..... It has been listed on the xxx Stock Exchange since January 1, 1975.

The principal activity of the company and its subsidiary and associated companies is to provide the following services in ____ countries:

List services provided here ____________
____
____

Head Office
Address
Phone
Telex, Cable
Telefax

Table of Contents

1. Financial Summary

Five-Year Financial Summary					
	1988	1987	1986	1985	1984
Year Ending MM/DD (Millions of ______)					
Total Revenues	xxx	xxx	xxx	xxx	xxx
Interest Expense	xxx	xxx	xxx	xxx	xxx
Earnings Before Income Taxes	xxx	xxx	xxx	xxx	xxx
Income Taxes	xxx	xxx	xxx	xxx	xxx
Net Income	xxx	xxx	xxx	xxx	xxx
Cash Flow Generated	xxx	xxx	xxx	xxx	xxx
Share Data					
Earnings per Share	x.x	x.x	x.x	x.x	x.x
Dividends per Share	x.x	x.x	x.x	x.x	x.x
Cash Flow per Share	x.x	x.x	x.x	x.x	x.x
Book Value per Share	x.x	x.x	x.x	x.x	x.x
Stock Price at MM/DD	x.x	x.x	x.x	x.x	x.x
At MM/DD (Millions of ______)					
Current Assets	xxx	xxx	xxx	xxx	xxx
Property, Plant and Equipment	xxx	xxx	xxx	xxx	xxx
Total Assets	xxx	xxx	xxx	xxx	xxx
Long-Term Liabilities	xxx	xxx	xxx	xxx	xxx
Total Stockholders' Equity	xxx	xxx	xxx	xxx	xxx
Other Information (Millions of ___except*)	xxx	xxx	xxx	xxx	xxx
No. of Shares Outstanding* (thousands)	xxx	xxx	xxx	xxx	xxx
No. of Shareholders*	xxx	xxx	xxx	xxx	xxx
Capital Expenditures	xxx	xxx	xxx	xxx	xxx
Depreciation and Amortization Expenses	xxx	xxx	xxx	xxx	xxx
Research and Development Expenses	xxx	xxx	xxx	xxx	xxx
Total Employees*	xxx	xxx	xxx	xxx	xxx
Year End Backlog of Orders	xxx	xxx	xxx	xxx	xxx
Selected Financial Ratios					
*See details in Supplementary Information B					

2. Group's Organization

May Include the Following:

- Provide a chart outlining the group's organization including important consolidated subsidiaries.
- Separate consolidated subsidiaries by business segment.
- Separate consolidated subsidiaries by geographic distribution.
- Specify ownership of the subsidiaries.
- Include unconsolidated companies if the non-consolidation is due to material differences in industry classification,, and the unconsolidated companies are important to the group (e.g., banking group in oil company).

3. Key Executives and Board of Directors

Chairman	Variables e.g.,:	Name, Age, Years in the Office,
President		Past and Present Relevant Functions,
Directors		Re-election date, Special Tasks...

Senior Executives
Chief Accountant
Secretary

a. Board of Directors

. For each member of the board of the company, there should be further information about his affiliation, background in brief, length of time on the company's board and the expiration date of his term.

. Membership on each of the Board's committees should be clearly noted.

b. Senior Executives

Principal Executive Officers of the companies, including the Officers of the major divisions and subsidiaries, should be listed with title, age and length of time with the company.

4. Management Reports

- Macroeconomic analysis by Chief Executive Officer (includes strategic planning for near future)
- Detailed operating results by Finance Director

This section usually reviews a company's activities and is broken down as follows:

- A Letter from the President or Chief Executive
- Overview of the Year
- Macro Trends of the Marketplace
- Research and Development
- International Activities

In addition, the management's financial review is also provided. The review outlines the following:

- Factors contributing to increase/decrease in key accounts such as sales, earnings, total assets, current liabilities and shareholders' equity
- Unusual financial items (such as discontinued operations, extraordinary gains/losses, disposal of assets, etc.)
- Mergers/acquisitions undertaken during the year
- The impact of broader economic events on the company's activities

5. Non-Financial Analysis of Major Subsidiaries and Sectors

May Include the Following:

- New Services
- Major Activities
- Labor Relations
- Social Activities

. <u>Capital Expenditures</u>

The total amount of capital expenditures undertaken during the year should be disclosed (along with a description of major projects in the management letter).

. <u>Research & Development</u>

If the company is in a research intensive industry or has substantial R & D expenditures, total amount spent during the year should be disclosed.

6. Auditor's Report

   Should Include the Following:

   To the Board of Directors and Shareholders

   - Scope
   - Opinion
   - Auditor's Signature
   - Local Audit Firm and International Auditing Firm, if any
   - Address of the Auditor
   - Date

7. Financial Statements

   Annual reports should include four basic consolidated financial statements:

   - Income Statement
   - Balance Sheet
   - Statement of Cash Flow
   - Statement of Changes in Shareholders' Equity

   a. Income Statement

      - Suggested Income Statement is provided.

   b. Balance Sheet

      - Suggested format of Balance Sheet is provided.
      - It should be in descending order of liquidity on the asset side and ascending order of maturity on the liability side.

   c. Statement of Cash Flow

      - Suggested format of Statement of Cash Flow is provided.

   d. Statement of Shareholders' Equity

      - Suggested format of Statement of Shareholders' Equity is provided.

ABC Company

Consolidated Income Statement

(For the Year Ending MM/DD/1988)

(Millions of Local Currency)

	Notes	1988	1987
Sales		XXX	XXX
Revenue from Other Operating Activities		XXX	XXX
Total Revenue		XXXX	XXXX
Cost of Goods Sold		XXX	XXX
Gross Margin		XXX	XXX
Selling, General and Administrative Expenses	1	XXX	XXX
Operating Income		XXX	XXX
Non-Operating Expenses/Income, Net	2	XXX	XXX
Income before Taxes		XXX	XXX
Income Taxes		XX	XX
Income before Extraordinary Items and Minority Interest		XX	XX
Extraordinary Items	4	XX	XX
Minority Interest		XX	XX
Net Income Attributable to the Group		XX	XX
Dividend Declared	14	XX	XX
Earnings per Share:	15		
Basic EPS		XX.XX	XX.XX
Fully Diluted EPS		XX.XX	XX.XX

ABC Company
Consolidated Balance Sheet

(As of MM/DD/1988)

(Millions of Local Currency)

Assets	Notes	1988	1987
Current Assets:			
. Cash and Bank Deposits		XXX	XXX
. Marketable Securities	5	XXX	XXX
. Current Accounts Receivable (Net of		XXX	XXX
Allowance for Bad Debt)		XXX	XXX
. Inventories (Net of Obsolescence	6		
Reserve)		XXX	XXX
. Prepaid Expenses & Other Current Assets		XXX	XXX
Total Current Assets		XXX	XXX
Investment in Non-Consolidated			
Subsidiaries and Affiliates	7	XXX	XXX
Long-Term Receivables and Investments	8	XXX	XXX
Property, Plant and Equipment			
. Land		XXX	XXX
. Building		XXX	XXX
. Machinery and Equipment		XXX	XXX
. Construction in Progress		XXX	XXX
Total: Property Plant & Equipment		XXX	XXX
Less: Accumulated Depreciation		XXX	XXX
Net Property, Plant & Equipment	9	XXX	XXX
Intangibles and Other Assets		XXX	XXX
Total Assets		XXXX	XXXX

ABC Company
Consolidated Balance Sheet (Continued)

(As of MM/DD/1988)

(Millions of Local Currency)

LIABILITIES & SHAREHOLDERS' EQUITY	Notes	1988	1987
Current Liabilities:			
. Short-Term Borrowings	10	xxx	xxx
. Long-Term Debt Due Within One Year	10	xxx	xxx
. Notes and Accounts Payable		xxx	xxx
. Wages and Other Expenses Accrued		xxx	xxx
. Taxes Accrued to be Paid Within One Year		xxx	xxx
Total Current Liabilities		xxx	xxx
Long-Term Liabilities and Provisions:			
. Long-Term Debt Due After One Year	10	xxx	xxx
. Long-Term Provisions		xxx	xxx
. Deferred Income Taxes (to be paid after one year)		xxx	xxx
. Subordinated Loans		xxx	xxx
. Minority Interests in Consolidated Subsidiaries		xxx	xxx
Total Liabilities & Provisions		xxx	xxx
Shareholders' Equity:			
. Preferred Stocks	12	xxx	xxx
. Common Stocks at Par	13	xxx	xxx
. Additional Paid in Capital		xxx	xxx
. Legal Reserves		xxx	xxx
. Retained Earnings		xxx	xxx
Shareholders' Equity		xxx	xxx
Less: Treasury Stock at Cost		xx	xx
Total Shareholders' Equity		xxx	xxx
Total Liabilities and Shareholders' Equity		xxxx	xxxx

ABC Company

Consolidated Statements of Cash Flow

(For the Year Ending MM/DD/1988)

(Millions of Local Currency)

	Notes	1988	1987
Operating Activities:			
Income from Continuing Operations		XXX	XXX
Non-cash Items Included in Income:			
.Depreciation and Amortization		XX	XX
.Reserves, Deferred Liabilities and Deferred Income Tax		XX	XX
.Undistributed Earnings of Equity Investments		(XX)	(XX)
.Outside Minority Interests		XX	XX
Change in Accounts Receivable, Inventories and Trade Payables		XX	XX
Other Changes in Working Capital, Net		XX	XX
Funds from Operating Activities		XXX	XXX
Investing Activities:			
Sales of (Additions to) Property, Plant and Equipment		XXX	XXX
Proceeds from Dispositions and Discontinued Operations		XXX	XXX
Investments in and Advances to Unconsolidated Subsidiaries		XXX	XXX
Other Investing Activities, Net		XXX	XXX
Funds from (used for) Investing Activities		XXX	XXX
Financing Activities:			
Issuance of Long-Term Debt		XXX	XXX
(Repayments) of Long-Term Debt		XXX	XXX
Issuance of Capital Stock		XXX	XXX
Dividends (Paid)		XXX	XXX
Funds from (used for) Financing Activities		XXX	XXX
Exchange Rate Effects		XXX	XXX
Increase in Cash and Marketable Securities During the Year		XXX	XXX
Cash and Equivalents - Beginning of Year		XXX	XXX
Cash and Equivalents - End of Year		XXX	XXX

ABC Company
Consolidated Statement of Changes in Shareholders' Equity
(For the Year Ending MM/DD/1988)

(Millions of Local Currency)

	1988	1987
Preferred Stock		
Balance at Beginning of Year	xxx	xxx
Increase (Decrease) in the Year	xx	xx
Balance at End of Year	xxx	xxx
Common Stock		
Balance at Beginning of Year	xxx	xxx
Increase (Decrease) 1	xx	xx
2	(xx)	(xx)
Balance at End of Year	xxx	xxx
Additional Paid in Capital		
Balance at Beginning of Year	xxx	xxx
Increase (Decrease) from Preferred Stock	xxx	xxx
Increase (Decrease) from Common Stock	xxx	xxx
Balance at End of Year	xxx	xxx
Legal Reserves		
Balance at Beginning of Year	xxx	xxx
Increase (Decrease) during the Year	xxx	xxx
Balance at End of Year	xxx	xxx
Retained Earnings		
Balance at Beginning of Year	xxx	xxx
Dividends Declared	(xxx)	(xxx)
Net Income during the Year	xxx	xxx
Balance at End of Year	xxx	xxx
Common Stock in Treasury, at Cost		
Balance at Beginning of Year	xxx	xxx
Increase (Decrease) during the Year	xxx	xxx
Balance at End of Year	xxx	xxx
Total Stockholders' Equity	xxx	xxx

8. Major Accounting Policies

- This section outlines the basic accounting policies used for preparing financial statements.
- Many international users are familiar with key accounting concepts in their home country, but are not well versed in the accounting practices of other countries. This brief summary of local accounting standards used by the company should help international users in analyzing foreign company reports.
- Guidance statements for the reader are included below for certain items (see, for example, item a). In most cases, however, the descriptions simply illustrate a type of policy which a given company could follow. A company's specific policy should be described in the report.

a. Basis of Presentation

Each country has different regulations on reporting the results of operations. This section should identify the regulatory bodies and related regulations. If the reporting differs from the home country's regulations, the differences should be summarized here.

b. Basis of Consolidation

The consolidated financial statements include the accounts of the parent company and its majority-owned domestic and foreign subsidiaries, except the subsidiaries in finance and unrelated business which are included on an equity basis. Subsidiaries and affiliates that are 20% to 50% owned by the company are included in the consolidated financial statements on an equity basis. Accordingly, the company's share of the earnings of these companies is included in its consolidated net income. Investments in other companies are carried at cost.

Inter-company transactions are eliminated and net earnings are reduced by the portion of the earnings of subsidiaries applicable to minority shareholders.

c. Foreign Currency Translation

Assets and liabilities of most foreign subsidiaries are translated at current exchange rates, and the effects of these translation adjustments are reported as a separate component of stockholders' equity.

Exchange gains and losses from transactions in a currency other than the local currency of the entity involved, and translation adjustments in countries with highly inflationary economies (primarily in Latin America), are included in income.

d. Inventory Valuation

The cost of inventories is determined by the first-in, first-out (FIFO) method. Certain inventories, primarily materials and supplies, are valued generally at average cost. At the balance sheet date, inventories are stated at the lower of cost or market.

e. Property, Plant and Equipment

Depreciation is computed using an accelerated method that results in accumulated depreciation of approximately two-thirds of asset costs during the first half of the asset's estimated useful life.

On average, buildings and land improvements are depreciated based on a 30-year life; machinery, equipment, and office furniture are depreciated based on a 12-year life.

All maintenance, repairs, and rearrangement expenses are expensed as incurred. Expenditures that increase the value of productive capacity of assets are capitalized.

The costs of special tools are amortized over periods of time representing the short productive use of such tools.

Pre-production costs incurred in connection with new facilities are expensed as incurred.

f. Advertising and Sales Promotion

Advertising and sales promotion costs are expensed as incurred.

g. Product Warranty Costs

Estimated costs related to product warranty are recorded as expenses at the time of the sale of the products.

h. Research and Development Costs

Research and development costs are expensed as incurred.

i. Income Taxes

Income taxes are recognized during the year in which transactions enter into the determination of financial statement income, with deferred taxes being provided for timing differences.

Investment tax credits, if applicable, are recorded using the flow-through method. Under this method, these credits reduce income tax expense in the year they arise.

j. Marketable Securities

Equity securities are stated at the lower of cost or market. All other marketable securities are carried at cost.

k. Goodwill and Other Intangible Assets

Goodwill, trademarks, and other intangibles are amortized using the straight-line method over periods of up to _ years.

l. Earnings Per Share

Earnings per share are based on the weighted average shares of outstanding common stock and additional common stock equivalents.

m. Pensions and Other Retirement Benefits

The company's general policy is to accrue and fund the actuarially determined pension cost for the year.

The company accrues its liability for vacations earned but not taken. The company and many of its subsidiaries provide certain post-retirement health care and life insurance benefits for most of their retirees, if they are working for the company when they become eligible for retirement. These post-retirement and similar benefits for active employees are provided through programs where the costs are based on the benefits paid during the year.

n. Major Changes During the Year

- Changes in Accounting Principles
- Corporate Changes

If major acquisitions have taken place, the company name has changed or any other major change in corporate structure has occurred, such changes should be disclosed in a footnote. The beginning of the Summary of the Accounting Principles section is found to be the most suitable place for this footnote.

o. Foreign Currency Rates Used

Exchange rates used for major currencies in translating financial statements of foreign subsidiaries should be provided.

9. Notes to the Financial Statements

Note 1. Selling, General and Administrative Expenses

(Millions of Local Currency)

	1988	1987
Salaries	xxx	xxx
Depreciation Expenses	xxx	xxx
Allowance for Doubtful Accounts	xxx	xxx
Advertising Expenses	xxx	xxx
R & D Expenses	xxx	xxx
Allowance for Retirement Benefits	xxx	xxx
Rent	xxx	xxx
Taxes other than Income Taxes	xxx	xxx
Other Selling, General and Administrative Expenses	xxx	xxx
Total Selling, General and Administrative Expenses	xxx	xxx

Note 2. Non-Operating Expenses/Income, Net

(Millions of Local Currency)

	1988	1987
Interest Expenses	xxx	xxx
Interest and Dividends	(xxx)	(xxx)
Foreign Exchange Loss (Gain)	xxx	xxx
Loss (Gain) on Sale of Fixed Assets	xxx	xxx
Equity Loss (Income) or Investment in Unconsolidated Subsidiaries and Affiliates	xxx	xxx
Other Non-Operating Expenses (Income)	xxx	xxx
Non-Operating Expenses (Income), Net	xxx	xxx

Note 3. Income Taxes

The components of income before income taxes and the provision for income taxes are as follows:

(Millions of Local Currency)

	1988	1987
Income before Income Taxes		
Home Country	xxx	xxx
Foreign	xxx	xxx
Total Income Before Income Taxes	xxx	xxx
Home Country Income Taxes:	xxx	xxx
Current Provision	xxx	xxx
Deferred Provision, Net	xxx	xxx
Foreign Income Taxes:	xxx	xxx
Current Provision	xxx	xxx
Deferred Provision, Net		
Total Income Taxes	xxx	xxx
Reconciliation of Legal Tax Rate & Effective Tax Rate should be presented here.		

Note 4. <u>Extraordinary Items</u> (Net of taxes)

(Millions of Local Currency)

	1988	1987
Gain or Loss on Disposal of Fixed Assets (net of tax xxx)	xxx	
Provision Reserves for Possible Losses (net of tax xxx)	xxx	
Changes in Regulations (net of tax xxx)		xxx
Total Extraordinary Items (Net of tax xxx in 1988, xxx in 1987)	xxx	xxx

Note 5. <u>Marketable Securities</u>

Example:

<u>Marketable Securities</u>

The amount shown for marketable securities consists of:

(Millions of Local Currency)

	1988	1987
Equity Securities at Cost	xxx	xxx
Less: Valuation Allowance	(xx)	(xx)
Other Marketable Securities at Cost (Approximate market value yyy, and yyy in 1988 and 1987, respectively)	xxx	xxx
Total Marketable Securities	xxx	xxx

Note 6. <u>Inventory</u>

Inventories as of December 31, 1988 and 1987 comprise the following:

(Millions of Local Currency)

	1988	1987
Raw Materials	xxx	xxx
Work in Process	xxx	xxx
Finished Goods	xxx	xxx
Sub Total	xxx	xxx
Less: Obsolescence and Other Inventory Valuation Reserves	xx	xx
Total Inventory	xxx	xxx

Note 7. Investments in Unconsolidated Subsidiaries and Affiliates

Valuation method for specific investments is disclosed, if significant.

(Millions of Local Currency)

	1988		1987	
	Book Value	Valuation	Book Value	Valuation
Unconsolidated Subsidiaries				
Listed	xx	xx	xx	xx
Unlisted	xx	xx	xx	xx
Associated Companies				
Listed	xx	xx	xx	xx
Unlisted	xx	xx	xx	xx
Total Investments	xxx	xxx	xxx	xxx
Equity Earnings by Equity Method	xxx		xxx	

List of companies disclosed at page xx

Note 8. Long-Term Receivables and Investments

(Millions of Local Currency)

	1988	1987
Long-Term Receivables		
Related Companies	xxx	xxx
Unrelated Companies	xxx	xxx
Long-Term Receivables	xxx	xxx
Less: Allowance for Doubtful Accounts	xx	xx
Net Long-Term Receivables	xxx	xxx
Long-Term Investments		
Listed		
In Domestic Market	xxx	xxx
In Foreign Market	xxx	xxx
Unlisted	xxx	xxx
Total Long-Term Investments	xxx	xxx
Total Long-Term Receivables and Investments	xxx	xxx
Estimated Market Value of Long-Term Investments	xxx	xxx

Note 9. Property, Plant and Equipment

(Millions of Local Currency)

	1988	1987
Balance at Beginning of Year	XXX	XXX
Adjustments	XX	XX
Balance after Adjustment	XXX	XXX
Less Depreciation for the Year	XXX	XXX
Balance at End of Year	XXX	XXX
Depreciation Expenses:		
Cost of Goods Sold	XXX	XXX
Selling, General and Administrative Expense	XXX	XXX

	Gross Amount	Accumulated Depreciation	Net
1987			
Building	XXX	XXX	XXX
Machinery and Equipment	XXX	XXX	XXX
Land	XXX	XXX	XXX
Construction in Progress	XXX	XXX	XXX
Total Amount	XXX	XXX	XXX
Estimated Market Value			XXX
1988			
Building	XXX	XXX	XXX
Machinery and Equipment	XXX	XXX	XXX
Land	XXX	XXX	XXX
Construction in Progress	XXX	XXX	XXX
Total Amount	XXX	XXX	XXX
Estimated Market Value			XXX

Note 10. Short-Term Borrowings and Long-Term Debt

Example:

- Short-term borrowings of _____ (in millions of local currency) were outstanding as of December 31, 1988, with interest rates ranging from ___% to ___% per year.
- Unused line of credit as of December 31, 1988 was ____ (in millions of local currency).
- Long-term debt as of December 31, 1988 is comprised of the following:

Type of Long-Term Debt	Due Date	Interest Rate	Currency	Amount of Borrowings in Millions of Currency

Note 11. Subordinated Loans

(Millions of Local Currency)

	1988	1987
Subordinated Notes (8 1/2% interest, No date)	xx	xx
Loan Capital (6 1/2%....)	xx	xx
(Subordinated Capital Notes)		
Total Subordinated Loans	xxx	xxx

Note 12. Preferred Stocks

(Millions of Local Currency)

	1988	1987
Redeemable Preferred Stocks		
Redeemable Preferred A, 8%	xx	xx
Redeemable Preferred B, 7%, Convertible	xx	xx
Total Redeemable Preferred Stocks	xxx	xxx
Unredeemable Preferred Stocks		
Name 1	xx	xx
Name 2	xx	xx
Total Unredeemable Preferred Stocks	xxx	xxx
Total Preferred Stocks	xxx	xxx

Note 13. Common Stocks

If additional stocks are issued in the year, the issuances may be explained here.

(Millions of Local Currency)

	1988	1987
Authorized Capital (xxx shares, x.x in par)	xxx	xxx
Common Stocks Issued		
Balance at Beginning of Year (number of shares issued)	xxx	xxx
Conversion of Convertible Debentures (number of shares)	xx	xx
Exercising Option by Executives (number of shares)	xx	xx
New Issuance (number of shares)	xx	-
Balance at End of Year (number of shares)	xxx	xxx

* Common Stock in Treasury could be entered here.

Note 14. Dividends Declared

	1988		1987	
	Per Share	Millions of Local Currency	Per Share	Millions of Local Currency
Preferred Shares:				
Preferred Share A	x.x	xx	x.x	xx
Preferred Share B				
Interim	x.x	xx	x.x	xx
Final	x.x	xx	x.x	xx
Total Amount	x.x	xx	x.x	xx
Common Shares:				
Interim	x.x	xx	x.x	xx
Final	x.x	xx	x.x	xx
Total Amount	x.x	xx	x.x	xx
Total Dividends Declared		xxx		xxx

Note 15. Earnings per Share

	1988	1987
Basic EPS Net Income Attributable to Group xx and Weighted Average Number Common Stocks in Issue During 1988	x.x	
Net Income Attributable to Group xxx and Weighted Average Number Common Stocks in Issue During 1987		x.x
Fully Diluted (Earnings xxx and number shares in 1988)	x.x	
(Earnings xxx and number shares in 1987)		x.x

Note 16. Lease Commitments

Rental Expense:

(Millions of Local Currency)

	1988	1987	1986
Gross Rentals	xxx	xxx	xxx
Deduct: Sublease Income	xxx	xxx	xxx
Total Rental Expense	xxx	xxx	xxx

The approximate amounts of noncancellable lease commitments with terms of more than one year, principally for the rental of real property, are as follows:

Minimum Rental Commitments

(Millions of Local Currency)

	1988	1987	1986
1989	xx	xx	xx
1990	xx	xx	xx
1991	xx	xx	xx
1992	xx	xx	xx
1993	xx	xx	xx
1994 and beyond	xx	xx	xx
Total Minimum Rental Commitments	xxx	xxx	xxx

Note 17. Employee Retirement Plans

Example:
The worldwide charge to ABC Company's income for pension plans was ________ million in 1988, _________ million in 1987, and ________ million in 1986.

Pension expense for 1988 was based on an assumed discount rate of ____%, an assumed average rate of increase in future compensation level of ______%, and an expected average rate of return on pension fund assets of _____%.

Note 18. Contingent Liabilities

- Litigation on pending lawsuits
- Contingent liabilities not from operating activities

Example:

The Company has guaranteed approximately ____ (in millions of local currency), for the obligations of others, made with other responsible companies in the ordinary course of business. If these companies are unable to meet certain obligations, the Company may be required to advance funds against future charges. No material loss is anticipated under these guarantees.

The Company and its subsidiaries are engaged in litigation and have a number of unresolved claims pending. While the amounts claimed are substantial and the ultimate liability in respect of such litigation and claims cannot be determined at this time, the company is of the opinion that such liability, to the extent not provided for through insurance or otherwise, is not likely to be of material importance in relation to its accounts.

In its accounts, the Company has provided for items and issues not yet resolved, based on the management's best judgment.

Note 19. Subsequent Events

All key events occurring between the year-end date and the date of the annual report which have an impact on financial data or the further viability of the firm should be disclosed.

A note such as "no events with material financial consequences have occurred since the year-end date of the report" would also be appropriate.

Example:

On _______, the company acquired all of the outstanding common stock of XYZ Company. The cost of the acquisition was approximately ___ and will be accounted for as a purchase. Results of XYZ Company will be included in the Consolidated Statement of Earnings from the date of acquisition. XYZ company had net sales of ____ million and net earnings from continuing operations of ___ for the 12 months ended last year-end. XYZ Company had total shareholders' equity of ____ million at the last year-end.

The following summarizes the unaudited pro forma combined results of operations, as though an acquisition had occurred at the beginning of the company's current fiscal year.

Sales _____

Net Earnings*_____

Net Earnings Per Share _____

* (Adjusted for the amortization of estimated excess purchase price and interest on debt in connection with the acquisition)

The unaudited pro forma financial information is not necessarily indicative either of the results of operations that would have occurred had the two companies actually been combined during the period presented, or of future results of operations of the combined companies.

Note 20. Pending Accounting Changes

This note should explain if there are any accounting changes which are required by local accounting standards and, if so, that they will be implemented by the company in the near future .

This note should disclose an explanation of any changes in accounting standards, date of implementation, and the potential impact on the company's Income Statement and Balance Sheet .

ABC Industrial Company

Supplementary Information A

Operating Results by Segment and Geographic Area

1. Results by Business Segment

   . For diversified companies, key financial indicators (such as sales, assets employed and operating profit) should be disclosed by business segment.

   . A brief definition (i.e., which major product lines or divisions are included) should be provided on each business segment.

   . Inter-company transactions should be eliminated.

   . Capital expenditures and depreciation by segment would also be useful to investors.

2. Results by Geographic Area

   The company should also provide key financial variables (such as sales, assets employed and operating profit) by geographic area.

   Several options can be explored to decide geographic classification.

   a. Define geographic areas along conventional geographic lines (i.e., North America, South America, Western Europe, Middle East, Africa, Far East and Australia/New Zealand).

   b. Provide results by country, if the company has significant operations in a few countries, and combine other small operations as other foreign business.

   c. Mix key countries and regions.

   Inter-area transfers should be eliminated.

   Exports from the home country, if substantial, should be reported separately in a footnote to geographic disclosures.

   Companies operating in several business segments in several international regions may want to combine their segment and geographic disclosures into one table.

ABC Industrial Company

Integrated Segment and Geographic Disclosure
A-1. Sales

Sales	Product Groups					Eliminations	Net Sales by Geographic Area
	A	B	C	D	E		
By Geographic Areas 1 2 3 4 5							
Eliminations							
Net Sales by Segment							

A-2. Assets Employed

Assets Employed	Product Group					Eliminations	Net Assets Employed by Geographic Area
	A	B	C	D	E		
By Geographic Areas 1 2 3 4 5							
Eliminations							
Net Assets Employed by Segment							

A-3. Operating Income

Operating Income	Product Group					Eliminations	Operating Income by Geographic Area
	A	B	C	D	E		
By Geographic Areas 1 2 3 4 5							
Eliminations							
Net Operating Income by Segment							

ABC Industrial Company

Supplementary Information B

Selected Financial Ratios

1. Profitability Ratios

   a. Gross Profit Margin = Gross Profit divided by Sales

   b. Pre-Tax Margin = Pre-Tax Income divided by Sales

   c. Net Income Margin = Net Income divided by Sales

   d. Cash Flow as % of Sales = (Net Income + Non-Cash Expenses) divided by Sales

   e. Sales Growth = (Sales This Year less Sales Last Year) divided by (Sales Last Year)

   f. Net Income Growth = (Net Income This Year Less Net Income Last Year) divided by Net Income Last Year

   g. Sales Per Employee = Sales divided by Total Employees

2. Asset Utilization Ratios

   a. Asset Turnover = Sales divided by Total Assets

   b. Capital Expenditures as % of Total Assets = Capital Expenditures divided by Total Assets

   c. Age of Fixed Assets = Accumulated Depreciation divided by Gross Depreciable Assets

   d. Assets Per Employee = Total Assets divided by Total Employees

3. Liquidity Ratios

   a. Current Ratio = Current Assets divided by Current Liabilities

   b. Quick Ratio = (Current Assets - Inventories) divided by Current Liabilities

4. Leverage Ratios

   a. Debt to Assets = Total Debt divided by Total Assets

   b. Debt to Equity = Total Debt divided by Total Shareholders' Equity

5. Per Share Ratios (for common shares)

   a. Earnings per share

   b. Dividends per share

   c. Cash flow per share

   d. Market price per share

   e. Book value per share

6. Capital Market-Related Ratios

   a. Dividend Yield = Dividend Per Share divided by Market Price Per Share

   b. Dividend Payout = Total Dividend divided by Net Income

   c. Total Shareholders' Return = (End of Year Stock Price - Beginning of Year Stock Price + Dividend Paid During the Year) divided by Beginning of Year Stock Price

   d. Price to Earnings = Market Price Per Share divided by Earnings Per Share

   e. Price to Book = Market Price Per Share divided by Book Value Per Share

   f. Dividend Growth = (Dividend Per Share This Year - Dividend Per Share Last Year) divided by Dividend Per Share Last Year

   g. Net Worth Growth = (Net Worth Per Share This Year - Net Worth Per Share Last Year) divided by Net Worth Per Share Last Year

   h. Cash Dividend Coverage = Net Income Available to Common Shareholders divided by Dividends Paid This Year

7. International Business-Related Ratios

   a. Foreign Sales as % of Total Worldwide Sales

   b. Foreign Income as % of Total Worldwide Income

   c. Foreign Assets as % of Total Worldwide Assets

   d. Exports as % of Total Home Country Sales

Supplementary Information C

Quarterly Analysis of Financial Results

(Millions of Local Currency, except per share data)

	4th Quarter	3rd Quarter	2nd Quarter	1st Quarter
Sales				
1988	xxx	xxx	xxx	xxx
1987	xxx	xxx	xxx	xxx
Earnings before Income Taxes				
1988	xxx	xxx	xxx	xxx
1987	xxx	xxx	xxx	xxx
Provision for Taxes				
1988	xxx	xxx	xxx	xxx
1987	xxx	xxx	xxx	xxx
Net Earnings				
1988	xxx	xxx	xxx	xxx
1987	xxx	xxx	xxx	xxx
Per Share Earnings				
1988	x.x	x.x	x.x	x.x
1987	x.x	x.x	x.x	x.x

Note: Per share earnings should be restated for stock splits and/or stock dividends which occurred during these quarters.

Supplementary Information D

Value Added Statement

Breakdown of total revenues in terms of various beneficiaries (i.e., suppliers, employees, tax agencies, lenders and shareholders), should be provided. Such disclosure can be provided as a value added statement.

(Millions of Local Currency)

	1988	1987
Sources of Total Value Added		
Sales and Service Revenues		
Less: Purchases of Material and Services		
Total Value Added by Manufacturing and Trading		
Disposal of Total Value Added		
Employees (Wages, Bonus, Retirement Benefits)		
Government Taxes		
Net Interest Cost		
Dividends to Shareholders		
Minority Shareholders in Subsidiaries		
Sub-total Disposed		
Reinvestment in the Business:		
Depreciation		
Retained Profit in the Business		
Sub-total Reinvested		
Total Disposed and Reinvested		

ABC Industrial Company

Supplementary Information E

Selected Financial Data Adjusted for Changes in General Price Level

(Millions of Local Currency)

	1988	1987	1986	1985	1984
Sales					
As Reported	XXX	XXX	XXX	XXX	XXX
Adjusted	XXX	XXX	XXX	XXX	XXX
Operating Income					
As Reported	XXX	XXX	XXX	XXX	XXX
Adjusted	XXX	XXX	XXX	XXX	XXX
Net Income					
As Reported	XXX	XXX	XXX	XXX	XXX
Adjusted	XXX	XXX	XXX	XXX	XXX
Total Assets					
As Reported	XXX	XXX	XXX	XXX	XXX
Adjusted	XXX	XXX	XXX	XXX	XXX
Per Share Data:					
Earnings					
As Reported	X.XX	X.XX	X.XX	X.XX	X.XX
Adjusted	X.XX	X.XX	X.XX	X.XX	X.XX
Dividends					
As Reported	X.XX	X.XX	X.XX	X.XX	X.XX
Adjusted	X.XX	X.XX	X.XX	X.XX	X.XX
Price Index*	XXX	XXX	XXX	XXX	XXX

*Explain the Price Index Used

ABC Industrial Company

Supplementary Information F

Restatement into Accounting Standards of a Foreign Country

- In order to assist international users, companies should identify key differences between local accounting standards used in preparing their annual reports and widely used international accounting standards. Such a disclosure can be done in footnote form.

- If shareholders from a given country own a large percentage of the company, then the company may want to consider restating their key financial numbers into the accounting standards of a particular foreign country, or into the International Accounting Standards issued by the International Accounting Standards Committee (41 Kingsway, London WC2 B6YU, United Kingdom). Such restatement can be done in footnote format.

  Standards of the International Accounting Standards Committee contain several options. This note should clearly state which options are used.

Supplementary Information G

Selected Financial Data for Major Subsidiaries

- Parent Bank: Condensed Income Statement and Balance Sheet
- Major Subsidiaries: Selected Financial Data, Address, Phone, Fax, Telex, Major Business Area, % of Ownership
- Unconsolidated Subsidiaries: Majority Owned and Significant to the Group; Selected Financial Data, Address, Phone, Fax, Telex, Major Business Area, % of Ownership

1. ABC Company (Parent Company Only)

ABC Company
Condensed Income Statement
(Parent Company Only)

(Millions of Local Currency)

	1988	1987
Sales	XXXX	XXXX
Cost of Goods Sold	XXXX	XXXX
Selling, General and Administrative Expenses	XXX	XXX
Operating Income	XXX	XXX
Non-Operating Expenses/Income	XXX	XXX
Income Before Taxes and Extraordinary Items	XXX	XXX
Income Taxes	XXX	XXX
	XXX	XXX
Extraordinary Items	XX	XX
Net Income	XXX	XXX

ABC Company
Condensed Balance Statement
(Parent Company Only)

(Millions of Local Currency)

	1988	1987
Assets		
Current Assets	XXX	XXX
Long-Term Investments and Receivables	XXX	XXX
Property, Plant and Equipment	XXX	XXX
Intangibles and Other Assets	XXX	XXX
Total Assets	XXXX	XXXX
Current Liabilities	XXX	XXX
Long-Term Debt	XXX	XXX
Long-Term Provisions	XXX	XXX
Other Long-Term Liabilities	XXX	XXX
Total Liabilities	XXX	XXX
Shareholders' Equity	XXX	XXX
Total Liabilities and Shareholders' Equity	XXXX	XXXX

Major Subsidiaries

2. ABCP Company

ABC Company Group's Holdings: 100% Address, Phone, Fax, Telex, Major Business Area

(Millions of Local Currency)

	1988	1987
Sales	xxx	xxx
Operating Income	xxx	xxx
Net Income	xxx	xxx
Dividends Paid	xxx	xxx
EPS	x.xx	x.xx
Current Assets	xxx	xxx
Total Assets	xxx	xxx
Current Liabilities	xxx	xxx
Total Liabilities	xxx	xxx
Shareholders' Equity	xxx	xxx

3. ABCQ Company

ABC Company Group's Holdings: 90% Address, Phone, Fax, Telex, Major Business Area

(Millions of Local Currency)

	1988	1987
Sales	xxx	xxx
Operating Income	xxx	xxx
Net Income	xxx	xxx
Dividends Paid	xxx	xxx
EPS	x.xx	x.xx
Current Assets	xxx	xxx
Total Assets	xxx	xxx
Current Liabilities	xxx	xxx
Total Liabilities	xxx	xxx
Shareholders' Equity	xxx	xxx

Consolidated Subsidiaries, which are not significant to the group's operating results may disclose only significant information. - Address, Phone, Fax, Telex, Major Business - % of Ownership - Total Assets, Total Revenue, Net Income, and Contributions to the Group.

[Example]

	Total Assets	Sales	Net Income	Contributions To Group
ABCR Financial Services Address, Phone, Fax, Telex, 100% Owned	xxx	xxx	xx	xx

Associated Companies

Name	Address, Phone, Fax Telex	% of Ownership	Total Assets	Purchase Price	Estimated Market Value
ABCS		45%	xxx	xxx	xxx
ABCT		40%	xxx	xxx	xxx
ABCU		25%	xxx	xxx	xxx

Other Long-Term Investment

Name (Country)	Purchase Price	Estimated Market Value
ABCV Company (France)	xxx	xxx
ABCW Company (U.S.)	xxx	xxx

ABC Industrial Company

Supplementary Information H

Major Branches and Offices

- Domestic Branches and Offices
    - Responsible Person
    - Address, Phone, Fax, Telex

- Foreign Branches and Offices
    - Responsible Person
    - Address, Phone, Fax, Telex

Supplementary Information I

Shareholder-Related Information

In this section, items pertaining to common shares and shareholders are covered:

1. Capital Change Information

   Changes in common shareholders' equity should be provided for the last five years on items such as stock dividends, stock splits, rights issues and new stock issues.

   Such disclosure would allow users to convert share related ratios such as earnings per share, dividends per share and book value per share on a common denominator historically.

2. Analysis of Shareholdings

   Shareholders should be classified by type (i.e., individuals, financial institutions, pension funds, others) and number of shares owned (i.e., 1-100, 101-500, 501-1,000, etc.)

   Geographic distribution of shareholders would also be useful.

   If major changes have taken place in ownership, two years' comparative data would be useful.

   Shareholdings by the key officials and members of the board should also be provided along with any options granted to these individuals.

Shareholders by Number of Shares Owned on MM/DD/1988

Category	Number of Shareholders	Number of Shares	% of Capital
1- 1,000 sh	40,000	15,000,000	3
1,001- 5,000 sh	30,000	70,000,000	14
5,001-10,000 sh	3,000	30,000,000	6
10,001-	250	400,000,000	77
Total	73,250	515,000,000	100%

Shareholders by Type of Organization on MM/DD/1988

Category	Number of Shareholders	Number of Shares	% of Shares Outstanding
Individuals	xxx	xxx	x.x
Financial Institution	xx	xxx	x.x
Pension Funds	xx	xxx	x.x
Other Organizations	xx	xxx	x.x
Total	xxxx	xxxx	100%

Major Shareholders

Name	Number of Shares	%
Top xx Shareholders:		
A. ABC Company	xxx	x.x
B. Person (Director)	xxx	x.x
C. Case Society	xxx	x.x
Total for Top xx Shareholders	xxx	x.x
Other Directors' Shareholdings:		
F.	xxx	x.x
G.	xxx	x.x
H.	xxx	x.x
Total for Other Directors' Shareholdings	xxx	x.x
Total for Major Shareholders and Directors	xxx	x.x

3. Multiple Classes of Common Shares

In several countries (i.e., Belgium, Canada, Denmark, Italy, Sweden and Switzerland), multiple classes of common shares are allowed. Brief descriptions of each type of share, along with key items such as the number of shares outstanding, dividends per share, earnings per share (if different), as well as capital change information should be provided.

4. Capital Market Information

A list of stock exchanges (both domestic and foreign) where the company's securities are listed along with the appropriate ticker symbol would be useful.

Closing price for the year, high low for the last five years as well as monthly for the last six months, and the volume of shares traded should be reported.

Address and phone numbers of the company's share registrar and/or transfer agent would also be useful information for shareholders.

Stock Exchange(s) Listed: Stock Exchange 1; Ticker Symbol ABC

Principal Registrar or Transfer Agent: <Address 1, Phone 1>

Other Registrars or Transfer Agents <Address 2, Phone 2>

Recent Stock Prices

Closing, and High-Low Prices for Last 5 Years Common Stock - Stock Exchange-1					
	1988	1987*	1986*	1985*	1984*
Closing	xxx	xxx	xxx	xxx	xxx
High	xxx	xxx	xxx	xxx	xxx
Low	xxx	xxx	xxx	xxx	xxx
Volume	xxx	xxx	xxx	xxx	xxx

* Price has been adjusted by stock splits in 1984-87.

Closing, and High-Low Prices and Volume for Last 6 Months Common Stock - Stock Exchange-1						
1988	12	11	10	9	8	7
Closing	xxx	xxx	xxx	xxx	xxx	xxx
High	xxx	xxx	xxx	xxx	xxx	xxx
Low	xxx	xxx	xxx	xxx	xxx	xxx
Volume	xxx	xxx	xxx	xxx	xxx	xxx

These tables should be repeated for multiple shares, if they exist.

5. Financial Calendar

This item should include the following dates:

- Dividend Announcement Date
- Preliminary Results Announcement Date
- Annual General Meeting Date
- Interim Results Announcement Date

6. Availability of Additional Information About the Company

Any of the following items, if applicable, should be disclosed:

- A list of investment houses who follow the company and have issued reports on the company over the last 12 months.
- Name of Local Stock Exchange Authority or Securities and Exchange Commission where additional information about the company is on file and accessible to the public.
- Availability of a printed transcript (or audio cassette recording) of proceedings at Annual General Meeting of Shareholders.
- Availability of annual reports in different languages.
- Names of Investor Relations Executives with their addresses and phone numbers.

APPENDIX B

A GUIDE FOR PREPARING AN ANNUAL REPORT FOR A MULTINATIONAL COMMERCIAL BANK

INTRODUCTION

This appendix provides a suggested format for preparing the annual report of a multinational commercial bank. It is recommended that the reader should first review the information in the Introduction to the Appendices A, B and C before starting to read Appendix B.

The appendix includes an appropriate format for each section of the report. Where possible, descriptive or narrative comments have been avoided. In certain instances, descriptive comments are made to provide specific guidance. Readers are encouraged to consult local authorities concerning any areas for which further guidance is needed.

XYZ Bank

[inside of cover]

- Brief Description of Business
- Brief History
- Address of Headquarters

- The XYZ Bank was founded in 1900..... It has been listed on the xxx Stock Exchange since January 1, 1975.

The principal activity of the bank and its subsidiary and associated companies is to provide commercial banking and other financial services through 250 offices in 15 countries in Europe and North America.

Head Office
Address
Phone
Telex, Cable
Telefax

Table of Contents

1. Financial Summary

Five-Year Financial Summary						
Year Ending MM/DD		1988	1987	1986	1985	1984
(In Millions of Local Currency)						
Total Interest Income		xxx	xxx	xxx	xxx	xxx
Total Interest Expense		xxx	xxx	xxx	xxx	xxx
Net Interest Revenue		xxx	xxx	xxx	xxx	xxx
Provision for Possible Loan Losses		xxx	xxx	xxx	xxx	xxx
Operating Income		xxx	xxx	xxx	xxx	xxx
Income Before Extraordinary Item		xxx	xxx	xxx	xxx	xxx
Net Income Attributable to the Group		xxx	xxx	xxx	xxx	xxx
At MM/DD						
Loans and Due from Banks, Net		xxx	xxx	xxx	xxx	xxx
Total Investments		xxx	xxx	xxx	xxx	xxx
Adjusted Total Assets(*)		xxx	xxx	xxx	xxx	xxx
Deposits and Due to Banks		xxx	xxx	xxx	xxx	xxx
Interest Bearing Debt		xxx	xxx	xxx	xxx	xxx
Total Shareholders' Equity		xxx	xxx	xxx	xxx	xxx
Total Capital(**)		xxx	xxx	xxx	xxx	xxx
Number of Employees		xxx	xxx	xxx	xxx	xxx
Per Share Data						
Dividends per Share		x.x	x.x	x.x	x.x	x.x
Earnings per Share		x.x	x.x	x.x	x.x	x.x
Book Value per Share		x.x	x.x	x.x	x.x	x.x
Market Value per Share at MM/DD		x.x	x.x	x.x	x.x	x.x
Selected Ratios (%)***						
Rate of Return on Average:						
Adjusted Total Assets	1-g	x.xx	x.xx	x.xx	x.xx	x.xx
Common Shareholders' Equity	1-h	x.xx	x.xx	x.xx	x.xx	x.xx
Return on Earning Assets	1-i	x.xx	x.xx	x.xx	x.xx	x.xx
Interest Expense to Interest Bearing Liabilities	1-l	x.xx	x.xx	x.xx	x.xx	x.xx
Earning Assets to Adj. Total Assets	3-c	x.xx	x.xx	x.xx	x.xx	x.xx
Capital to Adjusted Total Assets	3-d	x.xx	x.xx	x.xx	x.xx	x.xx
Dividend Payout Ratio	4-b	x.xx	x.xx	x.xx	x.xx	x.xx
Reserve for Possible Loan Losses to Total Loans	1-k	x.xx	x.xx	x.xx	x.xx	x.xx
Net Charge-offs to Avg. Total Loans	1-j	x.xx	x.xx	x.xx	x.xx	x.xx

* Adjusted Total Assets equals total assets, excluding customers' liabilities for acceptances and guarantees.

** Total Capital is the sum of Long-Term Debt and Subordinated Debt, Minority Interests, and Total Shareholders' Equity

*** See details in Supplementary Information B

2. Group's Organization

May Include the Following:

- Provide a chart outlining the group's organization for important consolidated subsidiaries.

- Separate consolidated subsidiaries by business segment (i.e., commercial banking, investment banking, other financial services, etc.).

- Separate consolidated subsidiaries by geographic distribution.

- Specify ownership of the subsidiaries.

- Include unconsolidated companies if the non-consolidation is due to material differences in industry classification, and the unconsolidated companies are important to the group (e.g., oil company in banking group).

3. Key Executives and Board of Directors

Chairman President Directors	Variables: e.g.,	Name, Age, Years in the Office, Past and Present Relevant Functions, Re-election Date, Special Tasks, etc.

Senior Executives
Chief Accountant
Secretary

a. Board of Directors

. For each member of the board of the company, there should be further information about his affiliation, background in brief, length of time on the company's board and the expiration date of his term.

. Membership on each of the Board's committees should be clearly noted.

b. Senior Executives

Principal executive officers of the companies, including officers of the major divisions and subsidiaries, should be listed with title, age and length of time with the company.

4. Management Reports

   - Macroeconomic analysis by Chief Executive Officer (includes strategic planning for near future)

   - Detailed operating results by Finance Director

   This section usually reviews the company's activities grouped in the following sections:

   . A Letter from the President or Chief Executive

   . Overview of the Year

   . Macro Trends of the Marketplace

   . International Activities

   In addition, the management's financial review is provided. The review outlines the following:

   . Factors contributing to increase/decrease in key accounts such as revenues, earnings, total assets, loans, deposits, and shareholders' equity

   . Unusual financial items (such as discontinued operations, extraordinary gains/losses, disposal of assets, etc.)

   . Mergers/acquisitions undertaken during the year

   . Impact of broader economic events on the company's activities

5. Non-Financial Analysis of Major Subsidiaries and Sectors

   May Include the Following:

   - New Services

   - Major Activities

   - Labor Relations

   - Social Activities

6. Auditor's Report

Should include the following:

To Board of Directors and Shareholders:

- Scope
- Opinion
- Auditor's Signature
- Local Audit Firm and International Auditing Firm, if any
- Address of the Auditor
- Date

7. Financial Statements

XYZ Bank Consolidated Income Statement (For the Year Ending MM/DD/1988) (Millions of Local Currency)			
	Notes	1988	1987
Interest Income and Equivalents			
From Loans and Due from Banks		xxx	xxx
From Security Investments		xxx	xxx
Total Interest Income and Equivalents	15	xxxx	xxxx
Interest Expense			
For Amounts Due to Banks		xxx	xxx
For Deposits from Customers		xxx	xxx
For Interest Bearing Debt and Subordinated Loans		xxx	xxx
Total Interest Expenses		xxxx	xxxx
Net Interest Income		xxxx	xxxx
Provisions for Possible Loan Losses	3	(xx)	(xx)
Net Interest Income after Provisions for Possible Loan Losses		xxx	xxx
Commissions and Fees Received	16	xxx	xxx
Gain (Loss) on Foreign Exchange Transaction		xxx	xxx
Gain (Loss) on Trading Account Securities		xxx	xxx
Other Operating Income	17	xxx	xxx
		xxxx	xxxx
Other Operating Expenses	18	xxx	xxx
Operating Income		xxx	xxx
Non-Operating Expenses/Income, Net	19	xxx	xxx
		xxx	xxx
Income Taxes	20	xxx	xxx
Net Income Before Extraordinary Items and Minority Interest		xx	xx
Extraordinary Items (Net of Tax xxx)	21	xx	xx
Minority Interest		xx	xx
Net Income Attributable to the Group		xx	xx
Dividends Declared	22	xx	xx
Earnings Per Share:	23		
(Basic EPS)		xx.xx	xx.xx
(Fully Diluted EPS)		xx.xx	xx.xx

XYZ Bank
Consolidated Balance Sheet
(At MM/DD/1988)
(Millions of Local Currency)

	Notes	1988	1987
Assets			
Cash and Cash Equivalents	1	xxx	xxx
Deposits and Due from Banks		xxx	xxx
Loans and Advances to Customers		xxx	xxx
Total Loans and Due from Banks, Gross		xxxx	xxxx
Less Reserves for Possible Loan Losses		(xx)	(xx)
Total Loans and Due from Banks, Net	2,3	xxxx	xxxx
Trading Account Securities	4	xxx	xxx
Long-Term Investments	5	xxx	xxx
Investments in Unconsolidated Subsidiaries and Associated Companies	6	xxx	xxx
Property and Equipment	7	xxx	xxx
Intangible and Other Assets		xxx	xxx
Customers' Liabilities for Acceptances and Guarantees	8	xxx	xxx
Total Assets		xxxx	xxxx
Liabilities & Stockholders' Equity			
Deposits from Customers		xxx	xxx
Deposits and Due to Banks		xxx	xxx
Total Deposits and Due to Banks	9	xxxx	xxxx
Short-Term Interest-Bearing Debt	10	xxx	xxx
Other Liabilities	11	xxx	xxx
Acceptances and Guarantees	8	xxx	xxx
Long Term Interest-Bearing Debt	10	xxx	xxx
Subordinated Loans	12	xxx	xxx
Minority Interest		xxx	xxx
Total Liabilities		xxxx	xxxx
Preferred Stock	13	xxx	xxx
Common Stock	14	xxx	xxx
Additional Paid in Capital		xxx	xxx
Legal Reserves		xxx	xxx
Retained Earnings		xxx	xxx
Common Stock in Treasury, at Cost		(xx)	(xx)
Total Shareholders' Equity		xxxx	xxxx
Total Liabilities & Shareholders' Equity		xxxx	xxxx

XYZ Bank
Consolidated Statement of Changes in Financial Position
For the Year Ending MM/DD/1988)

(Millions of Local Currency)

	Notes	1988	1987
Funds Provided by			
Net Income		xxx	xxx
Addition (Reduction) of Non-Cash Items			
Depreciation and Amortization		xxx	xxx
Gain on Disposal of Fixed Assets		(xxx)	(xxx)
Minority Interest		xxx	xxx
Deferred Tax Charges		xxx	xxx
Funds provided by Operations		xxx	xxx
Sale of Fixed Assets		xxx	xxx
Sale of Long-Term Investments		xxx	xxx
Increase in Bonds		xxx	xxx
Increase in Capital Stock		xxx	xxx
Total Funds Provided		xxxx	xxxx
Funds Used For			
Acquisition of Fixed Assets		xxx	xxx
Repayment of Long-Term Debt		xxx	xxx
Total Funds Used		xxxx	xxxx
Net Increase (Decrease) in Funds		xx	xx
Net Increase (Decrease) in funds is represented by:			
Increase (Decrease) in Cash and Near Cash		xx	xx
Increase (Decrease) in Loans and Due from Bank		xx	xx
Increase (Decrease) in Trading Accounts		xx	xx
Decrease (Increase) in Deposits and Due to Bank		xx	xx
Decrease (Increase) in Short-Term Debt		xx	xx
Net Increase (Decrease) in Funds		xx	xx

XYZ Bank
Consolidated Statement of Changes in Shareholders' Equity
(For the Year Ending MM/DD/1988)

(Millions of Local Currency)

	1988	1987
Preferred Stocks		
Balance at Beginning of Year	xxx	xxx
Increase (Decrease) During the Year	xx	xx
Balance at End of Year	xxx	xxx
Common Stocks		
Balance at Beginning of Year	xxx	xxx
Increase (Decrease) 1	xx	xx
2	(xx)	(xx)
Balance at End of Year	xxx	xxx
Additional Paid-in Capital		
Balance at Beginning of Year	xxx	xxx
Increase (Decrease) from Preferred Stock	xxx	xxx
Increase (Decrease) from Common Stock	xxx	xxx
Balance at End of Year	xxx	xxx
Legal Reserves		
Balance at Beginning of Year	xxx	xxx
Increase (Decrease) During the Year	xxx	xxx
Balance at End of Year	xxx	xxx
Retained Earnings		
Balance at Beginning of Year	xxx	xxx
Dividends Declared	(xxx)	(xxx)
Net Income in the Year	xxx	xxx
Balance at End of Year	xxx	xxx
Common Stock in Treasury, at Cost		
Balance at Beginning of Year	xxx	xxx
Increase (Decrease) During the Year	xxx	xxx
Balance at End of Year	xxx	xxx
Total Shareholders' Equity	xxx	xxx

8. Major Accounting Policies

- This section outlines the basic accounting policies used for preparing financial statements.

- Many international users are familiar with key accounting concepts in their home country, but are not well versed in the accounting practices of other countries. This brief summary of local accounting standards used by the company should help international users in analyzing foreign company reports.

- The descriptions given for the following items illustrate policies which could be followed. A company's specific policy should be described in the report.

a. Basis of Presentation

The consolidated financial statements of the XYZ Bank are prepared in accordance with accounting principles prescribed by the regulations and related rules issued by the Regulatory Authorities and other prevailing practices of the banking industry. These regulations require the bank to carry its assets and liabilities on the historical cost basis and to follow the accrual method of accounting.

The accounting principles followed in determining net income conform in all material respects with accounting principles generally accepted in the home country except for (i) the deferral of gains and losses on the disposal of debt securities, (ii) the accounting for losses on loans and (iii) the translation of foreign currencies.

b. Basis of Consolidation

The consolidated financial statements include the assets and liabilities and results of operations of all subsidiaries after elimination of intercompany transactions and balances. The Bank accounts for the acquisition of subsidiaries using the purchase method; any difference between the cost of the investment and the fair value of assets acquired is amortized over appropriate periods varying from 5 to 25 years.

Investments in associated corporations (of which the bank owns between 20% and 50%) are accounted for using the equity method. The Bank's share of earnings of these associated corporations and gains and losses realized on dispositions of investments in associated corporations are included in income from securities investments.

c. Translation of Foreign Currencies

Assets, liabilities and operating results denominated in foreign currencies are translated into the home currency at the spot rate on the balance sheet date. The operating results denominated in foreign currencies for which transactions are concluded as a hedge against foreign exchange risks are translated at the rates of the relevant hedging contracts.

Foreign exchange differences are included in the Income Statement, with the exception of those differences arising from investments in foreign equity participations and branches, which are included in the foreign exchange translation differences under Reserves.

Forward exchange transactions related to funds borrowed and invested in light of Eurodeposit business are translated at the spot rate and the resultant balance is included in other assets or other liabilities. The corresponding swap results, which are determined by the difference between the spot rate and the forward rate on the date of closing these forward exchange contracts, are placed under the Income Statement.

The other forward exchange transactions are carried net in the balance sheet under Loans and Due from Banks, or they are included under Deposits and Due to Banks in the amount of the difference between the rate of the remaining term at the balance sheet date and the rate of the forward contract.

The 5 1/2% subordinated debentures in US dollars convertible into ordinary shares are, in accordance with the loan conditions, translated at an exchange rate of U.S. $x.xx to home currency 1.00.

d. Loans and Due from Banks

Loans and Due from Banks are the outstanding amount, net of unearned discount. Interest on non-discounted loans is generally recognized based upon the principal amount outstanding. Interest on discounted loans is recognized based on methods which generally approximate the interest method.

The accrual of interest ceases on commercial loans when principal or interest is past due 90 days or more and collateral is inadequate to cover principal and interest. The accrual of interest also ceases immediately if, in the opinion of the Management, full collection is doubtful. Interest accrued but not collected as of the date of placement on non-accrual status is reversed and charged against current income, unless fully collateralized. Subsequent cash payments received are either applied to the outstanding principal balance or recorded as interest income, depending upon Management's assessment of the ultimate collectibility of principal.

The reserves for possible loan losses are based upon analyses of the loan portfolio and reflect an amount which, in managements' judgment, is adequate to provide for potential losses. The analyses include management's consideration of such factors as economic conditions, loan portfolio characteristics, prior loan loss experience and results of periodic reviews of the portfolio. The reserve for possible loan losses is increased by charges to operations and reduced by charge-offs, net of recoveries.

e. Valuation of Investment Assets

- Trading Account Securities

Trading account securities are carried at market value. Trading account securities include debt securities and certain money market instruments held for trading purposes. Realized gains and losses on sales of trading account assets, and unrealized gains and losses on sales of trading account assets representing market value adjustments of the portfolio, are included in trading account profits and commissions.

- Long-Term Investments

Debt securities held for investment are carried at cost, reduced by the amortization of premium and increased by the accretion of discount, both computed by the straight-line method. Marketable equity securities are carried, as determined on an aggregate basis, at the lower of cost or market. The specific identification method is used to determine realized gains and losses on sales of investment securities which are reported under other operating revenue-investment securities gains (losses).

- Investments in Unconsolidated Subsidiaries and Associated Companies

Investments in unconsolidated subsidiaries and associated companies are carried on the basis of net asset value. Determination of the net asset value of subsidiaries not consolidated is effected so far as possible in accordance with the principles used in these financial statements.

Valuation differences other than exchange differences are accounted for in the Income Statement under other operating income.

Goodwill on the acquisition of investments in unconsolidated subsidiaries and associated companies, which is the difference between the purchase consideration and net asset value determined in accordance with the applicable bases of valuation, is charged directly to the general reserve.

f. Depreciation

The bank's office equipment is depreciated according to a special schedule. The difference between scheduled depreciation and depreciation for tax purposes is reported as an extra depreciation reserve. Bank premises are depreciated at the highest percentages permissible for tax purposes.

g. Special Reserves (If necessary under the country's regulations)

Untaxed Reserves

Swedish banks are allowed to make income tax-deductible appropriations to reserves for lending, bonds/interest rate risks and foreign currencies. Transfers between these untaxed reserves may be made via the profit and loss account. Current losses -- lending, bond and currency losses -- are charged directly to earnings. The untaxed reserves are thus purely a means of financial consolidation.

h. Income Taxes

The bank and its subsidiaries file a consolidated income tax return. The income taxes related to the individual entities are generally computed as if each one had filed a separate return.

Deferred income taxes are provided for revenue and expense items that are reported in different periods for financial reporting purposes as opposed to tax purposes.

i. Provision for Retirement Allowances

The provision for retirement allowances of the bank's employees are based upon the final pay system. All retirement allowances are covered and funded by means of annual level premiums from the time of recognition or the improvement of retirement allowances, to the retirement date. Post-retirement allowances are discounted on the basis of interest at 4% for active participants and 4 1/2% for pensioners.

Contributions by the Bank to the retirement fund are fixed annually at the sum needed by the fund to maintain its premium reserve at the level required to cover the aforementioned commitments. They are increased by an extra guarantee reserve.

j. Interest Rate Futures

The Bank uses interest rate futures contracts as part of its overall interest rate risk management strategy and in its securities trading operations. Outstanding financial futures contracts represent future commitments and are not included in the consolidated balance sheet. Gains and losses on the liquidation of futures contracts designated as hedges in the asset/liability management function are deferred and amortized over the life of the items hedged as an adjustment to interest income or interest expense. Futures contracts used in securities trading operations are adjusted to market value and the resulting gains and losses are recognized currently and included in other operating income.

k. Interest Rate Swaps

The bank takes trading positions for its interest rate swap transactions and in connection with its asset/liability management program. Interest rate swaps held as trading positions are carried at market value. Credit fees related to these interest rate swaps are separately identified and recorded as income over the term of the swap agreements. The net swap settlements on interest rate swap transactions entered into as part of the Bank's asset/liability management program are accrued as an adjustment of interest expense.

l. Changes in Accounting Principles

The bank changed to a scheduled depreciation method. Previously, a standard annual amount of 20 percent based on acquisition value was charged as depreciation expense. The new method means that depreciation expense for office equipment is lower in the current year than would have been reported according to the old standard.

9. Notes to the Financial Statements

Note 1. Cash and Cash Equivalents

- Elements to be included:

  - Coins, bank notes on hand
  - Balances or deposits with Central bank or regulatory banks
  - Other cash equivalents with high liquidity
  - Receivables in transit may be treated as cash equivalents

- May not need extra footnote for cash unless a certain item is significant

(Millions of Local Currency)

	1988	1987
Cash on Hand	xxx	xxx
Deposits with Central Bank	xxx	xxx
Receivables in Transit	xxx	xxx
	xxx	xxx

Note 2. Total Loans and Due from Banks

- Include deposits and due from banks and other financial institutions, money at call on short notice, as well as loans and advances to customers.

- Specify relationships between the total loans and due from banks and the reserves for possible loan losses.

[Example]

(Millions of Local Currency)

	1988		1987	
Deposits and Due from Banks		xxx		xxx
Consumer Loans				
Mortgage and Real Estate	xxx		xxx	
Installment and Other Consumer Loans	xxx	xxx	xxx	xxx
Commercial Loans				
Commercial and Industrial	xxx		xxx	
Mortgage and Real Estate	xxx		xxx	
Loans to Financial Institutions	xxx		xxx	
Government and Official Institutions	xxx	xxx	xxx	xxx
Total Loans and Due from Banks, Gross		xxxx		xxxx
Reserves for Possible Loan Losses (Note 3)		xxx		xxx
Total Loan and Due from Banks, Net		xxxx		xxxx

(Millions of Local Currency)

By Maturity	1988 -1 yr	1988 1-5 yr	1988 5 yr-	1988 Total	1987 -1 yr	1987 1-5 yr	1987 5 yr-	1987 Total
Deposits and Due from Banks	xx	xx	xx	xxx	xx	xx	xx	xxx
Consumer Loans	xx	xx	xx	xxx	xx	xx	xx	xxx
Commercial Loans	xx	xx	xx	xxx	xx	xx	xx	xxx
Total Loans and Due from Banks, Net	xxx	xxx	xxx	xxx	xxx	xxx	xxx	xxx

(Millions of Local Currency)

By Geographic Area	1988 Domestic	1988 Foreign	1988 Total	1987 Domestic	1987 Foreign	1987 Total
Deposits and Due from Banks	xx	xx	xxx	xx	xx	xxx
Consumer Loans						
Mortgage and Real Estate	xx	xx	xxx	xx	xx	xxx
Installment and Other	xx	xx	xxx	xx	xx	xxx
Commercial Loans						
Commercial and Industrial	xx	xx	xxx	xx	xx	xxx
Mortgage and Real Estate	xx	xx	xxx	xx	xx	xxx
Financial Institutions	xx	xx	xxx	xx	xx	xxx
Government and Official Institutions	xx	xx	xxx	xx	xx	xxx
Total Loans and Due from Banks, Net	xxx	xxx	xxxx	xxx	xxx	xxxx
By Origination						
From Domestic Office			xxx			xxx
From Foreign Office			xxx			xxx
Total Loans and Due from Banks			xxxx			xxx
By Currency Denominated						
In Local Currency			xxx			xxx
In Foreign Currencies			xxx			xxx
Total Loans and Due from Banks			xxxx			xxxx
Of Which, Non-performing Loans (Net of Provision)						
Domestic Loans			xxx			xxx
Foreign Loans			xxx			xxx
Total Loans and Due from Banks			xxxx			xxxx

Note 3. <u>Reserves for Possible Loan Losses</u>

(Millions of Local Currency)

	1988		1987	
Balance at Beginning of Year		xxx		xxx
Deductions (Net of Recovery)				
Deposits and Due from Banks	xx		xx	
Consumer Loans	xx		xx	
Commercial Loans	xx	xx	xx	xx
Total Amount before Additions		xxx		xxx
Additions:				
Provisions for Possible Loan Losses*		xxx		xxx
Balance at End of Year		xxx		xxx

*<u>Provisions for Possible Loan Losses</u>

(Millions of Local Currency)

	1988		1987	
Deposits and Due from Banks		xx		xx
Consumer Loans				
Mortgage and Real Estate	xx		xx	
Installment and Other Consumer Loans	xx	xx	xx	xx
Commercial Loans				
Commercial and Industrial	xx		xx	
Mortgage and Real Estate	xx		xx	
Loans to Financial Institutions	xx		xx	
Government and Official Institutions	xx	xx	xx	xx
Total Provisions for Possible Loan Losses		xxx		xxx
Specific Provisions		xx		xx
General Provisions		xx		xx
Total Amounts		xxx		xxx

Note 4. Trading Account Securities

- Valuation method used is ABC method. The market value method is not used, but may be disclosed by the date of fiscal year-end.

- Foreign exchange for Short-Term investment purposes should be included here.

(Millions of Local Currency)

	1988	1987
Listed		
- in domestic market	XX	XX
- in foreign market	XX	XX
	XXX	XXX
Unlisted	XXX	XXX
Total Trading Account Securities	XXX	XXX

Note 5. Long-Term Investments

(Millions of Local Currency)

	1988	1987
Government and Municipal Bonds	XX	XX
Corporate Bonds	XX	XX
Stocks and Shares	XX	XX
Other Investments	XX	XX
Total Long-Term Investments	XXX	XXX

	1988		1987	
	Book Value	Market Value	Book Value	Market Value
Listed				
- on domestic market	XX	XX	XX	XX
- on foreign market	XX	XX	XX	XX
Total Listed Securities	XXX	XXX	XXX	XXX
Unlisted	XXX	XXX	XXX	XXX
Total Listed and Unlisted Securities	XXX	XXX	XXX	XXX

Note 6. Investments in Unconsolidated Subsidiaries and Associated Companies

- Valuation method for specific investments is disclosed, if significant.

(Millions of Local Currency)

	1988		1987	
	Book Value	Valuation	Book Value	Valuation
Unconsolidated Subsidiary				
Listed	xx	xx	xx	xx
Unlisted	xx	xx	xx	xx
Associated Companies				
Listed	xx	xx	xx	xx
Unlisted	xx	xx	xx	xx
Total	xxx	xxx	xxx	xxx

List of Companies disclosed at page xx

Note 7. Property and Equipment

(Millions of Local Currency)

	1988	1987
Premises, Sites and Leasehold Improvement		
Balance at Beginning of Year	xxx	xxx
Adjustments*	xx	xx
Beginning Balance after Adjustments	xxx	xxx
Less Depreciation, Amortization for the Year	(xx)	(xx)
Balance at End of Year	xxx	xxx
Accumulated Depreciation	xxx	xxx
Estimated Market Value	xxx	xxx
Furniture and Equipment		
Balance at Beginning of Year	xxx	xxx
Adjustments*	xx	xx
Beginning Balance after Adjustments	xxx	xxx
Less Depreciation, Amortization for the Year	(xx)	(xx)
Balance at End of Year	xxx	xxx
Accumulated Depreciation	xxx	xxx
Estimated Market Value	xxx	xxx
Total Property and Equipment at end of year	xxx	xxx

* Adjustments may include "Adjustments for exchange rate fluctuations", "Revaluations", or "Additions or disposals during the year".

Note 8. <u>Customers' Liabilities for Acceptances and Guarantees</u>

- All commitments and contingent liabilities of a material nature may be included here.

  (Examples)

  <u>Acceptances</u>

  . Fiduciary Investments
  . Endorsement Liabilities from Re-discountings
  . Leasing Commitments
  . Commitments Arising from Fixed Forward Transactions
  . Confirmed Lines of Credit
  . Other Commitments

  <u>Letters of Credit</u>

  . Commitments Arising from Letters of Credit

  <u>Guarantees</u>

  . Aval, Surety and Guarantee Liabilities
  . Guarantees on Behalf of Other Financial Institutions
  . Guarantees on Behalf of Customers
  . Other Guarantees

- If any isolated item is significant and able to be broken down, or any other item is appropriate to be included, they may be included.

- If any item is regulated by special regulation(s), the regulation(s) should be explained.

(Millions of Local Currency)

	1988	1987
Acceptances	XXX	XXX
Letters of Credit	XXX	XXX
Guarantees	XXX	XXX
Total Customers' Liability for Acceptance and Guarantees	XXX	XXX

Note 9. Total Deposits and Due to Banks

(Millions of Local Currency)

	1988		1987	
Due to Banks				
Due to Banks on Demand	xx		xx	
Due to Banks at Fixed Dates	xx	xxx	xx	xxx
Deposits from Customers				
Demand Deposits	xx		xx	
Savings Deposits	xx		xx	
Time Deposits	xx		xx	
Other Deposits	xx	xxx	xx	xxx
Total Deposits and Due to Banks		xxx		xxx
By Geographical Area:				
Due to Banks				
Domestic	xx		xx	
Country 1	xx		xx	
Country 2	xx		xx	
Other Countries	xx	xxx	xx	xxx
Deposits from Customers				
Domestic	xx		xx	
Country 1	xx		xx	
Country 2	xx		xx	
Other Countries	xx	xxx	xx	xxx
Total Deposits and Due to Banks		xxx		xxx
By Currency Denominated:				
Domestic Currency		xx		xx
Foreign Currencies		xx		xx
Total Deposits and Due to Banks		xxx		xxx

Note 10. <u>Interest-Bearing Debt</u>

(Millions of Local Currency)

	1988				1987
	< 1yr- 1 yr	1-5 yr	5 yr - > 5 yr	Total	Total
Bank Debentures (1)	xx	xx	xx	xxx	xxx
Bond Issues (2)	xx	xx	xx	xxx	xxx
Total	xxx	xxx	xxx	xxx	xxx

1. Bank Debentures

Issues	Due	Amount
Issue 1 (Interest rate, callable features, if any)	mm/dd/yy	xxx
etc.		
Total Bank Debentures		xxx

2. Bond Issues

Issues	Due	Amount
Issue A (Interest rate, callable features, if any)	mm/dd/yy	xxx
etc.		
Total Bond Issues		xxx

Note 11. <u>Other Liabilities</u>

(Millions of Local Currency)

	1988	1987
<u>Current Liabilities:</u>		
Interest Payable	xx	xx
Dividend Payable	xx	xx
Current Taxation	xx	xx
Other Current Liabilities	xx	xx
Total Current Liabilities	xxx	xxx
<u>Non-Current Liabilities:</u>		
Deferred Taxation	xx	xx
Provision for Retirement Allowances	xx	xx
Total Non-Current Liabilities	xxx	xxx
Total Current and Non-Current Liabilities	xxx	xxx

Note 12. Subordinated Loans

(Millions of Local Currency)

	1988	1987
Subordinated Notes (8 1/2% interest, No date)	xx	xx
Loan Capital (6 1/2%....) (Subordinated Capital Notes)	xx	xx
Total Subordinated Loans	xxx	xxx

Note 13. Preferred Stocks

(Millions of Local Currency)

	1988	1987
Redeemable Preferred Stock		
Redeemable Preferred A, 8%	xx	xx
Redeemable Preferred B, 7%, Convertible	xx	xx
Total Redeemable Preferred Stock	xxx	xxx
Unredeemable Preferred Stock		
Name 1	xx	xx
Name 2	xx	xx
Total Unredeemable Preferred Stock	xxx	xxx
Total Preferred Stock	xxx	xxx

Note 14. Common Stocks

- If additional stock is issued during the year, the issues may be explained here.

(Millions of Local Currency)

	1988	1987
Authorized Capital (xxx shares, x.x in par)	xxx	xxx
Common Stocks Issued		
Balance at Beginning of Year (number of shares issued)	xxx	xxx
Conversion of Convertible Debenture (number of shares)	xx	xx
Exercising Option by Executives (number of shares)	xx	xx
New Issue (number of shares)	xx	-
Balance at End of Year (number of shares)	xxx	xxx

* Common Stock in Treasury could be entered here.

Note 15. Total Interest Income and its Equivalents

(Millions of Local Currency)

	1988		1987	
Interest Income From:				
Deposits and Due from Banks		xxx		xxx
Consumer Loans				
Mortgage and Real Estate	xx		xx	
Installment and Other Consumer Loans	xx	xxx	xx	xxx
Commercial Loans				
Commercial and Industrial	xx		xx	
Mortgage and Real Estate	xx		xx	
Loans to Financial Institutions	xx		xx	
Government and Official Institutions	xx	xxx	xx	xxx
Total Interest Income From Loans and Due from Banks		xxx		xxx
Interest Income from Fixed Income Securities Investment		xx		xx
Dividends Received from Equity Securities Investment		xx		xx
Total Interest Income and its Equivalents		xxx		xxx

Note 16. Commissions and Fees Received

- May include Commissions and Fees Received in Gross

(Millions of Local Currency)

	1988	1987
Trust Fees	xx	xx
Fees on Checking Accounts	xx	xx
Fees on Letter of Credit Services	xx	xx
Total Commissions and Fees Received	xxx	xxx

Note 17. Other Operating Income

- Capital gains on disposal of investments
- Equity earnings on unconsolidated subsidiaries and associated companies

(Millions of Local Currency)

	1988	1987
Capital Gain (Loss) on Disposal of Investment Assets	xx	xx
Equity Earnings on Unconsolidated Subsidiary and Associated Companies	xx	xx
Income from Insurance Brokerage	xx	xx
Sundry Operating Income	xx	xx
Total Other Operating Income	xxx	xxx

Note 18. Other Operating Expenses

(Millions of Local Currency)

	1988	1987
Salaries and other Personnel Expenses (*)	xx	xx
Depreciation and Amortization (Note 7)	xx	xx
Indirect Taxes (other than income taxes)	xx	xx
Commissions and Fees Paid	xx	xx
Sundry Operating Expenses	xx	xx
Total Other Operating Expenses	xxx	xxx

* Number of Employees

	1988		1987	
Domestic				
Foreign		xxx		xxx
North America	xxx		xxx	
Europe	xxx		xxx	
Asia	xxx		xxx	
Other Area	xxx	xxx	xxx	xxx
Total Number of Employees at Year-End		xxx		xxx
Full-Time		xxx		xxx
Full-Time Equivalents of Part-Time		xx		xx
Total Full-Time Equivalents		xxx		xxx

Note 19. Non-Operating Expenses/Income, Net

(Millions of Local Currency)

	1988	1987
Non-Operating Income:		
Gain on Sale of Fixed Assets	xx	xx
Item 2	xx	xx
Total Non-Operating Income	xx	xx
Non-Operating Expenses:		
Loss on Sale of Fixed Assets	xx	xx
Item 2	xx	xx
Total Non-Operating Expenses	xx	xx
Non-Operating Expenses/Income, Net	xx	xx

Note 20. Income Tax Expense

(Millions of Local Currency)

	1988	1987
Current Income Taxes	xx	xx
Deferred Income Taxes	xx	xx
Total Income Tax Expense	xxx	xxx

Note 21. Extraordinary Items (Net of taxes)

(Millions of Local Currency)

	1988	1987
Gain or Loss on Disposal of Fixed Assets (net of tax xxx)	xxx	
Provision Reserves for Possible Losses (Net of tax xxx)	xxx	
Changes in Regulation (Net of tax xxx)		xxx
Total Extraordinary Items (Net of tax xxx in 1988, xxx in 1987)	xxx	xxx

Note 22. Dividends Declared

	1988		1987	
	Per Share	Millions of Local Currency	Per Share	Millions of Local Currency
Preferred Shares:				
Preferred Share A	x.x	xx	x.x	xx
Preferred Share B				
Interim	x.x	xx	x.x	xx
Final	x.x	xx	x.x	xx
Total Amount	x.x	xx	x.x	xx
Common Shares:				
Interim	x.x	xx	x.x	xx
Final	x.x	xx	x.x	xx
Total Amount	x.x	xx	x.x	xx
Total Dividends Declared		xxx		xxx

Note 23. Earnings per Share

	1988	1987
Basic EPS		
Net Income Attributable to Group xx and weighted average xxx Common Stocks in issue during 1988	x.x	
Net Income Attributable to Group xxx and weighted average xxxx Common Stocks in issue during 1987		x.x
Fully Diluted		
(Earnings xxx and xxxx Shares in 1988)	x.x	
(Earnings xxx and xxxx shares in 1987)		x.x

Note 24. Contingent Liabilities

- Litigation on pending lawsuits

- Contingent liabilities not from operating activities which are not quantified contra items in the Customers' Liabilities for Acceptances

- Contra items in the Customers' Liabilities for Acceptances and Guarantees

Example:

The Company has guaranteed approximately __, (in millions of local currency), for the obligations of others, made with other responsible companies in the ordinary course of business. If these companies are unable to meet certain obligations, the Company may be required to advance funds against future charges. No material loss is anticipated under these guarantees.

The Company and its subsidiaries are engaged in litigation and have a number of unresolved claims pending. While the amounts claimed are substantial and the ultimate liability in respect of such litigation and claims cannot be determined at this time, the company is of the opinion that such liability, to the extent not provided for through insurance or otherwise, is not likely to be of material importance in relation to its accounts.

The Company has provided in its accounts for items and issues not yet resolved based on management's best judgment.

Note 25. Subsequent Events

All key events occurring between the year end-date and the date of the annual report which have an impact on the financial data or further viability of the firm should be disclosed.

A note such as "no events with material financial consequences have occurred since the year-end date of the report" would also be appropriate.

Example:

On ______, the company acquired all of the outstanding common stock of XYZ Company. The cost of the acquisition was approximately ___ and will be accounted for as a purchase. Results of XYZ Company will be included in the Consolidated Statement of Earnings from the date of acquisition. XYZ company had total assets of ____ million and net earnings from continuing operations of ___ for the 12 months at last year-end. XYZ Company had total shareowners' equity of ____ million at last year-end.

The following summarizes the unaudited pro forma combined results of operations adjusted for the amortization of estimated excess purchase price and interest on debt in connection with the acquisition. It is stated as though the acquisition had occurred at the beginning of the company's current fiscal year.

Net Earnings	_____
Net Earnings Per Share	_____
Total Assets	_____
Total Shareowners' Equity	_____

The unaudited pro forma financial information is not necessarily indicative of the results of operations that would have occurred had the two companies actually been combined during the period presented. Pro forma information does not indicate the future results of operations of the combined companies.

Note 26. Pending Accounting Changes

This note should disclose an explanation of the changes in accounting standards, date of implementation, and the potential impact on the company's financial statements.

X Y Z Bank

Supplementary Information A

Operating Results by Segment and Geographic Area

1. Results by Business Segment

   - For diversified companies, key financial indicators (such as total revenues, assets employed and operating profit) should be disclosed by business segment.

   - A brief definition (i.e., which major product lines or divisions are included) should be provided for each business segment.

   - Inter-company transactions should be eliminated.

   - Capital expenditures and depreciation by segment would also be useful to investors.

2. Results by Geographic Area

   The company should also provide key financial variables (such as total revenues, assets employed and operating profit) by geographic area.

   Several options can be explored to decide geographic classification.

   a. Define geographic areas along conventional geographic lines (i.e., North America, South America, Europe, Asia, Africa, and Australia/New Zealand).

   b. Provide results by country, if the company has significant operations in a few countries, and combine other small operations as other foreign business.

   c. Mix key countries and regions.

   Inter-area transfers should be eliminated.

   Companies operating in several business segments in several international regions may want to combine their segment and geographic disclosures into one table.

Supplementary Information B

Selected Financial Ratios

1. Profitability Ratios

   a. Gross Operating Margin = Operating Income divided by Total Revenue

      Total Revenue = Total Interest and Investment Income and its Equivalents + Commission and Fees Received + Gains (Losses) on Foreign Exchange Transactions + Gains (Losses) on Trading Account Securities + Other Operating Income

   b. Pre-Tax Income Margin = Pre-Tax Income divided by Total Revenue

   c. Net Income Margin = Net Income divided by Total Revenue

   d. Total Revenue Growth = (Total Revenue This Year - Total Revenue Last Year) divided by Total Revenue Last Year

   e. Net Income Growth = (Net Income This Year - Net Income Last Year) divided by Net Income Last Year

   f. Total Revenue per Employee = Total Revenue divided by Total Employees

   g. Return on Average Total Assets = Net Income divided by Average Adjusted Total Assets

   h. Return on Average Common Shareholders' Equity = Net Income divided by Average Shareholders' Equity

   i. Return on Earning Assets = Income from Earning Assets divided by Average Earning Assets

      Income from Earning Assets = Interest Income and its Equivalents + Gain (Losses) on Foreign Exchange Transactions + Gains(Losses) on Trading Account Securities - Provision for Possible Loan Losses

      Earning Assets = Total Loans and Due from Banks, Net + Trading Account Securities and Long-Term Investments

   j. Net Charge-offs to Average Total Loans = Actual Loan Losses divided by Average Total Loans and Due from Banks, Gross

   k. Reserve for Possible Loan Losses to Total Loans = Reserve for Possible Loan Losses divided by Total Loans and Due from Banks, Gross

l. Interest Expenses to Interest-Bearing Liabilities = Total Interest Expenses divided by Average Interest-Bearing Liabilities

Interest-Bearing Liabilities = Total Deposits and Due to Banks + Short-Term and Long-Term Interest-Bearing Debt + Subordinated Loans

Dividends on redeemable preferred stock may be added to the numerator, and redeemable preferred stock may be added to the denominator.

2. Asset Utilization Ratios

   a. Asset Utilization = Total Revenue divided by Average Total Assets

   b. Assets per Employee = Total Assets divided by Total Employees

3. Leverage Ratios

   a. Debt to Assets = Total Debt divided by Total Assets

   b. Debt to Equity = Total Debt divided by Total Shareholders' Equity

   c. Earning Assets to Adjusted Total Assets = Earning Assets divided by Adjusted Total Assets

   d. Capital to Adjusted Total Assets = Total Capital divided by Adjusted Total Assets

   e. Total Loans to Total Deposits = Total Loans divided by Total Deposits

   f. Total Earning Assets to Total Interest-Bearing Liabilities = Total Earning Assets divided by Total Interest-Bearing Liabilities

4. Capital Market-Related Ratios

   a. Dividend Yield = Dividend Per Share divided by Market Price Per Share

   b. Dividend Payout = Total Dividend divided by Net Income

   c. Total Shareholders' Return = (End of Year Stock Price - Beginning of Year Stock Price + Dividend Paid During the Year) divided by Beginning of Year Stock Price

   d. Price to Earnings = Market Price Per Share divided by Earnings Per Share

   e. Price to Book = Market Price Per Share divided by Book Value Per Share

f. Dividend Growth = (Dividend Per Share This Year - Dividend Per Share Last Year) divided by Dividend Per Share Last Year

g. Net Worth Growth = (Net Worth Per Share This Year - Net Worth Per Share Last Year) divided by Net Worth Per Share Last Year

h. Cash Dividend Coverage = Net Income Available to Common Shareholders divided by Dividends Paid This Year

5. International Business-Related Ratios

a. Foreign Total Revenues as % of Total Worldwide Revenues

b. Foreign Operating Income as % of Total Worldwide Operating Income

c. Foreign Assets as % of Total Worldwide Assets

Supplementary Information C

Analysis of Loans and Due from Banks

(Millions of Local Currency)

	1988			1987		
	Average Balance	Interest Income	Yield (%)	Average Balance	Interest Income	Yield (%)
Deposits and Due from Banks	XXX	XX	X.X	XXX	XX	X.X
Consumer Loans:	XXX	XX	X.X	XXX	XX	X.X
Mortgage and Real Estate	XXX	XX	X.X	XXX	XX	X.X
Installment and Others	XXX	XX	X.X	XXX	XX	X.X
Domestic	XXX	XX	X.X	XXX	XX	X.X
Foreign	XXX	XX	X.X	XXX	XX	X.X
Total Consumer Loans	XXX	XX	X.X	XXX	XX	X.X
Commercial Loans	XXX	XX	X.X	XXX	XX	X.X
Commercial and Industrial	XXX	XX	X.X	XXX	XX	X.X
Mortgage and Real Estate	XXX	XX	X.X	XXX	XX	X.X
Financial Institutions	XXX	XX	X.X	XXX	XX	X.X
Government and Official Institutions	XXX	XX	X.X	XXX	XX	X.X
Domestic	XXX	XX	X.X	XXX	XX	X.X
Foreign	XXX	XX	X.X	XXX	XX	X.X
Total Commercial Loans	XXX	XX	X.X	XXX	XX	X.X
Total Loans and Due from Banks	XXXX	XXX	X.X	XXXX	XX	X.X

Supplementary Information D

Analysis of Earning Assets

(Millions of Local Currency)

	1988			1987		
	Average Balance	Interest Income	Yield (%)	Average Balance	Interest Income	Yield (%)
Total Loans and Due from Banks	XXXX	XX	X.X	XXXX	XX	X.X
Trading Account Securities	XXX	XX	X.X	XXX	XX	X.X
Long-Term Investments	XXX	XX	X.X	XXX	XX	X.X
Investments in Unconsolidated Subsidiary and Associated Co.	XXX	XX	X.X	XXX	XX	X.X
Total Earning Assets	XXXX	XXX	X.X	XXXX	XXX	X.X

Supplementary Information E

Analysis of Interest-Bearing Liabilities

(Millions of Local Currency)

	1988			1987		
	Average Balance	Interest Income	%	Average Balance	Interest Income	%
Due to Banks	xxx	xx	x.x	xxx	xx	x.x
Deposits from Customers						
Demand Deposits	xxx	xx	x.x	xxx	xx	x.x
Savings Deposits	xxx	xx	x.x	xxx	xx	x.x
Time Deposits	xxx	xx	x.x	xxx	xx	x.x
Other Deposits	xxx	xx	x.x	xxx	xx	x.x
Domestic	xxx	xx	x.x	xxx	xx	x.x
Foreign	xxx	xx	x.x	xxx	xx	x.x
Total Deposits and Due to Banks	xxxx	xxx	x.x	xxxx	xxx	x.x
Short-Term Debt	xxx	xx	x.x	xxx	xx	x.x
Long-Term Debt	xxx	xx	x.x	xxx	xx	x.x
Subordinated Loans	xxx	xx	x.x	xxx	xx	x.x
Domestic	xxx	xx	x.x	xxx	xx	x.x
Foreign	xxx	xx	x.x	xxx	xx	x.x
Total Interest-Bearing Debt	xxxx	xxx	x.x	xxxx	xxx	x.x
Domestic	xxx	xx	x.x	xxx	xx	x.x
Foreign	xxx	xx	x.x	xxx	xx	x.x
Total Interest-Bearing Liabilities	xxxx	xxx	x.x	xxxx	xx	x.x
Redeemable Preferred Stock	xxx	xx	x.x	xxx	xx	x.x

Supplementary Information F

Analysis of Capital Requirement

a. Conventional Capital

Long-Term Debt, Minority Interests, Preferred Stock and Common Shareholders' Equity.

(Millions of Local Currency)

Components of Conventional Capital	1988	1987	% Change
Long-Term Debt	xxx	xxx	x.x
Minority Interest	xxx	xxx	x.x
Preferred Stock	xxx	xxx	x.x
Common Shareholders' Equity	xxx	xxx	x.x
Total Conventional Capital	xxx	xxx	x.x

b. Primary Capital

Qualified Long-Term Debt, Minority Interests, Preferred Stocks and Common Shareholders' Equity

Qualified long-term debt is classified as such under the Capital Adequacy Guidelines of the Federal Reserve Board if it matures within twelve years and is mandatorily convertible to equity or if it includes a commitment to redeem the debt through a subsequent issuance of common or perpetual preferred stock. (These guidelines are required in the US only, although they provide useful information.)

(Millions of Local Currency)

Components of Primary Capital	1988	1987	% Change
Qualified Long-Term Debt	xxx	xxx	x.x
Minority Interests	xxx	xxx	x.x
Qualified Preferred Stocks	xxx	xxx	x.x
Common Shareholders' Equity	xxx	xxx	x.x
Total Primary Capital	xxx	xxx	x.x

Supplementary Information G

Quarterly Selected Financial Data

(Millions of Local Currency)

	1988				1987			
	4th	3rd	2nd	1st	4th	3rd	2nd	1st
Total Interest Income and its Equivalents	xxx	xxx	xxx	xxx	xxx	xxx	xxx	xxx
Total Interest Expenses	xxx	xxx	xxx	xxx	xxx	xxx	xxx	xxx
Provision for Possible Loan Losses	xx	xx	xx	xx	xx	xx	xx	xx
Net Interest Income	xxx	xxx	xxx	xxx	xxx	xxx	xxx	xxx
Other Operating Income	xxx	xxx	xxx	xxx	xxx	xxx	xxx	xxx
Other Operating Expenses	xxx	xxx	xxx	xxx	xxx	xxx	xxx	xxx
Operating Income	xxx	xxx	xxx	xxx	xxx	xxx	xxx	xxx
Income Taxes	xxx	xxx	xxx	xxx	xxx	xxx	xxx	xxx
Net Income	xx	xx	xx	xx	xx	xx	xx	xx
Earnings Per Share	x.xx	x.xx	x.xx	x.xx	x.xx	x.xx	x.xx	x.xx
Total Loans & Due from Banks, Net	xxx	xxx	xxx	xxx	xxx	xxx	xxx	xxx
Total Investments	xxx	xxx	xxx	xxx	xxx	xxx	xxx	xxx
Total Assets	xxx	xxx	xxx	xxx	xxx	xxx	xxx	xxx
Cash Dividends Declared	x.xx	x.xx	x.xx	x.xx	x.xx	x.xx	x.xx	x.xx

X Y Z Bank

Supplementary Information H

Selected Financial Data Adjusted for Changes in General Price Level

(Millions of Local Currency)

	1988	1987	1986	1985	1984
Net Interest Income					
As Reported	XXX	XXX	XXX	XXX	XXX
Adjusted	XXX	XXX	XXX	XXX	XXX
Operating Income					
As Reported	XXX	XXX	XXX	XXX	XXX
Adjusted	XXX	XXX	XXX	XXX	XXX
Net Income					
As Reported	XXX	XXX	XXX	XXX	XXX
Adjusted	XXX	XXX	XXX	XXX	XXX
Total Assets					
As Reported	XXX	XXX	XXX	XXX	XXX
Adjusted	XXX	XXX	XXX	XXX	XXX
<u>Per Share Data:</u>					
Earnings					
As Reported	X.XX	X.XX	X.XX	X.XX	X.XX
Adjusted	X.XX	X.XX	X.XX	X.XX	X.XX
Dividends					
As Reported	X.XX	X.XX	X.XX	X.XX	X.XX
Adjusted	X.XX	X.XX	X.XX	X.XX	X.XX
Price Index*	XXX	XXX	XXX	XXX	XXX

*Explain the Price Index Used

Supplementary Information I

Selected Financial Data for Major Subsidiaries

- Parent Bank: Condensed Balance Sheet and Income Statement
- Major Subsidiaries: Selected Financial Data, Address, Phone, Fax, Telex, Major Business Area, % of Ownership
- Unconsolidated Subsidiaries: Majority Owned and Significant to the Group; Selected Financial Data, Address, Phone, Fax, Telex, Major Business Area, % of Ownership

1. XYZ Bank (Parent Bank Only)

XYZ Bank
Condensed Balance Sheet
(Parent Bank Only)

(Millions of Local Currency)

	1988	1987
Assets		
Cash and its Equivalents	xxx	xxx
Deposits and Due from Banks	xxx	xxx
Loans and Advances to Customers	xxx	xxx
Total Loans and Due from Banks	xxx	xxx
Reserves for Possible Loan Losses	xx	xx
Net Loans and Due from Banks	xxx	xxx
Investment Assets	xxx	xxx
Investment in Subsidiary Companies	xxx	xxx
Other Assets	xxx	xxx
Customers' Acceptances and Guarantees	xxx	xxx
Total Assets	xxxx	xxxx
Liabilities and Shareholders' Equity		
Deposits from Customers	xxx	xxx
Deposits and Due to Banks	xxx	xxx
Total Interest-Bearing Debt	xxx	xxx
Other Liabilities	xxx	xxx
Acceptances and Guarantees	xxx	xxx
Total Liabilities	xxx	xxx
Shareholders' Equity	xxx	xxx
Total Liabilities and Shareholders' Equity	xxxx	xxxx

XYZ Bank
Condensed Income Statement
(Parent Bank Only)

(Millions of Local Currency)

	1988	1987
Interest Income from Customers	xxx	xxx
Interest Income from Subsidiaries	xxx	xxx
Total Interest Income and Equivalents	xxx	xxx
Interest Expense		
On Due to Banks	xxx	xxx
On Deposits from Customers	xxx	xxx
On Debt and Subordinated Loans	xxx	xxx
Total Interest Expenses	xxx	xxx
Net Interest Income	xxx	xxx
Provision for Possible Loan Losses	xxx	xxx
Net Interest Income after Provision for Possible Loan Losses	xxx	xxx
Other Operating Income	xxx	xxx
Other Operating Expenses	xxx	xxx
Operating Income	xxx	xxx
Non-Operating Expense/Revenue	xx	xx
	xxx	xxx
Income Taxes	xx	xx
Income before Extraordinary Items	xxx	xxx
Extraordinary Items	xx	xx
Net Income	xx	xx

Major Subsidiaries

2. XYZA Bank

XYZ Bank Group's Holdings: 100%
Address, Phone, Fax, Telex, Major Business Area

(Millions of Local Currency)

	1988	1987
Total Loans	xxx	xxx
Total Investments	xxx	xxx
Total Assets	xxx	xxx
Total Deposits and Due to Banks	xxx	xxx
Shareholders' Equity	xxx	xxx
Total Revenue	xxx	xxx
Operating Income	xxx	xxx
Net Income	xxx	xxx
Dividends Paid	xx	xx
EPS	x.x	x.x

3. XYZL Bank

XYZ Bank Group's Holdings: 90%
Address, Phone, Fax, Telex, Major Business Area

(Millions of Local Currency)

	1988	1987
Total Loans	xxx	xxx
Total Investments	xxx	xxx
Total Assets	xxx	xxx
Total Deposits and Due to Banks	xxx	xxx
Shareholders' Equity	xxx	xxx
Total Revenue	xxx	xxx
Operating Income	xxx	xxx
Net Income	xx	xx
Dividends Paid	xx	xx
EPS	x.x	x.x

Consolidated subsidiaries which are not significant to the group's operating results, may disclose only significant information.

- Address, Phone, Fax, Telex, Major Business
- % of Ownership
- Total Assets, Total Revenue, Net Income, and Contributions to the Group.

[Example]

	Total Assets	Total Revenue	Net Income	Contributions To Group
XYZR Financial Services Address, Phone, Fax, Telex, 100% Owned	XXX	XXX	XX	XX

<u>Associated Companies</u>

Name	Address, Phone, Fax Telex	% of Ownership	Total Assets	Purchase Price	Estimated Market Value
XYZP		45%	XXX	XXX	XXX
XYZQ		40%	XXX	XXX	XXX
XYZR		25%	XXX	XXX	XXX

<u>Other Long-Term Investment</u>

Name (Country)	Purchase Price	Estimated Market Value
XYZS Company (France)	XXX	XXX
XYZT Company (U.S.)	XXX	XXX

Supplementary Information J

Major Branches and Offices

- Domestic Branches and Offices
  - Responsible Person
  - Address, Phone, Fax, Telex

- Foreign Branches and Offices
  - Responsible Person
  - Address, Phone, Fax, Telex

Supplementary Information K

Shareholder-Related Information

In this section, items pertaining to common shares and shareholders are covered:

1. Capital Change Information

   Changes in common shareholders' equity should be provided for the last five years on items such as stock dividends, stock splits, rights issues and new stock issues.

   Such disclosure would allow users to convert share-related ratios such as earnings per share, dividends per share, and book value per share on a common denominator historically.

2. Analysis of Shareholdings

   . Shareholders should be classified by type (i.e., individuals, financial institutions, pension funds, others) and number of shares owned (i.e., 1-100, 101-500, 501-1,000, etc.)

   . Geographic distribution of shareholders would be useful.

   . If major changes have taken place in ownership, two years' comparative data would be useful.

   Shareholdings by the key officials and members of the board should also be provided, along with any options granted to these individuals.

Shareholders and Number of Shares Owned on MM/DD/1988

Category	Number of Shareholders	Number of Shares	% of Capital
1- 1,000 sh	40,000	15,000,000	3
1,001- 5,000 sh	30,000	70,000,000	14
5,001-10,000 sh	3,000	30,000,000	6
10,001-	250	400,000,000	77
Total	73,250	515,000,000	100%

Shareholders by Type of Organization on MM/DD/1988

Category	Number of Shareholders	Number of Shares	% of Total Shares
Individuals	xxx	xxx	x.x
Financial Institutions	xx	xxx	x.x
Pension Funds	xx	xxx	x.x
Other Organizations	xx	xxx	x.x
Total	xxxx	xxxx	100%

Major Shareholders

Name	Number of Shares	%
Top xx Shareholders:		
A. ABC Company	xxx	x.x
B. Individual Shareholder (Director)	xxx	x.x
C. Pension Funds	xxx	x.x
Total for Top xx Shareholders	xxx	x.x
Other Directors' Shareholdings:		
F.	xxx	x.x
G.	xxx	x.x
H.	xxx	x.x
Total for Other Directors	xxx	x.x
Total for Major Shareholders and Directors	xxx	x.x

3. Multiple Classes of Common Shares

In several countries (i.e., Belgium, Canada, Denmark, Italy, Sweden and Switzerland), multiple classes of common shares are allowed. Brief descriptions of each type of share, along with key items such as the number of shares outstanding, dividends per share, earnings per share (if different), as well as capital change information should be provided.

4. Capital Market Information

A list of stock exchanges (both domestic and foreign) where the company's securities are listed, along with the appropriate ticker symbol, would be useful.

Closing price for the year, high low for the last five years as well as the last six months, and the volume of shares traded should be reported.

Address and phone numbers of the company's share registrar and/or transfer agent would also be useful information for shareholders.

Stock Exchange(s) Listed: Stock Exchange 1, Ticker Symbol XYZ

Principal Registrar or
Transfer Agent: <Address 1, Phone 1>

Other Registrars or
Transfer Agents: <Address 2, Phone 2>

Recent Stock Prices

Closing, and High-Low Prices for Last 5 Years Common Stock - Stock Exchange-1					
	1988	1987	1986	1985	1984
Closing	xxx	xxx	xxx	xxx	xxx
High	xxx	xxx	xxx	xxx	xxx
Low	xxx	xxx	xxx	xxx	xxx
Volume	xxx	xxx	xxx	xxx	xxx

Price has been adjusted by stock splits in 1984-87.

Closing, and High-Low Prices and Volume for Last 6 Months Common Stock						
1988	12	11	10	9	8	7
Closing	xxx	xxx	xxx	xxx	xxx	xxx
High	xxx	xxx	xxx	xxx	xxx	xxx
Low	xxx	xxx	xxx	xxx	xxx	xxx
Volume	xxx	xxx	xxx	xxx	xxx	xxx

These tables should be repeated for multiple shares, if they exist.

5. Financial Calendar

This item should include the following dates:

- Dividend Announcement Date
- Preliminary Results Announcement Date
- Annual General Meeting Date
- Interim Results Announcement Date

6. Availability of Additional Information About the Company

Any of the following items, if applicable, should be disclosed:

- A list of investment houses who follow the company and have issued reports on the company over the last 12 months.

- Name of Local Stock Exchange Authority or Securities and Exchange Commission where additional information about the company is on file and accessible to the public.

- Availability of a printed transcript (or audio cassette recording) of proceedings at the Annual General Meeting of Shareholders.

- Availability of annual reports in different languages.

- Names of Investor Relations Executives with their addresses and phone numbers.

APPENDIX C

A GUIDE FOR PREPARING AN ANNUAL REPORT FOR A MULTINATIONAL INSURANCE COMPANY

INTRODUCTION

This appendix provides a suggested format for preparing the annual report of a multinational insurance company. It is recommended that the reader should first review the information in the Introduction to the Appendices A, B and C before starting to read Appendix C.

The appendix includes an appropriate format for each section of the report. Where possible, descriptive or narrative comments have been avoided. In certain instances, descriptive comments are made to provide specific guidance. Readers are encouraged to consult local authorities concerning any areas for which further guidance is needed.

PQR Insurance Company

[inside of cover]

- Brief Description of Business
- Brief History
- Address of Headquarters

- The PQR Insurance Company was founded in 1900..... It has been listed on the xxx Stock Exchange since January 1, 1975.

  The principal activity of the Insurance Company and its subsidiary and associated companies is to provide insurance and other financial services through 250 offices in 15 countries in Europe and North America.

  Head Office
  Address
  Phone
  Telex, Cable
  Telefax

PQR Insurance Company

Table of Contents

1. Financial Summary

Financial Summary

Five-Year Financial Summary						
Year Ending MM/DD		1988	1987	1986	1985	1984
(In Millions of Local Currency)						
Life Insurance In Force		XXX	XXX	XXX	XXX	XXX
Net Premium Income						
Life		XXX	XXX	XXX	XXX	XXX
Non-Life		XXX	XXX	XXX	XXX	XXX
Total Net Premium Income		XXX	XXX	XXX	XXX	XXX
Investment Income		XXX	XXX	XXX	XXX	XXX
Total Revenue		XXX	XXX	XXX	XXX	XXX
Operating Income		XXX	XXX	XXX	XXX	XXX
Net Income		XXX	XXX	XXX	XXX	XXX
At MM/DD						
Investment Assets		XXX	XXX	XXX	XXX	XXX
Total Assets		XXX	XXX	XXX	XXX	XXX
Insurance Reserves		XXX	XXX	XXX	XXX	XXX
Shareholders' Equity		XXX	XXX	XXX	XXX	XXX
Total Capital (*)		XXX	XXX	XXX	XXX	XXX
Number of Employees		XXX	XXX	XXX	XXX	XXX
Per share Data						
Dividends per Share		X.X	X.X	X.X	X.X	X.X
Earnings per Share		X.X	X.X	X.X	X.X	X.X
Book Value per Share		X.X	X.X	X.X	X.X	X.X
Market Value per Share at Year-End		X.X	X.X	X.X	X.X	X.X
Selected Ratios (%)**						
Rate of Return on Average:						
Total Assets	1-h	X.XX	X.XX	X.XX	X.XX	X.XX
Common Shareholders' Equity	1-i	X.XX	X.XX	X.XX	X.XX	X.XX
Loss Ratio	1-j	X.XX	X.XX	X.XX	X.XX	X.XX
Expense Ratio	1-k	X.XX	X.XX	X.XX	X.XX	X.XX
Combined Ratio	1-l	X.XX	X.XX	X.XX	X.XX	X.XX
Profitability of Investment Assets	1-m	X.XX	X.XX	X.XX	X.XX	X.XX
Investment Assets to Total Assets	3-c	X.XX	X.XX	X.XX	X.XX	X.XX
Insurance Reserves to Total Assets	3-d	X.XX	X.XX	X.XX	X.XX	X.XX
Capital to Total Assets	3-e	X.XX	X.XX	X.XX	X.XX	X.XX
Dividend Payout Ratio	4-b	X.XX	X.XX	X.XX	X.XX	X.XX

* Total Capital is the sum of Long-Term Debt and Subordinated Loans, Minority Interests, and Total Shareholders' Equity

** See details in Supplementary Information B

2. Group's Organization

May Include the Following:

- Provide a chart outlining the group's organization for important consolidated subsidiaries.
- Separate consolidated subsidiaries by business segment (i.e., Life Insurance, Non-Life Insurance, other financial services....).
- Separate consolidated subsidiaries by geographic distribution.
- Specify ownership of the subsidiaries.
- Include unconsolidated companies if the non-consolidation is by material difference in industry classification, and the unconsolidated companies are important to the group (e.g., oil company in insurance group).

3. Key Executives and Board of Directors

Chairman President Directors	Variables: e.g.	Name, Age, Years in Office, Past and Present Relevant Functions Re-election Date, Special Tasks, etc.

Senior Executives
Chief Accountant
Secretary

a. Board of Directors

. For each member of the board of the company, there should be further information about his affiliation, background in brief, length of time on the company's board and the expiration date of his term.

. Membership on each of the Board's committees should be clearly noted.

b. Senior Executives

Principal executive officers of the companies, including officers of the major divisions and subsidiaries should be listed with title, age and length of time with the company.

4. Management Reports

   - Macroeconomic analysis by Chief Executive Officer (Includes strategic planning in near future)

   - Detailed operating results by Finance Director

This section usually reviews the company's activities grouped in the following sections:

- A Letter from the President or Chief Executive
- Overview of the Year
- Macro Trends of the Marketplace
- International Activities

In addition, the management's financial review is also provided. The review outlines the following:

- Factors contributing to an increase/decrease in key accounts such as revenues, earnings, total assets, current liabilities and shareholders' equity
- Unusual financial items (such as discontinued operations, extraordinary gains/losses, disposal of assets, etc.)
- Mergers/acquisitions undertaken during the year
- Impact of broader economic events on the company's activities

5. Non-Financial Analysis of Major Subsidiaries and Sectors

   May Include the Following:

   - New Services
   - Major Activities
   - Labor Relations
   - Social Activities

6. Auditor's Report

   Should include the following:

   To Board of Directors and Shareholders:

   - Scope
   - Opinion
   - Auditor's Signature
   - Local Audit Firm and International Auditing Firm, if any
   - Address
   - Date

7. Appraiser's Report

To the Policyholders and Shareholders of PQR Insurance Company

. Scope - What areas are Reviewed

.   - Which Criteria are Used

. Opinion

. Appraiser
  (Address)

. Date

8. Financial Statements

PQR Insurance Company
Consolidated Income Statement
(For the Year Ending MM/DD/1988)
(Millions of Local Currency)

	Notes	1988	1987
Premium Written		xxx	xxx
Unearned Premium and Reinsurance Adjustments		(xx)	(xx)
Net Premium Income	11,12	xxx	xxx
Investment Income	13	xxx	xxx
Other Operating Income	14	xxx	xxx
Total Revenue		xxxx	xxxx
Claims and Losses		xxx	xxx
Underwriting Expenses		xxx	xxx
Provision for Long-Term Policyholders' Reserves		xxx	xxx
Distributions to Policyholders		xxx	xxx
Other Operating Expenses	15	xxx	xxx
Operating Income		xxx	xxx
Non-Operating Expenses/Income	16	xxx	xxx
		xxx	xxx
Income Tax Expenses	17	xxx	xxx
Extraordinary Items (Net of Tax xxx)	18	xxx	xxx
Net Income Before Minority Interest		xxx	xxx
Minority Interest		xxx	xxx
Net Income Attributable to the Group		xxx	xxx
Dividends Declared	19	xx	xx
Earnings per Share:	20		
Basic EPS		xx.xx	xx.xx
Fully Diluted EPS		xx.xx	xx.xx

PQR Insurance Company
Consolidated Income Statement of Life Insurance Business
(For the Year Ending MM/DD/1988)
(Millions of Local Currency)

	Notes	1988	1987
Premium Income	11	xxx	xxx
Investment Income	13	xxx	xxx
Other Operating Income		xxx	xxx
Total Revenue		xxxx	xxxx
Claims and Losses		xxx	xxx
Underwriting Expenses		xxx	xxx
Provision for Long-Term Policyholders' Reserves		xxx	xxx
Distributions to Policyholders		xxx	xxx
Other Operating Expenses		xxx	xxx
Operating Income		xxx	xxx
Non-Operating Expenses/Income		xxx	xxx
Income Before Tax and Extraordinary Items		xxx	xxx
Income Tax Expenses		xxx	xxx
Extraordinary Items (Net of Tax xxx)		xxx	xxx
Net Income Attributable to the Shareholders		xxx	xxx

PQR Insurance Company
Consolidated Income Statement of Non-Life Insurance Business
(For the Year Ending MM/DD/1988)

(Millions of Local Currency)

	Notes	1988	1987
Premiums Written		xxx	xxx
Unearned Premiums		xxx	xxx
Reinsurance		xxx	xxx
Net Premium Income	12	xxx	xxx
Investment Income	13	xxx	xxx
Other Operating Income		xxx	xxx
Total Revenue		xxxx	xxxx
Claims and Losses		xxx	xxx
Underwriting Expenses		xxx	xxx
Other Operating Expenses		xxx	xxx
Operating Income		xxx	xxx
Non-Operating Expenses/Income		xxx	xxx
Income Before Taxes and Extraordinary Items		xxx	xxx
Income Tax Expenses		xxx	xxx
Extraordinary Items (Net of Tax xxx)		xxx	xxx
Net Income Attributable to the Shareholders		xxx	xxx

PQR Insurance Company
Consolidated Balance Sheet
(At MM/DD/1988)
(Millions of Local Currency)

	Notes	1988	1987
Assets			
Cash and Cash Equivalents		xxx	xxx
Trading Account Securities	1	xxx	xxx
Government and Municipal Securities		xxx	xxx
Corporate Fixed Income Securities		xxx	xxx
Preferred Shares		xxx	xxx
Ordinary Shares		xxx	xxx
Real Estate Investments		xxx	xxx
Loans on Policies		xxx	xxx
Mortgages and Loans		xxx	xxx
Other Investments		xxx	xxx
Total Investment Assets	2	xxxx	xxxx
Receivables		xxx	xxx
Property and Equipment	4	xxx	xxx
Investments in Unconsolidated Subsidiaries and Associated Companies	3	xxx	xxx
Other Assets		xxx	xxx
Total Assets		xxxx	xxxx
Liabilities and Stockholders' Equity			
Outstanding Claims and Losses		xxx	xxx
Unearned Premium		xxx	xxx
Long-Term Policyholders' Reserves		xxx	xxx
Other Insurance Reserves		xxx	xxx
Total Insurance Reserves	5	xxxx	xxxx
Short-Term Interest-Bearing Debt	6	xxx	xxx
Other Liabilities	7	xxx	xxx
Long-Term Interest-Bearing Debt	6	xxx	xxx
Subordinated Loans	8	xxx	xxx
Minority Interest		xxx	xxx
Total Liabilities		xxxx	xxxx
Preferred Stocks	9	xxx	xxx
Common Stocks	10	xxx	xxx
Additional Paid in Capital		xxx	xxx
Legal Reserves		xxx	xxx
Retained Earnings		xxx	xxx
Common Stock in Treasury, at Cost		(xxx)	(xxx)
Total Shareholders' Equity		xxxx	xxxx
Total Liabilities and Shareholders' Equity		xxxx	xxxx

PQR Insurance Company
Consolidated Statement of Changes in Financial Position

(Millions of Local Currency)

	Notes	1988	1987
Funds Provided by:			
Net Income		xxx	xxx
Addition (Deduction) of Non-Cash Items			
Depreciation and Amortization		xxx	xxx
Gain/Loss on Securities Transactions		xxx	xxx
Funds Provided by Operations		xxx	xxx
Decrease in Investment Assets		xxx	xxx
Decrease in Fixed Assets		xxx	xxx
Increase in Insurance Reserves		xxx	xxx
Increase in Shareholders' Equity		xxx	xxx
Total Funds Provided		xxx	xxx
Funds Used for:			
Increase in Investment Assets		xxx	xxx
Decrease in Insurance Reserve		xxx	xxx
Decrease in Shareholders' Equity		xxx	xxx
Dividends Paid		xxx	xxx
Total Funds Used		xxx	xxx
Net Increase (Decrease) in Funds		xxx	xxx

PQR Insurance Company
Consolidated Statement of Changes in Shareholders' Equity
(For the Year Ending MM/DD/1988)

(Millions of Local Currency)

	1988	1987
Preferred Stocks		
Balance at Beginning of Year	xxx	xxx
Increase (Decrease) in the Year	xx	xx
Balance at End of Year	xxx	xxx
Common Stocks		
Balance at Beginning of Year	xxx	xxx
Increase (Decrease) 1	xx	xx
2	(xx)	(xx)
Balance at End of Year	xxx	xxx
Additional Paid-in Capital		
Balance at Beginning of Year	xxx	xxx
Increase (Decrease) from Preferred Stock	xxx	xxx
Increase (Decrease) from Common Stock	xxx	xxx
Balance at End of Year	xxx	xxx
Legal Reserves		
Balance at Beginning of Year	xxx	xxx
Increase (Decrease) during the Year	xxx	xxx
Balance at End of Year	xxx	xxx
Retained Earnings		
Balance at Beginning of Year	xxx	xxx
Dividends Declared	(xxx)	(xxx)
Net Income during the Year	xxx	xxx
Balance at End of Year	xxx	xxx
Common Stock in Treasury, at Cost		
Balance at Beginning of Year	xxx	xxx
Increase (Decrease) during the Year	xxx	xxx
Balance at End of Year	xxx	xxx
Total Shareholders' Equity	xxx	xxx

9. Major Accounting Policies

- This section outlines the basic accounting policies used for preparing financial statements.

- Many international users are familiar with key accounting concepts in their home country, but are not well versed in the accounting practices of other countries. This brief summary of local accounting standards used by the company should help international users in analyzing foreign company reports.

- The descriptions given for the following items illustrate policies which could be followed. A company's specific policy should be described in the report.

a. Basis of Presentation

The consolidated financial statements of PQR Insurance Company are prepared in accordance with accounting principles prescribed by the (Regulations) and its related rules issued by the (Regulatory Authorities), and other prevailing practices of the insurance industry.

As many of the Company's subsidiaries are insurance companies, the group accounts do not disclose certain information, some of which relates to provisions and reserves. The company is exempt from disclosing such information under provisions of the (Regulations).

b. Basis of Consolidation

(i) Subsidiaries

The consolidated financial statements are prepared in accordance with (Regulations) and consequently include all subsidiaries in which PQR Company directly or indirectly owns more than 50 percent of the equity capital and exercises management control. They also include the subsidiaries in which PQR Insurance Company owns 50 percent or less of the equity capital but exercises control under a management contract.

Subsidiaries are consolidated on the basis of audited accounts through 31st December each year, employing uniform accounting policies.

(ii) Participations

Investments in associated companies (companies of which PQR owns between 20% and 50%) are accounted for using the equity method. The company's share of earnings of these associated companies and gains and losses realized on disposition of investments in associated companies are included as part of other operating income.

c. Foreign Currency Translation

Amounts recorded in foreign currencies relating to assets and liabilities, as well as to revenue and expenditure of non-domestic units, are translated into reporting currency at the exchange rates prevailing at fiscal year-end.

Balance Sheet items recorded in foreign currencies which relate to direct activities abroad are translated into reporting currency at the exchange rates prevailing at fiscal year-end. Exchange differences are credited or debited to the relevant components of capital and surplus. Income and expenditures recorded in foreign currencies are translated at the rate on the date of the transaction.

Forward exchange transactions not yet completed, concluded with respect to assets and liabilities recorded in foreign currencies, are translated at the spot rate on the balance sheet date. Realized and unrealized foreign exchange gains or losses are included in capital and surplus.

d. Income and Expense Recognition

(i) General

The Income Statement reflects all non-life income and expenditure (together with life profits due to shareholders), other than items charged to provisions set up in earlier years.

The non-life underwriting result is determined after taking account of unearned premiums, deferred acquisition costs and outstanding claims. Net premium income is stated after payments or recoveries in respect to outward reinsurance.

Premium income from life operations, after allowance for outward reinsurance, is reflected in the movement of life funds.

(ii) Unearned Premium

Unearned premiums are those portions of the premiums written in a year that relate to the periods of risk subsequent to the balance sheet date. They are computed principally on either the daily or monthly prorated basis.

(iii) Reinsurance Adjustment

Net results from reinsurance transactions have reduced the premium written to arrive at net premium income.

(iv) Investment Income

Investment income is comprised of interest, dividends and rents receivable for the year, after adding back any related tax credit; expenses incurred in the management of investments are deducted from investment income. No depreciation charge is made with respect to investment property occupied by the Group since such property represents an immaterial proportion of total assets.

(v) Outstanding Claims

Full provision is made for outstanding claims, including claim settlement expenses, and claims incurred but not reported.

(vi) Expenses and Commissions

Expenses and commissions are written off in the year in which they are incurred, except to the extent that they relate to unearned premiums.

(vii) Life Profits and Policyholders' Reserves

Life profits accrue to the shareholders as a result of annual actuarial valuations of the Long-Term policyholders' reserves. These are based on local practice and are subject to movements to or from investment reserves which are made on the advice of the group actuary. The profits included in the Income Statement are stated before taxation, with the related taxation being included in the taxation charge.

e. Investment Assets

(i) General

Revaluation of investments above cost is not permitted under the regulations.

Regulations do not require the disclosure of market value or other valuation information.

Profits and losses on the realization of investments and amounts written off are credited or charged to the Income Statement and not taken directly to reserves.

(ii) Trading Account Securities are valued at market value.

(iii) Fixed income securities are stated principally as follows: Government, municipal and corporate bonds at amortized cost, preferred stocks at cost.

(iv) Common stock and segregated funds are valued at market value.

(v) Loans on policies and mortgages are valued at their unpaid principal balances.

(vi) Real estate investments are valued at cost, less accumulated depreciation.

(vii) Joint ventures, included in other investments, are valued at net equity in partnerships.

(viii) Unconsolidated subsidiaries and associated companies are valued using the equity method.

f. Depreciation and Amortization

(i) Fixed Assets and Depreciation:

Major items of capital expenditure, such as computer equipment and developmental cost vehicles, and for non-life insurance companies, items such as furniture and office equipment, are capitalized and depreciated by equal annual installments over their estimated useful lives. Other assets are written off in the year of purchase. All properties within the group are regarded as investment properties and, therefore, are not depreciated.

(ii) Leased Assets:

In cases where assets are financed by leasing agreements that give rights approximating ownership ("finance leases"), the assets are capitalized as if they had been purchased outright. Commitments under finance leases are included in "other creditors." Depreciation on the relevant assets is charged to the Income Statement. Lease payments are comprised of capital and interest elements, and the interest is charged to the Income Statement.

For other leases, the annual rentals payable/receivable are charged/credited to the appropriate revenue account or to the Income Statement.

g. Special Reserves

Investment Reserves (Only if Allowed by Local Regulations):

Investment reserves are held in the long-term funds of the company's insurance subsidiaries. From time to time, transfers may be made between the revenue account and insurance fund. Reserves are combined with revaluation reserves.

h. Taxation

The income tax expenses in the Income Statement are based on the taxable profits for the year, and include the amount of taxation attributable to the shareholders' proportion of life profits. In the movement in policyholders' reserve, the tax expenses are based on the method of assessing taxation for life funds applicable in the relevant territory of operation. Provision is made for deferred taxation where it is expected that a liability will crystallize. No amount is provided if a liability or relief is not expected to arise and if timing differences are of a continuing nature.

i. Pension Costs

The Group operates defined benefit pension schemes covering the majority of employees, and contributions are made on a going concern basis as recommended by actuaries. The pension schemes are fully funded on a discontinuance actuarial valuation basis.

The Company provides certain life insurance and health care benefits for its retired employees. All of the Company's employees are potentially eligible if they reach retirement age while working for the Company.

j. Insurance Reserves

(i) Policyholders' Reserves

These reserves are determined in accordance with the tables and methods which are locally accepted. The methods must be approved by the government authorities responsible for supervision of the life insurance industry.

(ii) Future Profit Participation of Policyholders

This relates to the amounts reserved for future entitlements of policyholders; allotment takes place in the future years, often by means of addition to the sums insured.

k. Prior Year Figures

Any change in the classification of insurance transacted or other items relevant to the annual accounts for the period will involve a corresponding adjustment to the figures of the prior year.

10. Notes to the Financial Statements

Note 1. Trading Account Securities

(Millions of Local Currency)

	1988	1987
Listed		
- In Domestic Market	XXX	XXX
- In Foreign Market	XXX	XXX
	XXX	XXX
Unlisted	XXX	XXX
Total Trading Account Securities	XXX	XXX

Note 2. Investment Assets other than Trading Account Securities

(Millions of Local Currency)

	1988			1987
	Life	Non-Life	Total	Total
Investment Securities				
Government and Municipal Securities	XXX	XXX	XXX	XXX
Corporate Fixed-Income Securities	XXX	XXX	XXX	XXX
Preferred Shares	XXX	XXX	XXX	XXX
Ordinary Shares	XXX	XXX	XXX	XXX
Other Securities	XXX	XXX	XXX	XXX
Total Investment Securities	XXXX	XXXX	XXXX	XXXX
Real Estate Investments	XXX	XXX	XXX	XXX
Loans on Policies	XXX	XXX	XXX	XXX
Mortgage and Loans	XXX	XXX	XXX	XXX
Other Investments	XXX	XXX	XXX	XXX
Total Investment Assets other than Trading Account Securities	XXXX	XXXX	XXXX	XXXX
Investment Securities				
Listed				
On Domestic Market	XXX	XXX	XXX	XXX
On Foreign Market	XXX	XXX	XXX	XXX
	XXX	XXX	XXX	XXX
Unlisted	XXX	XXX	XXX	XXX
Total Investment Securities	XXX	XXX	XXX	XXX

Note 3. Investments in Unconsolidated Subsidiaries and Associated Companies

- Valuation method for specific investments is disclosed, if significant.

(Millions of Local Currency)

	1988		1987	
	Book Value	Valuation	Book Value	Valuation
Unconsolidated Subsidiary				
Listed	xx	xx	xx	xx
Unlisted	xx	xx	xx	xx
Associated Companies				
Listed	xx	xx	xx	xx
Unlisted	xx	xx	xx	xx
Total	xxx	xxx	xxx	xxx

List of Companies disclosed on page xx

Note 4. Property and Equipment

(Millions of Local Currency)

	1988	1987
Premises, Sites and Leasehold Improvement		
Balance at Beginning of Year	xxx	xxx
Adjustments*	xx	xx
Beginning Balance after Adjustments	xxx	xxx
Less Depreciation, Amortization for the Year	(xx)	(xx)
Balance at End of Year	xxx	xxx
Accumulated Depreciation	xxx	xxx
Estimated Market Value	xxx	xxx
Furniture and Equipment		
Balance at Beginning of Year	xxx	xxx
Adjustments*	xx	xx
Beginning Balance after Adjustments	xxx	xxx
Less Depreciation, Amortization for the Year	(xx)	(xx)
Balance at End of Year	xxx	xxx
Accumulated Depreciation	xxx	xxx
Estimated Market Value	xxx	xxx
Total Property and Equipment at End of Year	xxx	xxx

* Adjustments may include "Adjustments for exchange rate fluctuations", "Revaluations", or "Additions or disposals during the year".

Note 5. Insurance Reserves

(Millions of Local Currency)

	1988			1987
	Life	Non-Life	Total	Total
Insurance Reserves				
Outstanding Claims and Losses	xxx	xxx	xxx	xxx
Unearned Premium	-	xxx	xxx	xxx
Long-Term Policyholders' Reserves	xxx	-	xxx	xxx
Other Insurance Reserves	xxx	xxx	xxx	xxx
Total Insurance Reserves	xxxx	xxxx	xxxx	xxxx

	1988	1987
Long-Term Policyholders' Reserves:		
Balance at Beginning of Year	xxx	xxx
Foreign Currency Adjustments	xxx	xxx
Adjustments due to Changes in Price Level	xxx	xxx
Balance at Beginning of Year After Adjustments	xxx	xxx
Provision for the Year	xxx	xxx
Balance at End of Year	xxx	xxx
Other Insurance Reserves:		
Reserves for Distributions to Policyholders	xxx	xxx
Reserves for Segregated Funds	xxx	xxx
Total Other Insurance Reserves	xxx	xxx

Note 6. Interest-Bearing Debt

(Millions of Local Currency)

	1988				1987
	-1 yr	1-5 yr	5 yr +	Total	Total
Bank Debentures (1)	xx	xx	xx	xxx	xxx
Bond Issues (2)	xx	xx	xx	xxx	xxx
Total	xxx	xxx	xxx	xxx	xxx

1. Bank Debentures

Issues	Due	Amount
Issue 1 (Interest rate, callable feature, if any) etc.	mm/dd/yy	xxx
Total Bank Debentures		xxx

2. Bond Issues

Issues	Due	Amount
Issue A (Interest rate, callable feature, if any) etc.	mm/dd/yy	xxx
Total Bond Issues		xxx

Note 7. Other Liabilities

(Millions of Local Currency)

	1988	1987
Current Liabilities:		
Payables to Reinsurers	xxx	xxx
Payables to Agent	xxx	xxx
Payables to Policyholders	xxx	xxx
Taxes Payable	xxx	xxx
Dividends Payable	xxx	xxx
Other Current Liabilities	xxx	xxx
Total Current Liabilities	xxxx	xxxx
Non-Current Liabilities		
Deferred Taxation	xxx	xxx
Provision for Retirement Allowances	xxx	xxx
Other Non-Current Liabilities	xxx	xxx
Total Non-Current Liabilities	xxxx	xxxx
Total Other Liabilities	xxxx	xxxx

Note 8. Subordinated Loans

(Millions of Local Currency)

	1988	1987
Subordinated Notes (x% interest, No date)	xx	xx
Loan Capital (x%....)	xx	xx
(Subordinated Capital Notes)		
Total Subordinated Loans	xxx	xxx

Note 9. Preferred Stock

(Millions of Local Currency)

	1988	1987
Redeemable Preferred Stock		
Redeemable Preferred A, x%	xx	xx
Redeemable Preferred B, y%, Convertible	xx	xx
Total Redeemable Preferred Stock	xxx	xxx
Unredeemable Preferred Stock		
Name 1	xx	xx
Name 2	xx	xx
Total Unredeemable Preferred Stock	xxx	xxx
Total Preferred Stock	xxx	xxx

Note 10. Common Stocks

- If additional stock is issued during the year, the issue may be explained here.

(Millions of Local Currency)

	1988	1987
Authorized Capital (xxx shares)	xxx	xxx
Common Stock Issued		
Balance at Beginning of Year x.x in par, xxx shares issued	xxx	xxx
Conversion of Convertible Debenture (xxx shares)	xx	xx
Exercising Options by Executives (xxx shares)	xx	xx
New Issuance (xxx shares)	xx	-
Balance at End of Year (xxx shares)	xxx	xxx

* Common Stock in Treasury may be disclosed here.

Note 11. Life Premium Income

(Millions of Local Currency)

	1988	1987
Individual		
Individual Life	xx	xx
Individual Annuity	xx	xx
Total Premiums from Individuals	xxx	xxx
Group		
Group Life	xx	xx
Group Annuity	xx	xx
Total Premiums from Groups	xxx	xxx
Total Life Premium Income	xxx	xxx

PQR Insurance Company

Note 12. Non-Life Premium Income, Net

(Millions of Local Currency)

	Fire		Accident		Health		Other		Total	
	1988	1987	1988	1987	1988	1987	1988	1987	1988	1987
Premiums Written, Gross	xxx	xxx	xxx	xxx	xxx	xxx	xxx	xxx	xxx	xxx
Reinsurance Results	xxx	xxx	xxx	xxx	xxx	xxx	xxx	xxx	xxx	xxx
Premiums for Company's Account	xxx	xxx	xxx	xxx	xxx	xxx	xxx	xxx	xxx	xxx
Unearned Premium	xxx	xxx	xxx	xxx	xxx	xxx	xxx	xxx	xxx	xxx
Net Premium Income	xxx	xxx	xxx	xxx	xxx	xxx	xxx	xxx	xxx	xxx
Reinsurance Results										
Premiums Ceded to Reinsurance	xxx	xxx	xxx	xxx	xxx	xxx	xxx	xxx	xxx	xxx
Income from Reinsurance Ceded										
Underwriting Expenses	xxx	xxx	xxx	xxx	xxx	xxx	xxx	xxx	xxx	xxx
Claims and Losses	xxx	xxx	xxx	xxx	xxx	xxx	xxx	xxx	xxx	xxx
Net Reinsurance Results	xxx	xxx	xxx	xxx	xxx	xxx	xxx	xxx	xxx	xxx

Note 13. Investment Income

(Millions of Local Currency)

	1988	1987
Investment Income:		
Interest Income from Government and Municipal Bonds, Corporate Bonds and Loans	xxx	xxx
Dividend Income from Equity Investments	xxx	xxx
Income from Other Investments	xxx	xxx
	xxx	xxx
Gains/Losses on Trading Account Securities	xxx	xxx
Gains/Losses on Disposal of Investment Securities	xxx	xxx
Total Investment Income	xxx	xxx

Note 14. Other Operating Income

- Capital gains on disposal of investments
- Equity earnings on unconsolidated subsidiaries and associated companies

(Millions of Local Currency)

	1988	1987
Commission and Fees Received	xx	xx
Equity earnings from unconsolidated subsidiary and associated companies	xx	xx
Sundry Operating Income	xx	xx
Total Other Operating Income	xxx	xxx

Note 15. Other Operating Expenses

- Number of Employees (full-time, part-time; average for the year)
- Salaries to Directors

(Millions of Local Currency)

	1988	1987
Salaries and other Personnel Expenses (*)	xx	xx
Depreciation and Amortization (Note 7)	xx	xx
Indirect Taxes (other than income taxes)	xx	xx
Commissions and Fees Paid	xx	xx
Sundry Operating Expenses	xx	xx
Total Other Operating Expenses	xxx	xxx

*Number of Employees:

	1988		1987	
Domestic				
Foreign		xxx		xxx
North America	xxx		xxx	
Europe	xxx		xxx	
Asia	xxx		xxx	
Other Area	xxx	xxx	xxx	xxx
Total Number of Employees at Year End		xxx		xxx
Full-Time		xxx		xxx
Full-Time Equivalent of Part-Time		xx		xx
Total Full and Full-Time Equivalents		xxx		xxx

Note 16. Non-Operating Expenses/Income, Net

(Millions of Local Currency)

	1988	1987
Non-Operating Income:		
Gain on Sale of Fixed Assets	xx	xx
Item 2	xx	xx
Total Non-Operating Income	xx	xx
Non-Operating Expenses:		
Loss on Sale of Fixed Assets	xx	xx
Item 2	xx	xx
Total Non-Operating Expenses	xx	xx
Non-Operating Expenses/Income, Net	xx	xx

Note 17. Income Tax Expenses

(Millions of Local Currency)

	1988	1987
Current Income Taxes	xx	xx
Deferred Income Taxes	xx	xx
Total Income Tax Expenses	xxx	xxx

Note 18. Extraordinary Items (Net of Taxes)

(Millions of Local Currency)

	1988	1987
Gain or Loss on Disposal of Fixed Assets (Net of tax xxx)	xxx	
Provision Reserves for Possible Losses (Net of tax xxx)	xxx	
Changes in Regulation (Net of tax xxx)		xxx
Total Extraordinary Items (Net of tax xxx in 1988, xxx in 1987)	xxx	xxx

PQR Insurance Company

Note 19. Dividends Declared

	1988		1987	
	Per Share	Millions of Local Currency	Per Share	Millions of Local Currency
Preferred Shares:				
Preferred Share A	x.x	xx	x.x	xx
Preferred Share B				
Interim	x.x	xx	x.x	xx
Final	x.x	xx	x.x	xx
Total Amount	x.x	xx	x.x	xx
Common Shares:				
Interim	x.x	xx	x.x	xx
Final	x.x	xx	x.x	xx
Total Amount	x.x	xx	x.x	xx
Total Dividends Declared		xxx		xxx

Note 20. Earnings per Share

	1988	1987
Basic EPS		
Net Income Attributable to Group xx and Weighted Average xxx Common Stocks in Issue During 1988	x.x	
Net Income Attributable to Group xxx and Weighted Average xxx Common Stocks in Issue During 1987		x.x
Fully Diluted		
(Earnings xxx and xxx Shares in 1988)	x.x	
(Earnings xxx and xxx Shares in 1987)		x.x

Note 21. Contingent Liabilities

- Litigation on pending lawsuits

- Contingent liabilities not from operating activities

Example:

The Company has guaranteed approximately __, (in millions of local currency), for the obligations of others, made with other responsible companies in the ordinary course of business. If these companies are unable to meet certain obligations, the Company may be required to advance funds against future charges. No material loss is anticipated under these guarantees.

The Company and its subsidiaries are engaged in litigation and have a number of unresolved claims pending. While the amounts claimed are substantial and the ultimate liability in respect of such litigation and claims cannot be determined at this time, the company is of the opinion that such liability, to the extent not provided for through insurance or otherwise, is not likely to be of material importance in relation to its accounts.

The Company has provided in its accounts for items and issues not yet resolved based on management's best judgment.

Note 22. Post-Balance Sheet Events

- Acquisition(s) of new company(ies) after balance sheet date

- Any other important event after balance sheet date

All key events occurring between the year-end date and the date of the annual report which have an impact on financial data or the further viability of the firm should be disclosed.

A note such as "no events with material financial consequences have occurred since the year-end date of the report" would also be appropriate.

Example:

On ______, the company acquired all of the outstanding common stock of XYZ Company. The cost of the acquisition was approximately ___ and will be accounted for as a purchase. Results of XYZ Company will be included in the Consolidated Statement of Earnings from the date of acquisition. XYZ company had total assets of ____ million and net earnings from continuing operations of ___ for the 12 months ended last year-end. XYZ Company had total shareholders' equity of ___ million at last year-end.

PQR Insurance Company

The following summarizes the unaudited pro forma combined results of operations adjusted for the amortization of estimated excess purchase price and interest on debt in connection with the acquisition. It is stated as though the acquisition had occurred at the beginning of the company's current fiscal year.
Net Earnings_____
Net Earnings Per Share _____
Total Assets _____
Total Shareholders' Equity _____
The unaudited pro forma financial information is not necessarily indicative of the results of operations that would have occurred had the two companies actually been combined during the period presented. Pro forma information does not indicate the future results of operations of the combined companies.

Supplementary Information A

Operating Results by Segment and Geographic Area

1. Results by Business Segment

- For diversified companies, key financial indicators (such as total revenues, assets employed and operating profit) should be disclosed by business segment.

- A brief definition (i.e., which major product lines or divisions are included) should be provided for each business segment.

- Inter-company transactions should be eliminated.

- Capital expenditures and depreciation by segment would also be useful to investors.

2. Results by Geographic Area

The company should also provide key financial variables (such as total revenues, assets employed and operating profit) by geographic area.

Several options can be explored to decide geographic classification.

a. Define geographic areas along conventional geographic lines (i.e., North America, South America, Western Europe, Middle East, Africa, Far East and Australia/New Zealand).

b. Provide results by country, if the company has significant operations in a few countries, and combine other small operations as other foreign business.

c. Mix key countries and regions.

Inter-area transfers should be eliminated.
Companies operating in several business segments in several international regions may want to combine their segment and geographic disclosures into one table.

PQR Insurance Company

Supplementary Information B

Selected Financial Ratios

1. Profitability Ratios

   a. Gross Operating Margin = Operating Income divided by Total Revenue

   b. Profit Margin = Pre-Tax Income divided by Total Revenue

   c. Net Income Margin = Net Income divided by Total Revenue

   d. Funds for Operations % Total Revenue = Funds for Operation divided by Total Revenue

   e. Total Revenue Growth = (Total Revenue This Year - Total Revenue Last Year) divided by Total Revenue Last Year

   f. Net Income Growth = (Net Income This Year - Net Income Last Year) divided by Net Income Last Year

   g. Total Revenue per Employee = Total Revenue divided by Total Employees

   h. Return on Average Total Assets = Net Income divided by Average Total Assets

   i. Return on Average Shareholders' Equity = Net Income divided by Average Shareholders' Equity

   j. Loss Ratio = Claims and Loss Expense + Provision for Long-Term Policyholders' Reserve divided by Total Net Premium Income

   k. Expense Ratio = Underwriting Expenses divided by Total Net Premium Income

   l. Combined Ratio = Loss Ratio plus Expenses Ratio

   m. Profitability of Investment Assets = Investment Income divided by Average Total Investment Assets

2. Asset Utilization Ratios

   a. Asset Utilization = Total Revenue divided by Average Total Assets

   b. Assets per Employee = Total Assets divided by Total Employees

3. Leverage Ratios

   a. Debt to Assets = Total Debt divided by Total Assets

   b. Debt to Equity = Total Debt divided by Total Shareholders' Equity

   c. Investment Assets to Total Assets = Investment Assets divided by Total Assets

   d. Insurance Reserves to Total Assets = Total Insurance Reserves divided by Total Assets

   e. Total Capital to Total Assets = Total Capital divided by Total Assets

4. Capital Market-Related Ratios

   a. Dividend Yield = Dividend Per Share divided by Market Price Per Share

   b. Dividend Payout = Total Dividend divided by Net Income

   c. Total Shareholders' Return = (End of Year Stock Price - Beginning of Year Stock Price + Dividend Paid During the Year) divided by Beginning of Year Stock Price

   d. Price to Earnings = Market Price Per Share divided by Earnings Per Share

   e. Price to Book = Market Price Per Share divided by Book Value Per Share

   f. Dividend Growth = (Dividend Per Share This Year - Dividend Per Share Last Year) divided by Dividend Per Share Last Year

   g. Net Worth Growth = (Net Worth Per Share This Year - Net Worth Per Share Last Year) divided by Net Worth Per Share Last Year

   h. Cash Dividend Coverage = Net Income Available to Common Shareholders divided by Dividends Paid This Year

5. International Business-Related Ratios

   a. Foreign Total Revenues as % of Total Worldwide Revenues

   b. Foreign Operating Income as % of Total Worldwide Operating Income

   c. Foreign Assets as % of Total Worldwide Assets

PQR Insurance Company

Supplementary Information C

Analysis of Investment Assets

(Millions of Local Currency)

	1988			1987		
	Average Balance	Interest Income	Yield (%)	Average Balance	Interest Income	Yield (%)
Trading Account Securities	xxx	xx	x.x	xxx	xx	x.x
Investment Securities						
Government and Municipal Securities	xxx	xx	x.x	xxx	xx	x.x
Corporate Securities	xxx	xx	x.x	xxx	xx	x.x
Preferred Shares	xxx	xx	x.x	xxx	xx	x.x
Ordinary Shares	xxx	xx	x.x	xxx	xx	x.x
Other Securities	xxx	xx	x.x	xxx	xx	x.x
Total Investment Securities	xxx	xx	x.x	xxx	xx	x.x
Real Estate Investments	xxx	xx	x.x	xxx	xx	x.x
Loans to Policies	xxx	xx	x.x	xxx	xx	x.x
Mortgage and Loans	xxx	xx	x.x	xxx	xx	x.x
Other Investments	xxx	xx	x.x	xxx	xx	x.x
Total Investment Assets	xxxx	xxx	x.x	xxxx	xx	x.x

Supplementary Information D

Analysis of Premium Income, Underwriting Results

(Millions of Local Currency)

	1988			1987		
	Life	Non-Life	Total	Life	Non-Life	Total
Net Premium Income	xxx	xxx	xxx	xxx	xxx	xxx
Insurance Expenses						
Claims and Losses	xxx	xxx	xxx	xxx	xxx	xxx
Insurance Reserve Changes	xxx	-	xxx	xxx	-	xxx
Underwriting Expenses	xxx	xxx	xxx	xxx	xxx	xxx
Other Insurance Expenses	xxx	xxx	xxx	xxx	xxx	xxx
Underwriting Results	xxx	xxx	xxx	xxx	xxx	xxx

PQR Insurance Company

Supplementary Information E

Analysis of Interest-Bearing Liabilities

(Millions of Local Currency)

	1988			1987		
	Average Balance	Interest Income	Yield (%)	Average Balance	Interest Income	Yield (%)
Short-Term Debts	xxx	xx	x.x	xxx	xx	x.x
Long-Term Debts	xxx	xx	x.x	xxx	xx	x.x
Subordinated Loans	xxx	xx	x.x	xxx	xx	x.x
Domestic	xxx	xx	x.x	xxx	xx	x.x
Foreign	xxx	xx	x.x	xxx	xx	x.x
Total Interest-Bearing Debts	xxxx	xxx	x.x	xxxx	xxx	x.x
Domestic	xxx	xx	x.x	xxx	xx	x.x
Foreign	xxx	xx	x.x	xxx	xx	x.x
Total Interest-Bearing Liabilities	xxxx	xxx	x.x	xxxx	xx	x.x
Redeemable Preferred Stock	xxx	xx	x.x	xxx	xx	x.x

PQR Insurance Company

Supplementary Information F

Quarterly Selected Financial Data

(Millions of Local Currency)

	1988				1987			
	4th	3rd	2nd	1st	4th	3rd	2nd	1st
Net Premium Income	xxx	xxx	xxx	xxx	xxx	xxx	xxx	xxx
Investment Income	xxx	xxx	xxx	xxx	xxx	xxx	xxx	xxx
Other Operating Income	xxx	xxx	xxx	xxx	xxx	xxx	xxx	xxx
Total Revenue	xxx	xxx	xxx	xxx	xxx	xxx	xxx	xxx
Claims and Losses	xxx	xxx	xxx	xxx	xxx	xxx	xxx	xxx
Underwriting Expenses	xxx	xxx	xxx	xxx	xxx	xxx	xxx	xxx
Provision for Long-Term Policyholders' Reserves	xxx	xxx	xxx	xxx	xxx	xxx	xxx	xxx
Other Operating Expenses	xxx	xxx	xxx	xxx	xxx	xxx	xxx	xxx
Operating Income	xxx	xxx	xxx	xxx	xxx	xxx	xxx	xxx
Income Taxes	xxx	xxx	xxx	xxx	xxx	xxx	xxx	xxx
Net Income	xx	xx	xx	xx	xx	xx	xx	xx
Earnings Per Share	x.xx	x.xx	x.xx	x.xx	x.xx	x.xx	x.xx	x.xx
Total Investment Assets	xxx	xxx	xxx	xxx	xxx	xxx	xxx	xxx
Total Assets	xxx	xxx	xxx	xxx	xxx	xxx	xxx	xxx
Total Insurance Revenue	xxx	xxx	xxx	xxx	xxx	xxx	xxx	xxx
Total Shareholders' Equity	xxx	xxx	xxx	xxx	xxx	xxx	xxx	xxx
Dividends Declared	x.xx	x.xx	x.xx	x.xx	x.xx	x.xx	x.xx	x.xx

PQR Insurance Company

Supplementary Information G

Selected Financial Data Adjusted for Changes in General Price Level

(Millions of Local Currency)

	1988	1987	1986	1985	1984
Net Premium Income					
As Reported	xxx	xxx	xxx	xxx	xxx
Adjusted	xxx	xxx	xxx	xxx	xxx
Operating Income					
As Reported	xxx	xxx	xxx	xxx	xxx
Adjusted	xxx	xxx	xxx	xxx	xxx
Net Income					
As Reported	xxx	xxx	xxx	xxx	xxx
Adjusted	xxx	xxx	xxx	xxx	xxx
Investment Assets	xxx	xxx	xxx	xxx	xxx
As Reported	xxx	xxx	xxx	xxx	xxx
Adjusted	xxx	xxx	xxx	xxx	xxx
Total Assets					
As Reported	xxx	xxx	xxx	xxx	xxx
Adjusted	xxx	xxx	xxx	xxx	xxx
Total Insurance Reserve					
As Reported	xxx	xxx	xxx	xxx	xxx
Adjusted	xxx	xxx	xxx	xxx	xxx
Per Share Data:					
Earnings					
As Reported	x.xx	x.xx	x.xx	x.xx	x.xx
Adjusted	x.xx	x.xx	x.xx	x.xx	x.xx
Dividends					
As Reported	x.xx	x.xx	x.xx	x.xx	x.xx
Adjusted	x.xx	x.xx	x.xx	x.xx	x.xx
Price Index*	xxx	xxx	xxx	xxx	xxx

*Explain the Price Index Used

PQR Insurance Company

Supplementary Information H

Selected Financial Data for Major Subsidiaries

- Parent Insurance Co.: Condensed Balance Sheet and Income Statement
- Major Subsidiaries: Selected Financial Data, Address, Phone, Fax, Telex, Business Area, % of Ownership
- Unconsolidated Subsidiaries: Majority Owned and Significant to the Group; Selected Financial Data, Address, Phone, Fax, Telex, Business Area, % of Ownership

A. PQR Insurance Company (Parent Company Only)

PQR Insurance Company
(H-1) Condensed Balance Sheet (Parent Company Only)

(Millions of Local Currency)

	1988	1987
Assets		
Cash and Cash Equivalents	xxx	xxx
Trading Account Securities	xxx	xxx
Fixed Income Securities	xxx	xxx
Ordinary Stocks	xxx	xxx
Real Estate Investments	xxx	xxx
Policy Loans and Mortgage Loans	xxx	xxx
Other Investments	xxx	xxx
Total Investment Assets	xxx	xxx
Receivables	xxx	xxx
Property and Equipment	xxx	xxx
Investments in Companies	xxx	xxx
Other Assets	xxx	xxx
Total Assets	xxxx	xxxx
Liabilities and Shareholders' Equity		
Outstanding Claims and Losses	xxx	xxx
Unearned Premiums	xxx	xxx
Long Term Policyholders' Reserve	xxx	xxx
Other Insurance Reserve	xxx	xxx
Total Insurance Reserve	xxx	xxx
Interest-Bearing Liabilities	xxx	xxx
Other Liabilities	xxx	xxx
Subordinated Loans	xxx	xxx
Minority Interest	xxx	xxx
Total Liabilities	xxx	xxx
Shareholders' Equity	xxx	xxx
Total Liabilities and Shareholders' Equity	xxxx	xxxx

PQR Insurance Company
(H-2) Condensed Income Statement
(Parent Company Only)

(Millions of Local Currency)

	1988	1987
Premium Written	xxx	xxx
Unearned Premium & Reinsurance Adjustment	xxx	xxx
Net Premium Written	xxx	xxx
Investment Income	xxx	xxx
Other Operating Income	xxx	xxx
Total Revenue	xxx	xxx
Claims and Losses	xxx	xxx
Underwriting Expenses	xxx	xxx
Provision for Long-Term Policyholders' Reserve	xxx	xxx
Distribution to Policyholders	xxx	xxx
Other Operating Expenses	xxx	xxx
Operating Income	xxx	xxx
Non-Operating Revenue/Expense	xx	xx
	xxx	xxx
Income Taxes	xx	xx
Income Before Extraordinary Items	xxx	xxx
Extraordinary Items	xx	xx
Net Income	xx	xx

Major Subsidiaries

B. PQRA Insurance Company

PQRA Insurance Group's Holdings: 100%
Address, Phone, Fax, Telex, Major Business Area

(Millions of Local Currency)

	1988	1987
Total Investment Assets	xxx	xxx
Total Assets	xxx	xxx
Total Insurance Reserves	xxx	xxx
Shareholders' Equity	xxx	xxx
Total Revenue	xxx	xxx
Net Premium Income	xxx	xxx
Operating Income	xxx	xxx
Net Income	xxx	xxx
Dividends Paid	xx	xx
EPS	x.x	x.x

C. PQRL Life Insurance

PQRL Insurance Group's Holdings: 90%
Address, Phone, Major Business Area

(Millions of Local Currency)

	1988	1987
Total Investment Assets	xxx	xxx
Total Assets	xxx	xxx
Total Insurance Reserve	xxx	xxx
Shareholders' Equity	xxx	xxx
Total Revenue	xxx	xxx
Net Premium Income	xxx	xxx
Operating Income	xxx	xxx
Net Income	xxx	xxx
Dividends Paid	xx	xx
EPS	x.x	x.x

Consolidated Subsidiaries, which are not significant to the group's operating results, may disclose only significant information.

- Address, Phone, Fax, Telex, Major Business
- % of Ownership
- Total Assets, Total Revenue, Net Income, and Contributions to the Group.

[Example]

	Total Assets	Total Revenue	Net Income	Contributions To Group
PQRM Financial Services Address, Phone, 100% Owned	xxx	xxx	xx	xx

Associated Companies

Name	Address, Phone Fax, Telex	% of Ownership	Total Assets	Purchase Price	Estimated Market Value
PQRP		45%	xxx	xxx	xxx
PQRQ		40%	xxx	xxx	xxx
PQRR		25%	xxx	xxx	xxx

Other Long-Term Investment

Name (Country)	Purchase Price	Estimated Market Value
PQRS Company (France)	xxx	xxx
PQRT Company (U.S.)	xxx	xxx

PQR Insurance Company

Supplementary Information I

Major Branches and Offices

- Domestic Branches and Offices
  - Responsible Person(s)
  - Address, Phone, Fax, Telex

- Foreign Branches and Offices
  - Responsible Person(s)
  - Address, Phone, Fax, Telex

Supplementary Information J

Shareholder-Related Information

In this section, items pertaining to common shares and shareholders are covered:

1. <u>Capital Change Information</u>

   Changes in common shareholders' equity should be provided for the last five years on items such as stock dividends, stock splits, rights issues and new stock issues.

   Such disclosure would allow users to convert share related ratios such as earnings per share, dividends per share and book value per share on a common denominator historically.

2. <u>Analysis of Shareholdings</u>

   . Shareholders should be classified by type (i.e., individuals, financial institutions, pension funds, others), and number of shares owned (i.e., 1-100, 101-500, 501-1,000, etc.)

   . Geographic distribution of shareholders would be useful.

   . If major changes have taken place in ownership, two years' comparative data would be useful.

   Shareholdings by the key officials and members of the board should also be provided along with any options granted to these individuals.

Shareholders by Number of Shares Owned on MM/DD/1988

Category	Number of Shareholders	Number of Shares	% of Capital
1- 1,000 sh	40,000	15,000,000	3
1,001- 5,000 sh	30,000	70,000,000	14
5,001-10,000 sh	3,000	30,000,000	6
10,001-	250	400,000,000	77
Total	73,250	515,000,000	100%

Shareholders by Type of Organization on MM/DD/1988

Category	Number of Shareholders	Number of Shares	% of Shares Outstanding
Individuals	xxx	xxx	x.x
Financial Institution	xx	xxx	x.x
Pension Funds	xx	xxx	x.x
Other Organizations	xx	xxx	x.x
Total	xxxx	xxxx	100%

Major Shareholders

Name	Number of Shares	%
Top xx Shareholders:		
A. ABC Company	xxx	x.x
B. Individual Shareholder (Director)	xxx	x.x
C. Pension Funds	xxx	x.x
Total for Top xx Shareholders	xxx	x.x
Other Directors' Shareholdings:		
F.	xxx	x.x
G.	xxx	x.x
H.	xxx	x.x
Total for Other Directors	xxx	x.x
Total for Major Shareholders and Directors	xxx	x.x

3. Multiple Classes of Common Shares

In several countries (i.e., Belgium, Canada, Denmark, Italy, Sweden and Switzerland), multiple classes of common shares are allowed. Brief descriptions of each type of share, along with key items such as the number of shares outstanding, dividends per share, earnings per share (if different), as well as capital change information should be provided.

4. Capital Market Information

A list of stock exchanges (both domestic and foreign) where the company's securities are listed along with the appropriate ticker symbol would be useful.

Closing price for the year, high low for the last five years as well as monthly for the last six months, and volume of shares traded should be reported.

Addresses and phone numbers of the company's share registrar and/or transfer agent would also be useful information for shareholders.

Stock Exchange(s) Listed: Stock Exchange 1; Ticker Symbol PQR

Principal Registrar or Transfer Agent: <Address 1, Phone 1>

Other Registrars or Transfer Agents <Address 2, Phone 2>

Recent Stock Prices

Closing, and High-Low Prices for Last 5 Years Common Stock - Stock Exchange-1					
	1988	1987*	1986*	1985*	1984*
Closing	xxx	xxx	xxx	xxx	xxx
High	xxx	xxx	xxx	xxx	xxx
Low	xxx	xxx	xxx	xxx	xxx
Volume	xxx	xxx	xxx	xxx	xxx

* Price has been adjusted by stock splits in 1984-87.

Closing, and High-Low Prices and Volume for Last 6 Months Common Stock						
1988	12	11	10	9	8	7
Closing	xxx	xxx	xxx	xxx	xxx	xxx
High	xxx	xxx	xxx	xxx	xxx	xxx
Low	xxx	xxx	xxx	xxx	xxx	xxx
Volume	xxx	xxx	xxx	xxx	xxx	xxx

These tables should be repeated for multiple shares, if they exist.

5. Financial Calendar

This item should include the following dates:

- Dividend Announcement Date
- Preliminary Results Announcement Date
- Annual General Meeting Date
- Interim Results Announcement Date

6. Availability of Additional Information About the Company

Any of the following items, if applicable, should be disclosed:

- A list of investment houses who follow the company and have issued reports on the company over the last 12 months

- The name of the Local Stock Exchange Authority or Securities and Exchange Commission where additional information about the company is on file and accessible to the public

- Availability of a printed transcripts (or audio cassette recordings) of proceedings at Annual General Meeting of Shareholders

- Availability of annual reports in different languages

- Names of Investor Relations Executives with their address and phone numbers

APPENDIX D

ACCOUNTING LEXICON IN EIGHT LANGUAGES WITH ENGLISH TRANSLATION

Appendix D presents a list of over 800 frequently used accounting and auditing terms and phrases appearing in the English language. The translations for these items are listed in eight different languages, namely, Dutch, French, German, Italian, Korean, Japanese, Portuguese and Spanish. These particular languages were included in this manual because they represent the languages of the majority of the non-English language company annual reports.

Specific words and phrases were chosen to describe essentially all of the principal components of the Balance Sheet, Income Statement, Statement of Changes in Financial Position and Statement of Changes in Owner's Equity, plus some of the more common terminology used in financial transactions as well as in accounting and in the auditing process.

The primary source for this appendix has been a representative sample of fiscal year 1987 reports of the leading industrial companies, banks and insurance companies which publish reports in English as well as their native language. Reference books available in libraries (mentioned in the acknowledgement section) were consulted as secondary sources.

For the users' convenience, the lexicon is indexed in each language as well as in English.

Page Index - Appendix D

ACCOUNTING LEXICON : DUTCH - ENGLISH

DUTCH	ENGLISH
à pari	par value
aandeel in het verlies van deelnemingen	share in loss of affiliates
aandeelhouders	stockholders
aandelen	shares
aandelenkapitaal	capital stock
aanloopkosten	start-up cost
aanpassing	adjustment
aanspraken	claims
aanvullende informatie	disclosure
aanvullende informatie	supplementary information
aard	nature
accijns	excise tax
accountant	auditor
accountantscontrole	audit
accountantsonderzoek	audit
accountantsrapport	auditor's report
accountantsverklaring	audit opinion
achtergestelde financiering	subordinated financing
achtergestelde schuld	subordinated debt
achterstallig	overdue
achterwaartse verliescompensatie	carryback
acid-test ratio	acid test ratio
activa	assets
activeren van lease-contracten	capitalization of leases
activeren van rente	capitalization of interests
activering van financieringskosten	capitalization of financial costs
actuariele waarde	actuarial value
administratie	accounting
administreren	record (verb)
adviesverschaffende diensten	consulting services
advocaat	lawyer
afdelingshoofd	officer
afgebroken activiteiten	discontinued operations
afhankelijk van	subject to
aflosbaar	redeemable
afschrijven	write down
afschrijvingen	depreciation expense
afschrijvingen (gebouwen)	depreciation - buildings
afschrijvingen volgens de jaarnummer-methode	sum of the years'-digits method
afschrijvingsmethode volgens een vast percentage van de aanschafwaarde	sum of the years'-digits method
afwisselende procedures	straight-line method
agio	straight-line method
agio	alternate procedures
agio bij aandelenemissie	premium
agioreserve	debt premium
	premium on issue of capital
	capital surplus

DUTCH	ENGLISH
algemeen aanvaard	generally accepted
algemeen directeur	general manager
algemene en administratieve kosten	general and administrative expense
algemene kosten	overhead expenses
algemene reserves	retained earnings
algemene verzekering	general insurance
alloceren	allocate
als geheel genomen	taken as a whole
alternatieve procedures	alternative procedures
analytische controle	analytical review
andere bedrijfswinsten/verliezen	other operating profits (losses)
andere leningen	other loans
andere winsten uit verleende diensten	other income for services
anticipatie-posten activa	deferred charges
april	April
arbeidswet	labor law
assurantie eigen risico	self-insurance
augustus	August
auteursrecht	copyright
balans	balance sheet
balansdatum	balance sheet date
bank	bank
bedrijf	industry
bedrijfscyclus	operating cycle
bedrijfstak	business segment
bedrijfstak	industry
bedrijfsuitrustingen	furniture and fixtures
bedrijfsuitrustingen	machinery and equipment
begroting	budget
behalve voor	except for
beheerskosten	administrative expenses
beinvloeden	impact (verb)
belangrijkheid	material (significant)
belangrijkste klanten	major customers
belastbaar inkomen	taxable income
belasting	tax
belasting toegevoegde waarde (btw)	value added tax (VAT)
belastingaangifte	tax return
belastingbesparing	tax savings
belastingdienst	tax authorities
belastinglatenties	deferred taxes
belastingplichtige	taxpayer
belastingvermindering	tax credits
belastingvoet	tax rates
belegging	investment
(beleggingen (kt) + debiteuren + kas): (vlottende schulden)	acid test
	acid test

DUTCH	ENGLISH
beperkingen van de reikwijdte	restrictions on the scope
beroepsnormen	professional standards
besteding van middelen	uses of funds
bestendig toegepast	consistently applied
bestendige gedragslijn	consistency
bestendigheid	consistency
betaalbaar dividend	dividends payable
betalingen	disbursement
betalingen	payments
betalingscyclus	payments cycle
beurscommissie (USA)	Securities and Exchange Commission
bewijsstuk	voucher
bieden	bid (verb)
bijprodukten	by-products
binnenlandse dochtermaatschappijen	domestic subsidiaries
bod	bid
boeken	record
boekhouder	accountant
boekhouding	accounting
boekwaarde	book value
bon	voucher
borgtochten	guarantee deposits
break even point	break even point
breuk	severance
bruto marge	gross margin
bruto nationaal produkt	gross national product
bruto omzetbelasting	gross revenue tax
bruto winstratio	gross profit ratio
budget	budget
buitengewone posten	extraordinary items
buitenlandse dochtermaatschappij	foreign subsidiary
call prijs	call price
carry forward periode	carryforward period
cash flow	cash flow
ceteris paribus	ceteris paribus
claims	claims
clienten	customers
coderen	code (verb)
commerciele bank	commercial bank
commissarissen	directors
communicatiekosten	communications expense
compenseren	offset
completed-contract methode	completed-contract method
concessies	licences
consolideren door middel van het samen	pooling of interest
voegen van jaarrekeningen	pooling of interest
contant dividend	cash dividends

DUTCH	ENGLISH
continuiteit	going concern
controle personeel	audit staff
controle procedure	auditing procedures
controle standaarden	auditing standards
controle strategie	audit strategy
controleaanpak	audit approach
controlebenadering	audit approach
controleleider	audit manager
controleopdracht	audit engagement
controlerisiko	audit risk
controlesteekproef	audit sampling
converteerbare schulden	convertible debt
copyright	copyright
correctie	adjustment
correcties met betrekking tot vorige	prior period adjustments
boekingsperiode	prior period adjustments
crediteuren	accounts payable
cumulatief effect	cumulative effect
dagboekrekeningen	subsidiary records
datum einde boekjaar	year-end closing date
december	December
debiteuren	receivables
debiteuren	accounts receivable
deelneming	investment
deelneming in andere ondernemingen	equity in other companies
deelnemingen	affiliates
deelnemingen	investment in subsidiaries
deelnemingen 20-50% van de aandelen zijn	affiliated firms
in handen van een andere onderneming	affiliated firms
degressieve belasting	regressive tax
dekking door termijntransactie	hedge
depositocertificaten	certificate of deposit
deviezen	foreign exchange
direct opeisbare deposito's	demand deposits
directe kosten	direct cost
disagio	debt discount
disconteringsrente	discount rate
dividend	dividend
dividend per aandeel	dividend per share
dochtermaatschappij	subsidiary
document	form
dollars	dollars
doorlopende inventarisatie	perpetual inventory system
doteren	allocate
driemaandelijks	quarterly
driemaandelijks (4 maal per jaar)	quarterly (4 times a year)
dubbele belasting	double taxation

DUTCH	ENGLISH
duizend	thousand
duizenden	thousands
economische levensduur	useful life (of an asset)
economische omgeving	economic environment
effect	effect
effecten van prijsveranderingen	effects of changing prices
effectenbeurs	stock exchange
effectenmakelaar	stockbroker
eigen vermogen	shareholders' equity
eigen vermogen	stockholders' equity
eigen vermogen	net worth
eisen met betrekking tot het verpanden	pledging requirements
equity-methode	equity method
exploitatie huur	operating leases
export	export
factuur	invoice
fallissement	bankruptcy
februari	February
financiele samenvatting	financial summary
financien	finance
financieren	finance (verb)
financieringmaatschappijen	financial entities
first in, first out (FIFO)	first in, first out (FIFO)
fiscale winst	taxable income
flexibele koersen	floating rate
fondsen	funds
formulier	form
fouten	errors
fusie	merger
fusies	business combinations
fysieke voorraad	physical inventory
garanties	guarantees
gebonden reserve	appropriated retained earnings
gebouwen	buildings and structures
geconsolideerde jaarrekening	consolidated accounts
geconsolideerde jaarrekening	consolidated financial statements
gecumuleerde afschrijvingen	accumulated depreciation
gecumuleerde amortizaties	accumulated amortization
gecumuleerde correcties	cumulative adjustment
gegevensverwerkende apparatuur	data processing equipment
geldboete	fine
gemiddeld	average
gereed produkt	finished goods
geregistreerde obligaties	listed bonds
gestort vermogen	paid-in capital
getrouwe weergave	feasibility
gewogen gemiddelde	weighted average

DUTCH	ENGLISH
gewoon aandelenkapitaal	common stock
goederen in bewerking	goods in process
goederen ter wederverkoop	resale merchandise
goodwill	goodwill
groep	group (of companies)
grond	land
grondslagen voor de verslaggeving	accounting principles
grondstoffen	raw materials
grootboek	general ledger
halffabrikaten	semi-finished goods
handelsdebiteuren	trade receivables -
handelsmerken	trade marks
handelsmerken	trademarks
handelsvorderingen	trade receivables
hedge	hedge
herfinanciering	refinancing
herkomst van middelen	sources of funds
herstructureren	restructure
herverzekering en premiecorrecties	reinsurance and premium adjustments
herwaardering	revaluation
herwaarderingsreserve	revaluation reserve
het vlottende gedeelte van ...	current portion of ...
historische kostprijs	historical cost
holdingmaatschappij	holding company
honderden	hundreds
honorarium	fee
honorarium geleverde diensten aan derden	fees for services by third party
houder	bearer
hulpmiddelen	supplies
huur en verhuur	lease
huurder	lessee
huurovereenkomst	lease
hypotheek	mortgage
hypotheekbank	mortgage bank
immateriele activa	intangible assets
in overeenstemming met	in accordance with
in- en uitvoerrechten	customs duty
indirecte belasting	excise tax
indirecte kosten	overhead expenses
inflatie	inflation
inflatiecorrectie	adjustment for inflation
ingehouden winst	retained earnings
ingekochte, eigen aandelen,	treasury stock
nog niet ingetrokken	treasury stock
inhoud	contents
initiele kosten	start-up costs
inkomen uit dividend	dividend income

DUTCH	ENGLISH
inkomen uit verleende diensten	income for services rendered
inkomstenbelasting	income tax
inningen	collections
inschrijving	subscription
inter-company leningen	inter-company loans
internationale dochtermaatschappijen	international subsidiaries
internationale handel	international trade
interne accountants	internal auditors
interne controle	internal controls
investeringen op lange termijn	long-term investments
investeringspremie	investment tax credit
investment bank/merchant bank	investment bank/merchant bank
invloed	impact
jaarlijks	annually
jaarlijkse vergadering	annual meeting
jaarlijkse vergadering van aandeel	annual shareholders' meeting
houders	annual shareholders' meeting
jaarrekening	financial statements
januari	January
joint venture	joint venture
journaal (boekhouding)	journal
journaalpost	journal entry
juli	July
juni	June
kantoorbehoeften	office supplies
kapitaaltoename	capital increase
kas	cash
kas en banktegoeden	cash and banks
kasstroom	cash flow
kastransacties	monetary transactions
kleine kas	petty cash
kleine ondernemingen	small companies
korte termijn banklening	short-term bank loans
korte termijn investering/belegging	short-term investments
korte termijn leningen	short-term loans
kosten	expenses
kosten van accountantscontrole	audit fees
kosten van de verkochte goederen	cost of goods sold
kosten van de verkopen	cost of sales
kosten van personeelswerving	recruiting expense
kosten voor bankdiensten	bank service charges
kosten voor opleiding	training expenditure
krediet op lange termijn	long-term credits
kredietplafond	credit line
kwalificatie	qualification(of an audit opinion)
kwaliteitscontrole	quality control
kwart	quarter

DUTCH	ENGLISH
kwartaal	quarter
kwartaalbericht	quarterly financial statements
land	land
landenrisico	country risk
lang lopende schulden	non-current liabilities
lange termijn contracten	long-term contracts
last in, first out (LIFO)	last in, first out (LIFO)
lasten	expenses
latente belasting	deferred income tax
leaseback	leaseback
leenvemrogen	debenture
lening	debenture
leningen	loans
levensverzekering	life insurance
leveranciers	suppliers
leveranties	supplies
liability methode	liability method
licenties	licences
lid van dagelijks bestuur	officer
liquide middelen	cash
liquide middelen	liquid assets
liquiditeit	liquidity
liquiditeitsratio	liquidity ratio
liquiditeitsrisiko	liquidity risk
locale valuta	local currency
lonen en salarissen	salaries and wages
loon	fee
loonlijst	payroll
lopende belastingen	accrued taxes
lopende kosten	accrued expenses
lopende onderneming	going concern
maandelijks	monthly
maart	March
magazijn	warehouse
marge	spread (between rates)
marginale kosten	marginal cost
marktprijs	market price
mate	extent
materialen	materials
materialiteit	materiality
materiality	materiality
materiele duurzame activa	tangible fixed assets
mei	May
merken	trade marks
miljarden	billions
miljoenen	millions
minderheidsbelang	minority interest

DUTCH	ENGLISH
minimumwaarderingsregel	lower of cost or market
minimumwaarderingsregel	cost or market
misleidende informatie	misleading information
moedermaatschappij	parent company
monetaire activa	monetary assets
monetaire transacties	monetary transactions
multinational	multinational enterprise
multionationale onderneming	multinational enterprise
multipele regressie	multiple regression
mutual fund	mutual fund
natuur	nature
negatieve goodwill	negative goodwill
netto contante waarde	net present value
netto directe opbrengstwaarde	net realizable value
netto handelsdebiteuren	net trade accounts receivable
netto omzet	net sales
netto vaste activa	net fixed assets
netto verdiende premies	net premiums earned
netto verkopen	net sales
netto winst	net income
niet door accountants gecontroleerd	unaudited
niet gekwalificeerd	unqualified
niet-belastbaar inkomen	non-taxable income
niet-geld transacties	non-monetary transactions
nog te betalen / nog te ontvangen posten	accrual
nominale waarde	face value
nota	invoice
november	November
obligatie	debenture
obligatie	bond
obligaties zonder zekerheidsstelling	unsecured bonds
obligo's	commitments
octrooien	patents
oktober	October
omloopsnelheid ratio	turnover ratio
omloopsnelheid van crediteuren	credits turnover ratio
omloopsnelheid van de voorraden	inventory turnover ratio
omloopsnelheid werkkapitaal	working capital turnover
omrekening van valuta	currency translation
omrekening van vreemde valuta	foreign currency translation
omstandigheden	circumstances
omvang van de steekproef	sample size
omzet	sales (turnover)
omzetbelasting	sales tax
onafhankelijk	independence
onderaanbesteden	sublet
onderhoud	repairs

DUTCH	ENGLISH
ondernemingsstatuten	company by-laws
onderpand	collateral
onderverhuren	sublet
onderworpen aan	subject to
onderzoek- en ontwikkelingskosten	research and development costs
onderzoeken	examine
ongebruikte capaciteit	idle capacity
ongewoon	remote
oninbaar	uncollectible
onregelmatigheid	irregularity
ontdekken	detect
onverdeelde winst	unappropriated retained earnings
onzekerheid	uncertainty
opbrengst	yield
opbrengst der geproduceerde goederen	sale of manufactured goods
opdeling (van een onderneming)	split (of a company)
opeenvolgende gebeurtenissen	subsequent events
operating leases	operating laeses
opgebouwde vakantierechten	accrued vacations
opnemen	record
opportunity cost	opportunity cost
opstellen van jaarrekening	compilation of financial statements
opties	options
organisatiediagram	organization chart
organisatiekosten	organization expenses
organisatieplan	flowchart
over the counter-transactie	over the counter transaction
overboekingen via de bank	bank overdrafts
overeenstemmen met	comply with
overschrijving	overdraft
pacht	lease
pakhuis	warehouse
pand	pledge
pariwaarde	par value
partner	partner
passief	liability
patenten	patents
pensioen	pension
pensioentoezegging	pension plan
percentage	percentage
periodewinst (-verlies)	net income (loss) of the period
permanente voorraadregistratie	perpetual inventory system
persoonlijke inkomstenbelasting	personal income tax
plaatsing	placement
populatie	population
populatie (statistische betekenis)	population (in a statist. environ.)
preferent aandeel	preference share (UK)

DUTCH	ENGLISH
preferent aandeel	preferred share (USA)
preferent aandeel	preference share
premie	premium
president	chairman
president-directeur	chief executive officer
primair vermogen	primary capital
private sector	private sector
procesvoering	litigation
produktfinanciering	product financing
produktgarantie	product warranties
produktie capaciteit	production capacity
produktie-eenheden	units of production
produktiecyclus	production cycle
produktiecyclus	operating cycle
produktiekosten	production cost
proefbalans	trial balance
professionele beoordeling	professional judgment
progressieve belasting	progressive tax
projectie	projection
promotiekosten	promotional costs
provisie	bank service charges
provisie-winsten-(-veriezen)	commissions & fees profits (losses)
publieke sector	public sector
publikatie	disclosure
raad van commissarissen	board of directors
recessie	recession
recu	voucher
redelijk waarschijnlijk	reasonably possible
regels	rules
reglementen	regulations
reikwijdte	scope
rekening	invoice
rekeningstelsel	chart of accounts
relatieve betekenis	material (significant)
rendement	yield
rentabiliteit op eigen vermogen	return on equity
rentabiliteit op totaal vermogen	return on assets
rentebaten	interest income
rentelasten	interest expense
rentevoet	interest rate
reparaties	repairs
reparaties en onderhoud	repairs and maintenance
reproduktiekosten	reproduction cost
research and development kosten	research and development costs
resultaat	net income
resultaten voortvloeiende uit steekproef	sampling results
resultatenrekening	profit & loss accounts

DUTCH	ENGLISH
salderen	offset
samengevatte jaarrekening	condensed financial statements
samenstelling van een portfolio	portfolio composition
schadeloosstellingen	indemnities
schuld	liability
schuld herstructurering	debt restructuring
schuld op lange termijn	long-term debt
schulden	loans
schulden op korte termijn	current liabilities
schuldverhouding	indebtedness ratio
secundaire markt	secondary market
september	September
servicekosten	cost of services rendered
sociale lasten	social security expense
spaargelden	saving deposits
speciale bonus	special bonus
speciale verslagen	special reports
staat van herkomst en besteding van middelen	statement changes in fin. position
	statement changes in fin. position
staat van herkomst en besteding van middelen	statement sources & uses of funds
	statement sources & uses of funds
standaardkosten	standard cost
statistisch verantwoorde steekproef	statistical sampling
statutair vereist accountantsverslag	statutory audit report
statutaire reserves	statutory reserve
steekproef nemen (-trekken)	sampling
steekproefrisico	sampling risk
steekproeftrekken (niet statistisch)	non-statistical sampling
stelselwijziging (van de financiele administratie)	accounting changes
	accounting changes
stock dividend	stock dividends
stock optie-plan	stock option plans
stroomdiagram	flowchart
successierechten	inheritance tax
sum of the years'-digits methode	sum of the years'-digits method
te betalen promessen	notes payable
te betalen rente	interest payable
te vorderen rente	interest receivable
technische voorzieningen	life policy benefits
ter beurze genoteerde aandelen	marketable stocks
ter beurze genoteerde effecten	marketable securities
ter beurze genoteerde obligaties	listed bonds
termijncontracten	future contracts
termijndepositos	time deposits
terrein	land
terugkoopovereenkomst	repurchase agreement
testen	tests

DUTCH	ENGLISH
tijdelijke verschillen	temporary differences
timing	timing
toelichting	disclosure
toelichting bij de jaarrekening	footnotes to financial statements
toepassingsgebied	scope
toerekenen	allocate
toerekenen van baten en lasten aan een	accrual (acc. method)
bepaalde periode	accrual (acc. method)
toerekenen van opbrengsten en kosten	percentage-of-completion-method
naar de rato van de werkvoortgang	percentage-of-completion-method
toets	test
toetsen	tests
toevallig	random
toezeggingen	commitments
totale herkomst uit bedrijfsvoering	total funds from operations
totale opbrengsten	total revenue
totale voorziening voor verzekering	total insurance reserves
transacties	transactions
transacties met verbonden partijen	related party transactions
transitoria en anticipatie posten	accrual
transitoria en anticipatieposten/activa	accrued income
transitoria en anticipatieposten/passiva	accrued liabilities
transitorische passiva	deferred income
trend	trend
tussentijds financieel bericht	interim financial statements
tweede verzoek	second request
uiteenzetting van grondslagen voor	statement of accounting policy
waardering en winstbepaling	statement of accounting policy
uitgaafprijs	historical cost
uitgaven	expenses
uitgaven	disbursements
uitgaven voor liefdadigheid	charity expense
uitgezonderd	except for
uitrustingen	fittings
uitstaande aandelen	outstanding shares
uitstelmethode	deferral method
uitvoer	export
uitvoerbaarheidsstudie	feasibility study
uitvoerrechten	export duties
valutakoers	exchange rate
valutakoersrisiko	exchange rate risk
variabele kosten	variable cost
vaste activa	fixed assets
vaste activa	non-current assets
vaste activa in aanbouw	construction in progress
vennoot	partner
verantwoordelijkheid van de accountant	auditor's responsibility

DUTCH	ENGLISH
verbetering van land	land improvements
verbonden	affiliate
verbonden vennootschap/onderneming	associated firm
verbreking (van contracten)	severance
verbruiksduur	useful life (of an asset)
vergelijkende financiele overzichten	comparative financial statements
vergunningen	licences
verhoudingsgetal voor liquiditeit van	acid test ratio
de eerste orde	acid test ratio
verhuurder	lessor
verkoop	disposition
verkoop op afbetaling	sales on installments
verkoopkosten	selling expenses
verkopers	vendors (USA)
verlies	loss
verliescompensatie	carry forward
vermeldingen	disclosure
vermogensbelasting	capital tax
vermogensbelasting	capital gains tax
vernietiging	disposition
veroudering	obsolescence
verpakkingsmateriaal	packaging material
verplichting	liability
verplichtingen	commitments
verslag	report
verslaggeving	accounting
verslaggeving aan het management	report to management
versnelde afschrijvingen	accelerated depreciation
vervaldag	maturity
vervaldag	due date
vervallen leningen	matured loans
vervangingskosten	replacement cost
vervroegde aflossing van schuld	early extinguishment of debt
vervroegde pensionering,- uittreding	early retirement
verwachte restwaarde	expected salvage value
verwerving (van een onderneming)	acquisition (of a company)
verwervingskosten	acquisition cost
verzameling uitgangspunten voor de	accounting policies
verslaggeving	accounting policies
verzekeringsmaatschappij	insurance company
vice-president	vice-chairman
vice-voorzitter	vice-chairman
vlottende activa	current assets
(vlottende activa : vlottende passiva)	current ratio
voertuigen	vehicles
volgorde van produktie	production order
volmacht (recht van gevolmachtigde)	proxy (power of attorney)

DUTCH	ENGLISH
voor belastingdoeleinden	for taxation purposes
voor seizoensinvloeden gecorrigeerd	seasonally adjusted
voor uitkering beschikbare winst	unappropriated retained earnings
voorbehoud (van accountantsverklaring)	qualification(of an audit opinion)
voorraad en reserveonderdelen	supplies and spare parts
voorraden	inventories -(USA) (stocks-UK)
voorschriften	rules
voorspelling	forecast
vooruit betaald aan leveranciers	advances to suppliers
vooruitbetaalde kosten	prepaid expense
vooruitbetaalde lasten	deferred expense
vooruitontvangen baten	deferred income
vooruitontvangen rente	unearned interests
voorwaardelijke baten en lasten	contingencies
voorwaartse verliescompensatie	carry forward
voorziening	provision
voorziening	allowance
voorziening uit hoofde van krediet	reserve for loan losses
verlening	reserve for loan losses
voorziening uit hoofde van krediet	allowance for loan losses
verlening	allowance for loan losses
voorziening voor algemene risico's	reserve for general risks
voorziening voor dubieuze debiteuren	allowance for doubtful accounts
voorziening voor dubieuze debiteuren	allowance for doubtful accounts
voorziening voor waardeverminderingen	allowance for devaluation of inv't
van beleggingen	allowance for devaluation of inv't
voorziening wisselkoersveranderingen	reserve for exch. rate fluctuations
voorzitter	chairman
vorm	form
vreemde valuta	foreign currency
waarderingsgrondslagen	valuation principles
waardevermindering	depreciation expense
waardeverminderingen	write down
waarschijnlijk	probable
wederhuur	leaseback
wederverkoopovereenkomst	resale agreements
werkelijke verliezen op leningen	actual loan losses
werkkapitaal	working capital
werkkapitaal-ratio	working capital ratio
werknemer	employee
werkuren	labor hours
wettelijke reserve	legal reserve
wettelijke vereisten	legal requirements
wijze van waarderen van lang lopende	percentage-of-completion-method
contracten met het doel de winsten te	percentage-of-completion-method
spreiden over de looptijd van het	percentage-of-completion-method
contract	percentage-of-completion-method

DUTCH	ENGLISH
willekeurig	at random
willekeurig	random
winst	profit
winst	gain
winst (verlies) op vreemde valuta	foreign exchange gains (losses)
winst door herwaardering van effecten	gain on revaluation of securities
winst door verkoop van vaste activa	gain on sale of fixed assets
winst per aandeel	earnings per share
winst- en verliesrekening	profit & loss accounts
winstbelasting	income tax
winstmarge	profit margin
winstuitkering in de vorm van aandelen	stock dividends
winstverdeling	profit sharing
wisselkoers	exchange rate
zakelijke kredieten	commercial & industrial loans
zegelrecht	stamp duty
zekerheden	guarantees
zero base budget	zero base budget
zero base budgeting	zero base budgeting
zonder voorbehoud	unqualified
zonder winststreven	non-profit
zwevende koers	floating rate

ENGLISH	DUTCH
accelerated depreciation	versnelde afschrijvingen
accountant	boekhouder
accounting	administratie
accounting	boekhouding
accounting	verslaggeving
accounting changes	stelselwijziging (van de financiele
accounting changes	administratie)
accounting policies	verzameling uitgangspunten voor de
accounting policies	verslaggeving
accounting principles	grondslagen voor de verslaggeving
accounts payable	crediteuren
accounts receivable	debiteuren
accrual	nog te betalen / nog te ontvangen posten
accrual	transitoria en anticipatie posten
accrual (acc. method)	toerekenen van baten en lasten aan een
accrual (acc. method)	bepaalde periode
accrued expenses	lopende kosten
accrued income	transitoria en anticipatieposten/activa
accrued liabilities	transitoria en anticipatieposten/passiva
accrued taxes	lopende belastingen
accrued vacations	opgebouwde vakantierechten
accumulated amortization	gecumuleerde amortizaties
accumulated depreciation	gecumuleerde afschrijvingen
acid test	(beleggingen (kt) + debiteuren + kas):
acid test	(vlottende schulden)
acid test ratio	acid-test ratio
acid test ratio	verhoudingsgetal voor liquiditeit van
acid test ratio	de eerste orde
acquisition (of a company)	verwerving (van een onderneming)
acquisition cost	verwervingskosten
actual loan losses	werkelijke verliezen op leningen
actuarial value	actuariele waarde
adjustment	aanpassing
adjustment	correctie
adjustment for inflation	inflatiecorrectie
administrative expenses	beheerskosten
advances to suppliers	vooruit betaald aan leveranciers
affiliate	verbonden
affiliated firms	deelnemingen 20-50% van de aandelen zijn
affiliated firms	in handen van een andere onderneming
affiliates	deelnemingen
allocate	alloceren
allocate	doteren
allocate	toerekenen
allowance	voorziening
allowance for devaluation of inv't	voorziening voor waardeverminderingen
allowance for devaluation of inv't	van beleggingen

ENGLISH	DUTCH
allowance for doubtful accounts	voorziening voor dubieuze debiteuren
allowance for doubtful accounts	voorziening voor dubieuze debiteuren
allowance for loan losses	voorziening uit hoofde van krediet
allowance for loan losses	verlening
alternate procedures	afwisselende procedures
alternative procedures	alternatieve procedures
analytical review	analytische controle
annual meeting	jaarlijkse vergadering
annual shareholders' meeting	jaarlijkse vergadering van aandeel
annual shareholders' meeting	houders
annually	jaarlijks
appropriated retained earnings	gebonden reserve
April	april
assets	activa
associated firm	verbonden vennootschap/onderneming
at random	willekeurig
audit	accountantscontrole
audit	accountantsonderzoek
audit approach	controleaanpak
audit approach	controlebenadering
audit engagement	controleopdracht
audit fees	kosten van accountantscontrole
audit manager	controleleider
audit opinion	accountantsverklaring
audit risk	controlerisiko
audit sampling	controlesteekproef
audit staff	controle personeel
audit strategy	controle strategie
auditing procedures	controle procedure
auditing standards	controle standaarden
auditor	accountant
auditor's report	accountantsrapport
auditor's responsibility	verantwoordelijkheid van de accountant
August	augustus
average	gemiddeld
balance sheet	balans
balance sheet date	balansdatum
bank	bank
bank overdrafts	overboekingen via de bank
bank service charges	kosten voor bankdiensten
bank service charges	provisie
bankruptcy	fallissement
bearer	houder
bid	bod
bid (verb)	bieden
billions	miljarden
board of directors	raad van commissarissen

ENGLISH	DUTCH
bond	obligatie
book value	boekwaarde
break even point	break even point
budget	begroting
budget	budget
buildings and structures	gebouwen
business combinations	fusies
business segment	bedrijfstak
by-products	bijprodukten
call price	call prijs
capital gains tax	vermogensbelasting
capital increase	kapitaaltoename
capital stock	aandelenkapitaal
capital surplus	agioreserve
capital tax	vermogensbelasting
capitalization of financial costs	activering van financieringskosten
capitalization of interests	activeren van rente
capitalization of leases	activeren van lease-contracten
carry forward	verliescompensatie
carry forward	voorwaartse verliescompensatie
carryback	achterwaartse verliescompensatie
carryforward period	carry forward periode
cash	kas
cash	liquide middelen
cash and banks	kas en banktegoeden
cash dividends	contant dividend
cash flow	cash flow
cash flow	kasstroom
certificate of deposit	depositocertificaten
ceteris paribus	ceteris paribus
chairman	president
chairman	voorzitter
charity expense	uitgaven voor liefdadigheid
chart of accounts	rekeningstelsel
chief executive officer	president-directeur
circumstances	omstandigheden
claims	aanspraken
claims	claims
code (verb)	coderen
collateral	onderpand
collections	inningen
commercial & industrial loans	zakelijke kredieten
commercial bank	commerciele bank
commissions & fees profits (losses)	provisie-winsten-(-veriezen)
commitments	obligo's
commitments	toezeggingen
commitments	verplichtingen

ENGLISH	DUTCH
common stock	gewoon aandelenkapitaal
communications expense	communicatiekosten
company by-laws	ondernemingsstatuten
comparative financial statements	vergelijkende financiele overzichten
compilation of financial statements	opstellen van jaarrekening
completed-contract method	completed-contract methode
comply with	overeenstemmen met
condensed financial statements	samengevatte jaarrekening
consistency	bestendige gedragslijn
consistency	bestendigheid
consistently applied	bestendig toegepast
consolidated accounts	geconsolideerde jaarrekening
consolidated financial statements	geconsolideerde jaarrekening
construction in progress	vaste activa in aanbouw
consulting services	adviesverschaffende diensten
contents	inhoud
contingencies	voorwaardelijke baten en lasten
convertible debt	converteerbare schulden
copyright	auteursrecht
copyright	copyright
cost of goods sold	kosten van de verkochte goederen
cost of sales	kosten van de verkopen
cost of services rendered	servicekosten
cost or market	minimumwaarderingsregel
country risk	landenrisico
credit line	kredietplafond
credits turnover ratio	omloopsnelheid van crediteuren
cumulative adjustment	gecumuleerde correcties
cumulative effect	cumulatief effect
currency translation	omrekening van valuta
current assets	vlottende activa
current liabilities	schulden op korte termijn
current portion of ...	het vlottende gedeelte van ...
current ratio	(vlottende activa : vlottende passiva)
customers	clienten
customs duty	in- en uitvoerrechten
data processing equipment	gegevensverwerkende apparatuur
December	december
debenture	leenvemrogen
debenture	lening
debenture	obligatie
debt discount	disagio
debt premium	agio
debt restructuring	schuld herstructurering
deferral method	uitstelmethode
deferred charges	anticipatie-posten activa
deferred expense	vooruitbetaalde lasten

ENGLISH	DUTCH
deferred income	transitorische passiva
deferred income	vooruitontvangen baten
deferred income tax	latente belasting
deferred taxes	belastinglatenties
demand deposits	direct opeisbare deposito's
depreciation - buildings	afschrijvingen (gebouwen)
depreciation expense	afschrijvingen
depreciation expense	waardevermindering
detect	ontdekken
direct cost	directe kosten
directors	commissarissen
disbursement	betalingen
disbursements	uitgaven
disclosure	aanvullende informatie
disclosure	publikatie
disclosure	toelichting
disclosure	vermeldingen
discontinued operations	afgebroken activiteiten
discount rate	disconteringsrente
disposition	verkoop
disposition	vernietiging
dividend	dividend
dividend income	inkomen uit dividend
dividend per share	dividend per aandeel
dividends payable	betaalbaar dividend
dollars	dollars
domestic subsidiaries	binnenlandse dochtermaatschappijen
double taxation	dubbele belasting
due date	vervaldag
early extinguishment of debt	vervroegde aflossing van schuld
early retirement	vervroegde pensionering,- uittreding
earnings per share	winst per aandeel
economic environment	economische omgeving
effect	effect
effects of changing prices	effecten van prijsveranderingen
employee	werknemer
equity in other companies	deelneming in andere ondernemingen
equity method	equity-methode
errors	fouten
examine	onderzoeken
except for	behalve voor
except for	uitgezonderd
exchange rate	valutakoers
exchange rate	wisselkoers
exchange rate risk	valutakoersrisiko
excise tax	accijns
excise tax	indirecte belasting
expected salvage value	verwachte restwaarde
expenses	kosten
expenses	lasten
expenses	uitgaven
export	export
export	uitvoer
export duties	uitvoerrechten
extent	mate
extraordinary items	buitengewone posten
face value	nominale waarde
feasibility	getrouwe weergave
feasibility study	uitvoerbaarheidsstudie
February	februari
fee	honorarium
fee	loon
fees for services by third party	honorarium geleverde diensten aan derden
finance	financien
finance (verb)	financieren
financial entities	financieringmaatschappijen
financial statements	jaarrekening
financial summary	financiele samenvatting
fine	geldboete
finished goods	gereed produkt
first in, first out (FIFO)	first in, first out (FIFO)
fittings	uitrustingen
fixed assets	vaste activa
floating rate	flexibele koersen
floating rate	zwevende koers
flowchart	organisatieplan
flowchart	stroomdiagram
footnotes to financial statements	toelichting bij de jaarrekening
for taxation purposes	voor belastingdoeleinden
forecast	voorspelling
foreign currency	vreemde valuta
foreign currency translation	omrekening van vreemde valuta
foreign exchange	deviezen
foreign exchange gains (losses)	winst (verlies) op vreemde valuta
foreign subsidiary	buitenlandse dochtermaatschappij
form	document
form	formulier
form	vorm
funds	fondsen
furniture and fixtures	bedrijfsuitrustingen
future contracts	termijncontracten
gain	winst
gain on revaluation of securities	winst door herwaardering van effecten
gain on sale of fixed assets	winst door verkoop van vaste activa

ENGLISH	DUTCH
general and administrative expense	algemene en administratieve kosten
general insurance	algemene verzekering
general ledger	grootboek
general manager	algemeen directeur
generally accepted	algemeen aanvaard
going concern	continuiteit
going concern	lopende onderneming
goods in process	goederen in bewerking
goodwill	goodwill
gross margin	bruto marge
gross national product	bruto nationaal produkt
gross profit ratio	bruto winstratio
gross revenue tax	bruto omzetbelasting
group (of companies)	groep
guarantee deposits	borgtochten
guarantees	garanties
guarantees	zekerheden
hedge	dekking door termijntransactie
hedge	hedge
historical cost	historische kostprijs
historical cost	uitgaafprijs
holding company	holdingmaatschappij
hundreds	honderden
idle capacity	ongebruikte capaciteit
impact	invloed
impact (verb)	beinvloeden
in accordance with	in overeenstemming met
income for services rendered	inkomen uit verleende diensten
income tax	inkomstenbelasting
income tax	winstbelasting
indebtedness ratio	schuldverhouding
indemnities	schadeloosstellingen
independence	onafhankelijk
industry	bedrijf
industry	bedrijfstak
inflation	inflatie
inheritance tax	successierechten
insurance company	verzekeringsmaatschappij
intangible assets	immateriele activa
inter-company loans	inter-company leningen
interest expense	rentelasten
interest income	rentebaten
interest payable	te betalen rente
interest rate	rentevoet
interest receivable	te vorderen rente
interim financial statements	tussentijds financieel bericht
internal auditors	interne accountants

ENGLISH	DUTCH
internal controls	interne controle
international subsidiaries	internationale dochtermaatschappijen
international trade	internationale handel
inventories -(USA) (stocks-UK)	voorraden
inventory turnover ratio	omloopsnelheid van de voorraden
investment	belegging
investment	deelneming
investment bank/merchant bank	investment bank/merchant bank
investment in subsidiaries	deelnemingen
investment tax credit	investeringspremie
invoice	factuur
invoice	nota
invoice	rekening
irregularity	onregelmatigheid
January	januari
joint venture	joint venture
journal	journaal (boekhouding)
journal entry	journaalpost
July	juli
June	juni
labor hours	werkuren
labor law	arbeidswet
land	grond
land	land
land	terrein
land improvements	verbetering van land
last in, first out (LIFO)	last in, first out (LIFO)
lawyer	advocaat
lease	huur en verhuur
lease	huurovereenkomst
lease	pacht
leaseback	leaseback
leaseback	wederhuur
legal requirements	wettelijke vereisten
legal reserve	wettelijke reserve
lessee	huurder
lessor	verhuurder
liability	passief
liability	schuld
liability	verplichting
liability method	liability methode
licences	concessies
licences	licenties
licences	vergunningen
life insurance	levensverzekering
life policy benefits	technische voorzieningen
liquid assets	liquide middelen

ENGLISH	DUTCH
liquidity	liquiditeit
liquidity ratio	liquiditeitsratio
liquidity risk	liquiditeitsrisiko
listed bonds	geregistreerde obligaties
listed bonds	ter beurze genoteerde obligaties
litigation	procesvoering
loans	leningen
loans	schulden
local currency	locale valuta
long-term contracts	lange termijn contracten
long-term credits	krediet op lange termijn
long-term debt	schuld op lange termijn
long-term investments	investeringen op lange termijn
loss	verlies
lower of cost or market	minimumwaarderingsregel
machinery and equipment	bedrijfsuitrustingen
major customers	belangrijkste klanten
March	maart
marginal cost	marginale kosten
market price	marktprijs
marketable securities	ter beurze genoteerde effecten
marketable stocks	ter beurze genoteerde aandelen
material (significant)	belangrijkheid
material (significant)	relatieve betekenis
materiality	materialiteit
materiality	materiality
materials	materialen
matured loans	vervallen leningen
maturity	vervaldag
May	mei
merger	fusie
millions	miljoenen
minority interest	minderheidsbelang
misleading information	misleidende informatie
monetary assets	monetaire activa
monetary transactions	kastransacties
monetary transactions	monetaire transacties
monthly	maandelijks
mortgage	hypotheek
mortgage bank	hypotheekbank
multinational enterprise	multinational
multinational enterprise	multionationale onderneming
multiple regression	multipele regressie
mutual fund	mutual fund
nature	aard
nature	natuur
negative goodwill	negatieve goodwill

ENGLISH	DUTCH
net fixed assets	netto vaste activa
net income	netto winst
net income	resultaat
net income (loss) of the period	periodewinst (-verlies)
net premiums earned	netto verdiende premies
net present value	netto contante waarde
net realizable value	netto directe opbrengstwaarde
net sales	netto omzet
net sales	netto verkopen
net trade accounts receivable	netto handelsdebiteuren
net worth	eigen vermogen
non-current assets	vaste activa
non-current liabilities	lang lopende schulden
non-monetary transactions	niet-geld transacties
non-profit	zonder winststreven
non-statistical sampling	steekproeftrekken (niet statistisch)
non-taxable income	niet-belastbaar inkomen
notes payable	te betalen promessen
November	november
obsolescence	veroudering
October	oktober
office supplies	kantoorbehoeften
officer	afdelingshoofd
officer	lid van dagelijks bestuur
offset	compenseren
offset	salderen
operating cycle	bedrijfscyclus
operating cycle	produktiecyclus
operating laeses	operating leases
operating leases	exploitatie huur
opportunity cost	opportunity cost
options	opties
organization chart	organisatiediagram
organization expenses	organisatiekosten
other income for services	andere winsten uit verleende diensten
other loans	andere leningen
other operating profits (losses)	andere bedrijfswinsten/verliezen
outstanding shares	uitstaande aandelen
over the counter transaction	over the counter-transactie
overdraft	overschrijving
overdue	achterstallig
overhead expenses	algemene kosten
overhead expenses	indirecte kosten
packaging material	verpakkingsmateriaal
paid-in capital	gestort vermogen
par value	à pari
par value	pariwaarde

ENGLISH	DUTCH
parent company	moedermaatschappij
partner	partner
partner	vennoot
patents	octrooien
patents	patenten
payments	betalingen
payments cycle	betalingscyclus
payroll	loonlijst
pension	pensioen
pension plan	pensioentoezegging
percentage	percentage
percentage-of-completion-method	toerekenen van opbrengsten en kosten
percentage-of-completion-method	naar de rato van de werkvoortgang
percentage-of-completion-method	wijze van waarderen van lang lopende
percentage-of-completion-method	contracten met het doel de winsten te
percentage-of-completion-method	spreiden over de looptijd van het
percentage-of-completion-method	contract
perpetual inventory system	doorlopende inventarisatie
perpetual inventory system	permanente voorraadregistratie
personal income tax	persoonlijke inkomstenbelasting
petty cash	kleine kas
physical inventory	fysieke voorraad
placement	plaatsing
pledge	pand
pledging requirements	eisen met betrekking tot het verpanden
pooling of interest	consolideren door middel van het samen
pooling of interest	voegen van jaarrekeningen
population	populatie
population (in a statist. environ.)	populatie (statistische betekenis)
portfolio composition	samenstelling van een portfolio
preference share	preferent aandeel
preference share (UK)	preferent aandeel
preferred share (USA)	preferent aandeel
premium	agio
premium	premie
premium on issue of capital	agio bij aandelenemissie
prepaid expense	vooruitbetaalde kosten
primary capital	primair vermogen
prior period adjustments	correcties met betrekking tot vorige
prior period adjustments	boekingsperiode
private sector	private sector
probable	waarschijnlijk
product financing	produktfinanciering
product warranties	produktgarantie
production capacity	produktie capaciteit
production cost	produktiekosten
production cycle	produktiecyclus

ENGLISH	DUTCH
production order	volgorde van produktie
professional judgment	professionele beoordeling
professional standards	beroepsnormen
profit	winst
profit & loss accounts	resultatenrekening
profit & loss accounts	winst- en verliesrekening
profit margin	winstmarge
profit sharing	winstverdeling
progressive tax	progressieve belasting
projection	projectie
promotional costs	promotiekosten
provision	voorziening
proxy (power of attorney)	volmacht (recht van gevolmachtigde)
public sector	publieke sector
qualification(of an audit opinion)	kwalificatie
qualification(of an audit opinion)	voorbehoud (van accountantsverklaring)
quality control	kwaliteitscontrole
quarter	kwart
quarter	kwartaal
quarterly	driemaandelijks
quarterly (4 times a year)	driemaandelijks (4 maal per jaar)
quarterly financial statements	kwartaalbericht
random	toevallig
random	willekeurig
raw materials	grondstoffen
reasonably possible	redelijk waarschijnlijk
receivables	debiteuren
recession	recessie
record	boeken
record	opnemen
record (verb)	administreren
recruiting expense	kosten van personeelswerving
redeemable	aflosbaar
refinancing	herfinanciering
regressive tax	degressieve belasting
regulations	reglementen
reinsurance and premium adjustments	herverzekering en premiecorrecties
related party transactions	transacties met verbonden partijen
remote	ongewoon
repairs	onderhoud
repairs	reparaties
repairs and maintenance	reparaties en onderhoud
replacement cost	vervangingskosten
report	verslag
report to management	verslaggeving aan het management
reproduction cost	reproduktiekosten
repurchase agreement	terugkoopovereenkomst

ENGLISH	DUTCH
resale agreements	wederverkoopovereenkomst
resale merchandise	goederen ter wederverkoop
research and development costs	onderzoek- en ontwikkelingskosten
research and development costs	research and development kosten
reserve for exch. rate fluctuations	voorziening wisselkoersveranderingen
reserve for general risks	voorziening voor algemene risico's
reserve for loan losses	voorziening uit hoofde van krediet
reserve for loan losses	verlening
restrictions on the scope	beperkingen van de reikwijdte
restructure	herstructureren
retained earnings	algemene reserves
retained earnings	ingehouden winst
return on assets	rentabiliteit op totaal vermogen
return on equity	rentabiliteit op eigen vermogen
revaluation	herwaardering
revaluation reserve	herwaarderingsreserve
rules	regels
rules	voorschriften
salaries and wages	lonen en salarissen
sale of manufactured goods	opbrengst der geproduceerde goederen
sales (turnover)	omzet
sales on installments	verkoop op afbetaling
sales tax	omzetbelasting
sample size	omvang van de steekproef
sampling	steekproef nemen (-trekken)
sampling results	resultaten voortvloeiende uit steekproef
sampling risk	steekproefrisico
saving deposits	spaargelden
scope	reikwijdte
scope	toepassingsgebied
seasonally adjusted	voor seizoensinvloeden gecorrigeerd
second request	tweede verzoek
secondary market	secundaire markt
Securities and Exchange Commission	beurscommissie (USA)
self-insurance	assurantie eigen risico
selling expenses	verkoopkosten
semi-finished goods	halffabrikaten
September	september
severance	breuk
severance	verbreking (van contracten)
share in loss of affiliates	aandeel in het verlies van deelnemingen
shareholders' equity	eigen vermogen
shares	aandelen
short-term bank loans	korte termijn banklening
short-term investments	korte termijn investering/belegging
short-term loans	korte termijn leningen
small companies	kleine ondernemingen

ENGLISH	DUTCH
social security expense	sociale lasten
sources of funds	herkomst van middelen
special bonus	speciale bonus
special reports	speciale verslagen
split (of a company)	opdeling (van een onderneming)
spread (between rates)	marge
stamp duty	zegelrecht
standard cost	standaardkosten
start-up cost	aanloopkosten
start-up costs	initiele kosten
statement changes in fin. position	staat van herkomst en besteding van
statement changes in fin. position	middelen
statement of accounting policy	uiteenzetting van grondslagen voor
statement of accounting policy	waardering en winstbepaling
statement sources & uses of funds	staat van herkomst en besteding van
statement sources & uses of funds	middelen
statistical sampling	statistisch verantwoorde steekproef
statutory audit report	statutair vereist accountantsverslag
statutory reserve	statutaire reserves
stock dividends	stock dividend
stock dividends	winstuitkering in de vorm van aandelen
stock exchange	effectenbeurs
stock option plans	stock optie-plan
stockbroker	effectenmakelaar
stockholders	aandeelhouders
stockholders' equity	eigen vermogen
straight-line method	afschrijvingsmethode volgens een vast
straight-line method	percentage van de aanschafwaarde
subject to	afhankelijk van
subject to	onderworpen aan
sublet	onderaanbesteden
sublet	onderverhuren
subordinated debt	achtergestelde schuld
subordinated financing	achtergestelde financiering
subscription	inschrijving
subsequent events	opeenvolgende gebeurtenissen
subsidiary	dochtermaatschappij
subsidiary records	dagboekrekeningen
sum of the years'-digits method	afschrijvingen volgens de jaarnummer-
sum of the years'-digits method	methode
sum of the years'-digits method	sum of the years'-digits methode
supplementary information	aanvullende informatie
suppliers	leveranciers
supplies	hulpmiddelen
supplies	leveranties
supplies and spare parts	voorraad en reserveonderdelen
taken as a whole	als geheel genomen

ENGLISH	DUTCH
tangible fixed assets	materiele duurzame activa
tax	belasting
tax authorities	belastingdienst
tax credits	belastingvermindering
tax rates	belastingvoet
tax return	belastingaangifte
tax savings	belastingbesparing
taxable income	belastbaar inkomen
taxable income	fiscale winst
taxpayer	belastingplichtige
temporary differences	tijdelijke verschillen
test	toets
tests	testen
tests	toetsen
thousand	duizend
thousands	duizenden
time deposits	termijndepositos
timing	timing
total funds from operations	totale herkomst uit bedrijfsvoering
total insurance reserves	totale voorziening voor verzekering
total revenue	totale opbrengsten
trade marks	handelsmerken
trade marks	merken
trade receivables	handelsvorderingen
trade receivables -	handelsdebiteuren
trademarks	handelsmerken
training expenditure	kosten voor opleiding
transactions	transacties
treasury stock	ingekochte, eigen aandelen,
treasury stock	nog niet ingetrokken
trend	trend
trial balance	proefbalans
turnover ratio	omloopsnelheid ratio
unappropriated retained earnings	onverdeelde winst
unappropriated retained earnings	voor uitkering beschikbare winst
unaudited	niet door accountants gecontroleerd
uncertainty	onzekerheid
uncollectible	oninbaar
unearned interests	vooruitontvangen rente
units of production	produktie-eenheden
unqualified	niet gekwalificeerd
unqualified	zonder voorbehoud
unsecured bonds	obligaties zonder zekerheidsstelling
useful life (of an asset)	economische levensduur
useful life (of an asset)	verbruiksduur
uses of funds	besteding van middelen
valuation principles	waarderingsgrondslagen

ENGLISH	DUTCH
value added tax (VAT)	belasting toegevoegde waarde (btw)
variable cost	variabele kosten
vehicles	voertuigen
vendors (USA)	verkopers
vice-chairman	vice-president
vice-chairman	vice-voorzitter
voucher	bewijsstuk
voucher	bon
voucher	recu
warehouse	magazijn
warehouse	pakhuis
weighted average	gewogen gemiddelde
working capital	werkkapitaal
working capital ratio	werkkapitaal-ratio
working capital turnover	omloopsnelheid werkkapitaal
write down	afschrijven
write down	waardeverminderingen
year-end closing date	datum einde boekjaar
yield	opbrengst
yield	rendement
zero base budget	zero base budget
zero base budgeting	zero base budgeting

ACCOUNTING LEXICON : FRENCH - ENGLISH

FRENCH	ENGLISH
à l'exception de	except for
abattement fiscal pour investissement	investment tax credit
accord de financement	financing arrangement
accord de rachat	repurchase agreement
accord de revente	resale agreement
accumulation	accrual
acquisition (d'une entreprise)	acquisition (of a company)
actif	assets
actif circulant	current assets
actif de roulement	current assets
actif immobilisé	non-current assets
actif monétaire	monetary assets
actif realisable à court terme	current assets
actifs incorporels	intangible assets
action de priorité	preference share
action preferée	preference share (UK)
action preferée	preferred share (USA)
action privilegiée	preference share
actionnaires	stockholders
actions	shares
actions ordinaires	common stock
actions preferées non remboursables	non-redeemable preferred stock
actions preferées remboursables	redeemable preferred stock
actions propres en portefeuille	treasury stock
actions émises	outstanding shares
activité	industry
administrateurs	directors
affecter	allocate
affilié(e)	affiliate
agent de bourse	stockbroker
ajustement	adjustment
ajustement cumulé	cumulative adjustment
aléatoire	random
aléatoirement	at random
amende	fine
amendements des sols	land improvements
amortissement accéléré	accelerated depreciation
amortissement anticipé de la dette	early extinguishment of debt
amortissement de la dette à long terme	retirement of long-term debt
amortissements cumulés	accumulated amortization
amortissements cumulés	accumulated depreciation
amplitude de l'échantillon	sample size
annuellement	annually
août	August
appel d'offres	bid (noun)

FRENCH	ENGLISH
appliqués de façon constante	consistently applied
assemblée générale d'actionnaires	annual shareholders' meeting
assemblée générale ordinaire	annual meeting
associé	partner
assurance sur la vie	life insurance
assurances générales	general insurance
attestation	auditor's report
auditeur associé	audit partner
auditeurs internes	internal auditors
augmentation de capital	capital increase
autoassurance	self-insurance
autoassurer	self-insure
autorités fiscaux	tax authorities
autres procedures de contrôle	alternative procedures
autres prêts	other loans
autres revenus (pertes) d'exploitation	other operating profits (losses)
autres revenus pour des services	other income for services
aux effets fiscaux	for taxation purposes
avances à fournisseurs	advances to suppliers
avantages sociaux	employee benefits
avocat	lawyer
avoirs invisibles	intangible assets
avril	April
bail	lease
bailleur	lessor
balance de soldes	trial balance
banque	bank
banque commerciale	commercial bank
banque d'affaires	investment bank/merchant bank
banque d'investissement	investment bank/merchant bank
banque de crédit hypothècaire	mortgage bank
banqueroute	bankruptcy
banques,caisse,chèques postaux	liquid assets
biens immobiliers	fixed assets
bilan	balance sheet
billet garanti	secured note
bon	bond
bon	voucher
bourse (des valeurs)	stock exchange
brevets	patents
budget	budget
budget base zero	zero base budget
bénéfice	profit
bénéfice attribuable aux assurés	policyholders' surplus
bénéfice distribué	appropriated retained earnings

ACCOUNTING LEXICON : FRENCH - ENGLISH

FRENCH	ENGLISH
bénéfice net	net income
bénéfice net de l'exercice	net income of the period
bénéfice net par action	earnings per share
bénéfice non distribué	unappropriated retained earnings
bénéfices accumulés	retained earnings
bénéfices affectés	appropriated retained earnings
bénéfices imposables	taxable income
bénéfices non distribués	retained earnings
bénéfices prêtés par assurances de vie	life policy benefits
bénéfices realisés	accrued income
caisse	cash
caisse,banques et chèques postaux	cash and banks
capacité de production	production capacity
capacité oisive	idle capacity
capital	capital stock
capital de base	primary capital
capital versé	paid-in capital
capitalisation des intérêts	capitalization of interest
capitaux propres	shareholders' equity
capitaux propres	stockholders' equity
cents	hundreds
certificat de dépôt	certificate of deposit
certification	opinion
cession (d'un actif)	disposal (of an asset)
cession-bail	leaseback
ceteris paribus	ceteris paribus
changement des méthodes comptables	accounting changes
charges	expenses
charges constatées d'avance	prepaid expense
charges de structure	overhead expenses
charges differées	deferred charges
charges operationnelles	overhead expenses
charges payées d'avance	prepaid expense
charges à payer	accrued expenses
chiffre d'affaires	sales (turnover)
chiffre d'affaires net	net sales
circonstances	circumstances
clients	customers
clients principaux	major customers
codifier	code (verb)
coefficient de liquidité	liquidity ratio
coefficient de rotation de stocks	inventory turnover ratio
coefficient des encaissements	collection ratio
coefficient du bénéfice brut	gross profit ratio
collaborateurs du commissaire	audit staff

FRENCH	ENGLISH
combinaison des intérêts	pooling of interest
combinaisons commerciaux	business combinations
commerce international	international trade
commissaire aux comptes	auditor
commission des opérations de bourse	Securities and Exchange Commission
commissions et honoraires-revenus	commissions & fees-profits(losses)
(pertes)	commissions & fees-profits(losses)
compagnie d'assurances	insurance company
compensation	offset (noun)
compilation des états financiers	compilation of financial statements
composition du portefeuille	portfolio composition
comptabilité	accounting
comptabilité d'exercice	accrual method of accounting
comptabilité par valeurs échues	accrual method of accounting
comptable	accountant
compte de pertes et profits	profit & loss account
compte de pertes et profits	income statement
comptes consolidés	consolidated accounts
comptes de regularisation	prepaid expenses & deferred charges
comptes de regularisation	accrued expenses
comptes de regularisation	deferred income/expense
comptes financiers	financial statements
comptes ordinaires	demand deposits
comptes transitoires	prepaid expense
comtes de tiers débiteurs	accounts receivable
confirmation directe	confirmation of accounts
congés payés	vacation with pay
conseil d'administration	board of directors
conseil juridique	lawyer
constructions	buildings and structures
contenu	contents
contexte économique	economic environment
contracts à long terme	long-term contracts
contribuable	taxpayer
contrôle de qualité	quality control
contrôle des comptes	audit
contrôle interne	internal control
contrôle operationnel	operational auditing
contrôles operationnels	operational controls
contrôles opératifs	operating controls
conversion des devises	foreign currency translation
conversion monetaire	currency translation
cours de change	exchange rate
couverture	hedge
couverture	collateral

FRENCH	ENGLISH
coût d'achat	acquisition cost
coût d'achat des marchandises vendues	cost of goods sold
coût d'acquisition	acquisition cost
coût d'opportunité	opportunity cost
coût de prestations des services	cost of services rendered
coût de production	production cost
coût de remplacement	replacement cost
coût de reproduction	reproduction cost
coût des ventes	cost of sales
coût direct	direct cost
coût historique	historical cost
coût marginal	marginal cost
coût ou valeur actuelle	lower of cost or market method
coût ou valeur de marché	lower of cost or market method
coût standard	standard cost
coût variable	variable cost
créances	accounts receivable
créances	receivables
créances clients et comptes rattachés	net trade accounts receivable
crédit d'impôts	tax credits
crédits commerciaux	trade receivables
crédits syndiqués	syndicated loans
crédits à long terme	long-term credits
cycle de production	production cycle
cycle des paiements	payments cycle
cycle opératif	operating cycle
d'accord avec	in accordance with
dans son ensemble	taken as a whole
date d'arrêt du bilan	balance sheet date
date de clôture de l'exercice	year-end closing date
décembre	December
debenture	debenture
decaissements	disbursements
demandes	claims
dernier entré, premier sorti	last in, first out (LIFO)
dessaisonalisé	seasonally adjusted
dette prioritaire	senior debt
dettes aux fournisseurs	trade payables
dettes non récupérables	troubled debt
dettes à court terme	current liabilities
dettes à court terme	accounts payable
dettes à long terme	long-term debt
deuxième demande	second request
devises	foreign exchange
diagramme de circulation	flowchart

FRENCH	ENGLISH
différences temporaires	temporary differences
directeur général	general manager
directeurs	directors
directoire	board of directors
dirigeant (d'une société)	officer (of a company)
disponibilités	cash equivalents
dividende	dividend
dividende par action	dividend per share
dividende sous forme d'actions	stock dividends
dividendes en effectif	cash dividends
dividendes reçues	dividend income
dividendes à payer	dividends payable
dollars	dollars
donner une image fidèle	fairly present
dossier permanent	permanent file
dotation aux amortissements	depreciation expense
dotation aux comptes d'amortissements pour constructions	depreciation on buildings
double imposition	depreciation on buildings
droit d'accise	double taxation
droit de l'auteur	excise tax
droit de successions	copyright
droit de timbre	inheritance tax
droits d'exportation	stamp duty
droits de douane	export duties
débiteurs	customs duties
déclaration d'impôts	receivables
découvert	tax return
découvert	bank overdraft
dépendants	overdraft
dépenses	dependents
dépenses administratives	expenses
dépenses de charité	administrative expenses
dépenses de recherche et développement	charity expense
dépôt à terme	research and development costs
dépôts de banques	time deposit
dépôts en compte d'épargne	interbank assets/funds
dépôts en garantie	savings deposits
dépôts interbancaires	guarantee deposits
écart de réévaluation	interbank deposits
écart à la norme	revaluation surplus
échantillonnage	departure from a pronouncement
échantillonnage de revision	sampling
échantillonnage non statistique	audit sampling
échantillonnage statistique	non-statistical sampling
	statistical sampling

ACCOUNTING LEXICON : FRENCH - ENGLISH

FRENCH	ENGLISH
échu	overdue
échéance	due date
échéance	maturity
économies fiscaux	tax savings
écritures au journal	journal entry
éléments probants	evidential matter
épreuve concluante	acid test
épreuves substantives	substantive tests
établissement de crédit hypothècaire	mortgage bank
états financiers	financial statements
états financiers comparés	comparative financial statements
états financiers consolidés	consolidated financial statements
états financiers intérimaires	interim financial statements
états financiers resumés	condensed financial statements
états financiers schematiques	financial summary
états financiers trimestriels	quarterly financial statements
étude de praticabilité	feasibility study
événements postérieurs	subsequent events
être en concordance avec	comply with
effectif	employee
effet	effect
effet cumulatif	cumulative effect
effet de la variation des prix	effects of changing prices
effets à payer	notes payable
effets à recevoir	notes receivable
emplois des fonds	uses of funds
emprunts banquiers à court terme	short-term bank loans
emprunts subordonnés	subordinated debt
emprunts à moins d'un an	short-term loans
encaissements	collections
engagements	commitments
engagements des clients	customers'liability for acceptances
engagements à terme	future contracts
enregistrements comptables	accounting records
enregistrer	post entries to the ledger
enregistrer	record (verb)
entreprise commune	joint venture
entreprise en activité	going concern
entreprise multinationale	multinational enterprise
entreprises affiliées	affiliated firms
entreprises correspondantes	correspondent firms
entreprises en voie de développement	development stage companies
entreprises liées	affiliated firms
entrepôt	warehouse
erreurs	errors

FRENCH	ENGLISH
examiner	examine
expert comptable	accountant
exportation	export
exposition à la risque	risk exposure
facture	invoice
faillite	bankruptcy
feuille de paie	payroll
filiale	subsidiary
filiales	affiliates
filiales internationaux	international subsidiaries
filiales nationaux	domestic subsidiaries
filiales étrangères	foreign subsidiaries
finance	finance (noun)
financement de l'achat d'un produit	product financing
financement subordonné	subordinated financing
financier	finance (verb)
flux de fonds	cash flow
flux de trésorerie	cash flow
fond commun de placement	mutual fund
fonds	funds
fonds d'exploitation	total funds from operations
fonds de commerce	goodwill
fonds de roulement	working capital
formulaire	form
fournisseurs	suppliers
fournisseurs	vendors (USA)
fournitures	supplies (noun)
frais	expenses
frais bancaires	bank service charges
frais courus	accrued expenses
frais d'amortissement	depreciation expense
frais d'entretien et réparations	repair and maintenance expense
frais d'exhibitions	exhibitions and events expense
frais d'organisation	organization expenses
frais d'émission des polices	underwriting policy acquis. costs
frais d`augmentation de capital	expenses on capital increase
frais d`établissement	start-up costs
frais de contrôle	audit fees
frais de formation du personnel	training expenditure
frais de promotion	promotional costs
frais de recherche et développement	research and development costs
frais de recherche et mise au point	research and development costs
frais de recrutement (de personnel)	recruiting expense
frais de représentation	entertainment expense
frais de securité sociale	social security expense

FRENCH	ENGLISH
frais de télécommunications	communications expense
frais de ventes	selling expenses
frais divers de gestion	general and administrative expense
frais financiers	interest expense
frais généraux	overhead expenses
fusion	merger
février	February
gains (pertes) sur investissements en titres	investment securities gains(losses)
	investment securities gains(losses)
garantie	guarantee
garantie	collateral
garanties sur produits	product warranties
grand livre	general ledger
groupe (de sociétés)	group (of companies)
généralement admis	generally accepted
généralement reconnu	generally accepted
gérant de la société de revision	audit manager
homme-heures	labor hours (man-hours)
honoraires	fees
honoraires pour services extérieurs	fees for services by third party
hypothèque	mortgage
immobilisations	fixed assets
immobilisations corporelles	fixed assets
immobilisations corporelles	tangible fixed assets
immobilisations en cours	construction in progress
immobilisations financières	long-term investments
immobilisations incorporelles	intangible assets
immobilisations net	net fixed assets
impayé	overdue
importance relative	materiality
imputation à un exercice antérieur	carryback
imputer	allocate
impôt	tax
impôt differé	deferred taxes
impôt progressif	graduated tax
impôt progressif	progressive tax
impôt regressif	regressive tax
impôt sur le revenu	income tax
impôt sur le résultat	income tax
impôt sur les bénéfices	income tax
impôt sur les bénéfices des personnes physiques	personal income tax
	personal income tax
impôt sur les bénéfices differé	deferred income taxes
impôt sur les fondes propres	capital tax
impôt sur les plus-values de cession	capital gains tax

FRENCH	ENGLISH
impôt sur les sociétés	corporation tax
impôts courus	accrued taxes
impôts retenues	withheld taxes
incertitude	uncertainty
incorporation des charges financières au coût d'un bien	capitalization of financial costs
	capitalization of financial costs
incorporation à l'actif d'un bien donné en crédit-bail	capitalization of leases
	capitalization of leases
indemnité pour retraite	post-retirement benefits
indemnités	indemnities
indemnités de départ	severance indemnities
indexation	adjustment for inflation
industrie	industry
inflation	inflation
informations trompeuses	misleading information
installations	fittings
intention de la direction	management intention
intérêts créditeurs	interest income
intérêts débiteurs	interest expense
intérêts passifs	unearned interest
intérêts payés	interest expense
intérêts à payer	interest payable
intérêts à recevoir	interest receivable
investissement	investment
investissements en filiales	investment in subsidiaries
investissements à court terme	short-term investments
irregularité	irregularity
irrécupérable	uncollectible
janvier	January
jugement professionnel	professional judgment
juillet	July
juin	June
lettre de recommandations	report to management
lettre de représentation	client representation letter
licenciement	severance
ligne de crédit	credit line
limite	extent
liquidité	liquidity
litiges	litigation
livre journal	journal
livres auxiliaires	subsidiary records
locataire	lessee
location (crédit-bail)	leasing
location opérative	operating lease
loi du travail	labor law

FRENCH	ENGLISH
machines et outillage	machinery and equipment
magasin	warehouse
mai	May
marchandises de revente	resale merchandise
marchandises en route	goods in transit
marge	spread (between rates)
marge brute	gross margin
marge brute d'autofinancement	cash flow
marge bénéficiaire	profit margin
marge pour risque d'échantillonnage	allowance for sampling risk
marque de fabrique	trade mark
mars	March
matières premières	raw materials
matériel	material (noun)
mensuellement	monthly
mettre en gage	pledge (verb)
mille	thousand
milliards	billions
milliers	thousands
millions	millions
mise en équivalence	equity method
mobiliers,aménagements,installations	furniture and fixtures
monnaie nationale	local currency
monnaies étrangères	foreign currency
moyenne	average (mean)
moyenne ponderée	weighted average
méthode de "avec et sans"	with and without method
méthode de la somme des chiffres	sum of the years' digits method
méthode de pourcentage d'achèvement	percentage-of-completion-method
méthode du contrat achevé	completed-contract method
méthode du contrôle	audit approach
méthode linéaire	straight-line method
nantissement	collateral
nature	nature
normes de revision	auditing standards
note explicative sur les principes comptables appliqués	statement of accounting policy
	statement of accounting policy
notes aux états financiers	footnotes to financial statements
notes réescomptés	rediscounted notes
novembre	November
obligation	bond
obligation	debenture
obligation perpétuelle	perpetual bond
obligations convertibles	convertible bonds
obligations de gager	pledging requirements
obligations légaux	legal requirements
obligations sans garantie	unsecured bonds
obligations à coupon zéro	zero coupon bonds
obligations à payer	bonds payable
octobre	October
offrir	bid (verb)
operation de couverture à terme	hedging
opinion	opinion
oppportunité	timing
options	options
opération sur options	options
opérations cessées	discontinued operations
opérations sur futures	future contracts
ordre de production	production order
organigramme	organization chart
paiements	payments
pair	par value
papiers de travail	working papers
par mois	monthly
paragraphe d'opinion	opinion paragraph
paragraphe de portée	scope paragraph
participation des salariés aux bénéfices	profit sharing
participation en perte des affiliées	share in loss of affiliates
participation minoritaire	minority interests
participations en autres sociétés	equity in other companies
partie courante de...	current portion of ...
passer par pertes et profits	write off (verb)
passif	liability
passifs transitoires	accrued liabilities
passifs à court terme	current liabilities
passifs à long terme	non-current liabilities
patrimoine attribuable aux assurés	policyholders' equity
pension	pension
perte	loss
perte cumulée	loss carry-forward
perte nette de l'exercice	net loss of the period
petite caisse	petty cash
petites entreprises	small companies
pièces de rechange	supplies and spare parts
pièces justificatives	supporting documentation
placement	placement
placements au jour le jour	overnight funds
placements intersociétaires	inter-company loans
plan comptable général	chart of accounts
plan d'option sur actions	stock option plan

FRENCH	ENGLISH
planification de la revision	audit strategy
plus-value	gain
plus-value sur titres	gain on revaluation of securities
point mort	break even point
points faibles du système	control weakness
population	population
porteur	bearer
portée	scope
pourcentage	percentage
praticabilité	feasibility
premier entré, premier sorti	first in, first out (FIFO)
prime	premium
prime d'acquisition	goodwill
prime d'émission	premium on issue of capital
prime d'émission	capital surplus
prime sur dette	debt premium
primes d'assurance émises	total premiums written
primes et gratifications	special bonus
primes nettes	net premiums earned
principes comptables	accounting principles
prix de rachat	call price
prix du marché	market price
probable	probable
produit d'exploitation	operating profit
produit national brut	gross national product
produits constatés d'avance	deferred income
produits en cours de production	goods in process
produits et charges exceptionnelles	extraordinary items
produits financiers	interest income
produits finis	finished goods
produits non taxés	non-taxable income
produits semi-terminés	semi-finished goods
profits et produits non incorporés	non-operating income and expense
profits sur exercices antérieurs	prior period adjustments
projection	projection
provision	provision
provision	allowance
provision pour créances douteuses	allowance for doubtful accounts
provision pour dépréciation	accumulated depreciation
provision pour dépréciation sur immobilisations financières	allowance for devaluation of inv't
	allowance for devaluation of inv't
provision pour pertes sur créances irregulières	allowance for uncollectible acc'ts
	allowance for uncollectible acc'ts
provision pour prêts irrécupérables	allowance for loan losses
provision pour vacances	accrued vacations

FRENCH	ENGLISH
président du conseil d'administration	chairman
président directeur général	chief executive officer
préséntation	disclosure
prévision	forecast
prêts	loans
prêts commerciaux et industriels	commercial & industrial loans
prêts en crédit-bail	lease financing loans
prêts hypothécaires	real estate and mortgage loans
prêts non productifs	non-performing earning assets
prêts non récupérables	actual loan losses
prêts échus	matured loans
période ecoulée	intervening period
questionnaire de contrôle interne	internal control questionnaire
raisonnablement possible	reasonably possible
rapport	report
rapport de vérification	auditor's report
rapport des commissaires aux comptes	auditors' report
rapport des commissaires aux comptes	statutory audit report
rapport du commissaire aux comptes	auditor's report
rapport général	audit opinion
rapports spéciaux	special reports
rapprochement bancaire	bank reconciliation (statement)
ratio d'endettement	indebtedness ratio
ratio d'exploitation	operating ratio
ratio de liquidité immediate	acid test ratio
ratio de rotation	turnover ratio
ratio de rotation des crédits	credit turnover ratio
ratio du capital circulant	working capital ratio
ratio du court terme	current ratio
rattacher	accrue
recettes totales	total revenue
redressement	audit
refinancement	refinancing
refus de certification	adverse opinion
refus de la certification	disclaimer of opinion
regression multiple	multiple regression
relever	detect
remboursable	redeemable
remboursement	refund
remote	remote
rendement	yield
renseignements supplémentaires	supplementary information
report à nouveau	balance carried forward
requisition d'achat	purchase requisition
reserve pour risques	reserve for general risks

ACCOUNTING LEXICON : FRENCH - ENGLISH

FRENCH	ENGLISH
responsabilité du commissaire aux comptes	auditor's responsibility
ressources de fonds	auditor's responsibility
restrictions sur la portée	sources of funds
restructuration	restrictions on the scope
restructuration de la dette	restructuring
retention des impôts	debt restructuring
retention à taux fixe	withholding of tax
retraite anticipé	flat tax withholding
revenu par action	early retirement
revenus (pertes) de change	earnings per share
revenus (pertes) pour administration des fonds de tiers	foreign exchange gains (losses)
revenus de cession d`immobilisations	trust operations profits (losses)
revenus imposables	trust operations profits (losses)
revenus pour services	gain on sale of fixed assets
reviseur	taxable income
revision analytique	income for services rendered
revision aux états financiers	auditor
risque d'échantillonnage	analytical review
risque de change	review of financial statements
risque de contrôle	sampling risk
risque de pénurie de liquidité	exchange rate risk
risque du pays	audit risk
risque éloigné de l'échantillonnage	liquidity risk
risques divers	country risk
rotation du capital circulant	non-sampling risk
réassurances et ajustements des primes	contingencies
récession	working capital turnover
réclamation non realisée	reinsurance and premium adjustments
réclamations et pertes pour sinistres	recession
réescompte de la dette	unasserted claim
régime de retraite	total insurance claims and losses
réparations	debt discount
réseau operationnel	pension plan
réserve	repairs
réserve de réévaluation	operational network
réserve légale	qualification(of an audit opinion)
réserve légale	revaluation reserve
réserve pour différences de change	legal reserve
réserve pour débiteurs douteux	statutory reserve
réserve pour prêts irrécupérables	reserve for exch. rate fluctuations
réserve pour réclamations et pertes	reserve for loan losses/bad debts
réserves non patrimoniales	reserve for loan losses
réserves à long terme pour sinistres	reserve for o/s claims and losses
	non-equity reserves
	long-term insurance reserve charges

FRENCH	ENGLISH
résultat net	net income
résultats d'échantillonnage	sampling results
résultats financiers	financial summary
révélation	disclosure
réévaluation	revaluation
règlements	regulations
règles	rules
règles comptables particulières à une entreprise	accounting policies
règles d'évaluation	accounting policies
règles de rachat	valuation principles
règles professionnelles	redemption features
salaires	professional standards
salarié	salaries and wages
sans but lucratif	employee
sans contrôler	non-profit
sans réserve	unaudited
sauf	unqualified
scission (d'une société)	except for
second marché	split (of a company)
secteur privé	secondary market
secteur publique	private sector
segment du commerce	public sector
septembre	business segment
services de consultation	September
seuil de rentabilité	consulting services
SICAV	break even point
significatif	mutual fund
signification	material (significant)
sinistres	materiality
situation comptable intérimaire	claims
situation nette	interim accounts
situation nette	shareholders' equity
situation nette	stockholders' equity
société affiliée	net worth
société associée	subsidiary
société de portefeuille	associated firm
société dominante	holding company
société mère	parent company
sociétés financières	parent company
soldes des comptes	financial entities
sous produit	account balances
sous-facturation	by-product
souscription	underinvoicing
souslocation	subscription
	sublet (noun)

FRENCH	ENGLISH
spread	spread (between rates)
statuts sociaux	company by-laws
stocks	inventory (USA) stocks(UK)
stocks physiques	physical inventory
sujet à	subject to
suppléant	proxy (noun)
surfacturation	overinvoicing
surtaxe à l'importation	import surcharges
survaleur non amortisé	unamortized premium
survaloir	goodwill
systeme d'inventaire permanent	perpetual inventory system
tableau de financement	statement changes in fin. position
tableau des ressources et des emplois des fonds	statement sources & uses of funds
	statement sources & uses of funds
taux d'escompte	discount rate
taux d'imposition	tax rate
taux d'intérêt	interest rate
taux de change	exchange rate
taux de change flottant	floating rate
taux de parité	exchange rate
taux de rentabilité des actifs	return on assets
taux de rentabilité des fonds propres	return on equity
taux interbancaire	interbank rate
taxe sur des produits determinés	excise tax
taxe sur la valeur ajoutée (TVA)	value added tax (VAT)
taxe sur le chiffre d'affaires	gross revenue tax
taxe sur les ventes	sales tax
techniques de contrôle	auditing procedures
tendance	trend
terrains	land
test	test
titre	bond
titres cotés	marketable securities
titres cotés en bourse	marketable stocks
titres cotés-monnaie nationale	listed bonds-local currency
titres de participation	investment in subsidiaries
titres de placement	marketable securities
titres de tiers	custody securities
titres et valeurs de tiers	trust securities
titres negociables	marketable securities
totale des réserves pour risques	total insurance reserves
traitement fiscale	tax treatment
transaction hors coté	over-the-counter transaction
transactions	transactions
transactions avec des intéressés	related party transactions

FRENCH	ENGLISH
transactions monétaires	monetary transactions
transactions non monétaires	non-monetary transactions
transports sur achats	freight on purchases of materials
travaux de contrôle	audit engagement
trimestre	quarter
trimestriellement	quarterly
trimestriellement (4 fois par an)	quarterly (4 times a year)
uniformité	consistency
unités de production	units of production
valeur actuariel	actuarial value
valeur actuelle net	net present value
valeur comptable	book value
valeur historique	historical cost
valeur net de réalisation	net realizable value
valeur nominal	face value
valeur nominale	par value
valeur récupérable presumé	expected salvage value
valeur venale	market price
valeurs d'exploitation	inventory -(USA) (stocks-UK)
valeurs immobilisées	fixed assets
valeurs mobilières de placement	marketable securities
vente de produits (finis)	sale of (manufactured) goods
ventes	sales (turnover)
ventes nettes	net sales
ventes à tempérament	sales on installments
vice-président	vice-chairman
vie utile	useful life (of an asset)
vieillissement	obsolescence
véhicules	vehicles
vérification fiscale	tax audit
vérifier	examine

ENGLISH	FRENCH
accelerated depreciation	amortissement accéléré
account balances	soldes des comptes
accountant	comptable
accountant	expert comptable
accounting	comptabilité
accounting changes	changement des méthodes comptables
accounting policies	règles comptables particulières à une entreprise
accounting policies	principes comptables
accounting principles	enregistrements comptables
accounting records	dettes à court terme
accounts payable	créances
accounts receivable	comtes de tiers débiteurs
accounts receivable	accumulation
accrual	comptabilité par valeurs échues
accrual method of accounting	comptabilité d'exercice
accrual method of accounting	rattacher
accrue	frais courus
accrued expenses	charges à payer
accrued expenses	comptes de regularisation
accrued expenses	bénéfices realisés
accrued income	passifs transitoires
accrued liabilities	impôts courus
accrued taxes	provision pour vacances
accrued vacations	amortissements cumulés
accumulated amortization	amortissements cumulés
accumulated depreciation	provision pour dépréciation
accumulated depreciation	épreuve concluante
acid test	ratio de liquidité immediate
acid test ratio	acquisition (d'une entreprise)
acquisition (of a company)	coût d'acquisition
acquisition cost	coût d'achat
acquisition cost	prêts non récupérables
actual loan losses	valeur actuariel
actuarial value	ajustement
adjustment	indexation
adjustment for inflation	dépenses administratives
administrative expenses	avances à fournisseurs
advances to suppliers	refus de certification
adverse opinion	affilié(e)
affiliate	entreprises affiliées
affiliated firms	entreprises liées
affiliated firms	filiales
affiliates	affecter
allocate	imputer
allocate	

ENGLISH	FRENCH
allowance	provision
allowance for devaluation of inv't	provision pour dépréciation sur immobilisations financières
allowance for devaluation of inv't	provision pour créances douteuses
allowance for doubtful accounts	provision pour prêts irrécupérables
allowance for loan losses	marge pour risque d'échantillonnage
allowance for sampling risk	provision pour pertes sur créances irregulières
allowance for uncollectible acc'ts	autres procedures de contrôle
allowance for uncollectible acc'ts	revision analytique
alternative procedures	assemblée générale ordinaire
analytical review	assemblée générale d'actionnaires
annual meeting	annuellement
annual shareholders' meeting	bénéfice distribué
annually	bénéfices affectés
appropriated retained earnings	avril
appropriated retained earnings	actif
April	société associée
assets	aléatoirement
associated firm	contrôle des comptes
at random	redressement
audit	méthode du contrôle
audit	travaux de contrôle
audit approach	frais de contrôle
audit engagement	gérant de la société de revision
audit fees	rapport général
audit manager	auditeur associé
audit opinion	risque de contrôle
audit partner	échantillonnage de revision
audit risk	collaborateurs du commissaire
audit sampling	planification de la revision
audit staff	techniques de contrôle
audit strategy	normes de revision
auditing procedures	commissaire aux comptes
auditing standards	reviseur
auditor	attestation
auditor	rapport du commissaire aux comptes
auditor's report	rapport de vérification
auditor's report	comptes
auditor's report	responsabilité du commissaire aux
auditor's responsibility	rapport des commissaires aux comptes
auditor's responsibility	août
auditors' report	moyenne
August	report à nouveau
average (mean)	bilan
balance carried forward	
balance sheet	

ENGLISH	FRENCH
balance sheet date	date d'arrêt du bilan
bank	banque
bank overdraft	découvert
bank reconciliation (statement)	rapprochement bancaire
bank service charges	frais bancaires
bankruptcy	banqueroute
bankruptcy	faillite
bearer	porteur
bid (noun)	appel d'offres
bid (verb)	offrir
billions	milliards
board of directors	conseil d'administration
board of directors	directoire
bond	obligation
bond	bon
bond	titre
bonds payable	obligations à payer
book value	valeur comptable
break even point	seuil de rentabilité
break even point	point mort
budget	budget
buildings and structures	constructions
business combinations	combinaisons commerciaux
business segment	segment du commerce
by-product	sous produit
call price	prix de rachat
capital gains tax	impôt sur les plus-values de cession
capital increase	augmentation de capital
capital stock	capital
capital surplus	prime d'émission
capital tax	impôt sur les fondes propres
capitalization of financial costs	incorporation des charges financières
capitalization of financial costs	au coût d'un bien
capitalization of interest	capitalisation des intérêts
capitalization of leases	incorporation à l'actif d'un bien donné
capitalization of leases	en crédit-bail
carryback	imputation à un exercice antérieur
cash	caisse
cash and banks	caisse,banques et chèques postaux
cash dividends	dividendes en effectif
cash equivalents	disponibilités
cash flow	flux de fonds
cash flow	marge brute d'autofinancement
cash flow	flux de trésorerie
certificate of deposit	certificat de dépôt
ceteris paribus	ceteris paribus
chairman	président du conseil d'administration
charity expense	dépenses de charité
chart of accounts	plan comptable général
chief executive officer	président directeur général
circumstances	circonstances
claims	demandes
claims	sinistres
client representation letter	lettre de représentation
code (verb)	codifier
collateral	nantissement
collateral	couverture
collateral	garantie
collection ratio	coefficient des encaissements
collections	encaissements
commercial & industrial loans	prêts commerciaux et industriels
commercial bank	banque commerciale
commissions & fees-profits(losses)	commissions et honoraires-revenus
commissions & fees-profits(losses)	(pertes)
commitments	engagements
common stock	actions ordinaires
communications expense	frais de télécommunications
company by-laws	statuts sociaux
comparative financial statements	états financiers comparés
compilation of financial statements	compilation des états financiers
completed-contract method	méthode du contrat achevé
comply with	être en concordance avec
condensed financial statements	états financiers resumés
confirmation of accounts	confirmation directe
consistency	uniformité
consistently applied	appliqués de façon constante
consolidated accounts	comptes consolidés
consolidated financial statements	états financiers consolidés
construction in progress	immobilisations en cours
consulting services	services de consultation
contents	contenu
contingencies	risques divers
control weakness	points faibles du système
convertible bonds	obligations convertibles
copyright	droit de l'auteur
corporation tax	impôt sur les sociétés
correspondent firms	entreprises correspondantes
cost of goods sold	coût d'achat des marchandises vendues
cost of sales	coût des ventes
cost of services rendered	coût de prestations des services

ENGLISH	FRENCH
country risk	risque du pays
credit line	ligne de crédit
credit turnover ratio	ratio de rotation des crédits
cumulative adjustment	ajustement cumulé
cumulative effect	effet cumulatif
currency translation	conversion monetaire
current assets	actif de roulement
current assets	actif circulant
current assets	actif realisable à court terme
current liabilities	passifs à court terme
current liabilities	dettes à court terme
current portion of ...	partie courante de...
current ratio	ratio du court terme
custody securities	titres de tiers
customers	clients
customers'liability for acceptances	engagements des clients
customs duties	droits de douane
December	décembre
debenture	obligation
debenture	debenture
debt discount	réescompte de la dette
debt premium	prime sur dette
debt restructuring	restructuration de la dette
deferred charges	charges differées
deferred income	produits constatés d'avance
deferred income taxes	impôt sur les bénéfices différé
deferred income/expense	comptes de regularisation
deferred taxes	impôt différé
demand deposits	comptes ordinaires
departure from a pronouncement	écart à la norme
dependents	dépendants
depreciation expense	dotation aux amortissements
depreciation expense	frais d'amortissement
depreciation on buildings	dotation aux comptes d'amortissements pour constructions
depreciation on buildings	relever
detect	entreprises en voie de développement
development stage companies	coût direct
direct cost	directeurs
directors	administrateurs
directors	decaissements
disbursements	refus de la certification
disclaimer of opinion	révélation
disclosure	présentation
disclosure	opérations cessées
discontinued operations	

ENGLISH	FRENCH
discount rate	taux d'escompte
disposal (of an asset)	cession (d'un actif)
dividend	dividende
dividend income	dividendes reçues
dividend per share	dividende par action
dividends payable	dividendes à payer
dollars	dollars
domestic subsidiaries	filiales nationaux
double taxation	double imposition
due date	échéance
early extinguishment of debt	amortissement anticipé de la dette
early retirement	retraite anticipé
earnings per share	bénéfice net par action
earnings per share	revenu par action
economic environment	contexte économique
effect	effet
effects of changing prices	effet de la variation des prix
employee	effectif
employee	salarié
employee benefits	avantages sociaux
entertainment expense	frais de représentation
equity in other companies	participations en autres sociétés
equity method	mise en équivalence
errors	erreurs
evidential matter	éléments probants
examine	examiner
examine	vérifier
except for	à l'exception de
except for	sauf
exchange rate	cours de change
exchange rate	taux de parité
exchange rate	taux de change
exchange rate risk	risque de change
excise tax	droit d'accise
excise tax	taxe sur des produits determinés
exhibitions and events expense	frais d'exhibitions
expected salvage value	valeur récupérable presumé
expenses	charges
expenses	frais
expenses	dépenses
expenses on capital increase	frais d`augmentation de capital
export	exportation
export duties	droits d'exportation
extent	limite
extraordinary items	produits et charges exceptionnelles

ENGLISH	FRENCH
face value	valeur nominal
fairly present	donner une image fidèle
feasibility	praticabilité
feasibility study	étude de praticabilité
February	février
fees	honoraires
fees for services by third party	honoraires pour services extérieurs
finance (noun)	finance
finance (verb)	financier
financial entities	sociétés financières
financial statements	comptes financiers
financial statements	états financiers
financial summary	états financiers schematiques
financial summary	résultats financiers
financing arrangement	accord de financement
fine	amende
finished goods	produits finis
first in, first out (FIFO)	premier entré, premier sorti
fittings	installations
fixed assets	biens immobiliers
fixed assets	immobilisations corporelles
fixed assets	immobilisations
fixed assets	valeurs immobilisées
flat tax withholding	retention à taux fixe
floating rate	taux de change flottant
flowchart	diagramme de circulation
footnotes to financial statements	notes aux états financiers
for taxation purposes	aux effets fiscaux
forecast	prévision
foreign currency	monnaies étrangères
foreign currency translation	conversion des devises
foreign exchange	devises
foreign exchange gains (losses)	revenus (pertes) de change
foreign subsidiaries	filiales étrangères
form	formulaire
freight on purchases of materials	transports sur achats
funds	fonds
furniture and fixtures	mobiliers,aménagements,installations
future contracts	engagements à terme
future contracts	opérations sur futures
gain	plus-value
gain on revaluation of securities	plus-value sur titres
gain on sale of fixed assets	revenus de cession d`immobilisations
general and administrative expense	frais divers de gestion
general insurance	assurances générales

ENGLISH	FRENCH
general ledger	grand livre
general manager	directeur général
generally accepted	généralement admis
generally accepted	généralement reconnu
going concern	entreprise en activité
goods in process	produits en cours de production
goods in transit	marchandises en route
goodwill	fonds de commerce
goodwill	survaloir
goodwill	prime d'acquisition
graduated tax	impôt progressif
gross margin	marge brute
gross national product	produit national brut
gross profit ratio	coefficient du bénéfice brut
gross revenue tax	taxe sur le chiffre d'affaires
group (of companies)	groupe (de sociétés)
guarantee	garantie
guarantee deposits	dépôts en garantie
hedge	couverture
hedging	operation de couverture à terme
historical cost	coût historique
historical cost	valeur historique
holding company	société de portefeuille
hundreds	cents
idle capacity	capacité oisive
import surcharges	surtaxe à l'importation
in accordance with	d'accord avec
income for services rendered	revenus pour services
income statement	compte de pertes et profits
income tax	impôt sur les bénéfices
income tax	impôt sur le revenu
income tax	impôt sur le résultat
indebtedness ratio	ratio d'endettement
indemnities	indemnités
industry	activité
industry	industrie
inflation	inflation
inheritance tax	droit de successions
insurance company	compagnie d'assurances
intangible assets	actifs incorporels
intangible assets	immobilisations incorporelles
intangible assets	avoirs invisibles
inter-company loans	placements intersociétaires
interbank assets/funds	dépôts de banques
interbank deposits	dépôts interbancaires

ACCOUNTING LEXICON : ENGLISH - FRENCH

ENGLISH	FRENCH
interbank rate	taux interbancaire
interest expense	intérêts débiteurs
interest expense	frais financiers
interest expense	intérêts payés
interest income	intérêts créditeurs
interest income	produits financiers
interest payable	intérêts à payer
interest rate	taux d'intérêt
interest receivable	intérêts à recevoir
interim accounts	situation comptable intérimaire
interim financial statements	états financiers intérimaires
internal auditors	auditeurs internes
internal control	contrôle interne
internal control questionnaire	questionnaire de contrôle interne
international subsidiaries	filiales internationaux
international trade	commerce international
intervening period	période ecoulée
inventory (USA) stocks(UK)	stocks
inventory (USA) stocks(UK)	valeurs d'exploitation
inventory turnover ratio	coefficient de rotation de stocks
investment	investissement
investment bank/merchant bank	banque d'investissement
investment bank/merchant bank	banque d'affaires
investment in subsidiaries	investissements en filiales
investment in subsidiaries	titres de participation
investment securities gains(losses)	gains (pertes) sur investissements en titres
investment securities gains(losses)	
investment tax credit	abattement fiscal pour investissement
invoice	facture
irregularity	irregularité
January	janvier
joint venture	entreprise commune
journal	livre journal
journal entry	écritures au journal
July	juillet
June	juin
labor hours (man-hours)	homme-heures
labor law	loi du travail
land	terrains
land improvements	amendements des sols
last in, first out (LIFO)	dernier entré, premier sorti
lawyer	conseil juridique
lawyer	avocat
lease	bail
lease financing loans	prêts en crédit-bail
leaseback	cession-bail
leasing	location (crédit-bail)
legal requirements	obligations légaux
legal reserve	réserve légale
lessee	locataire
lessor	bailleur
liability	passif
life insurance	assurance sur la vie
life policy benefits	bénéfices prêtés par assurances de vie
liquid assets	banques,caisse,chèques postaux
liquidity	liquidité
liquidity ratio	coefficient de liquidité
liquidity risk	risque de pénurie de liquidité
listed bonds-local currency	titres cotés-monnaie nationale
litigation	litiges
loans	prêts
local currency	monnaie nationale
long-term contracts	contracts à long terme
long-term credits	crédits à long terme
long-term debt	dettes à long terme
long-term insurance reserve charges	réserves à long terme pour sinistres
long-term investments	immobilisations financières
loss	perte
loss carry-forward	perte cumulée
lower of cost or market method	coût ou valeur de marché
lower of cost or market method	coût ou valeur actuelle
machinery and equipment	machines et outillage
major customers	clients principaux
management intention	intention de la direction
March	mars
marginal cost	coût marginal
market price	prix du marché
market price	valeur venale
marketable securities	titres cotés
marketable securities	titres negociables
marketable securities	titres de placement
marketable securities	valeurs mobilières de placement
marketable stocks	titres cotés en bourse
material (noun)	matériel
material (significant)	significatif
materiality	importance relative
materiality	signification
matured loans	prêts échus
maturity	échéance
May	mai

ENGLISH	FRENCH
merger	fusion
millions	millions
minority interests	participation minoritaire
misleading information	informations trompeuses
monetary assets	actif monétaire
monetary transactions	transactions monétaires
monthly	par mois
monthly	mensuellement
mortgage	hypothèque
mortgage bank	établissement de crédit hypothècaire
mortgage bank	banque de crédit hypothècaire
multinational enterprise	entreprise multinationale
multiple regression	regression multiple
mutual fund	fond commun de placement
mutual fund	SICAV
nature	nature
net fixed assets	immobilisations net
net income	bénéfice net
net income	résultat net
net income of the period	bénéfice net de l'exercice
net loss of the period	perte nette de l'exercice
net premiums earned	primes nettes
net present value	valeur actuelle net
net realizable value	valeur net de réalisation
net sales	chiffre d'affaires net
net sales	ventes nettes
net trade accounts receivable	créances clients et comptes rattachés
net worth	situation nette
non-current assets	actif immobilisé
non-current liabilities	passifs à long terme
non-equity reserves	réserves non patrimoniales
non-monetary transactions	transactions non monétaires
non-operating income and expense	profits et produits non incorporés
non-performing earning assets	prêts non productifs
non-profit	sans but lucratif
non-redeemable preferred stock	actions preferées non remboursables
non-sampling risk	risque éloigné de l'échantillonnage
non-statistical sampling	échantillonnage non statistique
non-taxable income	produits non taxés
notes payable	effets à payer
notes receivable	effets à recevoir
November	novembre
obsolescence	vieillissement
October	octobre
officer (of a company)	dirigeant (d'une société)

ENGLISH	FRENCH
offset (noun)	compensation
operating controls	contrôles opératifs
operating cycle	cycle opératif
operating lease	location opérative
operating profit	produit d'exploitation
operating ratio	ratio d'exploitation
operational auditing	contrôle operationnel
operational controls	contrôles operationnels
operational network	réseau operationnel
opinion	opinion
opinion	certification
opinion paragraph	paragraphe d'opinion
opportunity cost	coût d'opportunité
options	opération sur options
options	options
organization chart	organigramme
organization expenses	frais d'organisation
other income for services	autres revenus pour des services
other loans	autres prêts
other operating profits (losses)	autres revenus (pertes) d'exploitation
outstanding shares	actions émises
over-the-counter transaction	transaction hors coté
overdraft	découvert
overdue	impayé
overdue	échu
overhead expenses	frais généraux
overhead expenses	charges de structure
overhead expenses	charges operationnelles
overinvoicing	surfacturation
overnight funds	placements au jour le jour
paid-in capital	capital versé
par value	pair
par value	valeur nominale
parent company	société mère
parent company	société dominante
partner	associé
patents	brevets
payments	paiements
payments cycle	cycle des paiements
payroll	feuille de paie
pension	pension
pension plan	régime de retraite
percentage	pourcentage
percentage-of-completion-method	méthode de pourcentage d'achèvement
permanent file	dossier permanent

ENGLISH	FRENCH
perpetual bond	obligation perpétuelle
perpetual inventory system	systeme d'inventaire permanent
personal income tax	impôt sur les bénéfices des personnes physiques
personal income tax	petite caisse
petty cash	stocks physiques
physical inventory	placement
placement	mettre en gage
pledge (verb)	obligations de gager
pledging requirements	patrimoine attribuable aux assurés
policyholders' equity	bénéfice attribuable aux assurés
policyholders' surplus	combinaison des intérêts
pooling of interest	population
population	composition du portefeuille
portfolio composition	enregistrer
post entries to the ledger	indemnité pour retraite
post-retirement benefits	action de priorité
preference share	action privilegiée
preference share	action preferée
preference share (UK)	action preferée
preferred share (USA)	prime
premium	prime d'émission
premium on issue of capital	charges payées d'avance
prepaid expense	comptes transitoires
prepaid expense	charges constatées d'avance
prepaid expense	comptes de regularisation
prepaid expenses & deferred charges	capital de base
primary capital	profits sur exercices antérieurs
prior period adjustments	secteur privé
private sector	probable
probable	financement de l'achat d'un produit
product financing	garanties sur produits
product warranties	capacité de production
production capacity	coût de production
production cost	cycle de production
production cycle	ordre de production
production order	jugement professionnel
professional judgment	règles professionnelles
professional standards	bénéfice
profit	compte de pertes et profits
profit & loss account	marge bénéficiaire
profit margin	participation des salariés aux bénéfices
profit sharing	impôt progressif
progressive tax	projection
projection	frais de promotion
promotional costs	

ENGLISH	FRENCH
provision	provision
proxy (noun)	suppléant
public sector	secteur publique
purchase requisition	requisition d'achat
qualification(of an audit opinion)	réserve
quality control	contrôle de qualité
quarter	trimestre
quarterly	trimestriellement
quarterly (4 times a year)	trimestriellement (4 fois par an)
quarterly financial statements	états financiers trimestriels
random	aléatoire
raw materials	matières premières
real estate and mortgage loans	prêts hypothécaires
reasonably possible	raisonnablement possible
receivables	créances
receivables	débiteurs
recession	récession
record (verb)	enregistrer
recruiting expense	frais de recrutement (de personnel)
redeemable	remboursable
redeemable preferred stock	actions preferées remboursables
redemption features	règles de rachat
rediscounted notes	notes réescomptés
refinancing	refinancement
refund	remboursement
regressive tax	impôt regressif
regulations	règlements
reinsurance and premium adjustments	réassurances et ajustements des primes
related party transactions	transactions avec des intéressés
remote	remote
repair and maintenance expense	frais d'entretien et réparations
repairs	réparations
replacement cost	coût de remplacement
report	rapport
report to management	lettre de recommandations
reproduction cost	coût de reproduction
repurchase agreement	accord de rachat
resale agreement	accord de revente
resale merchandise	marchandises de revente
research and development costs	dépenses de recherche et développement
research and development costs	frais de recherche et mise au point
research and development costs	frais de recherche et développement
reserve for exch. rate fluctuations	réserve pour différences de change
reserve for general risks	reserve pour risques
reserve for loan losses	réserve pour prêts irrécupérables

ENGLISH	FRENCH
reserve for loan losses/bad debts	réserve pour débiteurs douteux
reserve for o/s claims and losses	réserve pour réclamations et pertes
restrictions on the scope	restrictions sur la portée
restructuring	restructuration
retained earnings	bénéfices accumulés
retained earnings	bénéfices non distribués
retirement of long-term debt	amortissement de la dette à long terme
return on assets	taux de rentabilité des actifs
return on equity	taux de rentabilité des fonds propres
revaluation	réévaluation
revaluation reserve	réserve de réévaluation
revaluation surplus	écart de réévaluation
review of financial statements	revision aux états financiers
risk exposure	exposition à la risque
rules	règles
salaries and wages	salaires
sale of (manufactured) goods	vente de produits (finis)
sales (turnover)	chiffre d'affaires
sales (turnover)	ventes
sales on installments	ventes à tempérament
sales tax	taxe sur les ventes
sample size	amplitude de l'échantillon
sampling	échantillonnage
sampling results	résultats d'échantillonnage
sampling risk	risque d'échantillonnage
savings deposits	dépôts en compte d'épargne
scope	portée
scope paragraph	paragraphe de portée
seasonally adjusted	dessaisonalisé
second request	deuxième demande
secondary market	second marché
secured note	billet garanti
Securities and Exchange Commission	commission des opérations de bourse
self-insurance	autoassurance
self-insure	autoassurer
selling expenses	frais de ventes
semi-finished goods	produits semi-terminés
senior debt	dette prioritaire
september	septembre
severance	licenciement
severance indemnities	indemnités de départ
share in loss of affiliates	participation en perte des affiliées
shareholders' equity	capitaux propres
shareholders' equity	situation nette
shares	actions

ENGLISH	FRENCH
short-term bank loans	emprunts banquiers à court terme
short-term investments	investissements à court terme
short-term loans	emprunts à moins d'un an
small companies	petites entreprises
social security expense	frais de securité sociale
sources of funds	ressources de fonds
special bonus	primes et gratifications
special reports	rapports spéciaux
split (of a company)	scission (d'une société)
spread (between rates)	marge
spread (between rates)	spread
stamp duty	droit de timbre
standard cost	coût standard
start-up costs	frais d`établissement
statement changes in fin. position	tableau de financement
statement of accounting policy	note explicative sur les principes comptables appliqués
statement of accounting policy	tableau des ressources et des emplois des fonds
statement sources & uses of funds	échantillonnage statistique
statement sources & uses of funds	rapport des commissaires aux comptes
statistical sampling	réserve légale
statutory audit report	dividende sous forme d'actions
statutory reserve	bourse (des valeurs)
stock dividends	plan d'option sur actions
stock exchange	agent de bourse
stock option plan	actionnaires
stockbroker	capitaux propres
stockholders	situation nette
stockholders' equity	méthode linéaire
stockholders' equity	sujet à
straight-line method	souslocation
subject to	emprunts subordonnés
sublet (noun)	financement subordonné
subordinated debt	souscription
subordinated financing	événements postérieurs
subscription	filiale
subsequent events	société affiliée
subsidiary	livres auxiliaires
subsidiary	épreuves substantives
subsidiary records	méthode de la somme des chiffres
substantive tests	renseignements supplémentaires
sum of the years' digits method	fournisseurs
supplementary information	fournitures
suppliers	pièces de rechange
supplies (noun)	
supplies and spare parts	

ENGLISH	FRENCH
supporting documentation	pièces justificatives
syndicated loans	crédits syndiqués
taken as a whole	dans son ensemble
tangible fixed assets	immobilisations corporelles
tax	impôt
tax audit	vérification fiscale
tax authorities	autorités fiscaux
tax credits	crédit d'impôts
tax rate	taux d'imposition
tax return	déclaration d'impôts
tax savings	économies fiscaux
tax treatment	traitement fiscale
taxable income	bénéfices imposables
taxable income	revenus imposables
taxpayer	contribuable
temporary differences	différences temporaires
test	test
thousand	mille
thousands	milliers
time deposit	dépôt à terme
timing	oppportunité
total funds from operations	fonds d'exploitation
total insurance claims and losses	réclamations et pertes pour sinistres
total insurance reserves	totale des réserves pour risques
total premiums written	primes d'assurance émises
total revenue	recettes totales
trade mark	marque de fabrique
trade payables	dettes aux fournisseurs
trade receivables	crédits commerciaux
training expenditure	frais de formation du personnel
transactions	transactions
treasury stock	actions propres en portefeuille
trend	tendance
trial balance	balance de soldes
troubled debt	dettes non récupérables
trust operations profits (losses)	revenus (pertes) pour administration
trust operations profits (losses)	des fonds de tiers
trust securities	titres et valeurs de tiers
turnover ratio	ratio de rotation
unamortized premium	survaleur non amortisé
unappropriated retained earnings	bénéfice non distribué
unasserted claim	réclamation non realisée
unaudited	sans contrôler
uncertainty	incertitude
uncollectible	irrécupérable
underinvoicing	sous-facturation
underwriting policy acquis. costs	frais d'émission des polices
unearned interest	intérêts passifs
units of production	unités de production
unqualified	sans réserve
unsecured bonds	obligations sans garantie
useful life (of an asset)	vie utile
uses of funds	emplois des fonds
vacation with pay	congés payés
valuation principles	règles d'évaluation
value added tax (VAT)	taxe sur la valeur ajoutée (TVA)
variable cost	coût variable
vehicles	véhicules
vendors (USA)	fournisseurs
vice-chairman	vice-président
voucher	bon
warehouse	entrepôt
warehouse	magasin
weighted average	moyenne pondérée
with and without method	méthode de "avec et sans"
withheld taxes	impôts retenues
withholding of tax	retention des impôts
working capital	fonds de roulement
working capital ratio	ratio du capital circulant
working capital turnover	rotation du capital circulant
working papers	papiers de travail
write off (verb)	passer par pertes et profits
year-end closing date	date de clôture de l'exercice
yield	rendement
zero base budget	budget base zero
zero coupon bonds	obligations à coupon zéro

GERMAN	ENGLISH
Abfindungen	indemnities
Abgang	disposition
abgebrochener Betrieb	discontinued operations
abschreiben	write down
Abschreibung (Gebäude)	depreciation - buildings
Abschreibungsaufwand	depreciation expense
Abzinsungssatz	discount rate
Abzugsteuern	withheld taxes
Änderungen in der Buchführungsmethode	accounting changes
Agio	premium
Agio	debt premium
Aktien	shares
Aktienbörse	stock exchange
Aktionär	shareholder
Aktionäre	stockholders
Aktiva	current assets
Aktiva	assets
aktive Rechnungsabgrenzung	deferred charges
Aktivierung der Finanzierungskosten	capitalization of financial costs
Aktivierung der Leasingverträge	capitalization of leases
Aktivierung der Zinsen	capitalization of interests
Allgemeine Versicherung	general insurance
allgemeine und Verwaltungskosten	general and administrative expense
als Ganzes genommen	taken as a whole
alternative Verfahren	alternative procedures
an der Börse notierte Schuld -	listed bonds-local currency
verschreibungen	listed bonds-local currency
analytischer Überblick	analytical review
andere Gewinne aus Dienstleistungen	other income for services
Angestellter	employee
Anlagen im Bau	construction in progress
Anlagevermögen	fixed assets
Anlaufkosten	start-up costs
Anleihe	debenture
Anpassung	adjustment
Anschaffungskosten	acquisition cost
Anschaffungskosten	historical cost
Ansprüche	claims
Anteil der Minderheitsaktionäre	minority interest
Anteile in Fremdbesitz	minority interests
antizipative Aktiva	accrued income
antizipative Passiva	accrued liabilities
antizipative Passiva	accrued expenses
Anzahlungen	advances to suppliers
April	April

GERMAN	ENGLISH
Arbeitnehmer	employee
Arbeitsablaufplan	flowchart
Arbeitsrecht	labor law
Arbeitsstunden	labor hours
Art	nature
assoziiertes Unternehmen	associated firm
aufgelaufener Urlaubsanspruch	accrued vacations
Aufgeld	premium
aufgeschobene Einkommensteuer -	deferred income tax
verbindlichkeit	deferred income tax
Aufsichtsrat	board of directors
Aufsichtsrat	supervisory board
Aufsichtsratsmitglieder	directors
Aufwand für Wohltätigkeit	charity expense
Aufwendungen	expenses
Aufwendungen für Bankdienste	bank service charges
Aufwertung	revaluation
August	August
Ausbeute	yield
Ausfuhr	export
Ausfuhrzölle	export duties
ausländische Tochtergesellschaft	foreign subsidiary
ausser	except for
ausserbörslicher Handel	over the counter transaction
ausserordentliche Posten	extraordinary items
Ausstattungen	fittings
ausstehende Aktien	outstanding shares
Auswirkung	effect
Auszahlung	disbursements
Bank	bank
Bankausgleichung	bank reconciliation
Bankkontoüberziehung	bank overdrafts
Bankrott	bankruptcy
Bardividende	cash dividends
Bargeld	cash
bargeldlose Transaktionen	non-monetary transactions
Bedarfsmeldung	purchase requisition
beeinflussen	impact (verb)
Beleg	voucher
beratende Dienstleistungen	consulting services
Bericht	report
Berichtigung	adjustment
Berufsgrundsätze	professional standards
Bestellobligo	commitments
Beteiligungen	investments

GERMAN	ENGLISH
Beteiligungen an Tochtergesellschaften	investment in subsidiaries
Beteiligungsgesellschaft	holding company
betrieblich nicht genutzte Kapazität	idle capacity
Betriebs- und Hilfsstoffe	supplies
Betriebs- und Geschäftsausstattung	furniture and fixtures
betriebsfremder Ertrag und Aufwand	non-operating income and expense
Betriebsgewinn	operating profit
Betriebskapitalsratio	working capital ratio
Betriebskontrollen	operating controls
Betriebskreislauf	operating cycle
Betriebsmieten	operating leases
Betriebsstoffe und Ersatzteile	supplies and spare parts
Bewertungsgrundsätze	valuation principles
Bewirtungskosten	entertainment expense
Bezahlung mit Bargeld	disbursements
bieten	bid (verb)
Bilanz	balance sheet
Bilanzgewinn	unappropriated retained earnings
Bilanzierungsgrundsätze	accounting principles
Bilanzierungspolitik	accounting policies
Bilanzierungsprinzipien	accounting principles
Bilanzstichtag	balance sheet date
Bilanzsumme	total assets
Bilanzsumme	total liabilities + shareh. equity
break even point	break even point
Bruttogewinnmesszahl	gross profit ratio
Bruttomarge	gross margin
Bruttosozialprodukt	gross national product
Bruttoumsatzsteuer	gross revenue tax
Buchführer	accountant
Buchführung	accounting
Buchhalter	accountant
Buchhaltung	accounting
Buchwert	book value
Budget	budget
Busse	fine
Bürgschaften	guarantee deposits
Bürobedarf	office supplies
Börsenaufsichtsbehörde (USA)	Securities and Exchange Commission
börsengängige Aktien	marketable stocks
börsengängige Wertpapiere	marketable securities
cash flow	cash flow
ceteris paribus	ceteris paribus
consolidierter Jahresabschluss	consolidated accounts
Copyright	copyright

GERMAN	ENGLISH
Darlehen	loans
Datenverarbeitungsanlage	data processing equipment
Debitoren	accounts receivable
Depositenzertifikat	certificate of deposit
Devisen	foreign exchange
Devisengewinne (Verluste)	foreign exchange gains (losses)
Dezember	December
Dienstleistungskosten	cost of services rendered
digitale Abschreibungsmethode	sum of the years'-digits method
Disagio	debt discount
Diskontsatz	discount rate
Dividende	dividend
Dividende pro Aktie	dividend per share
Dividenden in Form von Aktien	stock dividends
Dividendenertrag	dividend income
Dokument	form
Dollars	dollars
Doppelbesteuerung	double taxation
Durchführbarkeit	feasibility
Durchschnitt	average
Effekt	effect
Effekt von Preisänderungen	effects of changing prices
eigene Aktien	treasury stock
eigene Mittel	capital and reserves
Eigenkapital	capital and reserves
Eigenkapital	net worth
Eigenkapital	shareholders' equity
Eigenkapital	stockholders' equity
Einfluss	impact
eingeschränkter Bestätigungsvermerk des Prüfers	qualification (of an audit opinion)
	qualification (of an audit opinion)
eingezahltes Kapital	paid-in capital
Einkommen für geleistete Dienste	income for services rendered
Einkommensteuer	income tax
Einkommensteuer	personal income tax
einlösbar	redeemable
eintragen	record (verb)
Einzahlungsverpflichtungen	commitments
Einzelkosten	direct cost
Einzüge	collections
entdecken	detect
Enthüllung	disclosure
entsprechend	in accordance with
Equity-Methode	equity method
Erbschaftssteuer	inheritance tax

GERMAN	ENGLISH
Erfolgsrechnung	profit & loss accounts
Erläuterungen zum Jahresabschluss	footnotes to financial statements
Ersatzkosten	replacement cost
Erträge aus der Auflösung von Wert -	prior period adjustments
berichtigungen und Rückstellungen	prior period adjustments
Ertragsschwelle	break even point
Ertragssteuer	income tax
Erträge	revenue
Erträge	income
Erträge aus Aufwertung von Wertpapieren	gain on revaluation of securities
Erträge aus dem Abgang von Sachanlagen	gain on sale of fixed assets
Erwerb einer Gesellschaft	acquisition (of a company)
Etat	budget
Export	export
Februar	February
Fehler	errors
fehlleitende Information	misleading information
fertige Erzeugnisse	finished goods
Fertigungskosten	production cost
Festgeld	time deposits
Finanzen	finance
Finanzieren	finance (verb)
Finanzierungsinstitute	financial entities
Finanzverwaltung	tax authorities
Firmenwert	goodwill
first in, first out (FIFO)	first in, first out (FIFO)
flüssige Mittel	cash
flüssige Mittel	liquid assets
Fonds	funds
Forderungen	claims
Forderungen	receivables
Forderungen an Kreditinstitute	claims on banks
Forderungen aus Lieferungen und	trade receivables
Leistungen	trade receivables
Formular	form
Forschungs- und Entwicklungskosten	research and development costs
freie Rücklagen	unappropriated retained earnings
Freiverkehr	over the counter transaction
fremde Währung	foreign currency
Fremdwährungsumrechnung	foreign currency translation
Fuhrpark	vehicles
Fusion	merger
Fusionen	business combinations
fällige Obligationen	matured loans
Fälligkeit	maturity

GERMAN	ENGLISH
Fälligkeitstermin	due date
Garantiekaution	guarantee deposits
Garantien	guarantees
Gebühren	fees
Gebühren für Leistungen an Dritte	fees for services by third party
Gebäude	buildings and structures
gegensätzliche Meinung	adverse opinion
Gehaltsabrechnung	payroll
Gehälter und Löhne	salaries and wages
Geldstrafe	fine
Gemeinkosten	overhead expenses
gemeinnützig	non-profit
Generalbevollmächtigter	executive vice president
Generaldirektor	general manager
Geschäfts - und Industrie Kredite	commercial & industrial loans
Geschäftsbank	commercial bank
Geschäftsbereich	business segment
Geschäftsbericht	annual report
Geschäftsführer	general manager
Geschäftsleiter	general manager
Geschäftswert	goodwill
Gesellschafter	partner
Gesellschaftsstatuten	company by-laws
gesetzliche Rücklage	legal reserve
gesetzliche Vorschriften	legal requirements
gewerbliche Schutzrechte	trade marks
Gewinn	gain
Gewinn	profit
Gewinn pro Aktie	earnings per share
Gewinn- und Verlustrechnung	profit & loss accounts
Gewinnbeteiligung	profit sharing
Gewinnbeteilung der Versicherungsnehmer	policyholders' equity
Gewinnspanne	profit margin
Gewinnverwendung	appropriation of profit
Gewinnvortrag	retained earnings
Grad	extent
Grenzkosten	marginal cost
Grundbuch	journal
Grundkapital	capital stock
Grundstücke	land
Grundstückverbesserungen	land improvements
Gruppe	group (of companies)
halbfertige Erzeugnisse	semi-finished goods
Handlungsvollmacht	proxy (power of attorney)
Hauptbuch	general ledger

GERMAN	ENGLISH
Hauptkunden	major customers
Herstellkosten der verkauften Ware	cost of goods sold
Herstellungskosten	production cost
Hinweis in der Bilanz	disclosure
Holdinggesellschaft	holding company
Honorare	fees
Hunderte	hundreds
Hypothek	mortgage
Hypothekenbank	mortgage bank
im Range nachstehende Schuld	subordinated debt
immaterielle Anlagen	intangible assets
immaterielle Vermögensgegenstände	intangible assets
in Übereinstimmung mit	in accordance with
Industrie	industry
Inflation	inflation
Inflationskorrektur	adjustment for inflation
Ingangsetzungskosten	start-up costs
Inhaber	bearer
Inhalt	contents
Inkassos	collections
inländische Tochtergesellschaften	domestic subsidiaries
Innenrevisoren	internal auditors
innerbetriebliche Kontrolle	internal controls
innerbetrieblicher Kontrollfragebogen	internal control questionnaire
Instandhaltung	repairs and maintenance
Interessengemeinschaft	pooling of interest
internationale Tochtergesellschaft	international subsidiaries
internationaler Handel	international trade
Inventar	inventory
Investition	investment
Investitionszuschuss	investment tax credit
Investmentbank	investment bank/merchant bank
Jahresabschluss	financial statements
Jahresabschluss mit Vergleichszahlen	comparative financial statements
Jahresabschlussdatum	year-end closing date
Jahresbericht	annual report
Jahresversammlung	annual meeting
Jahresüberschuss	net income
Jahresübersicht	financial summary
Januar	January
Joint Venture	joint venture
Journal	journal
Journalbuchung	journal entry
Juli	July
Juni	June

GERMAN	ENGLISH
jährlich	annually
jährliche Hauptversammlung der Aktionäre	annual shareholders' meeting
Kapitalanlage	investment
Kapitalanlagegesellschaft auf Gegenseitigkeit	mutual fund
Kapitalanlagegesellschaft auf Gegenseitigkeit	mutual fund
Kapitalerhöhung	capital increase
Kapitalgewinnsteuer	capital gains tax
Kapitalsteuer	capital tax
Kasse und Bankguthaben	cash and banks
Kassenbestand	cash on hand
kleine Firmen	small companies
kleine Kasse	petty cash
kodieren	code (verb)
Kommunikationskosten	communications expense
Kompagnon	partner
Konkurs	bankruptcy
Konsolidierungsausgleichposten (Passiva)	negative goodwill
Konsortialkredit	syndicated loans
Kontenplan	chart of accounts
Kontenrahmen	chart of accounts
konvertierbare Schuld	convertible debt
Konzern	group
Konzernabschluss	consolidated financial statements
Konzernbilanz	consolidated balance sheet
Konzerngewinn	consolidated profit
Kreditoren	accounts payable
Kreditvolumen	total lending
kumulative Korrektur	cumulative adjustment
kumulativer Effekt	cumulative effect
kumulierte Abschreibungen	accumulated depreciation
kumulierte Amortisation	accumulated amortization
Kunden	customers
Kurzbericht	condensed financial statements
kurzfristige Verbindlichkeiten	short-term loans
kurzfristige Verbindlichkeiten	current liabilities
kurzfristiger Bankkredit	short-term bank loans
kurzfristiges Betriebskapital	working capital
körperliche Inventur	physical inventory
Lager	warehouse
Landeswährung	local currency
langfristige Aktiva	non-current assets
langfristige Beteiligungen	long-term investments
langfristige Kredite	long-term credits
langfristige Verbindlichkeit	long-term debt
langfristige Verbindlichkeiten	non-current liabilities

GERMAN	ENGLISH
langfristige Verträge	long-term contracts
last in, first out (LIFO)	last in, first out (LIFO)
latente Steuerschulden	deferred taxes
Lebensdauer	useful life (of an asset)
Lebensversicherung	life insurance
Lieferanten	suppliers
lineare Abschreibungsmethode	straight-line method
liquide Aktiva	liquid assets
Liquidität	liquidity
Liquidität ersten Grades	acid test
Liquiditätskennzahl	current ratio
Liquiditätskennzahl	liquidity ratio
Liquiditätsrisiko	liquidity risk
Lizenzen	licences
Lohnabrechnung	payroll
Lohnliste	payroll
Länderrisiko	country risk
Mai	May
Makler	stockbroker
Marge	spread (between rates)
Markenzeichen	trade marks
Marktpreis	market price
maschinelle Anlagen und Ausrüstung	machinery and equipment
Mass	extent
Materialaufwand	cost of material
Materialien	materials (sust.)
Mehrwertsteuer	value added tax (VAT)
Meinung	opinion
Miete	lease
Mieter	lessee
Milliarde	billions
Millionen	millions
Mitglied der Geschäftsleitung	officer
Mittelherkunft	sources of funds
Mittelherkunfts -und Verwendungsrechnung	statement sources & uses of funds
monatlich	monthly
monetare Aktiva	monetary assets
multinationales Unternehmen	multinational enterprise
Muttergesellschaft	parent company
März	march
Natur	nature
Nebenprodukte	by-products
Nennwert	par value
Nennwert	face value
Nettoerlöswert	net realizable value

GERMAN	ENGLISH
Nettogegenwartswert	net present value
Nettoumsatz	net sales
nicht ausgeschütteter Gewinn	retained earnings
nicht besteuerbares Einkommen	non-taxable income
Niederstwertprinzip	lower of cost or market
Niederstwertprinzip	cost or market
noch nicht verdientes Einkommen	deferred income
Nominalbetrag	face value
November	November
Null-Coupon Bonds	zero coupon bonds
Nutzungsdauer	useful life (of an asset)
Obligation	debenture
Obligation	bond
Öffentlichkeitsbereich	public sector
ohne Gewinnabsicht	non-profit
Oktober	october
Option	options
ordnungsgemäss	generally accepted
Organisationskosten	organization expenses
Organisationsplan	flowchart
Organisationsplan	organization chart
Pacht	lease
Passiva	liabilities
Passiva	liabilities + shareholder's equity
passive Rechnungsabgrenzung	accrued expenses
Patente	patents
Pauschalwert Berichtigung	reserve for general risks
Pension	pension
Pensionsplan	pension plan
periodische Abgrenzung von Aufwand und Ertrag	accrual (acc. method)
	accrual (acc. method)
Pfand	pledge
Pflichtprüfung	statutory audit report
Planungstudie	feasibility study
Plazierung	placement
Population	population
Preisangebot	bid
Privatbereich	private sector
Produktfinanzierung	product financing
Produktgarantie	product warranties
Produktionsauftrag	production order
Produktionseinheiten	units of production
Produktionskapazität	production capacity
Produktionskosten	production cost
Produktionszyklus	production cycle

GERMAN	ENGLISH
professionelle Bewertung	professional judgment
proportionale Kosten	variable cost
Provisionen und Erträge für geleistete	commissions & fees profits (losses)
Dienste (Verluste)	commissions & fees profits (losses)
Prozentsatz	percentage
Prozess	litigation
prüfen	examine
Prüfer	auditor
Prüfung	audit
Prüfung der Rechnungslegung	audit
Prüfungsauftrag	audit engagement
Prüfungsbericht	auditor's report
Prüfungsbewertung	audit opinion
Prüfungsgebühren	audit fees
Prüfungsgrundsätze	auditing standards
Prüfungsleiter	audit manager
Prüfungspersonal	audit staff
Prüfungsprobe	audit sampling
Prüfungsrisiko	audit risk
Prüfungsstrategie	audit strategy
Prüfungsverfahren	auditing procedures
Qualitätskontrolle	quality control
Quartal	quarter
Quartalbericht	quarterly financial statements
Rabatt	allowance
Rahmenkredit	credit line
Rechnung	invoice
Rechnungsabgrenzungsposten	prepaid expense
Rechnungszinsfuss	discount rate
Rechtsanwalt	lawyer
Rechtsstreit	litigation
Refinanzierung	refinancing
Regeln	rules
regressive Steuer	regressive tax
Reichweite	scope
Reinvermögen	net worth
Reinvermögen der Gesellschafter	stockholders' equity
Reinvermögen der Gesellschafter	shareholders' equity
Rekrutierungsaufwand	recruiting expense
Rendite	yield
Rente	pension
Reserven	retained earnings
Rezession	recession
Rohbilanz	trial balance
Rohstoffe	raw materials

GERMAN	ENGLISH
Rücklage aus Agio	capital surplus
Rücklagen	retained earnings
Rückstellung	accrual
Rückstellung	accrued liabilities
Rückstellung im Kreditgeschäft	reserve for loan losses
Rückvergütung	refund
Sachanlagen	tangible fixed assets
Sachanlagevermögen	tangible fixed assets
Saldo	account balances
Saldovortrag	carryforward
satzungsgemässe Rücklage	statutory reserve
Schatzwechsel	treasury bills
Schulden	loans
Schuldmesszahl	indebtedness ratio
Schuldschein	debenture
Schuldverschreibung	debenture
Schuldverschreibung	bond
schwebender Kurs	floating rate
Sekundarmarkt	secondary market
Selbstversicherung	self-insurance
Selbständigkeit	independence
September	September
Sicherheit	collateral
Sonderabschreibung	accelerated depreciation
Sonderabschreibung	write down
Sonderzuwendung	special bonus
sonstige Darlehen	other loans
sonstige Passivposten	other liabilities
sonstige Vermögensgegenstände	other assets
sonstige betriebliche Gewinne	other operating profits (losses)
soziale Aufwendungen	social security expense
Sozialleistungen	employee benefits
Spareinlagen	saving deposits
Stammaktien	common stock
Stammkapital	capital stock
Standardkosten	standard cost
Stempelsteuer	stamp duty
stetig verwendet	consistently applied
Stetigkeit	consistency
Steuer	tax
Steuererklärung	tax return
Steuerersparnis	tax savings
Steuergutschrift	tax credit
steuerlicher Verlustnachtrag	carryback
steuerlicher Verlustvortrag	carryforward

GERMAN	ENGLISH
Steuerpflichtiger	taxpayer
steuerpflichtiges Einkommen	taxable income
Steuersätze	tax rates
Steuervergünstigung	tax credits
Stockdividenden	stock dividends
Summe der Aktiven	total assets
Summe der Passiven	total liabilities + shareh. equity
Tausend	thousand
Tausende	thousands
Teilnahme an anderen Unternehmen	equity in other companies
Termineinlagen	time deposits
Termingeschaft	hedge
Termingeschäfte	future contracts
Test	test
Tilgungselemente	redemption features
Timing	timing
Tochtergesellschaft	subsidiary
Transaktionen	transactions
transitorisches Passivum	deferred income
Trend	trend
täglich fällig	payable on demand
täglich fällige Gelder	demand deposits
übereinstimmen mit	comply with
überfällig	overdue
Überschuss	net income
Überziehung	overdraft
Umlaufvermögen	current assets
Umsatz	sales (turnover)
Umsatzerlöse	sales (turnover)
Umsatzkosten	cost of sales
Umsatzsteuer	sales tax
Umschlagsratio	turnover ratio
Umschuldung	debt restructuring
Umstände	circumstances
uneinbringlich	uncollectible
uneingeschränkt	unqualified
unfertige Erzeugnisse	goods in process
ungeprüft	unaudited
ungesicherte Schuldverschreibungen	unsecured bonds
Unregelmässigkeit	irregularity
untersuchen	examine
untervermieten	sublet
Unterwegsware	goods in transit
unterwerfen	subject to
unverteilter Reingewinn	retained earnings
Urheberrecht	copyright
ursprüngliche Kosten	historical cost
Veralterung	obsolescence
Verantwortlichkeit des Prüfers	auditor's responsibility
Verbindlichkeit	liability
Verbindlichkeiten	accounts payable
Verbindlichkeiten aus erklärten	dividends payable
Dividenden	dividends payable
Verbrauchssteuer	excise tax
verbunden	affiliate
verbundene Unternehmen	affiliated firms
verbundene Unternehmen	affiliates
vereinnahmte Aufwendungen	deferred expense
Verfalltag	due date
Vergütung für Investmentabwertung	allowance for devaluation of inv'ts
Verhältnis der Barmittel und Forderungen	acid test
zu kurzfristigen Verbindlichkeiten	acid test
Verhältnisse	circumstances
Verkauf	disposition
Verkauf auf Abbezahlung	sales on installments
Verkauf von hergestellter Ware	sale of manufactured goods
Verkaufskosten	selling expenses
Verkäufer	vendors (USA)
Verlust	loss
Verlustvortrag	loss carry-forward
Vermieter	lessor
Verordnungen	regulations
Verpackungsmaterial	packaging material
verrechnen	offset
Versicherungsgesellschaft	insurance company
Vertriebskosten	selling expenses
Verwaltungsbeirat	advisory board
Verwaltungskosten	administrative expenses
Verwaltungsrat	advisory board
Verwendung	appropriation
vierteljährlich	quarterly
Vizepräsident	vice-chairman
vorausbezahlte Aufwendungen	prepaid expense
voraussichtlicher Bergungswert	expected salvage value
Vorauszahlung an Lieferanten	advances to suppliers
Vorräte	inventories -(USA) (stocks-UK)
Vorschau	forecast
Vorschriften	rules
Vorsitzender	chairman
Vorsitzender des Aufsichtsrates	chairman of the supervisory board

GERMAN	ENGLISH
Vorstand	board of managing directors
Vorstand	executive board
Vorstandsmitglied	officer
Vorstandsvorsitzender	chief executive officer
vorzeitige Pensionierung	early retirement
vorzeitige Schuldentilgung	early extinguishment of debt
Vorzugsaktie	preferred share (USA)
vorübergehende Unterschiede	temporary differences
Wahrenlager	warehouse
wahrscheinlich	probable
Wandelschuld	convertible debt
Warenzeichen	trade marks
Wechselkurs	exchange rate
Wechselkursrisiko	exchange rate risk
wechselnde Verfahren	alternate procedures
Wechselverbindlichkeiten	notes payable
Werbekosten	promotional costs
Wertberichtigung	allowance
Wertberichtigung für Kreditverluste	allowance for loan losses
Wertberichtigung für nicht einholbare	allowance for uncollectible acct's
Forderungen	allowance for uncollectible acct's
Wertberichtigung für zweifelhafte	allowance for doubtful accounts
Forderungen	allowance for doubtful accounts
Wertpapierbörse	stock exchange
Wertpapiere	securities
Wertpapiere des Umlaufvermögens	short-term investments
Wertpapierprovisionen	securities commissions
wesentlich	material (significant)
Wesentlichkeit	materiality
Wichtigkeit	materiality
Wiederherstellungskosten	reproduction cost
willkürlich	at random
willkürlich	random
wirkliche Kreditverluste	actual loan losses
wirtschaftliches Umfeld	economic environment
Wirtschaftsprüfer	auditor
Währungsumrechnung	currency translation
Zahlungen	payments
Zahlungsrythmus	payments cycle
Zahlungsverkehr	monetary transactions
Zeichnung von Aktien	subscription
Zinsaufwand	interest expense
Zinsenforderungen	interest receivable
Zinsertrag	interest income
Zinssatz	interest rate

GERMAN	ENGLISH
Zinsschulden	interest payable
Zollabgabe	customs duty
zu Steuerzwecken	for taxation purposes
Zufälle	contingencies
Zugewinn aus Lebensversicherung	life policy benefits
zuordnen	allocate
zuteilen	allocate
zweckgebundene Rücklagen	appropriated retained earnings
Zwischenbericht	interim financial statements
zwischenbetriebliche Darlehen	inter-company loans

ENGLISH	GERMAN
accelerated depreciation	Sonderabschreibung
account balances	Saldo
accountant	Buchhalter
accountant	Buchführer
accounting	Buchführung
accounting	Buchhaltung
accounting changes	Änderungen in der Buchführungsmethode
accounting policies	Bilanzierungspolitik
accounting principles	Bilanzierungsgrundsätze
accounting principles	Bilanzierungsprinzipien
accounts payable	Kreditoren
accounts payable	Verbindlichkeiten
accounts receivable	Debitoren
accrual	Rückstellung
accrual (acc. method)	periodische Abgrenzung von Aufwand und
accrual (acc. method)	Ertrag
accrued expenses	passive Rechnungsabgrenzung
accrued expenses	antizipative Passiva
accrued income	antizipative Aktiva
accrued liabilities	Rückstellung
accrued liabilities	antizipative Passiva
accrued vacations	aufgelaufener Urlaubsanspruch
accumulated amortization	kumulierte Amortisation
accumulated depreciation	kumulierte Abschreibungen
acid test	Liquidität ersten Grades
acid test	Verhältnis der Barmittel und Forderungen
acid test	zu kurzfristigen Verbindlichkeiten
acquisition (of a company)	Erwerb einer Gesellschaft
acquisition cost	Anschaffungskosten
actual loan losses	wirkliche Kreditverluste
adjustment	Anpassung
adjustment	Berichtigung
adjustment for inflation	Inflationskorrektur
administrative expenses	Verwaltungskosten
advances to suppliers	Anzahlungen
advances to suppliers	Vorauszahlung an Lieferanten
adverse opinion	gegensätzliche Meinung
advisory board	Verwaltungsrat
advisory board	Verwaltungsbeirat
affiliate	verbunden
affiliated firms	verbundene Unternehmen
affiliates	verbundene Unternehmen
allocate	zuteilen
allocate	zuordnen
allowance	Rabatt

ENGLISH	GERMAN
allowance	Wertberichtigung
allowance for devaluation of inv'ts	Vergütung für Investmentabwertung
allowance for doubtful accounts	Wertberichtigung für zweifelhafte
allowance for doubtful accounts	Forderungen
allowance for loan losses	Wertberichtigung für Kreditverluste
allowance for uncollectible acct's	Wertberichtigung für nicht einholbare
allowance for uncollectible acct's	Forderungen
alternate procedures	wechselnde Verfahren
alternative procedures	alternative Verfahren
analytical review	analytischer Überblick
annual meeting	Jahresversammlung
annual report	Jahresbericht
annual report	Geschäftsbericht
annual shareholders' meeting	jährliche Hauptversammlung der Aktionäre
annually	jährlich
appropriated retained earnings	zweckgebundene Rücklagen
appropriation	Verwendung
appropriation of profit	Gewinnverwendung
April	April
assets	Aktiva
associated firm	assoziiertes Unternehmen
at random	willkürlich
audit	Prüfung
audit	Prüfung der Rechnungslegung
audit engagement	Prüfungsauftrag
audit fees	Prüfungsgebühren
audit manager	Prüfungsleiter
audit opinion	Prüfungsbewertung
audit risk	Prüfungsrisiko
audit sampling	Prüfungsprobe
audit staff	Prüfungspersonal
audit strategy	Prüfungsstrategie
auditing procedures	Prüfungsverfahren
auditing standards	Prüfungsgrundsätze
auditor	Prüfer
auditor	Wirtschaftsprüfer
auditor's report	Prüfungsbericht
auditor's responsibility	Verantwortlichkeit des Prüfers
August	August
average	Durchschnitt
balance sheet	Bilanz
balance sheet date	Bilanzstichtag
bank	Bank
bank overdrafts	Bankkontoüberziehung
bank reconciliation	Bankausgleichung

ENGLISH	GERMAN
bank service charges	Aufwendungen für Bankdienste
bankruptcy	Bankrott
bankruptcy	Konkurs
bearer	Inhaber
bid	Preisangebot
bid (verb)	bieten
billions	Milliarde
board of directors	Aufsichtsrat
board of managing directors	Vorstand
bond	Obligation
bond	Schuldverschreibung
book value	Buchwert
break even point	break even point
break even point	Ertragsschwelle
budget	Etat
budget	Budget
buildings and structures	Gebäude
business combinations	Fusionen
business segment	Geschäftsbereich
by-products	Nebenprodukte
capital and reserves	Eigenkapital
capital and reserves	eigene Mittel
capital gains tax	Kapitalgewinnsteuer
capital increase	Kapitalerhöhung
capital stock	Stammkapital
capital stock	Grundkapital
capital surplus	Rücklage aus Agio
capital tax	Kapitalsteuer
capitalization of financial costs	Aktivierung der Finanzierungskosten
capitalization of interests	Aktivierung der Zinsen
capitalization of leases	Aktivierung der Leasingverträge
carryforward	Saldovortrag
carryforward	steuerlicher Verlustvortrag
carryback	steuerlicher Verlustnachtrag
cash	Bargeld
cash	flüssige Mittel
cash and banks	Kasse und Bankguthaben
cash dividends	Bardividende
cash flow	cash flow
cash on hand	Kassenbestand
certificate of deposit	Depositenzertifikat
ceteris paribus	ceteris paribus
chairman	Vorsitzender
chairman of the supervisory board	Vorsitzender des Aufsichtsrates
charity expense	Aufwand für Wohltätigkeit

ENGLISH	GERMAN
chart of accounts	Kontenrahmen
chart of accounts	Kontenplan
chief executive officer	Vorstandsvorsitzender
circumstances	Verhältnisse
circumstances	Umstände
claims	Forderungen
claims	Ansprüche
claims on banks	Forderungen an Kreditinstitute
code (verb)	kodieren
collateral	Sicherheit
collections	Einzüge
collections	Inkassos
commercial & industrial loans	Geschäfts - und Industrie Kredite
commercial bank	Geschäftsbank
commissions & fees profits (losses)	Provisionen und Erträge für geleistete
commissions & fees profits (losses)	Dienste (Verluste)
commitments	Einzahlungsverpflichtungen
commitments	Bestellobligo
common stock	Stammaktien
communications expense	Kommunikationskosten
company by-laws	Gesellschaftsstatuten
comparative financial statements	Jahresabschluss mit Vergleichszahlen
comply with	übereinstimmen mit
condensed financial statements	Kurzbericht
consistency	Stetigkeit
consistently applied	stetig verwendet
consolidated accounts	consolidierter Jahresabschluss
consolidated balance sheet	Konzernbilanz
consolidated financial statements	Konzernabschluss
consolidated profit	Konzerngewinn
construction in progress	Anlagen im Bau
consulting services	beratende Dienstleistungen
contents	Inhalt
contingencies	Zufälle
convertible debt	konvertierbare Schuld
convertible debt	Wandelschuld
copyright	Copyright
copyright	Urheberrecht
cost of goods sold	Herstellkosten der verkauften Ware
cost of material	Materialaufwand
cost of sales	Umsatzkosten
cost of services rendered	Dienstleistungskosten
cost or market	Niederstwertprinzip
country risk	Länderrisiko
credit line	Rahmenkredit

ENGLISH	GERMAN
cumulative adjustment	kumulative Korrektur
cumulative effect	kumulativer Effekt
currency translation	Währungsumrechnung
current assets	Aktiva
current assets	Umlaufvermögen
current liabilities	kurzfristige Verbindlichkeiten
current ratio	Liquiditätskennzahl
customers	Kunden
customs duty	Zollabgabe
data processing equipment	Datenverarbeitungsanlage
debenture	Schuldschein
debenture	Schuldverschreibung
debenture	Anleihe
debenture	Obligation
debt discount	Disagio
debt premium	Agio
debt restructuring	Umschuldung
December	Dezember
deferred charges	aktive Rechnungsabgrenzung
deferred expense	vereinnahmte Aufwendungen
deferred income	noch nicht verdientes Einkommen
deferred income	transitorisches Passivum
deferred income tax	aufgeschobene Einkommensteuer -
deferred income tax	verbindlichkeit
deferred taxes	latente Steuerschulden
demand deposits	täglich fällige Gelder
depreciation - buildings	Abschreibung (Gebäude)
depreciation expense	Abschreibungsaufwand
detect	entdecken
direct cost	Einzelkosten
directors	Aufsichtsratsmitglieder
disbursements	Bezahlung mit Bargeld
disbursements	Auszahlung
disclosure	Hinweis in der Bilanz
disclosure	Enthüllung
discontinued operations	abgebrochener Betrieb
discount rate	Rechnungszinsfuss
discount rate	Abzinsungssatz
discount rate	Diskontsatz
disposition	Abgang
disposition	Verkauf
dividend	Dividende
dividend income	Dividendenertrag
dividend per share	Dividende pro Aktie
dividends payable	Verbindlichkeiten aus erklärten

ENGLISH	GERMAN
dividends payable	Dividenden
dollars	Dollars
domestic subsidiaries	inländische Tochtergesellschaften
double taxation	Doppelbesteuerung
due date	Fälligkeitstermin
due date	Verfalltag
early extinguishment of debt	vorzeitige Schuldentilgung
early retirement	vorzeitige Pensionierung
earnings per share	Gewinn pro Aktie
economic environment	wirtschaftliches Umfeld
effect	Auswirkung
effect	Effekt
effects of changing prices	Effekt von Preisänderungen
employee	Arbeitnehmer
employee	Angestellter
employee benefits	Sozialleistungen
entertainment expense	Bewirtungskosten
equity in other companies	Teilnahme an anderen Unternehmen
equity method	Equity-Methode
errors	Fehler
examine	prüfen
examine	untersuchen
except for	ausser
exchange rate	Wechselkurs
exchange rate risk	Wechselkursrisiko
excise tax	Verbrauchssteuer
executive board	Vorstand
executive vice president	Generalbevollmächtigter
expected salvage value	voraussichtlicher Bergungswert
expenses	Aufwendungen
export	Export
export	Ausfuhr
export duties	Ausfuhrzölle
extent	Mass
extent	Grad
extraordinary items	ausserordentliche Posten
face value	Nennwert
face value	Nominalbetrag
feasibility	Durchführbarkeit
feasibility study	Planungstudie
February	Februar
fees	Gebühren
fees	Honorare
fees for services by third party	Gebühren für Leistungen an Dritte
finance	Finanzen

ENGLISH	GERMAN
finance (verb)	Finanzieren
financial entities	Finanzierungsinstitute
financial statements	Jahresabschluss
financial summary	Jahresübersicht
fine	Busse
fine	Geldstrafe
finished goods	fertige Erzeugnisse
first in, first out (FIFO)	first in, first out (FIFO)
fittings	Ausstattungen
fixed assets	Anlagevermögen
floating rate	schwebender Kurs
flowchart	Organisationsplan
flowchart	Arbeitsablaufplan
footnotes to financial statements	Erläuterungen zum Jahresabschluss
for taxation purposes	zu Steuerzwecken
forecast	Vorschau
foreign currency	fremde Währung
foreign currency translation	Fremdwährungsumrechnung
foreign exchange	Devisen
foreign exchange gains (losses)	Devisengewinne (Verluste)
foreign subsidiary	ausländische Tochtergesellschaft
form	Dokument
form	Formular
funds	Fonds
furniture and fixtures	Betriebs- und Geschäftsausstattung
future contracts	Termingeschäfte
gain	Gewinn
gain on revaluation of securities	Erträge aus Aufwertung von Wertpapieren
gain on sale of fixed assets	Erträge aus dem Abgang von Sachanlagen
general and administrative expense	allgemeine und Verwaltungskosten
general insurance	Allgemeine Versicherung
general ledger	Hauptbuch
general manager	Geschäftsführer
general manager	Generaldirektor
general manager	Geschäftsleiter
generally accepted	ordnungsgemäss
goods in process	unfertige Erzeugnisse
goods in transit	Unterwegsware
goodwill	Geschäftswert
goodwill	Firmenwert
gross margin	Bruttomarge
gross national product	Bruttosozialprodukt
gross profit ratio	Bruttogewinnmesszahl
gross revenue tax	Bruttoumsatzsteuer
group	Konzern

ENGLISH	GERMAN
group (of companies)	Gruppe
guarantee deposits	Garantiekaution
guarantee deposits	Bürgschaften
guarantees	Garantien
hedge	Termingeschaft
historical cost	Anschaffungskosten
historical cost	ursprüngliche Kosten
holding company	Beteiligungsgesellschaft
holding company	Holdinggesellschaft
hundreds	Hunderte
idle capacity	betrieblich nicht genutzte Kapazität
impact	Einfluss
impact (verb)	beeinflussen
in accordance with	in Übereinstimmung mit
in accordance with	entsprechend
income	Erträge
income for services rendered	Einkommen für geleistete Dienste
income tax	Ertragssteuer
income tax	Einkommensteuer
indebtedness ratio	Schuldmesszahl
indemnities	Abfindungen
independence	Selbständigkeit
industry	Industrie
inflation	Inflation
inheritance tax	Erbschaftssteuer
insurance company	Versicherungsgesellschaft
intangible assets	immaterielle Vermögensgegenstände
intangible assets	immaterielle Anlagen
inter-company loans	zwischenbetriebliche Darlehen
interest expense	Zinsaufwand
interest income	Zinsertrag
interest payable	Zinsschulden
interest rate	Zinssatz
interest receivable	Zinsenforderungen
interim financial statements	Zwischenbericht
internal auditors	Innenrevisoren
internal control questionnaire	innerbetrieblicher Kontrollfragebogen
internal controls	innerbetriebliche Kontrolle
international subsidiaries	internationale Tochtergesellschaft
international trade	internationaler Handel
inventories -(USA) (stocks-UK)	Vorräte
inventory	Inventar
investment	Investition
investment	Kapitalanlage
investment bank/merchant bank	Investmentbank

ENGLISH	GERMAN
investment in subsidiaries	Beteiligungen an Tochtergesellschaften
investment tax credit	Investitionszuschuss
investments	Beteiligungen
invoice	Rechnung
irregularity	Unregelmässigkeit
January	Januar
joint venture	Joint Venture
journal	Grundbuch
journal	Journal
journal entry	Journalbuchung
July	Juli
June	Juni
labor hours	Arbeitsstunden
labor law	Arbeitsrecht
land	Grundstücke
land improvements	Grundstückverbesserungen
last in, first out (LIFO)	last in, first out (LIFO)
lawyer	Rechtsanwalt
lease	Miete
lease	Pacht
legal requirements	gesetzliche Vorschriften
legal reserve	gesetzliche Rücklage
lessee	Mieter
lessor	Vermieter
liabilities	Passiva
liabilities + shareholder's equity	Passiva
liability	Verbindlichkeit
licences	Lizenzen
life insurance	Lebensversicherung
life policy benefits	Zugewinn aus Lebensversicherung
liquid assets	flüssige Mittel
liquid assets	liquide Aktiva
liquidity	Liquidität
liquidity ratio	Liquiditätskennzahl
liquidity risk	Liquiditätsrisiko
listed bonds-local currency	an der Börse notierte Schuld -
listed bonds-local currency	verschreibungen
litigation	Rechtsstreit
litigation	Prozess
loans	Schulden
loans	Darlehen
local currency	Landeswährung
long-term contracts	langfristige Verträge
long-term credits	langfristige Kredite
long-term debt	langfristige Verbindlichkeit

ENGLISH	GERMAN
long-term investments	langfristige Beteiligungen
loss	Verlust
loss carry-forward	Verlustvortrag
lower of cost or market	Niederstwertprinzip
machinery and equipment	maschinelle Anlagen und Ausrüstung
major customers	Hauptkunden
March	März
marginal cost	Grenzkosten
market price	Marktpreis
marketable securities	börsengängige Wertpapiere
marketable stocks	börsengängige Aktien
material (significant)	wesentlich
materiality	Wesentlichkeit
materiality	Wichtigkeit
materials (sust.)	Materialien
matured loans	fällige Obligationen
maturity	Fälligkeit
May	Mai
merger	Fusion
millions	Millionen
minority interest	Anteil der Minderheitsaktionäre
minority interests	Anteile in Fremdbesitz
misleading information	fehlleitende Information
monetary assets	monetare Aktiva
monetary transactions	Zahlungsverkehr
monthly	monatlich
mortgage	Hypothek
mortgage bank	Hypothekenbank
multinational enterprise	multinationales Unternehmen
mutual fund	Kapitalanlagegesellschaft auf
mutual fund	Gegenseitigkeit
nature	Art
nature	Natur
negative goodwill	Konsolidierungsausgleichposten (Passiva)
net income	Jahresüberschuss
net income	Überschuss
net present value	Nettogegenwartswert
net realizable value	Nettoerlöswert
net sales	Nettoumsatz
net worth	Eigenkapital
net worth	Reinvermögen
non-current assets	langfristige Aktiva
non-current liabilities	langfristige Verbindlichkeiten
non-monetary transactions	bargeldlose Transaktionen
non-operating income and expense	betriebsfremder Ertrag und Aufwand

ENGLISH	GERMAN
non-profit	ohne Gewinnabsicht
non-profit	gemeinnützig
non-taxable income	nicht besteuerbares Einkommen
notes payable	Wechselverbindlichkeiten
November	November
obsolescence	Veralterung
October	Oktober
office supplies	Bürobedarf
officer	Mitglied der Geschäftsleitung
officer	Vorstandsmitglied
offset	verrechnen
operating controls	Betriebskontrollen
operating cycle	Betriebskreislauf
operating leases	Betriebsmieten
operating profit	Betriebsgewinn
opinion	Meinung
options	Option
organization chart	Organisationsplan
organization expenses	Organisationskosten
other assets	sonstige Vermögensgegenstände
other income for services	andere Gewinne aus Dienstleistungen
other liabilities	sonstige Passivposten
other loans	sonstige Darlehen
other operating profits (losses)	sonstige betriebliche Gewinne
outstanding shares	ausstehende Aktien
over the counter transaction	Freiverkehr
over the counter transaction	ausserbörslicher Handel
overdraft	Überziehung
overdue	überfällig
overhead expenses	Gemeinkosten
packaging material	Verpackungsmaterial
paid-in capital	eingezahltes Kapital
par value	Nennwert
parent company	Muttergesellschaft
partner	Gesellschafter
partner	Kompagnon
patents	Patente
payable on demand	täglich fällig
payments	Zahlungen
payments cycle	Zahlungsrythmus
payroll	Gehaltsabrechnung
payroll	Lohnabrechnung
payroll	Lohnliste
pension	Rente
pension	Pension
pension plan	Pensionsplan
percentage	Prozentsatz
personal income tax	Einkommensteuer
petty cash	kleine Kasse
physical inventory	körperliche Inventur
placement	Plazierung
pledge	Pfand
policyholders' equity	Gewinnbeteilung der Versicherungsnehmer
pooling of interest	Interessengemeinschaft
population	Population
preferred share (USA)	Vorzugsaktie
premium	Agio
premium	Aufgeld
prepaid expense	Rechnungsabgrenzungsposten
prepaid expense	vorausbezahlte Aufwendungen
prior period adjustments	Erträge aus der Auflösung von Wert -
prior period adjustments	berichtigungen und Rückstellungen
private sector	Privatbereich
probable	wahrscheinlich
product financing	Produktfinanzierung
product warranties	Produktgarantie
production capacity	Produktionskapazität
production cost	Produktionskosten
production cost	Herstellungskosten
production cost	Fertigungskosten
production cycle	Produktionszyklus
production order	Produktionsauftrag
professional judgment	professionelle Bewertung
professional standards	Berufsgrundsätze
profit	Gewinn
profit & loss accounts	Gewinn- und Verlustrechnung
profit & loss accounts	Erfolgsrechnung
profit margin	Gewinnspanne
profit sharing	Gewinnbeteiligung
promotional costs	Werbekosten
proxy (power of attorney)	Handlungsvollmacht
public sector	Öffentlichkeitsbereich
purchase requisition	Bedarfsmeldung
qualification (of an audit opinion)	eingeschränkter Bestätigungsvermerk des
qualification (of an audit opinion)	Prüfers
quality control	Qualitätskontrolle
quarter	Quartal
quarterly	vierteljährlich
quarterly financial statements	Quartalbericht
random	willkürlich

ENGLISH	GERMAN
raw materials	Rohstoffe
receivables	Forderungen
recession	Rezession
record (verb)	eintragen
recruiting expense	Rekrutierungsaufwand
redeemable	einlösbar
redemption features	Tilgungselemente
refinancing	Refinanzierung
refund	Rückvergütung
regressive tax	regressive Steuer
regulations	Verordnungen
repairs and maintenance	Instandhaltung
replacement cost	Ersatzkosten
report	Bericht
reproduction cost	Wiederherstellungskosten
research and development costs	Forschungs- und Entwicklungskosten
reserve for general risks	Pauschalwert Berichtigung
reserve for loan losses	Rückstellung im Kreditgeschäft
retained earnings	Reserven
retained earnings	nicht ausgeschütteter Gewinn
retained earnings	Gewinnvortrag
retained earnings	Rücklagen
retained earnings	unverteilter Reingewinn
revaluation	Aufwertung
revenue	Erträge
rules	Regeln
rules	Vorschriften
salaries and wages	Gehälter und Löhne
sale of manufactured goods	Verkauf von hergestellter Ware
sales (turnover)	Umsatzerlöse
sales (turnover)	Umsatz
sales on installments	Verkauf auf Abbezahlung
sales tax	Umsatzsteuer
saving deposits	Spareinlagen
scope	Reichweite
secondary market	Sekundarmarkt
securities	Wertpapiere
Securities and Exchange Commission	Börsenaufsichtsbehörde (USA)
securities commissions	Wertpapierprovisionen
self-insurance	Selbstversicherung
selling expenses	Vertriebskosten
selling expenses	Verkaufskosten
semi-finished goods	halbfertige Erzeugnisse
September	September
shareholder	Aktionär

ENGLISH	GERMAN
shareholders' equity	Reinvermögen der Gesellschafter
shareholders' equity	Eigenkapital
shares	Aktien
short-term bank loans	kurzfristiger Bankkredit
short-term investments	Wertpapiere des Umlaufvermögens
short-term loans	kurzfristige Verbindlichkeiten
small companies	kleine Firmen
social security expense	soziale Aufwendungen
sources of funds	Mittelherkunft
special bonus	Sonderzuwendung
spread (between rates)	Marge
stamp duty	Stempelsteuer
standard cost	Standardkosten
start-up costs	Ingangsetzungskosten
start-up costs	Anlaufkosten
statement sources & uses of funds	Mittelherkunfts -und Verwendungsrechnung
statutory audit report	Pflichtprüfung
statutory reserve	satzungsgemässe Rücklage
stock dividends	Dividenden in Form von Aktien
stock dividends	Stockdividenden
stock exchange	Aktienbörse
stock exchange	Wertpapierbörse
stockbroker	Makler
stockholders	Aktionäre
stockholders' equity	Reinvermögen der Gesellschafter
stockholders' equity	Eigenkapital
straight-line method	lineare Abschreibungsmethode
subject to	unterwerfen
sublet	untervermieten
subordinated debt	im Range nachstehende Schuld
subscription	Zeichnung von Aktien
subsidiary	Tochtergesellschaft
sum of the years'-digits method	digitale Abschreibungsmethode
supervisory board	Aufsichtsrat
suppliers	Lieferanten
supplies	Betriebs- und Hilfsstoffe
supplies and spare parts	Betriebsstoffe und Ersatzteile
syndicated loans	Konsortialkredit
taken as a whole	als Ganzes genommen
tangible fixed assets	Sachanlagen
tangible fixed assets	Sachanlagevermögen
tax	Steuer
tax authorities	Finanzverwaltung
tax credit	Steuergutschrift
tax credits	Steuervergünstigung

ENGLISH	GERMAN
tax rates	Steuersätze
tax return	Steuererklärung
tax savings	Steuerersparnis
taxable income	steuerpflichtiges Einkommen
taxpayer	Steuerpflichtiger
temporary differences	vorübergehende Unterschiede
test	Test
thousand	Tausend
thousands	Tausende
time deposits	Festgeld
time deposits	Termineinlagen
timing	Timing
total assets	Bilanzsumme
total assets	Summe der Aktiven
total liabilities + shareh. equity	Summe der Passiven
total liabilities + shareh. equity	Bilanzsumme
total lending	Kreditvolumen
trade marks	Markenzeichen
trade marks	gewerbliche Schutzrechte
trade marks	Warenzeichen
trade receivables	Forderungen aus Lieferungen und
trade receivables	Leistungen
transactions	Transaktionen
treasury bills	Schatzwechsel
treasury stock	eigene Aktien
trend	Trend
trial balance	Rohbilanz
turnover ratio	Umschlagsratio
unappropriated retained earnings	freie Rücklagen
unappropriated retained earnings	Bilanzgewinn
unaudited	ungeprüft
uncollectible	uneinbringlich
units of production	Produktionseinheiten
unqualified	uneingeschränkt
unsecured bonds	ungesicherte Schuldverschreibungen
useful life (of an asset)	Nutzungsdauer
useful life (of an asset)	Lebensdauer
valuation principles	Bewertungsgrundsätze
value added tax (VAT)	Mehrwertsteuer
variable cost	proportionale Kosten
vehicles	Fuhrpark
vendors (USA)	Verkäufer
vice-chairman	Vizepräsident
voucher	Beleg
warehouse	Lager

ENGLISH	GERMAN
warehouse	Wahrenlager
withheld taxes	Abzugsteuern
working capital	kurzfristiges Betriebskapital
working capital ratio	Betriebskapitalsratio
write down	abschreiben
write down	Sonderabschreibung
year-end closing date	Jahresabschlussdatum
yield	Ausbeute
yield	Rendite
zero coupon bonds	Null-Coupon Bonds

ACCOUNTING LEXICON : ITALIAN - ENGLISH

ITALIAN	ENGLISH
a caso	at random
accantonamenti a lungo termine per risarcimenti	long-term insurance reserve charges
accantonamento	long-term insurance reserve charges
accantonamento	provision
accantonamento per vacanze	allowance
accantonare	accrued vacations
accordo di finanziamento	allocate
accordo di riacquisito	financing arrangement
accordo di rivendita	repurchase agreement
accumularsi	resale agreement
acquisizione (di una impresa)	accrue
agente di cambio	acquisition (of a company)
aggio	stockbroker
aggiustamento cumulativo	premium
agosto	cumulative adjustment
alternato	August
altri prestiti	proxy (noun)
altri proventi (perditi) di gestione	other loans
altri proventi per servizi	other operating profits (losses)
ammenda	other income for services
amministratori	fine
ammortamenti di costruzioni	directors
ammortamento accelerato	depreciation of buildings
ammortamento dei debiti a lungo termine	accelerated depreciation
ammortamento economico	retirement of long term debt
ammortamento maturato	depreciation expense
ampiezza del campione	accumulated depreciation
annualmente	sample size
anticipi a fornitori	annually
applicato uniformemente	advances to suppliers
applicazioni dei fondi	consistently applied
aprile	uses of funds
archivio permanente	April
area d'affari	permanent file
assegnare	business segment
assemblea annuale	allocate
assemblea annuale degli azionisti	annual meeting
assicurazione generale	annual shareholders' meeting
assicurazione sulla vita	general insurance
attività a lungo termine	life insurance
attività correnti	non-current assets
attività fisse nette	current assets
attività immateriali	net fixed assets
attività liquide	intangible assets
attività monetaria	liquid assets
attivo	monetary assets
	assets

ITALIAN	ENGLISH
attivo fisso	fixed assets
attivo realizzabile	current assets
attrezzature	fittings
attribuzione	accrual
auditore	auditor
aumento di capitale	capital increase
autoassicurare	self-insure
autoassicurazione	self-insurance
autorità fiscali	tax authorities
autorizzazione di pagamento	voucher
avviamento	goodwill
avviamento negativo	negative goodwill
avvocato	lawyer
azienda affiliata	affiliate
azienda collegata	affiliate
azienda consociata	associated firm
azienda in attività	going concern
aziende corrispondente	correspondent firms
azione preferenziale	preference share
azione privilegiata	preference share (UK)
azione privilegiata	preferred share (USA)
azioni	shares
azioni di tesoreria	treasury stock
azioni in circolazione	outstanding shares
azioni ordinari	common stock
azioni privilegiati non riscattabili	non-redeemable preferred stock
azioni privilegiati riscattabili	redeemable preferred stock
azionisti	stockholders
banca	bank
banca commerciale	commercial bank
banca d'investimento	investment bank/merchant bank
banca di credito ordinario	commercial bank
benefici prestati per l'assicurazione sulla vita	life policy benefits
beni immobili	life policy benefits
bilancio	fixed assets
bilancio	financial statements
bilancio comparato	balance sheet
bilancio consolidato	comparative financial statements
bilancio de previsione	consolidated financial statements
bilancio di verifica per saldi	budget
bilancio riclassificato	trial balance
bilancio riclassificato	financial summary
bilancio sintetico	condensed financial statements
bilione	condensed financial statements
borsa valori	billions
brevetti	stock exchange
	patents

ITALIAN	ENGLISH
buono	voucher
cambiali attivi	notes receivable
cambio dei metodi contabili	accounting changes
cambio flessibile	floating rate
campionatura	sampling
campionatura di revisione	audit sampling
campionatura non statistica	non-statistical sampling
campionatura statistica	statistical sampling
capacità di produzione	production capacity
capacità inutilizatta	idle capacity
capitale circolante netto	working capital
capitale conferito	paid-in capital
capitale di risparmio	retained earnings
capitale netto	net worth
capitale primario	primary capital
capitale sociale	capital stock
capitalizzazione dei costi finanziari	capitalization of financial costs
capitalizzazione dei interessi	capitalization of interest
capitalizzazione dei locazioni	capitalization of leases
cash flow	cash flow
cassa	cash
cassa e depositi bancari	cash and banks
castelletto	credit line
casuale	random
centi	hundreds
certificato di deposito	certificate of deposit
ceteris paribus	ceteris paribus
ciclo dei pagamenti	payments cycle
ciclo di produzione	production cycle
ciclo operativo	operating cycle
cifrare	code (verb)
circostanze	circumstances
clienti	customers
clienti principali	major customers
collegio sindacale	internal auditors
collocamenti alla giornata	overnight funds
collocamenti interaziendali	inter-company loans
collocamento	placement
combinazioni d'affari	business combinations
commercio internazionale	international trade
commissione per le società e la borsa	Securities and Exchange Commission
commissioni e onorari-profitti(perditi)	commissions & fees-profits(losses)
compensazione	offset (noun)
compenso del revisore contabile	audit fees
compilazione dei bilanci	compilation of financial statements
composizione delle portafoglio	portfolio composition
concordanza	consistency

ITALIAN	ENGLISH
condizioni di riscatto	redemption features
conferma dei conti	confirmation of accounts
conformemente a	in accordance with
consiglieri	directors
consiglio di amministrazione	board of directors
contabile	accountant
contabilità	accounting
contabilità per competenze	accrual method of accounting
contenuto	contents
conti attivi netti di credito mercantile	net trade accounts receivable
	net trade accounts receivable
conti correnti	demand deposits
conti impegni	customers'liability for acceptances
conto economico	profit & loss account
conto profitti e perditi	profit & loss account
conto profitti e perditi	income statement
contrati a termine	future contracts
contratti a lungo termine	long-term contracts
contratto a premio	option
contribuente	taxpayer
contributo di previdenza sociale	social security expense
controlli di gestione	operating controls
controlli operativi	operational controls
controllo del bilancio	audit
controllo della qualità	quality control
controllo interno	internal control
conversione dei valuta estera	foreign currency translation
conversione della moneta	currency translation
conversione valutaria	currency translation
copertura verso flutazioni	hedge
correzione	adjustment
correzione per inflazione	adjustment for inflation
corso del cambio	exchange rate
costi	expenses
costi di riparazione e manutenzione	repair and maintenance expense
costi di trasporto sulle acquisti	freight on purchases of materials
costi pluriennali	deferred charges
costo dei prodotti venduti	cost of goods sold
costo dei servizi prestati	cost of services rendered
costo del venduto	cost of sales
costo delle merci vendute	cost of goods sold
costo di acquisizione	acquisition cost
costo di avviamento	start-up costs
costo di opportunità	opportunity cost
costo di produzione	production cost
costo di reproduzione	reproduction cost
costo di rimpiazzo	replacement cost

ITALIAN	ENGLISH
costo diretto	direct cost
costo marginale	marginal cost
costo o prezzo di mercato	lower of cost or market method
costo o valore di mercato	lower of cost or market method
costo o valore di realizzo	lower of cost or market method
costo standard	standard cost
costo storico	historical cost
costo variabile	variable cost
costruzioni in corso	construction in progress
crediti	accounts receivable
crediti	receivables
crediti a lungo termine	long-term credits
crediti commerciali	trade receivables
credito d'imposta	tax credit
credito d'imposta per investimento	investment tax credit
credito scoperto	bank overdraft
criteri di valutazione	valuation principles
cumulo di interessi	pooling of interest
dall'effetto fiscale	for taxation purposes
dare in garanzia	pledge (verb)
data del bilancio	year-end closing date
data di chiusura del bilancio	balance sheet date
dazi di esportazione	export duties
dazi doganali	customs duties
debiti	accounts payable
debiti a breve termine	short-term loans
debiti a lungo termine	long-term debt
debiti commerciali	trade payables
debiti di primo grado	senior debt
debiti irrecuperabili	troubled debt
debiti verso fornitori	trade payables
debito subordinato	subordinated debt
debitori	receivables
deboli di controlle	control weakness
delega	proxy (noun)
denaro liquido	cash
depositi a risparmio	savings deposits
depositi in garanzia	guarantee deposits
depositi interbancari	interbank deposits
deposito a termine	time deposit
destagionalizato	seasonally adjusted
deviazione di una dichiarazione	departure from a pronouncement
diagramma di flusso	flowchart
dicembre	December
dichiarazione d'imposta	tax return
dichiarazione dei principi contabili	statement of accounting policy
adottati	statement of accounting policy

ITALIAN	ENGLISH
differenzi temporanei	temporary differences
dipendente	employee
direttore della revisione	audit manager
direttore generale	general manager
direttore generale	chief executive officer
diritto di autore	copyright
disponibilità	current assets
disponibilità	cash equivalents
dividendi da pagare	dividends payable
dividendi in azioni	stock dividends
dividendi in contanti	cash dividends
dividendi ricevuti	dividend income
dividendo	dividend
dividendo per azione	dividend per share
divise	foreign exchange
documenti contabili	accounting records
documenti giustificativi	supporting documentation
documenti riscontati	rediscounted notes
dollari	dollars
doppia imposizzione	double taxation
eccedenza di rivalutazione	revaluation surplus
effetti attivi	notes receivable
effetti da esigere	notes receivable
effetti della variazione dei prezzi	effects of changing prices
effetti passivi	notes payable
effetto	impact
effetto	effect
effetto cumulativo	cumulative effect
effetto garantito	secured note
equipaggio di revisione	audit staff
errori	errors
esaminare	examine
esito (di una attività)	disposal (of an asset)
esportazione	export
esposizione al rischio	risk exposure
eventi successivi alla data del bilancio	subsequent events
evidenza	evidential matter
fabbricati	buildings and structures
fallimento	bankruptcy
fatto eccezione di	except for
fattura	invoice
fatturato	sales (turnover)
fatturato netto	net sales
febbraio	February
ferie pagate	vacation with pay
filiale	subsidiary
filiale estera	foreign subsidiary

ITALIAN	ENGLISH
filiali internazionali	international subsidiaries
finanza	finance (noun)
finanziamento dell'acquisto di un prodotto	product financing
	product financing
finanziamento subordinato	subordinated financing
finanziare	finance (verb)
flusso dei fonti e degli impieghi dei fondi	statement sources & uses of funds
	statement sources & uses of funds
flusso di cassa	cash flow
flussogramma	flowchart
foco della revisione	audit approach
fogli di lavoro	working papers
fondi	funds
fondi interbancari	interbank assets/funds
fondi non patrimoniali	non-equity reserves
fondo	allowance
fondo	provision
fondo comune d'investimento	mutual fund
fondo di ammortamento	accumulated depreciation
fondo di rappresentanza	entertainment expense
fondo di riserva legale	statutory reserve
fondo per crediti irrecuperabili	allowance for uncollectible acc'ts
fondo per oscillazione del cambio	reserve exchange rate fluctuations
fondo per risarcimenti e perditi	reserve for o/s claims and losses
fondo per rischi diversi	reserve for general risks
fondo per rischi su crediti	allowance for loan losses
fondo per rischi su crediti	allowance for doubtful accounts
fondo rischi su crediti	reserve for loan losses/bad debts
fondo rivalutazione	revaluation reserve
fondo svalutazione investimenti	allowance for devaluation of inv't
fonti di finanziamento	sources of funds
fornitori	vendors (USA)
fornitori	suppliers
funzionario (di una società)	officer (of a company)
fusione	merger
garanzia	guarantee
garanzia collaterale	collateral
garanzia reale	collateral
garanzie sulle prodotti	product warranties
gennaio	January
giudizio professionale	professional judgment
giugno	June
(grado di) rilevanza	materiality
gruppo (d'imprese)	group (of companies)
immobilizzazioni	fixed assets
immobilizzazioni immateriali	intangible assets
immobilizzazioni in corso	construction in progress

ITALIAN	ENGLISH
immobilizzazioni materiali	tangible fixed assets
impegnare	pledge (verb)
impegni	commitments
impiegato	employee
imposta	tax
imposta progressiva	graduated tax
imposta progressiva	progressive tax
imposta regressiva	regressive tax
imposta sui consumi	excise tax
imposta sul capitale	capital tax
imposta sul fatturato lordo	gross revenue tax
imposta sul reddito	income tax
imposta sul reddito personale	personal income tax
imposta sul valore aggiunto (IVA)	value added tax (VAT)
imposta sulle plus-valenze derivanti da cessioni	capital gains tax
	capital gains tax
imposta sulle società	corporation tax
imposta sulle successioni	inheritance tax
imposta sulle vendite	sales tax
imposte differite	deferred taxes
imposte sul reddito differite	deferred income taxes
imposti maturati	accrued taxes
impresa in collaborazione	joint venture
imprese collegate	affiliated firms
imprese in via de sviluppo	development stage companies
incassi	collections
incertezza	uncertainty
indennità	indemnities
indennità di buonuscita	post retirement benefits
indennità di licenziamento	severance indemnities
indice di dilazione dei pagamenti	collection ratio
indice di indebitamento	indebtedness ratio
indice di proffito lordo	gross profit ratio
indice di rotazione	turnover ratio
indice di rotazione dei crediti	credit turnover ratio
indice di rotazione del capitale circolante	working capital turnover
	working capital turnover
indice di rotazione delle scorte	inventory turnover ratio
indipendenza	independence
industria	industry
inesigibile	uncollectible
inflazione	inflation
informazione fuorviante	misleading information
informazione supplementare	supplementary information
intenzione della direzione	management intention
interessi attivi	interest income
interessi esigibili	interest receivable

ACCOUNTING LEXICON : ITALIAN - ENGLISH

ITALIAN	ENGLISH
interessi pagabili	interest payable
interessi passivi	unearned interests
interessi passivi	interest expense
inventario fisico	physical inventory
investimenti a breve termine	short-term investments
investimenti a lungo termine	long-term investments
investimenti in filiali	investment in subsidiaries
investimento	investment
ipoteca	mortgage
irrecuperabile	uncollectible
irregolarità	irregularity
istituto di credito ipotecario	mortgage bank
lavoro di revisione	audit engagement
leasing immobiliare	leaseback
legge di lavoro	labor law
lettera di rappresentazione	client representation letter
libri sussidiari	subsidiary records
libro giornale	journal
licenziamento	severance
licitazione	bid (noun)
limite	extent
linea di credito	credit line
liquidità	liquidity
lite	litigation
locatario	lessee
locatore	lessor
locazione	leasing
locazione	lease
locazione operativa	operating lease
luglio	July
macchine ed attrezzature fisse	machinery and equipment
magazzino	warehouse
maggio	May
marca di fabbrica	trade mark
margine	spread (between rates)
margine di profitto	profit margin
margine di rischio della campionatura	allowance for sampling risk
margine lordo	gross margin
marzo	March
mastro generale	general ledger
materiale	material (noun)
materie prime	raw materials
maturare	accrue
media	average (mean)
media ponderata	weighted average
mensilmente	monthly
mercato secondario	secondary market

ITALIAN	ENGLISH
merci in lavorazione	goods in process
merci in transito	goods in transit
merci per rivendita	resale merchandise
metodo del patrimonio neto	equity method
metodo del risconto	deferral method
metodo della somma degli anni di prevista durata	sum of the years' digits method sum of the years' digits method
metodo di "con e senza"	with and without method
metodo di contratto compiuto	completed-contract method
metodo di passività	liability method
metodo di percentuale di compimento	percentage-of-completion-method
metodo di quote constanti	straight-line method
mezzi propri	shareholders' equity
migliaio(a)	thousands
miglioramenti fondiari	land improvements
milioni	millions
mille	thousand
mobili e arredi	furniture and fixtures
modulo	form
multa	fine
mutui	loans
mutui commerciali e industriali	commercial & industrial loans
mutui di locazione	lease financing loans
mutui ipotecari	real estate and mortgage loans
natura	nature
nell'insieme	taken as a whole
nomi	payroll
normi	rules
normi di contabilità	accounting principles
normi professionali	professional standards
note al bilancio	footnotes to financial statements
novembre	November
obbligazione	debenture
obbligazione	bond
obbligazione perpetua	perpetual bond
obbligazioni convertibili	convertible bonds
obbligazioni per pagare	bonds payable
obbligazioni senza garantia	unsecured bonds
obsolescenza	obsolescence
offrire	bid (verb)
oneri finanziari	interest expense
onorari	fees
onorari per servizi di terzi	fees for services by third party
operazione di copertura	hedging
operazione fuori di borsa	over the counter transaction
operazioni cessati	discontinued operations
operazioni commerciali	transactions

ITALIAN	ENGLISH
operazioni monetari	monetary transactions
operazioni non monetari	non-monetary transactions
opinione	opinion
opportunità	timing
opzione	option
ordine di produzione	production order
ore-uomo	labor hours (man-hours)
organigramma	organization chart
ottobre	October
pagamenti	payments
pagamento anticipato dei debiti	early extinguishment of debt
paragrafo di opinione	opinion paragraph
paragrafo di portata	scope paragraph
parere	opinion
parere con eccezioni	adverse opinion
parte della perdita degli società affiliate	share in loss of affiliates
partecipazione di minoranza	minority interests
partecipazioni in altre società	equity in other companies
partecipazioni in società controllate	investment in subsidiaries
participazione agli utili	profit sharing
particolari criteri contabili	accounting policies
partite straordinari	extraordinary items
passività	liability
passività a breve termine	current liabilities
passività a lungo termine	non-current liabilities
passività correnti	current liabilities
patrimonio corrispondente agli assicurati	policyholders' equity
	policyholders' equity
patrimonio netto	stockholders' equity
patrimonio netto	shareholders' equity
patrimonio netto	net worth
pensione	pension
per mese	monthly
percentuale	percentage
perdita	loss
perdita accumulata	loss carry-forward
perdita netta dell'esercizio	net loss of the period
perditi su crediti	actual loan losses
periodo intercorrente	intervening period
persona a carico	dependent
pezzi di ricambio	supplies and spare parts
piani di diritto di opzione sul azioni	stock option plans
piano contabile	chart of accounts
piano de pensionamiento	pension plan
piano previdenziale	employee benefit plan
piccola cassa	petty cash

ITALIAN	ENGLISH
piccole imprese	small companies
plusvalenza	gain
plusvalenze sul titoli	gain on revaluation of securities
popolazione	population
popolazione	population (in a statist. environ.)
portata	scope
portatore	bearer
practicabilità	feasibility
premi d'assicurazione emessi	total premiums written
premi netti	net premiums earned
premio sul debito	debt premium
presidente del consiglio di amministrazione	chairman
	chairman
prestare osservanza a	comply with
prestiti	loans
prestiti bancari a breve termine	short-term bank loans
prestiti infruttiferi	non performing earning assets
prestiti scaduti	matured loans
prestiti sindicati	syndicated loans
prestito obbligazionario	debenture
previsione	forecast
prezzo di mercato	market price
prezzo di riscatto	call price
primo entrato, primo uscito	first in, first out (FIFO)
principi di revisione contabile	auditing standards
probabile	probable
procedura alternativa	alternative procedure
procedure di revisione	auditing procedures
prodotti finiti	finished goods
prodotti semilavorati	semi-finished goods
prodotto nazionale lordo	gross national product
profitti(perditi) sulle investimenti in titoli	investment securities gains(losses)
	investment securities gains(losses)
profitto	profit
proiezione	projection
prospetto delle variazioni nella situazione patrimoniale-finanziaria	statement changes in fin. position
	statement changes in fin. position
prospetto riepilogativo dei dati essenziali dei bilanci	financial summary
	financial summary
prova	test
prova con la cartina al tornasole	acid test
prova sostantiva	substantive test
proventi (perditi) del conto merci	trading account profits (losses)
proventi (perditi) per amministrazione dei fondi di terzi	trust operations profits (losses)
	trust operations profits (losses)
proventi finanziari	interest income
punto di pareggio	break even point

ITALIAN	ENGLISH
punto morto	break even point
quadro economico	economic environment
questionario di controllo interno	internal control questionnaire
quote corrente dei...	current portion of ...
quoziente di disponibilità	current ratio
ragionevolmente possible	reasonably possible
ragioniere	accountant
rapporto	report
rapporto alla direzione	report to management
rapporto di liquidità	working capital ratio
rapporto di liquidità	liquidity ratio
rapporto operativo	operating ratio
rapporto secco di liquidità	acid test ratio
rappresentare ragionevolmente	fairly present
ratei e risconti attivi	prepaid expenses & deferred charges
ratei e risconti passivi	accrued liabilities
ratei e risconti passivi	accrued expenses
rateo attivo	accrued income
recessione	recession
reclami e perditi per risarcimenti	total insurance claims and losses
redditi e spese non operative	non-operating income and expense
reddito differito	deferred income
reddito imponibile	taxable income
reddito netto	net income
reddito non imponibile	non-taxable income
reddito operativo	operating profit
reddito per azione	earnings per share
reddito per servizi prestati	income for services rendered
redimibile	redeemable
registrare	record (verb)
regolamenti	regulations
regoli	rules
regressione multipla	multiple regression
relazione	report
relazione dei sindaci	auditor's report
relazione del revisore dei conti	auditor's report
relazione di verifica	audit opinion
relazione di verifica	auditors' report
relazione interinale	interim financial statements
relazione speciale	special reports
remoto	remote
rendiconti consolidati	consolidated accounts
rendiconti finanziari	financial statements
rendiconti finanziari trimestrali	quarterly financial statements
rendiconto delle fonti e degli impieghi dei fondi	statement sources & uses of funds
	statement sources & uses of funds
rendiconto di reconciliazione	bank reconciliation (statement)

ITALIAN	ENGLISH
rendiconto finanziario	statement changes in fin. position
rendimento	yield
rendimento del capitale netto	return on equity
rendimento delle attività	return on assets
requisiti di pegno	pledging requirements
requisiti legali	legal requirements
responsabilità del revisore	auditor's responsibility
restrizioni sulla portata	restrictions on the scope
rete operativa	operational network
revisione analitica	analytical review
revisione contabile	audit
revisione dei bilanci	review of financial statements
revisione fiscale	tax audit
revisione operativa	operational auditing
revisore dei conti	auditor
riassicurazione e correzione dei premi	reinsurance and premium adjustments
ricavo di gestione	total funds from operations
ricavo totale	total revenue
richiesta di approvvigionamento	purchase requisition
richiesta non asserita	unasserted claim
riduzione contabile	write down (noun)
rifinanziamento	refinancing
rifiuto di certificazione	disclaimer of opinion
rilevante	material (significant)
rimborso	refund
riparazioni	repairs
ripartizione su esercizi precedenti	carryback
riportare a mastro	post entries to the ledger
riporto a nuovo	balance carried forward
ripresa su accantonamenti precedenti	prior period adjustment
risarcimenti	claims
riscattabili	redeemable
rischio d'illiquidità	liquidity risk
rischio dei cambi	exchange rate risk
rischio del paese	country risk
rischio della revisione	audit risk
rischio di campionatura	sampling risk
rischio estraneo alla campionatura	non-sampling risk
risconti attivi	prepaid expenses
risconti attivi	deferred expense
risconti passivi	deferred income
riserva	qualification(of an audit opinion)
riserva di capitale	capital surplus
riserva legale	legal reserve
risparmio fiscale	tax savings
ristrutturazioni	restructuring
ristrutturazioni dei debiti	debt restructuring

ITALIAN	ENGLISH
risultati di campionatura	sampling results
ritenuta di acconto	withheld taxes
ritiro anticipato	early retirement
rivalutazione	revaluation
rivelazione	disclosure
saldi dei conti	account balances
sborsi	disbursements
scadenza	maturity
scadenza	due date
scaduto	overdue
scarto	spread (between rates)
scelto a caso	random
scissione (di una società)	split (of a company)
sconto sul valore dei debiti	debt discount
scoperto	bank overdraft
scoperto di conto	overdraft
scoprire	detect
scorte	inventory -(USA) (stocks-UK)
scorti	supplies (noun)
scrittura	journal entry
seconda domanda	second request
secondo	in accordance with
senza revisare	unaudited
senza riserva	unqualified
senza scopo di lucro	non-profit
servizi di consulenza	consulting services
settembre	September
settore privato	private sector
settore pubblico	public sector
sistema d'inventario permanente	perpetual inventory system
situazione contabile interina	interim accounts
società - madre	parent company
società affiliata	subsidiary
società collegate	affiliated firms
società controllante	parent company
società controllata	subsidiary
società controllate nazionale	domestic subsidiaries
società di assicurazione	insurance company
società di credito ipotecario	mortgage bank
società di finanziamento	financial entities
società finanziaria	holding company
società multinazionale	multinational enterprise
socio	partner
socio della revisione	audit partner
soggeto a	subject to
soppravenienze passive	contingent liabilities
sopraddazio d'importazione	import surcharge
soprafatturazione	overinvoicing
sopraprezzo	premium
sopraprezzo azioni	premium on issue of capital
sopraprezzo non ammortizzato	unamortized premium
sottofatturazione	underinvoicing
sottoprodotto	by-product
sottoscrizione	subscription
spese	expenses
spese amministrative	administrative expenses
spese amministrative e generali	general and administrative expense
spese bancari	bank service charges
spese da pagare	accrued expenses
spese dall'emissione di polizza	underwriting and policy acq. costs
spese di addestramento	training expenditure
spese di ammortamento	depreciation expense
spese di aumento di capitale	expenses on capital increase
spese di carità	charity expense
spese di communicazioni	communications expense
spese di esposizione	exhibitions and events expense
spese di organizzazione	organization expenses
spese di reclutamento (di personale)	recruiting expense
spese di ricerca e sviluppo	research and development costs
(spese di) vendita	selling expenses
spese generali	overhead expenses
spese maturate	accrued expenses
spese prepagate	prepaid expenses
spese promozionali	promotional costs
statuto della società	company by-laws
stipendi e salari	salaries and wages
stornare	write off (verb)
storno	write off (noun)
strategia della revisione	audit strategy
studio della praticabilità	feasibility study
subaffitto	sublet (noun)
svalutare	write down (verb)
tasso d'imposta	tax rate
tasso d'interesse	interest rate
tasso di cambio	exchange rate
tasso di sconto	discount rate
tasso interbancario	interbank rate
tendenza	trend
terreni	land
titoli a reddito fisso	marketable securities
titoli di credito con interesse	zero coupon bonds
anticipato	zero coupon bonds
titoli di terzi	custody securities
titoli e valori dei terzi	trust securities

ITALIAN	ENGLISH
titoli quotati in borsa	marketable stocks
titoli quotati-valuta nazionale	listed bonds-local currency
titolo a reddito fisso	bond
totale dei fondi per rischi	total insurance reserves
tranne (per)	except for
transazione con parti collegati	related party transactions
transazioni	transactions
trattamento fiscale	tax treatment
trattenuta fiscale	withholding of tax
trattenuta fiscale unica e definitiva	flat tax withholding
trimestralmente	quarterly
trimestralmente (4 volte per anno)	quarterly (4 times a year)
trimestre	quarter
ultimo entrato, primo uscito	last in, first out (LIFO)
unità di produzione	units of production
universo	population (in a statist. environ.)
utile	profit
utile (perdita) di cambio	foreign exchange gains (losses)
utile corrispondente agli assicurati	policyholders' surplus
utile dell'esercizio	net income
utile della vendita di beni immobili	gain on sale of fixed assets
utile di gestione	operating profit
utile distribuito	appropriated retained earnings
utile netto	net income
utile netto dell'esercizio	net income of the period
utile non impegnate	unappropriated retained earnings
utile per azione	earnings per share
utili non distribuiti	retained earnings
valore attuale neto	net present value
valore attuariale	actuarial value
valore contabile	book value
(valore di) parità	par value
valore netto di presunto realizo	net realizable value
valore nominale	face value
valore presunto di ricupero	expected salvage value
valore storico	historical cost
valore venale	market price
valori mobiliari	marketable securities
valori negoziabili	marketable securities
valuta estera	foreign exchange
valuta estera	foreign currency
valuta nazionale	local currency
veicoli	vehicles
vendita de prodotti	sale of (manufactured) goods
vendite	sales (turnover)
vendite nette	net sales
vendite rateali	sales on installment
verifica di legge della contabilità	statutory audit report
verificare	examine
vice-presidente	vice-chairman
vita economica	useful life (of an asset)

ENGLISH	ITALIAN
accelerated depreciation	ammortamento accelerato
account balances	saldi dei conti
accountant	contabile
accountant	ragioniere
accounting	contabilità
accounting changes	cambio dei metodi contabili
accounting policies	particolari criteri contabili
accounting principles	normi di contabilità
accounting records	documenti contabili
accounts payable	debiti
accounts receivable	crediti
accrual	attribuzione
accrual method of accounting	contabilità per competenze
accrue	maturare
accrue	accumularsi
accrued expenses	spese maturate
accrued expenses	ratei e risconti passivi
accrued expenses	spese da pagare
accrued income	rateo attivo
accrued liabilities	ratei e risconti passivi
accrued taxes	imposti maturati
accrued vacations	accantonamento per vacanze
accumulated depreciation	ammortamento maturato
accumulated depreciation	fondo di ammortamento
acid test	prova con la cartina al tornasole
acid test ratio	rapporto secco di liquidità
acquisition (of a company)	acquisizione (di una impresa)
acquisition cost	costo di acquisizione
actual loan losses	perditi su crediti
actuarial value	valore attuariale
adjustment	correzione
adjustment for inflation	correzione per inflazione
administrative expenses	spese amministrative
advances to suppliers	anticipi a fornitori
adverse opinion	parere con eccezioni
affiliate	azienda affiliata
affiliate	azienda collegata
affiliated firms	imprese collegate
affiliated firms	società collegate
allocate	accantonare
allocate	assegnare
allowance	fondo
allowance	accantonamento
allowance for devaluation of inv'ts	fondo svalutazione investimenti
allowance for doubtful accounts	fondo per rischi su crediti
allowance for loan losses	fondo per rischi su crediti
allowance for sampling risk	margine di rischio della campionatura

ENGLISH	ITALIAN
allowance for uncollectible acc'ts	fondo per crediti irrecuperabili
alternative procedure	procedura alternativa
analytical review	revisione analitica
annual meeting	assemblea annuale
annual shareholders' meeting	assemblea annuale degli azionisti
annually	annualmente
appropriated retained earnings	utile distribuito
April	aprile
assets	attivo
associated firm	azienda consociata
at random	a caso
audit	controllo del bilancio
audit	revisione contabile
audit approach	foco della revisione
audit engagement	lavoro di revisione
audit fees	compenso del revisore contabile
audit manager	direttore della revisione
audit opinion	relazione di verifica
audit partner	socio della revisione
audit risk	rischio della revisione
audit sampling	campionatura di revisione
audit staff	equipaggio di revisione
audit strategy	strategia della revisione
auditing procedures	procedure di revisione
auditing standards	principi di revisione contabile
auditor	auditore
auditor	revisore dei conti
auditor's report	relazione dei sindaci
auditor's report	relazione del revisore dei conti
auditor's responsibility	responsabilità del revisore
auditors' report	relazione di verifica
August	agosto
average (mean)	media
balance carried forward	riporto a nuovo
balance sheet	bilancio
balance sheet date	data di chiusura del bilancio
bank	banca
bank overdraft	credito scoperto
bank overdraft	scoperto
bank reconciliation (statement)	rendiconto di reconciliazione
bank service charges	spese bancari
bankruptcy	fallimento
bearer	portatore
bid (noun)	licitazione
bid (verb)	offrire
billions	bilione
board of directors	consiglio di amministrazione

ENGLISH	ITALIAN
bond	obbligazione
bond	titolo a reddito fisso
bonds payable	obbligazioni per pagare
book value	valore contabile
break even point	punto morto
break even point	punto di pareggio
budget	bilancio de previsione
buildings and structures	fabbricati
business combinations	combinazioni d'affari
business segment	area d'affari
by-product	sottoprodotto
call price	prezzo di riscatto
capital gains tax	imposta sulle plus-valenze derivanti da cessioni
capital gains tax	aumento di capitale
capital increase	capitale sociale
capital stock	riserva di capitale
capital surplus	imposta sul capitale
capital tax	capitalizzazione dei costi finanziari
capitalization of financial costs	capitalizzazione dei interessi
capitalization of interest	capitalizzazione dei locazioni
capitalization of leases	ripartizione su esercizi precedenti
carryback	cassa
cash	denaro liquido
cash	cassa e depositi bancari
cash and banks	dividendi in contanti
cash dividends	disponibilità
cash equivalents	flusso di cassa
cash flow	cash flow
cash flow	certificato di deposito
certificate of deposit	ceteris paribus
ceteris paribus	presidente del consiglio di amministrazione
chairman	spese di carità
chairman	piano contabile
charity expense	direttore generale
chart of accounts	circostanze
chief executive officer	risarcimenti
circumstances	lettera di rappresentazione
claims	cifrare
client representation letter	garanzia reale
code (verb)	garanzia collaterale
collateral	indice di dilazione dei pagamenti
collateral	incassi
collection ratio	mutui commerciali e industriali
collections	banca commerciale
commercial & industrial loans	banca di credito ordinario
commercial bank	
commercial bank	

ENGLISH	ITALIAN
commissions & fees-profits(losses)	commissioni e onorari-profitti(perditi)
commitments	impegni
common stock	azioni ordinari
communications expense	spese di communicazioni
company by-laws	statuto della società
comparative financial statements	bilancio comparato
compilation of financial statements	compilazione dei bilanci
completed-contract method	metodo di contratto compiuto
comply with	prestare osservanza a
condensed financial statements	bilancio riclassificato
condensed financial statements	bilancio sintetico
confirmation of accounts	conferma dei conti
consistency	concordanza
consistently applied	applicato uniformemente
consolidated accounts	rendiconti consolidati
consolidated financial statements	bilancio consolidato
construction in progress	costruzioni in corso
construction in progress	immobilizzazioni in corso
consulting services	servizi di consulenza
contents	contenuto
contingent liabilities	soppravenienze passive
control weakness	deboli di controlle
convertible bonds	obbligazioni convertibili
copyright	diritto di autore
corporation tax	imposta sulle società
correspondent firms	aziende corrispondente
cost of goods sold	costo dei prodotti venduti
cost of goods sold	costo delle merci vendute
cost of sales	costo del venduto
cost of services rendered	costo dei servizi prestati
country risk	rischio del paese
credit line	linea di credito
credit line	castelletto
credit turnover ratio	indice di rotazione dei crediti
cumulative adjustment	aggiustamento cumulativo
cumulative effect	effetto cumulativo
currency translation	conversione valutaria
currency translation	conversione della moneta
current assets	attività correnti
current assets	attivo realizzabile
current assets	disponibilità
current liabilities	passività a breve termine
current liabilities	passività correnti
current portion of ...	quote corrente dei...
current ratio	quoziente di disponibilità
custody securities	titoli di terzi
customers	clienti

ENGLISH	ITALIAN
customers'liability for acceptances	conti impegni
customs duties	dazi doganali
debenture	obbligazione
debenture	prestito obbligazionario
debt discount	sconto sul valore dei debiti
debt premium	premio sul debito
debt restructuring	ristrutturazioni dei debiti
December	dicembre
deferral method	metodo del risconto
deferred charges	costi pluriennali
deferred expense	risconti attivi
deferred income	risconti passivi
deferred income	reddito differito
deferred income taxes	imposte sul reddito differite
deferred taxes	imposte differite
demand deposits	conti correnti
departure from a pronouncement	deviazione di una dichiarazione
dependent	persona a carico
depreciation expense	ammortamento economico
depreciation expense	spese di ammortamento
depreciation of buildings	ammortamenti di costruzioni
detect	scoprire
development stage companies	imprese in via de sviluppo
direct cost	costo diretto
directors	consiglieri
directors	amministratori
disbursements	sborsi
disclaimer of opinion	rifiuto di certificazione
disclosure	rivelazione
discontinued operations	operazioni cessati
discount rate	tasso di sconto
disposal (of an asset)	esito (di una attività)
dividend	dividendo
dividend income	dividendi ricevuti
dividend per share	dividendo per azione
dividends payable	dividendi da pagare
dollars	dollari
domestic subsidiaries	società controllate nazionale
double taxation	doppia imposizzione
due date	scadenza
early extinguishment of debt	pagamento anticipato dei debiti
early retirement	ritiro anticipato
earnings per share	utile per azione
earnings per share	reddito per azione
economic environment	quadro economico
effect	effetto
effects of changing prices	effetti della variazione dei prezzi

ENGLISH	ITALIAN
employee	dipendente
employee	impiegato
employee benefit plan	piano previdenziale
entertainment expense	fondo di rappresentanza
equity in other companies	partecipazioni in altre società
equity method	metodo del patrimonio neto
errors	errori
evidential matter	evidenza
examine	esaminare
examine	verificare
except for	fatto eccezione di
except for	tranne (per)
exchange rate	corso del cambio
exchange rate	tasso di cambio
exchange rate risk	rischio dei cambi
excise tax	imposta sui consumi
exhibitions and events expense	spese di esposizione
expected salvage value	valore presunto di ricupero
expenses	costi
expenses	spese
expenses on capital increase	spese di aumento di capitale
export	esportazione
export duties	dazi di esportazione
extent	limite
extraordinary items	partite straordinari
face value	valore nominale
fairly present	rappresentare ragionevolmente
feasibility	practicabilità
feasibility study	studio della praticabilità
February	febbraio
fees	onorari
fees for services by third party	onorari per servizi di terzi
finance (noun)	finanza
finance (verb)	finanziare
financial entities	società di finanziamento
financial statements	bilancio
financial statements	rendiconti finanziari
financial summary	bilancio riclassificato
financial summary	prospetto riepilogativo dei dati essenziali dei bilanci
financial summary	
financing arrangement	accordo di finanziamento
fine	ammenda
fine	multa
finished goods	prodotti finiti
first in, first out (FIFO)	primo entrato, primo uscito
fittings	attrezzature
fixed assets	beni immobili

ENGLISH	ITALIAN
fixed assets	attivo fisso
fixed assets	immobilizzazioni
flat tax withholding	trattenuta fiscale unica e definitiva
floating rate	cambio flessibile
flowchart	diagramma di flusso
flowchart	flussogramma
footnotes to financial statements	note al bilancio
for taxation purposes	dall'effetto fiscale
forecast	previsione
foreign currency	valuta estera
foreign currency translation	conversione dei valuta estera
foreign exchange	divise
foreign exchange	valuta estera
foreign exchange gains (losses)	utile (perdita) di cambio
foreign subsidiary	filiale estera
form	modulo
freight on purchases of materials	costi di trasporto sulle acquisti
funds	fondi
furniture and fixtures	mobili e arredi
future contracts	contrati a termine
gain	plusvalenza
gain on revaluation of securities	plusvalenze sul titoli
gain on sale of fixed assets	utile della vendita di beni immobili
general and administrative expense	spese amministrative e generali
general insurance	assicurazione generale
general ledger	mastro generale
general manager	direttore generale
going concern	azienda in attività
goods in process	merci in lavorazione
goods in transit	merci in transito
goodwill	avviamento
graduated tax	imposta progressiva
gross margin	margine lordo
gross national product	prodotto nazionale lordo
gross profit ratio	indice di proffito lordo
gross revenue tax	imposta sul fatturato lordo
group (of companies)	gruppo (d'imprese)
guarantee	garanzia
guarantee deposits	depositi in garanzia
hedge	copertura verso flutazioni
hedging	operazione di copertura
historical cost	costo storico
historical cost	valore storico
holding company	società finanziaria
hundreds	centi
idle capacity	capacità inutilizatta
impact	effetto

ENGLISH	ITALIAN
import surcharge	sopraddazio d'importazione
in accordance with	conformemente a
in accordance with	secondo
income for services rendered	reddito per servizi prestati
income statement	conto profitti e perditi
income tax	imposta sul reddito
indebtedness ratio	indice di indebitamento
indemnities	indennità
independence	indipendenza
industry	industria
inflation	inflazione
inheritance tax	imposta sulle successioni
insurance company	società di assicurazione
intangible assets	attività immateriali
intangible assets	immobilizzazioni immateriali
inter-company loans	collocamenti interaziendali
interbank assets/funds	fondi interbancari
interbank deposits	depositi interbancari
interbank rate	tasso interbancario
interest expense	oneri finanziari
interest expense	interessi passivi
interest income	interessi attivi
interest income	proventi finanziari
interest payable	interessi pagabili
interest rate	tasso d'interesse
interest receivable	interessi esigibili
interim accounts	situazione contabile interina
interim financial statements	relazione interinale
internal auditors	collegio sindacale
internal control	controllo interno
internal control questionnaire	questionario di controllo interno
international subsidiaries	filiali internazionali
international trade	commercio internazionale
intervening period	periodo intercorrente
inventory -(USA) (stocks-UK)	scorte
inventory turnover ratio	indice di rotazione delle scorte
investment	investimento
investment bank/merchant bank	banca d'investimento
investment in subsidiaries	partecipazioni in società controllate
investment in subsidiaries	investimenti in filiali
investment securities gains(losses)	profitti(perditi) sulle investimenti in titoli
investment securities gains(losses)	
investment tax credit	credito d'imposta per investimento
invoice	fattura
irregularity	irregolarità
January	gennaio
joint venture	impresa in collaborazione

ENGLISH	ITALIAN
journal	libro giornale
journal entry	scrittura
July	luglio
June	giugno
labor hours (man-hours)	ore-uomo
labor law	legge di lavoro
land	terreni
land improvements	miglioramenti fondiari
last in, first out (LIFO)	ultimo entrato, primo uscito
lawyer	avvocato
lease	locazione
lease financing loans	mutui di locazione
leaseback	leasing immobiliare
leasing	locazione
legal requirements	requisiti legali
legal reserve	riserva legale
lessee	locatario
lessor	locatore
liability	passività
liability method	metodo di passività
life insurance	assicurazione sulla vita
life policy benefits	benefici prestati per l'assicurazione
life policy benefits	sulla vita
liquid assets	attività liquide
liquidity	liquidità
liquidity ratio	rapporto di liquidità
liquidity risk	rischio d'illiquidità
listed bonds-local currency	titoli quotati-valuta nazionale
litigation	lite
loans	prestiti
loans	mutui
local currency	valuta nazionale
long-term contracts	contratti a lungo termine
long-term credits	crediti a lungo termine
long-term debt	debiti a lungo termine
long-term insurance reserve charges	accantonamenti a lungo termine per
long-term insurance reserve charges	risarcimenti
long-term investments	investimenti a lungo termine
loss	perdita
loss carry-forward	perdita accumulata
lower of cost or market method	costo o valore di realizzo
lower of cost or market method	costo o prezzo di mercato
lower of cost or market method	costo o valore di mercato
machinery and equipment	macchine ed attrezzature fisse
major customers	clienti principali
management intention	intenzione della direzione
March	marzo

ENGLISH	ITALIAN
marginal cost	costo marginale
market price	valore venale
market price	prezzo di mercato
marketable securities	titoli a reddito fisso
marketable securities	valori negoziabili
marketable securities	valori mobiliari
marketable stocks	titoli quotati in borsa
material (noun)	materiale
material (significant)	rilevante
materiality	(grado di) rilevanza
matured loans	prestiti scaduti
maturity	scadenza
May	maggio
merger	fusione
millions	milioni
minority interests	partecipazione di minoranza
misleading information	informazione fuorviante
monetary assets	attività monetaria
monetary transactions	operazioni monetari
monthly	mensilmente
monthly	per mese
mortgage	ipoteca
mortgage bank	istituto di credito ipotecario
mortgage bank	società di credito ipotecario
multinational enterprise	società multinazionale
multiple regression	regressione multipla
mutual fund	fondo comune d'investimento
nature	natura
negative goodwill	avviamento negativo
net fixed assets	attività fisse nette
net income	reddito netto
net income	utile netto
net income	utile dell'esercizio
net income of the period	utile netto dell'esercizio
net loss of the period	perdita netta dell'esercizio
net premiums earned	premi netti
net present value	valore attuale neto
net realizable value	valore netto di presunto realizo
net sales	fatturato netto
net sales	vendite nette
net trade accounts receivable	conti attivi netti di credito
net trade accounts receivable	mercantile
net worth	patrimonio netto
net worth	capitale netto
non performing earning assets	prestiti infruttiferi
non-current assets	attività a lungo termine
non-current liabilities	passività a lungo termine

ENGLISH	ITALIAN
non-equity reserves	fondi non patrimoniali
non-monetary transactions	operazioni non monetari
non-operating income and expense	redditi e spese non operative
non-profit	senza scopo di lucro
non-redeemable preferred stock	azioni privilegiati non riscattabili
non-sampling risk	rischio estraneo alla campionatura
non-statistical sampling	campionatura non statistica
non-taxable income	reddito non imponibile
notes payable	effetti passivi
notes receivable	effetti attivi
notes receivable	effetti da esigere
notes receivable	cambiali attivi
November	novembre
obsolescence	obsolescenza
October	ottobre
officer (of a company)	funzionario (di una società)
offset (noun)	compensazione
operating controls	controlli di gestione
operating cycle	ciclo operativo
operating lease	locazione operativa
operating profit	utile di gestione
operating profit	reddito operativo
operating ratio	rapporto operativo
operational auditing	revisione operativa
operational controls	controlli operativi
operational network	rete operativa
opinion	opinione
opinion	parere
opinion paragraph	paragrafo di opinione
opportunity cost	costo di opportunità
option	opzione
option	contratto a premio
organization chart	organigramma
organization expenses	spese di organizzazione
other income for services	altri proventi per servizi
other loans	altri prestiti
other operating profits (losses)	altri proventi (perditi) di gestione
outstanding shares	azioni in circolazione
over the counter transaction	operazione fuori di borsa
overdraft	scoperto di conto
overdue	scaduto
overhead expenses	spese generali
overinvoicing	soprafatturazione
overnight funds	collocamenti alla giornata
paid-in capital	capitale conferito
par value	(valore di) parità
parent company	società controllante
parent company	società - madre
partner	socio
patents	brevetti
payments	pagamenti
payments cycle	ciclo dei pagamenti
payroll	nomi
pension	pensione
pension plan	piano de pensionamiento
percentage	percentuale
percentage-of-completion-method	metodo di percentuale di compimento
permanent file	archivio permanente
perpetual bond	obbligazione perpetua
perpetual inventory system	sistema d'inventario permanente
personal income tax	imposta sul reddito personale
petty cash	piccola cassa
physical inventory	inventario fisico
placement	collocamento
pledge (verb)	impegnare
pledge (verb)	dare in garanzia
pledging requirements	requisiti di pegno
policyholders' equity	assicurati
policyholders' equity	patrimonio corrispondente agli
policyholders' surplus	utile corrispondente agli assicurati
pooling of interest	cumulo di interessi
population	popolazione
population (in a statist. environ.)	popolazione
population (in a statist. environ.)	universo
portfolio composition	composizione delle portafoglio
post entries to the ledger	riportare a mastro
post retirement benefits	indennità di buonuscita
preference share	azione preferenziale
preference share (UK)	azione privilegiata
preferred share (USA)	azione privilegiata
premium	aggio
premium	sopraprezzo
premium on issue of capital	sopraprezzo azioni
prepaid expenses	spese prepagate
prepaid expenses	risconti attivi
prepaid expenses & deferred charges	ratei e risconti attivi
primary capital	capitale primario
prior period adjustment	ripresa su accantonamenti precedenti
private sector	settore privato
probable	probabile
product financing	finanziamento dell'acquisto di un
product financing	prodotto
product warranties	garanzie sulle prodotti
production capacity	capacità di produzione

ENGLISH	ITALIAN
production cost	costo di produzione
production cycle	ciclo di produzione
production order	ordine di produzione
professional judgment	giudizio professionale
professional standards	normi professionali
profit	utile
profit	profitto
profit & loss account	conto profitti e perditi
profit & loss account	conto economico
profit margin	margine di profitto
profit sharing	participazione agli utili
progressive tax	imposta progressiva
projection	proiezione
promotional costs	spese promozionali
provision	fondo
provision	accantonamento
proxy (noun)	alternato
proxy (noun)	delega
public sector	settore pubblico
purchase requisition	richiesta di approvvigionamento
qualification(of an audit opinion)	riserva
quality control	controllo della qualità
quarter	trimestre
quarterly	trimestralmente
quarterly (4 times a year)	trimestralmente (4 volte per anno)
quarterly financial statements	rendiconti finanziari trimestrali
random	casuale
random	scelto a caso
raw materials	materie prime
real estate and mortgage loans	mutui ipotecari
reasonably possible	ragionevolmente possible
receivables	crediti
receivables	debitori
recession	recessione
record (verb)	registrare
recruiting expense	spese di reclutamento (di personale)
redeemable	redimibile
redeemable	riscattabili
redeemable preferred stock	azioni privilegiati riscattabili
redemption features	condizioni di riscatto
rediscounted notes	documenti riscontati
refinancing	rifinanziamento
refund	rimborso
regressive tax	imposta regressiva
regulations	regolamenti
reinsurance and premium adjustments	riassicurazione e correzione dei premi
related party transactions	transazione con parti collegati
remote	remoto
repair and maintenance expense	costi di riparazione e manutenzione
repairs	riparazioni
replacement cost	costo di rimpiazzo
report	rapporto
report	relazione
report to management	rapporto alla direzione
reproduction cost	costo di reproduzione
repurchase agreement	accordo di riacquisito
resale agreement	accordo di rivendita
resale merchandise	merci per rivendita
research and development costs	spese di ricerca e sviluppo
reserve exchange rate fluctuations	fondo per oscillazione del cambio
reserve for general risks	fondo per rischi diversi
reserve for loan losses/bad debts	fondo rischi su crediti
reserve for o/s claims and losses	fondo per risarcimenti e perditi
restrictions on the scope	restrizioni sulla portata
restructuring	ristrutturazioni
retained earnings	capitale di risparmio
retained earnings	utili non distribuiti
retirement of long term debt	ammortamento dei debiti a lungo termine
return on assets	rendimento delle attività
return on equity	rendimento del capitale netto
revaluation	rivalutazione
revaluation reserve	fondo rivalutazione
revaluation surplus	eccedenza di rivalutazione
review of financial statements	revisione dei bilanci
risk exposure	esposizione al rischio
rules	normi
rules	regoli
salaries and wages	stipendi e salari
sale of (manufactured) goods	vendita de prodotti
sales (turnover)	fatturato
sales (turnover)	vendite
sales on installment	vendite rateali
sales tax	imposta sulle vendite
sample size	ampiezza del campione
sampling	campionatura
sampling results	risultati di campionatura
sampling risk	rischio di campionatura
savings deposits	depositi a risparmio
scope	portata
scope paragraph	paragrafo di portata
seasonally adjusted	destagionalizato
second request	seconda domanda
secondary market	mercato secondario
secured note	effetto garantito

ENGLISH	ITALIAN
Securities and Exchange Commission	commissione per le società e la borsa
self-insurance	autoassicurazione
self-insure	autoassicurare
selling expenses	(spese di) vendita
semi-finished goods	prodotti semilavorati
senior debt	debiti di primo grado
September	settembre
severance	licenziamento
severance indemnities	indennità di licenziamento
share in loss of affiliates	affiliate
share in loss of affiliates	parte della perdita degli società
shareholders' equity	mezzi propri
shareholders' equity	patrimonio netto
shares	azioni
short-term bank loans	prestiti bancari a breve termine
short-term investments	investimenti a breve termine
short-term loans	debiti a breve termine
small companies	piccole imprese
social security expense	contributo di previdenza sociale
sources of funds	fonti di finanziamento
special reports	relazione speciale
split (of a company)	scissione (di una società)
spread (between rates)	margine
spread (between rates)	scarto
standard cost	costo standard
start-up costs	costo di avviamento
statement changes in fin. position	rendiconto finanziario
statement changes in fin. position	prospetto delle variazioni nella
statement changes in fin. position	situazione patrimoniale-finanziaria
statement of accounting policy	dichiarazione dei principi contabili
statement of accounting policy	adottati
statement sources & uses of funds	flusso dei fonti e degli impieghi dei
statement sources & uses of funds	fondi
statement sources & uses of funds	rendiconto delle fonti e degli
statement sources & uses of funds	impieghi dei fondi
statistical sampling	campionatura statistica
statutory audit report	verifica di legge della contabilità
statutory reserve	fondo di riserva legale
stock dividends	dividendi in azioni
stock exchange	borsa valori
stock option plans	piani di diritto di opzione sul azioni
stockbroker	agente di cambio
stockholders	azionisti
stockholders' equity	patrimonio netto
straight-line method	metodo di quote constanti
subject to	soggeto a
sublet (noun)	subaffitto

ENGLISH	ITALIAN
subordinated debt	debito subordinato
subordinated financing	finanziamento subordinato
subscription	sottoscrizione
subsequent events	eventi successivi alla data del bilancio
subsidiary	filiale
subsidiary	società controllata
subsidiary	società affiliata
subsidiary records	libri sussidiari
substantive test	prova sostantiva
sum of the years' digits method	metodo della somma degli anni di
sum of the years' digits method	prevista durata
supplementary information	informazione supplementare
suppliers	fornitori
supplies (noun)	scorti
supplies and spare parts	pezzi di ricambio
supporting documentation	documenti giustificativi
syndicated loans	prestiti sindicati
taken as a whole	nell'insieme
tangible fixed assets	immobilizzazioni materiali
tax	imposta
tax audit	revisione fiscale
tax authorities	autorità fiscali
tax credit	credito d'imposta
tax rate	tasso d'imposta
tax return	dichiarazione d'imposta
tax savings	risparmio fiscale
tax treatment	trattamento fiscale
taxable income	reddito imponibile
taxpayer	contribuente
temporary differences	differenzi temporanei
test	prova
thousand	mille
thousands	migliaio(a)
time deposit	deposito a termine
timing	opportunità
total funds from operations	ricavo di gestione
total insurance claims and losses	reclami e perditi per risarcimenti
total insurance reserves	totale dei fondi per rischi
total premiums written	premi d'assicurazione emessi
total revenue	ricavo totale
trade mark	marca di fabbrica
trade payables	debiti verso fornitori
trade payables	debiti commerciali
trade receivables	crediti commerciali
trading account profits (losses)	proventi (perditi) del conto merci
training expenditure	spese di addestramento
transactions	operazioni commerciali

ENGLISH	ITALIAN
transactions	transazioni
treasury stock	azioni di tesoreria
trend	tendenza
trial balance	bilancio di verifica per saldi
troubled debt	debiti irrecuperabili
trust operations profits (losses)	proventi (perditi) per amministrazione
trust operations profits (losses)	dei fondi di terzi
trust securities	titoli e valori dei terzi
turnover ratio	indice di rotazione
unamortized premium	sopraprezzo non ammortizzato
unappropriated retained earnings	utile non impegnate
unasserted claim	richiesta non asserita
unaudited	senza revisare
uncertainty	incertezza
uncollectible	irrecuperabile
uncollectible	inesigibile
underinvoicing	sottofatturazione
underwriting and policy acq. costs	spese dall'emissione di polizza
unearned interests	interessi passivi
units of production	unità di produzione
unqualified	senza riserva
unsecured bonds	obbligazioni senza garantia
useful life (of an asset)	vita economica
uses of funds	applicazioni dei fondi
vacation with pay	ferie pagate
valuation principles	criteri di valutazione
value added tax (VAT)	imposta sul valore aggiunto (IVA)
variable cost	costo variabile
vehicles	veicoli
vendors (USA)	fornitori
vice-chairman	vice-presidente
voucher	buono
voucher	autorizzazione di pagamento
warehouse	magazzino
weighted average	media ponderata
with and without method	metodo di "con e senza"
withheld taxes	ritenuta di acconto
withholding of tax	trattenuta fiscale
working capital	capitale circolante netto
working capital ratio	rapporto di liquidità
working capital turnover	indice di rotazione del capitale
working capital turnover	circolante
working papers	fogli di lavoro
write down (noun)	riduzione contabile
write down (verb)	svalutare
write off (noun)	storno
write off (verb)	stornare
year-end closing date	data del bilancio
yield	rendimento
zero coupon bonds	titoli di credito con interesse
zero coupon bonds	anticipato

※ 「あいうえお」語順は、清音の最後に濁音、半濁音の順に配列してあります。

【あ】

後入先出法(ATOIRE SAKIDASHI-HOO)	LAST IN, FIRST OUT (LIFO)

【い】

一月(ICHI-GATSU)	JANUARY
一時所有の有価証券(ICHIJI SHOYUU NO YUUKA SHOOKEN)	MARKETABLE SECURITIES
一時的不一致(ICHIJI-TEKI FUICCHI)	TEMPORARY DIFFERENCES
一年以内に返済する(ICHINEN-INAI NI HENSAI SURU)	CURRENT PORTION OF ...
一定率の源泉税徴収(ITTEI-RITSU NO GENSEN-ZEI CHOOSHUU)	FLAT TAX WITHHOLDING
一般管理費(IPPAN KANRI-HI)	ADMINISTRATIVE EXPENSES
一般に公正妥当と認められる(IPPAN NI KOOSEI-DATOO TO MITOMERARERU)	GENERALLY ACCEPTED
印紙税(INSHI-ZEI)	STAMP DUTY
インフレ(INFURE)	INFLATION
インフレ調整(INFURE CHOOSEI)	ADJUSTMENT FOR INFLATION

【う】

受取債券(UKETORI SAIKEN)	RECEIVABLES
受取手形(UKETORI TEGATA)	NOTES RECEIVABLE
受取配当金(UKETORI HAITOO-KIN)	DIVIDEND INCOME
受取利息(UKETORI RISOKUU)	INTEREST INCOME
売上原価(URIAGE GENKA)	COST OF GOODS SOLD
売上総利益(URIAGE SOORIEKI)	GROSS MARGIN
売上総利益率(URIAGE SOO-RIEKI-RITSU)	GROSS PROFIT RATIO
売掛金(URIKAKE-KIN)	ACCOUNTS RECEIVABLE TRADE RECEIVABLES
売掛債権回転率(URIKAKE SAIKEN KAITEN-RITSU)	CREDITS TURNOVER RATIO
運営監査(UNEI KANSA)	OPERATIONAL AUDITING
運営管理(UNEI KANRI)	OPERATIONAL CONTROLS
運転資本(UNTEN SHIHON)	WORKING CAPITAL
運転資本回転率(UNTEN SHIHON KAITEN-RITSU)	WORKING CAPITAL TURNOVER
運搬具(UNPANGU)	VEHICLES
運搬中の商品(UNPANCHUU NO SHOOHIN)	GOODS IN TRANSIT

【え】

永久社債(EIKYUU SHASAI)	PERPETUAL BOND
永久保存(EIKYUU-HOZON)	PERMANENT FILE
営業活動より生じた運転資本金(EIGYOOKATSUDOO YORI SHOOJITA UNTENSHIHONKIN)	TOTAL FUNDS FROM OPERATIONS
営業外収益一費用(EIGYOO-GAI SHUUEKI HIYOO)	NON-OPERATING INCOME AND EXPENSES
営業権(EIGYOO-KEN)	GOODWILL
営業収益合計(EIGYOO SHUUEKI GOOKEI)	TOTAL REVENUE
営業周期(EIGYOO SHUUKI)	OPERATING CYCLE
営業賃貸借(EIGYOO CHINTAISHAKU)	OPERATING LEASES
営業利益(EIGYOO-RIEKI)_	OPERATING PROFIT
益(EKI)	GAIN

【お】

送り状(OKURI-JOO)	INVOICE
オプション(OPUSHON)	OPTIONS
親会社(OYA-GAISHA)	PARENT COMPANY
卸売業者(OROSHIURI GYOOSHA)	VENDORS (USA)

【か】

買掛金(KAIKAKE-KIN)	ACCOUNTS PAYABLE
海外汚職行為防止法(KAIGAI OSHOKU-KOOI BOOSHI-HOO)	FOREIGN CORRUPT PRACTICES ACT
海外子会社(KAIGAI KO-GAISHA)	FOREIGN SUBSIDIARY INTERNATIONAL SUBSIDIARIES
開業準備中の企業(KAIGYOO JUNBI CHUU NO KIGYOO)	DEVELOPMENT STAGE COMPANIES
開業費(KAIGYOO-HI)	START-UP COSTS
会計監査(KAIKEI-KANSA)	AUDIT
会計監査上のリスク(KAIKEI-KANSA-JOO NO RISUKU)	AUDIT RISK
会計監査人(KAIKEI KANSA-NIN)	AUDITOR
会計監査人の責任範囲(KAIKEI KANSA-NIN NO SEKININ HAN'I)	AUDITOR'S RESPONSIBILITY
会計学(KAIKEI-GAKU)	ACCOUNTING
会計記録(KAIKEI-KIROKU)	ACCOUNTING RECORDS
会計検査(KAIKEI-KENSA)	AUDIT
会計検査官(KAIKEI KENSA-KAN)	AUDITOR
会計原則(KAIKEI-GENSOKU)	ACCOUNTING PRINCIPLES

Japanese	English
会計士 (KAIKEI-SHI)	ACCOUNTANT
会計年度末日 (KAIKEI-NENDO MATSUJITSU)	YEAR-END CLOSING DATE
会計方針 (KAIKEI-HOOSHIN)	ACCOUNTING POLICIES
会計方針説明書 (KAIKEI HOOSHIN SETSUMEI-SHO)	STATEMENT OF ACCOUNTING POLICY
会計方針の変更 (KAIKEI-HOOSHIN NO HENKOO)	ACCOUNTING CHANGES
解雇 (KAIKO)	SEVERANCE
会社更正 (KAISHA KOOSEI)	RESTRUCTURE
回収不能 (KAISHUU FUNOO)	UNCOLLECTIBLE
回収率 (KAISHUU-RITSU)	COLLECTION RATIO
開示 (KAIJI)	DISCLOSURE
会長 (KAICHOO)	CHAIRMAN
回転率 (KAITEN-RITSU)	TURNOVER RATIO
価格変動財務情報 (KAKAKU HENDOO ZAIMU JOOHOO)	EFFECTS OF CHANGING PRICES
隔差 (KAKUSA)	SPREAD (BETWEEN RATES)
貸倒引当金 (KASHIDAORE-HIKIATEKIN)	ALLOWANCE FOR DOUBTFULL ACCOUNTS
	ALLOWANCE FOR LOAN LOSSES
	ALLOWANCE FOR UNCOLLECTIBLE ACCOUNTS
	RESERVE FOR LOAN LOSSES
貸付け金 (KASHI TSUKE-KIN)	LOANS
貸付金損準備金 (KASHITSUKE-KIN-SON JUNBI-KIN)	RESERVE FOR LOAN LOSSES
貸主 (KASHINUSHI)	LESSOR
加重平均法 (総平均法) KAJUU HEIKIN-HOO (SOO-HEIKIN-HOO)	WEIGHTED AVERAGE
課税処理法 (KAZEI SHORI-HOO)	TAX TREATMENT
課税対象所得 (KAZEI TAISHOO SHOTOKU)	TAXABLE INCOME
課税対象目的で (KAZEI TAISHOO MOKUTEKI DE)	FOR TAXATION PURPOSES
割賦販売 (KAPPU-HANBAI)	SALES ON INSTALLMENTS
稼働率、営業比率 (KADOO-RITSU, EIGYOO-HIRITSU)	OPERATING RATIO
かなり可能性の高い (KANARI KANOO-SEI NO TAKAI)	REASONABLY POSSIBLE
過不足請求 (KAFUSOKU SEIKYUU)	OVERINVOICING
株 (KABU)	SHARES
株式再評価利益 (KABUSHIKI SAIHYOOKA RIEKI)	GAIN ON REVALUATION OF SECURITIES
株式投資信託 (KABUSHIKI TOOSHI SHINTAKU)	MUTUAL FUND
株式配当 (KABUSHIKI HAITOO)	STOCK DIVIDENDS
株主 (KABUNUSHI)	STOCKHOLDERS
株式仲買人 (KABUNUSHI NAKAGAI-NIN)	STOCKBROKER
株主持分 (KABUNUSHI MOCHIBUN)	SHAREHOLDERS' EQUITY
貨幣資産 (KAHEI SHISAN)	MONETARY ASSETS
為替換算 (KAWASE KANSAN)	CURRENCY TRANSLATION

Japanese	English
為替換算益(損) KAWASE KANSANEKI (SON)	FOREIGN EXCHANGE GAINS (LOSS)
為替換算調整方法 (KAWASE KANSAN CHOOSEI HOOHOO)	FOREIGN CURRENCY TRANSLATION METHOD
為替換算変動準備金 (KAWASE KANSAN HENDOO JUNBI-KIN)	RESERVE FOR EXCH. RATE FLUCTUATIONS
為替相場 (KAWASE SOOBA)	EXCHANGE RATE
関係会社 (KANKEI GAISHA)	ASSOCIATED FIRM
関係会社貸付金 (KANKEI-GAISHA KASHITSUKE-KIN)	INTER-COMPANY LOANS
関係会社株式 (KANKEI-GAISHA KABUSHIKI)	INVESTMENT IN SUBSIDIARIES
関係会社出資金 (KANKEI-GAISHA SHUSSHI-KIN)	INVESTMENT IN SUBSIDIARIES
関係者間取引 (KANKEI-SHA-KAN TORIHIKI)	RELATED PARTY TRANSACTIONS
関係資料 (KANKEI SHIRYOO)	SUPPORTING DOCUMENTATION
監査意見 (KANSA IKEN)	AUDIT OPINION
	OPINION
監査意見欄 (KANSA IKEN-RAN)	OPINION PARAGRAPH
監査基準 (KANSA KIJUN)	AUDITING STANDARDS
監査契約 (KANSA-KEIYAKU)	AUDIT ENGAGEMENT
監査職員 (KANSA SHOKUIN)	AUDIT STAFF
監査戦略 (KANSA SENRYAKU)	AUDIT STATEGY
監査調書 (KANSA CHOOSHO)	WORKING PAPERS
監査手順 (KANSA-TEJUN)	AUDIT APPROACH
	AUDITING PROCEDURES
監査人の報告書 (KANSA-NIN NO HOOKOKU-SHO)	AUDITORS' REPORT
監査範囲の限定 (KANSA HAN'I NO GENTEI)	RESTRICTIONS ON THE SCOPE
監査標本抽出 (KANSA HYOOHON CHUUSHUTSU)	AUDIT SAMPLING
監査報告書 (KANSA HOOKOKU-SHO)	AUDITOR'S REPORT
監査料 (KANSA-RYOO)	AUDIT FEES
換算損失リスク (KANSAN SONSHITSU RISUKU)	EXCHANGE RATE RISK
換算レート (KANSAN REETO)	EXCHANGE RATE
勘定課目表 (KANJOO KAMOKU-HYOO)	CHART OF ACCOUNTS
勘定残高 (KANJOO-ZANDAKA)	ACCOUNT BALANCES
関税 (KANZEI)	CUSTOMS DUTY
カントリーリスク (KANTORII RISUKU)	COUNTRY RISK
看破 (KANPA)	DETECT
関連 (KANREN)	AFFILIATE
関連会社 (KANREN-GAISHA)	AFFILIATED FIRMS
関係団体 (KANKEI-DANTAI)	AFFILIATED FIRMS
外貨 (GAIKA)	FOREIGN CURRENCY
外貨建取引の換算方法 (GAIKA-DATE TORIHIKI NO KANSAN HOOHOO)	CURRENCY TRANSLATION METHOD
外国為替 (GAIKOKU KAWASE)	FOREIGN EXCHANGE

Japanese	English
外部要託費(GAIBU YOOTAKU-HI)	FEES FOR SVS. RENDERED BY 3R PARTY
額面(GAKUMEN)	PAR VALUE
額面価格(GAKUMEN KAKAKU)	FACE VALUE
合併(GAPPEI)	BUSINESS COMBINATIONS
	MERGER
合併一取得（企業） GAPPEI-SHUTOKU (KIGYOO)	ACQUISITION (OF A COMPANY)

【き】

Japanese	English
機械及び装置(KIKAI OYOBI SOOCHI)	MACHINERY AND EQUIPMENT
機会原価(KIKAI GENKA)	OPPORTUNITY COST
期間(KIKAN)	TIMING
基金、資本（相互保険会社）KIKIN,SHIHON(SOOGO-HOKEN-GAISHA)	POLICYHOLDERS' EQUITY
棄権(KIKEN)	DISCLAIMER OF OPINION
既償却高(KI-SHOOKYAKU-DAKA)	ACCUMULATED DEPRECIATION
季節変動調整(KISETSU HENDOO CHOOSEI)	SEASONALLY ADJUSTED
起訴(KISO)	LITIGATION
規則(KISOKU)	RULES
基礎事実(KISO JIJITSU)	EVIDENTIAL MATTER
寄付(KIFU)	CHARITY EXPENSE
キャシュフロー(KYASSHU FUROO)	CASH FLOW
キャピタルタックス(KYAPITARU TAKKUSU)	CAPITAL TAX
救済債務(KYUUSAI SAIMU)	TROUBLED DEBT
求人費(KYUU-JIN-HI)	RECRUITING EXPENSE
給料、賃金(KYUURYOO, CHINJIN)	PAYROLL
	SALARIES AND WAGES
供給者(KYOOKYUU-SHA)	SUPPLIERS
共同監査人(KYOODOO KANSA-NIN)	AUDIT PARTNER
記録する(KIROKU SURU)	RECORD (VERB)
金庫株(KINKO-KABU)	TREASURY STOCK
金融会社(KINYUU-GAISHA)	FINANCIAL ENTITIES
ギャップ違反（一般に認められた会計原則）(GYAPPU IHAN)	DEPARTURE FROM A PRONOUNCEMENTS
業者への前渡金(GYOOSHA E NO MAEWATASHI-KIN)	ADVANCES TO SUPPLIERS
業務収入(GYOOMU SHUUNYUU)	INCOME FOR SERVICES RENDERED
銀行(GINKOO)	BANK
銀行借り入れ短期借入金(GINKOO KARI-IRE TANKI SHAKUNYUU-KIN)	SHORT-TERM BANK LOANS
銀行勘定調整(GINKOO KANJOO CHOOSEI)	BANK RECONCILIATION
銀行手数料(GINKOO-TESUURYOO)	BANK SERVICE CHARGES

【く】

Japanese	English
九月(KU-GATSU)	SEPTEMBER
繰り越し期間(KURIKOSHI KIKAN)	CARRYFORWARD PERIOD
繰延資産(KURINOBE SHISAN)	DEFERRED CHARGES
繰延税金(KURINOBE ZEIKIN)	DEFERRED TAXES
繰延前受利息(KURINOBE MAEUKE RISOKU)	UNEARNED INTERESTS
繰延利益(費用) KURINOBE RIEKI(HIYOO)	DEFERRED INCOME(EXPENSE)
繰り戻し(KURIMODOSHI)	CARRYBACK
繰り戻し期間(KURIMODOSHI KIKAN)	CARRYFORWARD PERIOD
偶発債務(GUUHATSU SAIMU)	CONTINGENCIES
偶発利益(GUUHATSU RIEKI)	GAIN CONTINGENCY
グループ(GURUUPU)	GROUP (OF COMPANIES)

【け】

Japanese	English
経営者への報告(KEIEI-SHA E NO HOOKOKU)	REPORT TO MANAGEMENT
経営陣の意図(KEIEI-JIN NO ITO)	MANAGEMENT INTENTION
経営組織(KEIEI SOSHIKI)	OPERATIONAL NETWORK
景気後退(KEIKI KOOTAI)	RECESSION
傾向(KEIKOO)	TREND
経済環境(KEIZAI KANKYOO)	ECONOMIC ENVIRONMENT
継続して適用する(KEIZOKU SHITE TEKIYOO SURU)	CONSISTENTLY APPLIED
継続性(KEIZOKUSEI)	CONSISTENCY
継続の原則(KEIZOKU NO GENSOKU)	GOING CONCERN
経費(KEIHI)	OVERHEAD EXPENSES
契約義務(KEIYAKU GIMU)	COMMITMENTS
計理士(KEIRI-SHI)	ACCOUNTANT
欠損の繰越(KESSON NO KURIKOSHI)	LOSS CARRY-FORWARD
検査(KENSA)	EXAMINE
建設仮勘定(KENSETSU KARIKANJOO)	CONSTRUCTION IN PROGRESS
限界原価(GENKAI GENKA)	MARGINAL COST
原価か時価(GENKA KA JIKA)	COST OR MARKET
減価償却一建物(GENKASHOOKYAKU-TATEMONO)	DEPRECIATION - BUILDINGS
減価償却費(GENKASHOOKYAKU-HI)	DEPRECIATION EXPENSE
減価償却累計額(GENKA SHOOKYAKU RUIKEI-GAKU)	ACCUMULATED AMORTIZATION
	ACCUMULATED DEPRECIATION
現金(GENKIN)	CASH

Japanese	English
現金及び預金(GENKIN OYOBI YOKIN)	CASH AND BANKS
現金配当(GENKIN HAITOO)	CASH DIVIDENDS
原材料(GENZAIRYO)	RAW MATERIALS
源泉課税(GENSEN KAZEI)	WITHHOLDING TAX
源泉課税額(GENSEN KAZEI-GAKU)	WITHHELD TAXES
現地通貨(GENCHI TSUUKA)	LOCAL CURRENCY
限定(意見)[GENTEI (IKEN)]	QUALIFICATION(OF AN AUDIT OPINION)
現預金(GENYOKIN)	CASH EQUIVALENTS
原料（資材） GENRYOO(SHIZAI)	MATERIALS (SUST.)

【こ】

Japanese	English
効果(KOOKA)	EFFECT
公開(KOOKAI)	DISCLOSURE
公共部門(KOOKYOO-BUMON)	PUBLIC SECTOR
工業(KOOGYOO)	INDUSTRY
工具、器具、備品(KOOGU-KIGU-BIHIN)	FURNITURE AND FIXTURES
広告宣伝費(KOOKOKU SENDEN-HI)	PROMOTIONAL COSTS
交際費(KOOSAI-HI)	ENTERTAINMENT EXPENSE
工事完成基準(KOOJI KANSEI KIJUN)	COMPLETED-CONTRACT METHOD
工事進行基準(KOOJI SHINKOO KIJUN)	PERCENTAGE-OF-COMPLETION-METHOD
購入要望書(KOONYUU YOOBOOSHO)	PURCHASE REQUISITION
後発事象(KOOHATSU JISHOO)	SUBSEQUENT EVENTS
子会社(KO-GAISHA)	SUBSIDIARY
顧客(KOKYAKU)	CUSTOMERS
国際貿易(KOKUSAI BOOEKI)	INTERNATIONAL TRADE
国内子会社(KOKUNAI KO-GAISHA)	DOMESTIC SUBSIDIARIES
国民総生産(KOKUMIN SOO-SEISAN)	GROSS NATIONAL PRODUCT
小口現金(KOGUCHI GENKIN)	PETTY CASH
個人所得税(KOJIN SHOTOKU-ZEI)	PERSONAL INCOME TAX
固定資産(KOTEI SHISAN)	FIXED ASSETS
	NON-CURRENT ASSETS
固定資産処分益(KOTEI SHISAN SHOBUN-EKI)	GAIN ON SALE OF FIXED ASSETS
固定負債(KOTEI FUSAI)	NON-CURRENT LIABILITIES
顧問業務(KOMON GYOOMU)	CONSULTING SERVICES
根抵当(KON-TEITOO)	COLLATERAL
合同企業体(GOODOO KIGYOO-TAI)	JOINT VENTURE
五月(GO-GATSU)	MAY
誤謬(GOBYUU)	ERRORS

【さ】

Japanese	English
債券(SAI-KEN)	BOND
再購入契約(SAI-KOO NYUU KEIYAKU)	REPURCHASE AGREEMENT
再生産費(SAI-SEISAN-HI)	REPRODUCTION COST
再調達原価(SAI-CHOOTATSU GENKA)	REPLACEMENT COST
再販売契約(SAI-HANBAI KEIYAKU)	RESALE AGREEMENTS
再販売用商品(SAI-HANBAI-YOO SHOOHIN)	RESALE MERCHANDISE
再評価(SAIHYOOKA)	REVALUATION
再評価剰余金(SAI-HYOOKA JOOYOKIN)	REVALUATION SURPLUS
再保険と保険料調整(SAIHOKEN TO HOKEN-RYOO CHOOSEI)	REINSURANCE AND PREMIUM ADJUSTMENTS
債務の繰上返還(SAIMU NO KURIAGE HENKIN)	EARLY EXTINGUISHMENT OF DEBT
債務の再構成(SAIMU NO SAI-KOOSEI)	DEBT RESTRUCTURING
再割引手形(SAIWARIBIKI TEGATA)	REDISCOUNTED NOTES
先入先出法(SAKIIRE SAKIDASHI-HOO)	FIRST IN, FIRST OUT(FIFO)
先物契約(SAKIMONO KEIYAKU)	FUTURE CONTRACTS
三月(SAN-GATSU)	MARCH
産業(SANGYOO)	INDUSTRY
算術級数法(SANJUTSU KYUUSUU-HOO)	SUM OF THE YEARS'-DIGITS METHOD
酸性比率(SANSEI HIRITSU)	ACID TEST RATIO
酸性比率分析(SANSEI HIRITSU BUNSEKI)	ACID TEST
在職証明(ZAISHOKU SHOOMEI)	CERTIFICATE OF GOOD STANDING
財政(ZAISEI)	FINANCE
財政状態変動表(ZAISEI JOOTAI HENDOOHYOO)	STATEMENT OF CHANGES IN FIN'L POSITION
財務諸表(ZAIMUSHOHYOO)	FINANCIAL STATEMENTS
財務諸表項目の監査手続(ZAIMU SHOHYOO KOOMOKU NO KANSA TEJUN)	SUBSTANTIVE TEST
財務諸表注記(ZAIMU SHOHYOO CHUUKI)	FOOTNOTES TO THE FINANCIAL STATEMENTS
財務諸表の再考査(ZAIMU SHOHYOO NO SAI-KOOSA)	REVIEW OF FINANCIAL STATEMENTS
財務諸表の編集(ZAIMUSHOHYOO NO HENSHUU)	COMPILATION OF FINANCIAL STATEMENTS
材料購入副費-運搬(ZAIRYOO KOONYUU FUKUHI-UNPAN)	FREIGHT ON PURCHASES OF MATERIALS
残高確認状(ZANDAKA KAKUNIN-JOO)	CONFIRMATION OF ACCOUNTS

【し】

Japanese	English
仕掛品(SHIKAKE-HIN)	GOODS IN PROCESS
四月(SHIGATSU)	APRIL

Japanese	English
私企業 (SHIKIGYOO)	PRIVATE SECTOR
資金 (SHIKIN)	FUNDS
資金運用表 (SHIKIN UNYOO-HYOO)	STATEMENT OF SOURCES & USES OF FUNDS
資金収支 (SHIKIN SHUUSHI)	CASH FLOW
資金調達 (SHIKIN CHOOTATSU)	REFINANCING
資金の運用 (SHIKIN NO UNYOO)	USES OF FUNDS
資金の源泉 (SHIKIN NO GENSEN)	SOURCES OF FUNDS
試験 (SHIKEN)	TEST
試験研究費 (SHIKEN KENKYUU-HI)	RESEARCH AND DEVELOPMENT COSTS
資産 (SHISAN)	ASSETS
資産売却所得税 (SHISAN BAIKYAKU SHOTOKU-ZEI)	CAPITAL GAINS TAX
試算表 (SHISAN-HYOO)	TRIAL BALANCE
市場価格 (SHIJOO-KAKAKU)	MARKET PRICE
市場性のある株式 (SHIJOOSEI NO ARU KABUSHIKI)	MARKETABLE STOCKS
市場性のある有価証券 (SHIJOOSEI NO ARU YUUKA SHOOKEN)	MARKETABLE SECURITIES
従う (SHITAGAU)	COMPLY WITH
七月 (SHICHIGATSU)	JULY
市中銀行 (SHICHUUN-GINKOO)	COMMERCIAL BANK
支払い (SHIHARAI)	DISBURSEMENTS
	PAYMENTS
支払期限の過ぎた (SHIHARAI KIGEN NO SUGITA)	OVERDUE
支払い周期 (SHIHARAI SHUUKI)	PAYMENTS CYCLE
支払承諾見返う (SHIHARAI SHOODAKU MIKAERI)	CUSTOMERS' LIABILIT FOR ACCEPTANCES
支払準備金 (SHIHARAI JUNBIKIN)	RESERVE FOR O/S CLAIMS AND LOSSES
支払手形 (SHIHARAI TEGATA)	NOTES PAYABLE
支払利息 (SHIHARAI RISOKU)	INTEREST EXPENSE
支払利息の資産原価算入 (SHIHARAI-RISOKU NO SHISANGENKASANNYUU)	CAPITALIZATION OF INTEREST EXPENSES
四半期 (SHIHAN-KI)	QUARTER
四半期の (SHIHAN-KI NO)	QUARTERLY
四半期報告書 (SHIHAN-KI HOOKOKUSHO)	QUARTERLY FINANCIAL STATEMENTS
資本 (SHIHON)	SHAREHOLDERS' EQUITY
資本金 (SHIHON-KIN)	CAPITAL STOCK
資本再評価準備金 (SHIHON SAI-HYOOKA JUNBI-KIN)	REVALUATION RESERVE
資本準備金 (SHIHON JUNBI-KIN)	PREMIUM ON ISSUE OF CAPITAL
資本の部 (SHIHON NO BU)	STOCKHOLDERS' EQUITY
資本剰余金 (SHIHON JOOYO-KIN)	CAPITAL SURPLUS
社員教育費 (SHA-IN KYOOIKU-HI)	TRAINING EXPENDITURE
社会保障費 (SHAKAI HOSHOO-HI)	SOCIAL SECURITY EXPENSE

Japanese	English
借地契約 (SHAKUCHI-KEIYAKU)	LEASE
借地人 (SHAKUCHI-NIN)	LESSEE
借用証書 (SHAKUYOO-SHOOSHO)	BOND
社債 (SHA-SAI)	BOND
	BONDS PAYABLE
車輌 (SHARYOO)	VEHICLES
謝礼 (SHAREI)	FEES
集金 (SHUUKIN)	COLLECTIONS
修繕と維持 (SHUUZEN TO IJI)	REPAIRS AND MAINTENANCE
修理 (SHUURI)	REPAIRS
取得価格 (SHUTOKU-KAKAKU)	ACQUISITION COST
取得原価 (SHUTOKU GENKA)	HISTORICAL COST
主要財務情報 (SHUYOO ZAIMUJOOHOO)	FINANCIAL SUMMARY
主要な顧客 (SHUYOO NA KOKYAKU)	MAJOR CUSTOMERS
償還券付優先株 (SHOOKAN-KEN-TSUKI YUUSEN-KABU)	REDEEMABLE PREFERRED STOCK
償還できる (SHOOKAN DEKIRU)	REDEEMABLE
償却条件 (SHOOKYAKU JOOKEN)	REDEMPTION FEATURES
消極的暖簾 (SHOOKYOKU-TEKI NOREN)	NEGATIVE GOODWILL
商業貸付 (SHOOGYOO-KASHITSUKE)	COMMERCIAL & INDUSTRIAL LOAN
商業銀行 (SHOOGYOO-GINKOO)	COMMERCIAL BANK
証券会社 (SHOOKEN GAISHA)	INVESTMENT BANK/MERCHANT BANK
証券取引所 (SHOOKEN TORIHIKISHO)	STOCK EXCHANGE
小数株主持分 (SHOOSUU KABUNNUSHI MOCHIBUN)	MINORITY INTEREST
消費税 (SHOOHI-ZEI)	EXCISE TAX
商標権 (SHOOHYOO-KEN)	TRADE MARKS
商品有価証券売買益（損）SHOOHIN YUUKA SHOOKEN BAIBAI-EKI (SON)	TRADING ACCOUT PROFITS (LOSSES)
正味売上金 (SHOOMI URIAGE-KIN)	NET TRADE ACCOUNTS RECEIVABLE
正味現在価値 (SHOOMI GENZAI KACHI)	NET PRESENT VALUE
正味実現可能価額 (SHOOMI JITSUGEN-KANOO KAKAKU)	NET REALIZABLE VALUE
正味保険料収入 (SHOOMI HOKEN-RYOO SHUUNYUU)	NET PREMIUMS EARNED
正味有形固定資産 (SHOOMI YUUKEI KOTEI SHISAN)	NET FIXED ASSETS
消耗品と予備部分品 (SHOOMOO-HIN TO YOBI BUBUN-HIN)	SUPPLIES AND SPARE PARTS
証文 (SHOO-MON)	BOND
職員 (SHOKU-IN)	OFFICER
所得税 (SHOTOKU-ZEI)	INCOME TAX
処分 (SHOBUN)	DISPOSITION
処分利益余剰金 (SHOBUN RIEKI YOJOOKIN)	APPROPRIATED RETAINED EARNINGS
仕訳 (SHIWAKE)	JOURNAL ENTRY

Japanese	English
仕訳帳(SHIWAKE-CHOO)	JOURNAL
シンジケートローン(SHINJIKEETO ROON)	SYNDICATED LOANS
信託証券(SHINTAKU SHOOKEN)	TRUST SECURITIES
信託報酬益(SHINTAKU HOOSHUU-EKI)	TRUST OPERATIONS PROFITS (LOSSES)
時価(JIKA)	MARKET PRICE
自家保険(JIKA-HOKEN)	SELF-INSURANCE
事業費(JIGYOO-HI)	COST OF SERVICES RENDERED
事業部門別(JIGYOO-BUMON-BETSU)	BUSINESS SEGMENT
自己株式(JIKO KABUSHIKI)	TREASURY STOCK
自己資本(JIKO-SHIHON)	NET WORTH
自己資本利益率(JIKO SHIHON RIEKI-RITSU)	RETURN ON EQUITY
持参人(小切手ー手形の) JISAN-NIN(KOGITTE-TEGATA NO)	BEARER
実現可能かどうかの調査(JITSUGEN KANOO KA DOOKA NO CHOOSA)	FEASIBILITY STUDY
実行出来る可能性(JIKKOO DEKIRU KANOOSEI)	FEASIBILITY
事務用品(JIMU-YOOHIN)	OFFICE SUPPLIES
十一月(JUUICHI-GATSU)	NOVEMBER
十億(JUU-OKU)	BILLIONS
十月(JUU-GATSU)	OCTOBER
従業員(JYUUGYOO-IN)	EMPLOYEE
従属債務(JUUZOKU SAIMU)	SUBORDINATED DEBT
重大な(JUUDAI NA)	MATERIAL (SIGNIFICANT)
重役(JUUYAKU)	DIRECTORS
重要性(JUUYOO-SEI)	MATERIALITY
純売上高(JUN-URIAGE-DAKA)	NET SALES
〜に準拠し(NI JUNKYO SHI)	IN ACCORDANCE WITH
純利益(JUN-RIEKI)	NET INCOME
状況(JYOOKYOO)	CIRCUMSTANCES
〜を条件とする(O JOOKEN TO SURU)	SUBJECT TO
上場社債ー現地通貨による(JOOJOO-SHASAI-GENCHI TSUUKA NI YORU)	LISTED BONDS-LOCAL CURRENCY
剰余金(JOOYO-KIN)	RETAINED EARNINGS
剰余金（相互保険会社）JOOYO-KIN(SOOGO-HOKEN-GAISHA)	POLICYHOLDERS' SURPLUS
条例、規則(JOOREI KISOKU)	REGULATIONS
人口(JINKOO)	POPULATION

【す】

Japanese	English
スットックオプション(SUTOKKU OPUSSHON)	STOCK OPTION PLANS

【せ】

Japanese	English
生産原価(SEISAN GENKA)	PRODUCTION COST
生産工程順序一覧表(SEISAN KOOTEI JUNJO ICHIRAN-HYOO)	FLOWCHART
生産周期(SEISAN SHUUKI)	PRODUCTION CYCLE
生産順序(SEISAN JUNJO)	PRODUCTION ORDER
生産高比例法(SEISAN-DAKA HIREI-HOO)	UNITS OF PRODUCTION
生産能力(SEISAN NOORYOKU)	PRODUCTION CAPACITY
製品(SEIHIN)	FINISHED GOODS
製品原価(SEIHIN GENKA)	PRODUCTION COST
製品販売(SEIHIN HANBAI)	SALE OF MANUFACTURED GOODS
生命保険(SEIMEI HOKEN)	LIFE INSURANCE
生命保険金(SEIMEI-HOKEN-KIN)	LIFE POLICY BENEFITS
誓約(SEIYAKU)	PLEDGE
節税(SETSU-ZEI)	TAX SAVINGS
千(SEN)	THOUSANDS
専門家基準(SENMON-KA KIJUN)	PROFESSIONAL STANDARDS
専門家による判断(SENMONKA NI YORU HANDAN)	PROFESSIONAL JUDGMENT
税額減免(ZEIGAKU GENMEN)	TAX CREDITS
税金(ZEIKIN)	TAX
税効果期間配分額(ZEIKOOKA KIKAN HAIBUNGAKU)	DEFERRED INCOME TAX
税務監査(ZEIMU KANSA)	TAX AUDIT
税務署(ZEIMU-SHO)	TAX AUTHORITIES
税率(ZEI-RITSU)	TAX RATES
ゼロー クーポン債券(ZERO KUUPON SAI-KEN)	ZERO COUPON BONDS
ゼロベース予算(ZERO BEESU YOSAN)	ZERO BASE BUDGET
前期損益修正(ZENKI SON-EKI SHUUSEI)	PRIOR PERIOD ADJUSTMENTS
全体としてとらえる(ZENTAI TO SHITE TORAERU)	TAKEN AS A WHOLE

【そ】

Japanese	English
総売上高(SOO-URIAGE-DAKA)	SALES (TURNOVER)
総勘定元帳(SOO-KANJOO MOTOCHOO)	GENERAL LEDGER
早期隠退(SOOKI INTAI)	EARLY RETIREMENT
倉庫(SOOKO)	WAREHOUSE
相殺(SOOSAI)	OFFSET
総資本収益率(SOO-SHIHON SHUUEKI-RITSU)	RETURN ON ASSETS
総資本純運転資本率(SOOSHIHON JUN-UNTEN SHIHON-RITSU)	WORKING CAPITAL RATIO

Japanese	English
相続税(SOOZOKU-ZEI)	INHERITANCE TAX
総保険料収入(SOOHOKEN-RYOO SHUUNYUU)	TOTAL PREMIUMS WRITTEN
創立費(SOORITSU-HI)	ORGANIZATION EXPENSES
組識図(SOSHIKI-ZU)	ORGANIZATION CHART
訴訟(SOSHOO)	LITIGATION
その他の営業利益（損失）SONO TA NO EIGYOO RIEKI (SONSHITSU)	OTHER OPERATING INCOME(EXPENSES)
その他の貸付金(SONO TA NO KASHITSUKE-KIN)	OTHER LOANS
その他の業務利益(SONO TA NO GYOOMU RIEKI)	OTHER INCOME FOR SERVICES
損益計算書(SONEKI KEISAN-SHO)	PROFIT & LOSS ACCOUNTS
損益分岐点(SONEKI-BUNKI-TEN)	BREAK EVEN POINT
損益法(SON-EKI-HOO)	DEFERRAL METHOD
損害保険(SONGAI HOKEN)	GENERAL INSURANCE
損失(SONSHITSU)	LOSS
損失額(SONSHITSU-GAKU)	LOSS
増資(ZOOSHI)	CAPITAL INCREASE
増資に伴う費用(ZOOSHI NI TOMONAU HIYOO)	EXPENSES ON CAPITAL INCREASE
【た】	
貸借対照表(TAISHAKU-TAISHOO-HYOO)	BALANCE SHEET
貸借対照表の日付(TAISHAKU-TAISHOO-HYOO NO HIZUKE)	BALANCE SHEET DATE
貸出金償却(TAISHUTSU-KIN SHOOKYAKU)	ACTUAL LOAN LOSSES
退職給与(TAISHOKU KYUUYO)	SEVERANCE INDEMNITIES
退職年金(TAISHOKU NENKIN)	POST RETIREMENT BENEFITS
耐用年数(TAI-YOO NENSUU)	USEFUL LIFE (OF AN ASSET)
他国籍企業(TAKOKU-SEKI KIGYOO)	MULTINATIONAL ENTERPRISE
建物、構築物(TATEMONO,KOOCHIKU-BUTSU)	BUILDINGS STRUCTURES
棚卸し資産(TANAOROSHI SHISAN)	INVENTORIES -(USA) (STOCKS-UK)
棚卸し資産回転率(TANAOROSHI SHISAN KAITEN-RITSU)	INVENTORY TURNOVER RATIO
棚卸資産継続記録法(TANAOROSHI SHISAN KEIZOKU KIROKU-HOO)	PERPETUAL INVENTORY
棚卸資産の実地棚卸(TANA-OROSHI SHISAN NO JICCHI TANAOROSHI)	PHYSICAL INVENTOR
他の事情が同じならば(TANO JIJOO GA ONAJI NARABA)	CETERIS PARIBUS
短期貸付金(TANKI KASHITSUKE-KIN)	SHORT-TERM LOANS
短期投資(TANKI TOOSHI)	SHORT-TERM INVESTMENTS
担保(TANPO)	COLLATERAL
担保付き支払手形(TANPO-TSUKI SHIHARAI TEGATA)	SECURED NOTE
代案(DAIAN)	ALTERNATIVE PROCEDURES
第一次資本(DAI-ICHIJI SHIHON)	PRIMARY CAPITAL

Japanese	English
代表監査人(DAIHYOO KANSA-NIN)	AUDIT MANAGER
代表取締役(DAIHYOO-TORISHIMARI-YAKU)	CHIEF EXECUTIVE OFFICER
代理権(DAIRI-KEN)	PROXY (POWER OF ATTORNEY)
【ち】	
中間財務諸表(CHUUKAN ZAIMU SHOHYOO)	INTERIM FINANCIAL STATEMENTS
仲裁期間(SHUUSAI KIKAN)	INTERVENING PERIOD
長期契約(CHOOKI KEIYAKU)	LONG-TERM CONTRACTS
長期借入金(CHOOKI-SHAKUNYUU-KIN)	LONG-TERM DEBT
長期借入金返済(CHOOKI SHAKUNYUU-KIN HENSAI)	LONG TERM DEBT RETIRED
長期信用(CHOOKI SHINYOO)	LONG-TERM CREDITS
長期投資(CHOOKI TOOSHI)	LONG-TERM INVESTMENTS
長期保険契約に係わる準備金繰入(CHOOKI HOKEN-KEIYAKU NI KAKAWARU JUNBI KURIIRO)	LONG TERM INSUANCE RESERVE CHARG
徴収(CHOOSHUU)	COLLECTIONS
徴収率(CHOOSHUU-RITSU)	COLLECTION RATIO
調整(CHOOSEI)	ADJUSTMENT
帳簿価格(CHOOBO-KAKAKU)	BOOK VALUE
帳簿価値低下(CHOOBO KACHI TEIKA)	WRITE DOWN
直接費用(CHOKUSETSU HIYOO)	DIRECT COST
直線法(CHOKUSEN-HOO)	STRAIGHT-LINE METHOD
著作権(CHOSAKU-KEN)	COPYRIGHT
賃借人(CHINSHAKU-NIN)	LESSEE
賃貸借(CHINTAISHAKU)	LEASE
賃貸人(CHINTAI-NIN)	LESSOR
陳腐化(CHINPU-KA)	OBSOLESCENCE
【つ】	
通信費(TSUUSHIN-HI)	COMMUNICATIONS EXPENSE
通知預金(TSUUCHI YOKIN)	SAVING DEPOSITS
月の（月間の） TSUKINO (GEKKAN NO)	MONTHLY
付ける（値を） TSUKERU(NE O)	BID (VERB)
【て】	
低価法(TEEKA-HOO)	LOWER OF COST OR MARKET

Japanese	English
定額法(TEIGAKU-HOO)	STRAIGHT-LINE METHOD
定期購読契約(TEIKI KOODOKU KEIYAKU)	SUBSCRIPTION
定期預金(TEIKI YOKIN)	TIME DEPOSITS
逓減税(TEIGEN-ZEI)	REGRESSIVE TAX
定時株主総会(TEIJI KABUNUSHI-SOOKAI)	ANNUAL SHAREHOLDERS' MEETING
抵当権付き(TEITOO-KEN-TSUKI)	MORTGAGE
抵当物件(TEITOO BUKKEN)	PLEDGING REQUIREMENTS
定率法(TEIRITSU-HOO)	ACCELERATED DEPRECIATION
適正(意見) TEKISEI (IKEN)	UNQUALIFIED (OPINION)
適正に表示する(TEKISEI NI HYOOJI-SURU)	FAIRLY PRESENT
手数料益(損) TESUURYOO-EKI(SON)	COMMISSIONS & FEES PROFITS(EXPENSES)
テスト(TESUTO)	TESTS
転換社債(TENKAN SHASAI)	CONVERTIBLE DEBT
展示会出展費(TENJI-KAI SHUTTEN-HI)	EXHIBITIONS AND EVENTS EXPENPENSES
転貸(TENTAI)	SUBLET
データ処理装置(DEETA SHORI SOOCHI)	DATA PROCESSING EQUIPMENT

【と】

Japanese	English
当期純利益(TOOKI JUN-RIEKI)	NET INCOME (LOSS) OF THE PERIOD
統計上の標本抽出(TOOKEI-JOO NO HYOOHON CHUUSHUTSU)	STATISTICAL SAMPLING
倒産(TOOSAN)	BANKRUPTCY
当座貸越(TOOZA-KASHIKOSHI)	BANK OVERDRAFATS
	OVERDRAFT
当座預金、普通預金(TOOZA-YOKIN, FUTSUU-YOKIN)	DEMAND DEPOSITS
投資(TOOSHI)	INVESTMENT
投資再評価引当金(TOOSHI SAIHYOOKA HIKIATE-KIN)	ALLOWANCE FOR DEVALUATION OF INVESTMENTS
投資資産の構成(TOOSHI-SHISAN NO KOOSEI)	PORTFOLIO COMPOSITION
投資税額控除(TOOSHI ZEIGAKU KOOJO)	INVESTMENT TAX CREDIT
投資有価証券益(損) TOOSHI YUUKA SHOOKEN-EKI(SON)	INVESTMENT SECURITIES GAINS(LOSSES)
特大の(TOKUDAINO)	OVERSIZE(D)
特別損益項目(TOKUBETSU SONEKI KOOMOKU)	EXTRAORDINARY ITEMS
特別報告書(TOKUBETSU HOOKOKU)	SPECIAL REPORTS
特別法上の引当金(TOKUBETSU-HOO-JOO NO HIKIATE-KIN)	STATUTORY RESERVE
特別ボーナス(TOKUBETSU BOONASU)	SPECIAL BONUS
土地(TOCHI)	LAND
土地改良費(TOCHI KAIRYOO-HI)	LAND IMPROVEMENTS
特許権(TOKKYO-KEN)	PATENTS

Japanese	English
とても起こりそうにない(TOTEMO OKORISOO NINAI)	REMOTE
取引(TORIHIKI)	TRANSACTIONS
取引会社(TORIHIKI-GAISHA)	CORRESPONDENT FIRMS
独立性(DOKURITSU-SEI)	INDEPENDENCE
ドル(DORU)	DOLLARS

【な】

Japanese	English
内規(NAIKI)	COMPANY BY-LAWS
内部監査(NAIBU KANSA)	INTERNAL AUDITORS
内部統制質問書(NAIBU TOOSEI SHITSUMON-SHO)	INTERNAL CONTROL QUESTIONNAIRES
内部統制制度(NAIBU TOOSEI SEIDO)	INTERNAL CONTROLS
内部統制における弱点(NAIBU-TOOSEI NI OKERU JAKUTEN)	CONTROL WEAKNESS

【に】

Japanese	English
二月(NIGATSU)	FEBRUARY
二重課税(NIJUU-KAZEI)	DOUBLE TAXATION
二度目の催促(NIDO ME NO SAISOKU)	SECOND REQUEST
入札(NYUUSATSU)	BID

【ね】

Japanese	English
年金(NEN-KIN)	PENSION
年金制度(NENKIN SEIDO)	PENSION PLAN
年次定例会(NENJI TEIREI-KAI)	ANNUAL MEETING
一年に一度の(NEN NI ICHIDO NO)	ANNUALLY

【の】

Japanese	English
納税者(NOOZEI-SHA)	TAXPAYER
納税報告書(NOOZEI HOOKOKU-SHO)	TAX RETURN
～を除いては(O NOZOITE WA)	EXCEPT FOR
暖簾(NOREN)	GOODWILL

【は】

廃止事業(HAISHI JIGYOO)	DISCONTINUED OPERATIONS
配置(HAICHI)	PLACEMENT
配当金(HAITOO-KIN)	DIVIDEND
破産(HASAN)	BANKRUPTCY
八月(HACHI-GATSU)	AUGUST
発行済株式(HAKKOO-ZUMI KABUSHIKI)	OUTSTANDING SHARES
発生(HASSEI)	ACCRUAL
発生基準(HASSEI-KIJUN)	ACCRUAL (ACCT METHOD)
払い込み剰余金(HARAIKOMI JOOYOKIN)	PAID IN CAPITAL
払い戻し(HARAI MODOSHI)	REFUND
範囲(HAN' I)	EXTENT
	SCOPE
範囲区分(HAN' I-KUBUN)	SCOPE PARAGRAPH
半製品(HANSEIHIN)	SEMI-FINISHED GOODS
販売原価(HANBAI GENKA)	COST OF SALES
販売費(HANBAI-HI)	SELLING EXPENSES
販売費及び一般管理費(HANBAI-HI OYOBI IPPPAN KANRI-HI)	GENERAL AND ADMINISTRATIVE EXPENSES
売却(BAIKYAKU)	DISPOSITION
場外取引(BAGAI TORIKI)	OVER THE COUNTER TRANSACTION
罰金(BAKKIN)	FINE
パートナー(PAARTONAA)	PARTNER
パテント(PATENTO)	PATENTS

【ひ】

非営利（法人） HI-EIRI (HOOJIN)	NON-PROFIT
比較財務諸表(HIKAKU ZAIMU SHOHYOO)	COMPARATIVE FINANCIAL STATEMENTS
非課税収益(HIKAZEI SHUUEKI)	NON-TAXABLE INCOME
引当金(HIKIATEKIN)	ALLOWANCE
	PROVISION
非償還付優先株(HISHOOKAN-TSUKI YUUSEN-KABU)	NON-REDEEMABLE PREFERRED STOCKS
一株当り純利益(HITOKABU ATARI JUNRIEKI)	EARNINGS PER SHARE
一株当り配当額(HITOKABU ATARI HAITOOGAKU)	DIVIDEND PER SHARE
一株当り利益(HITOKABU ATARA RIEKI)	EARNINGS PER SHARE
百(HYAKU)	HUNDREDS
百分率(HYAKUBUN-RITSU)	PERCENTAGE
百万(HYAKU-MAN)	MILLIONS

評価基準(HYOOKA KIJUN)	VALUATION PRINCIPLES
評価方法(HYOOKA HOOHOO)	VALUATION PRINCIPLES
標準原価(HYOOJUN GENKA)	STANDARD COST
標本規模(HYOOHON KIBO)	SAMPLE SIZE
標本抽出(HYOOHON CHUUSHUTSU)	SAMPLING
標本抽出の結果(HYOOHON CHUUSHUTSU NO KEKKA)	SAMPLING RESULTS
標本抽出リスク(HYOOHON CHUUSHUTSU RISUKU)	SAMPLING RISK
費用(HIYOO)	EXPENSES
品質管理(HINSHITSU KANRI)	QUALITY CONTROL
品質保証(HINSHITSU HOSHOO)	PRODUCT WARRANTIES
備品(BIHIN)	FITTINGS

【ふ】

付加価値税（バット）FUKAKACHI-ZEI(BATTO)	VALUE ADDED TAX (VAT)
副会長(FUKU-KAICHOO)	VICE-CHAIRMAN
副産物(FUKUSAN-BUTSU)	BY-PRODUCTS
福利厚生(FUKURI KOOSEI)	EMPLOYEE BENEFITS
符号をつける(FUGOO O TSUKERU)	CODE (VERB)
負債(FUSAI)	LIABILITY
負債比率(FUSAI HIRITSU)	INDEBTNESS RATIO
普通株(FUTSUU-KABU)	COMMON STOCK
不適正意見(FUTEKISEI IKEN)	ADVERSE OPINION
不動産と抵当権付きローン(FUDOOSAN TO TEITOO-KEN-TSUKI ROON)	REAL ESTATE AND MORTGAGE LOANS
浮動レート(FUDOO-REETO)	FLOATING RATE
扶養家族(FUYOO KAZOKU)	DEPENDENTS
フローチャート(FUROO-CHAATO)	FLOWCHART
部長（支店長）(BUCHOO(SHITENCHOO))	GENERAL MANAGER
物品税(BUPPIN-ZEI)	SALES TAX
分割(BUNKATSU)	SPLIT (OF A COMPANY)
分析再調査(BUNSEKI SAI-CHOOSA)	ANALYTICAL REVIEW
プーリングーオブーインタレスト方式[PUURINGU OBU INTARESUTO HOOSHIKI]	POOLING OF INTEREST METHOD

【へ】

平均(HEIKIN)	AVERAGE
変則(HENSOKU)	IRREGULARITY
変動費(HENDOO-HI)	VARIABLE COST

【べ】

米国証券取引委員会 (BEIKOKU SHOOKEN TORIHIKI IIN-KAI)	SECURITIES AND EXCHANGE COMMISSION
弁護士 (BENGO-SHI)	LAWYER

【ほ】

報告 (HOOKOKU)	REPORT
法人税 (HOOJIN-ZEI)	INCOME TAX
包装材料 (HOOSOO ZAIRYOO)	PACKAGING MATERIAL
法定監査報告書 (HOOTEI KANSA HOOKOKU-SHO)	STATUTORY AUDIT REPORT
法定準備金 (HOOTEI JUNBI-KIN)	LEGAL RESERVE
法律上の必要条件 (HOORITSU-JOO NO HITSUYOO JOOKEN)	LEGAL REQUIREMENTS
保管有価証券 (HOKAN YUUKASHOOKEN)	CUSTODY SECURITIES
保険会社 (HOKEN-GAISHA)	INSURANCE COMPANY
保険数理原価 (HOKENSUURI GENKA)	ACTUARIAL VALUE
保険手数料 (HOKEN TESUU-RYOO)	UNDERWRITING AND POLICY ADQ. COSTS
保険料 (HOKENRYOO)	PREMIUM
保証 (HOSHOO)	GUARANTEES
補償 (HOSHOO)	INDEMNITIES
保証金 (HOSHOO-KIN)	GUARANTEE DEPOSITS
補助記録 (HOJO KIROKU)	SUBSIDIARY RECORDS
補足財務情報 (HOJO ZAIMU JOOHOO)	SUPPLEMENTARY INFORMATION
本質 (HONSHITSU)	NATURE
母集団 (BO-SHUUDAN)	POPULATION (IN A STATIST. ENVIRONMENT)

【ま】

前受収益 (MAEUKE SHUUEKI)	DEFERRED INCOME
前払資用 (MAEBARAI SHIYOO)	PREPAID EXPENSE
前払費用 (MAEBARAI HIYOO)	PREPAID EXPENSE
まぎらわしい情報 (MAGIRAWASHII JOOHOO)	MISLEADING INFORMATION
マネージメントによる誓約書 (MANEEGIMENTO NI YORU SEIYAKUSHO)	CLIENT REPRESENTATION LETTER
満期 (MANKI)	MATURITY
満期日 (MANKIJITSU)	DUE DATE
満期となったローン (MANKI TO NATTA ROON)	MATURED LOANS

【み】

未確定事項 (MIKAKUTEI JIKOO)	UNCERTAINTY
未監査 (MIKANSA)	UNAUDITED
未収収益 (MISHUU-SHUUEKI)	ACCRUED INCOME
未収利息 (MISHUU RISOKU)	INTEREST RECEIVABLE
未償却割増し金 (MISHOOKYAKU WARIMASHI-KIN)	UNAMORTIZED PREMIUM
未処理分利益金 (MISHORI-BUN RIEKI-KIN)	UNAPPROPRIATED RETAINED EARNINGS
未請求支払請求 (MISEIKYUU SHIHARAI SEIKYUU)	UNASSERTED CLAIM
見積り残存価格 (MITSUMORI ZANZON KAKAKU)	EXPECTED SALVAGE VALUE
未払配当金 (MIHARAI HAITOO-KIN)	DIVIDENDS PAYABLE
未払費用 (MIHARAI HIYOO)	ACCRUED EXPENSES
	ACCRUED LIABILITIES
未払法人税 (MIHARAI-HOOJIN-ZEI)	ACCRUED TAXES
未払利息 (MIHARAI RISOKU)	INTEREST PAYABLE

【む】

無形固定資産 (MUKEI KOTEI SHISAN)	INTANGIBLE ASSETS
無形資産 (MUKEI SHISAN)	INTANGIBLE ASSETS
無作為 (MUSAKUI)	RANDOM
無作為に (MUSAKUI NI)	AT RANDOM
無償株式配当 (MUSHOO KABUSHIKI HAITOO)	STOCK DIVIDENDS
無担保債券 (MUTANPO SAIKEN)	UNSECURED BONDS
無担保社債 (MUTANPO SHASAI)	DEBENTURE

【め】

免許 (MENKYO)	LICENCES

【も】

目次 (MOKUJI)	CONTENTS
持分 (MOCHIBUN)	EQUITY IN OTHER COMPANIES
持株会社 (MOCHIKABU GAISHA)	HOLDING COMPANY
持分法 (MOCHIBUN-HOO)	EQUITY METHOD
持分法による損失 (MOCHIBUN-HOO NI YORU SONSHITSU)	SHARE IN LOSS OF AFFILIATES
元帳への転記 (MOTO-CHO E NO TENKI)	POST ENTRIES TO THE LEDGER

【や】

役員会(YAKU-IN-KAI)	BOARD OF DIRECTORS

【ゆ】

有給休暇(YUUKYUU KYUUKA)	COMPENSATED ABSENCES
有給休暇引当金(YUUKYUU-KYUUKA HIKIATE-KIN)	ACCRUED VACATIONS
有形固定資産(YUUKEI KOTEI SHISAN)	TANGIBLE FIXED ASSETS
融資協定(YUUSHI KYOOTEI)	FINANCING ARRANGEMENT
融資する(YUUSHI SURU)	FINANCE (VERB)
融資枠(YUUSHIWAKU)	CREDIT LINE
優先株(YUUSEN-KABU)	PREFERRED SHARE (USA)
優先債務(YUUSEN SAIMU)	SENIOR DEBT
有望な(YUUBOO NA)	PROBABLE
輸出(YUSHUTSU)	EXPORT
輸入関税(YUNYUU KANZEI)	EXPORT DUTIES
輸入税(YUNYUU-ZEI)	IMPORT SURCHARGES

【よ】

要求(YOOKYUU)	CLAIMS
様式(YOOSHIKI)	FORM
要約財務諸表(YOOYAKU ZAIMUSHOHYOO)	CONDENSED FINANCIAL STATEMENTS
要約財務情報(YOOYAKU ZAIMU JOOHOO)	FINANCIAL SUMMARY
預金証書(YOKIN SHOOSHO)	CERTIFICATE OF DEPOSIT
翌日物資金(YOKUJITSU BUSSHIKIN)	OVERNIGHT FUNDS
予算(YOSAN)	BUDGET
余剰生産力(YOJOO SEISANRYOKU)	IDLE CAPACITY
予測(YOSOKU)	FORECAST
	PROJECTION
呼び値(YOBINE)	CALL PRICE

【り】

リースの資産原価算入(RIISU NO SHISAN GENKA SANNYUU)	CAPITALIZATION OF LEASES
リースバック(RI-SU BAKKU)	LEASEBACK
利益(RIEKI)	GAIN
利益(RIEKI)	NET INCOME
	PROFIT
利益金処分額(RIEKI-KIN SHOBUN-GAKU)	APPROPRIATED RETAINED EARNINGS
利益参与(RIEKI SANYO)	PROFIT SHARING
利益剰余金(RIEKI JOOYO-KIN)	RETAINED EARNINGS
理事会(RIJI-KAI)	BOARD OF DIRECTORS
利付きなし割引債券(RI-TSUKI NASHI WARIBIKI-SAIKEN)	ZERO COUPON BONDS
利幅(RIHABA)	PROFIT MARGIN
利回り(RIMAWARI)	YIELD
流動資産(RYUUDOO SHISAN)	CURRENT ASSETS
流動資産(RYUUDOO SHISAN)	LIQUID ASSETS
流動性(RYUUDOO-SEI)	LIQUIDITY
流動性水準リスク(RYUUDOO-SEI SUIJUN RISUKU)	LIQUIDITY RISK
流動比率(RYUUDOO HIRITSU)	CURRENT RATIO
流動負債(RYUUDOO FUSAI)	URRENT LIABILITIES
両掛け(RYOOGAKE)	HEDGE
領収書(RYOOSHUU-SHO)	VOUCHER
利率(RIRITSU)	INTEREST RATE

【る】

累進課税(RUISHIN KAZEI)	PROGRESSIVE TAX
累進税(RUISHIN-ZEI)	GRADUATED TAX
累積効果(RUISEKI KOOKA)	CUMULATIVE EFFECT
累積調整(RUISEKI CHOOSEI)	CUMULATIVE ADJUSMENT

【れ】

零細企業(REISAI KIGYOO)	SMALL COMPANIES
歴史的原価(REKISHITEKI GENKA)	HISTORICAL COST
連結勘定(RENKETSU KANJOO)	CONSOLIDATED ACCOUNTS
連結財務諸表(RENKETSU ZAIMUSHOHYOO)	CONSOLIDATED FINANCIAL STATEMENTS

【ろ】

労働時間(ROODOO-JIKAN)	LABOR HOURS
労働法(ROODOO-HOO)	LABOR LAW
六月(ROKU-GATSU)	JUNE

【わ】

割り当てる(WARIATERU)	ALLOCATE
割引債権(WARIBIKI SAIKEN)	DEBT DISCOUNT
割引率(WARIBIKI-RITSU)	DISCOUNT RATE
割増し金付き債券(WARIMASHI-KIN-TSUKI SAIKEN)	DEBT PREMIUM

English	Japanese
ACCELERATED DEPRECIATION	定率法（TEIRITSU-HOO)
ACCOUNT BALANCES	勘定残高 (KANJOO-ZANDAKA)
ACCOUNTANT	会計士 (KAIKEI-SHI)
	計理士 (KEIRI-SHI)
ACCOUNTING	会計学 (KAIKEI-GAKU)
ACCOUNTING CHANGES	会計方針の変更 (KAIKEI-HOOSHIN NO HENKOO)
ACCOUNTING POLICIES	会計方針 (KAIKEI-HOOSHIN)
ACCOUNTING PRINCIPLES	会計原則 (KAIKEI-GENSOKU)
ACCOUNTING RECORDS	会計記録 (KAIKEI-KIROKU)
ACCOUNTS PAYABLE	買掛金 (KAIKAKE-KIN)
ACCOUNTS RECEIVABLE	売掛金 (URIKAKE-KIN)
ACCRUAL	発生 (HASSEI)
ACCRUAL (ACC. METHOD)	発生基準 (HASSEI-KIJUN)
ACCRUED EXPENSES	未払費用 (MIHARAI HIYOO)
ACCRUED INCOME	未収収益 (MISHUU-SHUUEKI)
ACCRUED LIABILITIES	未払費用 (MIHARAI-HIYOO)
ACCRUED TAXES	未払法人税 (MIHARAI-HOOJIN-ZEI)
ACCRUED VACATIONS	有給休暇引当金 (YUUKYUU-KYUUKA HIKIATE-KIN)
ACCUMULATED AMORTIZATION	減価償却累計額 (GENKA SHOOKYAKU RUIKEI-GAKU)
ACCUMULATED DEPRECIATION	減価償却累計額 (GENKA SHOOKYAKU RUIKEI-GAKU)
	既償却高 (KI-SHOOKYAKU-DAKA)
ACID TEST	酸性比率分析 (SANSEI HIRITSU BUNSEKI)
ACID TEST RATIO	酸性比率 (SANSEI HIRITSU)
ACQUISITION (OF A COMPANY)	合併一取得（企業）(GAPPEI-SHUTOKU (KIGYOO))
ACQUISITION COST	取得価格 (SHUTOKU-KAKAKU)
ACTUAL LOAN LOSSES	貸出金償却 (TAISHUTSU-KIN SHOOKYAKU)
ACTUARIAL VALUE	保険数理原価 (HOKENSUURI GENKA)
ADJUSTMENT	調整 (CHOOSEI)
ADJUSTMENT FOR INFLATION	インフレ調整 (INFURE CHOOSEI)
ADMINISTRATIVE EXPENSES	一般管理費 (IPPAN KANRI-HI)
ADVANCES TO SUPPLIERS	業者への前渡金 (GYOOSHA E NO MAEWATASHI-KIN)
ADVERSE OPINION	不適正意見 (FUTEKISEI IKEN)
AFFILIATE	関連 (KANREN)
AFFILIATED FIRMS	関連会社 (KANREN-GAISHA)
	関係団体 (KANKEI-DANTAI)
ALLOCATE	割り当てる (WARIATERU)
ALLOWANCE	引当金 (HIKIATEKIN)
ALLOWANCE FOR DEVALUATION OF INVESTMENT	投資再評価引当金 (TOOSHI SAIHYOOKA HIKIATE-KIN)

English	Japanese
ALLOWANCE FOR DOUBTFULL ACCOUNTS	貸倒引当金 (KASHIDAORE-HIKIATEKIN)
ALLOWANCE FOR LOAN LOSSES	貸倒引当金 (KASHIDAORE-HIKIATEKIN)
ALLOWANCE FOR UNCOLLECTIBLE ACCOUNTS	貸倒引当金 (KASHIDAORE-HIKIATEKIN)
ALTERNATIVE PROCEDURES	代案 (DAIAN)
ANALYTICAL REVIEW	分析再調査 (BUNSEKI SAI-CHOOSA)
ANNUAL MEETING	年次定例会 (NENJI TEIREI-KAI)
ANNUAL SHAREHOLDERS' MEETING	定時株主総会 (TEIJI KABUNUSHI-SOOKAI)
ANNUALLY	一年に一度の (NEN NI ICHIDO NO)
APPROPRIATED RETAINED EARNINGS	利益金処分額 (RIEKI-KIN SHOBUN-GAKU)
	処分利益余剰金 (SHOBUN RIEKI YOJOOKIN)
APRIL	四月 (SHIGATSU)
ASSETS	資産 (SHISAN)
ASSOCIATED FIRM	関係会社 (KANKEI GAISHA)
AT RANDOM	無作為に (MUSAKUI NI)
AUDIT	会計検査 (KAIKEI-KENSA)
	会計監査 (KAIKEI-KANSA)
AUDIT APPROACH	監査手順 (KANSA-TEJUN)
AUDIT ENGAGEMENT	監査契約 (KANSA-KEIYAKU)
AUDIT FEES	監査料 (KANSA-RYOO)
AUDIT MANAGER	代表監査人 (DAIHYOO KANSA-NIN)
AUDIT OPINION	監査意見 (KANSA IKEN)
AUDIT PARTNER	共同監査人 (KYOODOO KANSA-NIN)
AUDIT RISK	会計監査上のリスク (KAIKEI-KANSA-JOO NO RISUKU)
AUDIT SAMPLING	監査標本抽出 (KANSA HYOOHON CHUUSHUTSU)
AUDIT STAFF	監査職員 (KANSA SHOKUIN)
AUDIT STATEGY	監査戦略 (KANSA SENRYAKU)
AUDITING PROCEDURES	監査手順 (KANSA TEJUN)
AUDITING STANDARDS	監査基準 (KANSA KIJUN)
AUDITOR	会計監査人 (KAIKEI KANSA-NIN)
	会計検査官 (KAIKEI KENSA-KAN)
AUDITOR'S REPORT	監査報告書 (KANSA HOOKOKU-SHO)
AUDITOR'S RESPONSIBILITY	会計監査人の責任範囲 (KAIKEI KANSA-NIN NO SEKININHAN I)
AUDITORS' REPORT	監査人の報告書 (KANSA-NIN NO HOOKOKU-SHO)
AUGUST	八月 (HACHI-GATSU)
AVERAGE	平均 (HEIKIN)
BALANCE SHEET	貸借対照表 (TAISHAKU-TAISHOO-HYOO)
BALANCE SHEET DATE	貸借対照表の日付 (TAISHAKU-TAISHOO-HYOO NO HIZUKE)
BANK	銀行 (GINKOO)

English	Japanese
BANK OVERDRAFATS	当座貸越(TOOZA-KASHIKOSHI)
BANK RECONCILIATION	銀行勘定調整(GINKOO KANJOO CHOOSEI)
BANK SERVICE CHARGES	銀行手数料(GINKOO-TESUURYOO)
BANKRUPTCY	破産(HASAN)
	倒産(TOOSAN)
BEARER	持参人(小切手一手形の) JISAN-NIN(KOGITTE-TEGATA NO)
BID	入札(NYUUSATSU)
BID (VERB)	付ける（値を）TSUKERU(NE O)
BILLIONS	十億(JUU-OKU)
BOARD OF DIRECTORS	理事会(RIJI-KAI)
	役員会(YAKU-IN-KAI)
BOND	債券(SAI-KEN)
	社債(SHA-SAI)
	借用証書(SHAKUYOO-SHOOSHO)
	証文(SHOO-MON)
BONDS PAYABLE	社債(SHASAI)
BOOK VALUE	帳簿価格(CHOOBO-KAKAKU)
BREAK EVEN POINT	損益分岐点(SONEKI-BUNKI-TEN)
BUDGET	予算(YOSAN)
BUILDINGS STRUCTURES	建物、構築物(TATEMONO,KOOCHIKU-BUTSU)
BUSINESS COMBINATIONS	合併(GAPPEI)
BUSINESS SEGMENT	事業部門別(JIGYOO-BUMON-BETSU)
BY-PRODUCTS	副産物(FUKUSAN-BUTSU)
CALL PRICE	呼び値(YOBINE)
CAPITAL GAINS TAX	資産売却所得税(SHISAN BAIKYAKU SHOTOKU-ZEI)
CAPITAL INCREASE	増資(ZOOSHI)
CAPITAL STOCK	資本金(SHIHON-KIN)
CAPITAL SURPLUS	資本剰余金(SHIHON JOOYO-KIN)
CAPITAL TAX	キャピタルタックス(KYAPITARU TAKKUSU)
CAPITALIZATION OF INTEREST ENPENSES	支払利息の資産原価算入 (SHIHARAI-RISOKU NO SHISANGENKASANNYUU)
CAPITALIZATION OF LEASES	リースの資産原価算入(RIISU NO SHISAN GENKA SANNYUU)
CARRYBACK	繰り戻し(KURIMODOSHI)
CARRYBACK PERIOD	繰り越し期間(KURIKOSHI KIKAN)
CARRYFORWARD PERIOD	繰り戻し期間(KURIMODOSHI KIKAN)
CASH	現金(GENKIN)
CASH AND BANKS	現金及び預金(GENKIN OYOBI YOKIN)
CASH DIVIDENDS	現金配当(GENKIN HAITOO)

English	Japanese
CASH EQUIVALENTS	現預金(GENYOKIN)
CASH FLOW	資金収支(SHIKIN SHUUSHI)
	キャシュフロー(KYASSHU FUROO)
CERTIFICATE OF DEPOSIT	預金証書(YOKIN SHOOSHO)
CERTIFICATE OF GOOD STANDING	在職証明(ZAISHOKU SHOOMEI)
CETERIS PARIBUS	他の事情が同じならば(TANO JIJOO GA ONAJI NARABA)
CHAIRMAN	会長(KAICHOO)
CHARITY EXPENSE	寄付(KIFU)
CHART OF ACCOUNTS	勘定課目表(KANJOO KAMOKU-HYOO)
CHIEF EXECUTIVE OFFICER	代表取締役(DAIHYOO-TORISHIMARI-YAKU)
CIRCUMSTANCES	状況(JYOOKYOO)
CLAIMS	要求(YOOKYUU)
CLIENT REPRESENTANTION LETTER	マネージメントによる誓約書 (MANEEGIMENTO NI YORU SEIYAKU SHOO)
CODE (VERB)	符号をつける(FUGOO O TSUKERU)
COLLATERAL	担保(TANPO)
	根抵当(KON-TEITOO)
COLLECTION RATIO	回収率(KAISHUU-RITSU)
	徴収率(CHOOSHUU-RITSU)
COLLECTIONS	集金(SHUUKIN)
	徴収(CHOOSHUU)
COMMERCIAL & INDUSTRIAL LOANS	商業貸付(SHOOGYOO-KASHITSUKE)
COMMERCIAL BANK	商業銀行(SHOOGYOO-GINKOO)
	市中銀行(SHICHUUN-GINKOO)
COMMISSIONS & FEES PROFITS (LOSSES)	手数料益（損）TESUURYOO-EKI(SON)
COMMITMENTS	契約義務(KEIYAKU GIMU)
COMMON STOCK	普通株(FUTSUU-KABU)
COMMUNICATIONS EXPENSE	通信費(TSUUSHIN-HI)
COMPANY BY-LAWS	内規(NAIKI)
COMPARATIVE FINANCIAL STATEMENTS	比較財務諸表(HIKAKU ZAIMU SHOHYOO)
COMPENSATED ABSENCES	有給休暇(YUUKYUU KYUUKA)
COMPILATION OF FINANCIAL STATEMENTS	財務諸表の編集(ZAIMUSHOHYOO NO HENSHUU)
COMPLETED-CONTRACT METHOD	工事完成基準(KOOJI KANSEI KIJUN)
COMPLY WITH	従う(SHITAGAU)
CONDENSED FINANCIAL STATEMENTS	要約財務諸表(YOOYAKU ZAIMUSHOHYOO)
CONFIRMATION OF ACCOUNTS	残高確認状(ZANDAKA KAKUNIN-JOO)
CONSISTENCY	継続性(KEIZOKUSEI)
CONSISTENTLY APPLIED	継続して適用する(KEIZOKU SHITE TEKIYOO SURU)

English	Japanese
CONSOLIDATED ACCOUNTS	連結勘定(RENKETSU KANJOO)
CONSOLIDATED FINANCIAL STATEMENTS	連結財務諸表(RENKETSU ZAIMUSHOHYOO)
CONSTRUCTION IN PROGRESS	建設仮勘定(KENSETSU KARIKANJOO)
CONSULTING SERVICES	顧問業務(KOMON GYOOMU)
CONTENTS	目次(MOKUJI)
CONTINGENCIES	偶発債務(GUUHATSU SAIMU)
CONTROL WEAKNESS	内部統制における弱点(NAIBU-TOOSEI NI OKERU JAKUTEN)
CONVERTIBLE DEBT	転換社債(TENKAN SHASAI)
COPYRIGHT	著作権(CHOSAKU-KEN)
CORRESPONDENT FIRMS	取引会社(TORIHIKI-GAISHA)
COST OF GOODS SOLD	売上原価(URIAGE GENKA)
COST OF SALES	販売原価(HANBAI GENKA)
COST OF SERVICES RENDERED	事業費(JIGYOO-HI)
COST OR MARKET	原価か時価(GENKA KA JIKA)
COUNTRY RISK	カントリーリスク(KANTORII RISUKU)
CREDIT LINE	融資枠(YUUSHIWAKU)
CREDITS TURNOVER RATIO	売掛債権回転率(URIKAKE SAIKEN KAITEN-RITSU)
CUMULATIVE ADJUSMENT	累積調整(RUISEKI CHOOSEI)
CUMULATIVE EFFECT	累積効果(RUISEKI KOOKA)
CURRENCY TRANSLATION	為替換算(KAWASE KANSAN)
	外貨建取引の換算方法(GAIKA-DATE TORIHIKI NO KANSAN HOOHOO)
CURRENT ASSETS	流動資産(RYUUDOO SHISAN)
CURRENT LIABILITIES	流動負債(RYUUDOO FUSAI)
CURRENT PORTION OF ...	一年以内に返済する(ICHINEN-INAI NI HENSAI SURU)
CURRENT RATIO	流動比率(RYUUDOO HIRITSU)
CUSTODY SECURITIES	保管有価証券(HOKAN YUUKASHOOKEN)
CUSTOMERS	顧客(KOKYAKU)
CUSTOMERS' LIABILIT FOR ACCEPTANCES	支払承諾見返り(SHIHARAI SHOODAKU MIKAERI)
CUSTOMS DUTY	関税(KANZEI)
DATA PROCESSING EQUIPMENT	データ処理装置(DEETA SHORI SOOCHI)
DEBENTURE	無担保社債(MUTANPO SHASAI)
DEBT DISCOUNT	割引債権(WARIBIKI SAIKEN)
DEBT PREMIUM	割増し金付き債券(WARIMASHI-KIN-TSUKI SAIKEN)
DEBT RESTRUCTURING	債務の再構成(SAIMU NO SAI-KOOSEI)
DEFERRAL METHOD	損益法(SON-EKI-HOO)
DEFERRED CHARGES	繰延資産(KURINOBE SHISAN)
DEFERRED INCOME	前受収益(MAEUKE SHUUEKI)
DEFERRED INCOME TAX	税効果期間配分額(ZEIKOOKA KIKAN HAIBUNGAKU)
DEFERRED INCOME(EXPENSE)	繰延利益(費用) KURINOBE RIEKI(HIYOU)
DEFERRED TAXES	繰延税金(KURINOBE ZEIKIN)
DEMAND DEPOSITS	当座預金、普通預金(TOOZA-YOKIN, FUTSUU-YOKIN)
DEPARTURE FROM A PRONOUNCEMENT	ギャップ違反（一般に認められた会計原則）GYAPPU I HAN (IPPAN NI MITOMERARETA KAIKEI GENSOKU)
DEPENDENTS	扶養家族(FUYOO KAZOKU)
DEPRECIATION - BUILDINGS	減価償却―建物(GENKASHOOKYAKU-TATEMONO)
DEPRECIATION EXPENSE	減価償却費(GENKASHOOKYAKU-HI)
DETECT	看破(KANPA)
DEVELOPMENT STAGE COMPANIES	開業準備中の企業(KAIGYOO JUNBI CHUU NO KIGYOO)
DIRECT COST	直接費用(CHOKUSETSU HIYOO)
DIRECTORS	重役(JUUYAKU)
DISBURSEMENTS	支払(SHIHARAI)
DISCLAIMER OF OPINION	棄権(KIKEN)
DISCLOSURE	開示(KAIJI)
	公開(KOOKAI)
DISCONTINUED OPERATIONS	廃止事業(HAISHI JIGYOO)
DISCOUNT RATE	割引率(WARIBIKI-RITSU)
DISPOSITION	処分(SHOBUN)
	売却(BAIKYAKU)
DIVIDEND	配当金(HAITOO-KIN)
DIVIDEND INCOME	受取配当金(UKETORI HAITOO-KIN)
DIVIDEND PER SHARE	一株当り配当額(HITOKABU ATARI HAITOOGAKU)
DIVIDENDS PAYABLE	未払配当金(MIHARAI HAITOO-KIN)
DOLLARS	ドル(DORU)
DOMESTIC SUBSIDIARIES	国内子会社(KOKUNAI KO-GAISHA)
DOUBLE TAXATION	二重課税(NIJUU-KAZEI)
DUE DATE	満期日(MANKIJITSU)
EARLY EXTINGUISHMENT OF DEBT	債務の繰上返還(SAIMU NO KURIAGE HENKAN)
EARLY RETIREMENT	早期隠退(SOOKI INTAI)
EARNINGS PER SHARE	一株当り純利益(HITOKABU ATARI JUNRIEKI)
	一株当り利益(HITOKABU ATARA RIEKI)
ECONOMIC ENVIRONMENT	経済環境(KEIZAI KANKYOO)
EFFECT	効果(KOOKA)
EFFECTS OF CHANGING PRICES	価格変動財務情報(KAKAKU HENDOO ZAIMU JOOHOO)
EMPLOYEE	従業員(JYUUGYOO-IN)
EMPLOYEE BENEFITS	福利厚生(FUKURI KOOSEI)
ENTERTAINMENT EXPENSE	交際費(KOOSAI-HI)

English	Japanese
EQUITY IN OTHER COMPANIES	持分 (MOCHIBUN)
EQUITY METHOD	持分法 (MOCHIBUN-HOO)
ERRORS	誤謬 (GOBYUU)
EVIDENTIAL MATTER	基礎事実 (KISO JIJITSU)
EXAMINE	検査 (KENSA)
EXCEPT FOR	～を除いては (O NOZOITE WA)
EXCHANGE RATE	為替相場 (KAWASE SOOBA)
	換算レート (KANSAN REETO)
EXCHANGE RATE RISK	換算損失リスク (KANSAN SONSHITSU RISUKU)
EXCISE TAX	消費税 (SHOOHI-ZEI)
EXHIBITIONS AND EVENTS EXPENSES	展示会出展費 (TENJI-KAI SHUTTEN-HI)
EXPECTED SALVAGE VALUE	見積り残存価格 (MITSUMORI ZANZON KAKAKU)
EXPENSES	費用 (HIYOO)
EXPENSES ON CAPITAL INCREASE	増資に伴う費用 (ZOOSHI NI TOMONAU HIYOO)
EXPORT	輸出 (YUSHUTSU)
EXPORT DUTIES	輸入関税 (YUNYUU KANZEI)
EXTENT	範囲 (HAN' I)
EXTRAORDINARY ITEMS	特別損益項目 (TOKUBETSU SONEKI KOOMOKU)
FACE VALUE	額面価格 (GAKUMEN KAKAKU)
FAIRLY PRESENT	適正に表示する (TEKISEI NI HYOOJI-SURU)
FEASIBILITY	実行出来る可能性 (JIKKOO DEKIRU KANOOSEI)
FEASIBILITY STUDY	実現可能かどうかの調査 (JITSUGEN KANOO KA DOOKA NO CHOOSA)
FEBRUARY	二月 (NIGATSU)
FEES	謝礼 (SHAREI)
FEES FOR SVS. RENDERED BY 3RD PARTY	外部委託費 (GAIBU YOOTAKU-HI)
FINANCE	財政 (ZAISEI)
FINANCE (VERB)	融資する (YUUSHI SURU)
FINANCIAL ENTITIES	金融会社 (KINYUU-GAISHA)
FINANCIAL STATEMENTS	財務諸表 (ZAIMUSHOHYOO)
FINANCIAL SUMMARY	要約財務情報 (YOOYAKU ZAIMU JOOHOO)
	主要財務情報 (SHUYOO ZAIMUJOOHOO)
FINANCING ARRANGEMENT	融資協定 (YUUSHI KYOOTEI)
FINE	罰金 (BAKKIN)
FINISHED GOODS	製品 (SEIHIN)
FIRST IN, FIRST OUT (FIFO)	先入先出法 (SAKIIRE SAKIDASHI-HOO)
FITTINGS	備品 (BIHIN)
FIXED ASSETS	固定資産 (KOTEI SHISAN)
FLAT TAX WITHHOLDING	一定率の源泉税徴収 (ITTEI-RITSU NO GENSEN-ZEI CHOOSHUU)

English	Japanese
FLOATING RATE	浮動レート (FUDOO-REETO)
FLOWCHART	フローチャート (FUROO-CHAATO)
	生産工程順序一覧表 (SEISAN KOOTEI JUNJO ICHIRAN-HYOO)
FOOTNOTES TO THE FINANCIAL STATEMENTS	財務諸表注記 (ZAIMU SHOHYOO CHUUKI)
FOR TAXATION PURPOSES	課税対象目的で (KAZEI TAISHOO MOKUTEKI DE)
FORECAST	予測 (YOSOKU)
FOREIGN CORRUPT PRACTICES ACT (USA)	海外汚職行為防止法 (KAIGAI OSHOKU-KOOI BOOSHI-HOO)
FOREIGN CURRENCY	外貨 (GAIKA)
FOREIGN CURRENCY TRANSLATION	為替換算調整方法 (KAWASE KANSAN CHOOSEI HOOHOO)
FOREIGN EXCHANGE	外国為替 (GAIKOKU KAWASE)
FOREIGN EXCHANGE GAINS (LOSSES)	為替換算益（損）(KAWASE KANSANEKI (SON))
FOREIGN SUBSIDIARY	海外子会社 (KAIGAI KO-GAISHA)
FORM	様式 (YOOSHIKI)
FREIGHT ON PURCHASES OF MATERIALS	材料購入副費－運搬 (ZAIRYOO KOONYUU FUKUHI-UNPAN)
FUNDS	資金 (SHIKIN)
FURNITURE AND FIXTURES	工具、器具、備品 (KOOGU-KIGU-BIHIN)
FUTURE CONTRACTS	先物契約 (SAKIMONO KEIYAKU)
GAIN	益 (EKI)
	利益 (RIEKI)
GAIN CONTINGENCY	偶発利益 (GUUHATSU RIEKI)
GAIN ON REVALUATION OF SECURITIES	株式再評価利益 (KABUSHIKI SAIHYOOKA RIEKI)
GAIN ON SALE OF FIXED ASSETS	固定資産処分益 (KOTEI SHISAN SHOBUN-EKI)
GENERAL AND ADMINISTRATIVE EXPENSES	販売費及び一般管理費 (HANBAI-HI OYOBI IPPPAN KANRI-HI)
GENERAL INSURANCE	損害保険 (SONGAI HOKEN)
GENERAL LEDGER	総勘定元帳 (SOO-KANJOO MOTOCHOO)
GENERAL MANAGER	部長（支店長）BUCHOO (SHITENCHOO)
GENERALLY ACCEPTED	一般に公正妥当と認められる
	(IPPAN NI KOOSEI-DATOO TO MITOMERARERU)
GOING CONCERN	継続の原則 (KEIZOKU NO GENSOKU)
GOODS IN PROCESS	仕掛品 (SHIKAKE-HIN)
GOODS IN TRANSIT	運搬中の商品 (UNPANCHUU NO SHOOHIN)
GOODWILL	暖簾 (NOREN)
	営業権 (EIGYOO-KEN)
GRADUATED TAX	累進税 (RUISHIN-ZEI)
GROSS MARGIN	売上総利益 (URIAGE SOORIEKI)
GROSS NATIONAL PRODUCT	国民総生産 (KOKUMIN SOO-SEISAN)
GROSS PROFIT RATIO	売上総利益率 (URIAGE SOO-RIEKI-RITSU)
GROUP (OF COMPANIES)	グループ (GURUUPU)

GUARANTEE DEPOSITS	保証金(HOSHOO-KIN)
GUARANTEES	保証(HOSHOO)
HEDGE	両掛け(RYOOGAKE)
HISTORICAL COST	取得原価(SHUTOKU GENKA)
	歴史的原価(REKISHITEKI GENKA)
HOLDING COMPANY	持株会社(MOCHIKABU GAISHA)
HUNDREDS	百(HYAKU)
IDLE CAPACITY	余剰生産力(YOJOO SEISANRYOKU)
IMPORT SURCHARGES	輸入税(YUNYUU-ZEI)
IN ACCORDANCE WITH	～に準拠し(NI JUNKYO SHI)
INCOME FOR SERVICES RENDERED	業務収入(HYOOMU SHUUNYUU)
INCOME TAX	法人税(HOOJIN-ZEI)
	所得税(SHOTOKU-ZEI)
INDEBTNESS RATIO	負債比率(FUSAI HIRITSU)
INDEMNITIES	補償(HOSHOO)
INDEPENDENCE	独立性(DOKURITSU-SEI)
INDUSTRY	工業(KOOGYOO)
	産業(SANGYOO)
INFLATION	インフレ(INFURE)
INHERITANCE TAX	相続税(SOOZOKU-ZEI)
INSURANCE COMPANY	保険会社(HOKEN-GAISHA)
INTANGIBLE ASSETS	無形固定資産(MUKEI KOTEI SHISAN)
	無形資産(MUKEI SHISAN)
INTER-COMPANY LOANS	関係会社貸付金(KANKEI-GAISHA KASHITSUKE-KIN)
INTEREST EXPENSE	支払利息(SHIHARAI RISOKU)
INTEREST INCOME	受取利息(UKETORI RISOKUU)
INTEREST PAYABLE	未払利息(MIHARAI RISOKU)
INTEREST RATE	利率(RIRITSU)
INTEREST RECEIVABLE	未収利息(MISHUU RISOKU)
INTERIM FINANCIAL STATEMENTS	中間財務諸表(CHUUKAN ZAIMU SHOHYOO)
INTERNAL AUDITORS	内部監査(NAIBU KANSA)
INTERNAL CONTROL QUESTIONNAIRE	内部統制質問書(NAIBU TOOSEI SHITSUMON-SHO)
INTERNAL CONTROLS	内部統制制度(NAIBU TOOSEI SEIDO)
INTERNATIONAL SUBSIDIARIES	海外子会社(KAIGAI KOGAISHA)
INTERNATIONAL TRADE	国際貿易(KOKUSAI BOOEKI)
INTERVENING PERIOD	仲裁期間(SHUUSAI KIKAN)
INVENTORIES -(USA) (STOCKS-UK)	棚卸し資産(TANAOROSHI SHISAN)
INVENTORY TURNOVER RATIO	棚卸し資産回転率(TANAOROSHI SHISAN KAITEN-RITSU)

INVESTMENT	投資(TOOSHI)
INVESTMENT BANK/MERCHANT BANK	証券会社(SHOOKEN GAISHA)
INVESTMENT IN SUBSIDIARIES	関係会社株式(KANKEI-GAISHA KABUSHIKI)
	関係会社出資金(KANKEI-GAISHA SHUSSHI-KIN)
INVESTMENT SECURITIES GAINS(LOSS)	投資有価証券益（損）TOOSHI YUUKA SHOOKEN-EKI(SON)
INVESTMENT TAX CREDIT	投資税額控除(TOOSHI ZEIGAKU KOOJO)
INVOICE	送り状(OKURI-JOO)
IRREGULARITY	変則(HENSOKU)
JANUARY	一月(ICHI-GATSU)
JOINT VENTURE	合同企業体(GOODOO KIGYOO-TAI)
JOURNAL	仕訳帳(SHIWAKE-CHOO)
JOURNAL ENTRY	仕訳(SHIWAKE)
JULY	七月(SHICHI-GATSU)
JUNE	六月(ROKU-GATSU)
LABOR HOURS	労働時間(ROODOO-JIKAN)
LABOR LAW	労働法(ROODOO-HOO)
LAND	土地(TOCHI)
LAND IMPROVEMENTS	土地改良費(TOCHI KAIRYOO-HI)
LAST IN, FIRST OUT (LIFO)	後入先出法(ATOIRE SAKIDASHI-HOO)
LAWYER	弁護士(BENGO-SHI)
LEASE	借地契約(SHAKUCHI-KEIYAKU)
	賃貸借(CHINTAISHAKU)
LEASEBACK	リースバック(RI-SU BAKKU)
LEGAL REQUIREMENTS	法律上の必要条件(HOORITSU-JOO NO HITSUYOO JOOKEN)
LEGAL RESERVE	法定準備金(HOOTEI JUNBI-KIN)
LESSEE	賃借人(CHINSHAKU-NIN)
	借地人(SHAKUCHI-NIN)
LESSOR	賃貸人(CHINTAI-NIN)
	貸主(KASHINUSHI)
LIABILITY	負債(FUSAI)
LICENCES	免許(MENKYO)
LIFE INSURANCE	生命保険(SEIMEI HOKEN)
LIFE POLICY BENEFITS	生命保険金(SEIMEI-HOKEN-KIN)
LIQUID ASSETS	流動資産(RYUUDOO SHISAN)
LIQUIDITY	流動性(RYUUDOO-SEI)
LIQUIDITY RISK	流動性水準リスク(RYUUDOO-SEI SUIJUN RISUKU)
LISTED BONDS-LOCAL CURRENCY	上場社債一現地通貨による(JOOJOO-SHASAI-GENCHI TSUUKA NI YORU)
LITIGATION	訴訟(SOSHOO) / 起訴(KISO)

English	Japanese
LOANS	貸付け金(KASHITSUKE-KIN)
LOCAL CURRENCY	現地通貨(GENCHI TSUUKA)
LONG TERM DEBT RETIRED	長期借入金返済(CHOOKI SHAKUNYUU-KIN HENSAI)
LONG TERM INSURANCE RESERVE CHARGES	長期保険契約に係わる準備金繰入 (CHOOKI HOKEN-KEIYAKU NI KAKAWARU JUNBIKIN KURIIRE)
LONG-TERM CONTRACTS	長期契約(CHOOKI KEIYAKU)
LONG-TERM CREDITS	長期信用(CHOOKI SHINYOO)
LONG-TERM DEBT	長期借入金(CHOOKI-SHAKUNYUU-KIN)
LONG-TERM INVESTMENTS	長期投資(CHOOKI TOOSHI)
LOSS	損失(SONSHITSU)
	損失額(SONSHITSU-GAKU)
LOSS CARRY-FORWARD	欠損の繰越(KESSON NO KURIKOSHI)
LOWER OF COST OR MARKET	低価法(TEIKA-HOO)
MACHINERY AND EQUIPMENT	機械及び装置(KIKAI OYOBI SOOCHI)
MAJOR CUSTOMERS	主要な顧客(SHUYOO NA KOKYAKU)
MANAGEMENT INTENTION	経営陣の意図(KEIEI-JIN NO ITO)
MARCH	三月(SAN-GATSU)
MARGINAL COST	限界原価(GENKAI GENKA)
MARKET PRICE	時価(JIKA)
	市場価格(SHIJOO-KAKAKU)
MARKETABLE SECURITIES	市場性のある有価証券(SHIJOOSEI NO ARU YUUKA SHOOKEN)
	一時所有の有価証券(ICHIJI SHOYUU NO YUUKA SHOOKEN)
MARKETABLE STOCKS	市場性のある株式(SHIJOOSEI NO ARU KABUSHIKI)
MATERIAL (SIGNIFICANT)	重大な(JUUDAI NA)
MATERIALITY	重要性(JUUYOO-SEI)
MATERIALS (SUST.)	原料（資材） GENRYOO(SHIZAI)
MATURED LOANS	満期となったローン(MANKI TONATTA ROON)
MATURITY	満期(MANKI)
MAY	五月(GO-GATSU)
MERGER	合併(GAPPEI)
MILLIONS	百万(HYAKU-MAN)
MINORITY INTEREST	小数株主持分(SHOOSUU KABUNUSHI MOCHIBUN)
MISLEADING INFORMATION	まぎらわしい情報(MAGIRAWASHII JOOHOO)
MONETARY ASSETS	貨幣資産(KAHEI SHISAN)
MONTHLY	月の（月間の）TSUKINO (GEKKAN NO)
MORTGAGE	抵当権付き(TEITOO-KEN-TSUKI)
MULTINATIONAL ENTERPRISE	他国籍企業(TAKOKU-SEKI KIGYOO)
MUTUAL FUND	株式投資信託(KABUSHIKI TOOSHI SHINTAKU)

English	Japanese
NATURE	本質(HONSHITSU)
NEGATIVE GOODWILL	消極的暖簾(SHOOKYOKU-TEKI NOREN)
NET FIXED ASSETS	正味有形固定資産(SHOOMI YUUKEI KOTEI SHISAN)
NET INCOME	純利益(JUN-RIEKI)
	利益(RIEKI)
NET INCOME (LOSS) OF THE PERIOD	当期純利益(TOOKI JUN-RIEKI)
NET PREMIUMS EARNED	正味保険料収入(SHOOMI HOKEN-RYOO SHUUNYUU)
NET PRESENT VALUE	正味現在価値(SHOOMI GENZAI KACHI)
NET REALIZABLE VALUE	正味実現可能価額(SHOOMI JITSUGEN-KAHOO KAKAKU)
NET SALES	純売上高(JUN-URIAGE-DAKA)
NET TRADE ACCOUNTS RECEIVABLE	正味売上金(SHOOMI URIAGE-KIN)
NET WORTH	自己資本(JIKO-SHIHON)
NON-CURRENT ASSETS	固定資産(KOTEI SHISAN)
NON-CURRENT LIABILITIES	固定負債(KOTEI FUSAI)
NON-OPERATING INCOME AND EXPENSE	営業外収益一費用(EIGYOO-GAI SHUUEKI HIYOO)
NON-PROFIT	非営利（法人）HI-EIRI (HOOJIN)
NON-REDEEMABLE PREFERRED STOCK	非償還付優先株(HISHOOKAN-TSUKI YUUSEN-KABU)
NON-TAXABLE INCOME	非課税収益(HIKAZEI SHUUEKI)
NOTES PAYABLE	支払手形(SHIHARAI TEGATA)
NOTES RECEIVABLE	受取手形(UKETORI TEGATA)
NOVEMBER	十一月(JUUICHI-GATSU)
OBSOLESCENCE	陳腐化(CHINPU-KA)
OCTOBER	十月(JUU-GATSU)
OFFICE SUPPLIES	事務用品(JIMU-YOOHIN)
OFFICER	職員(SHOKU-IN)
OFFSET	相殺(SOOSAI)
OPERATING CYCLE	営業周期(EIGYOO SHUUKI)
OPERATING LEASES	営業賃貸借(EIGYOO CHINTAISHAKU)
OPERATING PROFIT	営業利益(EIGYOO-RIEKI)
OPERATING RATIO	稼働率、営業比率(KADOO-RITSU, EIGYOO-HIRITSU)
OPERATIONAL AUDITING	運営監査(UNEI KANSA)
OPERATIONAL CONTROLS	運営管理(UNEI KANRI)
OPERATIONAL NETWORK	経営組織(KEIEI SOSHIKI)
OPINION	監査意見(KANSA IKEN)
OPINION PARAGRAPH	監査意見欄(KANSA IKEN-RAN)
OPPORTUNITY COST	機会原価(KIKAI GENKA)
OPTIONS	オプション(OPUSHON)
ORGANIZATION CHART	組織図(SOSHIKI-ZU)

English	Japanese
ORGANIZATION EXPENSES	創立費(SOORITSU-HI)
OTHER INCOME FOR SERVICES	その他の業務利益(SONO TA NO GYOOMU RIEKI)
OTHER LOANS	その他の貸付金(SONO TA NO KASHITSUKE-KIN)
OTHER OPERATING PROFITS	その他の営業利益（損失）SONO TA NO EIGYOO RIEKI (SONSHITSU)
OUTSTANDING SHARES	発行済株式(HAKKOO-ZUMI KABUSHIKI)
OVER THE COUNTER TRANSACTION	場外取引(BAGAI TORIKI)
OVERDRAFT	当座貸越(TOOZA KASHIKOSHI)
OVERDUE	支払期限の過ぎた(SHIHARAI KIGEN NO SUGITA)
OVERHEAD EXPENSES	経費(KEIHI)
OVERINVOICING	過不足請求(KAFUSOKU SEIKYUU)
OVERNIGHT FUNDS	翌日物資金(YOKUJITSU BUSSHIKIN)
OVERSIZE(D)	特大の(TOKUDAINO)
PACKAGING MATERIAL	包装材料(HOOSOO ZAIRYOO)
PAID IN CAPITAL	払い込み剰余金(HARAIKOMI JOOYOKIN)
PAR VALUE	額面(GAKUMEN)
PARENT COMPANY	親会社(OYA-GAISHA)
PARTNER	パートナー(PAATONAA)
PATENTS	特許権(TOKKYO-KEN)
	パテント(PATENTO)
PAYMENTS	支払い(SHIHARAI)
PAYMENTS CYCLE	支払い周期(SHIHARAI SHUUKI)
PAYROLL	給料、賃金(KYUURYOO, CHINGIN)
PENSION	年金(NEN-KIN)
PENSION PLAN	年金制度(NENKIN SEIDO)
PERCENTAGE	百分率(HYAKUBUN-RITSU)
PERCENTAGE-OF-COMPLETION-METHOD	工事進行基準(KOOJI SHINKOO KIJUN)
PERMANENT FILE	永久保存(EIKYUU-HOZON)
PERPETUAL BOND	永久社債(EIKYUU SHASAI)
PERPETUAL INVENTORY SYSTEM	棚卸資産継続記録法(TANAOROSHI SHISAN KEIZOKU KIROKU HOO)
PERSONAL INCOME TAX	個人所得税(KOJIN SHOTOKU-ZEI)
PETTY CASH	小口現金(KOGUCHI GENKIN)
PHYSICAL INVENTORY	棚卸資産の実地棚卸(TANA-OROSHI SHISAN NO JICCHI TANAOROSHI)
PLACEMENT	配置(HAICHI)
PLEDGE	誓約(SEIYAKU)
PLEDGING REQUIREMENTS	抵当物件(TEITOO BUKKEN)
POLICYHOLDERS' EQUITY	基金、資本（相互保険会社）KIKIN,SHIHON(SOOGO-HOKEN KAISHA)
POLICYHOLDERS' SURPLUS	剰余金（相互保険会社）JOOYO-KIN(SOOGO-HOKEN-GAISHA)
POOLING OF INTEREST METHOD	プーリングーオブーインタレスト方式

English	Japanese
POPULATION	人口(JINKOO)
POPULATION (IN A STATIST. ENVIRON.)	母集団(BO-SHUUDAN)
PORTFOLIO COMPOSITION	投資資産の構成(TOOSHI-SHISAN NO KOOSEI)
POST ENTRIES TO THE LEDGER	元帳への転記(MOTO-CHO E NO TENKI)
POST RETIREMENT BENEFITS	退職年金(TAISHOKU NENKIN)
PREFERRED SHARE (USA)	優先株(YUUSEN-KABU)
PREMIUM	保険料(HOKENRYOO)
PREMIUM ON ISSUE OF CAPITAL	資本準備金(SHIHON JUNBI-KIN)
PREPAID EXPENSE	前払資用(MAEBARAI SHIYOO)
	前払費用(MAEBARAI HIYOO)
PRIMARY CAPITAL	第一次資本(DAI-ICHIJI SHIHON)
PRIOR PERIOD ADJUSTMENTS	前期損益修正(ZENKI SON-EKI SHUUSEI)
PRIVATE SECTOR	私企業(SHIKIGYOO)
PROBABLE	有望な(YUUBOO NA)
PRODUCT WARRANTIES	品質保証(HINSHITSU HOSHOO)
PRODUCTION CAPACITY	生産能力(SEISAN NOORYOKU)
PRODUCTION COST	生産原価(SEISAN GENKA)
	製品原価(SEIHIN GENKA)
PRODUCTION CYCLE	生産周期(SEISAN SHUUKI)
PRODUCTION ORDER	生産順序(SEISAN JUNJO)
PROFESSIONAL JUDGMENT	専門家による判断(SENMONKA NI YORU HANDAN)
PROFESSIONAL STANDARDS	専門家基準(SENMON-KA KIJUN)
PROFIT	利益(RIEKI)
PROFIT & LOSS ACCOUNTS	損益計算書(SONEKI KEISAN-SHO)
PROFIT MARGIN	利幅(RIHABA)
PROFIT SHARING	利益参与(RIEKI SANYO)
PROGRESSIVE TAX	累進課税(RUISHIN KAZEI)
PROJECTION	予測(YOSOKU)
PROMOTIONAL COSTS	広告宣伝費(KOOKOKU SENDEN-HI)
PROVISION	引当金(HIKIATE-KIN)
PROXY (POWER OF ATTORNEY)	代理権(DAIRI-KEN)
PUBLIC SECTOR	公共部門(KOOKYOO-BUMON)
PURCHASE REQUISITION	購入要望書(KOONYUU YOOBOOSHO)
QUALIFICATION(OF AN AUDIT OPINION)	限定(意見)[GENTEI (IKEN)]
QUALITY CONTROL	品質管理(HINSHITSU KANRI)
QUARTER	四半期(SHIHAN-KI)
QUARTERLY	四半期の(SHIHAN-KI NO)
QUARTERLY FINANCIAL STATEMENTS	四半期報告書(SHIHAN-KI HOOKOKUSHO)

RANDOM	無作為 (MUSAKUI)
RAW MATERIALS	原材料 (GENZAIRYO)
REAL ESTATE AND MORTGAGE LOANS	不動産と抵当権付きローン (FUDOOSAN TO TEITOO-KEN-TSUKI ROON)
REASONABLY POSSIBLE	かなり可能性の高い (KANARI KANOO-SEI NO TAKAI)
RECEIVABLES	受取債券 (UKETORI SAIKEN)
RECESSION	景気後退 (KEIKI KOOTAI)
RECORD (VERB)	記録する (KIROKU SURU)
RECRUITING EXPENSE	求人費 (KYUU-JIN-HI)
REDEEMABLE	償還できる (SHOOKAN DEKIRU)
REDEEMABLE PREFERRED STOCK	償還券付優先株 (SHOOKAN-KEN-TSUKI YUUSEN-KABU)
REDEMPTION FEATURES	償却条件 (SHOOKYAKU JOOKEN)
REDISCOUNTED NOTES	再割引手形 (SAIWARIBIKI TEGATA)
REFINANCING	資金調達 (SHIKIN CHOOTATSU)
REFUND	払い戻し (HARAI MODOSHI)
REGRESSIVE TAX	逓減税 (TEIGEN-ZEI)
REGULATIONS	条例、規則 (JOOREI KISOKU)
REINSURANCE AND PREMIUM ADJUSTMENT	再保険と保険料調整 (SAIHOKEN TO HOKEN-RYOO CHOOSEI)
RELATED PARTY TRANSACTIONS	関係者間取引 (KANKEI-SHA-KAN TORIHIKI)
REMOTE	とても起こりそうにない (TOTEMO OKORISOO NI NAI)
REPAIRS	修理 (SHUURI)
REPAIRS AND MAINTENANCE	修繕と維持 (SHUUZEN TO IJI)
REPLACEMENT COST	再調達原価 (SAI-CHOOTATSU GENKA)
REPORT	報告 (HOOKOKU)
REPORT TO MANAGEMENT	経営者への報告 (KEIEI-SHA E NO HOOKOKU)
REPRODUCTION COST	再生産費 (SAI-SEISAN-HI)
REPURCHASE AGREEMENT	再購入契約 (SAI-KOONYUU KEIYAKU)
RESALE AGREEMENTS	再販売契約 (SAI-HANBAI KEIYAKU)
RESALE MERCHANDISE	再販売用商品 (SAI-HANBAI-YOO SHOOHIN)
RESEARCH AND DEVELOPMENT COSTS	試験研究費 (SHIKEN KENKYUU-HI)
RESERVE FOR EXCH. RATE FLUCTUATION	為替換算変動準備金 (KAWASE KANSAN HENDOO JUNBI-KIN)
RESERVE FOR LOAN LOSSES	貸付金損準備金 (KASHITSUKE-KIN-SON JUNBI-KIN)
	貸倒引当金 (KASHIDAORE HIKIATEKIN)
RESERVE FOR O/S CLAIMS AND LOSSES	支払準備金 (SHIHARAI JUNBIKIN)
RESTRICTIONS ON THE SCOPE	監査範囲の限定 (KANSA HAN'I NO GENTEI)
RESTRUCTURE	会社更正 (KAISHA KOOSEI)
RETAINED EARNINGS	剰余金 (JOOYO-KIN)
	利益剰余金 (RIEKI JOOYO-KIN)
RETURN ON ASSETS	総資本収益率 (SOO-SHIHON SHUUEKI-RITSU)

RETURN ON EQUITY	自己資本利益率 (JIKO SHIHON RIEKI-RITSU)
REVALUATION	再評価 (SAIHYOOKA)
REVALUATION RESERVE	資本再評価準備金 (SHIHON SAI-HYOOKA JUNBI-KIN)
REVALUATION SURPLUS	再評価剰余金 (SAI-HYOOKA JOOJOKIN)
REVIEW OF FINANCIAL STATEMENTS	財務諸表の再考査 (ZAIMU SHOHYOO NO SAI-KOOSA)
RULES	規則 (KISOKU)
SALARIES AND WAGES	給料,賃金 (KYUURYOO, CHINGIN)
SALE OF MANUFACTURED GOODS	製品販売 (SEIHIN HANBAI)
SALES (TURNOVER)	総売上高 (SOO-URIAGE-DAKA)
SALES ON INSTALLMENTS	割賦販売 (KAPPU-HANBAI)
SALES TAX	物品税 (BUPPIN-ZEI)
SAMPLE SIZE	標本規模 (HYOOHON KIBO)
SAMPLING	標本抽出 (HYOOHON CHUUSHUTSU)
SAMPLING RESULTS	標本抽出の結果 (HYOOHON CHUUSHUTSU NO KEKKA)
SAMPLING RISK	標本抽出リスク (HYOOHON CHUUSHUTSU RISUKU)
SAVING DEPOSITS	通知預金 (TSUUCHI YOKIN)
SCOPE	範囲 (HAN'I)
SCOPE PARAGRAPH	範囲区分 (HAN'I-KUBUN)
SEASONALLY ADJUSTED	季節変動調整 (KISETSU HENDOO CHOOSEI)
SECOND REQUEST	二度目の催促 (NIDOME NO SAISOKU)
SECURED NOTE	担保付き支払手形 (TANPO-TSUKI SHIHARAI TEGATA)
SECURITIES AND EXCHANGE COMMISSION	米国証券取引委員会 (BEIKOKU SHOOKEN TORIHIKI IIN-KAI)
SELF-INSURANCE	自家保険 (JIKA-HOKEN)
SELLING EXPENSES	販売費 (HANBAI-HI)
SEMI-FINISHED GOODS	半製品 (HANSEIHIN)
SENIOR DEBT	優先債務 (YUUSEN SAIMU)
SEPTEMBER	九月 (KU-GATSU)
SEVERANCE	解雇 (KAIKO)
SEVERANCE INDEMNITIES	退職給与 (TAISHOKU KYUUYO)
SHARE IN LOSS OF AFFILIATES	持分法による損失 (MOCHIBUN-HOO NI YORU SONSHITSU)
SHAREHOLDERS' EQUITY	株主持分 (KABUNUSHI MOCHIBUN)
	資本 (SHIHON)
SHARES	株 (KABU)
SHORT-TERM BANK LOANS	銀行借り入れ短期借入金 (GINKOO KARI-IRE TANKI SHAKUNYUUKIN)
SHORT-TERM INVESTMENTS	短期投資 (TANKI TOOSHI)
SHORT-TERM LOANS	短期貸付金 (TANKI KASHITSUKE-KIN)
SMALL COMPANIES	零細企業 (REISAI KIGYOO)
SOCIAL SECURITY EXPENSE	社会保障費 (SHAKAI HOSHOO-HI)

SOURCES OF FUNDS	資金の源泉(SHIKIN NO GENSEN)
SPECIAL BONUS	特別ボーナス(TOKUBETSU BOONASU)
SPECIAL REPORTS	特別報告書(TOKUBETSU HOOKOKUSHO)
SPLIT (OF A COMPANY)	分割(BUNKATSU)
SPREAD (BETWEEN RATES)	隔差(KAKUSA)
STAMP DUTY	印紙税(INSHI-ZEI)
STANDARD COST	標準原価(HYOOJUN GENKA)
START-UP COSTS	開業費(KAIGYOO-HI)
STATEMENT OF ACCOUNTING POLICY	会計方針説明書(KAIKEI HOOSHIN SETSUMEI-SHO)
STATEMENT OF CHANGES IN FIN POSITION	財政状態変動表(ZAISEI JOOTAI HENDOOHYOO)
STATEMENT OF SOURCES & USES OF FUNDS	資金運用表(SHIKIN UNYOO-HYOO)
STATISTICAL SAMPLING	統計上の標本抽出(TOOKEI-JOO NO HYOOHON CHUUSHUTSU)
STATUTORY AUDIT REPORT	法定監査報告書(HOOTEI KANSA HOOKOKU-SHO)
STATUTORY RESERVE	特別法上の引当金(TOKUBETSU-HOO-JOO NO HIKIATE-KIN)
STOCK DIVIDENDS	無償株式配当(MUSHOO KABUSHIKI HAITOO)
	株式配当(KABUSHIKI HAITOO)
STOCK EXCHANGE	証券取引所(SHOOKEN TORIHIKISHO)
STOCK OPTION PLANS	スットックオプション(SUTOKKU OPUSHON)
STOCKBROKER	株式仲買人(KABUNUSHI NAKAGAI-NIN)
STOCKHOLDERS	株主(KABUNUSHI)
STOCKHOLDERS' EQUITY	資本の部(SHIHON NO BU)
	資本(SHIHON)
STRAIGHT-LINE METHOD	定額法(TEIGAKU-HOO)
	直線法(CHOKUSEN-HOO)
SUBJECT TO	～を条件とする(O JOOKEN TO SURU)
SUBLET	転貸(TENTAI)
SUBORDINATED DEBT	従属債務(JUUZOKU SAIMU)
SUBSCRIPTION	定期購読契約(TEIKI KOODOKU KEIYAKU)
SUBSEQUENT EVENTS	後発事象(KOOHATSU JISHOO)
SUBSIDIARY	子会社(KO-GAISHA)
SUBSIDIARY RECORDS	補助記録(HOJO KIROKU)
SUBSTANTIVE TESTS	財務諸表項目の監査手続(ZAIMU SHOHYOO KOOMOKU NO KANSATETSUKI)
SUM OF THE YEARS'-DIGITS METHOD	算術級数法(SANJUTSU KYUUSUU-HOO)
SUPPLEMENTARY INFORMATION	補足財務情報(HOSOKU ZAIMU JOOHOO)
SUPPLIERS	供給者(KYOOKYUU-SHA)
SUPPLIES AND SPARE PARTS	消耗品と予備部分品(SHOOMOO-HIN TO YOBI BUBUN-HIN)
SUPPORTING DOCUMENTATION	関係資料(KANKEI SHIRYOO)
SYNDICATED LOANS	シンジケートローン(SHINJIKEETO ROON)

TAKEN AS A WHOLE	全体としてとらえる(ZENTAI TO SHITE TORAERU)
TANGIBLE FIXED ASSETS	有形固定資産(YUUKEI KOTEI SHISAN)
TAX	税金(ZEIKIN)
TAX AUDIT	税務監査(ZEIMU KANSA)
TAX AUTHORITIES	税務署(ZEIMU-SHO)
TAX CREDITS	税額減免(ZEIGAKU GENMEN)
TAX RATES	税率(ZEI-RITSU)
TAX RETURN	納税報告書(NOOZEI HOOKOKU-SHO)
TAX SAVINGS	節税(SETSU-ZEI)
TAX TREATMENT	課税処理法(KAZEI SHORI-HOO)
TAXABLE INCOME	課税対象所得(KAZEI TAISHOO SHOTOKU)
TAXPAYER	納税者(NOOZEI-SHA)
TEMPORARY DIFFERENCES	一次的不一致(ICHIJI-TEKI FUICCHI)
TEST	試験(SHIKEN)
TESTS	テスト(TESUTO)
THOUSANDS	千(SEN)
TIME DEPOSITS	定期預金(TEIKI YOKIN)
TIMING	期間(KIKAN)
TOTAL FUNDS FROM OPERATIONS	営業活動より生じた運転資本金
	(EIGYOOKATSUDOO YORI SHOOJITA UNTENSHIHONKIN)
TOTAL PREMIUMS WRITTEN	総保険料収入(SOOHOKEN-RYOO SHUUNYUU)
TOTAL REVENUE	営業収益合計(EIGYOO SHUUEKI GOOKEI)
TRADE MARKS	商標権(SHOOHYOO-KEN)
TRADE RECEIVABLES	売掛金(URIKAKE-KIN)
TRADING ACCOUNT PROFITS	商品有価証券売買益（損）SHOOHIN YUUKA SHOOKEN BAIBAI-EKI(SON)
TRAINING EXPENDITURE	社員教育費(SHA-IN KYOOIKU-HI)
TRANSACTIONS	取引(TORIHIKI)
TREASURY STOCK	自己株式(JIKO KABUSHIKI)
	金庫株(KINKO-KABU)
TREND	傾向(KEIKOO)
TRIAL BALANCE	試算表(SHISAN-HYOO)
TROUBLED DEBT	救済債務(KYUUSAI SAIMU)
TRUST OPERATIONS PROFITS (LOSSES)	信託報酬益(SHINTAKU HOOSHUU-EKI)
TRUST SECURITIES	信託証券(SHINTAKU SHOOKEN)
TURNOVER RATIO	回転率(KAITEN-RITSU)
UNAMORTIZED PREMIUM	未償却割増し金(MISHOOKYAKU WARIMASHI-KIN)
UNAPPROPRIATED RETAINED EARNINGS	未処理分利益金(MISHORI-BUN RIEKI-KIN)
UNASSERTED CLAIM	未請求支払請求(MISEIKYUU SHIHARAI SEIKYUU)

English	Japanese
UNAUDITED	未監査(HIKANSA)
UNCERTAINTY	未確定事項(HIKAKUTEI JIKOO)
UNCOLLECTIBLE	回収不能(KAISHUU FUNOO)
UNDERWRITING AND POLICY ADQ. COSTS	保険手数料(HOKEN TESUU-RYOO)
UNEARNED INTERESTS	繰延前受利息(KURINOBE MAEUKE RISOKU)
UNITS OF PRODUCTION	生産高比例法(SEISAN-DAKA HIREI-HOO)
UNQUALIFIED (OPINION)	適正（意見）TEKISEI (IKEN)
UNSECURED BONDS	無担保債券(MUTANPO SAIKEN)
USEFUL LIFE (OF AN ASSET)	耐用年数(TAI-YOO NENSUU)
USES OF FUNDS	資金の運用(SHIKIN NO UNYOO)
VALUATION PRINCIPLES	評価基準(HYOOKA KIJUN)
	評価方法(HYOOKA HOOHOO)
VALUE ADDED TAX (VAT)	付加価値税（バット）FUKAKACHI-ZEI(BATTO)
VARIABLE COST	変動費(HENDOO-HI)
VEHICLES	車輛(SHARYOO)
	運搬具(UNPANGU)
VENDORS (USA)	卸売業者(OROSHIURI GYOOSHA)
VICE-CHAIRMAN	副会長(FUKU-KAICHOO)
VOUCHER	領収書(RYOOSHUU-SHO)
WAREHOUSE	倉庫(SOOKO)
WEIGHTED AVERAGE	加重平均法(総平均法)KAJUU HEIKIN-HOO (SOO-HEIKIN-HOO)
WITHHELD TAXES	源泉課税額(GENSEN KAZEI-GAKU)
WITHHOLDING TAX	源泉課税(GENSEN KAZEI)
WORKING CAPITAL	運転資本(UNTEN SHIHON)
WORKING CAPITAL RATIO	総資本純運転資本率(SOOSHIHON JUN-UNTEN SHIHON-RITSU)
WORKING CAPITAL TURNOVER	運転資本回転率(UNTEN SHIHON KAITEN-RITSU)
WORKING PAPERS	監査調書(KANSA CHOOSHO)
WRITE DOWN	帳簿価値低下(CHOOBO KACHI TEIKA)
YEAR-END CLOSING DATE	会計年度末日(KAIKEI-NENDO MATSUJITSU)
YIELD	利回り(RIMAWARI)
ZERO BASE BUDGET	ゼロベース予算(ZERO BEESU YOSAN)
ZERO COUPON BONDS	利付きなし割引債券(RI-TSUKI NASHI WARIBIKI-SAIKEN)
	ゼロ- ク-ポン債券(ZERO KUUPON SAI-KEN)

Korean	English
가격변동 조정(GAKYUK BYUNDONG JOJUNG)	ADJUSTMENT FOR INFLATION
가격변동 효과(GAKYUK BYUNDONG HYOKWA)	EFFECT OF CHANGING PRICE
가능성 희박한(GANEUNGSUNG HEE-BAK-HAN)	REMOTE
가성(GAASUNG)	GOODWILL
가중평균(GAH-JOONG PYONG KYUN)	WEIGHTED AVERAGE
간접비용(GANJUP BEYONG)	OVERHEAD EXPENSES
감가상감비(GAMGA SANG-GAK-BEE)	DEPRECIATION EXPENSES
감가상각비-건물(GAMGA SANG-GAK-BEE ,GUNMOOL)	DEPRECIATION - BUILDINGS
감가상각 충당금(GAM-GA SANG-GAK CHUNGDANGKUM)	ACCUMULATED DEPRECIATION
감모상각 충당금(GAM-MO SANG-GAK CHUNGDANGKUM)	ACCUMULATED AMORTIZATION
감사(GAM SA)	AUDITOR
감사계약(GAM SA GEH YAK)	AUDIT ENGAGEMENT
감사공준(GAM SA GONG JOON)	AUDITING STANDARDS
감사되지 않은(GAMSA DWEJI AHNUN)	UNAUDITED
감사방법(GAM SA BANG BUP)	AUDIT APPROACH
감사범위 문단(GAMSA BUMWI MOONDAN)	SCOPE PARAGRAPH
감사보고서(GAM SA BO KO SUH)	AUDITOR'S REPORT
감사비(KAM SA BI)	AUDIT FEES
감사요원(KAM SA YO WON)	AUDIT STAFF
감사위험(KAM SA WI HEUM)	AUDIT RISK
감사의견(KAM SA UI KYUN)	AUDIT OPINION
	OPINION
감사의견문단(GAMSA UI-KYUN MOONDAN)	OPINION PARAGRAPH
감사의뢰서(KAMSA EUROESUH)	CLIENT REPRESENTATION LETTER
감사인(KAM SA IN)	AUDIT PARTNER
감사표본추출(KAM SA PYO BON CHOO CHOOL)	AUDIT SAMPLING
감정가치(GAMJUNG GACHI)	ACTUARIAL VALUE
개인소득세(GAEYIN SODEUK-SEH)	PERSONAL INCOME TAX
거래(GUH-RAE)	TRANSACTIONS
거래처(GUHRAE CHUR)	CORRESPONDENT FIRMS
건물 및 구축물(GUNMOOL MIT KOOCHOOKMOOL)	BUILDINGS AND STRUCTURES
건설가계정(GUNSUL GAGYEJUNG)	CONSTRUCTION IN PROGRESS
검사(GUHM-SA)	EXAMINE
검증(GUM JEONG)	TEST

Korean	English
격차(KYUK CHA)	SPREAD
경기후퇴(KYUNG-KI HU-TOI)	RECESSION
경영자의 의도(KYONG-YOUNG-JAH UI UIDO)	MANAGEMENT INTENTION
경영층에 보고(KYUNGYOUNG-CHEONG EH BOGO)	REPORT TO MANAGEMENT
경제 환경(KYUNG-JE HWAN-KYUNG)	ECONOMIC ENVIRONMENT
계속기업(GYESOK KI-UP)	GOING CONCERN
계속성(GYESOK SUNG)	CONSISTENCY
계절변동조정(GYEJHUL BYUNDONG JOJUNG)	SEASONALLY ADJUSTED
계정목록(GYEJUNG MOKLOK)	CHART OF ACCOUNTS
계정잔액(GYEJUNG JAN-AEK)	ACCOUNT BALANCES
계획(GYE-HWEK)	PROJECTION
고객(GO-GAK)	CUSTOMERS
고정부채(GOJUNG BOOCHAE)	NON-CURRENT LIABILITIES
고정세율징수(GOJUNG SEH-YUL JINGSU)	FLAT TAX WITHHOLDING
고정자산(GOJUNG JASAN)	FIXED ASSETS
	NON-CURRENT ASSETS
고정자산처분익(GOJUNG JASAN CHURBUN YIYIK)	GAIN ON SALE OF FIXED ASSET
공사완성법(GONGSA WANSUNG BUP)	COMPLETED-CONTRACT METHOD
공공부문(GONG GONG BOOMOON)	PUBLIC SECTOR
공급자(GONG-GUP-JA)	SUPPLIERS
공동경영자(GONGDONG KYUNG-YOUNG-JA)	PARTNER
공사진행기준(GONGSA JINHAENG GHIJUN)	PERCENTAGE OF-COMPLETION-METHOD
공시(GONG SI)	DISCLOSURE
공인회계사(GONG IN HOE GEH SA)	AUDITOR
공표기준일탈(GONGPYO KIJOON YIL-TAL)	DEPART. FROM A PRONOUNCEMENT
공제 세금(GONG-JEH SEH-KUM)	WITHHELD TAXES
과대한(GWA DAE HAN)	OVERSIZE(D)
과세소득(GWA-SEH SODEUK)	TAXABLE INCOME
과세처리법(GWA-SEH CHUR-RI-BOP)	TAX TREATMENT
관계단체(GWAN GEH DAN CHAE)	AFFILIATES
관계회사(GWAN GEH HOE SA)	ASSOCIATED FIRM
관계회사 손실지분(GWAN-GEH HOE SA SONSIL JIBUN)	SHARE IN LOSS OF AFFILIATES
주식(GWAN-GEH HOESAH JUSIK)	INVESTMENT IN SUBSIDIARIES
관련자료(GWALYON JA-RYO)	SUPPORTING DOCUMENTATION

Korean	English
관세(GWAN SEH)	CUSTOMS DUTY
구매청구서(GUMAE CHEUNGUSUH)	PURCHASE REQUISITION
구월(GU WOL)	SEPTEMBER
국가별 위험(GUK-KA-BYUL WIHUM)	COUNTRY RISK
국내 자회사 (GUK-NAE JA-HOE-SA)	DOMESTIC SUBSIDIARIES
국내통화(GUK-NAE TONG-HWA)	LOCAL CURRENCY
국내통화표시 상장채권(SANGJANG CHAEKWON (GUKNAE)	LISTED BOND-LOCAL CURRENCY
국민소득(GOOKMIN SODEUK)	GROSS NATIONAL PRODUCT
규칙(KYU-CHIK)	REGULATIONS
	RULES
그룹(GROUP)	GROUP (OF COMPANIES)
금융기업(KUMYUNG KI-UP)	FINANCIAL ENTITIES
금융거래(KUMYUNG GUHRAE)	MONETARY TRANSACTIONS
금융비용의 자본화(KUMYUNGBIYONG UI JABONWHA)	CAPITALIZATION FIN. COSTS
금융자산(KUMYUNG JASAN)	MONETARY ASSETS
기간 순이익(순손실)(KIGAN SOONYIYIK(SOONSONSIL)	NET INCOME (LOSS)
기계 및 장비(KI-GEH MIT JANGBEE)	MACHINERY AND EQUIPMENT
기구 및 비품(KIGU MIT BIPOOM)	FURNITURE AND FIXTURES
기금(KIKUM)	FUNDS
기록하다(GI-ROK-HADA)	RECORD (VERB)
기업결합(KI-UP KYULHAP)	BUSINESS COMBINATIONS
기장(KI JANG)	POST ENTRIES TO LEDGER
기준에 따라(KIJOONEH TTA RA)	IN ACCORDANCE WITH
기 처분 이익잉여금(KI CHUBOON YIYIK YING-YOKUM)	APPROPRIATED R/E
기타용역수익(KITA YONGYOG SUYIK)	OTHER INCOME FOR SERVICE
기타영업이익(KITA YOUNGUP YIYIK (SONSIL)	OTHER OPERATING PROF.(LOSS)
기타융자금(KITA YOONGJAKUM)	OTHER LOANS
기회비용(KIHOE BEYONG)	OPPORTUNITY COST
납세자(NAP-SEH-JA)	TAXPAYER
납입자본금(NAP YIP JABONKUM)	CAPITAL STOCK
내규(NAE KYU)	COMPANY BY-LAWS
내부감사(NAEBU GAMSA)	INTERNAL AUDITORS
내부거래(NAE-BU GEUHRAE)	RELATED PARTY TRANSACTION
내부통제(NAEBU TONGJEH)	INTERNAL CONTROLS

Korean	English
내부통제 관리약점(NAEBU TONGJAE GWAL-LEE YAKJEUM)	CONTROL WEAKNESS
내부통제 질문지(NAEBU TONGJEH JILMOONJI)	INTERNAL CTRL. QUESTIONNAIRE
내용연수(NAE-YONG YOUNSU)	USEFUL LIFE (OF AN ASSET)
노동법(NODONG BUP)	LABOR LAW
노동시간(NODONG SIGAHN)	LABOR HOURS
누적조정(NUJUK JOJUNG)	CUMULATIVE ADJUSTMENT
누적효과(NUJUK HYOKWA)	CUMULATIVE EFFECT
누진세(NOOJINSEH)	GRADUATED TAX
	PROGRESSIVE TAX
다국적기업(DAH GOOK JEOK KIUP)	MULTINATIONAL ENTERPRISE
다른상황이 불변이면(DALUN SAHANGYI BULBYUN YIMYUN)	CETERIS PARIBUS
다중회귀분석(DAHJOONG HOEGUI BUNSEOK)	MULTIPLE REGRESSION
단기 융자(DANKI YOONGJA)	SHORT-TERM LOANS
단기은행 융자(DANKI EUN-HAENG YOONGJA)	SHORT-TERM BANK LOANS
단기투자(DANKI TOOJA)	SHORT-TERM INVESTMENTS
담보(DAM BO)	COLLATERAL
담보성 어음(DAMBOSUNG UH-WOOM)	SECURED NOTE
당좌기금성(DANG-JWA-SUNG GHIKUM)	OVERNIGHT FUNDS
당좌대월(DANGJWA DAEWOL)	OVERDRAFT
당좌비율(DANGJWA BI-YUL)	ACID TEST RATIO
당좌비율 분석(DANGJWA BI-YUL BOONSUK)	ACID TEST
당좌자산(DANGJWA JASAN)	LIQUID ASSETS
당좌차월(DANG JWA CHA WOL)	BANK OVERDRAFTS
대리권(DAE-RI-KWON)	PROXY (POWER OF ATTORNEY)
대손상각(DAESOHN SANG-GAK)	ACTUAL LOAN LOSSES
대손충당금—외상매출금(DAESONCHUNGDANGKUM—WOISANGMACHUL)	ALLOW FOR DOUBTFUL A/C
	ALLOW FOR UNCOLLECTABLE A/C
대손충당금—융자금(DAESONCHUNGDANGKUM—YUNGJAKUM)	ALLOW FOR LOAN LOSSES
대손충당금 전입액(DAESON CHOONGDANGKUM JUNYIPAEK)	RESERVE FOR LOAN LOSSES
대안(DAE AHN)	ALTERNATIVE PROCEDURES
대차대조표(DAE CHA DAE JO PYO)	BALANCE SHEET
대차대조표 마감일(DAE CHA DAE JO MA KAM IL)	BALANCE SHEET DATE
대표이사(DAE PYO YI SA)	CHIEF EXECUTIVE OFFICER
대표회계사(DAEPYO HOE GEH SA)	AUDIT MANAGER

도매업자(DOMAE-UP-JA)	VENDORS (USA)
도표(DO PYO)	FLOWCHART
독립(DONGNIP)	INDEPENDENCE
리스의 자본화(LEASE UI JABONWHA)	CAPITALIZATION OF LEASES
만기(MAHNKI)	MATURITY
만기일(MAHN-GI YIL)	DUE DATE
운송료(MAEYIP WOLYO EUI WUNSONGRYO)	FREIGHT, PURCH. OF MATERIALS
매출액(MAECHUL-AEK)	SALES (TURNOVER)
매출원가(MAECHUL WONKA)	COST OF GOODS SOLD
매출이익(MAECHUL YIYIK)	GROSS MARGIN
명세서(MYUNG-SEH-SUH)	DISCLOSURE
모기업(MO KI UP)	PARENT COMPANY
모집단(MO-JIPDAN)	POPULATION (IN A STAT.)
모회사(MO HOE SA)	PARENT COMPANY
목차(MOK CHA)	CONTENTS
무담보 사채(MU DAMBO SACHAE)	DEBENTURE
무이자 채권(MOOYIJA CHAEKWON)	ZERO COUPON BONDS
무작위(MOO-JAG-WI)	RANDOM
무작위로(MOO JAK WI RO)	AT RANDOM
무형고정자산(MOO-HYONG KOJUNG JASAN)	INTANGIBLE ASSETS
무형자산(MOO-HYONG JASAN)	INTANGIBLE ASSETS
미상각할증금(MI-SANG-GAK HAL-JEUNG-KUM)	UNAMORTIZED PREMIUM
미수금(MISUKUM)	RECEIVABLES
미수 수익(MISOO SOOYIK)	ACCRUED INCOME
미수 이자(MISOO YIJA)	INTEREST RECEIVABLE
미실현 이자(MI-SIL-HYUN YI-JA)	UNEARNED INTERESTS
미지급 배당금(MI JIKUP BAEDANGKUM)	DIVIDENDS PAYABLE
미지급 비용(MIJIGUP BEEYONG)	ACCRUED EXPENSES
미지급 세금(MIGIGUP SEHKUM)	ACCRUED TAXES
미지급 이자(MIJIKUP YIJA)	INTEREST PAYABLE
미지급 휴가(MIGIGUP HYUGA)	ACCRUED VACATIONS
미착품(MI CHAK POOM)	GOODS IN TRANSIT
미처분 이익잉여금(MICHURBUN YIYIK YING-YUR-KUM)	UNAPPROPRIATED R/E
미처분 잉여금(MICHURBOON YI-YIK YING-YUR-KUM)	RETAINED EARNINGS

밀린(MILIN)	OVERDUE
반기재무재표(BANKI JAEMOO JAPYO)	INTERIM FINAN'L STATEMENT
반제품(BANJEPOOM)	WORK IN PROCESS
	SEMI-FINISHED GOODS
반환금(BAN-HWAN-KUM)	REFUND
받을어음(BAHDUL UH-WOOM)	NOTES RECEIVABLE
발생(BAL SAENG)	ACCRUAL
발생주의(BAL SAENG JOO-UI)	ACCRUAL (ACC. METHOD)
발생하다(BALSAENG HADA)	ACCRUE
발행주식(BALHAENG JUSIK)	OUTSTANDING SHARES
방어(BANG-UHR)	HEDGE
배당(BAE-DANG)	DIVIDEND
배분(BAEBOON)	ALLOCATE
배상(BAESANG)	INDEMNITIES
배상청구(BAE SANG CHUNG KU)	CLAIMS
배치(BAECHI)	PLACEMENT
백(BAIK)	HUNDREDS
백만(BAIK-MAHN)	MILLIONS
벌금(BUHL-KUM)	FINE
범위(BUMWI)	SCOPE
범위에 대한 제한(BUMWI EH DAEHAN JEH-HAN)	RESTRICTION ON THE SCOPE
법률적 요구사항(BUMYOOLJEOK YOGOO SAHANG)	LEGAL REQUIREMENTS
법인세전 순이익(BUP-YIN-SEH JEON SOON-YIYIK)	TAXABLE INCOME
법정 감사보고서(BUPJUNG GAMSA BOGOSUH)	STATUTORY AUDIT REPORT
법정 준비금(BUPJUNG JUN-BE-KUM)	STATUTORY RESERVE
법정 적립금(BUPJUNG JUNGNIPKUM)	LEGAL RESERVE
변동비 (BYUNDONG-BE)	VARIABLE COST
변동율(BYUNDONG YUL)	FLOATING RATE
변칙(BYUNCHIK)	IRREGULARITY
변호사(BYUNHOSA)	LAWYER
보고서(BOGOSUH)	REPORT
보관증권(BOGWAN JEUNG-GWON)	CUSTODY SECURITIES
보증(BOJEUNG)	GUARANTEES
보통주(BOTONG JOO)	COMMON STOCK

Korean	English
보험가입자 잉여분(BOHUM GAYIPJA YING–YUR–BOON)	POLICYHOLDERS' SURPLUS
보험가입자 자본(BOHUM GAYIPJA JABON)	POLICYHOLDERS' EQUITY
보험금(BO–HUM KUM)	TOTAL INS. CLAIMS & LOSSES
보험금지급 충당금(BOHUMKUM JIKUP CHOONGDANGKUM)	RESERVE, O/S CLAIM & LOSS
보험수수료(BO–HUM SU–SU–RYO)	UNDERWR. & POLICY ADQ. COSTS
보험료(BOHUMRYO)	PREMIUM
보험료 준비금(BOHUMRYO JOONBEEKUM)	LT INSURANCE RESERVE CHARGES
보험회사 (BOHUM HOESA)	INSURANCE COMPANY
복리후생비(BOKREE HOOSAENGBEE)	EMPLOYEE BENEFITS
부가가치세(BOO–GA GA–CHI–SEH)	VALUE ADDED TAX (VAT)
부동산융자(BUDONGSAN YOONGJA)	MORTGAGE
	REAL ESTATE & MORTGAGE LOANS
부록(BOO–ROK)	SUPPLEMENTARY INFORMATION
부산물(BOO SAN MOOL)	BY–PRODUCTS
부실투자자산(BUSIL TOOJA JASAN)	NON–PERFORMING EARNING ASSETS
부의 영업권(BOO–UI YOUNG–UP–KWON)	NEGATIVE GOODWILL
부적정 의견(BU JUKJUNG YUI–KYUN)	ADVERSE OPINION
부채(BOOCHAE)	LIABILITY
부채비율(BOOCHAE BEYOOL)	INDEBTNESS RATIO
부채재조정(BUCHAE JAEJOJONG)	DEBT RESTRUCTURING
부회장(BOO–HOE–JANG)	VICE–CHAIRMAN
분개(BOONGAE)	JOURNAL ENTRY
분개장(BOONGAEJANG)	JOURNAL
분기(BOON–KI)	QUARTER
분기별(BOON–KI–BYUL)	QUARTERLY
분기별 재무제표(BOON–KI–BYUL JAEMOO–JEH–PYO)	QUARTERLY FINANCIAL STATEMENT
분석적 개관(BOONSUKJUK KAEKWAN)	ANALYTICAL REVIEW
분할(BOON–HAL)	SPLIT (OF A COMPANY)
불(BUL)	DOLLARS
불입자본금(BOOLYIP JABONKUM)	PAID–IN CAPITAL
불확실성(BOOL HWAK–SIL–SUNG)	UNCERTAINTY
비과세 소득(BE–GWASEH SODEUK)	NON–TAXABLE INCOME
비교재무제표(BEEKYO JAEMOO JEHPYO)	COMPARATIVE FINANCIAL STAT.
비금융거래(BEKUMYOONG GUHRAE)	NON–MONETARY TRANSACTION
비담보 채권(BE–DAM–BO CHAE–KWON)	UNSECURED BONDS
비상환부 우선주(BEE SANGHWANBOO WOOSUNJU)	NON–REDEEMABLE PREF. STOCK
비영리(BE–YOUNG–REE)	NON–PROFIT
비용(BEE–YONG)	EXPENSES
비자본성 충당금(BEJABON–SUNG CHOONGDANGKUM)	NON–EQUITY RESERVES
비통계적 표본추출(BE–TONGGUEJEOK PYOBONCHUCHUL)	NON–STATISTICAL SAMPLING
비표본추출 위험(BE–PYOBONCHOOCHOOL WI HEUM)	NON–SAMPLING RISK
비품(BIPOOM)	FITTINGS
사경제부문(SA–KYUNG–JEH BOOMOON)	PRIVATE SECTOR
사무용 소모품(SAMOOYONG SOMOPOOM)	OFFICE SUPPLIES
사업부(SA UP BOO)	BUSINESS SEGMENT
사월(SAH WOL)	APRIL
사채(SA CHAE)	BOND
	BONDS PAYABLE
사회보장비용(SAHOE BOJANG BEYONG)	SOCIAL SECURITY EXPENSE
산술급수법(SANSUL GUPSU BOP)	SUM OF YRS'–DIGIT METHOD
산업(SANUP)	INDUSTRY
삼월(SAM–WOL)	MARCH
상각(SANG–GAK)	WRITE DOWN
상담(SANGDAM)	CONSULTING SERVICES
상당성(SANDANG–SEONG)	MATERIALITY
상당한(SANGDANGHAN)	MATERIAL (SIGNIFICANT)
상업 및 산업융자(SANG–UP MIT SAN–UP YUNG JA)	COMMERCIAL & INDUSTRIAL LOANS
상속세(SANG–SOK SEH)	INHERITANCE TAX
상쇄(SANG SWOE)	OFFSET
상업은행(SANG–UP EUN HAENG)	COMMERCIAL BANK
상품보증부 융자(SANGPOOM BOJEUNG BU YUNGJA)	PRODUCT FINANCING
상품유가증권(SANGPOOM YOOKAH JEUNG–KWON)	MARKETABLE SECURITIES
	MARKETABLE STOCKS
상품유가증권 매매손익(SANGPUM YUKAJUNGKON MAMAESONIK)	TRADING ACCT.PROF.(LOSS)
상표(SANG PYO)	TRADEMARKS
상호금융(SANGHO KUMYOONG)	MUTUAL FUND
상환부(SANG–HWAN–BOO)	REDEEMABLE
상환부 우선주(SANG–HWAN–BOO WOOSON–JOO)	REDEEMABLE PREFERRED STOCK

상환조건(SANG-HWAN JOKEON)	REDEMPTION FEATURES
생명보험(SAENGMYUNG BOHUM)	LIFE INSURANCE
생명보험금(SAENG-MYUNG BOHUMKUM)	LIFE POLICY BENEFITS
생산능력(SAENG-SAN NEUNG-LYUK)	PRODUCTION CAPACITY
생산단위(SAENG-SAN DAN-WUI)	UNITS OF PRODUCTION
생산비(SAENG-SAN-BE)	PRODUCTION COST
생산주기(SAENG-SAN JUKI)	PRODUCTION CYCLE
생산주문(SAENG-SAN JUMOON)	PRODUCTION ORDER
선급비용(SUNGUP BEYONG)	ADVANCES TO SUPPLIERS
	PREPAID EXPENSE
선입선출법(SUHNYIP SUHNCHOOL BUHP)	FIRST IN,FIRST OUT(FIFO)
선물계약(SUNMUL GEHYAK)	FUTURE CONTRACTS
세금(SEH-KUM)	TAX
세금보고(SEH-KUM BOGO)	TAX RETURN
세금분배효과(SEH KUM BUNBAE HYOKWA)	DEFERRED INCOME TAX
세금특혜(SEH KEUM TEUK HAE)	CREDIT FOR TAX BREAKS
세금혜택(SEH-KUM HEH-TAEK)	TAX CREDITS
세무감사(SEH-MOO GAMSA)	TAX AUDIT
세무당국(SEH-MOO DANG-GUK)	TAX AUTHORITIES
세무원칙에 입각한(SEMOO WONCHIK EH YIPGAKHAN)	FOR TAXATION PURPOSES
세율(SEH-YOOL)	TAX RATES
소규모 기업(SOKYUMO KIUP)	SMALL COMPANIES
소득세(SODEUK SEH)	INCOME TAX
소모품 및 비품(SOMOPOOM MIT BOOPOOM)	SUPPLIES AND SPARE PARTS
소비세(SOBEE SEH)	EXCISE TAX
소송(SOSONG)	LITIGATION
소액지급금(SOHAEK JIKEUP-KUM)	PETTY CASH
손실(SOHN-SIL)	LOSS
손익계정(SOHN-YHIK GEH-JUNG)	PROFIT & LOSS ACCOUNTS
손익분기점(SOHN YIK BOONKIJUM)	BREAK EVEN POINT
송장(SONGJANG)	INVOICE
수금(SU KUM)	COLLECTIONS
수금이 불가능한(SU-KUM-YI BOOL-GA-NEUNG HAN)	UNCOLLECTIBLE
수금비율(SU KUM BIYOOL)	COLLECTION RATIO

수당(SOODANG)	ALLOWANCE
수선(SUSON)	REPAIRS
수선 및 유지비(SUSON MIT YUJIBE)	REPAIRS AND MAINTENANCE
수수료(SUSU RYO)	FEES
수입배당금(SUYIP BAEDANGKUM)	DIVIDEND INCOME
수입수수료(SU-YIP SUSURYO)	COMM. & FEES PROF. (LOSSES)
수입이자(SUYIP YIJA)	INTEREST INCOME
수입특별관세(SUYIP TEUK-BYUL GWANSEH)	IMPORT SURCHARGES
수출(SU-CHOOL)	EXPORT
수출세(SU-CHOOL SEH)	EXPORT DUTIES
순고정자산(SOON GOJUNG JASAN)	NET FIXED ASSETS
순 판매액(SOON PAAN-MAE-AEK)	NET SALES
순수입 보험료(SOON SUYIP BOHUMRYO)	NET PREMIUMS EARNED
순 실현액(SOON SIL-HYUN AEK)	NET REALIZABLE VALUE
순 외상매출금(SOON WOESAN MAECHOOLKUM)	NET TRADE A/R
순이익(SOON YIYIK)	NET INCOME
시기(SI-GHI)	TIMING
시산표(SI-SAN-PYO)	TRIAL BALANCE
시월(SI-WOL)	OCTOBER
시장가격(SIJANG GAKYOK)	MARKET PRICE
시중은행(SIJOONG EUN HAENG)	COMMERCIAL BANK
시중가격(SIJOONG GAKYOK)	MARKET PRICE
신디케이트 융자(SYNDICATE YUNG JA)	SYNDICATED LOANS
신용거래액(SHIN YONG GUHRAE AEK)	CREDIT LINE
신용거래 회전율(SINYONG GUHRAE HOEJONYOOL)	CREDIT TURNOVER RATIO
신탁계정 손익(SINTAK GEH-JUNG SONYIK)	TRUST OPER. PROF. (LOSS)
신탁증권(SIN-TAK JEUNGKWON)	TRUST SECURITIES
실지재고자산(SILJI JAEGO JASAN)	PHYSICAL INVENTORY
십억(SIP-OUK)	BILLIONS
십일월(SIP-IL-WOL)	NOVEMBER
씨-디(CD)	CERTIFICATE OF DEPOSIT
악성부채(AHK-SUNG BOOCHAE)	TROUBLED DEBT
액면가(AEG-MYUN KA)	FACE VALUE
	PAR VALUE

Korean	English
약정(YAK JUNG)	COMMITMENTS
양도 소득세(YANG DO SODEUKSEH)	CAPITAL GAINS TAX
양식(YANGSIK)	FORM
역 리스(YOG LEASE)	LEASEBACK
연결계정(YOUNKYUL GYEJUNG)	CONSOLIDATED ACCOUNTS
연결재무제표(YOUNKYUL JAEMOO JAEPYO)	CONSOLIDATED F/S
연구개발비(YOUNGU KAEBALBEE)	RESEARCH & DEVELOPMENT COST
연금(YOUNKUM)	PENSION
연금제도(YOUNKUM JEHDO)	PENSION PLAN
연수 및 훈련비(YOUNSU MIT HUL-YUN-BE)	TRAINING EXPENDITURE
연차적으로(YONCHAJUKURO)	ANNUALLY
연차 주주총회(YONCHA JUJU CHONG-HOE)	ANNUAL S/H MEETING
연차총회(YONCHA CHONG-HOE)	ANNUAL MEETING
영구보존서류(YOUNG-GU BOJON SEORYU)	PERMANENT FILE
영구사채(YOUNG-GU SACHAE)	PERPETUAL BOND
영업권(YOUNG-UP-GWON)	GOODWILL
영업외 손익(YOUNG-UP WOE SOHN YIK)	NON-OPERATING INCOME & EXP.
영업임대차(YOUNG-UP YIMDAECHA)	OPERATING LEASES
영업이익(YOUNG-UP YIYIK)	OPERATING PROFIT
영업이익율(YOUNG-UP YIYIKYOOL)	OPERATING RATIO
영업조달 순운전 자금(YOUNGUP-JODAL SUN WUNJON JAKUM)	TOTAL FUND FROM OPERATION
영업주기(YOUNG-UP JUKI)	OPERATING CYCLE
영업활동의 중단(YOUNG-UP HWALDONG UI JOONGDAN)	DISCONTINUED OPERATIONS
영향(YOUNG-HYANG)	IMPACT
예산(YE SAN)	BUDGET
예측(YECHEUK)	FORECAST
예치보증금(YECHI BOJEUNGKUM)	GUARANTEE DEPOSITS
오류(ORYOU)	ERRORS
오월(OUWOL)	MAY
옵션(OPTION)	OPTIONS
완제품(WANJEPOOM)	FINISHED GOODS
왜곡된 정보(WAEKOK DOEN JUNGBO)	MISLEADING INFORMATION
외부주주 지분(WOEBOO JUJU JEEBOON)	MINORITY INTEREST
외상 매입금(WOESANG MAEYIPKUM)	ACCOUNTS PAYABLE
외상 매출금(WOESANG MAECHULKUM)	ACCOUNTS(TRADE) RECEIVABLE
외화(WOE HWA)	FOREIGN CURRENCY
외화자산의 평가(WOE WHA JASAN UI PYONGKA)	CURRENCY TRANSLATION
외화 환산(WOE HWA HWAN-SAN)	FOREIGN CURRENCY TRANSLATION
외환(WOE HWAN)	FOREIGN EXCHANGE
외환 매매익(손)(WOEHWAN MAEMAEYIK (SON)	FOREIGN EXCH. GAIN (LOSS)
요구불 예금(YOGOOBOOL YEKUM)	DEMAND DEPOSITS
요약 재무상태(YOYAK JAEMOO SANGTAE)	FINANCIAL SUMMARY
요약 재무제표(YOYAK JAEMOO JAEPYO)	CONDENSED F/S
용역비 (발생한)(YONGYUG-BEE (BALSANG HAN)	COST OF SERVICES RENDERED
용역 수수료(YONGYUG SUSURYO)	FEES, SVS. REND. BY 3RD PARTY
용역수입(YONGYUG SUYIP)	INCOME, SERVICES RENDERED
우발성(WOO BAL SEUNG)	CONTINGENCIES
우발차익(WOOBAL CHA YIK)	GAIN CONTINGENCY
우선자본(WOOSUN JABON)	PRIMARY CAPITAL
우선주(WOO-SON-JU)	PREFERRED SHARE (USA)
우선채무(WOO-SON CHAE-MOO)	SENIOR DEBT
운영감독(WOON-YOUNG GAMDOK)	OPERATING CONTROLS
운영감사(WOON-YOUNG GAMSA)	OPERATIONAL AUDITING
운영관리(WOON-YOUNG GWAL-LEE)	OPERATIONAL CONTROLS
운영관리조직(WOON-YOUNG GWAL-LEE JOJIK)	OPERATIONAL NETWORK
운전자본(WOON JEON JA-BON)	WORKING CAPITAL
운전자본 비율(WOON-JEON JA-BON BE-YOOL)	WORKING CAPITAL RATIO
운전자본 회전율(WOON-JEON JA-BON HOE-JEON YOOL)	WORKING CAPITAL TURNOVER
원가(WONKA)	HISTORICAL COST
원가 혹은 시가(WONKA HOGUN SITKA)	COST OR MARKET
원료(WOLYO)	RAW MATERIALS
원천징수세(WON-CHUN JING-SU SEH)	WITHHOLDING TAX
월별(WOL BYUL)	MONTHLY
월부판매(WOLBOO PAN-MAE)	SALES ON INSTALLMENT
위문금(WIMOONKUM)	CHARITY EXPENSES
위탁(WI-TAK)	PLEDGE
위탁조건(WI-TAK JOGUN)	PLEDGING REQUIREMENTS
위험성의 노출(WI-HUM-SUNG UI NOCHOOL)	RISK EXPOSURE

Korean	English
유가증권(YUKAH JEUNG-KWON)	MARKETABLE SECURITIES
유가증권처분익(손)(YUKAH JEUNGKWON CHOBOON YIK(SON)	INVESTMENT SECURITY GAIN(LOSS)
유급휴가(YU KUP HYUGA)	COMPENSATED ABSENCES
유동부분,단기부분(YUDONG BOOBOON, DANKI BOOBOON)	CURRENT PORTION OF
유동부채(YUDONG BOOCHAE)	CURRENT LIABILITIES
유동비율(YUDONG BEE YOOL)	CURRENT RATIO
유동성(YUDONG-SEONG)	LIQUIDITY
유동성비율(YUDONGSEUNG BEEYOOL)	LIQUIDITY RATIO
유동자산(YUDONG JASAN)	CURRENT ASSETS
유월(YOU-WOL)	JUNE
유형고정자산(YU-HYUNG GO-JUNG JA-SAN)	TANGIBLE FIXED ASSETS
유휴시설(YOOHYU SISUL)	IDLE CAPACITY
융자(YOONGJA)	LOANS
은행(EUN HAENG)	BANK
은행간 자산(EUNHANG GHAN JASAN)	INTERBANK ASSETS
은행간 저축(EUNHANG GHAN JUH-CHOOK)	INTERBANK DEPOSITS
은행간 이자율(EUNHANG GHAN YIJAYOOL)	INTERBANK RATE
은행계정 조정표(EUN HEANG GEH-JONG JOJONGPYO)	BANK RECONCILIATION
은행 수수료(EUN HAENG SUSURYO)	BANK SERVICE CHARGES
의견(UI-KYUN)	OPINION
의견거절(UIKYUN GUHJEOL)	DISCLAIMER OF OPINION
이사(YI-SA)	DIRECTORS
이사회(YISAHOE)	BOARD OF DIRECTORS
이연방법(YIYEUN BANG BEUP)	DEFERRAL METHOD
이연부채(YIYOUN BUCHAE)	ACCRUED LIABILITIES
이연자산(YIYEON JASAN)	DEFERRED CHARGES
이연수익(YIYEON SUYIK)	DEFERRED INCOME
이연세금(YI YEON SAE KUM)	DEFERRED TAXES
이월(YI WOL)	FEBRUARY
이월기간(YI WOL KI GAN)	CARRYFORWARD PERIOD
이월손실금(YIWOL SOHNSILKUM)	LOSS CARRYFORWARD
이월조정액(YI-WOL JOJUNG-AEK)	PRIOR PERIOD ADJUSTMENTS
이익(YIYIK)	PROFIT
이익잉여금 (YIYIK YING-YUR-KUM)	RETAINED EARNINGS

Korean	English
이익참여(YI-YIK CHAMYUR)	PROFIT SHARING
이자율(YIJAYOOL)	INTEREST RATE
이자의 자본화(YIJA UI JABONWHA)	CAPITALIZATION OF INTERESTS
이중과세(YIJOONG GWA-SEH)	DOUBLE TAXATION
이중세(YIJOONG SEH)	DOUBLE TAXATION
인건비(YIN-KON-BE)	PAYROLL
	SALARIES AND WAGES
인구(IN GU)	POPULATION
인지 세(YINJISEH)	STAMP DUTY
인플레이션(INFLATION)	INFLATION
일관성있게 적용한(YILKWANSUNG YITGEH JUGYONGHAN)	CONSISTENTLY APPLIED
일반 관리비(YILBAN GWAL-LEE-BE)	ADMINISTRATIVE EXPENSES
일반보험(YILBAN BOHUM)	GENERAL INSURANCE
일반적으로 인정되는(YILBANJUGURO YINJUNG-DOENEUN)	GENERALLY ACCEPTED
일시적 불일치(YILSI-JEOK BOOL-YIL-CHI)	TEMPORARY DIFFERENCES
일월(YIL-WOL)	JANUARY
일주당 배당금(YIL JU-DANG BAEDANGKUM)	DIVIDEND PER SHARE
일주당 순이익(YIL JUDANG SOON YI-YIK)	EARNINGS PER SHARE
임대인(YIM-DAE-YIN)	LESSOR
임대차 (YIMDAECHA)	LEASE
임대차 융자금(YIMDAECHA YOONGJAKUM)	LEASE FINANCING LOANS
임원(YIMWON)	OFFICER
임차인(YIM-CHA-YIN)	LESSEE
입찰(YIP CHAL)	BID
입찰하다(YIP-CHAL HADA)	BID(VERB)
자격증(JA-KYUK JEUNG)	LICENSES
자금계획(JAKUM GEH-HOEK)	FINANCING ARRANGEMENT
자금동원하다(JAKUM DONGWON HADA)	FINANCE (VERB)
자금모집비용(JAKUM MOJIP BIYONG)	EXPENSES ON CAPITAL INCREASE
자금운영표(JAKUM WUNYONG PYO)	STAT OF SOURCES & USES OF FUNDS
자기자본(JAKI JABON)	NET WORTH
자기자본 이익율(JAKI JABON YI-YIK-YOOL)	RETURN ON EQUITY
자기주식(JAKI JU-SIK)	TREASURY STOCK
자료수집철(JARYO SOOJIP CHUL)	WORKING PAPERS

자본(JABON)	STOCKHOLDERS' EQUITY
자본잉여금(JABON YING YO KUM)	CAPITAL SURPLUS
자본증식(JABON JUNGSIK)	CAPITAL INCREASE
자본총계(JABON CHONG-GEH)	SHAREHOLDERS' EQUITY
자산(JA SAN)	ASSETS
자산구성(JASAN KUSUNG)	PORTFOLIO COMPOSITION
자산재평가(JASAN JAE PYONG-KA)	REVALUATION
자산재평가 준비금(JASAN JAE PYONG-KA JUNBE-KUM)	REVALUATION RESERVES
자체보험(JACHE BOHUM)	SELF INSURANCE
자회사(JA HOESA)	SUBSIDIARY
잔존가격(JANJON GAKYUK)	EXPECTED SALVAGE VALUE
장기계약(JANG-GHEE GEH-YAK)	LONG-TERM CONTRACTS
장기부채(JANG-GHEE BOOCHAE)	LONG-TERM DEBT
장기부채의 변제(JANG-GHEE BOOCHAE UI BYUNJAE)	LONG-TERM DEBT RETIRED
장기신용(JANG GHEE SINYONG)	LONG-TERM CREDITS
장기투자(JANG-GHEE TOOJAH)	LONG-TERM INVESTMENTS
장부(JANG-BOO)	VOUCHER
장부가격(JANG-BOO KAKYUK)	BOOK VALUE
장외거래(JANGWOE GUHRAE)	OVER THE COUNTER TRANSACTION
재고자산(JAEGO JASAN)	INVENTORIES-USA(STOCKS-UK)
재고자산회전율(JAEGO JASAN HOEJUHN YOOL)	INVENTORY TURNOVER RATIO
재구매계약(JAE GU-MAE KEH-YAK)	REPURCHASE AGREEMENT
재료(JAERYO)	MATERIALS (SUST.)
재무관리(JAEMOO GWALEE)	FINANCE
재무상태변동표(JAEMOO SANG-TAI BYUNDONG PYO)	STAT OF CHANGES IN FIN'L POSIT.
재무자원원천 및 운영표(JAEMUJAWON WONCHUN/WUNYON PYO)	STAT OF SOUR. & USES OF FUNDS
재무자원의 운용(JAEMOO JAWON UI WOONYONG)	USES OF FUNDS
재무자원의 원천(JAEMOO JAWON UI WONCHUN)	SOURCES OF FUNDS
재무제표(JAEMOO JEPYO)	FINANCIAL STATEMENTS
재무제표의 개관(JAEMOO JEHPYO UI GAE-GWAN)	REVIEW OF FINANCIAL STATEMENTS
재무제표의 주석(JAEMOO JEHPYO UI JOOSUK)	FOOTNOTES (FIN'L STATEMENT)
재무제표의 편집(JAEMU JAEPYO UI PYUN JIP)	COMPILATION OF FIN'L STATEMENT
재보험 조정액(JAE-BOHUM JOJUNG-AEK)	REINSURANCE & PREMIUM ADJUST.
재생산비(JAE SAENGSANBE)	REPRODUCTION COST
재요구(JAE YOKU)	SECOND REQUEST
재자금 조달(JAE JA-KUM JODAL)	REFINANCING
재조정(JAE JOJUNG)	RESTRUCTURE
재직증명서(JAEJIK JUNGMUNGSEH)	CERTIFICATE OF GOOD STANDING
재판매계약(JAE PAN-MAE KEH-YAK)	RESALE AGREEMENTS
재판매용 상품(JAE PAN-MAE-YONG SANGPOOM)	RESALE MERCHANDISE
재평가 잉여금(JAE PYONG-KA YING-YUR-KUM)	REVALUATION SURPLUS
재할인 어음(JAE HAL-YIN UHR-WOOM)	REDISCOUNTED NOTES
저가법(JUH-KA BOP)	LOWER OF COST OR MARKET
저당(JUH DANG)	COLLATERAL
저작권(JUH JAK KWON)	COPYRIGHT
저축예금(JUHCHOOK YEKUM)	SAVING DEPOSIT
적정(JUK-JEONG)	UNQUALIFIED
적정 가능한(JUK JUNG KANEUNG HAN)	REASONABLY POSSIBLE
적정하게 표시하다 (JUK-JUNG HAGEH PYOSIHADA)	FAIRLY PRESENTED
전기이월(JUHNGI YI WOL)	CARRYFORWARD
전기이월조정액(JUHNGI YIWOL JOJUNG AEK)	PRIOR PERIOD ADJUSTMENT
전대(JUHNDAI)	SUBLET
전무(JUHN MOO)	GENERAL MANAGER
전문가의 기준(JUHN-MOON-GA UI KIJOON)	PROFESSIONAL STANDARDS
전문가의 판단(JUHN-MOON-GA UI PANDAN)	PROFESSIONAL JUDGEMENT
전시비용(JUHN-SI BIYONG)	EXHIBITION EVENT EXPENSES
전자계산장비(JUHNJA GUESAN JANGBE)	DATA PROCESSING EQUIPMENT
전체적으로(JUHN CHE JEUK UI RO)	TAKEN AS A WHOLE
전표확인(JUHNPYO WHAKIN)	CONFIRMATION OF ACCOUNTS
전환사채(JUHNWHAN SA CHAE)	CONVERTIBLE DEBT
절세(JUHL-SEH)	TAX SAVINGS
접대비(JUPDAE BEE)	ENTERTAINMENT EXPENSES
정기예금(JUHNG-KI YEKUM)	TIME DEPOSIT
정액법(JUNG-AEK-BOP)	STRAIGHT LINE METHOD
정율법(JUNG YOOL BUP)	ACCELERATED DEPRECIATION
제2차 담보부 부채(JEH YEE CHA DAMBOBU BUCHAE)	SUBORDINATED DEBT
제2차 담보부 융자(JEH YEE CHA DAMBOBU YOONGJA)	SUBORDINATED FINANCING
제로베이스 예산(ZERO BASE YE-SAN)	ZERO BASE BUDGET

Korean	English
제이 시장권(JE-YI SIJANG-KWON)	SECONDARY MARKET
제외하고(JEWOE HAGO)	EXCEPT FOR
제품판매(JEH-POOM PAN-MAE)	SALE OF MANUFACTURED GOODS
조건부로(JOKUNBOO KO)	SUBJECT TO
조기부채변제(JOKI BOOCHAE BYUNJE)	EARLY EXTINGUISHMENT OF DEBT
조기은퇴(JOKI EUN-TOE)	EARLY RETIREMENT
조정(JOJUNG)	ADJUSTMENT
조직비용(JOJIK BEYONG)	ORGANIZATION EXPENSES
조직표(JOJIK PYO)	ORGANIZATION CHART
종속법인(JONGSOK BUB IN)	AFFILIATED FIRMS
종속회사(JONGSOK HOESA)	SUBSIDIARY
종업원(JONG-UP WON)	EMPLOYEE
주식, 주권(JUSIK, JUKWON)	SHARES
주식배당(JUSIK BAEDANG)	STOCK DIVIDENDS
주식 옵션안(JUSIK OPTION AHN)	STOCK OPTION PLANS
주식재평가이익(JUSIK JAEPYONGKA YIYIK)	GAIN ON REVAL.OF SECURITIES
주식중매인(JUSIK JOONGMAEYIN)	STOCK BROKERS
주요 고객(JUYO GOGAEK)	MAJOR CUSTOMERS
주주(JUJU)	STOCKHOLDERS
주택융자(JUTAEK YOONGJA)	MORTGAGE
주택융자은행(JUTAEK YOONGJA EUN-HAENG)	MORTGAGE BANK
준비금(JOON-BE-KUM)	PROVISION
준수하다(JOONSU HADA)	COMPLY WITH
준현금(JOON HYUNKUM)	CASH EQUIVALENTS
중간재무제표(JOONG-GHAN JAEMOO JEPYO)	INTERIM FINANCIAL STATEMENTS
중대성에 관한 검증(JOONGDAESUNG EH GWANHAN GUMJEUG)	SUBSTANTIVE TESTS
중요성(JOONGYO-SEONG)	MATERIALITY
중요한(JOONGYOHAN)	MATERIAL
중재기간(JOONGJAE KIGHAN)	INTERVENING PERIOD
증권감독원(JEUNGKWON GAMDOKWON)	SECUR. & EXCH. COMMISSION
증권거래(JEUNG-KWON GUHRAE)	STOCK EXCHANGE
증권거래소(JEUNG-KWON GUHRAESO)	STOCK EXCHANGE
증권회사(JEUNG KWON HOI SA)	INVESTMENT BANK/MERCHANT BANK
증빙서류(JEUNG-BING SUHRYOU)	EVIDENTIAL MATTER

Korean	English
지급보증 대충(JIGUP BO-JEUNG DAECHOONG)	CUSTOMERS'LIAB. FOR ACCEPTANCE
지급어음(JIGUP UH-WOOM)	NOTES PAYABLE
지급이자(JIGUP YI-JA)	INTEREST EXPENSES
지배권 취득(JIBAEKWON CHUIDUK)	ACQUISITION(OF A COMPANY)
지배회사(JIBAE HOESA)	HOLDING COMPANY
지분(JIBOON)	EQUITY IN OTHER COMPANIES
지분공동계산법(JIBOON GONGDONG GYE-SAN-BUP)	POOLING OF INTEREST METHOD
지불(JIBOOL)	DISBURSEMENTS
	PAYMENTS
지불만기된 융자(JIBUL MAHNKIDOEN YOONG-JAH)	MATURED LOANS
지불주기(JIBOOL JUGHI)	PAYMENT CYCLE
지분법(JIBOON BUP)	EQUITY METHOD
지불불능위험(JIBOOL BOOLNEUNG WUIHEUM)	LIQUIDITY RISK
지참인(JICHAM YIN)	BEARER
직접비용(JIK-JEOP-BE-YONG)	DIRECT COST
진부성(JINBOO-SUNG)	OBSOLESCENCE
차기이월(CHAGI YI WOL)	CARRYBACK
차량(CHA-RYANG)	VEHICLES
차익(CHAYIK)	GAIN
차입금(CHAYIPKUM)	DEBENTURE
차후발생사항(CHAHOO BAL-SAENG SAHANG)	SUBSEQUENT
창업비(CHANG-UP BEE)	START-UP COST
창업회사(CHANG UP HOE SA)	DEVELOPMENT STAGE COMPANIES
창고(CHANG-GO)	WAREHOUSE
찾아내다(CHAJANAEDA)	DETECT
채권(CHAE KWON)	BOND
채용비용(CHAE YONG BEYONG)	RECRUITING EXPENSE
처분(CHUR BOON)	DISPOSITION
천(CHUN)	THOUSAND
	THOUSANDS
청약(CHUNG-YAK)	SUBSCRIPTION
체감세(CHE-GAM-SEH)	REGRESSIVE TAX
총계정원장(CHONG GEHJUNG WONJANG)	GENERAL LEDGER
총보험준비금(CHONG BO-HUM JUN-BE-KUM)	TOTAL INSURANCE RESERVES

Korean	English
총수익(CHONG SU-YIK)	TOTAL REVENUE
총수익세(CHONG SUYIKSEH)	GROSS REVENUE TAX
총수익율(CHONG SUYIKYOOL)	GROSS PROFIT RATIO
총수입 보험료(CHONG SU-YIP BO-HUM-RYO)	TOTAL PREMIUM WRITTEN
총자본 이익율(CHONG JABON YI-YIK-YOOL)	RETURN ON ASSETS
추세(CHOO-SEH)	TREND
취득가(CHUI-DEUK KA)	HISTORICAL COST
취득가격(CHUIDUK KAKYUK)	ACQUISITION COST
충당금(CHUNGDANGKUM)	ALLOWANCE
치환원가(CHI HWAN WON KA)	REPLACEMENT COST
칠월(CHIL-WOL)	JULY
타당성(TADANG-SUNG)	FEASIBILITY
타당성 연구(조사) (TADANG-SUNG YOUNKU)	FEASIBILITY STUDY
토지(TOH JI)	LAND
토지개발(TOH-JI GAEBAL)	LAND IMPROVEMENTS
통계적 표본추출(TONGGEHGEOK PYOBON CHOOCHOOL)	STATISTICAL SAMPLING
통신비용(TONG-SIN BI-YONG)	COMMUNICATIONS EXPENSES
퇴직연금(TWEJIK YOUNKUM)	POST RETIREMENT BENEFITS
투자(TOOJAH)	INVESTMENT
투자감면세(TOOJAH GAMMYUN SEH)	INVESTMENT TAX CREDIT
투자재평가충당금(TUJA JAEPYUNG-GA CHUNGDANGKUM)	ALLOW FOR DEVAL OF INVEST
특별상여금(TEUK-BYUL SANYURKUM)	SPECIAL BONUS
특별감사보고서(TEUK-BYUL KAMSA BOKOSEH)	SPECIAL REPORTS
특별항목(TEUK-BYUL HAHNGMOK)	EXTRAORDINARY ITEMS
특성(TEUK SUNG)	NATURE
특허권(TEUK-HER-KWON)	PATENTS
파산(PASAN)	BANKRUPTCY
판매 및 일반관리비(PANMAEBEE WA YILBANGWALEE BEE)	GENERAL & ADMIN. EXPENSES
판매비용(PAN-MAE BEYONG)	SELLING EXPENSES
판매세(PAN MAE SEH)	SALES TAXES
판매수익(PAN-MAE SU-YIK)	SALES(TURNOVER)
판매원가(PANMAE WONKA)	COST OF SALES
판촉비(PAN-CHOK-BE)	PROMOTIONAL COSTS
팔월(PAL WOL)	AUGUST

Korean	English
퍼센트(PERCENT)	PERCENTAGE
평가원칙(PYUNG-KA WONCHIK)	VALUATION PRINCIPLES
평균(PYUNG KYUN)	AVERAGE
포장재료(POJANG JAERYO)	PACKAGING MATERIAL
표본의 크기(PYOBON KU-GHI)	SAMPLE SIZE
표본추출(PYOBON CHOOCHOOL)	SAMPLING
표본추출결과(PYOBON CHOOCHOOL KYUL-GWA)	SAMPLING RESULTS
표본추출 위험(PYOBON CHOOCHOOL WUIHUM)	SAMPLING RISK
표본추출 위험보유액(PYOBON CHOOCHOOL WIHUM BOYUEIK)	ALLOW. FOR SAMPLING RISK
표준비용(PYOJUN BEYONG)	STANDARD COST
품질관리(POOMJIL GWALEE)	QUALITY CONTROL
품질보증(POOMJIL BOJEUNG)	PRODUCT WARRANTIES
피부양자(PI BU-YANG-JA)	DEPENDENTS
한계비용(HAN-GEH BE-YONG)	MARGINAL COST
한정의견(HANJUNG UI KYUN)	QUALIFIED OPINION
할인율(HAL-YIN YUL)	DISCOUNT RATE
할인채권(HAL-YIN CHAEKWON)	DEBT DISCOUNT
할증부 주식발행(HAL-JEUNG-BOO JUSIK BALHAENG)	PREMIUM ISSUE OF CAPITAL
할증부 채권(HAL-JEUNG-BOO BUCHAE)	DEBT PREMIUM
합병(HAAP-BYUNG)	MERGER
합작(HAAPJAK)	JOINT VENTURE
항구재고조사법(HANG KU JAEKOH JOSAH-BUP)	PERPETUAL INVENTORY SYSTEM
해고(HAE KO)	SEVERANCE
해고/퇴직 보상(HAE KO/TOEIJIK BOSANG)	SEVERANCE INDEMNITIES
해외무역(HAEWOE MOOYOK)	INTERNATIONAL TRADE
해외 부정방지법(HAEWOE BUJUNG BANGJIBUP)	FOREIGN CORRUPT PRACT ACT(USA)
해외자회사(HAEWOE JA-HOE-SA)	INTERNATIONAL SUBSIDIARY
해외종속법인(HAEWOE JONGSOK BUBYIN)	FOREIGN SUBSIDIARY
현금(HYUN KUM)	CASH
현금배당(HYUNKUM BAE DANG)	CASH DIVIDENDS
현금 및 예금(HYUNKUM MIT YAE KUM)	CASH AND BANKS
현금유입 총액(HYUNKUM YUYIP CHONG AEK)	CASH INFLOW
현금유출 총액(HYUNKUM YUCHUL CHONG AEK)	CASH OUTFLOW
현재가치(HYUNJAE GACHI)	NET PRESENT VALUE

Korean	English
호가(HOKA)	CALL PRICE
확률(HWAK-RYUL)	PROBABLE
환경(HWAN KYUNG)	CIRCUMSTANCE
환율(HWAN YOOL)	EXCHANGE RATE
환율변동 준비금(HWAN-YOOL BYUNDONG JUNBEKUM)	RESERVE FOR EXCH.RATE FLUCTUAT
환차손실 위험(HWAN-CHA SONSIL WI-HUM)	EXCHANGE RATE RISK
회계감사(HOE GEH KAMSA)	AUDIT
회계감사의 책임(HOE GEH KAM SA UI CHAEK YIM)	AUDITOR'S RESPONSIBILITY
회계기록(HOE-GEH KI ROK)	ACCOUNTING RECORDS
회계사(HOE-GEH-SAH)	ACCOUNTANT
회계연도말 이후의 사항(HOE GEH YOUNDOMAL YIHU-UI SAHANG)	SUBSEQUENT EVENTS
회계 연도 말일(HOE-GEH YOUNDO MAL-YIL)	YEAR END CLOSING DATE
회계원칙(HOE-GEH WON-CHIK)	ACCOUNTING PRINCIPLES
회계원칙 변경(HOE-GEH WON-CHIK BYUNKYUNG)	ACCOUNTING CHANGES
회계정책(HOE-GEH JUNG CHAEK)	ACCOUNTING POLICIES
회계정책 변경(HOE-GEH JUNG-CHAEK BYUNKYUNG)	ACCOUNTING CHANGES
회계정책사항(HOE GEH JUNGCHAEK SA-HANG)	STATEMENT OF ACCOUNTING POLICY
회계학(HOE-GEH-HAK)	ACCOUNTING
회사간 융자거래 (HOESAGHAN YOONGJA GUHRAE)	INTER-COMPANY LOANS
회장(HOE JANG)	CHAIRMAN
회전비율(HOE-JUHN BE-YOOL)	TURNOVER RATIO
후입선출법(HUYIP SUNCHOOL BUP)	LAST IN, FIRST OUT(LIFO)
효과(HYO KWA)	EFFECT
	YIELD

English	Korean
ACCELERATED DEPRECIATION	정율법(JUNG YOOL BUP)
ACCOUNT BALANCES	계정잔액(GYEJONG JAN-AEK)
ACCOUNTANT	회계사(HOE-GEH-SAH)
ACCOUNTING	회계학(HOE-GEH-HAK)
ACCOUNTING CHANGES	회계원칙 변경(HOE-GEH WON-CHIK BYUNKYUNG)
	회계정책 변경(HOE-GEH JUNG-CHAEK BYUNKYUNG)
ACCOUNTING POLICIES	회계정책(HOE-GEH JUNG CHAEK)
ACCOUNTING PRINCIPLES	회계원칙(HOE-GEH WON-CHIK)
ACCOUNTING RECORDS	회계기록(HOE-GEH KI ROK)
ACCOUNTS PAYABLE	외상 매입금(WOESANG MAEYIPKUM)
ACCOUNTS RECEIVABLE	외상 매출금(WOESANG MAECHULKUM)
ACCRUAL	발생(BAL SAENG)
ACCRUAL (ACCT. METHOD)	발생주의(BAL SAENG JOO-UI)
ACCRUE	발생하다(BALSAENG HADA)
ACCRUED EXPENSES	미지급 비용(MIJIGUP BEEYONG)
ACCRUED INCOME	미수 수익(MISOO SOOYIK)
ACCRUED LIABILITIES	이연부채(YIYOUN BUCHAE)
ACCRUED TAXES	미지급 세금(MIGIGUP SEHKUM)
ACCRUED VACATIONS	미지급 휴가(MIGIGUP HYUGA)
ACCUMULATED AMORTIZATION	감모상각 충당금(GAM-MO SANG-GAK CHUNGDANGKUM)
ACCUMULATED DEPRECIATION	감가상각 충당금(GAM-GA SANG-GAK CHUNGDANGKUM)
ACID TEST	당좌비율 분석(DANGJWA BI-YUL BOONSUK)
ACID TEST RATIO	당좌비율(DANGJWA BI-YUL)
ACQUISITION(OF A COMPANY)	지배권 취득(JIBAEKWON CHUIDUK)
ACQUISITION COST	취득가격(CHUIDUK KAKYUK)
ACTUAL LOAN LOSSES	대손상각(DAESOHN SANG-GAK)
ACTUARIAL VALUE	감정가치(GAMJUNG GACHI)
ADJUSTMENT	조정(JOJUNG)
ADJUSTMENT FOR INFLATION	가격변동 조정(GAKYUK BYUNDONG JOJUNG)
ADMINISTRATIVE EXPENSES	일반 관리비(YILBAN GWAL-LEE-BE)
ADVANCES TO SUPPLIERS	선급비용(SUNGUP BEYONG)
ADVERSE OPINION	부적정 의견(BU JUKJUNG YUI-KYUN)
AFFILIATED FIRMS	종속법인(JONGSOK BUB IN)
	관계회사(GWAN GEH HOE SA)

English	Korean
AFFILIATES	관계단체(GWAN GEH DAN CHAE)
ALLOCATE	배분(BAEBOON)
ALLOWANCE	충당금(CHUNGDANGKUM)
	수당(SOODANG)
ALLOW FOR DEVAL OF INVESTMENT	투자재평가충당금(TUJA JAEPYUNG-GA CHUNGDANGKUM)
ALLOW FOR DOUBTFULL A/C	대손충당금-외상매출금 (DAESONCHUNGDANGKUM-WOISANGMACHUL)
ALLOW FOR LOAN LOSSES	대손충당금-융자금(DAESONCHUNGDANGKUM-YUNGJAKUM)
ALLOW FOR SAMPLING RISK	표본추출 위험보유액(PYOBON CHUCHUL WIHUM BOYUAEK)
ALLOW FOR UNCOLLECT A/C	대손충당금-외상매출금 (DAESONCHUNGDANGKUM-WOSANGMACHULKUM)
ALTERNATIVE PROCEDURES	대안(DAE AHN)
ANALYTICAL REVIEW	분석적 개관(BOONSUKJUK KAEKWAN)
ANNUAL MEETING	연차총회(YONCHA CHONG-HOE)
ANNUAL S/H MEETING	연차 주주총회(YONCHA JUJU CHONG-HOE)
ANNUALLY	연차적으로(YONCHAJUKURO)
APPROPRIATED RETAINED EARNINGS	기 처분 이익잉여금(KI CHUBOON YIYIK YING-YOKUM)
APRIL	사월(SAH WOL)
ASSETS	자산(JA SAN)
ASSOCIATED FIRM	관계회사(KWAN GEH HOE SA)
AT RANDOM	무작위로(MOO JAK WI RO)
AUDIT	회계감사(HOE GEH KAMSA)
AUDIT APPROACH	감사방법(GAM SA BANG BUP)
AUDIT ENGAGEMENT	감사계약(GAM SA GEH YAK)
AUDIT FEES	감사비(GAM SA BI)
AUDIT MANAGER	대표회계사(DAEPYO HOE GEH SA)
AUDIT OPINION	감사의견(GAM SA UI KYUN)
AUDIT PARTNER	감사인(GAM SA IN)
AUDIT RISK	감사위험(GAM SA WI HUM)
AUDIT SAMPLING	감사표본추출(GAM SA PYO BON CHOO CHOOL)
AUDIT STAFF	감사요원(GAM SA YO WON)
AUDIT STRATEGY	감사전략(GAM SA JUL-YAK)
AUDITING PROCEDURES	감사절차(GAM SA JUL CHA)
AUDITING SHAREHOLDERS	주주감사(JOOJOO GAMSAH)

English	Korean
AUDITING STANDARDS	감사공준(GAM SA GONG JOON)
AUDITOR	공인회계사(GONG IN HOE GEH SA)
	감사(GAM SA)
AUDITOR'S REPORT	감사보고서(GAM SA BO KO SUH)
AUDITOR'S RESPONSIBILITY	회계감사의 책임(HOE GEH KAM SA UI CHAEK YIM)
AUGUST	팔월(PAL WOL)
AVERAGE	평균(PYUNG KYUN)
BALANCE SHEET	대차대조표(DAE CHA DAE JO PYO)
BALANCE SHEET DATE	대차대조표 마감일(DAE CHA DAE JO MA KAM IL)
BANK	은행(EUN HAENG)
BANK OVERDRAFTS	당좌차월(DANG JWA CHA WOL)
BANK RECONCILIATION	은행계정 조정표(EUN HEANG GEH–JONG JOJONGPYO)
BANK SERVICE CHARGES	은행 수수료(EUN HAENG SUSURYO)
BANKRUPTCY	파산(PASAN)
BEARER	지참인(JICHAM YIN)
BID	입찰(YIP CHAL)
BID (VERB)	입찰하다(YIP–CHAL HADA)
BILLIONS	십억(SIP–OUK)
BOARD OF DIRECTORS	이사회(YISAHOE)
BOND	채권(CHAE KWON)
	사채(SA CHAE)
BONDS PAYABLE	사채(SA CHAE)
BOOK VALUE	장부가격(JANG–BOO KAKYUK)
BREAK EVEN POINT	손익분기점(SOHN YIK BOONKIJUM)
BUDGET	예산(YE SAN)
BUILDINGS AND STRUCTURES	건물 및 구축물(GUNMOOL MIT KOOCHOOKMOOL)
BUSINESS COMBINATIONS	기업결합(KI–UP KYULHAP)
BUSINESS SEGMENT	사업부(SA UP BOO)
BY–PRODUCTS	부산물(BOO SAN MOOL)
CALL PRICE	호가(HOKA)
CAPITAL GAINS TAX	양도 소득세(YANG DO SODEUKSEH)
CAPITAL INCREASE	자본증식(JABON JUNGSIK)
CAPITAL STOCK	납입자본금(NAP YIP JABONKUM)
CAPITAL SURPLUS	자본잉여금(JABON YING YO KUM)

English	Korean
CAPITALIZATION OF FIN'L COSTS	금융비용의 자본화(KUMYUNGBIYONG UI JABONWHA)
CAPITALIZATION OF INTERESTS	이자의 자본화(YIJA UI JABONWHA)
CAPITALIZATION OF LEASES	리스의 자본화(LEASE UI JABONWHA)
CARRYBACK	전기이월(JEUNKI YI WOL)
CARRYFORWARD	차기이월(CHAKI YI WOL)
CARRYFORWARD PERIOD	이월기간(YI WOL KI GAN)
CASH	현금(HYUN KUM)
CASH AND BANKS	현금 및 예금(HYUNKUM MIT YAE KUM)
CASH DIVIDENDS	현금배당(HYUNKUM BAE DANG)
CASH EQUIVALENTS	준현금(JOON HYUNKUM)
CASH INFLOW	현금유입 총액(HYUNKUM YUYIP CHONG AEK)
CASH OUTFLOW	현금유출 총액(HYUNKUM YUCHUL CHONG AEK)
CERTIFICATE OF DEPOSIT	씨–디 (CD)
CERTIFICATE OF GOOD STANDING	재직증명서(JAIJIK JUNGMUNGSEH)
CETERIS PARIBUS	다른상황이 불변이면(DALUN SAHANGYI BULBYUN YIMYUN)
CHAIRMAN	회장(HOE JANG)
CHARITY EXPENSE	위문금(WIMOONKUM)
CHART OF ACCOUNTS	계정목록(GYEJUNG MOKLOK)
CHIEF EXECUTIVE OFFICER	대표이사(DAE PYO YI SA)
CIRCUMSTANCES	환경(HWAN KYUNG)
CLAIMS	배상청구(BAE SANG CHUNG KU)
CLIENT REPRESENTANTION LETTER	감사의뢰서(GAMSA EUROESUH)
COLLATERAL	저당(JUH DANG)
	담보(DAM BO)
COLLECTION RATIO	수금비율(SU KUM BIYOOL)
COLLECTIONS	수금(SU KUM)
COMMERCIAL & INDUSTRIAL LOANS	상업 및 산업융자(SANG–UP MIT SAN–UP YUNG JA)
COMMERCIAL BANK	상업은행(SANG–UP EUN HAENG)
	시중은행(SIJOONG EUN HAENG)
COMMISSIONS & FEES PROF.(LOSSES)	수입수수료(SU–YIP SUSURYO)
COMMITMENTS	약정(YAK JUNG)
COMMON STOCK	보통주(BOTONG JOO)
COMMUNICATIONS EXPENSE	통신비용(TONG–SIN BI–YONG)
COMPANY BY–LAWS	내규(NAE KYU)

English	Korean
COMPARATIVE FINANCIAL STATEMENT	비교재무제표(BEEKYO JAEMOO JEHPYO)
COMPENSATED ABSENCES	유급휴가(YU KUP HYUGA)
COMPILATION OF FINANCIAL STAT.	재무제표의 편집(JAEMOO JEHPYO UI PYUN JIP)
COMPLETED-CONTRACT METHOD	공사완성법(GONGSA WANSUNG BUP)
COMPLY WITH	준수하다(JOONSU HADA)
CONDENSED F/S	요약 재무제표(YOYAK JAEMOO JEHPYO)
CONFIRMATION OF ACCOUNTS	전표확인(JUHNPYO WHAKIN)
CONSISTENCY	계속성(GYESOK SUNG)
CONSISTENTLY APPLIED	일관성있게 적용한(YILKWANSUNG YITGEH JUGYONGHAN)
CONSOLIDATED ACCOUNTS	연결계정(YOUNKYUL GYEJUNG)
CONSOLIDATED F/S	연결재무제표(YOUNKYUL JAEMOO JAEPYO)
CONSTRUCTION IN PROGRESS	건설가계정(GUNSUL GAGYEJUNG)
CONSULTING SERVICES	상담(SANGDAM)
CONTENTS	목차(MOK CHA)
CONTINGENCIES	우발성(WOO BAL SEUNG)
CONTROL WEAKNESS	내부통제 관리약점(NAEBU TONGJEH GWAL-LEE YAKJEUM)
CONVERTIBLE DEBT	전환사채(JUHNWHAN SA CHAE)
COPYRIGHT	저작권(JUH JAK KWON)
CORRESPONDENT FIRMS	거래처(GUHRAE CHUR)
COST OF GOODS SOLD	매출원가(MAECHUL WONKA)
COST OF SALES	매출원가(MAICHUL WONKA)
	판매원가(PANMAE WONKA)
COST OF SERVICES RENDERED	용역비 (발생한) YONG-YUK-BEE (BALSANG HAN)
COST OR MARKET	원가 혹은 시가(WONKA HOGUN SITKA)
COUNTRY RISK	국가별 위험(GUK-KA-BYUL WIHUM)
CREDIT FOR TAX BREAKS	세금특혜(SAE KUM TEUK HYE)
CREDIT LINE	신용거래액(SHIN YONG GUHRAE AEK)
CREDITS TURNOVER RATIO	신용거래 회전율(SINYONG GUHRAE HOEJONYOOL)
CUMULATIVE ADJUSMENT	누적조정(NUJUK JOJUNG)
CUMULATIVE EFFECT	누적효과(NUJUK HYOKWA)
CURRENCY TRANSLATION	외화자산의 평가(WOE WHA JASAN UI PYONGKA)
CURRENT ASSETS	유동자산(YUDONG JASAN)
CURRENT LIABILITIES	유동부채(YUDONG BOOCHAE)
CURRENT PORTION OF ...	유동부분,단기부분(YUDONG BOOBOON, DANKI BOOBOON)

English	Korean
CURRENT RATIO	유동비율(YUDONG BEE YOOL)
CUSTODY SECURITIES	보관증권(BOGWAN JEUNG-GWON)
CUSTOMERS	고객(GO-GAK)
CUSTOMERS'LIAB FOR ACCEPTANCE	지급보증 대충(JIGUP BO-JEUNG DAECHOONG)
CUSTOMS DUTY	관세(GWAN SEH)
DATA PROCESSING EQUIPMENT	전자계산장비(JUHNJA GEHSAN JANGBE)
DEBENTURE	차입금(CHAYIPKUM)
	무담보 사채(MU DAMBO SACHAE)
DEBT DISCOUNT	할인채권(HAL-YIN CHAEKWON)
DEBT PREMIUM	할증부 채권(HAL-JEUNG-BOO BUCHAE)
DEBT RESTRUCTURING	부채재조정(BUCHAE JAEJOJONG)
DEFERRAL METHOD	이연방법(YIYEUN BANG BEUP)
DEFERRED CHARGES	이연자산(YIYEON JASAN)
DEFERRED INCOME	이연수익(YIYEON SUYIK)
DEFERRED INCOME TAX	세금분배효과(SEH KUM BUNBAE HYOKWA)
DEFERRED TAXES	이연세금(YI YEON SEH KUM)
DEMAND DEPOSITS	요구불 예금(YOGOOBOOL YEKUM)
DEPART.FROM A PRONOUNCEMENT	공표기준 일탈(GONGPYO KIJOON YIL-TAL)
DEPENDENTS	피부양자(PI BU-YANG-JA)
DEPRECIATION - BUILDINGS	감가상각비-건물(GAMGA SANG-GAK-BEE ,GUNMOOL)
DEPRECIATION EXPENSE	감가상각비(GAMGA SANG-GAK-BEE)
DETECT	찾아내다(CHAJANAEDA)
DEVELOPMENT STAGE COMPANIES	창업회사(CHANG UP HOE SA)
DIRECT COST	직접비용(JIK-JEOP-BE-YONG)
DIRECTORS	이사(YI-SA)
DISBURSEMENTS	지불(JI-BOOL)
DISCLAIMER OF OPINION	의견거절(UIKYUN GUHJEOL)
DISCLOSURE	공시(GONG SI)
	명세서(MYUNG-SEH-SUH)
DISCONTINUED OPERATIONS	영업활동의 중단(YOUNG-UP HWALDONG UI JOONGDAN)
DISCOUNT RATE	할인율(HAL-YIN YUL)
DISPOSITION	처분(CHUR BOON)
DIVIDEND	배당(BAE-DANG)
DIVIDEND INCOME	수입배당금(SUYIP BAEDANGKUM)

English	Korean
DIVIDEND PER SHARE	일주당 배당금(YIL JU-DANG BAEDANGKUM)
DIVIDENDS PAYABLE	미지급 배당금(MI JIKUP BAEDANGKUM)
DOLLARS	불(BUL)
DOMESTIC SUBSIDIARIES	국내 자회사(GUK-NAE JA-HOE-SA)
DOUBLE TAXATION	이중과세(YIJOONG GWA-SEH)
	이중세(YIJOONG SEH)
DUE DATE	만기일(MAH-GI YIL)
EARLY EXTINGUISHMENT OF DEBT	조기부채변제(JOKI BOOCHAE BYUNJE)
EARLY RETIREMENT	조기은퇴(JOKI EUN-TOE)
EARNINGS PER SHARE	일주당 순이익(YIL JUDANG SOON YI-YIK)
ECONOMIC ENVIRONMENT	경제 환경(KYUNG-JE HWAN-KYUNG)
EFFECT	효과(HYO KWA)
EFFECT OF CHANGING PRICE	가격변동 효과(GAKYUK BYUNDONG HYOKWA)
EMPLOYEE	종업원(JONG-UP WON)
EMPLOYEE BENEFITS	복리후생비(BOKREE HOOSAENGBEE)
ENTERTAINMENT EXPENSE	접대비(JUPDAE BEE)
EQUITY IN OTHER COMPANIES	지분(JIBOON)
EQUITY METHOD	지분법(JIBOON BUP)
ERRORS	오류(ORYOU)
EVIDENTIAL MATTER	증빙서류(JEUNG-BING SUHRYOU)
EXAMINE	검사(GUHM-SA)
EXCEPT FOR	제외하고(JEWOE HAGO)
EXCHANGE RATE	환율(HWAN YOOL)
EXCHANGE RATE RISK	환차손실 위험(HWAN-CHA SONSIL WI-HUM)
EXCISE TAX	소비세(SOBEE SEH)
EXHIBITION,EVENT EXPENSE	전시비용(JUHN-SI BIYONG)
EXPECTED SALVAGE VALUE	잔존가격(JANJON GAKYUK)
EXPENSES	비용(BEE-YONG)
EXPENSES ON CAPITAL INCREASE	자금모집비용(JA KUM MOJIP BIYONG)
EXPORT	수출(SU-CHOOL)
EXPORT DUTIES	수출세(SU-CHOOL SEH)
EXTRAORDINARY ITEMS	특별항목(TEUK-BYUL HAHNGMOK)
FACE VALUE	액면가(AEG-MYUN KA)
FAIRLY PRESENT	적정하게 표시하다 (JUHK-JUNG HAGEH PYOSIHADA)

English	Korean
FEASIBILITY	타당성(TADANG-SUNG)
FEASIBILITY STUDY	타당성 연구(조사)(TADANG-SUNG YOUNKU)
FEBRUARY	이월(YI WOL)
FEES	수수료(SUSU RYO)
FEES & SVS. REND.BY 3RD PARTY	용역 수수료(YONGYUG SUSURYO)
FINANCE	재무관리(JAEMOO GWALEE)
FINANCE (VERB)	자금동원하다(JAKUM DONGWON HADA)
FINANCIAL ENTITIES	금융기업(KUMYUNG KI-UP)
FINANCIAL STATEMENTS	재무제표(JAEMOO JEHYO)
FINANCIAL SUMMARY	요약 재무상태(YOYAK JAEMOO SANGTAE)
FINANCING ARRANGEMENT	자금계획(JAKUM GEH-HOEK)
FINE	벌금(BUHL-KUM)
FINISHED GOODS	완제품(WANJEPOOM)
FIRST IN, FIRST OUT(FIFO)	신입선출법(SUHNYIP SUHNCHOOL BUHP)
FITTINGS	비품(BIPOOM)
FIXED ASSETS	고정자산(GOJUNG JASAN)
FLAT TAX WITHHOLDING	고정세율징수(GOJUNG SEH-YUL JINGSU)
FLOATING RATE	변동율(BYUNDONG YUL)
FLOWCHART	도표(DO PYO)
FOOTNOTES(FIN'L STAT.)	재무제표의 주석(JAEMU JEPYO UI JOOSUK)
FOR TAXATION PURPOSES	세무원칙에 입각한(SEHMOO WONCHIK EH YIPGAKHAN)
FORECAST	예측(YECHEUK)
FOREIGN CORRUPT PRACT ACT(USA)	해외 부정방지법(HAEWOE BUJUNG BANGJIBUP)
FOREIGN CURRENCY	외화(WOE HWA)
FOREIGN CURRENCY TRANSLATION	외화 환산(WOE HWA HWAN-SAN)
FOREIGN EXCHANGE	외환(WOE HWAN)
FOREIGN EXCH. GAIN(LOSS)	외환 매매익(손) WOEHWAN MAEMAEYIK (SON)
FOREIGN SUBSIDIARY	해외종속법인(HAEWOE JONGSOK BUBYIN)
FORM	양식(YANGSIK)
FREIGHT ON PURCH. OF MATERIALS	매입원료의 운송료(MAEYIP WOLYO EUI WUNSONGRY0)
FUNDS	기금(KIKUM)
FURNITURE AND FIXTURES	기구 및 비품(KIGU MIT BIPOOM)
FUTURE CONTRACTS	선물계약(SUNMUL GEHYAK)
GAIN	차익(CHAYIK)

GAIN CONTINGENCY	우발차익(WOOBAL CHA YIK)
GAIN ON REVAL. OF SECURITIES	주식재평가이익(JUSIK JAEPYONGKA YIYIK)
GAIN ON SALE OF FIXED ASSET	고정자산 처분익(GOJUNG JASAN CHURBUN YIYIK)
GENERAL & ADMIN. EXPENSE	판매 및 일반관리비(PANMAEBEE WA YILBANGWALEE BEE)
GENERAL INSURANCE	일반보험(YILBAN BOHUM)
GENERAL LEDGER	총계정원장(CHONG GEHJUNG WONJANG)
GENERAL MANAGER	전무(JUHN MOO)
GENERALLY ACCEPTED	일반적으로 인정되는(YILBANJUGURO YINJUNG-DOENEUN)
GOING CONCERN	계속기업(GYE-SOK KI-UP)
GOODS IN PROCESS	반제품(BANJEPOOM)
GOODS IN TRANSIT	미착품 (MI CHAK POOM)
GOODWILL	영업권(YOUNG-UP-GWON)
	가성(GAASUNG)
GRADUATED TAX	누진세(NUJINSEH)
GROSS MARGIN	매출이익(MAECHUL YIYIK)
GROSS NATIONAL PRODUCT	국민소득(GOOKMIN SODEUK)
GROSS PROFIT RATIO	총수익율(CHONG SUYIKYOOL)
GROSS REVENUE TAX	총수익세(CHONG SUYIKSEH)
GROUP (OF COMPANIES)	그룹(GROUP)
GUARANTEE DEPOSITS	예치보증금(YECHI BOJEUNGKUM)
GUARANTEES	보증(BOJEUNG)
HEDGE	방어(BANG-UHR)
HISTORICAL COST	원가(WONKA)
	취득가(CHUI-DEUK KA)
HOLDING COMPANY	지배회사(JIBAE HOESA)
HUNDREDS	백(BAIK)
IDLE CAPACITY	유휴시설(YOOHYU SISUL)
IMPACT	영향(YOUNG-HYANG)
IMPORT SURCHARGES	수입특별관세(SUYIP TEUK-BYUL GWANSEH)
IN ACCORDANCE WITH	기준에 따라(KIJOONEH TTA RA)
INCOME FROM SERVICES RENDERED	용역수입(YONGYUG SUYIP)
INCOME TAX	소득세(SODEUK SEH)
INDEBTNESS RATIO	부채비율(BOOCHAE BEYOOL)
INDEMNITIES	배상(BAESANG)

INDEPENDENCE	독립(DONGNIP)
INDUSTRY	산업(SANUP)
INFLATION	인플레이션(INFLATION)
INHERITANCE TAX	상속세(SANG-SOK SEH)
INSURANCE COMPANY	보험회사(BOHUM HOESA)
INTANGIBLE ASSETS	무형고정자산(MOO-HYONG KOJUNG JASAN)
	무형자산(MOO-HYONG JASAN)
INTER-COMPANY LOANS	회사간 융자거래 (HOESAGHAN YOONGJA GUHRAE)
INTERBANK ASSETS	은행간 자산(EUNHANG GHAN JASAN)
INTERBANK DEPOSITS	은행간 저축(EUNHANG GHAN JUH-CHOOK)
INTERBANK RATE	은행간 이자율(EUNHANG GHAN YIJAYOOL)
INTEREST EXPENSE	지급이자(JIGUP YI-JA)
INTEREST INCOME	수입이자(SUYIP YIJA)
INTEREST PAYABLE	미지급이자(MIJIKUP YIJA)
INTEREST RATE	이자율(YIJAYOOL)
INTEREST RECEIVABLE	미수이자(MISOO YIJA)
INTERIM FINAN'L STATEMENTS	반기재무제표(BANKI JAEMOO JAPYO)
	중간재무제표(JOONG-GHAN JAEMOO JEPYO)
INTERNAL AUDITORS	내부감사(NAIBU GAMSA)
INTERNAL CTRL. QUESTIONNAIRE	내부통제 질문지 (NAEBU TONGJEH JILMOONJI)
INTERNAL CONTROLS	내부통제(NAEBU TONGJEH)
INTERNATIONAL SUBSIDIARY	해외자회사(HAEWOE JA-HOE-SA)
INTERNATIONAL TRADE	해외무역(HAEWOE MOOYOK)
INTERVENING PERIOD	중재기간(JOONGJAE KIGHAN)
INVENTORIES-USA (STOCKS-UK)	재고자산(JAEGO JASAN)
INVENTORY TURNOVER RATIO	재고자산회전율(JAEGO JASAN HOEJUHN YOOL)
INVESTMENT	투자(TOOJAH)
INVEST. BANK/MERCHANT BANK	증권회사(JEUNG KWON HOI SA)
INVESTMENT IN SUBSIDIARIES	관계회사 주식(GWAN-GEH HOESAH JUSIK)
INVEST.SECURITY GAIN(LOSS)	유가증권처분익(손) YUKA JEUNGKWON CHOBOON YIK(SON)
INVESTMENT TAX CREDIT	투자감면세 (TOOJAH GAMMYUN SEH)
INVOICE	송장(SONGJANG)
IRREGULARITY	변칙(BYUNCHIK)
JANUARY	일월(YIL-WOL)

English	Korean
JOINT VENTURE	합작(HAAPJAK)
JOURNAL	분개장(BOONGAEJANG)
JOURNAL ENTRY	분개(BOONGAE)
JULY	칠월(CHIL-WOL)
JUNE	유월(YOU-WOL)
LABOR HOURS	노동시간(NODONG SIGAHN)
LABOR LAW	노동법(NODONG BUP)
LAND	토지(TOH JI)
LAND IMPROVEMENTS	토지개발(TOH-JI GAEBAL)
LAST IN, FIRST OUT(LIFO)	후입선출법(HUYIP SUNCHOOL BUP)
LAWYER	변호사(BYUNHOSA)
LEASE	임대차(YIMDAECHA)
LEASE FINANCING LOANS	임대차 융자금(YIMDAECHA YOONGJAKUM)
LEASEBACK	역 리스(YOG LEASE)
LEGAL REQUIREMENTS	법률적 요구사항(BUMYOOLJEOK YOGOO SAHANG)
LEGAL RESERVE	법정 적립금 (BUPJUNG JUNGNIPKUM)
LESSEE	임차인(YIM-CHA-YIN)
LESSOR	임대인(YIM-DAE-YIN)
LIABILITY	부채(BOOCHAE)
LICENCES	자격증(JA-KYUK JEUNG)
LIFE INSURANCE	생명보험(SAENGMYUNG BOHUM)
LIFE POLICY BENEFITS	생명보험금(SAENG-MYUNG BOHUMKUM)
LIQUID ASSETS	당좌자산(DANGJWA JASAN)
LIQUIDITY	유동성(YUDONG-SEONG)
LIQUIDITY RATIO	유동비율(YUDONG BEYOOL)
LIQUIDITY RISK	지불 불능(JIBOOL BOOLNEUNG)
LISTED BOND-LOCAL CURRENCY	국내통화표시 상장채권 SANGJANG CHAEKWON (GOOK-NAE)
LITIGATION	소송(SOSONG)
LOANS	융자(YOONGJA)
LOCAL CURRENCY	국내통화(GUK-NAE TONG-HWA)
LONG TERM DEBT RETIRED	장기부채의 변제(JANG-GHEE BOOCHAE UI BYUNJAE)
LONG-TERM CONTRACTS	장기계약(JANG-GHEE GEH-YAK)
LONG-TERM CREDITS	장기신용(JANG GHEE SINYONG)
LONG-TERM DEBT	장기부채(JANG-GHEE BOOCHAE)

English	Korean
LONG-TERM INVESTMENTS	장기투자(JANG-GHEE TOOJAH)
LOSS	손실(SOHN-SIL)
LOSS CARRY-FORWARD	이월손실금 (YIWOL SOHNSILKUM)
LOWER OF COST OR MARKET	저가법(JUH-KA BOP)
LT INSURANCE RESERVE CHARGES	보험료 준비금(BOHUMRYO JOONBEEKUM)
MACHINERY AND EQUIPMENT	기계 및 장비(KI-GEH MIT JANGBEE)
MAJOR CUSTOMERS	주요고객(JUYO GOGAEK)
MANAGEMENT INTENTION	경영자의 의도(KYONG-YOUNG-JAH UI UIDO)
MARCH	삼월(SAM-WOL)
MARGINAL COST	한계비용(HAN-GEH BE-YONG)
MARKET PRICE	시중가격(SIJOONG GAKYUK)
	시장가격(SIJANG GAKYUK)
MARKETABLE SECURITIES	유가증권(YUKAH JEUNG-KWON)
	상품유가증권(SANGPOOM YOOKAH JEUNG-KWON)
MARKETABLE STOCKS	상품유가증권(SANGPOOM YOOKAH JEUNG-KWON)
MATERIAL (SIGNIFICANT)	중요한(JOONGYOHAN)
	상당한(SANGDANGHAN)
MATERIALITY	중요성(JOONGYO-SUNG)
	상당성(SANDANG-SUNG)
MATERIALS (SUST.)	재료(JAERYO)
MATURED LOANS	지불만기된 융자(JIBUL MAHNKIDOEN YOONG-JA)
MATURITY	만기(MAHNKI)
MAY	오월(OUWOL)
MERGER	합병(HAAP-BYUG MA)
MILLIONS	백만(BAIK-MAHN)
MINORITY INTEREST	외부주주 지분(WOEBOO JUJU JEEBOON)
MISLEADING INFORMATION	왜곡된 정보(WAEKOK DOEN JUNGBO)
MONETARY ASSETS	금융자산(KUMYUNG JASAN)
MONETARY TRANSACTIONS	금융거래(KUMYUNG GUHRAE)
MONTHLY	월별(WOL BYUL)
MORTGAGE	주택융자(JUTAEK YOONGJA)
	부동산융자(BUDONGSAN YOONGJA)
MORTGAGE BANK	주택융자은행(JUTAEK YOONGJA EUN-HAENG)
MULTINATIONAL ENTERPRISE	다국적기업 (DAH GOOK JEOK KIUP)

MULTIPLE REGRESSION	다중회귀분석(DAHJOONG HOEGUI BUNSEOK)
MUTUAL FUND	상호금융(SANGHO KUMYOONG)
NATURE	특성(TEUK SUNG)
NEGATIVE GOODWILL	부의 영업권(BOO-UI YOUNG-UP-KWON)
NET FIXED ASSETS	순고정자산(SOON GOJUNG JASAN)
NET INCOME	순이익(SOON YIYIK)
NET INCOME(LOSS), PERIOD	기간 순이익(순손실)KIGAN SOONYIYIK(SOONSONSIL)
NET PREMIUMS EARNED	순수입 보험료(SOON SUYIP BOHUMRYO)
NET PRESENT VALUE	불변가격(BOOLBYUN KAKYUK)
NET REALIZABLE VALUE	순 실현액(SOON SIL-HYUN AEK)
NET SALES	순 손실액(SOON PAAN-MAE-AEK)
NET TRADE A/R	순 외상매출금(SOON WOESAN MAECHOOLKUM)
NET WORTH	자기자본(JAKI JABON)
NON PERFORMING EARNING ASSETS	부실투자자산(BUSIL TOOJA JASAN)
NON-CURRENT ASSETS	고정자산(GOJUNG JASAN)
NON-CURRENT LIABILITIES	고정부채 (GOJUNG BOOCHAE)
NON-EQUITY RESERVES	비자본성 충당금(BEJABON-SUNG CHOONGDANGKUM)
NON-MONETARY TRANSACTION	비금융거래(BEKUMYOONG GUHRAE)
NONOPERATING INCOME & EXPENSES	영업외 손익 (YOUNG-UP WOE SOHN YIK)
NON-PROFIT	비영리(BE-YOUNG-REE)
NON-REDEEMABLE PREF STOCK	비상환부 우선주(BEE SANGHWANBOO WOOSUNJU)
NON-SAMPLING RISK	비표본추출 위험(BE-PYOBONCHOOCHOOL WI HUM)
NON-STATISTICAL SAMPLING	비통계적 표본추출(BE-TONGGUEJEOK PYOBONCHOOCHOOL)
NON-TAXABLE INCOME	비과세 소득(BE-GWASEH SODEUK)
NOTES PAYABLE	지급어음(JIGUP UH-WOOM)
NOTES RECEIVABLE	받을어음(BAHDUL UH-WOOM)
NOVEMBER	십일월(SIP-IL-WOL)
OBSOLESCENCE	진부성(JINBOO-SUNG)
OCTOBER	시월(SI-WOL)
OFFICE SUPPLIES	사무용 소모품(SAMOOYONG SOMOPOOM)
OFFICER	임원(YIMWON)
OFFSET	상쇄(SANG SWOE)
OPERATING CONTROLS	운영감독(WOON-YOUNG GAMDOK)
OPERATING CYCLE	영업주기(YOUNG-UP JUKI)
OPERATING LEASES	영업임대차(YOUNG-UP YIMDAECHA)
OPERATING PROFIT	영업이익(YOUNG-UP YIYIK)
OPERATING RATIO	영업이익율(YOUNG-UP YIYIKYOOL)
OPERATIONAL AUDITING	운영감사(WOON-YOUNG GAMSA)
OPERATIONAL CONTROLS	운영관리(WOON-YOUNG GWAL-LEE)
OPERATIONAL NETWORK	운영관리조직(WOON-YOUNG GWAL-LEE JOJIK)
OPINION	의견(UI-KYUN) 감사의견(GAMSA UI-KYUN)
OPINION PARAGRAPH	감사의견문단(GAMSA UI-KYUN MOONDAN)
OPPORTUNITY COST	기회비용(KIHOE BEYONG)
OPTIONS	선택권(SUHNTAK-KWON)
ORGANIZATION CHART	조직표(JOJIK PYO)
ORGANIZATION EXPENSES	조직비용(JOJIK BEYONG)
OTHER INCOME FOR SERVICE	기타용역수익(KITA YONGYOG SUYIK)
OTHER LOANS	기타융자금(KITA YOONGJAKUM)
OTHER OPERATING PROF.(LOSS)	기타영업이익(손실) KITA YOUNGUP YIYIK (SONSIL)
OUTSTANDING SHARES	발행주식(BALHAENG JUSIK)
OVER THE COUNTER TRANSACTION	장외거래(JANGWOE GUHRAE)
OVERDRAFT	당좌대월(DANGJWA DAEWOL)
OVERDUE	밀린(MILIN)
OVERHEAD EXPENSES	간접비용(GANJUP BEYONG)
OVERNIGHT FUNDS	당좌기금성(DANG-JWA-SUNG GHIKUM)
OVERSIZE(D)	과대한(GWA DAE HAN)
PACKAGING MATERIAL	포장재료(POJANG JAERYO)
PAID-IN CAPITAL	불입자본금(BOOLYIP JABONKUM)
PAR VALUE	액면가(AEK MYUN KA)
PARENT COMPANY	모기업(MO KI UP) 모회사(MO HOE SA)
PARTNER	공동경영자(GONGDONG KYUNG-YOUNG-JA)
PATENTS	특허권(TEUK-HER-KWON)
PAYMENTS	지불(JIBOOL)
PAYMENTS CYCLE	지불주기(JIBOOL JUGHI)
PAYROLL	인건비(YIN-KUHN-BE)
PENSION	연금(YOUNKUM)

English	Korean
PENSION PLAN	연금제도(YOUNKUM JEHDO)
PERCENTAGE	퍼센트(PERCENT)
PERCENTAGE OF-COMPLETION-METHOD	공사진행기준(GONGSA JINHAENG GHIJUN)
PERMANENT FILE	영구보존서류(YOUNG-GU BOJON SEORYU)
PERPETUAL BOND	영구사채(YOUNG-GU SACHAE)
PERPETUAL INVENTORY SYSTEM	항구재고조사법(HANG KU JAEKOH JOSAH-BUP)
PERSONAL INCOME TAX	개인소득세(GAEYIN SODEUK-SEH)
PETTY CASH	소액지급금(SOHAEK JIKEUP-KUM)
PHYSICAL INVENTORY	실지재고자산(SILJI JAEGO JASAN)
PLACEMENT	배치(BAECHI)
PLEDGE	위탁(WI-TAK)
PLEDGING REQUIREMENTS	위탁조건(WI-TAK JOGUN)
POLICYHOLDERS' EQUITY	보험가입자 자본(BOHUM GAYIPJA JABON)
POLICYHOLDERS' SURPLUS	보험가입자 잉여분(BOHUM GAYIPJA YING-YUR-BOON)
POOLING OF INTEREST	지분공동계산법(JIBOON GONGDONG GYE-SAN-BUP)
POPULATION	인구(YINGU)
POPULATION(IN A STATIST.)	모집단(MO-JIPDAN)
PORTFOLIO COMPOSITION	자산구성(JASAN KUSUNG)
POST ENTRIES TO LEDGER	기장(KI JANG)
POST RETIREMENT BENEFITS	퇴직연금(TWEJIK YOUNKUM)
PREFERRED SHARE (USA)	우선주(WOO-SON-JU)
PREMIUM	보험료(BOHUMRYO)
PREMIUM ON ISSUE OF CAPITAL	할증부 주식발행(HAL-JEUNG-BOO JUSIK BALHAENG)
PREPAID EXPENSE	선급비용(SONKUP BEYONG)
PRIMARY CAPITAL	우선자본(WOOSUN JABON)
PRIOR PERIOD ADJUSTMENTS	전기이월조정액(JUHN-GHI YIWOL JOJUNG AEK)
PRIVATE SECTOR	사경제부문(SA-KYUNG-JEH BOOMOON)
PROBABLE	확률(HWAK-RYUL)
PRODUCT FINANCING	상품보증부 융자(SANGPOOM BOJEUNG BU YUNGJA)
PRODUCT WARRANTIES	품질보증(POOMJIL BOJEUNG)
PRODUCTION CAPACITY	생산능력(SAENG-SAN NEUNG-LYUK)
PRODUCTION COST	생산비(SAENG-SAN-BE)
PRODUCTION CYCLE	생산주기(SAENG-SAN JUKI)
PRODUCTION ORDER	생산주문(SAENG-SAN JUMOON)
PROFESSIONAL JUDGMENT	전문가의 판단(JUHN-MOON-GA UI PANDAN)
PROFESSIONAL STANDARDS	전문가의 기준(JUHN-MOON-GA UI KIJOON)
PROFIT	이익(YIYIK)
PROFIT & LOSS ACCOUNTS	손익계정(SOHN-YHIK GEH-JUNG)
PROFIT SHARING	이익참여(YI-YIK CHAMYUR)
PROGRESSIVE TAX	누진세(NUJIN-SEH)
PROJECTION	계획(GYE-HWEK)
PROMOTIONAL COSTS	판촉비(PAN-CHOK-BE)
PROVISION	준비금(JOON-BE-KUM)
PROXY(POWER OF ATTORNEY)	대리권(DAE-RI-KWON)
PUBLIC SECTOR	공공부문(GONG GONG BOOMOON)
PURCHASE REQUISITION	구매요구서(GUMAE YOGUSUH)
QUALIFICATION(AUDIT OPINION)	한정의견(HANJUNG UI KYUN)
QUALITY CONTROL	품질관리(POOMJIL GWALEE)
QUARTER	분기(BOON-KI)
QUARTERLY	분기별 (BOON-KI-BYUL)
QUARTERLY FINANCIAL STAT	분기별 재무제표(BOON-KI-BYUL JAEMOO-JEH-PYO)
RANDOM	무작위(MOO-JAG-WI)
RAW MATERIALS	원료(WOLYO)
REAL ESTATE & MORTGAGE LOANS	부동산융자(BUDONGSAN YOONGJA)
REASONABLY POSSIBLE	적정 가능한(JUK JUNG KANEUNG HAN)
RECEIVABLES	미수금(MISUKUM)
RECESSION	경기후퇴(KYUNG-KI HU-TOI)
RECORD (VERB)	기록하다(GI-ROK-HADA)
RECRUITING EXPENSE	채용비용(CHAE YONG BEYONG)
REDEEMABLE	상환부(SANG-HWAN-BOO)
REDEEMABLE PREFERRED STOCK	상환부 우선주(SANG-HWAN-BOO WOOSON-JOO)
REDEMPTION FEATURES	상환조건(SANG-HWAN JOKEON)
REDISCOUNTED NOTES	재할인 어음(JAE HAL-YIN UHR-WOOM)
REFINANCING	재자금조달(JAE JA-KUM JODAL)
REFUND	반환금(BAN-HWAN-KUM)
REGRESSIVE TAX	체감세(CHE-GAM-SEH)
REGULATIONS	규칙(KYU-CHIK)
REINSURANCE & PREMIUM ADJUSTMENT	재보험 조정액(JAE-BOHUM JOJUNG-AEK)

English	Korean
RELATED PARTY TRANSACTION	내부거래(NAE-BOO GUHRAE)
REMOTE	가능성 희박한(GANEUNGSUNG HEE-BAK-HAN)
REPAIRS	수선(SUSON)
REPAIRS AND MAINTENANCE	수선 및 유지비(SUSON MIT YUJIBE)
REPLACEMENT COST	치환원가(CHI HWAN WON KA)
REPORT	보고서(BOGOSUH)
REPORT TO MANAGEMENT	경영층에 보고(KYUNGYOUNG-CHEUNG EH BOGO)
REPRODUCTION COST	재생산비(JAE SAENGSANBE)
REPURCHASE AGREEMENT	재구매계약(JAE GU-MAE KEH-YAK)
RESALE AGREEMENTS	재판매계약(JAE PAN-MAE KEH-YAK)
RESALE MERCHANDISE	재판매용 상품(JAE PAN-MAE-YONG SANGPOOM)
RESEARCH & DEVELOPMENT COST	연구개발비(YOUNGU KAEBALBEE)
RESERVE FOR EXCH. RATE FLUCT.	환율변동 준비금(HWAN-YOOL BYUNDONG JUNBEKUM)
RESERVE FOR LOAN LOSSES	대손충당금 전입액(DAESON CHOONGDANGKUM JUNYIPAEK)
RESERVE,O/S CLAIM & LOSS	보험금지급 충당금(BOHUMKUM JIKUP CHOONGDANGKUM)
RESTRICTION ON THE SCOPE	범위에 대한 제한(BUMWI EH DAEHAN JEH-HAN)
RESTRUCTURE	재조정 (JAE JOJUNG)
RETAINED EARNINGS	이익잉여금(YIYIK YING-YUR-KUM)
	미처분잉여금(MICHURBOON YI-YIK YING-YUR-KUM)
RETURN ON ASSETS	총자본 이익율(CHONG JABON YI-YIK-YOOL)
RETURN ON EQUITY	자기자본 이익율(JAKI JABON YI-YIK-YOOL)
REVALUATION	자산재평가(JASAN JAE PYONG-KA)
REVALUATION RESERVE	자산재평가 준비금(JASAN JAE PYONG-KA JUNBE-KUM)
REVALUATION SURPLUS	재평가 잉여금(JAE PYONG-KA YING-YUR-KUM)
REVIEW OF FINANCIAL STATEMENT	재무재표의 개관(JAEMOO JEHPYO UI GAE-GWAN)
RISK EXPOSURE	위험성의 노출(WI-HUM-SUNG UI NOCHOOL)
RULES	규칙(KYU CHIK)
SALARIES AND WAGES	인건비(YINKUHNBE)
SALE OF MANUFACTURED GOOD	제품판매(JEH-POOM PAN-MAE)
SALES (TURNOVER)	판매수익(PAN-MAE SU-YIK)
	매출액(MAECHUL-AEK)
SALES ON INSTALLMENTS	월부판매(WOLBOO PAN-MAE)
SALES TAX	판매세(PAN MAE SEH)
SAMPLE SIZE	표본의 크기(PYOBON KU-GHI)
SAMPLING	표본추출(PYOBON CHOOCHOOL)
SAMPLING RESULTS	표본추출결과(PYOBON CHOOCHOOL KYUL-GWA)
SAMPLING RISK	표본추출 위험(PYOBON CHOOCHOOL WUIHUM)
SAVING DEPOSITS	저축예금(JUHCHOOK YEKUM)
SCOPE	범위(BUMWI)
SCOPE PARAGRAPH	감사범위 문단(GAMSA BUMWI MOONDAN)
SEASONALLY ADJUSTED	계절변동조정(GYEJHUL BYUNDONG JOJUNG)
SECOND REQUEST	재요구(JAE YOKU)
SECONDARY MARKET	제이 시장권(JEH-YI SIJANG-KWON)
SECURED NOTE	담보성 어음(DAMBOSUNG UH-WOOM)
SECURI.& EXCH. COMMISSION	증권감독원(JEUNGKWON GAMDOKWON)
SELF-INSURANCE	자체보험(JACHE BOHUM)
SELLING EXPENSES	판매비용(PAN-MAE BEYONG)
SEMI-FINISHED GOODS	반제품(BANJEHPOOM)
SENIOR DEBT	우선채무(WOO-SON CHAE-MOO)
SEPTEMBER	구월(GU WOL)
SEVERANCE	해고(HAE KO)
SEVERANCE INDEMNITIES	해고/퇴직 보상(HAE KO/TOEIJIK BOSANG)
SHARE IN LOSS OF AFFILIATES	관계회사 손실지분(GWAN-GEH HOE SA SONSIL JIBOON)
SHAREHOLDERS' EQUITY	자본총계(JABON CHONG-GEH)
SHARES	주식, 주권(JUSIK, JUKWON)
SHORT-TERM BANK LOANS	단기은행 융자(DANKI EUN-HAENG YOONGJA)
SHORT-TERM INVESTMENTS	단기투자(DANKI TOOJA)
SHORT-TERM LOANS	단기 융자(DANKI YOONGJA)
SYNDICATED LOANS	신디케이트 융자(SYNDICATE YUNG JA)
SMALL COMPANIES	소규모 기업(SOKYUMO KIUP)
SOCIAL SECURITY EXPENSE	사회보장비용(SAHOE BOJANG BEYONG)
SOURCES OF FUNDS	재무자원의 원천(JAEMOO JAWON UI WONCHUN)
SPECIAL BONUS	특별상여금(TEUK-BYUL SANYURKUM)
SPECIAL REPORTS	특별감사보고서(TEUK-BYUL KAMSA BOKOSEH)
SPLIT (OF A COMPANY)	분할(BOON-HAL)
SPREAD (BETWEEN RATES)	격차(KYUK CHA)
STAMP DUTY	인지 세(YINJISEH)
STANDARD COST	표준비용(PYOJUN BEYONG)

English	Korean
START-UP COSTS	창업비(CHANG-UP BEE)
STAT OF CHANGES IN FIN POSITION	재무상태변동표(JAEMOO SANG-TAI BYUNDONG PYO)
STAT OF SOURCES & USES OF FUND	재무자원원천및 운영표 (JAEMUJAWON WONCHUN/WOONYONG PYO)
	자금운영표 (JAKUM WUNYONG PYO)
STATEMENT OF ACCOUNTING POLICY	회계정책사항(HOE GEH JUNGCHAEK SA-HANG)
STATISTICAL SAMPLING	통계적 표본추출(TONGGEHGEOK PYOBON CHOOCHOOL)
STATUTORY AUDIT REPORT	법정감사보고서(BUPJUNG GAMSA BOGOSUH)
STATUTORY RESERVE	법정준비금(BUPJUNG JUN-BE-KUM)
STOCK DIVIDENDS	주식배당(JUSIK BAEDANG)
STOCK EXCHANGE	증권거래(JEUNG-KWON GUHRAE)
	증권거래소(JEUNG-KWON GUHRAESO)
STOCK OPTION PLANS	주식 옵션안(JUSIK OPTION AHN)
STOCKBROKER	주식중매인(JUSIK JOONGMAEYIN)
STOCKHOLDERS	주주(JUJU)
STOCKHOLDERS' EQUITY	자본(JABON)
STRAIGHT-LINE METHOD	정액법(JUNG-AEK-BOP)
SUBJECT TO	조건부로(JOKUNBOO RO)
SUBLET	전대(JUHNDAI)
SUBORDINATED DEBT	제2차 담보부 부채(JEH YEE CHA DAMBOBU BUCHAE)
SUBORDINATED FINANCING	제2차 담보부 융자(JEH YEE CHA DAMBOBU YOONGJA)
SUBSCRIPTION	청약(CHUNG-YAK)
SUBSEQUENT EVENTS	회계연도말 이후의 사항 (HOEGEH YOUNDOMAL YIHU-UI SAHANG)
	차후발생사항(CHAHOO BAL-SAENG SAHANG)
SUBSIDIARY	자회사(JA HOESA) / 종속회사(JONGSOK HOESA)
SUBSTANTIVE TESTS	중대성에 관한 검증(JUNGDAESUNG EH GWANHAN GUMJUNG)
SUM OF YRS'-DIGIT METHOD	산술급수법(SANSUL GUPSU BOP)
SUPPLEMENTARY INFORMATION	부록(BOO-ROK)
SUPPLIERS	공급자(GONG-GUP-JA)
SUPPLIES AND SPARE PARTS	소모품 및 비품(SOMOPOOM MIT BOOPOOM)
SUPPORTING DOCUMENTATION	관련자료(GWALYON JA-RYO)
TAKEN AS A WHOLE	전체적으로(JUHN CHE JEUK UI RO)
TANGIBLE FIXED ASSETS	유형고정자산(YU-HYUNG GO-JUNG JA-SAN)

English	Korean
TAX	세금(SEH-KUM)
TAX AUDIT	세무감사(SEH-MOO GAMSA)
TAX AUTHORITIES	세무당국(SEH-MOO DANG-GUK)
TAX CREDITS	세금혜택(SEH-KUM HEH-TAEK)
TAX RATES	세율(SEH-YOOL)
TAX RETURN	세금보고(SEH-KUM BOGO)
TAX SAVINGS	절세(JUHL-SEH)
TAX TREATMENT	과세처리법(GWA-SEH CHUR-RI-BOP)
TAXABLE INCOME	법인세전 순이익(BUP-YIN-SEH JEON SOON-YIYIK)
	과세소득(GWA-SEH SODEUK)
TAXPAYER	납세자(NAP-SEH-JA)
TEMPORARY DIFFERENCES	일시적 불일치(YILSI-JEOK BOOL-YIL-CHI)
TEST	검증(GUM JEONG)
THOUSAND	천 (CHUN)
THOUSANDS	천 (CHUN)
TIME DEPOSITS	정기예금 (JUNG-KI YEKUM)
TIMING	시기 (SI-GHI)
TOTAL FUND FROM OPERATION	영업조달 순운전 자금 (YOUNG-UP-JODAL SUN WUNJON JAKUM)
TOTAL INSURANCE CLAIMS & LOSSES	보험금(BO-HUM KUM)
TOTAL INSURANCE RESERVES	총보험준비금(CHONG BO-HUM JUN-BE-KUM)
TOTAL PREMIUMS WRITTEN	총수입 보험료(CHONG SU-YIP BO-HUM-RYO)
TOTAL REVENUE	총수익(CHONG SU-YIK)
TRADE MARKS	상표(SANG PYO)
TRADE RECEIVABLES	외상매출금(WOE-SANG MAECHOOLKUM)
TRADING ACCOUNT PROF.(LOSS)	상품유가증권 매매손익 (SANGPUM YUKAJUNGKON MAMAE SONIK)
TRAINING EXPENDITURE	연수 및 훈련비(YEUNSU MIT HUL-YUN-BE)
TRANSACTIONS	거래(GUH-RAE)
TREASURY STOCK	자기주식(JA-KI JU-SIK)
TREND	추세(CHOO-SEH)
TRIAL BALANCE	시산표(SI-SAN-PYO)
TROUBLED DEBT	악성부채 (AHK-SUNG BOOCHAE)
TRUST OPERATION PROF.(LOSS)	신탁계정 손익(SINTAK GEH-JUNG SONYIK)

TRUST SECURITIES	신탁증권(SIN–TAK JEUNGKWON)
TURNOVER RATIO	회전비율(HOE–JUHN BE–YOOL)
UNAMORTIZED PREMIUM	미상각할증금(MI–SANG–GAK HAL–JEUNG–KUM)
UNAPPROPRIATED R/E	미처분 이익잉여금(MICHURBUN YIYIK YING–YUR–KUM)
UNAUDITED	감사되지 않은(GAMSA DWEJI AHNUN)
UNCERTAINTY	불확실성(BOOL HWAK–SIL–SUNG)
UNCOLLECTIBLE	수금이 불가능한(SU–KUM–YI BOOL–GA–NEUNG HAN)
UNDERWR.& POLICY ADQ. COSTS	보험수수료(BO–HUM SU–SU–RYO)
UNEARNED INTERESTS	미실현이자(MI–SIL–HYUN YI–JA)
UNITS OF PRODUCTION	생산단위(SAENG–SAN DAN–WUI)
UNQUALIFIED	적정의견(JUK–JEONG UIKEUN)
UNSECURED BONDS	비담보 채권 (BE–DAM–BO CHAE–KWON)
USEFUL LIFE (OF AN ASSET)	내용 연수(NAE–YONG YOUNSU)
USES OF FUNDS	재무자원의 운용(JAEMOO JAWON UI WOONYONG)
VALUATION PRINCIPLES	평가원칙(PYUNG–KA WONCHIK)
VALUE ADDED TAX (VAT)	부가가치세(BOO–GA GA–CHI–SEH)
VARIABLE COST	변동비(BYUNDONG–BE)
VEHICLES	차량(CHA–RYANG)
VENDORS (USA)	도매업자(DOMAE–UP–JA)
VICE–CHAIRMAN	부회장(BOO–HOE–JANG)
VOUCHER	장부(JANG–BOO)
WAREHOUSE	창고(CHANG–GO)
WEIGHTED AVERAGE	가중평균(GAH–JOONG PYONG KYUN)
WITHHELD TAXES	공제 세금(GONG–JEH SEH–KUM)
WITHHOLDING TAX	원천징수세(WON–CHUN JING–SU SEH)
WORKING CAPITAL	운전자본(WOON JEON JA–BON)
WORKING CAPITAL RATIO	운전자본 비율(WOON–JEON JA–BON BE–YOOL)
WORKING CAPITAL TURNOVER	운전자본 회전율(WOON–JEON JA–BON HOE–JEON YOOL)
WORKING PAPERS	자료수집철(JARYO SOOJIP CHUL)
WRITE DOWN	상각(SANG–GAK)
YEAR–END CLOSING DATE	회계 연도 말일(HOE–GEH YOUNDO MAL–YIL)
YIELD	실효(SIL–HYO)
ZERO BASE BUDGET	제로베이스 예산(ZERO BASE YE–SAN)
ZERO COUPON BONDS	무이자 채권(MOOYIJA CHAEKWON)

PORTUGUESE	ENGLISH
abril	April
abstenção de opinião	disclaimer of opinion
ação preferencial	preference share
ação preferencial	preference share (UK)
ação preferencial	preferred share (USA)
acionistas	stockholders
ações	shares
ações em tesouraria	treasury stock
ações emitidas	outstanding shares
ações preferenciais nao resgatáveis	non-redeemable preferred stock
ações preferenciais resgatáveis	redeemable preferred stock
acontecimentos posteriores	subsequent events
acordo de financiamento	financing arrangement
acordo de recompra	repurchase agreement
acordo de revenda	resale agreement
adiantamento a fornecedores	advances to suppliers
administrador geral	chief executive officer
advogado	lawyer
afiliada(o)	affiliate
agente de bolsa	stockbroker
agosto	August
ajustamento	adjustment
ajustamento acumulado	cumulative adjustment
ajustamento de exercícios anteriores	prior period adjustments
alcance	scope
alcance	extent
aleatóriamente	at random
aleatóriamente	random
alienação (de bens e direitos de ativo)	disposal (of an asset)
alocar	allocate
alocar a gastos	write off (verb)
amortização acumulada	accumulated depreciation
amortizações	depreciation expense
amostra de auditoria	audit sampling
amostragem	sampling
amostragem estadística	statistical sampling
amostragem não estadística	non-statistical sampling
anualmente	annually
aos efeitos fiscais	for taxation purposes
apartamento duma declaração (oficial)	departure from a pronouncement
aplicado consistentemente	consistently applied
aplicado uniformemente	consistently applied
aplicações de recursos	uses of funds
aposentadoria	pension
aposentadoria antecipada	early retirement
apreciação de títulos	gain on revaluation of securities
apresentar razoavelmente	fairly present
apresentação	disclosure
aquisição (duma empresa)	acquisition (of a company)
armazém	warehouse
assembléia anual	annual meeting
assembléia anual dos acionistas	annual shareholders' meeting
ativo	assets
ativo a curto prazo	current assets
ativo circulante	current assets
ativo corrente	current assets
ativo fixo	tangible fixed assets
ativo permanente	fixed assets
ativos imateriais	intangible assets
ativos interbancários	interbank assets/funds
ativos líquidos	liquid assets
ativos monetários	monetary assets
ativos não circolantes	non-current assets
auditoria	audit
auditoria fiscal	tax audit
auditoria operacional	operational auditing
aumento de capital	capital increase
auto-segurança	self-insurance
auto-segurar se	self-insure
autoridade fiscal	tax authorities
balançete de saldos	trial balance
balanço	balance sheet
banco	bank
banco comercial	commercial bank
banco de investimento	investment bank/merchant bank
banco hipotecário	mortgage bank
benefícios pos-aposentadoria	post-retirement benefits
benefícios prestados para seguro de vida	life policy benefits
bens imateriais	intangible assets
bilhões	billions
bolsa de valores	stock exchange
caixa	cash
caixa e bancos	cash and banks
calificação	qualification(of an audit opinion)
câmbio	exchange rate
capacidade de produção	production capacity
capacidade excedentória	idle capacity
capital circulante líquido	working capital
capital integralizado	paid-in capital
capital primário	primary capital

PORTUGUESE	ENGLISH
capital social	capital stock
capital social	common stock
capitalização de custos financeiros	capitalization of financial costs
capitalização de juros	capitalization of interest
capitalização de locaçoes financeiras	capitalization of leases
carta de representação	client representation letter
centos	hundreds
certificado de deposito	certificate of deposit
ceteris paribus	ceteris paribus
ciclo de pagamentos	payments cycle
ciclo de produção	production cycle
ciclo operacional	operating cycle
circunstâncias	circumstances
cisão (duma empresa)	split (of a company)
classificar	allocate
clientes	customers
clientes importantes	major customers
cobertura do risco financeiro	hedge
cobranças	collections
codificar	code (verb)
colateral	collateral
colocação	placement
colocações interempresárias	inter-company loans
colocações por um dia	overnight funds
combinação de interesses	pooling of interest
combinações de negócios	business combinations
comércio internacional	international trade
comissão de valores	Securities and Exchange Commission
comissões bancárias	bank service charges
comissões e honorários - receitas	commissions & fees profits (losses)
(dispesas)	commissions & fees profits (losses)
companhia de seguros	insurance company
companhia subsidiária	subsidiary
companhias em processo de	development stage companies
desenvolvimento	development stage companies
compensar	offset
compilação das demonstrações financeiras	compilation of financial statements
composição da carteira de títulos	portfolio composition
compromissos	commitments
comprovante	voucher
condições de resgate	redemption features
confirmação de contas	confirmation of accounts
conselheiros	directors
conselho de administração	board of directors
considerado em conjunto	taken as a whole
consistência	consistency
construções em curso	construction in progress
conta de perdas e ganhos	profit & loss account
conta de resultados de exercício	profit & loss account
conta de resultados de exercício	income statement
contabilidade	accounting
contabilidade de provisao	accrual method of accounting
contabilista	accountant
contas a pagar	accounts payable
contas a receber	receivables
contas a receber	accounts receivable
contas a receber comerciais	net trade accounts receivable
contas comerciais a pagar	trade payables
contas comerciais a receber	trade receivables
contas consolidadas	consolidated accounts
contas correntes	demand deposits
contexto econômico	economic environment
conteúdo	contents
contingência de ganho	gain contingency
contingências	contingencies
contratos a longo prazo	long-term contracts
contratos futuros	future contracts
contribuente	taxpayer
controle de qualidade	quality control
controles internos	internal control
controles operacionais	operating controls
controles operacionais	operational controls
conversão a moeda estrangeira	foreign currency translation
conversão monetária	currency translation
correção monetária	adjustment for inflation
costo de produçao	production cost
costo variável	variable cost
crédito de imposto	tax credit
crédito de imposto por investimento	investment tax credit
créditos	receivables
créditos	accounts receivable
créditos a longo prazo	long-term credits
créditos incobráveis	actual loan losses
créditos por desgravações fiscais	credit for tax breaks
critérios de valuação	valuation principles
cumprir com	comply with
custo das existências vendidas	cost of goods sold
custo de aquisição	acquisition cost
custo de oportunidade	opportunity cost
custo de reposição	replacement cost

ACCOUNTING LEXICON : PORTUGUESE - ENGLISH

PORTUGUESE	ENGLISH	PORTUGUESE	ENGLISH
custo de reprodução	reproduction cost	despesas de comunicações	communications expense
custo de vendas	cost of sales	despesas de exhibições e eventos	exhibitions and events expenses
custo direito	direct cost	despesas de juros	interest expense
custo dos produtos vendidos	cost of sales	despesas de promoção	promotional costs
custo dos serviços prestados	cost of services rendered	despesas diferidas	deferred charges
custo marginal	marginal cost	despesas diferidas	deferred expenses
custo ou valor de mercado	lower of cost or market method	(despesas em) formação de pessoal	training expenditure
custo standard	standard cost	despesas por reclutamento (de pessoal)	recruiting expense
custos de emissão de apólices	underwriting and policy acq. costs	detectar	detect
custos de reparação e manutenção	repair and maintenance expense	dezembro	December
data de fechamento do exercício	year-end closing date	diagrama de fluxos	flowchart
data de vençimento	due date	diário	journal
data do balanço	balance sheet date	diferença dada a revaliação	revaluation surplus
de acordo com	in accordance with	diferenças temporarias	temporary differences
debenture	debenture	direcção	board of directors
declaração da política contabilística	statement of accounting policy	direitos alfandegários	customs duties
declaração do imposto	tax return	direitos autorais	copyright
deduzir	write down (verb)	direitos de exportação	export duties
deficiência de controles	control weakness	diretor geral	general manager
demonstração das origens e aplicações	statement of sources&uses of funds	diretores	directors
de recursos	statement of sources&uses of funds	disconto sobre dívida	debt discount
demonstrações financeiras	financial statements	disminuição da dívida a longo prazo	retirement of long term debt
demonstrações financeiras a data	interim financial statements	disponibilidades	cash equivalents
interina	interim financial statements	dívida de primer grado	senior debt
demonstrações financeiras comparativas	comparative financial statements	dívida não cobrável	troubled debt
demonstrações financeiras consolidadas	consolidated financial statements	dívida subordinada	subordinated debt
demonstrações financeiras resumidas	condensed financial statements	dívidas a longo prazo	long-term debt
dependentes	dependents	dividendo	dividend
depreciação acelerada	accelerated depreciation	dividendo por ação	dividend per share
depreciação acumulada	accumulated depreciation	dividendos	cash dividends
depreciação de construcções	depreciation of buildings	dividendos a pagar	dividends payable
depósito	warehouse	dividendos em ações	stock dividends
depósito a prazo	time deposit	divisas	foreign exchange
depósitos em caderneta de poupança	saving deposits	documentação sustendadora	supporting documentation
depósitos em garantia	guarantee deposits	documentos descontados	rediscounted notes
depósitos interbancários	interbank deposits	dólares	dollars
descoberto	overdraft	donativos para caridade	charity expense
descoberto bancário	bank overdraft	economias fiscais	tax savings
desembolso	disbursements	edifícios e outras construções	buildings and structures
despedida	severance	efeito	impact
despesas	expenses	efeito	effect
despesas acumuladas a pagar	accrued expenses	efeito acumulado	cumulative effect
despesas administrativas	administrative expenses	efeito da alteração de preços	effects of changing prices
despesas antecipadas	accrued expenses	embalagem e vasilhame	packaging material
despesas de ampliação de capital	expenses on capital increase	empregado	employee

PORTUGUESE	ENGLISH
empresa controlada	subsidiary
empresa em andamento	going concern
empresa multinacional	multinational enterprise
empréstimo obrigacionista	bond
empréstimos	loans
empréstimos a curto prazo	short-term loans
empréstimos bancários a curto prazo	short-term bank loans
empréstimos comerciais e industriais	commercial & industrial loans
empréstimos convertíveis	convertible bonds
empréstimos de locação	lease financing loans
empréstimos hipotecários	real estate and mortgage loans
empréstimos que não ganham interesses	non-performing earning assets
empréstimos sindicados	syndicated loans
empréstimos vencidos	matured loans
entidades financeiras	financial entities
equipamento para processamento de datos	data processing equipment
equipo de trabalho de auditoria	audit staff
erros	errors
estatuto social	company by-laws
estoques	inventory -(USA) (stocks-UK)
estratégia de auditoria	audit strategy
estudo de viabilidade	feasibility study
evidência	evidential matter
examinar	examine
exceto	except for
existências	inventory -(USA) (stocks-UK)
exportação	export
exposição ao risco	risk exposure
falência	bankruptcy
fatura	invoice
fevereiro	February
finanças	finance (noun)
financiamento da compra dum produto	product financing
financiamento subordinado	subordinated financing
financiar	finance (verb)
firma associada	associated firm
firmas afiliadas	affiliated firms
firmas corresponsáveis	correspondent firms
fluxo financeiro	cash flow
folha de pagamentos do pessoal	payroll
formulário	form
fornecedores	suppliers
fornecedores	vendors (USA)
fretes por compra de materiais	freight on purchases of materials
funcionário (duma sociedade)	officer (of a company)

PORTUGUESE	ENGLISH
fundo comúm de investimento	mutual fund
fundo de comércio	goodwill
fundo de comércio negativo	negative goodwill
fundo de maneio	working capital
fundo fixo de caixa	petty cash
fundo para diferenças de câmbio	reserve for exch. rate fluctuations
fundo para riscos	reserve for general risks
fundos	funds
fundos gerados pelas operações	total funds from operations
fusão	merger
ganho	gain
ganho (perda) de câmbio	foreign exchange gains (losses)
ganho (perda) por investimentos em títulos	investment securities gains(losses)
ganho líquido	investment securities gains(losses)
ganho neto do exercício	net income
ganho por venda de imovilizado	net income (loss) of the period
ganhos	gain on sale of fixed assets
garantia	profit
garantia	collateral
garantias sobre produtos	guarantee
garantir	product warranties
gastos acumulados a pagar	pledge (verb)
gastos administrativos e gerais	accrued expenses
gastos de organização	general and administrative expense
gastos de pesquisas	organization expenses
gastos de pesquisas e desenvolvimento	research and development costs
gastos de representação	research and development costs
gastos de venda	entertainment expense
gastos gerais de fabrico	selling expenses
gastos pagos antecipadamente	overhead expenses
gastos pre-operativos	prepaid expenses & deferred charges
geralmente aceito	start-up costs
gerente de auditoria	generally accepted
gerente geral	audit manager
grupo (de empresas)	general manager
hipoteca	group (of companies)
honorários	mortgage
honorários de auditoria	fees
honorários por serviços de terceiros	audit fees
horas-homem	fees for services by third party
imobilizado	labor hours (man-hours)
imobilizado neto	fixed assets
imovilizado	net fixed assets
imposta de selos	tangible fixed assets
	stamp duty

PORTUGUESE	ENGLISH
imposto	tax
imposto ao valor agregado (IVA)	value added tax (VAT)
imposto de capital	capital tax
imposto de capital	capital gains tax
imposto de renda	income tax
imposto de renda diferido	deferred income taxes
imposto diferido	deferred taxes
imposto doações e sucessões	inheritance tax
imposto duplo	double taxation
imposto interno	excise tax
imposto progressivo	graduated tax
imposto progressivo	progressive tax
imposto regressivo	regressive tax
imposto sobre a receita bruta	gross revenue tax
imposto sobre as pessoas singulares	personal income tax
imposto sobre as sociedades	corporation tax
imposto sobre as vendas	sales tax
impostos e taxas a pagar	accrued taxes
impostos retidos	withheld taxes
impresso	form
incerteza	uncertainty
incobrável	uncollectible
indenizações	indemnities
indenizações por despedida	severance indemnities
independência	independence
índice de cobrança	collection ratio
índice de liquidez	liquidity ratio
índice de rotação de crédito	credit turnover ratio
índice de rotação de estoques	inventory turnover ratio
índice lucro bruto	gross profit ratio
índice operacional	operating ratio
indústria	industry
inflação	inflation
informação deturbada	misleading information
informações suplementares	supplementary information
ingresos diferidos	deferred income
ingressos não taxáveis	non-taxable income
instalações	fittings
intenção da gerência	management intention
interesses não ganhos	unearned interests
inventário físico	physical inventory
investimento	investment
investimento em empresas afiliadas	investment in subsidiaries
investimento em subsidiárias	investment in subsidiaries
investimentos a curto prazo	short-term investments

PORTUGUESE	ENGLISH
investimentos a longo prazo	long-term investments
irregularidade	irregularity
janeiro	January
joint-venture	joint venture
julgamento profissional	professional judgment
julho	July
junho	June
juros a pagar	interest payable
juros a receber	interest receivable
juros ganhos	interest income
juros pagos	interest expense
lançamento contabilístico	journal entry
lei de trabalho	labor law
letras enviadas a cobrança	customers'liability for acceptances
libro geral	general ledger
licenças	licences
licenças pagas	vacation with pay
licitar	bid (verb)
linha de crédito	credit line
liquidez	liquidity
litigio	litigation
locador	lessor
locatário	lessee
locação	lease
locação	leasing
locação financeira	operating lease
lucro	profit
lucro correspondente aos asegurados	policyholders' surplus
lucro em dividendos	dividend income
lucro líquido	net income
lucro líquido operacional	operating profit
lucro operacional	operating profit
lucro por ação	earnings per share
lucros acumulados	retained earnings
lucros acumulados	unappropriated retained earnings
lucros acumulados apropiados	appropriated retained earnings
lucros e despesas não operacionais	non-operating income and expense
lucros retidos	retained earnings
lucros retidos distribuidos	appropriated retained earnings
maio	May
máquinas i equipamentos	machinery and equipment
marcas registradas	trade mark
margem	spread (between rates)
margem bruta	gross margin
margem de lucro	profit margin

PORTUGUESE	ENGLISH
março	March
material	material (noun)
materialidade	materiality
matérias primas	raw materials
média	average (mean)
média ponderada	weighted average
melhoras sobre terrenos	land improvements
mensalmente	monthly
mercado de valores	stock exchange
mercado secundário	secondary market
mercadoria em processamento	goods in process
mercadoria em trânsito	goods in transit
mercadoria para revenda	resale merchandise
método da equivalência patrimonial	equity method
método da suma dos digitos	sum of the years' digits method
método de "com e sem"	with and without method
método de porcentagem de acabamento	percentage-of-completion-method
método do contrato completado	completed-contract method
método do diferido	deferral method
método do passivo	liability method
método linear	straight-line method
mil	thousand
milhares	thousands
milhões	millions
mobiliária e material escritório	furniture and fixtures
moeda estrangeira	foreign currency
moeda estrangeira	foreign exchange
moeda nacional	local currency
montante das vendas	sales (turnover)
movéis e utensilios	furniture and fixtures
multa	fine
natureza	nature
normas de auditoria	auditing standards
notas a cobrar	notes receivable
notas a pagar	notes payable
notas explicativas	footnotes to the financial statemts
novembro	November
obrigação	debenture
obrigação	bond
obrigação perpetua	perpetual bond
obrigações a pagar	bonds payable
obrigações sem garantia	unsecured bonds
obsolescência	obsolescence
oferta	bid (noun)
opções	options
operação de cobertura	hedging
operações descontinuadas	discontinued operations
opinião	opinion
opinião adversa	adverse opinion
opinião negativa	adverse opinion
oportunidade	timing
orçamento	budget
orçamento base zero	zero base budget
ordem de produção	production order
organigrama	organization chart
origens dos recursos	sources of funds
origens e aplicações de fundos	cash flow
outras receitas (despesas) operacionais	other operating profits (losses)
outras receitas por serviços	other income for services
outros empréstimos	other loans
outubro	October
pagamentos	payments
pagamentos antecipados	prepaid expense
papéis de trabalho	working papers
paragrafo de parecer	opinion paragraph
parecer	opinion
parecer de auditor	auditor's report
parrafo de alcance	scope paragraph
parte da perda dos afiliados	share in loss of affiliates
participação minoritária	minority interests
participação nos lucros	profit sharing
participações em outras companhias	equity in other companies
partidas extraordinárias	extraordinary items
passivo	liability
passivo a curto prazo	current liabilities
passivo circulante	current liabilities
passivos a pagar	accrued liabilities
passivos não circolantes	non-current liabilities
pasta permanente	permanent file
patentes	patents
patrimônio correspondente aos asegurados	policyholders' equity
patrimônio liquido	stockholders' equity
patrimônio líquido	shareholders' equity
peças sobressalentes	supplies and spare parts
pequenas empresas	small companies
perda	loss
perda acumulada	loss carry-forward
perda neta do exercício	net loss of the period
período compreendido	intervening period
planes de opção sobre ações	stock option plans

PORTUGUESE	ENGLISH
plano de aposentadoria	pension plan
plano de contas	chart of accounts
política contabilística	accounting policies
ponto de equilíbrio	break even point
popolação	population
por mes	monthly
porção corrente de...	current portion of ...
porcentagem	percentage
portador	bearer
preço de rescate	call price
preço do mercado	market price
prejuízo	loss
prémio	premium
prémio de emissão	capital surplus
prémio não amortizado	unamortized premium
prémios de emissão	premium on issue of capital
prémios de seguros reconhecidos	total premiums written
prémios líquidos reconhecidos	net premiums earned
presidente do conselho de administração	chairman(of the board of directors)
previsão	forecast
prima sobre dívida	debt premium
primeiro entrado, primeiro saido	first in, first out (FIFO)
princípios contabilísticos	accounting principles
princípios de contabilidade	accounting principles
procedimentos alternativos	alternative procedures
procedimentos de auditoria	auditing procedures
produto nacional bruto	gross national product
produtos acabados	finished goods
produtos semiacabados	semi-finished goods
projeção	projection
promissória garantizada	secured note
prova	test
prova ácida	acid test
provisão	allowance
provisão	provision
provisão	accrual
provisão para contas de cobrança duvidosa	allowance for doubtful accounts
	allowance for doubtful accounts
provisão para créditos incobráveis	reserve for loan losses/bad debts
provisão para créditos incobráveis	allowance for uncollectible acc'ts
provisão para desvalorização de investimentos	allowance for devaluation of inv'ts
	allowance for devaluation of inv'ts
provisão para férias e subsidio de férias	accrued vacations
	accrued vacations
provisão para perda em empréstimos	allowance for loan losses

PORTUGUESE	ENGLISH
provisão para risco de amostragem	allowance for sampling risk
provisionar	accrue
provável	probable
quadro de financiamento	statement of changes in fin positio
questionario de control interno	internal control questionnaire
racio de capital circulante	working capital ratio
racio de endívidamento	indebtedness ratio
racio de liquidez	current ratio
racio de liquidez reduzida	acid test ratio
racio de rotação	turnover ratio
razoavelmente possível	reasonably possible
receitas (perdas) por administração de fundos de terceiros	trust operations profits (losses)
	trust operations profits (losses)
receitas operacionais brutas	total revenue
receitas por serviços prestados	income for services rendered
receitas proporcionais auferidas	accrued income
recessão	recession
reclamação não realizada	unasserted claim
reclamações	claims
reclamações e perdas por sinistros	total insurance claims and losses
reconciliação bancária	bank reconciliation (statement)
rede operacional	operational network
reembolso	refund
reestruturar	restructuring
reestruturação da dívida	debt restructuring
refinanciamento	refinancing
regalias sociais	employee benefits
registrar	post entries to the ledger
registrar	record (verb)
registros auxiliares	subsidiary records
registros contabilísticos	accounting records
regras	rules
regras de valorização	valuation principles
regressão multiple	multiple regression
regulamentos	regulations
regulamentos profissionais	professional standards
relatório	report
relatório de auditoria	auditor's report
relatório de revisão de contas	audit opinion
relatório de verificação de contas	auditors' report
relatório do revisor	statutory audit report
relatório à gerência	report to management
relatórios especiais	special reports
relatórios financeiros	financial statements
relatórios financeiros trimestrais	quarterly financial statements

PORTUGUESE	ENGLISH
remoto	remote
renda líquida	net income
rendimento	yield
rendimento colectável	taxable income
rendimento diferido	deferred income(expense)
rendimento não colectável	non-taxable income
rentabilidade do ativo	return on assets
rentabilidade patrimonial	return on equity
reparações	repairs
requerimentos legais	legal requirements
requisição de compra	purchase requisition
requisitos de garantias	pledging requirements
requisitos legais	legal requirements
reserva de revaliação	revaluation reserve
reserva legal	legal reserve
reserva legal	statutory reserve
reserva para reclamos e perdas	reserve for o/s claims and losses
reservas de longo prazo por sinistros	long-term insurance reserve charge
reservas não patrimoniais	non-equity reserves
resgatável	redeemable
responsabilidade do auditor	auditor's responsibility
resseguros e ajustamentos de prêmios	reinsurance and premium adjustments
restricções ao alcance	restrictions on the scope
resultados da amostragem	sampling results
resumo financeiro	financial summary
retenção de impostos	withholding of tax
retenção única de impostos	flat tax withholding
revaliação	revaluation
revisão analítica	analytical review
revisão de contas	audit
revisão dos relatórios financeiros	review of financial statements
revisor	auditor
revisor oficial de contas	internal auditor
risco alheio da amostragem	non-sampling risk
risco da amostragem	sampling risk
risco de auditoria	audit risk
risco de iliquidez	liquidity risk
risco de pais	country risk
risco por variação de câmbio	exchange rate risk
rotação de capital circulante	working capital turnover
rubro de negócio	industry
saldo a descoberto	bank overdraft
saldo para o exercício seguinte	balance carried forward
saldos de contas	account balances
salários e ordenados	salaries and wages
segmento de negócio	business segment
segundo pedido	second request
segurança social	social security expense
seguro de vida	life insurance
seguros gerais	general insurance
sem auditar	unaudited
sem fins lucrativos	non-profit
sem reservas	unqualified
serviços de consultadoria	consulting services
setembro	September
setor privado	private sector
setor público	public sector
significativo	material (significant)
sistema de inventário permanente	perpetual inventory system
situação contabilística intermédia	interim accounts
sobrecargo à importação	import surcharges
sobrefaturação	overinvoicing
sociedade afiliada	subsidiary
sociedade de participações financeiras	holding company
sociedade dominante	parent company
sócio	partner
sócio de auditoria	audit partner
stocks	inventory -(USA) (stocks-UK)
subarrendamento	sublet (noun)
subfaturação	underinvoicing
subproduto	by-product
subscrição	subscription
subsidiária no exterior	foreign subsidiary
subsidiárias	affiliates
subsidiárias internacionais	international subsidiaries
subsidiárias locais	domestic subsidiaries
sujeito a	subject to
sumário financeiro	financial summary
suplente	proxy (noun)
suprimentos	supplies (noun)
tamanho da amostragem	sample size
taxa de câmbio	exchange rate
taxa de disconto	discount rate
taxa de imposto	tax rate
taxa flotante	floating rate
taxa interbancária	interbank rate
taxa social única	social security expense
taxas de juros	interest rate
tendência	trend
termino antecipado de dívida	early extinguishment of debt

PORTUGUESE	ENGLISH
terrenos	land
testes de substância	substantive tests
testes de validade	substantive tests
título	bond
títulos de terceiros	custody securities
títulos e valores de terceiros	trust securities
títulos e valores mobiliários	marketable securities
títulos negociáveis	marketable securities
títulos negociáveis-moeda nacional	listed bonds-local currency
títulos sem cupão de renda	zero coupon bonds
total das reservas para riscos	total insurance reserves
trabalho de auditoria	audit engagement
transação fora de bolsa	over the counter transaction
transações	transactions
transações entre partes interessadas	related party transactions
transações monetárias	monetary transactions
transações não monetárias	non-monetary transactions
traslado a um exercício anterior	carryback
tratamento fiscal	tax treatment
trimestralmente	quarterly
trimestralmente (4 vezes por ano)	quarterly (4 times a year)
trimestre	quarter
ultimo entrado, primeiro saido	last in, first out (LIFO)
unidades de produção	units of production
universo	population (in a statist. environ.)
valor actuarial	actuarial value
valor contabilístico	book value
valor contabilístico líquido	net present value
valor esperado de recuperação	expected salvage value
valor histórico	historical cost
valor líquido	net worth
valor líquido de realização	net realizable value
valor nominal	par value
valor nominal	face value
valor patrimonial	book value
valor patrimonial	book value
variações contabilísticas	accounting changes
veículos	vehicles
vencido	overdue
vencimento	maturity
venda de produtos	sale of (manufactured) goods
vendas	sales (turnover)
vendas a prestação	sales on installments
vendas netas	net sales
vender e arrendar	leaseback
viabilidade	feasibility
vice-presidente	vice-chairman
vida útil (dum ativo)	useful life (of an asset)

ENGLISH	PORTUGUESE
accelerated depreciation	depreciação acelerada
account balances	saldos de contas
accountant	contabilista
accounting	contabilidade
accounting changes	variações contabilísticas
accounting policies	política contabilística
accounting principles	princípios de contabilidade
accounting principles	princípios contabilísticos
accounting records	registros contabilísticos
accounts payable	contas a pagar
accounts receivable	contas a receber
accounts receivable	créditos
accrual	provisão
accrual method of accounting	contabilidade de provisão
accrue	provisionar
accrued expenses	despesas acumuladas a pagar
accrued expenses	despesas antecipadas
accrued expenses	gastos acumulados a pagar
accrued income	receitas proporcionais auferidas
accrued liabilities	passivos a pagar
accrued taxes	impostos e taxas a pagar
accrued vacations	provisão para férias e subsidio de férias
accrued vacations	amortização acumulada
accumulated depreciation	depreciação acumulada
accumulated depreciation	prova ácida
acid test	racio de liquidez reduzida
acid test ratio	aquisição (duma empresa)
acquisition (of a company)	custo de aquisição
acquisition cost	créditos incobráveis
actual loan losses	valor actuarial
actuarial value	ajustamento
adjustment	correção monetária
adjustment for inflation	despesas administrativas
administrative expenses	adiantamento a fornecedores
advances to suppliers	opinião adversa
adverse opinion	opinião negativa
adverse opinion	afiliada(o)
affiliate	firmas afiliadas
affiliated firms	subsidiárias
affiliates	alocar
allocate	classificar
allocate	provisão
allowance	provisão para desvalorização de investimentos
allowance for devaluation of inv'ts	
allowance for devaluation of inv'ts	

ENGLISH	PORTUGUESE
allowance for doubtful accounts	provisão para contas de cobrança duvidosa
allowance for doubtful accounts	provisão para perda em empréstimos
allowance for loan losses	provisão para risco de amostragem
allowance for sampling risk	provisão para créditos incobráveis
allowance for uncollectible acc'ts	procedimentos alternativos
alternative procedures	revisão analítica
analytical review	assembléia anual
annual meeting	assembléia anual dos acionistas
annual shareholders' meeting	anualmente
annually	lucros acumulados apropiados
appropriated retained earnings	lucros retidos distribuidos
appropriated retained earnings	abril
April	ativo
assets	firma associada
associated firm	aleatóriamente
at random	auditoria
audit	revisão de contas
audit	trabalho de auditoria
audit engagement	honorários de auditoria
audit fees	gerente de auditoria
audit manager	relatório de revisao de contas
audit opinion	sócio de auditoria
audit partner	risco de auditoria
audit risk	amostra de auditoria
audit sampling	equipo de trabalho de auditoria
audit staff	estratégia de auditoria
audit strategy	procedimentos de auditoria
auditing procedures	normas de auditoria
auditing standards	revisor
auditor	parecer de auditor
auditor's report	relatório de auditoria
auditor's report	responsabilidade do auditor
auditor's responsibility	relatório de verificação de contas
auditors' report	agosto
August	média
average (mean)	saldo para o exercício seguinte
balance carried forward	balanço
balance sheet	data do balanço
balance sheet date	banco
bank	descoberto bancário
bank overdraft	saldo a descoberto
bank overdraft	reconciliação bancária
bank reconciliation (statement)	comissões bancárias
bank service charges	falência
bankruptcy	

ENGLISH	PORTUGUESE
bearer	portador
bid (noun)	oferta
bid (verb)	licitar
billions	bilhoes
board of directors	direcção
board of directors	conselho de administração
bond	empréstimo obrigacionista
bond	obrigação
bond	título
bonds payable	obrigações a pagar
book value	valor patrimonial
book value	valor contabilístico
book value	valor patrimonial
break even point	ponto de equilíbrio
budget	orçamento
buildings and structures	edifícios e outras construções
business combinations	combinações de negócios
business segment	segmento de negócio
by-product	subproduto
call price	preço de rescate
capital gains tax	imposto de capital
capital increase	aumento de capital
capital stock	capital social
capital surplus	prémio de emissão
capital tax	imposto de capital
capitalization of financial costs	capitalização de custos financeiros
capitalization of interest	capitalização de juros
capitalization of leases	capitalização de locações financeiras
carryback	traslado a um exercício anterior
cash	caixa
cash and banks	caixa e bancos
cash dividends	dividendos
cash equivalents	disponibilidades
cash flow	fluxo financeiro
cash flow	origens e aplicações de fundos
certificate of deposit	certificado de deposito
ceteris paribus	ceteris paribus
chairman(of the board of directors)	presidente do conselho de administração
charity expense	donativos para caridade
chart of accounts	plano de contas
chief executive officer	administrador geral
circumstances	circunstâncias
claims	reclamações
client representation letter	carta de representação
code (verb)	codificar

ENGLISH	PORTUGUESE
collateral	garantia
collateral	colateral
collection ratio	índice de cobrança
collections	cobranças
commercial & industrial loans	empréstimos comerciais e industriais
commercial bank	banco comercial
commissions & fees profits (losses)	comissões e honorários - receitas
commissions & fees profits (losses)	(dispesas)
commitments	compromissos
common stock	capital social
communications expense	despesas de comunicações
company by-laws	estatuto social
comparative financial statements	demonstrações financeiras comparativas
compilation of financial statements	compilação das demonstrações financeiras
completed-contract method	método do contrato completado
comply with	cumprir com
condensed financial statements	demonstrações financeiras resumidas
confirmation of accounts	confirmação de contas
consistency	consistência
consistently applied	aplicado uniformemente
consistently applied	aplicado consistentemente
consolidated accounts	contas consolidadas
consolidated financial statements	demonstrações financeiras consolidadas
construction in progress	construções em curso
consulting services	serviços de consultadoria
contents	conteúdo
contingencies	contingências
control weakness	deficiência de controles
convertible bonds	empréstimos convertíveis
copyright	direitos autorais
corporation tax	imposto sobre as sociedades
correspondent firms	firmas corresponsáveis
cost of goods sold	custo das existências vendidas
cost of sales	custo dos produtos vendidos
cost of sales	custo de vendas
cost of services rendered	custo dos serviços prestados
country risk	risco de pais
credit for tax breaks	créditos por desgravações fiscais
credit line	linha de crédito
credit turnover ratio	índice de rotação de crédito
cumulative adjustment	ajustamento acumulado
cumulative effect	efeito acumulado
currency translation	conversão monetária
current assets	ativo circulante
current assets	ativo a curto prazo

ENGLISH	PORTUGUESE
current assets	ativo corrente
current liabilities	passivo a curto prazo
current liabilities	passivo circulante
current portion of ...	porção corrente de...
current ratio	racio de liquidez
custody securities	títulos de terceiros
customers	clientes
customers'liability for acceptances	letras enviadas a cobrança
customs duties	direitos alfandegários
data processing equipment	equipamento para processamento de datos
debenture	obrigação
debenture	debenture
debt discount	disconto sobre dívida
debt premium	prima sobre dívida
debt restructuring	reestruturação da dívida
December	dezembro
deferral method	método do diferido
deferred charges	despesas diferidas
deferred expenses	despesas diferidas
deferred income	ingresos diferidos
deferred income taxes	imposto de renda diferido
deferred income(expense)	rendimento diferido
deferred taxes	imposto diferido
demand deposits	contas correntes
departure from a pronouncement	apartamento duma declaração (oficial)
dependents	dependentes
depreciation expense	amortizações
depreciation of buildings	depreciação de construcções
detect	detectar
development stage companies	companhias em processo de
development stage companies	desenvolvimento
direct cost	custo direito
directors	diretores
directors	conselheiros
disbursements	desembolso
disclaimer of opinion	abstenção de opiniao
disclosure	apresentação
discontinued operations	operações descontinuadas
discount rate	taxa de disconto
disposal (of an asset)	alienação (de bens e direitos de ativo)
dividend	dividendo
dividend income	lucro em dividendos
dividend per share	dividendo por ação
dividends payable	dividendos a pagar
dollars	dólares

ENGLISH	PORTUGUESE
domestic subsidiaries	subsidiárias locais
double taxation	imposto duplo
due date	data de vençimento
early extinguishment of debt	termino antecipado de dívida
early retirement	aposentadoria antecipada
earnings per share	lucro por ação
economic environment	contexto econômico
effect	efeito
effects of changing prices	efeito da alteração de preços
employee	empregado
employee benefits	regalias sociais
entertainment expense	gastos de representação
equity in other companies	participações em outras companhias
equity method	método da equivalência patrimonial
errors	erros
evidential matter	evidência
examine	examinar
except for	exceto
exchange rate	câmbio
exchange rate	taxa de câmbio
exchange rate risk	risco por variação de câmbio
excise tax	imposto interno
exhibitions and events expenses	despesas de exhibições e eventos
expected salvage value	valor esperado de recuperação
expenses	despesas
expenses on capital increase	despesas de ampliação de capital
export	exportação
export duties	direitos de exportação
extent	alcance
extraordinary items	partidas extraordinárias
face value	valor nominal
fairly present	apresentar razoavelmente
feasibility	viabilidade
feasibility study	estudo de viabilidade
February	fevereiro
fees	honorários
fees for services by third party	honorários por serviços de terceiros
finance (noun)	finanças
finance (verb)	financiar
financial entities	entidades financeiras
financial statements	demonstrações financeiras
financial statements	relatórios financeiros
financial summary	sumário financeiro
financial summary	resumo financeiro
financing arrangement	acordo de financiamento

ENGLISH	PORTUGUESE
fine	multa
finished goods	produtos acabados
first in, first out (FIFO)	primeiro entrado, primeiro saido
fittings	instalações
fixed assets	imobilizado
fixed assets	ativo permanente
flat tax withholding	retenção única de impostos
floating rate	taxa flotante
flowchart	diagrama de fluxos
footnotes to the financial statemts	notas explicativas
for taxation purposes	aos efeitos fiscais
forecast	previsão
foreign currency	moeda estrangeira
foreign currency translation	conversão a moeda estrangeira
foreign exchange	moeda estrangeira
foreign exchange	divisas
foreign exchange gains (losses)	ganho (perda) de câmbio
foreign subsidiary	subsidiária no exterior
form	formulário
form	impresso
freight on purchases of materials	fretes por compra de materiais
funds	fundos
furniture and fixtures	mobiliária e material escritório
furniture and fixtures	movéis e utensilios
future contracts	contratos futuros
gain	ganho
gain contingency	contingência de ganho
gain on revaluation of securities	apreciação de títulos
gain on sale of fixed assets	ganho por venda de imovilizado
general and administrative expense	gastos administrativos e gerais
general insurance	seguros gerais
general ledger	libro geral
general manager	diretor geral
general manager	gerente geral
generally accepted	geralmente aceito
going concern	empresa em andamento
goods in process	mercadoria em processamento
goods in transit	mercadoria em trânsito
goodwill	fundo de comércio
graduated tax	imposto progressivo
gross margin	margem bruta
gross national product	produto nacional bruto
gross profit ratio	índice lucro bruto
gross revenue tax	imposto sobre a receita bruta
group (of companies)	grupo (de empresas)

ENGLISH	PORTUGUESE
guarantee	garantia
guarantee deposits	depósitos em garantia
hedge	cobertura do risco financeiro
hedging	operação de cobertura
historical cost	valor histórico
holding company	sociedade de participações financeiras
hundreds	centos
idle capacity	capacidade excedentória
impact	efeito
import surcharges	sobrecargo à importação
in accordance with	de acordo com
income for services rendered	receitas por serviços prestados
income statement	conta de resultados de exercício
income tax	imposto de renda
indebtedness ratio	racio de endívidamento
indemnities	indenizações
independence	independência
industry	indústria
industry	rubro de negócio
inflation	inflação
inheritance tax	imposto doações e sucessões
insurance company	companhia de seguros
intangible assets	ativos imateriais
intangible assets	bens imateriais
inter-company loans	colocações interempresárias
interbank assets/funds	ativos interbancários
interbank deposits	depósitos interbancários
interbank rate	taxa interbancária
interest expense	juros pagos
interest expense	despesas de juros
interest income	juros ganhos
interest payable	juros a pagar
interest rate	taxas de juros
interest receivable	juros a receber
interim accounts	situação contabilística intermédia
interim financial statements	demonstrações financeiras a data
interim financial statements	interina
internal auditor	revisor oficial de contas
internal control	controles internos
internal control questionnaire	questionario de control interno
international subsidiaries	subsidiárias internacionais
international trade	comércio internacional
intervening period	período compreendido
inventory -(USA) (stocks-UK)	estoques
inventory -(USA) (stocks-UK)	existências

ENGLISH	PORTUGUESE
inventory -(USA) (stocks-UK)	stocks
inventory turnover ratio	índice de rotação de estoques
investment	investimento
investment bank/merchant bank	banco de investimento
investment in subsidiaries	investimento em subsidiárias
investment in subsidiaries	investimento em empresas afiliadas
investment securities gains(losses)	ganho (perda) por investimentos em títulos
investment securities gains(losses)	
investment tax credit	crédito de imposto por investimento
invoice	fatura
irregularity	irregularidade
January	janeiro
joint venture	joint-venture
journal	diário
journal entry	lançamento contabilístico
July	julho
June	junho
labor hours (man-hours)	horas-homem
labor law	lei de trabalho
land	terrenos
land improvements	melhoras sobre terrenos
last in, first out (LIFO)	ultimo entrado, primeiro saido
lawyer	advogado
lease	locação
lease financing loans	empréstimos de locação
leaseback	vender e arrendar
leasing	locação
legal requirements	requerimentos legais
legal requirements	requisitos legais
legal reserve	reserva legal
lessee	locatário
lessor	locador
liability	passivo
liability method	método do passivo
licences	licenças
life insurance	seguro de vida
life policy benefits	benefícios prestados para seguro de vida
liquid assets	ativos líquidos
liquidity	liquidez
liquidity ratio	índice de liquidez
liquidity risk	risco de iliquidez
listed bonds-local currency	títulos negociáveis-moeda nacional
litigation	litigio
loans	empréstimos
local currency	moeda nacional

ENGLISH	PORTUGUESE
long-term contracts	contratos a longo prazo
long-term credits	créditos a longo prazo
long-term debt	dívidas a longo prazo
long-term insurance reserve charge	reservas de longo prazo por sinistros
long-term investments	investimentos a longo prazo
loss	perda
loss	prejuízo
loss carry-forward	perda acumulada
lower of cost or market method	custo ou valor de mercado
machinery and equipment	máquinas i equipamentos
major customers	clientes importantes
management intention	intenção da gerência
March	março
marginal cost	custo marginal
market price	preço do mercado
marketable securities	títulos e valores mobiliários
marketable securities	títulos negociáveis
material (noun)	material
material (significant)	significativo
materiality	materialidade
matured loans	empréstimos vencidos
maturity	vencimento
May	maio
merger	fusão
millions	milhões
minority interests	participação minoritária
misleading information	informação deturbada
monetary assets	ativos monetários
monetary transactions	transações monetárias
monthly	mensalmente
monthly	por mes
mortgage	hipoteca
mortgage bank	banco hipotecário
multinational enterprise	empresa multinacional
multiple regression	regressão multiple
mutual fund	fundo comúm de investimento
nature	natureza
negative goodwill	fundo de comércio negativo
net fixed assets	imobilizado neto
net income	lucro líquido
net income	ganho líquido
net income	renda líquida
net income of the period	ganho neto do exercício
net loss of the period	perda neta do exercício
net premiums earned	prémios líquidos reconhecidos

ENGLISH	PORTUGUESE
net present value	valor contabilístico líquido
net realizable value	valor líquido de realização
net sales	vendas netas
net trade accounts receivable	contas a receber comerciais
net worth	valor líquido
non performing earning assets	empréstimos que não ganham interesses
non-current assets	ativos não circolantes
non-current liabilities	passivos não circolantes
non-equity reserves	reservas não patrimoniais
non-monetary transactions	transações não monetárias
non-operating income and expense	lucros e despesas não operacionais
non-profit	sem fins lucrativos
non-redeemable preferred stock	ações preferenciais não resgatáveis
non-sampling risk	risco alheio da amostragem
non-statistical sampling	amostragem não estadística
non-taxable income	ingressos não taxáveis
non-taxable income	rendimento não colectável
notes payable	notas a pagar
notes receivable	notas a cobrar
November	novembro
obsolescence	obsolescência
October	outubro
officer (of a company)	funcionário (duma sociedade)
offset	compensar
operating controls	controles operacionais
operating cycle	ciclo operacional
operating lease	locação financeira
operating profit	lucro operacional
operating profit	lucro líquido operacional
operating ratio	índice operacional
operational auditing	auditoria operacional
operational controls	controles operacionais
operational network	rede operacional
opinion	parecer
opinion	opinião
opinion paragraph	paragrafo de parecer
opportunity cost	custo de oportunidade
options	opções
organization chart	organigrama
organization expenses	gastos de organização
other income for services	outras receitas por serviços
other loans	outros empréstimos
other operating profits (losses)	outras receitas (despesas) operacionais
outstanding shares	ações emitidas
over the counter transaction	transação fora de bolsa
overdraft	descoberto
overdue	vencido
overhead expenses	gastos gerais de fabrico
overinvoicing	sobrefaturação
overnight funds	colocações por um dia
packaging material	embalagem e vasilhame
paid-in capital	capital integralizado
par value	valor nominal
parent company	sociedade dominante
partner	sócio
patents	patentes
payments	pagamentos
payments cycle	ciclo de pagamentos
payroll	folha de pagamentos do pessoal
pension	aposentadoria
pension plan	plano de aposentadoria
percentage	porcentagem
percentage-of-completion-method	método de porcentagem de acabamento
permanent file	pasta permanente
perpetual bond	obrigação perpetua
perpetual inventory system	sistema de inventário permanente
personal income tax	imposto sobre as pessoas singulares
petty cash	fundo fixo de caixa
physical inventory	inventário físico
placement	colocação
pledge (verb)	garantir
pledging requirements	requisitos de garantias
policyholders' equity	patrimônio correspondente aos asegurados
policyholders' surplus	lucro correspondente aos asegurados
pooling of interest	combinação de interesses
population	popolação
population (in a statist. environ.)	universo
portfolio composition	composição da carteira de títulos
post entries to the ledger	registrar
post-retirement benefits	benefícios pos-aposentadoria
preference share	ação preferencial
preference share (UK)	ação preferencial
preferred share (USA)	ação preferencial
premium	prémio
premium on issue of capital	prémios de emissão
prepaid expense	pagamentos antecipados
prepaid expenses & deferred charges	gastos pagos antecipadamente
primary capital	capital primário
prior period adjustments	ajustamento de exercícios anteriores
private sector	setor privado

ENGLISH	PORTUGUESE
probable	provável
product financing	financiamento da compra dum produto
product warranties	garantias sobre produtos
production capacity	capacidade de produção
production cost	costo de produção
production cycle	ciclo de produção
production order	ordem de produção
professional judgment	julgamento profissional
professional standards	regulamentos profissionais
profit	lucro
profit	ganhos
profit & loss account	conta de resultados de exercício
profit & loss account	conta de perdas e ganhos
profit margin	margem de lucro
profit sharing	participação nos lucros
progressive tax	imposto progressivo
projection	projeção
promotional costs	despesas de promoção
provision	provisão
proxy (noun)	suplente
public sector	setor público
purchase requisition	requisição de compra
qualification(of an audit opinion)	calificação
quality control	controle de qualidade
quarter	trimestre
quarterly	trimestralmente
quarterly (4 times a year)	trimestralmente (4 vezes por ano)
quarterly financial statements	relatórios financeiros trimestrais
random	aleatóriamente
raw materials	matérias primas
real estate and mortgage loans	empréstimos hipotecários
reasonably possible	razoavelmente possível
receivables	contas a receber
receivables	créditos
recession	recessão
record (verb)	registrar
recruiting expense	despesas por reclutamento (de pessoal)
redeemable	resgatável
redeemable preferred stock	ações preferenciais resgatáveis
redemption features	condições de resgate
rediscounted notes	documentos descontados
refinancing	refinanciamento
refund	reembolso
regressive tax	imposto regressivo
regulations	regulamentos

ENGLISH	PORTUGUESE
reinsurance and premium adjustments	resseguros e ajustamentos de prêmios
related party transactions	transações entre partes interessadas
remote	remoto
repair and maintenance expense	custos de reparação e manutenção
repairs	reparações
replacement cost	custo de reposição
report	relatório
report to management	relatório à gerência
reproduction cost	custo de reprodução
repurchase agreement	acordo de recompra
resale agreement	acordo de revenda
resale merchandise	mercadoria para revenda
research and development costs	gastos de pesquisas e desenvolvimento
research and development costs	gastos de pesquisas
reserve for exch. rate fluctuations	fundo para diferenças de câmbio
reserve for general risks	fundo para riscos
reserve for loan losses/bad debts	provisão para créditos incobráveis
reserve for o/s claims and losses	reserva para reclamos e perdas
restrictions on the scope	restricções ao alcance
restructuring	reestruturar
retained earnings	lucros acumulados
retained earnings	lucros retidos
retirement of long term debt	disminuição da dívida a longo prazo
return on assets	rentabilidade do ativo
return on equity	rentabilidade patrimonial
revaluation	revaliação
revaluation reserve	reserva de revaliação
revaluation surplus	diferença dada a revaliação
review of financial statements	revisão dos relatórios financeiros
risk exposure	exposição ao risco
rules	regras
salaries and wages	salários e ordenados
sale of (manufactured) goods	venda de produtos
sales (turnover)	montante das vendas
sales (turnover)	vendas
sales on installments	vendas a prestação
sales tax	imposto sobre as vendas
sample size	tamanho da amostragem
sampling	amostragem
sampling results	resultados da amostragem
sampling risk	risco da amostragem
saving deposits	depósitos em caderneta de poupança
scope	alcance
scope paragraph	parrafo de alcance
second request	segundo pedido

ACCOUNTING LEXICON : ENGLISH - PORTUGUESE

ENGLISH	PORTUGUESE
secondary market	mercado secundário
secured note	promissória garantizada
Securities and Exchange Commission	comissão de valores
self-insurance	auto-segurança
self-insure	auto-segurar se
selling expenses	gastos de venda
semi-finished goods	produtos semiacabados
senior debt	dívida de primer grado
September	setembro
severance	despedida
severance indemnities	indenizações por despedida
share in loss of affiliates	parte da perda dos afiliados
shareholders' equity	patrimônio líquido
shares	ações
short-term bank loans	empréstimos bancários a curto prazo
short-term investments	investimentos a curto prazo
short-term loans	empréstimos a curto prazo
small companies	pequenas empresas
social security expense	taxa social única
social security expense	segurança social
sources of funds	origens dos recursos
special reports	relatórios especiais
split (of a company)	cisão (duma empresa)
spread (between rates)	margem
stamp duty	imposta de selos
standard cost	custo standard
start-up costs	gastos pre-operativos
statement of accounting policy	declaração da política contabilística
statement of changes in fin positio	quadro de financiamento
statement sources & uses of funds	demonstração das origens e aplicações de recursos
statement sources & uses of funds	
statistical sampling	amostragem estadística
statutory audit report	relatório do revisor
statutory reserve	reserva legal
stock dividends	dividendos em ações
stock exchange	bolsa de valores
stock exchange	mercado de valores
stock option plans	planes de opção sobre ações
stockbroker	agente de bolsa
stockholders	acionistas
stockholders' equity	patrimônio liquido
straight-line method	método linear
subject to	sujeito a
sublet (noun)	subarrendamento
subordinated debt	dívida subordinada
subordinated financing	financiamento subordinado
subscription	subscrição
subsequent events	acontecimentos posteriores
subsidiary	empresa controlada
subsidiary	companhia subsidiária
subsidiary	sociedade afiliada
subsidiary records	registros auxiliares
substantive tests	testes de validade
substantive tests	testes de substância
sum of the years' digits method	método da suma dos digitos
supplementary information	informações suplementares
suppliers	fornecedores
supplies (noun)	suprimentos
supplies and spare parts	peças sobressalentes
supporting documentation	documentação sustendadora
syndicated loans	empréstimos sindicados
taken as a whole	considerado em conjunto
tangible fixed assets	imovilizado
tangible fixed assets	ativo fixo
tax	imposto
tax audit	auditoria fiscal
tax authorities	autoridade fiscal
tax credit	crédito de imposto
tax rate	taxa de imposto
tax return	declaração do imposto
tax savings	economias fiscais
tax treatment	tratamento fiscal
taxable income	rendimento colectável
taxpayer	contribuente
temporary differences	diferenças temporarias
test	prova
thousand	mil
thousands	milhares
time deposit	depósito a prazo
timing	oportunidade
total funds from operations	fundos gerados pelas operações
total insurance claims and losses	reclamações e perdas por sinistros
total insurance reserves	total das reservas para riscos
total premiums written	prémios de seguros reconhecidos
total revenue	receitas operacionais brutas
trade mark	marcas registradas
trade payables	contas comerciais a pagar
trade receivables	contas comerciais a receber
training expenditure	(despesas em) formação de pessoal
transactions	transações

ENGLISH	PORTUGUESE
treasury stock	ações em tesouraria
trend	tendência
trial balance	balançete de saldos
troubled debt	dívida não cobrável
trust operations profits (losses)	receitas (perdas) por administração de
trust operations profits (losses)	fundos de terceiros
trust securities	títulos e valores de terceiros
turnover ratio	racio de rotação
unamortized premium	prémio não amortizado
unappropriated retained earnings	lucros acumulados
unasserted claim	reclamação não realizada
unaudited	sem auditar
uncertainty	incerteza
uncollectible	incobrável
underinvoicing	subfaturação
underwriting and policy acq. costs	custos de emissão de apólices
unearned interests	interesses não ganhos
units of production	unidades de produção
unqualified	sem reservas
unsecured bonds	obrigações sem garantia
useful life (of an asset)	vida útil (dum ativo)
uses of funds	aplicações de recursos
vacation with pay	licenças pagas
valuation principles	critérios de valuação
valuation principles	regras de valorização
value added tax (VAT)	imposto ao valor agregado (IVA)
variable cost	costo variável
vehicles	veículos
vendors (USA)	fornecedores
vice-chairman	vice-presidente
voucher	comprovante
warehouse	depósito
warehouse	armazém
weighted average	média ponderada
with and without method	método de "com e sem"
withheld taxes	impostos retidos
withholding of tax	retenção de impostos
working capital	capital circulante líquido
working capital	fundo de maneio
working capital ratio	racio de capital circulante
working capital turnover	rotação de capital circulante
working papers	papéis de trabalho
write down (verb)	deduzir
write off (verb)	alocar a gastos
year-end closing date	data de fechamento do exercício
yield	rendimento
zero base budget	orçamento base zero
zero coupon bonds	títulos sem cupão de renda

SPANISH	ENGLISH
a efectos de impositivos	for taxation purposes
abogado	lawyer
abril	April
abstención de opinión	disclaimer of opinion
acciones	shares
acciones con cotización	marketable stocks
acciones en circulación	outstanding shares
acciones ordinarias	common stock
acciones preferidas no rescatables	non-redeemable preferred stock
acciones preferidas rescatables	redeemable preferred stock
acciones propias en cartera	treasury stock
accionistas	stockholders
acción preferente	preference share
acción preferida	preference share (UK)
acción preferida	preferred share (USA)
acontecimientos posteriores	subsequent events
activo	assets
activo a corto plazo	current assets
activo circulante	current assets
activo corriente	current assets
activo fijo	fixed assets
activo fijo	tangible fixed assets
activos fijos netos	net fixed assets
activos intangibles	intangible assets
activos liquidos	liquid assets
activos monetarios	monetary assets
activos no corrientes	non-current assets
acuerdo de financiación	financing arrangement
adelantos a proveedores	advances to suppliers
adquisición (de una empresa)	acquisition (of a company)
afiliado(a)	affiliate
agente de bolsa	stockbroker
agosto	August
ahorros impositivos	tax savings
ajuste	adjustment
ajuste acumulado	cumulative adjustment
ajuste de ejercicios anteriores	prior period adjustments
ajuste por inflación	adjustment for inflation
al azar	at random
al azar	random
alcance	extent
alcance	scope
aleatorio	random
almacén	warehouse
amortizaciones	depreciation expense
amortización acumulada	accumulated depreciation
amortización acumulada	accumulated amortization
anticipos a proveedores	advances to suppliers
anualmente	annually
apartamiento de un pronunciamiento	departure from a pronouncement
aplicado consistentemente	consistently applied
aplicado uniformemente	consistently applied
apoderado	proxy (noun)
apreciación de inversiones negociables	gain on revaluation of securities
arrendador	lessor
arrendatario	lessee
asamblea anual ordinaria	annual meeting
asamblea anual ordinaria de accionistas	annual shareholders' meeting
asiento de diario	journal entry
auditores internos	internal auditors
auditoría	audit
auditoría impositiva	tax audit
auditoría operativa	operational auditing
aumento de capital	capital increase
autoasegurarse	self-insure
autoridad tributaria	tax authorities
autoseguro	self-insurance
aval	guarantee
balance (general)	balance sheet
balance de saldos	trial balance
bancarrota	bankruptcy
banco	bank
banco comercial	commercial bank
banco de inversión	investment bank/merchant bank
banco hipotecario	mortgage bank
banco para la vivienda	mortgage bank
beneficio	profit
beneficio de explotación	operating profit
beneficio neto	net income
beneficio por acción	earnings per share
beneficios aplicados	appropriated retained earnings
beneficios distribuidos	appropriated retained earnings
beneficios laborales	employee benefits
beneficios luego del retiro	post-retirement benefits
beneficios no distribuidos	retained earnings
beneficios prestados por seguros de vida	life policy benefits
beneficios retenidos	retained earnings
bienes de cambio	inventory -(USA) (stocks-UK)
bienes de uso	fixed assets
bienes de uso	tangible fixed assets

SPANISH	ENGLISH
bienes inmateriales	intangible assets
billones	billions
bolsa de valores	stock exchange
bono	bond
bono perpetuo	perpetual bond
bonos de cupón cero	zero coupon bonds
bonos sin cupón de renta	zero coupon bonds
caja	cash
caja chica	petty cash
calificación	qualification(of an audit opinion)
cambios contables	accounting changes
capacidad de producción	production capacity
capacidad ociosa	idle capacity
capital accionario	capital stock
capital básico	primary capital
capital circulante	working capital
capital de trabajo	working capital
capital integrado	paid-in capital
capital primario	primary capital
capital propio	stockholders' equity
capital social	capital stock
capitalización de arrendamientos	capitalization of leases
capitalización de costos financieros	capitalization of financial costs
capitalización de intereses	capitalization of interest
capitalización de locaciones	capitalization of leases
cargas de familia	dependents
cargos diferidos	deferred charges
carpeta permanente	permanent file
carta de manifestaciones del cliente	client representation letter
carta del comisario	statutory audit report
casa matriz	parent company
cash flow	cash flow
castigo	write down (noun)
censor	auditor
censor de cuentas	auditor
certificado de censura	auditor's report
certificado de depósito	certificate of deposit
certificado de libre deuda	certificate of good standing
ceteris paribus	ceteris paribus
ciclo de pagos	payments cycle
ciclo de producción	production cycle
ciclo operativo	operating cycle
cientos	hundreds
cifra de negocios	sales (turnover)
circunstancias	circumstances

SPANISH	ENGLISH
clasificar	allocate
clientes	customers
clientes significativos	major customers
cobertura de riscos financieros	hedge
cobranzas	collections
cobro	collections
codificar	code (verb)
coeficiente de rotación	turnover ratio
colateral	collateral
colocaciones interempresarias	inter-company loans
colocaciones por un dia	overnight funds
colocación	placement
combinaciones de negocios	business combinations
combinación de intereses	pooling of interest
comercio internacional	international trade
comisiones y honorarios-ingresos	commissions & fees profits (losses)
(gastos)	commissions & fees profits (losses)
comisión de valores	Securities and Exchange Commission
compañía controlada	subsidiary
compañía de seguros	insurance company
compañía matriz	holding company
compañías en proceso de desarrollo	development stage companies
compensar	offset (verb)
compilación de estados contables	compilation of financial statements
composición de la cartera	portfolio composition
comprobación	test
comprobante	voucher
compromiso de recompra	repurchase agreement
compromiso de reventa	resale agreement
compromisos	commitments
comunicaciones, telex y telefonos	communications expense
conciliación bancaria	bank reconciliation (statement)
condiciones de rescate	redemption features
confirmación de saldos	confirmation of accounts
consejeros	directors
consejo de administración	board of directors
considerado en su conjunto	taken as a whole
construcciones en proceso	construction in progress
contabilidad	accounting
contable	accountant
contador	accountant
contenido	contents
contexto económico	economic environment
contingencia de ganancia	gain contingency
contingencias	contingencies

SPANISH	ENGLISH
contratos a futuro	future contracts
contratos a largo plazo	long-term contracts
contratos a termino	future contracts
contribuyente	taxpayer
control de calidad	quality control
controles internos	internal control
controles operativos	operating controls
controles operativos	operational controls
conversión de monedas	currency translation
costo de adquisición	acquisition cost
costo de las mercaderías vendidas	cost of sales
costo de los productos vendidos	cost of goods sold
costo de los servicios prestados	cost of services rendered
costo de oportunidad	opportunity cost
costo de producción	production cost
costo de producción	production cost
costo de reposición	replacement cost
costo de reproducción	reproduction cost
costo de ventas	cost of sales
costo directo	direct cost
costo histórico	historical cost
costo marginal	marginal cost
costo o mercado	lower of cost or market method
costo o plaza	lower of cost or market method
costo standard	standard cost
costo variable	variable cost
costos de promoción	promotional costs
cotización	market price
crédito de impuestos	tax credit
crédito de impuestos por inversión	investment tax credit
créditos	receivables
créditos	accounts receivable
créditos a largo plazo	long-term credits
créditos por desgravaciones fiscales	credit for tax breaks
créditos por ventas clientela general	trade receivables
criterios de valoración	valuation principles
criterios de valuación	valuation principles
cuadro de financiamiento	statement changes in fin. position
cuadro de financiamiento	statement sources & uses of funds
cuenta de periodificación	deferred income/expense
cuenta de pérdidas y ganancias	profit & loss account
cuenta de pérdidas y ganancias	income statement
cuentas consolidadas	consolidated accounts
cuentas corrientes	demand deposits
cuentas de orden	customers'liability for acceptances

SPANISH	ENGLISH
cuentas por cobrar	accounts receivable
cuentas por cobrar	receivables
cuentas por cobrar comerciales	net trade accounts receivable
cuentas por pagar	accounts payable
cuestionario de control interno	internal control questionnaire
cumplir con	comply with
dar entrada en el libro mayor	post entries to the ledger
de acuerdo con	in accordance with
debentura	debenture
debilidad de control	control weakness
débitos por ventas clientela general	trade payables
declaración jurada de impuestos	tax return
deducción	write off (noun)
depreciaciones	depreciation expense
depreciaciones de construcciones	depreciation on buildings
depreciación acelerada	accelerated depreciation
depreciación acumulada	accumulated depreciation
depósito	warehouse
depósitos a plazo fijo	time deposit
depósitos en caja de ahorros	saving deposits
depósitos en garantía	guarantee deposits
depósitos interbancarios	interbank deposits
derechos aduaneros	customs duties
derechos de exportación	export duties
derechos de propiedad intelectual	copyright
descuento sobre deuda	debt discount
desembolsos	disbursements
desestacionalizado	seasonally adjusted
despido	severance
detectar	detect
deuda a largo plazo	long-term debt
deuda con problemas de cobro	troubled debt
deuda convertible en capital	convertible bonds
deuda de primer grado	senior debt
deuda subordinada	subordinated debt
devengado (método de lo)	accrual method of accounting
diagrama de circulación	flowchart
diciembre	December
dictamen del auditor	auditor's report
diferencia entre tasa pagada y cobrada	spread (between rates)
diferencia por revaluación	revaluation surplus
diferencias temporarias	temporary differences
director general	general manager
directores	directors
directorio	board of directors

ACCOUNTING LEXICON : SPANISH - ENGLISH

SPANISH	ENGLISH
disminución de la deuda a largo plazo	retirement of long-term debt
disponibilidades	cash equivalents
dividendo	dividend
dividendo por acción	dividend per share
dividendos a pagar	dividends payable
dividendos en acciones	stock dividends
dividendos en efectivo	cash dividends
dividendos percibidos	dividend income
divisas	foreign exchange
doble imposición	double taxation
documentación sustentatoria	supporting documentation
documentos descontados	rediscounted notes
documentos por cobrar	notes receivable
documentos por pagar	notes payable
dólares	dollars
donaciones y obras de caridad	charity expense
edificios y otras construcciones	buildings and structures
efectivo	cash
efectivo y bancos	cash and banks
efecto	effect
efecto	impact
efecto acumulado	cumulative effect
efecto de los cambios de precios	effects of changing prices
embalajes y envases	packaging material
empleado	employee
empresa en marcha	going concern
empresa multinacional	multinational enterprise
empréstito	bond
enajenación (de inmovilizado)	disposal (of an asset)
enero	January
enfoque de auditoría	audit approach
entidades financieras	financial entities
enunciado de política contable	statement of accounting policy
equipo de trabajo de auditoría	audit staff
errores	errors
escisión (de una empresa)	split (of a company)
estado de cambios de la posición financiera	statement changes in fin. position
estado de origen y aplicación de fondos	statement changes in fin. position
estados contables	statement sources & uses of funds
estados contables a fecha interina	financial statements
estados contables comparativos	interim financial statements
estados contables consolidados	comparative financial statements
estados contables interinos	consolidated financial statements
estados contables resumidos	interim accounts
	condensed financial statements

SPANISH	ENGLISH
estados contables trimestrales	quarterly financial statements
estados financieros	financial statements
estándares profesionales	professional standards
estatuto social	company by-laws
estimación	allowance
estratégia de auditoría	audit strategy
estudio de factibilidad	feasibility study
estudio de viabilidad	feasibility study
evidencia comprobatoria	evidential matter
examinar	examine
excepto por	except for
existencias	inventory -(USA) (stocks-UK)
exportación	export
exposición al riesgo	risk exposure
extinción temprana de la deuda	early extinguishment of debt
factibilidad	feasibility
factura	invoice
febrero	February
fecha de cierre del ejercicio	year-end closing date
fecha de vencimiento	due date
fecha del balance	balance sheet date
filial	subsidiary
financiaciones subordinadas	subordinated financing
financiación de la compra de un producto	product financing
financiar	finance (verb)
finanzas	finance (noun)
firma asociada	associated firm
firmas afiliadas	affiliated firms
firmas corresponsales	correspondent firms
fletes por compra de materiales	freight on purchases of materials
flujo de fondos	cash flow
flujograma	flowchart
fondo común de inversión	mutual fund
fondo de comercio	goodwill
fondo de comercio negativo	negative goodwill
fondo de maniobra	working capital
fondo de reserva para diferencias de cambio	reserve for exch. rate fluctuations
	reserve for exch. rate fluctuations
fondo de reserva para préstamos incobrables	reserve for loan losses/bad debts
	reserve for loan losses/bad debts
fondo de reserva para reclamos pendientes y pérdidas	reserve for o/s claims and losses
	reserve for o/s claims and losses
fondo de reserva para riesgos	reserve for general risks
fondos	funds
fondos generados por las operaciones	total funds from operations

SPANISH	ENGLISH
fondos interbancarios	interbank assets/funds
formulario	form
fuentes de fondos	sources of funds
funcionario (de una sociedad)	officer (of a company)
fusión	merger
ganancia	gain
ganancia	profit
ganancia (pérdida) por inversiones en	investment securities gains(losses)
títulos	investment securities gains(losses)
ganancia imponible	taxable income
ganancia neta	net income
ganancia neta del ejercicio	net income (loss) of the period
ganancia operativa	operating profit
ganancia por acción	earnings per share
ganancia por intereses no devengada	unearned interest
garantía	guarantee
garantía	collateral
garantías sobre productos	product warranties
garantizar	pledge (verb)
gastos	expenses
gastos a pagar	accrued expenses
gastos acumulados	accrued expenses
gastos administrativos	administrative expenses
gastos administrativos y generales	general and administrative expense
gastos bancarios	bank service charges
gastos de ampliación de capital	expenses on capital increase
gastos de capacitación al personal	training expenditure
gastos de comercialización	selling expenses
gastos de estructura	overhead expenses
gastos de estudios e investigación	research and development costs
gastos de investigación y desarrollo	research and development costs
gastos de organización	organization expenses
gastos de reparaciones y mantenimiento	repair and maintenance expense
gastos de representación	entertainment expense
gastos de ventas	selling expenses
gastos devengados	accrued expenses
gastos pagados por adelantado	prepaid expense
gastos por cargas sociales	social security expense
gastos por exhibiciones y eventos	exhibitions and events expense
gastos por generación de polizas	underwriting and policy acq. costs
gastos por intereses	interest expense
gastos por reclutamiento (del personal)	recruiting expense
gastos preoperativos	start-up costs
generalmente aceptado(s)	generally accepted
gerente del trabajo de auditoría	audit manager

SPANISH	ENGLISH
gerente general	general manager
gerente general	chief executive officer
giro en descubierto	bank overdraft
gratificaciones especiales	special bonus
grupo (de empresas)	group (of companies)
hechos posteriores	subsequent events
hipoteca	mortgage
holding	holding company
honorarios	fees
honorarios de auditoría	audit fees
honorarios por servicios de terceros	fees for services by third party
horas-hombre	labor hours (man-hours)
importante	material (significant)
impuesto	tax
impuesto a la herencia	inheritance tax
impuesto a las ganancias	income tax
impuesto a las ganancias diferido	deferred income taxes
impuesto a las ganancias eventuales	capital gains tax
impuesto a las ventas	sales tax
impuesto a los ingresos brutos	gross revenue tax
impuesto al valor agregado (IVA)	value added tax (VAT)
impuesto de sellos	stamp duty
impuesto de timbres	stamp duty
impuesto diferido	deferred taxes
impuesto doble	double taxation
impuesto interno	excise tax
impuesto progresivo	progressive tax
impuesto progresivo	graduated tax
impuesto regresivo	regressive tax
impuesto sobre la renta	income tax
impuesto sobre la renta de personas	personal income tax
físicas	personal income tax
impuesto sobre las sociedades	corporation tax
impuesto sobre los capitales	capital tax
impuesto sobre los ingresos	income tax
impuestos devengados	accrued taxes
impuestos retenidos	withheld taxes
imputar	allocate
imputar a gastos	write down (verb)
incertidumbre	uncertainty
incobrable	uncollectible
indemnizaciones	indemnities
indemnizaciones por despido	severance indemnities
independencia	independence
índice corriente	current ratio

SPANISH	ENGLISH
índice de cobranzas	collection ratio
índice de cobro	collection ratio
índice de endeudamiento	indebtedness ratio
índice de ganancia bruta	gross profit ratio
índice de liquidez	liquidity ratio
índice de liquidez reducida	acid test ratio
índice de líquidez	current ratio
índice de rotación de los créditos	credits turnover ratio
índice de rotación de los inventarios	inventory turnover ratio
índice del capital de trabajo	working capital ratio
índice operativo	operating ratio
industria	industry
inflación	inflation
información que lleva a confundir	misleading information
información suplementaria	supplementary information
informe	opinion
informe	report
informe a la gerencia	report to management
informe de auditoría	audit opinion
informe del auditor	auditor's report
informe del síndico	statutory audit report
informes especiales	special reports
ingresos (pérdidas) por administración	trust operations profits (losses)
de fondos de terceros	trust operations profits (losses)
ingresos diferidos	deferred income
ingresos imponibles	taxable income
ingresos no gravables	non-taxable income
ingresos no imponibles	non-taxable income
ingresos operativos totales	total revenue
ingresos por servicios prestados	income for services rendered
ingresos realizados	accrued income
ingresos y egresos no operativos	non-operating income and expense
inmovilizado	fixed assets
inmovilizado inmaterial	intangible assets
inmovilizado material	tangible fixed assets
instalaciones	fittings
intención de la gerencia	management intention
intereses a cobrar	interest receivable
intereses a pagar	interest payable
intereses ganados	interest income
intereses pagados	interest expense
intereses recibidos	interest income
inventario fisico	physical inventory
inventarios	inventory -(USA) (stocks-UK)
inversión	investment

SPANISH	ENGLISH
inversión en compañías afiliadas	investment in subsidiaries
inversión en subsidiarias	investment in subsidiaries
inversiones a corto plazo	short-term investments
inversiones a largo plazo	long-term investments
irregularidad	irregularity
joint venture	joint venture
juicio profesional	professional judgment
juicios	litigation
julio	July
junio	June
junta directiva	board of directors
ley de trabajo	labor law
libro diario	journal
libro mayor general	general ledger
licencias	licences
licencias pagas	vacation with pay
licitación	bid (noun)
línea de crédito	credit line
liquidez	liquidity
litigios	litigation
llave de negocio	goodwill
llave negativa	negative goodwill
locaciones operativas	operating lease
locación	lease
locación	leasing
locador	lessor
locatario	lessee
maquinaria y equipo	machinery and equipment
marcas	trade mark
margen	spread (between rates)
margen comercial	profit margin
margen de riesgo del muestreo	allowance for sampling risk
margen de utilidad	profit margin
margen de utilidad	gross margin
marzo	March
materiales	material (noun)
materiales de consumo y reposición	supplies and spare parts
materialidad	materiality
materias primas	raw materials
mayo	May
mayorizar	post entries to the ledger
media	average (mean)
mejoras sobre terrenos	land improvements
mensualmente	monthly
mercadería de reventa	resale merchandise

SPANISH	ENGLISH
mercadería en tránsito	goods in transit
mercado de valores	stock exchange
mercado secundario	secondary market
método de "con y sin"	with and without method
método de la línea recta	straight-line method
método de la suma de dígitos	sum of the years' digits method
método de lo diferido	deferral method
método del contrato completado	completed-contract method
método del grado de avance	percentage-of-completion method
método del pasivo	liability method
mil	thousand
miles	thousands
millones	millions
mobiliario y enseres	furniture and fixtures
moneda extranjera	foreign currency
moneda extranjera	foreign exchange
moneda local	local currency
muebles, útiles e instalaciones	furniture and fixtures
muestreo	sampling
muestreo de auditoría	audit sampling
muestreo estadístico	statistical sampling
muestreo no estadístico	non-statistical sampling
multa	fine
naturaleza	nature
nómina de empleados	payroll
normas de auditoría	auditing standards
notas a los estados financieros	footnotes to the financial statemts
noviembre	November
obligaciones por pagar	bonds payable
obligaciones sin garantía	unsecured bonds
obligación	debenture
obligación	bond
obsolescencia	obsolescence
octubre	October
oferta	bid (noun)
ofertar	bid (verb)
opciones	options
operaciones de cobertura	hedging
operaciones de leasing	lease financing loans
operaciones discontinuadas	discontinued operations
operación extrabursátil	over the counter transaction
opinión	opinion
opinión adversa	adverse opinion
opinión negativa	adverse opinion
oportunidad	timing

SPANISH	ENGLISH
orden de producción	production order
organigrama	organization chart
otros ingresos (egresos) operativos	other operating profits (losses)
otros ingresos por servicios	other income for services
otros préstamos	other loans
pagaré garantizado	secured note
pagos	payments
pagos anticipados	prepaid expense
papeles de trabajo	working papers
parrafo de alcance	scope paragraph
parrafo de opinión	opinion paragraph
participaciones en otras compañías	equity in other companies
participación en los beneficios	profit sharing
participación minoritaria	minority interests
partidas extraordinarias	extraordinary items
pasar a pérdidas y ganancias	write off (verb)
pasivo	liability
pasivo a corto plazo	current liabilities
pasivo corriente	current liabilities
pasivos acumulados	accrued liabilities
pasivos devengados	accrued liabilities
pasivos no corrientes	non-current liabilities
patentes	patents
patrimonio atribuible a los accionistas	stockholders' equity
patrimonio correspondiente a los asegurados	policyholder's equity
	policyholder's equity
patrimonio neto	shareholders' equity
patrimonio neto	stockholders' equity
pensión	pension
pequeñas empresas	small companies
pérdida	loss
pérdida acumulada	loss carry-forward
pérdida afiliados (valor pat. prop.)	share in loss of affiliates
pérdida neta del ejercicio	net loss of the period
periodo de traslado del crédito o de la pérdida impositiva	carryforward period
	carryforward period
período comprendido	intervening period
plan de cuentas	chart of accounts
plan de jubilaciones	pension plan
plan de pensiones	pension plan
planes de opción sobre acciones	stock option plans
plusvalía	gain
población	population
políticas contables	accounting policies
por mes	monthly

ACCOUNTING LEXICON : SPANISH - ENGLISH

SPANISH	ENGLISH
porcentaje	percentage
porción corriente de ...	current portion of ...
portador	bearer
precio de compra	acquisition cost
precio de mercado	market price
precio de rescate	call price
presentación	disclosure
presentar razonablemente	fairly present
presidente (de la junta directiva)	chairman(of board of directors)
presidente del directorio	chairman
préstamos	loans
préstamos a corto plazo	short-term loans
préstamos bancarios de corto plazo	short-term bank loans
préstamos comerciales e industriales	commercial & industrial loans
préstamos hipotecarios	real estate and mortgage loans
préstamos incobrables	actual loan losses
préstamos que no devengan intereses	non-performing earning assets
préstamos sindicados	syndicated loans
préstamos vencidos	matured loans
presupuestación base cero	zero base budgeting
presupuesto	budget
presupuesto base cero	zero base budget
previsión	accrual
previsión	allowance
previsión	forecast
previsión para cuentas de cobro dudoso	allowance for uncollectible acc'ts
previsión para deudas incobrables	allowance for doubtful accounts
previsión para devaluación de	allowance for devaluation of inv'ts
inversiones	allowance for devaluation of inv'ts
previsionar (devengar en libros)	accrue
prima	premium
prima de emisión	capital surplus
prima no amortizada	unamortized premium
prima sobre deuda	debt premium
primas de emisión	premium on issue of capital
primas de seguro emitidas	total premiums written
primas de seguro netas	net premiums earned
primero entrado, primero salido	first in, first out (FIFO)
principios de contabilidad	accounting principles
probable	probable
procedimientos alternativos	alternative procedures
procedimientos de auditoría	auditing procedures
producto bruto nacional	gross national product
productos en proceso	goods in process
productos semiterminados	semi-finished goods

SPANISH	ENGLISH
productos terminados	finished goods
promedio	average (mean)
promedio ponderado	weighted average
proporción corriente	current ratio
proveedores	vendors (USA)
proveedores	suppliers
provisión	provision
provisión para vacaciones	accrued vacations
proyección	projection
prueba	test
prueba ácida	acid test
pruebas de sustentación	substantive tests
pruebas de validación	substantive tests
punto de equilibrio	break even point
quiebra	bankruptcy
razonablemente posible	reasonably possible
reaseguros y ajustes de primas	reinsurance and premium adjustments
recargo a la importación	import surcharges
recesión	recession
reclamo no realizado (no concretado)	unasserted claim
reclamos	claims
reclamos y pérdidas totales por	total insurance claims and losses
siniestros	total insurance claims and losses
red operativa	operational network
redimible	redeemable
reembolso	refund
refinanciamiento	refinancing
registrar	record (verb)
registros auxiliares	subsidiary records
registros contables	accounting records
reglas	rules
regresión multiple	multiple regression
regulaciones	regulations
remoto	remote
rendimiento efectivo	yield
rentabilidad	yield
reparaciones	repairs
reporte de los auditores	auditors' report
requerimientos de garantías	pledging requirements
requerimientos legales	legal requirements
requisición de compra	purchase requisition
requisitos legales	legal requirements
rescatable	redeemable
reserva estatutaria	statutory reserve
reserva legal	legal reserve

SPANISH	ENGLISH
reserva para préstamos incobrables	allowance for loan losses
reserva por revaluación	revaluation reserve
reservas de largo plazo por siniestros	long term insurance reserve charges
reservas no patrimoniales	non-equity reserves
responsabilidad del auditor	auditor's responsibility
restricciones al alcance	restrictions on the scope
restructuración	restructuring
restructuración de deuda	debt restructuring
resultado negativo	loss
resultados acumulados	retained earnings
resultados del muestreo	sampling results
resultados no asignados	retained earnings
resumen financiero	financial summary
retención de impuestos	withholding of tax
retención única y definitiva	flat tax withholding
retiro anticipado	early retirement
retorno de la inversión social	return on equity
retorno sobre el patrimonio neto	return on equity
retorno sobre los activos	return on assets
revaluación	revaluation
revelación	disclosure
revisión analítica	analytical review
revisión de cuentas	audit
revisión de estados contables	review of financial statements
riesgo ajeno al muestreo	non-sampling risk
riesgo de auditoría	audit risk
riesgo de iliquidez	liquidity risk
riesgo inherente al muestreo	sampling risk
riesgo por variación de cambio	exchange rate risk
riesgo-país	country risk
rotación del capital de trabajo	working capital turnover
rubro de negocio	industry
salarios y jornales	salaries and wages
saldo a cuenta nueva	balance carried forward
saldos de cuentas	account balances
salvedad	qualification(of an audit opinion)
sector privado	private sector
sector público	public sector
segmento del negocio	business segment
segundo pedido	second request
seguro de vida	life insurance
seguros generales	general insurance
septiembre	September
servicios de consultoría	consulting services
significatividad	materiality

SPANISH	ENGLISH
significativo	material (significant)
sin auditar	unaudited
sin fines de lucro	non-profit
sin salvedades	unqualified
sistema de inventario permanente	perpetual inventory system
situación contable intermedia	interim accounts
sobrefacturación	overinvoicing
sobregiro	overdraft
sobregiro bancario	bank overdraft
sociedad dominante	parent company
sociedad matriz	parent company
socio	partner
socio del trabajo de auditoría	audit partner
subarrendamiento	sublet (noun)
subfacturación	underinvoicing
subproducto	by-product
subsidiaria	subsidiary
subsidiaria en el exterior	foreign subsidiary
subsidiarias	affiliates
subsidiarias internacionales	international subsidiaries
subsidiarias locales	domestic subsidiaries
sujeto a	subject to
sumario financiero	financial summary
suministradores	suppliers
suministros	supplies (noun)
suscripción	subscription
tamaño de la muestra	sample size
tarifa de cambio	exchange rate
tasa de cambio	exchange rate
tasa de descuento	discount rate
tasa de impuesto	tax rates
tasa de interés	interest rate
tasa flotante	floating rate
tasa interbancaria	interbank rate
tendencia	trend
tenedor	bearer
terrenos	land
tipo de cambio	exchange rate
título de deuda	bond
títulos con cotización oficial	marketable securities
títulos comercializables	marketable securities
títulos de terceros	custody securities
títulos negociables	marketable securities
títulos negociables-moneda local	listed bonds-local currency
títulos y valores de terceros	trust securities

SPANISH	ENGLISH
total de las reservas para riesgos	total insurance reserves
trabajo de auditoría	audit engagement
transacciones	transactions
transacciones entre partes relacionadas	related party transactions
transacciones monetarias	monetary transactions
transacciones no monetarias	non-monetary transactions
traslación a moneda extranjera	foreign currency translation
traslación entre monedas	currency translation
traslado a un ejercicio anterior	carryback
tratamiento a fines impositivos	tax treatment
tributo	excise tax
trimestralmente	quarterly
trimestralmente (4 veces por año)	quarterly (4 times a year)
trimestre	quarter
último entrado, primero salido	last in, first out (LIFO)
unidades de producción	units of production
uniformidad	consistency
universo	population (in a statist. environ.)
usos de fondos	uses of funds
útiles de librería	office supplies
utilidad	profit
utilidad (pérdida) de cambio	foreign exchange gains (losses)
utilidad (pérdida) por intermediación	trading account profits (losses)
con valores	trading account profits (losses)
utilidad correspondiente a los	policyholders' surplus
asegurados	policyholders' surplus
utilidad neta	net income
utilidad por acción	earnings per share
utilidad por enajenación de activo fijo	gain on sale of fixed assets
utilidades acumuladas	retained earnings
utilidades distribuidas	appropriated retained earnings
utilidades no distribuidas	unappropriated retained earnings
utilidades retenidas	retained earnings
utilidades retenidas aplicadas	appropriated retained earnings
utilidades retenidas no aplicadas	unappropriated retained earnings
valor actual neto	net present value
valor actuarial	actuarial value
valor contable	book value
valor de libros	book value
valor esperado de recupero	expected salvage value
valor histórico	historical cost
valor llave	goodwill
valor neto	net worth
valor neto de realización	net realizable value
valor nominal	par value

SPANISH	ENGLISH
valor nominal	face value
valor par	par value
valor par	face value
valor patrimonial neto	net worth
valor patrimonial proporcional	equity method
valor teórico	book value
valores realizables	marketable securities
vehículos	vehicles
vencido	overdue
vencimiento	maturity
vender y arrendar	leaseback
venta de productos	sale of (manufactured) goods
ventas	sales (turnover)
ventas a cobrar en cuotas	installment sales
ventas netas	net sales
viabilidad	feasibility
vice-presidente	vice-chairman
vida útil (de un activo)	useful life (of an asset)

ACCOUNTING LEXICON : ENGLISH - SPANISH

ENGLISH	SPANISH
accelerated depreciation	depreciación acelerada
account balances	saldos de cuentas
accountant	contador
accountant	contable
accounting	contabilidad
accounting changes	cambios contables
accounting policies	políticas contables
accounting principles	principios de contabilidad
accounting records	registros contables
accounts payable	cuentas por pagar
accounts receivable	créditos
accounts receivable	cuentas por cobrar
accrual	previsión
accrual method of accounting	devengado (método de lo)
accrue	previsionar (devengar en libros)
accrued expenses	gastos acumulados
accrued expenses	gastos a pagar
accrued expenses	gastos devengados
accrued income	ingresos realizados
accrued liabilities	pasivos acumulados
accrued liabilities	pasivos devengados
accrued taxes	impuestos devengados
accrued vacations	provisión para vacaciones
accumulated amortization	amortización acumulada
accumulated depreciation	amortización acumulada
accumulated depreciation	depreciación acumulada
acid test	prueba ácida
acid test ratio	índice de liquidez reducida
acquisition (of a company)	adquisición (de una empresa)
acquisition cost	costo de adquisición
acquisition cost	precio de compra
actual loan losses	préstamos incobrables
actuarial value	valor actuarial
adjustment	ajuste
adjustment for inflation	ajuste por inflación
administrative expenses	gastos administrativos
advances to suppliers	adelantos a proveedores
advances to suppliers	anticipos a proveedores
adverse opinion	opinión negativa
adverse opinion	opinión adversa
affiliate	afiliado(a)
affiliated firms	firmas afiliadas
affiliates	subsidiarias
allocate	imputar
allocate	clasificar
allowance	estimación
allowance	previsión
allowance for devaluation of inv'ts	previsión para devaluación de
allowance for devaluation of inv'ts	inversiones
allowance for doubtful accounts	previsión para deudas incobrables
allowance for loan losses	reserva para préstamos incobrables
allowance for sampling risk	margen de riesgo del muestreo
allowance for uncollectible acc'ts	previsión para cuentas de cobro dudoso
alternative procedures	procedimientos alternativos
analytical review	revisión analítica
annual meeting	asamblea anual ordinaria
annual shareholders' meeting	asamblea anual ordinaria de accionistas
annually	anualmente
appropriated retained earnings	beneficios aplicados
appropriated retained earnings	beneficios distribuidos
appropriated retained earnings	utilidades distribuidas
appropriated retained earnings	utilidades retenidas aplicadas
April	abril
assets	activo
associated firm	firma asociada
at random	al azar
audit	auditoría
audit	revisión de cuentas
audit approach	enfoque de auditoría
audit engagement	trabajo de auditoría
audit fees	honorarios de auditoría
audit manager	gerente del trabajo de auditoría
audit opinion	informe de auditoría
audit partner	socio del trabajo de auditoría
audit risk	riesgo de auditoría
audit sampling	muestreo de auditoría
audit staff	equipo de trabajo de auditoría
audit strategy	estratégia de auditoría
auditing procedures	procedimientos de auditoría
auditing standards	normas de auditoría
auditor	censor de cuentas
auditor	censor
auditor's report	dictamen del auditor
auditor's report	certificado de censura
auditor's report	informe del auditor
auditor's responsibility	responsabilidad del auditor
auditors' report	reporte de los auditores
August	agosto
average (mean)	media
average (mean)	promedio

ENGLISH	SPANISH
balance carried forward	saldo a cuenta nueva
balance sheet	balance (general)
balance sheet date	fecha del balance
bank	banco
bank overdraft	giro en descubierto
bank overdraft	sobregiro bancario
bank reconciliation (statement)	conciliación bancaria
bank service charges	gastos bancarios
bankruptcy	bancarrota
bankruptcy	quiebra
bearer	portador
bearer	tenedor
bid (noun)	licitación
bid (noun)	oferta
bid (verb)	ofertar
billions	billones
board of directors	directorio
board of directors	junta directiva
board of directors	consejo de administración
bond	empréstito
bond	bono
bond	obligación
bond	título de deuda
bonds payable	obligaciones por pagar
book value	valor teórico
book value	valor de libros
book value	valor contable
break even point	punto de equilibrio
budget	presupuesto
buildings and structures	edificios y otras construcciones
business combinations	combinaciones de negocios
business segment	segmento del negocio
by-product	subproducto
call price	precio de rescate
capital gains tax	impuesto a las ganancias eventuales
capital increase	aumento de capital
capital stock	capital social
capital stock	capital accionario
capital surplus	prima de emisión
capital tax	impuesto sobre los capitales
capitalization of financial costs	capitalización de costos financieros
capitalization of interest	capitalización de intereses
capitalization of leases	capitalización de arrendamientos
capitalization of leases	capitalización de locaciones
carryback	traslado a un ejercicio anterior

ENGLISH	SPANISH
carryforward period	periodo de traslado del crédito o de la
carryforward period	pérdida impositiva
cash	caja
cash	efectivo
cash and banks	efectivo y bancos
cash dividends	dividendos en efectivo
cash equivalents	disponibilidades
cash flow	flujo de fondos
cash flow	cash flow
certificate of deposit	certificado de depósito
certificate of good standing	certificado de libre deuda
ceteris paribus	ceteris paribus
chairman	presidente del directorio
chairman(of board of directors)	presidente (de la junta directiva)
charity expense	donaciones y obras de caridad
chart of accounts	plan de cuentas
chief executive officer	gerente general
circumstances	circunstancias
claims	reclamos
client representation letter	carta de manifestaciones del cliente
code (verb)	codificar
collateral	colateral
collateral	garantía
collection ratio	índice de cobranzas
collection ratio	índice de cobro
collections	cobranzas
collections	cobro
commercial & industrial loans	préstamos comerciales e industriales
commercial bank	banco comercial
commissions & fees profits (losses)	comisiones y honorarios-ingresos
commissions & fees profits (losses)	(gastos)
commitments	compromisos
common stock	acciones ordinarias
communications expense	comunicaciones, telex y telefonos
company by-laws	estatuto social
comparative financial statements	estados contables comparativos
compilation of financial statements	compilación de estados contables
completed-contract method	método del contrato completado
comply with	cumplir con
condensed financial statements	estados contables resumidos
confirmation of accounts	confirmación de saldos
consistency	uniformidad
consistently applied	aplicado consistentemente
consistently applied	aplicado uniformemente
consolidated accounts	cuentas consolidadas

ENGLISH	SPANISH
consolidated financial statements	estados contables consolidados
construction in progress	construcciones en proceso
consulting services	servicios de consultoría
contents	contenido
contingencies	contingencias
control weakness	debilidad de control
convertible bonds	deuda convertible en capital
copyright	derechos de propiedad intelectual
corporation tax	impuesto sobre las sociedades
correspondent firms	firmas corresponsales
cost of goods sold	costo de los productos vendidos
cost of sales	costo de las mercaderías vendidas
cost of sales	costo de ventas
cost of services rendered	costo de los servicios prestados
country risk	riesgo-país
credit for tax breaks	créditos por desgravaciones fiscales
credit line	línea de crédito
credits turnover ratio	índice de rotación de los créditos
cumulative adjustment	ajuste acumulado
cumulative effect	efecto acumulado
currency translation	conversión de monedas
currency translation	traslación entre monedas
current assets	activo a corto plazo
current assets	activo circulante
current assets	activo corriente
current liabilities	pasivo corriente
current liabilities	pasivo a corto plazo
current portion of ...	porción corriente de ...
current ratio	índice de líquidez
current ratio	índice corriente
current ratio	proporción corriente
custody securities	títulos de terceros
customers	clientes
customers'liability for acceptances	cuentas de orden
customs duties	derechos aduaneros
debenture	debentura
debenture	obligación
debt discount	descuento sobre deuda
debt premium	prima sobre deuda
debt restructuring	restructuración de deuda
December	diciembre
deferral method	método de lo diferido
deferred charges	cargos diferidos
deferred income	ingresos diferidos
deferred income taxes	impuesto a las ganancias diferido

ENGLISH	SPANISH
deferred income/expense	cuenta de periodificación
deferred taxes	impuesto diferido
demand deposits	cuentas corrientes
departure from a pronouncement	apartamiento de un pronunciamiento
dependents	cargas de familia
depreciation expense	depreciaciones
depreciation expense	amortizaciones
depreciation on buildings	depreciaciones de construcciones
detect	detectar
development stage companies	compañías en proceso de desarrollo
direct cost	costo directo
directors	directores
directors	consejeros
disbursements	desembolsos
disclaimer of opinion	abstención de opinión
disclosure	revelación
disclosure	presentación
discontinued operations	operaciones discontinuadas
discount rate	tasa de descuento
disposal (of an asset)	enajenación (de inmovilizado)
dividend	dividendo
dividend income	dividendos percibidos
dividend per share	dividendo por acción
dividends payable	dividendos a pagar
dollars	dólares
domestic subsidiaries	subsidiarias locales
double taxation	impuesto doble
double taxation	doble imposición
due date	fecha de vencimiento
early extinguishment of debt	extinción temprana de la deuda
early retirement	retiro anticipado
earnings per share	ganancia por acción
earnings per share	beneficio por acción
earnings per share	utilidad por acción
economic environment	contexto económico
effect	efecto
effects of changing prices	efecto de los cambios de precios
employee	empleado
employee benefits	beneficios laborales
entertainment expense	gastos de representación
equity in other companies	participaciones en otras compañías
equity method	valor patrimonial proporcional
errors	errores
evidential matter	evidencia comprobatoria
examine	examinar

ENGLISH	SPANISH
except for	excepto por
exchange rate	tipo de cambio
exchange rate	tarifa de cambio
exchange rate	tasa de cambio
exchange rate risk	riesgo por variación de cambio
excise tax	impuesto interno
excise tax	tributo
exhibitions and events expense	gastos por exhibiciones y eventos
expected salvage value	valor esperado de recupero
expenses	gastos
expenses on capital increase	gastos de ampliación de capital
export	exportación
export duties	derechos de exportación
extent	alcance
extraordinary items	partidas extraordinarias
face value	valor par
face value	valor nominal
fairly present	presentar razonablemente
feasibility	factibilidad
feasibility	viabilidad
feasibility study	estudio de viabilidad
feasibility study	estudio de factibilidad
February	febrero
fees	honorarios
fees for services by third party	honorarios por servicios de terceros
finance (noun)	finanzas
finance (verb)	financiar
financial entities	entidades financieras
financial statements	estados financieros
financial statements	estados contables
financial summary	sumario financiero
financial summary	resumen financiero
financing arrangement	acuerdo de financiación
fine	multa
finished goods	productos terminados
first in, first out (FIFO)	primero entrado, primero salido
fittings	instalaciones
fixed assets	bienes de uso
fixed assets	inmovilizado
fixed assets	activo fijo
flat tax withholding	retención única y definitiva
floating rate	tasa flotante
flowchart	flujograma
flowchart	diagrama de circulación
footnotes to the financial statemts	notas a los estados financieros

ENGLISH	SPANISH
for taxation purposes	a efectos de impositivos
forecast	previsión
foreign currency	moneda extranjera
foreign currency translation	traslación a moneda extranjera
foreign exchange	divisas
foreign exchange	moneda extranjera
foreign exchange gains (losses)	utilidad (pérdida) de cambio
foreign subsidiary	subsidiaria en el exterior
form	formulario
freight on purchases of materials	fletes por compra de materiales
funds	fondos
furniture and fixtures	muebles, útiles e instalaciones
furniture and fixtures	mobiliario y enseres
future contracts	contratos a termino
future contracts	contratos a futuro
gain	ganancia
gain	plusvalía
gain contingency	contingencia de ganancia
gain on revaluation of securities	apreciación de inversiones negociables
gain on sale of fixed assets	utilidad por enajenación de activo fijo
general and administrative expense	gastos administrativos y generales
general insurance	seguros generales
general ledger	libro mayor general
general manager	director general
general manager	gerente general
generally accepted	generalmente aceptado(s)
going concern	empresa en marcha
goods in process	productos en proceso
goods in transit	mercadería en tránsito
goodwill	fondo de comercio
goodwill	llave de negocio
goodwill	valor llave
graduated tax	impuesto progresivo
gross margin	margen de utilidad
gross national product	producto bruto nacional
gross profit ratio	índice de ganancia bruta
gross revenue tax	impuesto a los ingresos brutos
group (of companies)	grupo (de empresas)
guarantee	aval
guarantee	garantía
guarantee deposits	depósitos en garantía
hedge	cobertura de riscos financieros
hedging	operaciones de cobertura
historical cost	costo histórico
historical cost	valor histórico

ENGLISH	SPANISH
holding company	holding
holding company	compañía matriz
hundreds	cientos
idle capacity	capacidad ociosa
impact	efecto
import surcharges	recargo a la importación
in accordance with	de acuerdo con
income for services rendered	ingresos por servicios prestados
income statement	cuenta de pérdidas y ganancias
income tax	impuesto sobre la renta
income tax	impuesto a las ganancias
income tax	impuesto sobre los ingresos
indebtedness ratio	índice de endeudamiento
indemnities	indemnizaciones
independence	independencia
industry	industria
industry	rubro de negocio
inflation	inflación
inheritance tax	impuesto a la herencia
installment sales	ventas a cobrar en cuotas
insurance company	compañía de seguros
intangible assets	bienes inmateriales
intangible assets	inmovilizado inmaterial
intangible assets	activos intangibles
inter-company loans	colocaciones interempresarias
interbank assets/funds	fondos interbancarios
interbank deposits	depósitos interbancarios
interbank rate	tasa interbancaria
interest expense	intereses pagados
interest expense	gastos por intereses
interest income	intereses ganados
interest income	intereses recibidos
interest payable	intereses a pagar
interest rate	tasa de interés
interest receivable	intereses a cobrar
interim accounts	estados contables interinos
interim accounts	situación contable intermedia
interim financial statements	estados contables a fecha interina
internal auditors	auditores internos
internal control	controles internos
internal control questionnaire	cuestionario de control interno
international subsidiaries	subsidiarias internacionales
international trade	comercio internacional
intervening period	período comprendido
inventory -(USA) (stocks-UK)	existencias
inventory -(USA) (stocks-UK)	bienes de cambio
inventory -(USA) (stocks-UK)	inventarios
inventory turnover ratio	índice de rotación de los inventarios
investment	inversión
investment bank/merchant bank	banco de inversión
investment in subsidiaries	inversión en compañías afiliadas
investment in subsidiaries	inversión en subsidiarias
investment securities gains(losses)	ganancia (pérdida) por inversiones en títulos
investment securities gains(losses)	
investment tax credit	crédito de impuestos por inversión
invoice	factura
irregularity	irregularidad
January	enero
joint venture	joint venture
journal	libro diario
journal entry	asiento de diario
July	julio
June	junio
labor hours (man-hours)	horas-hombre
labor law	ley de trabajo
land	terrenos
land improvements	mejoras sobre terrenos
last in, first out (LIFO)	último entrado, primero salido
lawyer	abogado
lease	locación
lease financing loans	operaciones de leasing
leaseback	vender y arrendar
leasing	locación
legal requirements	requerimientos legales
legal requirements	requisitos legales
legal reserve	reserva legal
lessee	arrendatario
lessee	locatario
lessor	locador
lessor	arrendador
liability	pasivo
liability method	método del pasivo
licences	licencias
life insurance	seguro de vida
life policy benefits	beneficios prestados por seguros de vida
liquid assets	activos líquidos
liquidity	liquidez
liquidity ratio	índice de liquidez
liquidity risk	riesgo de iliquidez
listed bonds-local currency	títulos negociables-moneda local

ENGLISH	SPANISH
litigation	juicios
litigation	litigios
loans	préstamos
local currency	moneda local
long term insurance reserve charges	reservas de largo plazo por siniestros
long-term contracts	contratos a largo plazo
long-term credits	créditos a largo plazo
long-term debt	deuda a largo plazo
long-term investments	inversiones a largo plazo
loss	resultado negativo
loss	pérdida
loss carry-forward	pérdida acumulada
lower of cost or market method	costo o plaza
lower of cost or market method	costo o mercado
machinery and equipment	maquinaria y equipo
major customers	clientes significativos
management intention	intención de la gerencia
March	marzo
marginal cost	costo marginal
market price	cotización
market price	precio de mercado
marketable securities	títulos comercializables
marketable securities	tìtulos con cotización oficial
marketable securities	títulos negociables
marketable securities	valores realizables
marketable stocks	acciones con cotización
material (noun)	materiales
material (significant)	importante
material (significant)	significativo
materiality	materialidad
materiality	significatividad
matured loans	préstamos vencidos
maturity	vencimiento
May	mayo
merger	fusión
millions	millones
minority interests	participación minoritaria
misleading information	información que lleva a confundir
monetary assets	activos monetarios
monetary transactions	transacciones monetarias
monthly	mensualmente
monthly	por mes
mortgage	hipoteca
mortgage bank	banco hipotecario
mortgage bank	banco para la vivienda

ENGLISH	SPANISH
multinational enterprise	empresa multinacional
multiple regression	regresión multiple
mutual fund	fondo común de inversión
nature	naturaleza
negative goodwill	llave negativa
negative goodwill	fondo de comercio negativo
net fixed assets	activos fijos netos
net income	ganancia neta
net income	beneficio neto
net income	utilidad neta
net income (loss) of the period	ganancia neta del ejercicio
net loss of the period	pérdida neta del ejercicio
net premiums earned	primas de seguro netas
net present value	valor actual neto
net realizable value	valor neto de realización
net sales	ventas netas
net trade accounts receivable	cuentas por cobrar comerciales
net worth	valor patrimonial neto
net worth	valor neto
non-current assets	activos no corrientes
non-current liabilities	pasivos no corrientes
non-equity reserves	reservas no patrimoniales
non-monetary transactions	transacciones no monetarias
non-operating income and expense	ingresos y egresos no operativos
non-performing earning assets	préstamos que no devengan intereses
non-profit	sin fines de lucro
non-redeemable preferred stock	acciones preferidas no rescatables
non-sampling risk	riesgo ajeno al muestreo
non-statistical sampling	muestreo no estadístico
non-taxable income	ingresos no imponibles
non-taxable income	ingresos no gravables
notes payable	documentos por pagar
notes receivable	documentos por cobrar
November	noviembre
obsolescence	obsolescencia
October	octubre
office supplies	útiles de librería
officer (of a company)	funcionario (de una sociedad)
offset (verb)	compensar
operating controls	controles operativos
operating cycle	ciclo operativo
operating lease	locaciones operativas
operating profit	beneficio de explotación
operating profit	ganancia operativa
operating ratio	índice operativo

ENGLISH	SPANISH
operational auditing	auditoría operativa
operational controls	controles operativos
operational network	red operativa
opinion	informe
opinion	opinión
opinion paragraph	parrafo de opinión
opportunity cost	costo de oportunidad
options	opciones
organization chart	organigrama
organization expenses	gastos de organización
other income for services	otros ingresos por servicios
other loans	otros préstamos
other operating profits (losses)	otros ingresos (egresos) operativos
outstanding shares	acciones en circulación
over the counter transaction	operación extrabursátil
overdraft	sobregiro
overdue	vencido
overhead expenses	gastos de estructura
overinvoicing	sobrefacturación
overnight funds	colocaciones por un dia
packaging material	embalajes y envases
paid-in capital	capital integrado
par value	valor nominal
par value	valor par
parent company	casa matriz
parent company	sociedad dominante
parent company	sociedad matriz
partner	socio
patents	patentes
payments	pagos
payments cycle	ciclo de pagos
payroll	nómina de empleados
pension	pensión
pension plan	plan de jubilaciones
pension plan	plan de pensiones
percentage	porcentaje
percentage-of-completion-method	método del grado de avance
permanent file	carpeta permanente
perpetual bond	bono perpetuo
perpetual inventory system	sistema de inventario permanente
personal income tax	impuesto sobre la renta de personas físicas
personal income tax	caja chica
petty cash	inventario fisico
physical inventory	colocación
placement	

ENGLISH	SPANISH
pledge (verb)	garantizar
pledging requirements	requerimientos de garantías
policyholder's equity	patrimonio correspondiente a los asegurados
policyholder's equity	utilidad correspondiente a los asegurados
policyholders' surplus	combinación de intereses
policyholders' surplus	población
pooling of interest	universo
population	composición de la cartera
population (in a statist. environ.)	dar entrada en el libro mayor
portfolio composition	mayorizar
post entries to the ledger	beneficios luego del retiro
post entries to the ledger	acción preferente
post-retirement benefits	acción preferida
preference share	acción preferida
preference share (UK)	prima
preferred share (USA)	primas de emisión
premium	gastos pagados por adelantado
premium on issue of capital	pagos anticipados
prepaid expense	capital básico
prepaid expense	capital primario
primary capital	ajuste de ejercicios anteriores
primary capital	sector privado
prior period adjustments	probable
private sector	financiación de la compra de un producto
probable	garantías sobre productos
product financing	capacidad de producción
product warranties	costo de producción
production capacity	costo de producción
production cost	ciclo de producción
production cost	orden de producción
production cycle	juicio profesional
production order	estándares profesionales
professional judgment	beneficio
professional standards	ganancia
profit	utilidad
profit	cuenta de pérdidas y ganancias
profit	margen de utilidad
profit & loss account	margen comercial
profit margin	participación en los beneficios
profit margin	impuesto progresivo
profit sharing	proyección
progressive tax	costos de promoción
projection	provisión
promotional costs	
provision	

ENGLISH	SPANISH
proxy (noun)	apoderado
public sector	sector público
purchase requisition	requisición de compra
qualification(of an audit opinion)	calificación
qualification(of an audit opinion)	salvedad
quality control	control de calidad
quarter	trimestre
quarterly	trimestralmente
quarterly (4 times a year)	trimestralmente (4 veces por año)
quarterly financial statements	estados contables trimestrales
random	al azar
random	aleatorio
raw materials	materias primas
real estate and mortgage loans	préstamos hipotecarios
reasonably possible	razonablemente posible
receivables	créditos
receivables	cuentas por cobrar
recession	recesión
record (verb)	registrar
recruiting expense	gastos por reclutamiento (del personal)
redeemable	redimible
redeemable	rescatable
redeemable preferred stock	acciones preferidas rescatables
redemption features	condiciones de rescate
rediscounted notes	documentos descontados
refinancing	refinanciamiento
refund	reembolso
regressive tax	impuesto regresivo
regulations	regulaciones
reinsurance and premium adjustments	reaseguros y ajustes de primas
related party transactions	transacciones entre partes relacionadas
remote	remoto
repair and maintenance expense	gastos de reparaciones y mantenimiento
repairs	reparaciones
replacement cost	costo de reposición
report	informe
report to management	informe a la gerencia
reproduction cost	costo de reproducción
repurchase agreement	compromiso de recompra
resale agreement	compromiso de reventa
resale merchandise	mercadería de reventa
research and development costs	gastos de estudios e investigación
research and development costs	gastos de investigación y desarrollo
reserve for exch. rate fluctuations	fondo de reserva para diferencias de cambio
reserve for exch. rate fluctuations	
reserve for general risks	fondo de reserva para riesgos
reserve for loan losses/bad debts	fondo de reserva para préstamos incobrables
reserve for loan losses/bad debts	
reserve for o/s claims and losses	fondo de reserva para reclamos pendientes y pérdidas
reserve for o/s claims and losses	
restrictions on the scope	restricciones al alcance
restructuring	restructuración
retained earnings	beneficios no distribuidos
retained earnings	beneficios retenidos
retained earnings	utilidades acumuladas
retained earnings	utilidades retenidas
retained earnings	resultados no asignados
retained earnings	resultados acumulados
retirement of long-term debt	disminución de la deuda a largo plazo
return on assets	retorno sobre los activos
return on equity	retorno de la inversión social
return on equity	retorno sobre el patrimonio neto
revaluation	revaluación
revaluation reserve	reserva por revaluación
revaluation surplus	diferencia por revaluación
review of financial statements	revisión de estados contables
risk exposure	exposición al riesgo
rules	reglas
salaries and wages	salarios y jornales
sale of (manufactured) goods	venta de productos
sales (turnover)	cifra de negocios
sales (turnover)	ventas
sales tax	impuesto a las ventas
sample size	tamaño de la muestra
sampling	muestreo
sampling results	resultados del muestreo
sampling risk	riesgo inherente al muestreo
saving deposits	depósitos en caja de ahorros
scope	alcance
scope paragraph	parrafo de alcance
seasonally adjusted	desestacionalizado
second request	segundo pedido
secondary market	mercado secundario
secured note	pagaré garantizado
Securities and Exchange Commission	comisión de valores
self-insurance	autoseguro
self-insure	autoasegurarse
selling expenses	gastos de comercialización
selling expenses	gastos de ventas
semi-finished goods	productos semiterminados

ENGLISH	SPANISH
senior debt	deuda de primer grado
September	septiembre
severance	despido
severance indemnities	indemnizaciones por despido
share in loss of affiliates	pérdida afiliados (valor pat. prop.)
shareholders' equity	patrimonio neto
shares	acciones
short-term bank loans	préstamos bancarios de corto plazo
short-term investments	inversiones a corto plazo
short-term loans	préstamos a corto plazo
small companies	pequeñas empresas
social security expense	gastos por cargas sociales
sources of funds	fuentes de fondos
special bonus	gratificaciones especiales
special reports	informes especiales
split (of a company)	escisión (de una empresa)
spread (between rates)	margen
spread (between rates)	diferencia entre tasa pagada y cobrada
stamp duty	impuesto de sellos
stamp duty	impuesto de timbres
standard cost	costo standard
start-up costs	gastos preoperativos
statement changes in fin. position	cuadro de financiamiento
statement of accounting policy	enunciado de política contable
statement changes in fin. position	estado de cambios de la posición financiera
statement changes in fin. position	cuadro de financiamiento
statement sources & uses of funds	estado de origen y aplicación de fondos
statement sources & uses of funds	muestreo estadístico
statistical sampling	informe del síndico
statutory audit report	carta del comisario
statutory audit report	reserva estatutaria
statutory reserve	dividendos en acciones
stock dividends	bolsa de valores
stock exchange	mercado de valores
stock exchange	planes de opción sobre acciones
stock option plans	agente de bolsa
stockbroker	accionistas
stockholders	capital propio
stockholders' equity	patrimonio atribuible a los accionistas
stockholders' equity	patrimonio neto
stockholders' equity	método de la línea recta
straight-line method	sujeto a
subject to	subarrendamiento
sublet (noun)	deuda subordinada
subordinated debt	

ENGLISH	SPANISH
subordinated financing	financiaciones subordinadas
subscription	suscripción
subsequent events	hechos posteriores
subsequent events	acontecimientos posteriores
subsidiary	compañía controlada
subsidiary	filial
subsidiary	subsidiaria
subsidiary records	registros auxiliares
substantive tests	pruebas de validación
substantive tests	pruebas de sustentación
sum of the years' digits method	método de la suma de dígitos
supplementary information	información suplementaria
suppliers	suministradores
suppliers	proveedores
supplies (noun)	suministros
supplies and spare parts	materiales de consumo y reposición
supporting documentation	documentación sustentatoria
syndicated loans	préstamos sindicados
taken as a whole	considerado en su conjunto
tangible fixed assets	bienes de uso
tangible fixed assets	inmovilizado material
tangible fixed assets	activo fijo
tax	impuesto
tax audit	auditoría impositiva
tax authorities	autoridad tributaria
tax credit	crédito de impuestos
tax rates	tasa de impuesto
tax return	declaración jurada de impuestos
tax savings	ahorros impositivos
tax treatment	tratamiento a fines impositivos
taxable income	ganancia imponible
taxable income	ingresos imponibles
taxpayer	contribuyente
temporary differences	diferencias temporarias
test	comprobación
test	prueba
thousand	mil
thousands	miles
time deposit	depósitos a plazo fijo
timing	oportunidad
total funds from operations	fondos generados por las operaciones
total insurance claims and losses	reclamos y pérdidas totales por siniestros
total insurance claims and losses	total de las reservas para riesgos
total insurance reserves	primas de seguro emitidas
total premiums written	

ACCOUNTING LEXICON : ENGLISH - SPANISH

ENGLISH	SPANISH
total revenue	ingresos operativos totales
trade mark	marcas
trade payables	débitos por ventas clientela general
trade receivables	créditos por ventas clientela general
trading account profits (losses)	utilidad (pérdida) por intermediación con valores
trading account profits (losses)	gastos de capacitación al personal
training expenditure	transacciones
transactions	acciones propias en cartera
treasury stock	tendencia
trend	balance de saldos
trial balance	deuda con problemas de cobro
troubled debt	ingresos (pérdidas) por administración de fondos de terceros
trust operations profits (losses)	títulos y valores de terceros
trust operations profits (losses)	coeficiente de rotación
trust securities	prima no amortizada
turnover ratio	utilidades retenidas no aplicadas
unamortized premium	utilidades no distribuidas
unappropriated retained earnings	reclamo no realizado (no concretado)
unappropriated retained earnings	sin auditar
unasserted claim	incertidumbre
unaudited	incobrable
uncertainty	subfacturación
uncollectible	gastos por generación de polizas
underinvoicing	ganancia por intereses no devengada
underwriting and policy acq. costs	unidades de producción
unearned interest	sin salvedades
units of production	obligaciones sin garantía
unqualified	vida útil (de un activo)
unsecured bonds	usos de fondos
useful life (of an asset)	licencias pagas
uses of funds	criterios de valoración
vacation with pay	criterios de valuación
valuation principles	impuesto al valor agregado (IVA)
valuation principles	costo variable
value added tax (VAT)	vehículos
variable cost	proveedores
vehicles	vice-presidente
vendors (USA)	comprobante
vice-chairman	depósito
voucher	almacén
warehouse	promedio ponderado
warehouse	método de "con y sin"
weighted average	impuestos retenidos
with and without method	
withheld taxes	
withholding of tax	retención de impuestos
working capital	capital de trabajo
working capital	capital circulante
working capital	fondo de maniobra
working capital ratio	índice del capital de trabajo
working capital turnover	rotación del capital de trabajo
working papers	papeles de trabajo
write down (noun)	castigo
write down (verb)	imputar a gastos
write off (noun)	deducción
write off (verb)	pasar a pérdidas y ganancias
year-end closing date	fecha de cierre del ejercicio
yield	rendimiento efectivo
yield	rentabilidad
zero base budget	presupuesto base cero
zero base budgeting	presupuestación base cero
zero coupon bonds	bonos sin cupón de renta
zero coupon bonds	bonos de cupón cero